The Legacy of Vietnam Veterans and Their Families

Survivors of War: Catalysts for Change

Papers from the
1994 National Symposium

Edited by
Dennis K. Rhoades
Michael R. Leaveck
James C. Hudson

Agent Orange Class Assistance Program
Washington, DC
1995

Agent Orange Class Assistance Program

Printed in the United States of America

The symposium papers herein represent only the views of their respective authors and do not necessarily represent the views of the United States District Court for the Eastern District of New York or AOCAP. For more information about the AOCAP National Symposium or other AOCAP publications and materials, write AOCAP, P.O. Box 27413, Washington, DC 20038-7413.

Library of Congress Catalog Card Number: 95-78140

ISBN: Softcover— 0-9647667-1-X
Hardcover— 0-9647667-0-1

The painting reproduced on the cover is entitled "At The Wall." The artist is Arthur P. Hughes of Penngrove, California, who is a Vietnam veteran.

Editorial consulting by Joseph Foote

Design, keying, and layout by Norcott & Company

For sale by the U.S. Government Printing Office
Superintendent of Documents, Mail Stop: SSOP, Washington, DC 20402-9328

Dedication

This volume is dedicated to those American service men and women who lost their lives in the Vietnam War, and to their loved ones. And to the 220,000 Vietnam veterans and members of their families who have been served by the Agent Orange Class Assistance Program, the 85 agencies it has funded, and their hundreds of employees. And to all Vietnam veterans and their families, who have survived the terror and the aftermath of war and pressed on to create a better future.

Contents

Foreword

Throughout the course of American history, the federal government has made certain promises to the men and women who served and sacrificed in defense of the nation. We owe veterans and their families a tremendous debt and should not ever forget this obligation.

Today, there are more than 26 million veterans, and approximately 44 million family members of living veterans and survivors of deceased veterans, in the United States. Thus, almost 70 million individuals, or 27 percent of the total U.S. population, are potentially eligible for veterans' benefits.

The U.S. Department of Veterans Affairs (VA) is the agency charged with administering federal veterans' benefits programs, ranging from health care services to service-connected compensation and from vocational rehabilitation to education assistance. The VA's fiscal year 1995 budget was more than $38 billion.

In delivering health care and benefits to veterans, the VA typically follows a traditional model, viewing veterans as individuals rather than players in complex social systems, and providing care and services that are individual in nature. Although this approach may have had its place at one time, it is no longer always appropriate.

Veterans are not one-dimensional. They have significant relationships with other people who influence and are influenced by their daily lives. We must recognize that veterans are not simply men and women who served in the military. They are fathers and mothers, husbands and wives, sons and daughters, brothers and sisters, aunts and uncles, and employers and employees. They have interpersonal relationships that must be taken into account and addressed in order to serve their needs properly.

Although the government's legal obligation extends primarily to veterans, I believe the government also has a strong moral obligation to provide services to those family members who are affected by the veteran's experiences. Services should be offered to children with congenital disorders whose conditions are related to their parent's military service. Counseling should be offered to the family members of veterans with psychological or substance abuse problems related to their military service. By providing appropriate services and benefits, through either government or community-based organizations, the government would admit its responsibility and offer the assistance that some veterans and their families desperately need.

Fortunately, things are changing for the better. Acting as their own advocates, veterans have brought attention to the unique problems that they and their families face. They have forced the government to begin rethinking the way services and benefits are delivered to veterans. Today, many VA Readjustment Counseling Centers (Vet Centers) informally provide services to both veterans and their dependents.

Nevertheless, the VA has neither the financial resources nor the statutory authority to shift gears and fully address the needs of these veterans and their families. Accordingly, nongovernmental programs have been established in communities across the nation to fill the void. These programs play a critical role in meeting the needs of many veterans and their families who would otherwise be unable to access necessary services.

The programs make a wide range of services available to veterans and their families. They are usually operated by nonprofit, community-based or university-based organizations and staffed by dedicated and caring individuals. They receive funding primarily from nonprofit agencies, such as the Agent Orange Class Assistance Program (AOCAP), private corporations, and government agencies.

Since its inception, AOCAP has been instrumental in focusing public attention on the problems facing Vietnam veterans and their families. Through its guidance and financial support, AOCAP has helped thousands of Vietnam veterans and families across the nation. By fostering research and ensuring the delivery of services, AOCAP has saved many lives and made thousands much easier. The AOCAP staff and AOCAP grantees have done an outstanding job. On behalf of both Congress and the nation, I thank them for their efforts.

Concurrent with AOCAP's 1994 national symposium at which the papers in this volume were presented, I conducted a hearing of the House of Representatives' Veterans' Affairs Committee's Subcommittee on Oversight and Investigations. Several directors of programs funded by AOCAP testified about the services provided by their programs. They also spoke of problems veterans and their families have accessing services and the VA's inability to establish enough appropriate programs to meet the overwhelming demand for services. The hearing provided a great deal of information about what is being done today, what has been accomplished, and what remains to be done.

Unfortunately, AOCAP was established by the federal courts for a specific period of time and that period will soon be over. As AOCAP prepares to close its door, it is clear that its legacy will live on. The programs fostered by AOCAP are seeking new sources of financial assistance. Although a few may close, I believe that most programs will succeed and continue helping veterans and their families.

This volume is but a small chapter in AOCAP's history. Its contents provide valuable lessons for policy makers. It is an invaluable document for those of us who need to identify service strategies, methods, and programs that are effective in addressing the needs of veterans and their families. The volume expands the historical record of the legacy of the Vietnam War. Most important, however, it offers insights into the continuing personal cost of the Vietnam War. By detailing the personal struggles of Vietnam veterans and their families, it reveals an important part of their story as survivors and catalysts for change. This volume is the legacy of these brave men and women.

Lane Evans
Ranking Member
Subcommittee on Compensation, Pension,
Insurance, and Memorial Affairs
Committee on Veterans' Affairs
U.S. House of Representatives

Preface

Lessons from the Agent Orange Class Assistance Program for Families and Children of Vietnam Veterans

The papers in this compendium do not memorialize a battlefield or revisit the horrors and heroism of the Vietnam War—although our minds are branded with those memories. Nor do they recall, or attempt to explain, the failure of our society to appreciate fully what veterans did, or why and how much they and their families still suffer.

The papers record the experiences, insights, knowledge, and skills of thousands who have helped veterans and their families share healthier, more productive, and happier lives. These caregivers have been skilled, compassionate, and tender. They have much to teach the nation. Others need to absorb what they have learned. The federal government must reconsider its obligation to veterans' families. Out of an interchange of the ideas reflected in these papers has come a better understanding of those families and ways to help them.

We have had no illusions about the ability of the Agent Orange Settlement Fund to create a comprehensive system of services for Vietnam veterans and their families, nor can we hope that the programs funded through the Agent Orange Class Assistance Program (AOCAP) will reach all of those who are in need of help. We have, however, begun to break down the barriers between the isolated community of Vietnam veterans and the modern world of human services.

In general, the human services system in this country has evolved into a complex and sometimes frustrating web of independent agencies with widely varying eligibility requirements, confusing geographic coverage, and overly bureaucratic procedures. This is especially the case for families with needs relating to disabled children. The United States General Accounting Office found in 1989 that, on the whole, a wide range of services, especially medical services, was available to families with problems. One severe need singled out by the GAO was for case management to assist in providing information on, and coordinating access to, the array of resources already available to families.

It was decided early in the life of AOCAP to emphasize case management. Our intent was to leverage resources that were already available to Vietnam veterans and their families but were underused because of a lack of ability to obtain access to them or a lack of awareness of their existence.

The AOCAP network has also marked a useful path in redirecting the focus of veterans' services toward delivery that is more family oriented. Much has been written about the decline and disintegration of the American family. We have seen the consequences of this decline in many cases before our courts. The instabilities of the American family have been amplified among some Vietnam veterans because of the especially difficult experiences they have endured, their intense roles in combat, their poor reception upon their return, and the inadequate system of benefits and services available through the United States Department of Veterans Affairs to assist in their readjustment.

An important dimension to the negative experiences of Vietnam veterans, especially those with families, was the inadequate response of the conventional human services systems in this country. This unresponsiveness exacerbated the isolation of Vietnam veterans and their families. The VA has often failed to consider veterans' families relevant to services or benefits.

Conversely, few agencies that do treat families made efforts to tailor programs to fit the unique needs of Vietnam veterans. It was rare that a veteran's status was even noted in a family assessment profile. In some cases a veteran's status was used as a screening mechanism by human services agencies to reduce caseloads by making referrals back to the VA, even though there was no reason to believe help would be available from that agency to address the needs of the veteran's family.

I have been especially gratified that such a large share of the funds available through the settlement is being used to help the children of Vietnam veterans, especially those with disabilities and other physical or emotional problems. The original Agent Orange class action suit was based in large part on allegations that the veterans' exposure to herbicides in Vietnam was responsible for congenital disorders or developmental disabilities among their children. That concern continues today among Vietnam veterans and explains the high priority placed by AOCAP on funding programs to serve children.

It is in this area that some of the most useful programs have been developed. The total dollar value of services and adaptive and rehabilitative equipment provided by those projects to the children of Vietnam veterans has far exceeded AOCAP grants. Much the same kind of leveraging of the Agent Orange settlement has been accomplished in the area of veterans' benefits where, based on the work of an AOCAP-funded program, the VA's administrative process has been redirected so that Agent Orange–related VA compensation dwarfs the settlement itself.

Vietnam veterans are inclined, as a group, to mistrust government. Some have acquired a cynical view of the social and human services systems that have failed them or frozen them out. Building bridges of trust and confidence was the first challenge AOCAP faced. It was quickly found that, when a sincere effort was made to address long-standing needs by providing services tailored to address those needs, and when those services were delivered promptly and effectively, the positive responses of the veterans and their families were dramatic.

Providing assistance can make a noticeable difference in this population because of its long-standing isolation from the range of services available. We have received letters and oral statements from Vietnam veterans, spouses, children, and other family members expressing their gratitude for the services provided to them through AOCAP projects. Nothing could serve as more compelling evidence that we were on the right course.

It would have been a mistake for the Court and the Class Assistance Program to have created yet another isolated bureaucracy for Vietnam veterans, one that would wither and die when the settlement fund was exhausted. Thus it was decided during its early stages that AOCAP would seek out organizations experienced in delivering services needed by Vietnam veterans and their families.

AOCAP service providers have arranged to cooperate through the newly formed National Alliance of Veteran Family Service Organizations in continuing to serve families of veterans. Thus, their important work, as well as insights and experience acquired with the help of AOCAP grants, will continue.

Jack B. Weinstein
Senior United States District Judge
Eastern District of New York
Brooklyn, NY

Acknowledgments

The forty-one papers and the other contents of this volume are the culmination of a plan that began in 1992 and involved the contributions of scores of dedicated individuals. The Agent Orange Class Assistance Program (AOCAP) Board of Advisors recognized a need to examine the accomplishments and the lessons of the AOCAP experience through papers written by individuals involved in AOCAP projects across the country and by other interested authors. They believed that the papers would be of immediate practical use to those serving Vietnam veterans and their families, and that the papers would aid in considering public policy implications of the AOCAP network's experience and accomplishments.

Senior United States District Court Judge Jack B. Weinstein carefully examined the symposium proposal, and acted swiftly to authorize this unprecedented national meeting. A diverse team was appointed to the symposium planning committee and a call for abstracts was widely disseminated.

Each abstract was carefully reviewed by symposium domain committee and publication committee members. Authors whose abstracts were selected submitted their papers, which underwent rigorous committee review. Domain committee review teams thoughtfully studied the papers, aiding authors with their questions and suggestions. Mary E. Cadette and Joseph Foote contributed to the quality of the papers through their diligent fact checking, proofing, copyediting, and suggested revisions. They forged on after the symposium to work with authors to polish the papers for inclusion in this compendium. Norcott & Company designed and produced highly readable papers for the symposium, then produced this volume.

Grateful acknowledgment is given to the dedicated authors who contributed the forty-one papers that make up this volume. We also recognize the hard work of many others whose presentations are not included here, but whose efforts contributed to the stimulating exchange of ideas and the overall excellence of the symposium.

We also appreciate the Congressional delegates and their staff who participated in the symposium and ensured an opportunity for symposium participants to testify before the Subcommittee on Oversight and Investigations of the U.S. House of Representatives Committee on Veterans' Affairs on May 17, 1994, regarding the needs of Vietnam veterans and their families.

Special thanks to the symposium's keynote speakers: Charles R. Figley, director of the Marriage and Family Therapy Center, Florida State University, and Wilbur J. Scott, professor of sociology, University of Oklahoma, whose formal papers are included herein; and Commissioner Bob Williams, Administration on Developmental Disabilities, U.S. Department of Health and Human Services, who so generously offered his expertise and that of his staff in helping the AOCAP network of grantees identify financial resources.

We thank symposium guest speakers Hershel W. Gober, deputy secretary, U.S. Department of Veterans Affairs; Mary Lou Keener, general counsel, U.S. Department of Veterans Affairs; and Allan I. Bergman, deputy director, Community Services Division, and director, state-federal relations, United Cerebral Palsy Associations, Inc.

We are indebted to the symposium moderators, notetakers, timekeepers, registration personnel, and others who helped meet our administrative and logistical needs. High marks given the symposium by participants were earned in large part by their efforts.

We received remarkable support and active involvement before and during the symposium from officials of several federal, state, and other agencies and organizations including representatives of the U.S. Department of Health and Human Services, the National Center on Child Abuse and Neglect, the Maternal and Child Health Bureau, the Administration on Developmental Disabilities, and the U.S. Department of Veterans Affairs.

The AOCAP Board of Advisors was integral to the planning and execution of the symposium, as were the other Planning Committee members and AOCAP and American Association of University Affiliated Programs staff. They can be proud of their many contributions to the symposium.

We sincerely appreciate the support of Jan Scruggs and Wayne Smith of the Vietnam Veterans Memorial Fund, who coordinated with AOCAP in conducting the ceremony at The Wall honoring fellow Vietnam veteran Lewis Puller, Jr., who died just days before the symposium.

The success of AOCAP would not have been possible without the creativity and professionalism of Special Masters for to the Agent Orange Settlement Kenneth R. Feinberg and Deborah L. Greenspan. Their caring attitudes and efficiency enabled AOCAP to respond rapidly to the needs of individual families and grantees as well as to the Court. Special Master for Agent Orange Claims Appeals W. Bernard Richland has also been responsive to the needs and concerns of class members and was instrumental in obtaining important reference information, included in this volume as an appendix on cases related to the Agent Orange litigation.

Members of the advisory board to the Agent Orange Veteran Payment Program, and Maria Martinez, administrator of that program, and her staff, deserve recognition for their heartfelt and dedicated service to class members, and their wonderfully cooperative attitude toward AOCAP and the Vietnam Veterans Family Assistance Network.

No symposium can succeed without the enthusiastic involvement of its participants. We were especially impressed with the intensity of the participation of AOCAP grantee staff members, and we also thank their counterparts who remained at home offices to ensure client services would not be adversely affected by the week-long symposium.

Dennis K. Rhoades
Michael R. Leaveck
James C. Hudson
Editors

Introduction

The Vietnam Veterans Family Assistance Network and The Agent Orange Class Assistance Program

More than a decade ago, an out-of-court settlement was reached between the chemical companies that manufactured herbicides, including Agent Orange, that were used as defoliants in the Vietnam War, and Vietnam veterans who claimed that exposure to these herbicides caused injuries and death to veterans as well as miscarriages for their spouses and congenital disorders among their children. At the time, it was the largest settlement of its kind ever reached, and the distribution plan was both unique and controversial.

A major element in the distribution plan established by the United States District Court, Eastern District of New York, was the creation of a foundation to fund the delivery of broad-based social services for Vietnam veterans and their families, particularly those who had children with developmental or other chronic disabilities. That foundation, the Agent Orange Class Assistance Program (AOCAP), has developed a network of seventy-two programs that provide such services in all fifty states plus the District of Columbia and Puerto Rico. In the course of AOCAP's six years of operation, this network has provided services to nearly 200,000 persons, through the distribution of more than $60 million in grant funds.

In May 1994, AOCAP conducted a national symposium to assess and distill the experience of its Vietnam Veterans Family Assistance Network in providing services to Vietnam veterans and their families and to assess the public policy implications of the effort. This symposium, *The Legacy of Vietnam Veterans and Their Families: Survivors of War—Catalysts for Change,* was held precisely because the problems of the clients AOCAP serves necessitated the development of service methodologies that differ considerably from traditional veterans' program service models.

More than forty papers were presented at the symposium, most of which are published in this volume. To understand the issues and themes reflected in these papers, it may be useful to review in some detail AOCAP's development and the lawsuit settlement that created it.

Litigation, Settlement, and Distribution Plan

The Agent Orange Product Liability Litigation began in 1978, when a Vietnam veteran filed a lawsuit against the U.S. government and a number of chemical companies, claiming that the manufacture of Agent Orange and similar herbicides produced a dangerous impurity known as 2,3,7,8-tetrachloro-dibenzo-paradioxin. The suit alleged that exposure to this impurity caused injuries and death to veterans as well as miscarriages for their spouses and congenital disorders among their children. Many other veterans soon filed similar lawsuits. The lawsuits were transferred by the Multi-District Litigation Panel to the United States District Court, Eastern District of New York. Ultimately, the case was certified as a class action and the plaintiff class was defined as all persons who served in the U.S., New Zealand, and Australian armed forces between 1961 and 1971 and who were injured by exposure to Agent Orange or other phenoxy herbicides while in or near Vietnam. The class also includes the parents, spouses, and children of the veterans.

On May 7, 1984, the day the trial was to have begun, the attorneys for the plaintiff class and the chemical companies agreed to settle the case for $180 million, which was invested in U.S. Treasury notes. After conducting fairness hearings in five different cities throughout the country, the supervising judge, Jack B. Weinstein, worked with an advisory board of Vietnam veterans to design a distribution plan that made the best and fairest use of the limited settlement fund. The Court solicited and received advice from hundreds of individual veterans and veterans' organizations.

Throughout, the Court was constrained by the relatively small size of the settlement fund in comparison with a plaintiff class that included not only the 3 million veterans who served in Vietnam, but also their families. The Court initially announced the distribution plan in an opinion issued on May 28, 1985.

The plan had two major components. The larger component, the Agent Orange Veteran Payment Program, which operated from the beginning of 1989 to January 1995, distributed cash payments to totally disabled Vietnam veterans and to the spouses or children of deceased Vietnam veterans. To have been eligible for a payment, the applicant must have shown that the veteran met a Court-approved test of exposure to Agent Orange and that the disability or death was not caused by traumatic, accidental, or self-inflicted injury.

The smaller, and more unusual, component of the distribution plan was the creation of a foundation that would provide services to the class through grants to human service organizations. Although the United States Court of Appeals for the Second Circuit would later proscribe the use of an independent, private foundation, it upheld the concept of distribution of a portion of the settlement funds in the form of grants, as long as such funding was conducted under the supervision of the District Court. In June 1988, the Supreme Court of the United States upheld the settlement and distribution plan, as revised by the Second Circuit Court. By that time, the settlement fund had grown from $180 million to $240 million through accrued interest. The District Court appointed me executive director in December 1988, as well as an unpaid, ten member Board of Advisors, all but one of whom are Vietnam veterans. AOCAP began operations the following month.

Program Implementation

In developing the Class Assistance Program as the distribution plan envisioned it, we understandably faced several constraints. For example, no program that involved research into the causal relationship between Agent Orange exposure and health effects could be funded. This, in effect, removed us almost entirely from the ongoing debate about Agent Orange. In addition, the ruling of the Second Circuit Court of Appeals explicitly prohibited any political activity. For this reason, our relationship with the Congress, as well as other policy-making bodies in the federal government, has necessarily been very limited.

In addition to these constraints, we also confronted a number of challenges. First, because the settlement was the result of a nationwide class action, we were required to develop a program that was truly national in scope. Second, such a program had to serve the entire class, which included not only the 2.5 million to 3 million veterans who served in Vietnam, but also their parents, spouses, and children. Although the $52 million set aside by the Court for AOCAP represented a substantial investment in Vietnam veterans and their families, the very size of the class and the diversity of needs presented a formidable challenge in equitable distribution of these nonrenewable resources.

From AOCAP's earliest days, this latter question of need and program focus was central to our efforts. While both the advisory board and the Court recognized many worthy needs, they were at the same time concerned that if AOCAP distributed funds into too many service areas the settlement would not achieve a positive, lasting impact on the class. Our choices were numerous, as reflected in the proposals submitted in response to an August 1988 Request for Proposal (RFP) issued by the Court-appointed Special Master for the Settlement, Kenneth R. Feinberg, shortly after the Supreme Court ruling. In addition to requesting funding for local memorials and research projects, the 147 proposals we received posed solutions to many problems, such as homelessness, unemployment, and medical conditions.

The proposals we received were not, in their totality, an accurate barometer of need, but instead reflected institutional interests and issues that were not necessarily congruent with those needs. Working with our advisory board, we sought to discover those areas in which a demonstrable need was clearly unmet and in which, with AOCAP's limited resources, the funds could do the greatest good.

The need most apparent at the outset was for services for Vietnam veterans' children with disabilities or health problems. Throughout the course of the Agent Orange debate, veterans have expressed concern for the health of their children. Moreover, nearly 60 percent of all of the telephone calls and correspondence from the public as we began operation concerned child disability and health issues, most particularly the financial burden in providing adequate health care and adaptive equipment. I remember talking on the telephone with numerous families, many of whom were so far into debt, owing to hospital and doctor bills, that they were being evicted from their homes. While it was not, and is not, appropriate for the Class Assistance Program to judge the cause of any given disability or condition, we believed that it was AOCAP's responsibility to attempt to address the very real needs of these children and their families.

Assessing the universe of need among AOCAP-eligible veterans and their families is difficult, because the class itself does not conform to the veteran population cohorts that the federal government tracks through the decennial census. The Court has defined a member of the class as any person who served in Vietnam between 1961 and the end of 1971, which is the time period during which Agent Orange was used. However, the class also includes the veterans' parents, spouses, and children. For operational purposes, we have estimated that the class includes 2.5 million to 3 million veterans, as well as another 8 million to 10 million relatives. To estimate the number of persons in the class needing services, certain inferences can be made from available statistical data. First, according to the Research Triangle Institute, approximately 15 percent of veterans who served in Vietnam suffer from post-traumatic stress disorder (PTSD) to one degree or another. As many of the authors in this publication point out, PTSD is likely to have negative ramifications for the veteran's family. Second, data collected by the National Information System (NIS) at the University of South Carolina indicate that the families of Vietnam veterans differ from other families seeking services from NIS in that there is a higher rate of disability within the family (i.e., Vietnam veterans are likely to have more than one child with a disability) and that the children are more likely to have multiple disabilities.

Understandably, after five years of legal appeals, the expectations of Vietnam veterans and their families about our program's services were high. AOCAP thus began its grantmaking within three months of the program's January 1989 startup, before we had even acquired a permanent office. Still wrestling with establishing long-range goals, we developed criteria for our initial selections that have served us well for the past five years: (1) that grants reflect a broad geographic distribution; (2) that grants be made to organizations with proven records of successful services in the community; (3) that AOCAP funding neither duplicate existing services nor replace public funds; and (4) that initial grants place a special emphasis on services to families with children with developmental or other chronic disabilities or health conditions.

AOCAP Operating Principles

In consultation with our advisory board and the Court, we carefully studied and monitored the progress of those organizations to which we had distributed funding. The programs AOCAP funded provided a variety of services including counseling, provision of adaptive equipment, education, advocacy in regard to the U.S. Department of Veterans Affairs (VA), medical assistance, Supplemental Security Income (SSI), and family support groups. Nevertheless, as the number of grants we developed and supervised grew, the more apparent it became that there was a real commonality in service approaches among our most effective programs. These approaches were guided by four principles.

Family-Centered Service

The very nature of the plaintiff class—consisting of the Vietnam veteran and his or her family as co-equal partners—seemed to dictate a family-oriented approach to the provision of services. In this, AOCAP was not alone: for the past several years, human service providers have acknowledged that empowering the family empowers the individuals in the family. Several authors, including Dr. Charles R. Figley, discuss this issue in some detail in their papers. Moreover, our projects were finding that many veterans were accessible only through providing help to their families. After twenty years, many of the most disadvantaged Vietnam veterans had become mistrustful of agencies that purported to serve them as individuals. Although they might not seek or receive help for themselves, they would rarely, if ever, deny that assistance to their families, regardless of any institutional prejudices they might have. And because family-centered services are holistic by their very nature, the veteran received the help that he or she might otherwise have spurned.

Service Coordination

Many Vietnam veterans and their families who visited our projects had multiple needs: supplemental income for high doctor and hospitalization bills, basic preventive health care, mental health care, adaptive equipment, and respite care. Resources to meet these needs were available, but often difficult to access. Medicaid, for example, has been rightly characterized as the most user-unfriendly program ever adopted by Congress. In one state, the initial application for care is forty-two pages long. The need to maneuver through the welter of applications for service, changing eligibility requirements, and resistant bureaucracies is for many families an insurmountable barrier. Many have simply given up. The ability of a well-trained service coordinator to guide a family through the maze that leads to meeting multiple needs is therefore invaluable. In addition, given AOCAP's limited resources and the extent of the need for help, the ability of a project to leverage resources was clearly critical to its success. In this area, our projects have enjoyed considerable success. Dr. Bryan C. Smith's paper, "Impact Analysis of the AOCAP Network of Services," discusses the surprising extent to which the Vietnam Veterans Family Assistance Network has been able to find resources for its clients that far exceed AOCAP's funding investment.

Community-Based Service

Service coordination succeeds best when the services offered by an agency are a part of an integrated delivery system in the community. This is as true for veterans as it is for anyone else. Each community differs in its needs and systems designed to meet those needs. The trend toward decentralization of programs is now more than a generation old. Large-scale national categorical programs are becoming rarer as the end of this century approaches. Service coordinators need to have not only a basic generic understanding of available services, but a knowledge of eligibility requirements peculiar to a given program at the state or local level. Effective service coordinators constantly work to develop key agency contacts with whom they can establish good working relationships.

Cultural Competence

Each veteran and family member is also a product of his or her community. Their needs and attitudes are shaped by that community. This is particularly the case with minority veterans. Developing the cultural competence that acknowledges differences between and within communities to tailor effective programs for Vietnam veterans and their families has been a vital element in our grant-development efforts.

As we began to build these principles into our new grants and grant renewals, we discovered that, rather than operating in isolation, our projects were collaborating in serving individual clients, as well as working to resolve common problems. In New England, for example, AOCAP grantees formed a consortium and developed a common intake form. Similar collaborative systems were established in the Midwest, the Rocky Mountain states, and within the states of California and New York. Thus a coherent network of services, reaching from Fairbanks, Alaska, to Brevard County, Florida, began to emerge.

Profile of the Vietnam Veterans Family Assistance Network

Despite the close interaction among AOCAP projects, the network is not homogeneous. Nor were grants developed based on a rigid template. In fact, there is considerable diversity among the agencies that constitute the network. These organizations fall into four general categories: veterans' organizations, disability service agencies, family service programs, and national support projects.

Veterans' organizations make up about a third of current AOCAP grantees. In addition to the fifteen-state family assistance program of The American Legion, AOCAP provides funding to twenty-three community-based veterans projects, whose primary mission is to meet the service needs of Vietnam veterans. AOCAP grants have expanded the service capabilities of these organizations, which have traditionally provided help principally to individual veterans. AOCAP funding has permitted these agencies to serve the broader needs of Vietnam veterans and their families, with particular emphasis on services to children with disabilities.

Twenty-four AOCAP programs are operated by agencies serving persons with disabilities. They include University Affiliated Programs for Children with Developmental Disabilities (UAPs), national disability organizations, parent advocacy agencies, and local chapters of organizations such as United Cerebral Palsy Associations, Inc., and The Arc (formerly the Association for Retarded Citizens of the U.S.).

Twenty grantees are agencies whose primary mission is counseling, offering either general family therapy or problem-specific services such as substance abuse recovery programs. Family assistance agencies (many of which, incidentally, began as service agencies for the returning veterans of World War I and their families) have shown keen interest in participating in the Class Assistance Program since its beginning, and often specialize in service coordination, a critical need of Vietnam veterans and their families.

Five national support projects provide the core of the consultation, technical assistance, training, and other support services to the network of AOCAP-funded community projects in order for those projects to access the tools, skills, and expert advocacy necessary to serve individual clients. These projects range from the National Veterans Legal Services Project, with its expert knowledge of the veterans' benefits system and veterans law, to The Access Group, a project of the United Cerebral Palsy Associations that provides state-of-the-art knowledge regarding assistive technology for persons with disabilities. Each of these projects provides a significant level of direct services to Agent Orange class members as well.

Also included among the national support projects is the National Information System (NIS) at the University of South Carolina. The NIS is an advice and counseling system, accessible through a toll-free telephone line, that helps families develop strategies for serving the needs of their children and link up with appropriate resources in their communities or anywhere they may be available. NIS counselors are well trained and educated in the field of developmental disabilities, and they work from a nationwide database of more than 100,000 service providers in seeking out sources of help for Vietnam veterans' children.

Tied together through AOCAP's electronic mail system, called VETnet, the Vietnam Veterans Family Assistance Network is capable of providing services to Vietnam veterans and their families in need throughout the United States. The best example of that capability is found in our National Outreach Initiative. This initiative was designed to contact all of the original Agent Orange settlement claimants who submitted claims based on the health problems of their children, many of whom are now young adults.

Outreach to Original Claimants

Following the May 1984 settlement agreement, but prior to the development of the distribution plan, approximately 250,000 claims were filed against the settlement fund. Once the settlement was finally approved, all claimants were notified of the provisions of the Payment Program. Many claims were made not by veterans with medical conditions, but by families on behalf of their children. These claims were disaggregated from the larger group, and their addresses were sent to the NIS. Serving as a clearinghouse, the NIS two years ago began sending registered letters to the last known address of each family. Upon making contact with the family, the NIS screened that family's presenting needs and referred the family either to an AOCAP grantee or to another appropriate agency, depending on what services were being sought. By the end of 1994, we completed our effort to contact and provide services to all 76,000 families with claims filed on behalf of children.

The Legacy of Vietnam Veterans and Their Families

Although many have quarreled, and will continue to quarrel, about whether a settlement should have been reached at all, I believe we have accomplished some important tasks with the limited settlement resources at our disposal. But our efforts are time-limited: the settlement funds are finite and not renewable. Ultimately, the care that our veterans and their families need, like the problems associated with Agent Orange, is the responsibility of government.

AOCAP's program emphasis was developed precisely because many of the social service needs of Vietnam veterans and their families were not being met either through the veterans' services system or the broader human services system. Moreover, it is doubtful that any legislation, either pending or recently passed, addresses the broad spectrum of social service needs of Vietnam veterans and their families. In designing AOCAP's service network, we sought to fill gaps in the service system as evidenced by testimony from the Court's fairness hearings, the large numbers of letters and phone calls we took from members of the class, and the original claims made against the settlement fund. During the six years of AOCAP's operation, there has been little movement on the part of the federal government to fill these gaps. In part, this is attributable to the fact that the Vietnam Veterans Family Assistance Network has itself taken the initiative to meet the social services needs of the class. Yet, by the middle of 1996 funding for these services from the Agent Orange settlement will be exhausted, while the service needs of Vietnam veterans—indeed, all veterans—will remain. For these needs to be met on a long-term basis, changes in both the VA and the broader human services system need to be set in place in the near future.

Specifically, the VA should reexamine its mission with a view toward becoming a more family-oriented agency, adopting the family as the unit of care rather than the individual veteran. The concept of a "dependent" has a quaint, antiquated ring to it in our contemporary society. As the Gulf War clearly demonstrated, the family is the veteran's primary support system, and its dynamics are often vital to the readjustment and rehabilitation of the individual veteran.

The VA should also take a more holistic approach to service provision, i.e., service coordination. How many VA service providers are currently conversant with SSI or the peculiarities of Medicaid? Not many, I suspect. Once they have explored and exhausted the avenues of VA benefits and services, far too many veterans and their families in need are turned away rather than assisted in examining alternatives.

Veterans' services and programs are among a shrinking minority that are still operated directly by the federal government. The trend toward decentralization of programs is now over a generation old. Large-scale national categorical programs are becoming rarer as the end of this century approaches. This is not to suggest that the veterans' services system should in some way be defederalized, and responsibility for services shuffled out to the states. That particular avenue is fraught with dangers, as the Department of Labor has demonstrated with its system of state and locally operated employment and training programs. Federally mandated veterans preference has not fared well under these programs. What it does suggest is that the VA, its medical centers, counseling functions, and other programs need to become considerably more community oriented and community integrated. Effective coordination of services with state and local agencies can only be achieved if the VA becomes, either directly or through contracting out, an active, visible partner in the human services system at both the state and local levels.

But the VA is not the only agency that must change. Perhaps the first lesson that social service providers learn (and need to learn) is that the VA does not provide all of the services needed by veterans and their families. Too often, the VA is perceived as providing such a broad constellation of assistance that other public agencies view themselves as somehow absolved of the responsibility for serving what they perceive as this "special population group." The unfortunate result of this perception is that the families of veterans are an unrecognized, underserved population.

Within the social services system, it has become apparent that, in order to provide appropriate service coordination to veterans' families, agencies addressing a multitude of needs often must be dealt with, i.e., housing, developmental disabilities, veterans' issues, mental health, substance abuse, employment, and education. Many of these systems are interacting for the first time, and all have widely variant regulations and eligibility criteria, etc. Maneuvering among these groups to put together any kind of services package often requires innumerable hours of effort.

Within the developmental disability community in particular, it has been only recently that the needs and issues facing the entire family—rather than the individual—have been considered when providing services. This is particularly relevant when dealing with a veteran's family, because in addition to the disability factor, issues such as PTSD and secondary PTSD (as well as other problems specific to the veteran and his or her family) may be adding stressors to the family unit.

Finally, most human services symposia, by their nature, focus on problems and services—the impact of stresses, identifying individuals and groups at risk, recognizing personal and family dysfunction, and performing individual assessments; and, of course, they often examine solutions—new service approaches, therapies, treatments, and systemic change. The Vietnam War and the manifold adversities cascading from it demand this intense scrutiny as well as the consideration of thoughtfully designed solutions.

We would do well to remind ourselves, however, that Vietnam veterans and their families, as a group, have shown remarkable strength and resilience. Many Vietnam veterans were instrumental in the national debate that led to the end of the Vietnam War. It was Vietnam veterans, sometimes joined by veterans of earlier wars, who demanded and won education benefits comparable to those afforded World War II veterans, sued the Department of Labor when services were denied, forced improvements in VA medical centers, and initiated the call for judicial review of VA benefit decisions. And it was their actions and those of their families that resulted in the establishment of the settlement fund and aided the Court in shaping AOCAP's as well as the Direct Payment Program's goals and methods. As a group, even those who have experienced serious illness, disability, and economic hardship, have succeeded in holding their families together, and, as AOCAP grantees have learned, they continue to strive to help themselves. Vietnam veterans and their families have been, and undoubtedly will continue to be, the most powerful and effective catalysts for healthy and productive change, both within their families and in the sphere of national policy concerning Americans who served in the Vietnam War and their loved ones.

Dennis K. Rhoades
Executive Director
Agent Orange Class Assistance Program
Washington, DC

Part I

Vietnam Veterans Twenty Years After: Unmet Needs in a Family Systems Perspective

When Agent Orange Class Assistance Program grantees began their initiatives, they discovered a panoply of unresolved issues and concerns that affected those they hoped to reach—despite the passage of almost twenty years since the end of the Vietnam War. It soon became clear that chief among those issues were problems confronting the individual veteran as an integral part of his or her family.

Vietnam veterans had sought medical, income maintenance, educational, and other assistance from the U.S. Department of Veterans Affairs (VA) and other veterans' service delivery systems, but rarely had their concerns been considered in the context of the family as a unit. For example, a veteran having difficulties in making payments on his VA-insured home loan because his daughter had a severe physical disability was unlikely to learn from the VA or a veterans' service organization that Supplemental Security Income and Medicaid benefits were available to help with medical expenses. Even issues confronting Vietnam veterans' family members as a direct result of the veterans' war experiences have infrequently been evaluated and treated in the context of that experience and the very real psychological manifestations stemming from it. Domestic abuse—both emotional and physical—has been a concern of many families, including the adverse effects that a veteran's post-traumatic stress disorder can sometimes have on a spouse and children.

Ironically, veterans and their families who seek assistance from the social service agencies that serve the general population are often turned away because of the mistaken belief that the VA takes care of all veterans' problems. Not surprisingly, many veterans and their families have become alienated from traditional safety-net agencies as a result of their frustrations in dealing with both veteran- and nonveteran-related human service programs.

The papers in Part I reveal the enormous toll war takes not only on combatants, but also on their spouses and children.

Barriers to Services for Many Vietnam Veterans' Families

Bryan C. Smith, Ed.D.; Kathy L. Mayfield-Smith, M.A., M.B.A.; and Dawn Sudduth, M.Ed.

National Information System for Vietnam Veterans and Their Families
Center for Developmental Disabilities
Department of Pediatrics
School of Medicine
The University of South Carolina
Columbia, SC

Abstract

In the course of five years of assisting Vietnam veterans and their families, the National Information System (NIS) made referrals for a range of service needs. Despite the severity and urgency of many of the needs, veterans or other family members often failed to contact referral resources that were likely to resolve some of their problems. Using information gathered from families who had used NIS, a study was undertaken to explain this pattern of behavior.

Two random samples of veterans and their family members were drawn from NIS client records. In one sample, the referrals given to families included at least one service provider who was an Agent Orange Class Assistance Program (AOCAP) grantee. In the other sample, the referrals made to providers did not include an AOCAP grantee. Each member of these samples was contacted by telephone and interviewed to determine the outcomes of the referrals. A remarkable disparity was noted between the seemingly urgent need to solve problems and the failure to follow through with actions that might lead to solutions. In addition to these two samples, a group of service providers was asked to identify barriers that might prevent veteran families from obtaining needed services.

This paper examines some of the barriers that Vietnam veterans' families encounter in their efforts to obtain services. It explores possible reasons for the barriers and presents recommendations to help reduce or overcome some of them. The barriers have been grouped for discussion as the veteran or family itself as an obstacle as well as legal, geographic, and institutional barriers to obtaining services.

Bryan C. Smith, Ed.D., *is a research associate professor for the Department of Pediatrics of the University of South Carolina's School of Medicine, Columbia, SC.* ***Kathy L. Mayfield-Smith, M.A., M.B.A.,*** *is a research assistant professor and the project director of the National Clearinghouse for Infants and Children with Disabilities and Life Threatening Conditions. These authors and* ***Dawn Sudduth, M.Ed.,*** *are the administrative team that leads the National Information System for Vietnam Veterans and Their Families, which is part of the department's Center for Developmental Disabilities.*

The National Information System (NIS), an information systems project of the South Carolina University Affiliated Program, is a primary vehicle for helping Vietnam veteran families seeking information and service resources. This project, and seventy-one others, comprise the Agent Orange Class Assistance Program (AOCAP) network created to provide services for Vietnam veterans and their families, particularly families with a disabled child. The primary objectives of the NIS are to establish mechanisms by which effective communication and information sharing with these families can occur and to serve in a problem-solving capacity for these families. The program focuses on information related to disabilities and other health conditions and organizations that comprise the service delivery system.

The NIS began ten years ago as a federally funded demonstration project. Since then, the staff has concentrated on three target populations. The latest, and possibly the most challenging population served by the NIS, has been families who may have been affected by a veteran's exposure to Agent Orange during military service in Vietnam.

At the outset of providing information and referral services to this population, the NIS administration thought that working with veterans' families would be no different than working with other families who have children with disabilities. The information and referral process and method would be the same, with the only difference being that one or both parents were Vietnam veterans. It quickly became evident that the Vietnam experience placed unique strains on family structures. At that time, no one in the project realized how complex and diverse this population was and how complicated it would be to connect them with services. The characteristics of these families are quite different from other population groups helped by earlier components of the national system developed and operated by the University of South Carolina.

The referral process is also varied as are the Vietnam veterans' families' wide range of conditions and service needs. Usually, the final step in this process occurs when those who need a service connect with an appropriate service provider. It was most distressing to discover that many veterans' families who appeared to be in desperate need of services did not take this final step even in the absence of the usual obstacles—cost or availability of services, for example. A study was conducted to help explain this phenomenon. This paper discusses some barriers that Vietnam veteran families encounter in their efforts to obtain services, explores possible reasons for the barriers, and presents recommendations to help overcome some of them.

Study Method

Two random samples were drawn from the NIS client records by a computer-generated random set of files. Sample members were assigned numbers at the time of the call. The first was a sample of ninety family members who had been referred for services to at least one AOCAP grantee (hereafter referred to simply as a "grantee"). The second was a sample of ninety family members who had been referred to service providers that did not include a grantee. Each member of these samples was contacted by telephone and interviewed to determine the outcome of the referrals. Thirty service providers consisting of fifteen grantees and fifteen other agencies were asked to identify why veteran families did not obtain needed services.

The barriers to services were identified both directly and indirectly. The direct method was to ask the study population what they perceived as barriers and why they did not seek services for themselves or for other family members from service providers to whom they had been referred. Barriers to services were indirectly identified by making inferences based on self-reported behavior of the NIS callers contacted in the study. This approach compared those who accessed a service with those who did not, with the differences between the groups taken to represent a barrier or obstacle to obtaining services. For example, if a veteran living in an area with an active local, service-providing grantee was more likely to follow through with recommended referrals than a veteran living in an area without such a grantee, the absence of the grantee and the type of services they offered was presumed to be a barrier to obtaining services.

Results

Sample One

Two names were dropped from the first sample because the individuals had not given the NIS their telephone numbers or permission to transmit information about their call to a grantee. They were excluded out of respect for their desire for anonymity. Seventy-one of the remaining eighty-eight sample members were reached by telephone and were asked if they were willing to discuss the referral outcomes and process. Thirty-six members were unwilling, or unable, to recall or relate what had happened. Each remaining sample participant was interviewed to determine the extent of the follow-through and to assess the barriers or obstacles that limited their taking action beyond the initial telephone call to the NIS. The same interviewer contacted all the individuals and used the same protocol with all members of the sample.

From the thirty-five individuals interviewed, 84 percent followed through to contact at least one of the referral resources. Sixteen of the callers had failed to initiate contact with a referent grantee (a grantee to whom referrals were made), but in each case where the grantee had initiated the contact with the client, the follow-through for at least one other referral resource increased to 97 percent.

Sample Two

In the second random sample of ninety callers, twenty-four persons could not be reached by telephone, nine chose not to participate after they had been contacted, and one had died. The final study group of fifty-six participants had received an average of just over three referrals per family member. In ten cases, one referral resource was contacted and the others were not, even though the first call failed to produce the service the participant requested during the intake interview. In twenty-nine families, none of the referral resources had been contacted, although some study participants said they attempted to make a connection. The remaining seventeen either connected with some or all resources until they found the help they needed.

Slightly more than one in four clients (26 percent) followed through with referrals made by NIS. No correlation was found between the seriousness or urgency of the call and the likelihood of follow-through with the referrals by any family member.

Table 1 lists the reasons study respondents gave for not following through with referrals. Table 2 lists the reasons respondents gave for not following through when they were asked to identify the single most important reason for not trying to connect with the service provider.

Follow-through was not as likely to occur (20 percent) when veterans were seeking help for their own problems. A higher rate of follow-through did occur, however, when veterans were seeking services or help for their children. In general, fathers called NIS more frequently (60.4 percent of the child-related calls) than mothers (39.5 percent). This finding is unusual when compared with information and referral services that address children's health needs: nearly 95 percent of the calls for those services come from mothers. In this population, however, it seems logical that fathers called NIS because the father was usually the veteran in the family, and this program was identified with Vietnam veterans.

Table 1. Reasons Given for Not Following Through with Referrals

Interview Question	Percent of Respondents (n=35)
Reasons clients gave for not following through with referrals:	
1. Have not had time or gotten around to it	97
2. Want money, not more promises of services	86
3. Are afraid that they will lose some entitlements they are now receiving	83
4. Don't want to deal with "them" (what is perceived as either a social system or bureaucracy)	66
5. Felt there was too much hassle to get there	29
6. Were distrustful or turned off by the grantees' affiliation	29
7. Were promised money from attorneys and still want to get "what they have coming"	26
8. Were waiting for them (the grantee) to call	26
9. Were overwhelmed by the information given by the NIS (didn't know where to start)	26
10. Couldn't make the call (cost or no telephone)	26
11. Other	14

Table 2. Single Most Important Reason for Not Following Through with Referrals

Interview Question	Percent of Respondents (n=35)
The single most important reason clients gave for not following through with referrals:	
1. Want money, not more promises of services	17
2. Are afraid that they will lose some entitlements they are now receiving	17
3. Were promised money from attorneys and still want to get "what they have coming"	14
4. Were waiting for them (the grantee) to call	14
5. Were distrustful or turned off by the grantees' affiliation	9
6. Don't want to deal with "them" (what is perceived as either a social system or bureaucracy)	9
7. Have not had time or gotten around to it yet	6
8. Couldn't make the call (cost or no telephone)	6
9. Were overwhelmed by the information given by the NIS (didn't know where to start)	6
10. Felt there was too much hassle to get there	3

When service providers were asked to assess barriers to services by identifying all possible reasons that might prevent veterans' families from obtaining needed services, the reasons they gave were families were unable to pay for services (no insurance or Medicaid); families did not think the services were necessary; and families had difficulties getting transportation to the service provider.

Conclusions and Discussion

Vietnam veterans who made successful readjustments after the war and have families without complicated health problems were not likely to call NIS. Generally, this type of service is tapped by families who have been unable to find local resources that meet their service needs or the needs of family members. The low level of follow-through observed in this study may have been a phenomenon of socioeconomics, of Vietnam veterans' families, or both.

For many veterans, the nature of the war, their ages at the time of the tour of duty, readjustment issues, and negative attitudes toward Vietnam veterans seem to have compounded feelings of isolation and unsuccessful reassimilation into society. Many veteran callers seemed discouraged and emotionally overburdened. Some expressed feelings of depression and distrust and said the Vietnam experience had a negative impact on their lives. These feelings are counterproductive to problem solving; when it was shown that even when a match was made between their service needs and a service provider, the veteran was either reluctant or failed to contact the service provider. The reluctance to self-advocate and the wide array of unique problems are primary reasons why a specialized network of veterans' family-focused services is needed.

Service providers identified the veteran's motivational issues or attitudes as barriers rather than their own organizational procedures. From their perspective, the "fault" was the veteran's; yet, there appear to be many barriers to these families. Barriers may be present, not in relation to the Vietnam veteran status but as a consequence of belonging to a variety of subgroups, such as a minority group; being a resident of a rural area or the inner city; or being from a low socioeconomic group. Some obstacles are more problematic than others, but many can be overcome. For the purpose of discussion in this paper, barriers have been categorized as follows: the veteran or family, legal, geographic, and institutional.

The Veteran or Family as an Obstacle to Getting Services

Often veterans or their families were their own obstacle in accessing needed services, even when services were being sought for a family member other than the veteran. The apparent urgency of the problem had little bearing on whether the family followed through with the referrals. Families were, however, more likely to follow through with a resource if a local grantee was involved in a service coordination capacity.

Some reasons study participants gave for not following through with referrals seemed very weak when compared with the problem(s) that prompted their calls. The one reason identified, and one that appears to have been a major contributor to their lack of action, was a belief that if they pursued the referrals, they might lose entitlements they were currently receiving. Other possible and likely reasons for non-follow-through include a lack of encouragement; competition for family time and resources from other demands that appeared more important; apathy; and rejection of perceived institutional structures.

Findings from this study prompted a review of the observations made by NIS information specialists who have interviewed more than 15,000 Vietnam veterans' family members. The purpose of this review was to identify family characteristics that might help explain why veterans sought help from NIS but then neglected to pursue the recommended avenues to solutions. From their calls, the information specialists' records indicate that most Vietnam veterans' families:

- Were already on multiple waiting lists to receive services from community service providers;
- Had been denied help by an average of more than five agencies;
- Had low-income levels and limited financial resources;
- Lived in urban inner cities or in remote rural areas;
- Were not self-advocating; and
- Did not access some of the services to which they were entitled.

Information specialists' records also revealed that many Vietnam veteran families:

- Were frustrated and angry;
- Were divorced and remarried one or more times;

- Had feelings of helplessness;
- Felt themselves to be victims;
- Believed their situations were hopeless;
- Were disenfranchised and anti-institutional; and
- Were not members of a support network for their children.

Many of the attributes identified by NIS information specialists are also characteristics of a disadvantaged population. The lack of follow-through observed in this study could be a behavioral characteristic of a disadvantaged population. Health-related laws and policies in the United States have defined "disadvantaged" in various ways, but generally, the category includes those who, by virtue of racial or ethnic heritage, economic status, or other factors, do not have access to the health care system (Simpson, 1991). This definition would, in many cases, include the veteran families who contacted NIS.

If the Vietnam veteran's family was considered to be a disadvantaged family and not thought of as a veteran's family, their lack of follow-through is not unusual. Potential clients who are depressed, unhappy with life, consider themselves victims, or have feelings of helplessness may not believe the service provider can help to improve their situation. This perception may shape the decision of whether to seek the needed care (Lia-Hoagberg, Rode, and Skovholt, 1990). Kalmuss and Fennelly (1990) found that "feeling depressed and not up to going for care" and "needing time and energy to deal with other problems" were common reasons for seeking services late or not at all.

During the telephone interviews conducted for this study, reasons for action or inaction were often revealed by the way the client responded to questions. It appeared that those who insisted on revisiting the basic cause-and-effect issue of the Agent Orange problem perceived themselves as victims and felt helpless. It seemed that they had called to take issue but never intended to follow through with referrals that might lead to solutions. Others were unable to initiate the contact with providers when there appeared to be a commitment involved. The time commitment required for parent training is one example; some veterans' families were unwilling or unable to make a time or involvement commitment.

The situations many veterans find themselves in have understandably resulted in family distress. Basically, there are two types of distress reported in the literature (See, 1991) that seem to occur in the veteran family. First, there is distress caused by actions beyond the family's ability to avoid and brought on them by forces beyond their power, such as the inability to locate or maintain employment that provides adequate medical coverage. A feeling of victimization and consequent helplessness is a result of this type of distress. Second is the behavior demonstrated while attempting to attain a goal. For example, some families seem to perpetuate their distress by dwelling on the lack of support or the absence of helping resources in the community. According to See (1991), both types of distress on the family mirror the self-defeating behavior commonly observed in disadvantaged populations. They include a variety of actions and reactions ranging from depression, sabotage of success at work and in relationships, to neglect of physical health (Curtis, 1989, p. 6).

Barriers to Vietnam veterans' families may have occurred not because of the veteran status, but because of membership in other subgroups defined by race, ethnicity, occupation, or age. A variety of statistics shows that certain minority groups, including African Americans, Hispanics, and Native Americans, not only have more frequent and more severe health problems than Caucasians or other minority groups, but they also have inadequate financial resources and limited access to helping services, in part because many providers are reluctant to locate in low-income areas. Rudeness and other disrespectful behaviors by service providers may also contribute to noncompliant behaviors by members of minority groups (Haan and Kaplan, 1985) and to subsequent reluctance to follow through with seeking additional services.

Language differences can also present a barrier by preventing or limiting a family's understanding of services, particularly complex ones such as special-education procedures. Being unable to speak or read English proficiently frequently results in an inadequate transfer of information and increases the likelihood the family will have difficulty accessing a service. Hispanics often have found their access to Medicaid impeded by forms that have not been translated into Spanish or the absence of staff to help Spanish-speaking family members (National Coalition, 1990).

Veterans' families with strong ties to less familiar cultures, which includes some Native Americans and Hispanics, may find the services system alien. This can be a particular problem in the area of disability services that are unrelated to an episode of an acute illness or injury. Individuals from different cultures may place different values or timeframes on seeking assistance. As an example, some cultures believe that pregnant women need not be examined until after "quickening," the time when fetal movement can be felt. Some women may be reluctant or unwilling to seek reproductive health services from male providers. Others may prefer to seek services from healers that are customary to their culture (Institute of Medicine, 1988). Health status indicators suggest that, in many ways, the health of Native American women and children is worse than that of other Americans. Native American women generally receive fewer adequate services, and adolescents use fewer preventive health services (Blum, Harmon, and Harris, 1992). Health problems and underutilization of health services are probably attributable to many factors including poverty; racism; long travel times to service facilities in some areas where Native Americans live; inadequate information about the need for service; reliance on native healers; and abuse of certain substances, especially alcohol.

Veterans who change jobs frequently and subsequently become homeless have problems similar to those of migrant workers who have higher rates of health problems than other workers and face significant obstacles obtaining helping services (Rust, 1990). These obstacles include financial barriers—Medicaid status varies from state to state; incomes that are usually too low to purchase helping services out of pocket; discrimination; a work schedule that precludes seeking help during the day or on weekends; lack of familiarity with the service facilities in the different communities through which they travel; occasional language problems; and in some areas, long distances to facilities and an absence of public transportation.

All children, but particularly ones with disabilities, whether in parental homes, foster care, or institutions, depend on adults for services. School clinics are probably the only places where young children can ask for help until they reach an age at which they can initiate their requests for services. For children, this dependent age is in itself a barrier. Although adolescents are capable of seeking or initiating requests for services, costs, legal restrictions, and lack of transportation often prevent them from doing so (Zabin, Stark, and Emerson, 1991).

An additional problem faced by adolescents with disabilities is their in-between status with medical providers. Few adolescents feel comfortable in the offices of pediatricians because most of the other patients are infants or young children. One survey of suburban general pediatricians reported by Marks and others (1990) found that many were ambivalent about treating adolescents, citing problems with payment, time, lack of knowledge about adolescent health, and the adolescents' perception of them as "baby doctors" as reasons for their ambivalence. Few provided anticipatory guidance about sexuality; questioned adolescents about depression, incest, or child abuse; or had the equipment required for a gynecological examination (Marks, Fisher, and Lasker, 1990).

Legal Barriers

Many laws and regulations create barriers to obtaining services. Among the ones that have the greatest impact on veterans' families are regulations requiring frequent eligibility recertification for programs such as Medicaid and the Special Supplemental Food Program for Women, Infants, and Children (WIC). Additionally, mandated eligibility criteria often leave many cracks in the service system.

Even when only some family members receive financial entitlements, the resources often count as family income and thus, disqualify the family for other services. Many government-supported programs should consider the current costs for caring for persons with disabilities and factor those costs into qualification criteria. The current situation encourages dishonesty in income reporting. Moreover, when a family is disqualified, the family member with the disability is often blamed for the loss of benefits or assistance that could have helped the whole family (Klerman, 1992).

Geographic Barriers

Geographic barriers include those that result from inadequate numbers of providers relative to the population in a specific area and large distances between clients and providers in rural or nonmetropolitan areas. Many veterans live in inner cities or in rural areas where specialized medical services for a child with a disability may require traveling long distances. Rural areas are also typically populated by lower-income families who often have no health insurance. Rural states have more restrictive Aid to Families with Dependent Children (AFDC) programs and are less likely to adopt Medicaid eligibility and service options (Children's Defense Fund, 1991).

Specialists may not be accessible by public transportation, making automobile ownership or the ability to borrow a vehicle almost essential. Although city residents may find that inadequate or inaccessible public transportation is a barrier, travel-related problems are most frequently associated with rural areas. According to federal surveys, children in non-metropolitan areas are less likely to see a physician, and families in such areas are less likely to initiate prenatal services in the first trimester than those in metropolitan areas (McManus and Newacheck, 1989).

Despite the numbers of family and general practice physicians in this country, many veteran families, like other families, are faced with a shortage of providers where they live because these service providers are not distributed evenly in relation to the population that needs their services. This can be seen in the high concentration of physicians in metropolitan counties and a scarcity, or absence, of practitioners in many rural areas. In addition, within metropolitan areas, providers in private practice tend to concentrate in higher-income neighborhoods which may impose a travel burden on substantial populations of veterans' families living in rural areas or in poorer neighborhoods.

The number of Vietnam veterans who are homeless is estimated to be approximately 50,000 on any given night: one in ten of these homeless veterans are with their families (National Coalition for the Homeless, 1993). Homelessness is usually defined as having no permanent home, living in a temporary dwelling, in a shelter, or with another family. Mihaly (1991) estimates the number of American children who are homeless on any given night is between 60,000 and 500,000. The literature did not show how many of these children are veterans' children, but studies have found that homeless families receive less care than other poor families and homeless children have lower rates of immunization and increased rates of hospital admission, both suggesting problems with obtaining primary health care (Miller and Lin, 1988). Homeless families are also less likely to receive benefits under the WIC program.

Being without a permanent home is associated with several specific access barriers. Temporary housing and emergency shelters are frequently located in inner-city areas where the likelihood of coming in contact with violence and drugs is high. The depression and despair characteristic of homeless families compound anxiety about these problems. Also, homeless families may have been relocated from the areas in which they normally sought services and have little information about sources of helping services in unfamiliar areas (Wood, Valdez, Hayashi, and Shen, 1990).

Institutional Barriers

Institutional barriers include the policies, practices, and attitudes of persons who represent institutions such as hospitals and health centers as well as providers in private practice. Although some providers complain that veterans do not seek help, the reality is that too often they are not able to obtain it. Such providers are "blaming the victim" when the culprit may be the institution itself or another factor that the providers may control but not recognize.

Explicit provider policies, such as a refusal to accept Medicaid or to use a sliding fee schedule, often create obstacles to obtaining services. Policies of health maintenance organizations (HMOs), preferred provider organizations, and other programs of managed health care can impede access to services, despite the absence of financial disincentives. Studies have found that these programs may limit or even deny referrals to subspecialists or inpatient services; that in comparison with indemnity insurance plans, they may cover, without deductibles and copayments, fewer services needed by children with chronic illnesses, such as prescriptions, durable medical equipment, and mental health services. Additionally, they may ignore the benefits to which enrolled Medicaid children are entitled, especially the Early and Periodic Screening, Diagnosis, and Treatment (EPSDT) program (Rosenbaum, Hughes, Butler, and Howard, 1988). These barriers may result in substandard services, in delays in obtaining needed services, or in no help at all.

Many provider-imposed barriers are not based on explicit or intentional policies. Instead, they are the result of patterns of practice that have been adopted over the years, frequently with little attention to the impact they have on access. Service providers seldom recognize how difficult it may be for clients even to make an appointment, an initiative that most providers would consider simple. In reality, the provider may have insufficient telephone lines or staff to answer incoming calls. Parents report hearing a continual busy signal or having telephones ring for several minutes before being answered. Even if the telephone is answered promptly, the caller may be put on hold for extended periods. For an individual calling from home, these are minor annoyances, but they can be major barriers for someone trying to make a private call from work or from a public telephone. If the distance to the provider requires a long distance call, the problems are even greater, limiting the ability of the lowest-income families even to make the initial contact. Electronic-call routing systems can also present a barrier to persons who are unfamiliar with them. It can be difficult for the caller to know which option to choose when given many choices. Being transferred from one person to another is also potentially frustrating and may result in the caller abandoning the attempt. If, in the process of being transferred, the call is disconnected, the caller must begin the process all over again. The likelihood of follow-through diminishes if the first call was long distance or if the whole process was too lengthy or frustrating for the caller.

A long delay between making an appointment and being seen may also discourage help-seeking activities. The family member(s) who must take time from work or who are accompanied by small children and who experience a long wait at the time of the appointment may be less likely to return (Klerman, 1992). There are important nonmedical services that, when absent, may discourage use of medical services. These include on-site child care, bilingual staff, and assistance with transportation (Institute of Medicine, 1988).

The attitudes of service providers and their staffs, including technicians, receptionists, and others, can have a profound effect on a family's willingness to seek help. Negative attitudes toward Vietnam veterans can be detected in the way families are treated by service providers. Disrespect for economically disadvantaged clients or for those from racial or ethnic minority groups can be shown by calling them by their first names without asking their preference or by keeping them waiting for long periods. Leaving inadequate time to answer clients' questions and a generally hurried and hassled atmosphere also convey negative provider attitudes.

Recommendations

Family-related problems are compounded when the most severely affected families live within communities that have a multiplicity of problems: substandard schools; unsafe, deteriorating neighborhoods; isolation from services; and a pervasive drug culture and related violence. The study reported in this paper suggests that the ability of a family to overcome any of these is often seriously compromised or blocked outright by the inability to gain access to needed services in a coordinated and continuous fashion.

The efficacy of recognizing the family as the primary unit for service was verified in this study. When a veteran's family needed help and received some form of assistance or case management from a grantee, the family was more likely to follow through with recommended referrals than was a veteran's family not helped by a local grantee. The recommendations from this study include maintaining the family-focused approach to services and taking necessary actions to reduce a lack of follow-through in seeking needed services. It is particularly critical when the person who needs services is a child who must depend on other family members to take action to obtain those services. Many grantees were able to overcome this through their service coordination or case management strategies. When a grantee who had received a referral from the NIS initiated and contacted the veteran's family, there was a high likelihood of follow-through. Too many problems of the veteran impact the family, and too many problems of the family impact the veteran for there to be two totally separate systems of care, i.e., the VA for the veteran and public or private providers for other family members.

Geographic problems can be reduced by encouraging service providers to use telephone access through toll-free numbers and to establish offices in underserved areas. The federal government attempts to overcome personnel shortages in medical services by funding the National Health Service Corps as well as community and migrant health centers and special programs for the homeless. Sometimes, however, an isolated area may not have enough individuals to support a clinician in private practice or a clinic. In those instances, traveling teams of service providers or specialists, sometimes with specially equipped mobile vans, may be able to reduce some obstacles. When the absence of public transportation is the main barrier, something as simple as agency vans or taxi vouchers may be the answer (Redlener and Burke, 1992). Some grantees used vans successfully to provide direct services to families or to transport families to needed services.

Publicly supported service programs should decide whether services are best provided at a centralized site. Veterans' families in need of services might best be served in minimally equipped, community-based operations or even in their homes. The centralized and better-equipped facilities have obvious merits but could be reserved for those in need of specialists or laboratory and other services.

The process of changing provider policies, practices, and attitudes is very difficult, but it can be accomplished. There is a need to determine through systematic review what, or who, is making clients less eager to see the provider or to follow through with recommendations. Accompanying a veteran, particularly a first-time client, through a visit also may yield fresh insights as well as increase the likelihood of follow-through by the veteran's family.

Some grantees, including NIS, found that several forms of outreach succeeded in increasing the level of awareness or changing beliefs and attitudes of families. In many communities, veterans call local or regional information and referral systems to learn where and how they can obtain services. Local grantees are not only able to convey this type of information but also may provide the social support needed to increase the number of follow-throughs.

It is more effective to serve clients within the framework of their cultural beliefs than to try to change or ignore those beliefs. Providers should discuss cultural beliefs and, unless their practices would have an adverse impact, work with them to provide services that incorporate cultural differences. For example, in some cultures, when it comes to home care, actions that need to be taken by family members must be communicated through the maternal grandmother, or they will not get done.

State governments have several ways of reducing barriers. They regulate Medicaid and private health insurance within broad federal mandates, and with federal assistance, they fund or operate family planning clinics and other public facilities. Through these activities, states can establish minimum standards regarding what services are provided, where they are provided, and by whom. States also operate foster care programs, veterans' service programs, and programs for persons with disabilities. In several states, court orders were needed to ensure that veterans' children received the helping services to which they are entitled, suggesting obvious room for improvement in the delivery of these services.

Professional organizations should inform their members about the barriers that they, or the facilities in which they are employed, may be imposing, however unintentionally. Advocacy groups, particularly the Protection and Advocacy Programs for Persons With Developmental Disabilities, should keep the need for broad-based commitment to barrier reduction before legislators, professionals, and the public.

While financial barriers remain some of the most formidable obstacles, many other factors play an undeniably significant role. Removing barriers to services for the Vietnam veteran's family starts with recognizing that these obstacles exist. It is recommended that the obstacles identified in this paper be studied and a strategy developed so that action can be taken to reduce or eliminate barriers to services for Vietnam veterans and their families.

References

Blum, R.W., B. Harmon, and L. Harris. 1992. American Indian–Alaska Native youth health. *Journal of the American Medical Association* 267:1637-1644.

Children's Defense Fund. 1991. *Falling by the Wayside: Children in Rural America.* Washington, DC.

Curtis, R.C., ed. 1989. *Self-Defeating Behaviors: Experimental Research, Clinical Impressions, and Practical Implications*. New York: Plenum Press.

Haan, M., and G. Kaplan. 1985. Socioeconomic position and minority health: A summary of the evidence. In *Report of the Secretary's Task Force on Black and Minority Health.* U.S. Department of Health and Human Services, Task Force on Black and Minority Health. Washington, DC: U.S. Government Printing Office.

Institute of Medicine. 1988. *Care: Reaching Mothers, Reaching Infants,* ed. S.S. Brown. Washington, DC: National Academy Press.

Kalmuss, D., and K. Fennelly. 1990. Barriers to care among low-income women in New York City. *Family Planning Perspectives* 22:215-231.

Klerman, L.V. 1992. Non-financial barriers to the receipt of medical care. *The Future of Children* 2:177-178.

Lia-Hoagberg, B., P. Rode, and C.J. Skovholt. 1990. Barriers and motivators to care among low-income women. *Social Science and Medicine* 30:487-495.

Marks, A., M. Fisher, and S. Lasker. 1990. Adolescent medicine in pediatric practice. *Journal of Adolescent Health Care* 11:149-153.

McManus, M., and P. Newacheck. 1989. Rural maternal, child, and adolescent health. *Health Service's Research* 23:807-808.

Mihaly, L. 1991. *Homeless families: Failed policies and young victims*. Washington, DC: Children's Defense Fund.

Miller, D.S., and E.H.B. Lin. 1988. Children in sheltered homeless families: Reported health status and use of health services. *Pediatrics* 81:66-73.

National Coalition of Hispanic Health and Human Services Organizations. 1990. *And access for all: Medicaid and Hispanics*. Washington, DC: National Coalition of Hispanic Health and Human Services Organizations.

National Coalition for Homeless. 1993. Data supplied from Fact Sheet number 1, "Homeless Veterans." Washington, DC: National Coalition for Homeless.

Redlener, I., and K. Burke. 1992. Children's health project update. *Pediatrics* 89:801 (letter to the editor).

Rosenbaum, S., D.C. Hughes, E. Butler, and D. Howard. 1988. Incantations in the dark: Medicaid, managed care and maternity care. *The Milbank Quarterly* 66:661-693.

Rust, G.S. 1990. Health status of migrant farm workers: A literature review and commentary. *American Journal of Public Health* 80:117-121.

See, K.O. 1991. Comments from the special issue editor: Approaching poverty in the United States. *Social Problems* 38(4):427-432.

Simpson, C.E. 1991. *Health Status of Minorities and Low-income Groups.*, 3d ed. U.S. Department of Health and Human Services, Public Health Service, Health Resources and Services Administration, Bureau of Health Professions, Division of Disadvantaged Assistance.

Wood, D.L., R.B. Valdez, T. Hayashi, and A. Shen. 1990. Health of homeless children and housed, poor children. *Pediatrics* 86:85-86.

Zabin, L.S., H.A. Stark, and M.R. Emerson. 1991. Reasons for delay in contraceptive clinic utilization: Adolescent clinic and non-clinic populations compared. *Journal of Adolescent Health* 12:225-232.

Lingering Consequences of the Vietnam War: Veterans' Families with Children with Disabilities or Chronic Illnesses

Bryan C. Smith, Ed.D.; Kathy L. Mayfield-Smith, M.A., M.B.A.; and Dawn Sudduth, M.Ed.

National Information System for Vietnam Veterans and Their Families
Center for Developmental Disabilities
Department of Pediatrics
School of Medicine
The University of South Carolina
Columbia, SC

Abstract

How well does the traditional service delivery system meet the needs of Vietnam veterans and their families? The National Information System for Vietnam Veterans and Their Families (NIS) has amassed data on approximately 15,759 Vietnam veterans and their family members who contacted this organization for help in accessing services for themselves or for their children with disabilities.

The data indicated that these veterans showed patterns of disability and chronic illness, social problems, and poverty that seem unparalleled in comparison with other families. Veterans' families appear to face additional disadvantages in the form of isolation, economic deprivation, and lack of access to adequate services. The veterans' own disabling conditions placed additional strains on family structures.

As an alternative to the fragmented traditional service delivery system, compelling evidence exists that a service integration strategy offers a promising possibility worthy of careful and thorough exploration in the future. The Agent Orange Class Assistance Program (AOCAP) represents a change agent dedicated to developing a system based on the integration strategy.

Bryan C. Smith, Ed.D., *is a research associate professor for the Department of Pediatrics of the University of South Carolina's School of Medicine, Columbia, SC.* ***Kathy L. Mayfield-Smith, M.A., M.B.A.,*** *is a research assistant professor and the project director of the National Clearinghouse for Infants and Children with Disabilities and Life Threatening Conditions. These authors and* ***Dawn Sudduth, M.Ed.,*** *are the administrative team that leads the National Information System for Vietnam Veterans and Their Families, which is part of the department's Center for Developmental Disabilities.*

A bitter legacy of the Vietnam war has been the decades of concern over the health effects of Agent Orange and other herbicides used in Vietnam between 1961 and 1972. Many of the nearly 3 million Americans who served in or near Vietnam have come to suspect that their wartime exposure to these chemicals caused them, or their children, to develop serious health problems. This issue remains shrouded in controversy and mistrust, and is a source of great anguish for many veterans and their families.

This paper looks at three types of consequences of this controversy: tangible outcomes that have shown up in an analysis of the records of the people who have called the National Information System (NIS), a national information and referral system; some programmatic effects that have been positive and have produced some subtle, but monumental, results; and desirable goals of future actions.

Tangible Consequences

The National Information System is designed to connect families with children with disabilities who need services or information to the community resources that can provide them. The NIS is a part of the South Carolina University Affiliated Program that is currently funded by the Agent Orange Class Assistance Program (AOCAP). It began ten years ago as a federally funded demonstration project and since then it has concentrated efforts on three separate populations. The latest, and possibly the most challenging, has been families who believe they may have been affected by a veteran's exposure to Agent Orange during military service in Vietnam. The primary goals of the NIS are to establish mechanisms by which effective communication and information sharing can occur, and to serve in a problem-solving capacity for veterans and their families.

The staff of the NIS has helped families who have children with disabilities for more than fourteen years, and started working with Vietnam veterans' families in 1989. As their involvement with veterans' families progressed, NIS staff began to realize that they were trying to help a group of people decidedly different from those they had helped before, and they were amassing data that would clearly portray some of these differences.

NIS staff collected data from 15,759 client callers who were either veterans or family members seeking services for themselves or for their children with disabilities. Consequently, any conclusions from the NIS data can only be implied to the group being helped by the NIS, not to all Vietnam veterans or their family members. Therefore, the statistics used in this paper are descriptive, presenting what has been observed over the five years of this project.

One of the NIS staff's first observations was that many disabilities and severe chronic health conditions appeared to occur more frequently in these Vietnam veterans' families than in the general population. Autism, as one example, occurred in approximately 1.5 percent of the children served by the NIS, a rate that appears at first to be thirty times higher than the .05 percent prevalence experienced nationally by the general population (Thoene, 1992). Incidence and prevalence statistics require an accurate count of the number of people with a condition as well as an accurate tally of the persons who constitute the subpopulation to which the person with the condition belongs. Because neither the number of veterans' children who have autism nor the number of children in this subpopulation is known, incidence and prevalence data cannot be calculated. The basic error in the comparison of the NIS rate with the prevalence in the general population is that the 1.5 percent is a different statistic from the .05

percent, and the two cannot be compared. Even though the NIS data have such limitations, some other ways exist to get a sense of the data's unique character and meaning. For example, the data could be compared with data from another group of the general population who were also seeking help from the same kind of service system. This type of comparison can only produce an indicator of a difference and should not be interpreted as incidence or prevalence data that apply to the larger population of Vietnam veterans' families.

Before their involvement with Vietnam veterans' families, the NIS had operated other national information and referral programs. The one most comparable was the National Information System for Health Related Services (HRS) which served families with children from birth to age twenty-one who had disabilities and special health care needs. NIS staff collected data on the same forms and used the same interview techniques. Although some similarities appeared between the families and children in these two groups, differences and unique characteristics were readily apparent among Vietnam veterans' families.

The magnitude of these differences was not slight. In each characteristic cited, the other population (HRS users) had a very small number or rate. For example, almost all (nonveteran) families contacting the HRS to seek services had only *one* child with *one* disability. In contrast, 29.4 percent of the Vietnam veterans' families contacting the NIS to obtain services had more than one child with a disability, and 54.7 percent of the children with disabilities had multiple disabilities.

The NIS data reveal several unique characteristics in Vietnam veterans' families, some of which have corroborated the findings reported in the *1988 National Vietnam Veterans Readjustment Study* (NVVRS), which examined the health status of Vietnam veterans (Kulka et al., 1988). Some self-reported characteristics are:

- Of the veterans' children, 54.7 percent had multiple disabilities with an average of 2.9 conditions per child.
- Of the families, 29.4 percent had more than one child with disabilities. It was not uncommon for a veteran to have as many as six or seven children, all having disabling conditions.
- Most Vietnam veteran parents of a child with disabilities also had disabilities, usually service-connected.
- More than 40 percent were divorced (NVVRS, 1988) and in many remarriages, children in the new family also had disabilities.
- Occasionally, a veteran reported one or more children without disabilities born before the parent served in Vietnam and one or more children with disabilities born after the tour of duty.

Table 1 presents a categorical grouping of the frequency of more than 930 different diagnostic entities that callers reported to the NIS. This table shows the rates of reported conditions grouped into categories that reflect the expanded version of Medical Subject Headings (MeSH) created by the National Library of Medicine. All conditions falling under these categories have been grouped according to this taxonomy. In Table 1, the clients were placed in one of three groups based on their relationship to a veteran, i.e., a veteran's child (child by relationship, not age), the veteran, or a significant other, and tallied according to the condition(s) reported. A person with multiple conditions was tallied under each condition heading.

Collectively, the most common conditions fell into the skin abnormalities, learning disabilities, and immune deficiencies categories. The most common children's conditions were: birth defects (18.1 percent of the children who needed help from the NIS had conditions in this category); learning disabilities (17.6 percent), skin abnormalities (12.3 percent), immune deficiencies (12.0 percent), and asthma (7.8 percent).

Table 1. Rates of Conditions Categorically Grouped* by Relationship to a Veteran (n = 15,759)

	Rate per 100 Clients				
Condition	Child (n=10,845)	Veteran (n=4,656)	Significant Other (n=258)	Total Rate	n
Skin abnormalities	12.3	22.9	8.6	17.9	2,823
Learning disabilities	17.6	.5	.6	16.0	2,526
Immune deficiencies	12.0	5.3	8.7	13.5	2,128
Psychiatric/psychological	2.4	35.4	17.3	13.5	2,126
Birth defects	18.1	0	0	12.5	1,970
Asthma	7.8	1.4	3.3	6.9	1,094
Vision disorders	4.5	3.0	1.3	4.4	688
Attention deficit disorder	6.3	.2	0	4.4	687
Hearing disorders	3.1	4.4	3.3	3.9	620
Seizure disorders	3.3	2.0	3.3	3.6	568
Behavioral disorders	3.4	.2	0	3.3	519
Cancer	1.2	7.3	8.2	3.2	509
Mental retardation	2.9	.1	0	3.2	507
Speech disorders	4.0	.2	0	3.1	492
Neoplasms	1.8	3.5	4.7	3.0	470
Orthopedic disabilities	2.1	2.1	.7	2.9	452
Pregnancy outcomes	1.1	.6	7.3	2.3	365
Thyroid disorders	.3	.5	.7	2.1	327
Spinal disorders	1.7	.6	0	2.1	324
Heart disorders	1.0	3.9	8.0	1.9	298
Wounds/injuries	0	3.7	.7	1.7	260
Dental disorders	1.2	.6	.7	1.6	259
Cerebral palsy	1.8	0	0	1.6	255
Respiratory disorders	1.3	.8	0	1.5	233

* Categories were selected on the criteria of having a total rate above 1.4 per 100 clients.

When a veteran, rather than another family member, was the client, the most common categories of conditions that they reported were psychiatric and psychological disorders (35.4 percent), skin abnormalities (22.9 percent), and cancer (7.3 percent). More than 30 percent (30.1 percent) of the veteran clients were seeking services to address some aspect of their post-traumatic stress disorder (PTSD). The most common category for significant others was also the psychiatric and psychological disorders category (17.3 percent); immune deficiencies (8.7 percent) and skin abnormalities (8.6 percent) were second and third in ranking.

Table 2 lists the self-reported diagnosed rare conditions that went into some of the categories shown in Table 1. (Each condition was identified as rare by Thoene (1992), who defined a rare condition as one that affects fewer than 200,000 Americans.) There were 849 clients who reported that a family member had one of the 181 rare conditions that are alphabetically listed in Table 2.

The data related to service needs really reflect the callers' unmet needs, not their total needs. For example, if a child with attention deficit disorder needed special education services and was receiving such services at the time of the call, no referrals would have been made related to special education and, consequently, this service need would not be identified in the data. Table 3 gives the rates of services needed per 1,000 children, organized by broad grouping of service categories and listed by age groups. The greatest need was for services grouped under the medical services category. This grouping included cancer treatment, dental care,

Table 2. Rare Conditions and Their Frequency Identified from 15,759 NIS Clients, Self-Reported as Diagnosed (n = 849)

Condition	Number	Condition	Number
Aberfeld syndrome	1	Glomerulonephritis	2
Actinomycosis	1	Goodpasture syndrome	2
Adenocarcinoma	1	Goldenhar syndrome	6
Adnexitis	2	Graves disease (hyperthyroidism)	7
Alport syndrome	1	Guillain-Barre syndrome	6
Alpha I antitrypsin deficiency	2	Hallermann-Streiff syndrome	2
Angel syndrome	1	Hand-Schuller-Christian syndrome	1
Anosmia	2	Hirschsprung's disease	4
Aortic stenosis	3	Histiocytosis	2
Aortic valve insufficiency	3	Hodgkin's disease	25
Apert syndrome	1	Holoprosencephaly	1
Apnea	17	Huntington disease	1
Ataxia telangiectasia	1	Hygroma	1
Atelectasis	1	Hypercapnia	1
Autism	114	Hyperhidrosis	2
Bartter's disease	1	Hypoparathyroidism	1
Basal cell carcinoma	2	Idiopathic thrombocytohemia	1
Beckwith-Wiedemann syndrome	1	Ileal disease	1
Berylliosis	1	Joubert syndrome	1
Bistinidase deficiency	2	Kawasaki syndrome	2
Bladder exstrophy	1	Keratoconus	1
Bloch-Sulzberger syndrome	1	Klinefelter syndrome	3
Bowen disease	2	Klippel-Feil syndrome	2
Bronchogenic carcinoma	1	Kyphosis	1
Cafe au lait spots	1	Landau-Kleffner syndrome	1
Cat Eye syndrome	1	Larsen syndrome	1
Charcot-Marie Tooth disease	2	Legg-Calve-Perthes syndrome	7
CHARGE association	4	Lennox-Gastaut syndrome	1
Chyloperitoneum	1	Lesch-Nyhan syndrome	3
Coloboma	4	Letterer-Siwe disease	1
Cornelia de lange syndrome	3	Leukocytosis	2
Cri-du-chat syndrome	2	Leukopenia	1
Crouzon disease	6	Levers disease	4
Cushing syndrome	1	Lordosis	2
Dandy-Walker syndrome	2	Lymphosarcoma	1
Delaney syndrome	1	Maple syrup urine disease	7
Dermatomyositis	1	Marchiafava-Micheli syndrome	1
DiGeorge syndrome	3	Marcus Gunn's syndrome	1
Donohue syndrome	1	Marfan syndrome	8
Duane syndrome	1	Meniere disease	4
Dysautonomia, familial	1	Meningioma	4
Echolalia	1	Mobius syndrome	2
Ehlers-Danlos syndrome	2	Molluscum contagiosum virus	1
Elephantiasis	1	Morphea	1
Encephalocele	2	Moyamoya disease	4
Epidermolysis bullosa	2	Mucolipidosis	1
Epistaxis	39	Mucopolysaccharidosis	1
Erb Palsy	3	Multiple myeloma	3
Erythema, multiforme	1	Multiple sclerosis	23
Fetal alcohol syndrome	6	Munchausen syndrome	1
Fragile X syndrome	3	Myositis	2
Friedrich ataxia	5	Narcolepsy	8
Gangliosidosis	1	Nephrotic syndrome	3
Gigantism	1	Neutropenia	3

Table 2. Continued.

Condition	Number	Condition	Number
Non-Hodgkin's lymphoma	65	Sjogren's syndrome	1
Nonne syndrome	1	Soft-tissue sarcoma	45
Noonan syndrome	13	Sotos syndrome	3
Oculocerebrorenal dystrophy	3	Spherocytosis, hereditary	1
Oculodentodigital syndrome	2	Spondylitis, ankylosing	1
Opitz-Frias syndrome	4	Squamous cell carcinoma	2
Osgood-Schlatter disease	1	Stevens-Johnson syndrome	1
Osteitis	2	Sturge-Weber syndrome	2
Osteogenesis imperfecta	13	Sutton disease II	1
Osteopetosis	1	Synovioma	3
Paracoccidioidomycosis	14	Takayasu syndrome	2
Pelger-Huet anomaly	1	Tetracarcinoma	1
Pierre Robin syndrome	6	Thalassemia	3
Poland syndrome	3	Thrombocytopenia	7
Porphyria cutanea tarda	15	Thrombotic thrombocytopenia	1
Prader-Willi syndrome	9	Tietze's syndrome	1
Premotor cortex syndrome	1	Tinnitus	15
Proteus syndrome	1	Torticollis	2
Prune belly syndrome	2	Tourette syndrome	37
Purpura	3	Transverse myelitis	1
Pyelonephritis	1	Treacher-Collins syndrome	3
Pyloric stenosis	2	Trisomies	9
Raynaud's disease	5	Tuberculosis	10
Reflex sympathetic dystrophy syndrome	1	Tuberous sclerosis	9
Reiter's syndrome	1	Turner syndrome	13
Retinitis pigmentosa	3	Urethrophydronephrosis	1
Retinoblastoma	2	Usher syndrome	1
Rett syndrome	4	Vitiligo	16
Reye syndrome	1	Weaver's syndrome	1
Rhabdomyosarcoma	1	Weber Gubler syndrome	1
Romberg syndrome	1	Werdnig-Hoffmann disease	2
Rosacea	1	West syndrome	3
Sarcoidosis	6	William syndrome	2
Schamberg's disease	1	Wilms tumor	7
Schirmer's syndrome	1	Wilson disease	1
Shy-Drager syndrome	1	Wolff-Parkinson-White syndrome	1
Siderosis	1		
Silverskiold's syndrome	1		

dermatology services, immunotherapy, orthopedic care, respiratory therapy, and forty other subcategories. The next greatest need for the birth-to-five and six-to-ten age groups was for diagnosis and evaluation. The large numbers of children with learning disabilities, skin abnormalities, birth defects, and immune deficiencies account for this service need, which includes thirty-two subcategories of services. The second largest need of the eleven-to-fifteen and sixteen-to-twenty age groups was for special needs recreation.

Table 3 shows a high rate of services needed for children under the age of ten. The number of children in this age group contradicts a logical assumption that most Vietnam veterans' children are now young adults. The veterans' average age was approximately forty-eight years, but, like many middle-aged Americans, they are still having children. The average age of veterans' children helped by the NIS at the time of their initial contact was 14.2 years, with the actual ages ranging from birth to twenty-nine years. The average ages of the children

Table 3. **Services Needed According to Broad Grouping of Service Categories by Age of Veterans' Children (n = 6,851)**

	Rates per 1,000 According to Age Groups					
Service Need	0-5 (n=586)	6-10 (n=1,177)	11-15 (n=2,165)	16-20 (n=2,505)	20+ (n=418)	Total
Medical services	37.54	38.23	24.02	9.18	2.39	20.87
Special needs recreation	0	3.4	5.08	1.20	0	2.63
Diagnosis/evaluation	5.12	3.40	1.39	.40	0	1.61
Specialized equipment	1.71	3.4	.46	0	0	.88
Counseling	0	0	1.39	.80	0	.73
Financial assistance	0	2.55	.46	0	0	.58
Surgery	0	.85	.92	.40	0	.58
Support	0	1.70	.92	0	0	.58
Rehabilitation	1.17	.85	.92	0	0	.58
Education	0	.85	.46	0	0	.29
Psychological/psychiatric	0	0	.46	0	0	.15
Vocational rehabilitation	0	0	.46	0	0	.15

served in each of the five consecutive years rose by an average of 9.5 months annually. This average did not increase one year as one year lapsed because of the number of newborns that entered the population. Even more significant, these younger children had problems that caused one of their parents to initiate a search for help. The birth-to-five age group was 5.5 percent of all children helped by the NIS. Many of these very young children have disabilities and service needs that caused the family member to contact the NIS for help. Of the families calling the NIS, the average number of services needed per child was 4.4. The average number of referrals made to meet those service needs was 2.2 per child.

The data related to services needed by all callers, including veterans and significant others seeking help, show that the most frequently needed service was for client support services, such as support groups (92.8 percent). NIS staff made almost as many referrals (13,026) for support services as there were clients (15,759) (82.6 percent). Some referred clients needed more than one of the twenty-eight types of support services, including advocacy (13.8 percent). Next to support services, the greatest service need was for financial assistance services (79.7 percent), primarily to help pay medical bills (32.0 percent of those needing financial assistance), including both outstanding and future bills; followed by medical diagnosis and evaluation services (29.3 percent); and counseling, including psychiatric counseling (27.7 percent).

Discussion

The widespread assumption that veterans and their family members are cared for by the veterans' service system (primarily the programs run by the U.S. Department of Veterans Affairs) limits their inclusion in service planning and delivery from other human service systems. An obvious goal for further study is to determine the extent to which the conditions and service needs presented in this paper are a product of the fact of being a veteran or arise from socioeconomics or other related causes. The authors acknowledge that many of the characteristics identified are characteristics of low socioeconomic status and are probably a product of the combination of both. Kulka et al. (1988), as well as others (Bullman, Kang, and Thomas, 1991) have concluded that the nature of the war, the age of veterans during their service, readjustment issues, and the unpopular attitudes at home toward the war, appear to have compounded feelings in many Vietnam veterans of isolation and inability to reassimilate into society. Many veterans have feelings of depression and distrust and are leading lives that have been negatively affected by their Vietnam experience. Many veterans chose not to receive treatment for psychological disorders because of their anti-bureaucratic or institution-phobic feelings. This avoidance of institutional systems is reflected in part by the rate of veterans calling the NIS for help with their own problems. For example, 30.1 percent of them were seeking help for PTSD, a condition for which treatment is generally available through the existing veterans' service system.

That said, veterans' families encounter the usual issues that all families face in raising their children and, like any family with a child who has a disability, they have the additional challenge of dealing with their children's special needs. These needs may include solving the financial burdens of medical care, finding special equipment, learning about the child's condition and what the child needs, and identifying services to meet those needs. Problems for Vietnam veterans become even more complex than those of other parents because of the difficulty the veterans' service system has in addressing family health problems.

The families experienced conditions ranging from mild to severe, but generally families contacted the NIS when they perceived the problem to be beyond their ability to solve. Skin rashes and irregular immunological responses were commonly reported conditions that sound minor in comparison with many other acute or chronic diseases. But in this population, they are often very serious, even disabling, occurring in many family members and persisting for many years. Many veterans reported that their children were never without the conditions and that they could not find effective treatment.

A tally of the conditions and service needs described in this paper does not capture the toll that has been taken on families or how they have had to cope with the difficulties of PTSD; of children with complex health problems; of communities that rejected the Vietnam War veteran; and of bureaucratic barriers that limit help in some systems. Because of the interaction of these forces, the AOCAP network has responded to the challenges not of veterans or their children, but of their families. It is the family, whether or not the veteran remains a part of it, that has been seriously affected. It is the family that the NIS network strives to empower with information to help them meet the health needs of their children, both now and for years to come.

The complexity of the problems of Vietnam veterans' families is self-evident. The NIS caller is often in a family that is struggling with the debilitating consequences of primary and secondary PTSD. There may be two or three children with different types of disabilities who are medically underserved, emotionally overburdened, and living in an isolated rural area or an inner-city neighborhood that presents its own risk factors. Failure to address all dimensions of these problems may well result in diminished life opportunities and outcomes that could produce a generational consequence.

Callers identified patterns of disability and chronic illness, social problems, and poverty that seem unparalleled in comparison with other families helped by the NIS. The combination of the many and varied conditions, service needs, and the social milieu in which these families find themselves appears to be quite different from those who had used the HRS. In addition, the veterans' own disabling conditions seem to place strains on family structures that are decidedly severe, forcing the family to face isolation, economic deprivation, and the lack of access to adequate services. The data suggest that the frequency, diversity, and complexity of the conditions of Vietnam veterans' families who used the NIS appear to make them a unique group that deserves closer scientific scrutiny.

The data imply that Vietnam veterans' problems are problems of the whole family, and their resolution usually involves the whole family. Economic and interpersonal factors have often seriously eroded the integrity and functioning of the family. Goodwyn (1990) reported that Vietnam veterans who are married or living with a partner often demonstrate strained relations within the family unit. Their interpersonal conflicts are often manifested in domestic violence, psychological symptoms, indices of depression, political alienation, and adjustment problems. The rage and frustration felt by the veteran may precede a history of spousal abuse and violence in the home. Others, not so severely affected, may continue to live in isolation as partners, sharing little more than a common roof. West and Leon (1986) reported a study of the wives of Vietnam veterans in group therapy. Initially, the wives experienced feelings of isolation and depression and perceived their husbands as unavailable for support. These investigators found that the wife must often assume the role of primary financial supporter of the family.

It is now widely accepted that variables of the family affect the social and affective development of children (Sameroff and Chandler, 1975; Thomas and Chess, 1977). Research on children's learning shows that modeling and interactions with significant others strongly influence the child's perception of self (Bandura, 1977; Schunk, 1981). Piaget (1970) characterized children's development as a product of their innate abilities as affected by their environment. Accepting these perspectives, it can be assumed that many children of Vietnam veterans are developmentally at risk because their family environment may not have been particularly positive in their critical early years. The presence of PTSD appears to have strong influences that may have shaped a family's actions and reactions within a structured setting, such as the environment found in public education. Any child entering the educational system is at risk for failure when the family is less than functional. Add to this risk the possible sensory deprivation caused by high rates of impaired immunological responses and other systemic dysfunctions, and it is likely that the child will have trouble adjusting to any structured environment.

According to Klerman (1992), the kinds of problems this family milieu could pose for the children include: poor social and academic development; poor physical and mental health, including the existence of chronic conditions; abuse of drugs and alcohol, and conditions related to such abuse; exposure to domestic and community violence, and abuse; teenage pregnancy and the need to assume parental responsibilities prematurely; and limited employment opportunities. These multiple problems cut across categories of services and create needs for health, mental health, education, employment, housing, veterans' services, and social services.

Family-related problems are compounded when the most severely affected families live within severely or even mildly distressed rural or urban communities with their own deficiencies: weak labor markets, substandard schools, and unsafe, deteriorating neighborhoods with a pervasive drug culture and related violence. Access to services is impeded in a family where parental time may be severely limited, transportation is lacking, or family members simply cannot reach the place that offers the needed services.

Even when a match can be made between the veterans' family service needs and a service provider, the family often fails to connect because it does not advocate for itself effectively. (See Smith, Mayfield-Smith, and Sudduth (1994) for a discussion of these barriers.) Clearly, if the family-provider connection is to be made successfully, a specialized network of family-focused services for veterans is needed. The remainder of this paper discusses such a network as it pertains to veterans' families with children with disabilities or chronic illnesses.

Positive Consequences

One positive consequence of the Vietnam War for veterans and their families was that, through AOCAP, a new service delivery system was created that had an impact on veterans' families and on the broader service delivery system itself. AOCAP formed a two-tiered network of services to help those families most in need, primarily those with children with disabilities. Many of these families demonstrated an almost startling isolation from even the most fundamental publicly funded service systems that existed to address their needs. This new system had to be created quickly because of the delays caused by prolonged litigation and other factors. It had to encompass a wide array of programs that would serve a highly diverse population. As with many emerging social service approaches, the creation and expansion of this new system was nourished by a mixture of rational persuasion and passionate advocacy. The NIS believed that the Vietnam veteran's family presented special needs and had unusual barriers to overcome. The new system was formed to link community-based services with centralized specialty services to improve the delivery of comprehensive care to veterans' children with disabilities or chronic illnesses.

Designers of the system recognized early on that parents perceived existing services as fragmented, specialized, and complex. Whether based in reality or not, these perceptions deterred families from obtaining services. Perhaps the biggest failure was the apparent ineffectiveness of existing systems in providing services to children and families, particularly those with multiple needs. The large number of unserved children and the high frequency of multiple problems caused concern and helped shape the AOCAP network. It was apparent that the parents' problems exacerbated the children's problems, and to help the children often required helping the family.

Coincidentally, AOCAP came into existence on the heels of fundamental changes in the way that contemporary American medicine regards and treats children with disabilities or chronic illnesses. For many years, these children were placed in residential institutions permanently or kept in chronic health care facilities for extended periods of time. It was assumed that families could not, or would not, adequately care for them in their homes and that it was less expensive to care for them in institutions. Research has led experts to discard these assumptions, and practice today is based on the family as the caring and healing environment. Now it is families, including veterans' families, who—with appropriate supports—are regarded as capable of nurturing their children as well as managing their complex health problems.

AOCAP was not encumbered by years of stereotypical thinking on family limitations. Their programs, unlike many governmental policies and programs, were not based on the premise that a few common solutions could be uniformly applied to all home situations. Typically, families had to adapt to standard policies and service systems if their children were to receive any help. Many parents have had to make enormous sacrifices: give up career opportunities, pass up job promotions, deplete their financial resources, sacrifice quality time together, and experience extreme and sustained emotional, marital, and family stress trying to meet their family needs within the confines of the traditional service delivery system.

AOCAP realized that access to the array of services that a veteran's family may need was impeded by the common practice of specialized case management. A specialized system often meant that a family member received help only for his or her original problem. The services that were identified were determined by which human services port the family member entered. For example, if a child with a learning disability and a behavioral problem entered the juvenile justice system, he or she might receive all the services the court is able to deliver, but these may meet only a small part of his or her overall needs. Securing positive outcomes may require the provider to assess needs beyond the provider's own special competence, and link children and families with other providers who can supply the appropriate services.

Building on the family-centered care movement (Shelton, Jeppson, and Johnson, 1987), the AOCAP approach to case management was family-focused; it addressed the totality of needs of the entire family and did not rely on only one area of the service system. AOCAP adopted the attitude that families require essential information and support to help them understand and meet the diverse needs of their children. AOCAP recognized that veterans' families vary greatly in the ways they choose to live and to meet the needs of their children. Many families were very successful in responding to the problems or special concerns they must address, while they were far less efficacious in coping with immediate and long-term needs.

It was apparent to AOCAP that some veterans' families were not able to avail themselves of services, even when free. Families did not know what services to ask for, much less which option to take. Harris (1986) reported that, "no more than 13 percent of the persons with disabilities have used the available services which are generally available throughout the country." Because AOCAP had limited financial resources, it had to develop a system that would not duplicate, but would draw from, existing services. AOCAP saw an urgent need to inform families about key services that are available to them. It formed a network with strong national support systems, and attempted to eliminate or lessen one of the barriers that Bailey and Simeonsson (1988) described as "the greatest obstacle to information dissemination: the lack of a central resource center that can direct those in need of services to those who can provide the services."

AOCAP's strength lies in its ability to marshal or access resources beyond its immediate program boundaries for Vietnam veterans and their families. It has been apparent from the outset that the range of human services needed to meet their needs must come from existing providers that have had only minimal contact with veterans' families. The traditional system of veterans' benefits and services is veteran-focused and veteran-directed, providing services and benefits to the veteran with little regard to the veteran's family constellation. The lack of contact between the disabilities services system and the programs and personnel engaged in veterans' services had been nearly total until AOCAP created the network necessary to pull the two together.

Future Action

The lessons of the AOCAP experience could produce beneficial consequences not yet realized for the families of Vietnam veterans. From this five-year experience, the NIS has identified many service needs of veteran families that will remain after the last AOCAP dollar is spent.

Theoretically, two broad approaches to change could have the most significant, lasting effect of the Vietnam War on the lives of veterans and their families. One approach is radically to restructure human services legislation at the federal and state levels for wholesale replacement of organizations and funding. The magnitude and consequent political difficulty of replacement on this scale, however, would deter all but a few from the task. Even for those attracted to his approach, the lack of evidence that it will succeed or even improve the current system makes it difficult to sell, even on its theoretical merits.

In the other possible approach, existing categorical and targeted programs can be expanded. This strategy is popular, even though there is not much evidence that the current system is performing well enough to merit expansion, despite considerable effort over the past two decades to do so. The objectives of this approach are to correct the weaknesses of the existing system and develop a capacity simultaneously to deal with veterans' children and families holistically and promptly, and manage multiple family needs that cross professional and programmatic categories. This strategy seeks to reform rather than replace the existing system. It is a more practical, but no less fundamental or far-reaching approach to achieving change than the wholesale replacement approach. It should lead to legislative restructuring and more resources based on demonstrated performance.

The following recommendations would effect reform to accomplish a lasting beneficial effect for Vietnam veterans and their families:

- **Recommendation 1. Develop and maintain a single point of access with a supporting network of services**. This recommendation embodies service integration, which means far more than one national information and referral service. Faced with a complex web of agencies and professionals with vastly differing roles and missions, veterans' families are frequently unable to navigate the system successfully. Even sophisticated family members and experienced professionals may have difficulty determining which agency has the responsibility or expertise to respond to a particular family need. Adding to this confusion is the assumption of many providers that the veterans' system meets their service needs and that private providers therefore need not do so. Service integration rejects this view and, instead, draws on all providers from all systems, focusing on the needs of the service recipient rather than the jurisdiction of the provider. NIS experience shows that service integration has had a positive impact on consequences or services received by many Vietnam veterans and their families.

- **Recommendation 2. Individual agencies and programs need to use a unified, interrelated approach to meeting family needs.** Multiple services and programs are needed to meet a veteran's, as well as a family's, problems in a coordinated way. For instance, serving an individual child requires meeting the child's needs as well as the needs of family members whose own problems affect the child. Too many problems of the veteran affect the family, and too many problems of the family affect the veteran, for there to be two totally separate systems of care, that is, the VA for the veteran and public and private providers for the other family members. The traditional system of veterans' benefits and services is veteran-directed, providing services and benefits to the veteran directly and with little regard to the veteran's family configuration (except a variation in certain income allowances); few services are available to the veteran's family members from that system. Members of the veteran's family, characterized as "dependents," are generally recognized as having needs only if the veteran is disabled or deceased. Even the Vet Centers, which are designed to be more flexible and progress in their service delivery approach, deal with family issues only to the extent that they are an impediment to the veteran's "readjustment" counseling program.

  Most programs are organized to serve a person with a single condition; they cannot meet multiple needs. A veteran or family in need of health, education, counseling, employment, and other services must access four or more independent programs to meet these needs. These programs often have varying eligibility requirements, conflicting hours and locations, and, generally, no coordinated case management. This recommendation would help to reduce disjointed service planning, fragmentation of roles within the helping professions, and inappropriate program structures and procedures. Failure to address adequately the multiple dimensions of the complex, unique needs of these families may well create diminished life chances and ultimately have a negative generational consequence.

- **Recommendation 3. Establish a family advocacy responsibility with each service provider.** The primary reason that veterans' families need a network of services lies in their limited ability to advocate on their own behalf. Many agencies are not client- or family-friendly, and their policies often do not promote independence. Some categorical programs actively discourage or penalize efforts by families to assume personal responsibility for themselves: these programs may, for example, end services or benefits just when families are beginning to demonstrate success and independence. Assume, for instance, that a boy's primary source of support has been his mother, who receives Aid to Families with Dependent Children (AFDC). Once he is eighteen and has completed schooling, he "ages out" and his mother is no longer eligible for AFDC support for him. He is cut adrift at the point where job training programs are supposed to begin, perhaps before he can be employed and become self-supporting. During this critical transition in their lives, family members need bridge services. Family advocacy is needed because of the veterans' apparent inability to advocate on their own behalf. This recommendation may not change the attitude of many agencies that are not client- or family-friendly, but it would help the dependent child obtain needed services that a nonadvocating parent may choose not to pursue.

- **Recommendation 4. Establish a single point of accountability in the system.** When each program serves a specific group without formal connection or coordination among programs, the needs of different family members are not simultaneously recognized and addressed. Because of the fragmentation of agency responsibility, needed services and benefits are inappropriately delayed, interrupted, or stopped. For example, when child protective services removes a child from a veteran's home because of suspected or confirmed abuse, and places the child temporarily in foster care, the treatment for the abusive parent is provided by an entirely different program with no formal link to child protective services. It is likely that the child will eventually return to the same home with the same parent, a parent whose own problems may have not been adequately addressed. Ironically, the system that demands effective family functioning to use its services successfully rarely meets the needs of the families. Instead, it pressures the families to adapt to the service delivery system. This recommendation encourages the system to adapt to the family through service integration and agency accountability.

- **Recommendation 5. Require agency follow-up.** Even if intake and assessment of a veteran's family are well done, current follow-up is often weak or nonexistent. Contact to encourage return visits may or may not be part of the provider's protocol. Follow-up on referrals, particularly those to providers beyond the normal scope of the referring provider, may be perfunctory or nonexistent; in many cases, no one ensures that the child receives needed comprehensive services. Even when case management includes follow-up contact, it usually focuses on a specialized particular discipline rather than on all the needs of the child. The system assumes that the child or the child's family can find the means and the way to the other needed services. This assumption proves incorrect when the family does not understand what expectations the agency has for them, or has such limited resources that it is unable to follow up, or when the family cannot handle even one more demand on it. This recommendation would increase the likelihood that follow-through would occur and the persons who need services would get them.
- **Recommendation 6. Strongly encourage or require collaboration:** Collaboration requires concerted action among committed partners. Collaboration requires the blending of provider disciplines and usually involves multiple organizations and the family working together in a unified manner. These collaborations provide information and referral services, and they provide an integrated collection of primary services to both child and family in a way that addresses the whole family and its multiple problems and needs. The collaborations seek to strengthen or, where needed, supplement the family's ability to assess and meet the needs of their child. There has been strong interest in this linking, or integration, strategy at national, state, and local levels (Gerry and Certo, 1992).

Summary

The traditional service delivery system, which requires effective family functioning for successful use of services, often does not meet the needs of veterans' children and families; rather, it brings pressure on families to accommodate or adapt to the service delivery system as they find it. Neither more of the same, nor organizational restructuring of the system alone are strategies that can meet veterans' families' needs. Compelling evidence exists that a service integration strategy offers a promising alternative worthy of careful and thorough exploration for the future. AOCAP represents a change agent dedicated to developing a system based on the integration strategy. The general goal of AOCAP will continue; namely that veterans' children, particularly children who are at risk because of environmental or biological factors, will grow to adulthood able to function effectively and productively in the world around them.

References

Bailey, D.B., and R.J. Simeonsson. 1988. Assessing needs of families with handicapped infants. *Journal of Special Education* 22:117-127.

Bandura, A. 1977. *Social Learning Theory*. Englewood Cliffs, NJ: Prentice-Hall.

Bullman, T.A., H. Kang, and L.T. Thomas. 1991. Post-traumatic stress disorder among Vietnam veterans on the Agent Orange Registry: a case-control analysis. *Annals of Epidemiology* 1:505-512.

Center for Disease Control. 1988. Vietnam experience study. Health status of Vietnam veterans psychosocial characteristics. *Journal of the American Medical Association* 259:2701-2707.

Gerry, M., and N. Certo. 1992. Current activity at the federal level and the need for service integration. *The Future of Children* 2:118-126.

Goodwyn, I. 1990. *Readjustment Problems Among Vietnam Veterans.* Cincinnati, OH: Disabled American Veterans.

Harris, L., and Associates. 1986. *Disabled Americans' Self Perceptions: Bringing Disabled Americans into the Mainstream.* New York: International Center for the Disabled, Study No. 854009.

Klerman, L.V. 1992. Nonfinancial barriers to the receipt of medical care. *The Future of Children* 2:177-178.

Kulka, R.A., W.E. Schlenger, J.A. Fairbank, R.L. Hough, B.K. Jordan, C.R. Marmar, and D.S. Weiss. 1988. *Contractual Report of Findings from the National Vietnam Veterans Readjustment Study,* Vol. 1. Research Triangle Park, NC: Research Triangle Institute.

Piaget, I. 1970. Piaget's theory. In *Carmichael's Manual of Psychology,* ed. P.H. Mussen. New York: Wiley.

Sameroff, A.J., and M.J. Chandler. 1975. Reproductive risk and the continuum of caretaking casualty. In *Review of Child Development Research.* 4, ed. F.D. Horowitz. Chicago: University of Chicago Press.

Schunk, D.H. 1981. Modeling and attributional effects on children's achievement: A self-efficacy analysis. *Journal of Educational Psychology* 73:93-105.

Shelton, T.L., E.S. Jeppson, and B.H. Johnson. 1987. *Family-Centered Care for Children with Special Health Needs.* 2d ed. Washington, DC: Association for the Care of Children's Health.

Smith, B.C., K. L. Mayfield-Smith, and D. Sudduth. 1994. *Impact Analysis of the AOCAP Network of Services.* Washington, DC: AOCAP.

Thoene, J.G., ed. 1992. *Physicians' Guide to Rare Diseases.* Montvale, NJ: Dowden Publishing Co.

Thomas, A., and S. Chess. 1980. *The Dynamics of Psychological Development.* New York: Brunner/Mazel.

West, A.M., and C.A. Leon. 1986. Health needs of the Vietnam veteran exposed to Agent Orange. *Nurse Practitioner* 11:33-40.

I'm Really All Right

Marijane Goonan, B.S., T.R.T.
North Logan, UT

Abstract

The wives of many veterans of the Vietnam War may suffer under extremely stressful conditions at home as the veterans struggle to come to terms with the war and with themselves. Many wives live in fear and isolation and are anxious about their marriages and their children, especially when the children have birth defects. This paper explores the experiences of wives of Vietnam veterans.

The Agent Orange Class Assistance Program (AOCAP) has been a positive force in the lives of Vietnam veterans and their children. The program's network provides services for disabled children, but what about the unsung heroes. . . the wives? Services provided by AOCAP through the past few years have had a positive effect on wives. They have watched their children being served, but adequate support services have yet to be offered for distressed wives of Vietnam veterans in most projects. If families are to survive intact, the wife must have her own needs met apart from those of the veteran and children with birth defects. AOCAP has the strength and connections to channel services of this nature to support veterans' lives.

Marijane Goonan *holds a B.S. from Utah State University in health and physical education and a teaching certificate in secondary education. She is a licensed therapeutic recreation specialist and assistant department head, recreation therapy department, for Sunshine Terrace Foundation. Her husband, Tom, is a Vietnam veteran.*

My life in Vietnam started when I was transferred to 3rd Surgical Hospital (MASH) at Bihn Thuy, in the Mekong Delta. Nothing made sense, the smell of diesel fuel and rotten vegetables, the decay, the noise (especially choppers), JP4 jet fuel. At nineteen, terror had a certain appeal, it had no conscience or consequence. This was adventure in its most pure form.

By the time I got to Vietnam drugs were abundant and cheap. Pure heroin went for $10 per gram. Opium was less. Marijuana was $10 per kilo. It was all good quality. We got high every day. It was one good way of dealing with walking through the "nub ward" (amputees) and the burn unit. There were two twenty-bed wards that were full the whole time I was in-country.

There was a young Vietnamese girl who was under care who had been caught in an early morning strike in her village. She had third-degree burns over 65 percent of her body, mostly her head and chest. It makes me nauseated to think about her. It also makes me incredibly sad to think that she is perhaps still alive today. She was such a beautiful young girl who was turned into a mass of scar tissue with no future for marriage. Her family was killed in the raid. In a sense, so was she. I smell her from time to time.

I worked in a dental clinic, which was next to the flight deck and the ER, for a while. We occasionally worked with head wounds. I learned quite a bit about surgical techniques from the surgeon I worked with. We were a good team. We are still good friends today.

One day we were sitting around after smoking five or six joints. We got a call for incoming KIA. Two Americans, a captain and an E-7 (master sergeant). Someone from their unit had booby-trapped a Conex box (storage unit) with ten pounds of C-4. The captain opened the door, boom, no more captain. His head, arms, legs, and most of the soft tissue on his body was gone. The E-7 was twenty-five feet away. He lost one arm at the shoulder, half of his head, and a foot. They were both in body bags when they arrived. The dustoff crew chief told us what happened and advised us not to look.

I looked anyway. I threw up. I thought about my drill sergeant, who committed suicide. That night I went to a local opium den in Can Tho and got so high I threw up and slept on the bamboo tatami mat in this hut on the Mekong River. When I awoke in the morning, the papa-san was staring at me. I had nothing to say to him.

These are my treasures. They are like children who have grown to maturity. As horrible as some days may have been in my life, there is a hidden joy and mystery that continues to show itself. It centers on my family.

My children and wife have taught me to have pride in serving my country. My loving wife has tolerated me and supported me these past seven years. My sons, Michael and Jordan, taught me compassion when they were born with cleft lips and palates. My three stepsons don't realize how much joy they have brought me as they have grown to become men. And God, who promised He would not test any of us beyond our limits.

There is mystery in the morning when the light pours in the window and there is a new day.

Thomas M. Goonan

Chapter 1

On occasion people have exclaimed to me, "You are the wife of a Vietnam veteran. You have got to be crazy." I have often wondered about that statement, and I have just as often taken time to investigate my feelings concerning it. I have even questioned that statement. Is it crazy to be married to and stick with someone you love even if he is a Vietnam veteran? Is it crazy to observe growth and success of hundreds of not-so-young men as they struggle to find their place in life twenty years after the war? Is it crazy after twenty years to see a struggling adult woman trying to make sense of her lost years? Is it crazy to enjoy and in my own personal and proud way appreciate what my veteran and thousands like him did for me and a country I love? Is it crazy for me to feel defeat more than victory in a war I never went to, but that lives in my home every day? Is it crazy to feel a tinge of sadness and emptiness when one knows so much of life has been wasted and is now gone? And so I wonder. . . .

It is not easy to tell a story that could have so many titles. This story could be called War and Peace; Love Means You Never Have to Say You're Sorry or Say Anything At All; or Road Warrior. Or perhaps it could be titled, It Was The Best of Times, It Was the Worst of Times. It is even harder to think about telling a story that has thousands of beginnings but no ending. When the last chapter in this story is told, then maybe all of us together can figure out an ending.

I want to start with my beginning, as this is the one I am most familiar with. It started on a fall day on September 3, 1984. My nine-year-old son wanted to take karate lessons. A class at our local recreation center had been recommended. We walked into the room and there I met the most handsome man I had ever seen. He was tall, dark, and handsome and had control over an entire class of children. His looks and abilities were so enticing to me. Little did I know that on that beautiful fall day my life was about to change forever.

I was coming out of a bad marriage and had three little boys ages nine, seven, and five. My future husband was coming out of a bad life. During the first few months of my relationship with the handsome karate instructor, we put together a business that would house his karate school and my dance school. At the time all of this was happening, he exhibited several instances involving anger, violent outbursts, throwing things, foul language, lots of heavy drinking, and many times refusal to work at all. At the time, I brushed this behavior off. I was very hurt by this behavior and often felt like the burden of the two schools was mine. I always excused his behavior with the reasoning that he was in a new environment away from family, friends, and old surroundings. I just knew that, as soon as the school was up and running, life would get better.

Life did get better but the behaviors did not; they were only suppressed. Our relationship grew. We became best friends and then husband and wife. It was a joyous time, but I had feelings deep inside that the behaviors I had seen were just not right, but I could not figure out why. His reactions to simple life problems were catastrophic.

Our new marriage began just as many others begin, a one-day honeymoon and back to work. It was much more difficult in some ways, however, because of my having three children and an ex-husband to deal with. My new husband seemed content and happy. Things looked great for me and my family as his drinking stopped. One aspect of my life changed dramatically at this time. I returned to the work force full time after a period of ten years. We decided that my husband would run his karate school and take care of the children while I worked full time. It wasn't long, however, until old behaviors started creeping in. I became burdened with multiple roles in my family with little support for what I was doing.

There are always conflicts with roles. Any person, male or female, who is trying to manage several roles often has to juggle all of the demands, and so must make compromises.

As with all working women, conflicts with these roles are inevitable. It was not long before I found myself juggling a full-time job outside of home with all the pressure and stress of being a breadwinner as well as running the karate school after an eight-hour work day. I was responsible for paying the bills on time, talking to creditors, dressing appropriately, and producing quality work in order to receive promotions and pay raises. I often battled fatigue from interrupted sleep because of the children or my husband's endless sleep disturbances, anger, or depression. I found myself fulfilling the full-time role of wife and mother at home with little or no help and still being expected to be the stable emotional center of the home.

However, the important issue here is not the conflict itself but the reactions to the conflicts. Avoiding confrontation over repeated promises to help with chores that were rarely kept, trying to compensate for my husband's lack of involvement with the family, and being unable to afford services that make working easier all became a major source of contention and stress. Even though my husband suffered from stress and could recognize his anger, depression, and volatile temper, he was unable to recognize, respond to, or try to alleviate my stresses.

There were many days when neither I nor my three young boys even knew this stranger living in our house. My husband seemed to withdraw further and further. It is hard to describe the feelings that our family experienced. I knew he was a good person and I knew he had a lot of potential. I knew I loved him deeply and I knew he loved me and the boys, although he rarely expressed his feelings. The behaviors he displayed were upsetting and unnerving. Something was wrong. I knew it and he knew it but we never talked about it—except now he had started to dwell on Vietnam. All I knew was that I was tired of hearing his excuses. I hated Vietnam.

Chapter 2

We were expecting our first child. My husband was very excited and so proud, but it did not change his behaviors. If anything, the added stress only intensified them. During this time, he started describing his experiences as a medic in Vietnam. I had read a little and had experienced my own circumstances during the time he was at war, but nothing could have prepared me for the stories I was now beginning to hear. I also started getting the lectures about how tough it was in 'Nam and how easy my life was and not to bitch. I heard all about how he had suffered and how terrible things still were for him. I developed preeclampsia/toxemia with my pregnancy and was ordered to bed, but that was not to be. My husband was too stressed to work because of the pending added responsibility and much too stressed to help much at home. Everything became an issue. No one was more ill, stressed, or depressed than he. He totally blocked out everyone and everything but himself.

Things did change for awhile when our son Michael was born five weeks early. I almost died on the delivery table and so did our son. My husband was there with both of us. It was then that I saw an incredibly awesome side of my husband. We had the delivery videotaped. He was so tender and loving. Even watching the video six years later brings back overwhelming feelings. I just knew that as soon as our son was born my husband would forget this Vietnam thing and his heart would be with his new son and his family.

To our dismay, our son was born with a cleft lip. It is not easy to have an "imperfect" child even if everyone around you is telling you the imperfection is easy to repair. The tenderness that had been in the room only moments before soon disappeared. He went through the proper social things that every new dad goes through, but the shortness he was displaying was evidence that he was greatly disturbed. About thirty minutes later he left. I had expected him to return as he had promised me he would. I was frightened about almost dying and frightened about our new son. He did not return the entire evening. During the night I had another terrible seizure and almost died. After they stabilized me I tried to call home, no answer, no answer, no answer.

The next day about noon he showed up; he had gone out and gotten stone-faced drunk. Well, some may say that's all right, he deserved it, but once again, what about me? Where was my support system? During the next six weeks, I was to be on complete bed rest. That lasted hardly three weeks. My husband became resentful. Sharp remarks started, insults about how I needed to get up and going, and comments about how are we going to pay the bills were endless. His depression, anger, and mood swings intensified. At this time, his job was to teach karate classes three nights per week for three hours each night and two hours on Saturday. He had become so distraught that he threatened to stop teaching because he just couldn't handle it, so back to work I went. I was determined that, if I worked harder, didn't demand or ask him for help, and didn't above all ask for emotional support, everything would work out.

The verbal abuse intensified, and the children were starting to show signs of stress. They hated the verbal battles, but once again I covered up for his behaviors and decided that, if I just kept my mouth shut, there would be no more verbal battles. Every time there was a conflict I gave that theory a test run. It didn't work. Finally, I fought back. I defended the children and myself and raged at the name-calling and verbal abuse. And my children continued to withdraw. Our daily lives were centered on this mysterious war. There was not a day that went by that we didn't hear Vietnam this and Vietnam that.

Needless to say, as my husband's behavior worsened, so did my attitudes and behaviors. Depression and confusion were constant companions. I didn't know this person anymore; most days I didn't want to know him and wished I had never known him. No matter how bad things became or how many times I entertained the thought of packing up four children and leaving him, something in the deepest, innermost parts of my heart kept telling me I loved him and cared for him. Something always told me to hang on, hang on. It wasn't like I was going to save him or anything like that, it was just a real spiritual feeling that we belonged together.

The end of a person's rope many times depends on how big the knot is at the end and how much strength you have to hold on to the knot that you keep tying in the end. Well, the knot in the end of my rope nearly came untied when I found out I was going to start a new chapter.

Chapter 3

I was pregnant again. I cried for months, but my husband was elated. Elated and thrilled still didn't produce an attitude adjustment. My husband had been baptized into the Church of Jesus Christ of Latter Day Saints (Mormon), the predominant religion in Utah. My sons and I were members. This did help a great deal because this religion has such a strong belief in families. I am sure that some of his changes had come from there.

My pregnancy this time was uneventful except that they scheduled a C-section because Jordan was breeched. The morning of my onset of labor, all went well until Jordan was delivered. He had a unilateral cleft lip and palate and would need surgical repairs. My husband was not just angry and depressed, he was furious. The doctors could not figure out why we had two children back to back with clefts. My husband totally lost it. I was trying as hard as I could to keep this new child alive, recover from a C-section, work full time, maintain four other children, and try to understand the lack of help both physically and emotionally. Every time someone asked how we were doing, of course the answer was, "As soon as we get Jordan taken care of and things settle down, then everything will be all right."

There are miracles in this life and I am the product of several. At the suggestion of a good friend, my husband went for help. Our friend worked at our Utah State University and told us about the Agent Orange Family Assistance Program, a newly funded program for children of Vietnam veterans who had birth defects. So up to the university my husband went. The staff on the project saw a veteran with a full-blown case of post-traumatic stress disorder (PTSD). They did all they could to help us: not only did they say they could help Jordan, but they gave my husband a job. Finally, things started getting better. Tom seemed to settle in to his new job. He had a focus and was helping others and at the same time our son was being helped. The formal investigation and case study for our family was taken care of by Tom at the office. I never heard from the caseworker and was never questioned. I only knew Tom was getting counseling and had employment.

Our lives were intensely intertwined with Vietnam and children with birth defects. It was good to see my husband a little more focused, but as soon as the newness wore off the old behaviors appeared. Thank God they were not as bad, but things just did not feel right. We daily contended with depression, withdrawal, uncalled-for outbursts, anger, emotional withdrawal. It was extremely pleasing to see my son cared for and people around my husband trying to help him deal with our son's cleft lip and his behaviors. But I just could not shake the feeling that I didn't count. Was I to have no feelings and no emotions over the trials we had endured? No one seemed to care, and it became obvious to me that what had been reported to the caseworker had been viewed entirely from a viewpoint different from my own. Soon our file was closed; this case was taken care of. The project knew that our son had one surgery and others were planned and financed, and my husband was a perfect employee—charming everyone and every family he contacted. On the other hand, I felt abandoned, isolated, and more and more angry. When I interacted with Tom's co-workers I was the ultimate wife, always positive about my husband. Life outwardly appeared to be wonderful. Things were not right and I knew it, but I did not know how to put a stop to our Dr. Jekyll, Mr. Hyde existence.

Chapter 4

Life is always full of surprises. Our lives crashed just three months after Jordan was born and two-and-a-half months into my husband's new job. I was diagnosed with Hodgkin's lymphoma (a lymph cancer). Immediately, I had thoracic surgery. In the next two months, our lives turned upside-down and inside-out. Nine days after my surgery and confirmed diagnosis, my ten-year-old son was diagnosed with insulin-dependent diabetes. Twenty-eight days later, we started chemotherapy, sixty days out of surgery we had another palate repair, ninety days out of surgery another son had his appendix out, 120 days out of surgery I had more surgery, and in between all of this I went back to work two weeks out of surgery because our insurance was with my job.

During this time, my husband was a trouper. He did things that I never imagined he could or would. With all the added stress, the old behaviors still continued. They were not as frequent, but when they happened they were more intense than ever. Many days I wanted to die rather than have one more treatment or throw up one more time. Yet when my husband was depressed, angry, lashing out, it was I who was feeling guilty and still maintaining my superglue status with the family. I missed work that year only six half-days for chemotherapy and nine days for radiation sickness after my radiation therapy. I continued as before on the chemo days and I was feeling guilty. Is there something wrong with this picture? When one reads this story, one would say, "The poor man, he had a right to the way he dealt with all of this." Yes, he did, and I could not have survived without him, but something was still wrong with the intensity and degree of his reactions. They were unusual and always centered on Vietnam. Cancer, diabetes, appendicitis, birth defects were all secondary to Vietnam and his experiences. No one was ever sicker, more depressed, more angry than my husband, and so why should I complain? Well I'm here to tell you I didn't fight that damn war twenty-five years ago, but I was fighting it every day of my life as well as fighting my own war with cancer. Fighting to stay alive and fighting to keep my family intact and fighting to have a relationship with someone I really didn't know. What made all of this even more difficult was that I did start to think I was crazy. Maybe people were right. I was tired of the way I felt, but I had no one to talk to, and of course on the surface I worked overtime to let people know everything was wonderful.

I told you miracles do happen to ordinary people; well, another was to come my way. When my despair was darkest, the spring of 1990 dawned. The staff at the Agent Orange Class Assistance Program (AOCAP) had started to see me fraying around the edges and so decided I should travel to an American Legion meeting in Idaho. There AOCAP would be presented and it would be a fun-filled weekend with entertainment and socializing.

I guess it became crystal clear that I was at the end of my rope and there wasn't enough rope left to tie a knot. So off we went. What I experienced was not at all what I expected. For the first time in over three years, the pieces of my frustrating puzzle started coming together. The AOCAP presentation was formal. Speeches were made about what the program was, what it could do, and what it needed from the Legion. During the meeting, I looked around and saw row upon row of disabled veterans. More than half of the audience were Vietnam veterans with disabled children. They were there to find help for the husband and children. Later in the program, there was a formal meeting of the veterans, and so several of the wives got together to talk. At first, it was, "What can they do for my child or my husband or both?" When I shared what they had done for my family, it was amazing how those total strangers began to open up. I am not a miracle worker nor do I have a magnetic personality, but these women seemed to just talk and talk, and then I was questioned about my role.

I seemed so together. Suddenly, there was a room full of women telling stories and giving descriptions of their Vietnam veterans; they sounded identical to my own circumstances. What was going on here? I heard stories of PTSD, of physical disabilities, of depression, of anger, of isolation, of lack of emotions. Then came the heart-rending stories of birth-defect children. My heart ached and I counted my blessings that at least my children's cleft lips could be fixed and at least things were a little better at my house. As the conference wore on, several women told stories that jerked me up by my boot straps. Of the ten women in the group, not one had a different story. The characters had different names, but the scripts were all the same. One women told of how damn mad she was at her husband of twenty years: of never having a job, of the beatings she had received when he was out of sorts, and of living under his armed guard. But she concluded, "I will be all right now that my child's disabilities can be helped and my husband can get counseling."

Another told of not having a sexual relationship with her husband for over ten years, unless you call forced sex on his demand a relationship. She felt it was her fault for not being pretty enough or having the house spotless, as he wished. She told of the physical abuse on a weekly basis because she didn't get home before dark, dinner wasn't on the table, etc., etc. But she was all right because at least now her learning-disabled sons were going to be taken care of and she knew her husband would get better. All of these women shared experiences and always concluded they were all right. These women were as all right as I was—NOT! I realized I wasn't alone and I wanted to help, but what could I do about a situation I did not understand?

For the entire rest of the year, I traveled as much as my health would allow and made all the contacts with women that I could. I read everything I could get my hands on about Vietnam, its veterans, and the trauma it caused. A common thread ran through each contact. The initial interview with mom, dad, and kids was uneventful. Reports on the veteran and children along with some needs were requested. It became apparent that the father did all the talking. Each time a wife tried to insert something, she was cut off by the husband, and each time the veteran ended up talking about himself and his Vietnam experience rather than the children or their needs. The women of course were always all right. It took a lot of courage, but I finally discussed what I had been keeping track of with my husband. To my surprise, my husband already had deduced for himself what was going on. We had long talks on those trips about my role and my feelings and what could I do to help him do a better job. Together we devised a plan. He was pleased with my involvement and offered much support, and I was pleased because I was finally starting to understand my life and the man I loved.

After each formal visit, as the talk would turn to the war I would conveniently get the wives away from the room and conversation. Every contact I made was the same. I found women desperate for help. I don't mean for her husband or children, but for herself. These strangers would talk openly. I heard time after time the same desperate stories I had heard on my first trip.

Chapter 5

Jake and Sarah and their children lived in a trailer park out in the desert in a little town by the state prison. The roads were unpaved and the few trailers that were there were run-down. The children we saw playing were ill-kept and dirty. The only store within thirty miles was a convenience store. There were two churches and two schools. All were run-down and dirty.

When we entered the house, we found it to be immaculately clean. The children were snuggled by their mother on one side of the room. Jake sat on the sofa opposite them.

Sarah and the children had been to church and they were spit-shine clean. As we talked, the veteran sat playing with a large knife. There were weapons all over the house and, I later learned, several under the bed and one under his pillow.

The conversation was pleasant. Jake talked, Sarah and the children said nothing. After talking at length, we went outside. Sarah and I walked to where we could see the school. It did not take long to find out that the few medical problems of their children that Jake had mentioned were only the surface of the iceberg.

Jake worked graveyard or swing shift at the prison. There was only one car and he often did not return home until after lunch, so Sarah had no transportation. Jake often had bad dreams after falling asleep and had often gathered his family in one room with his weapons and would barricade them in for up to two hours at a time.

I found out that every member of that family had been abused physically when the father lost control. The oldest boy would not even speak if Jake was in the house. He demanded that the house be spotless and the children be spotless. If they weren't, there was always physical and verbal abuse.

This woman was given $20 per week for food for a family of six. Sarah had not had a birthday, Christmas, anniversary, or any present since their marriage. Sometimes the children got a small toy for Christmas. You know why? Because you should have seen men go without in Vietnam.

Our visit was a month before Thanksgiving. Sarah asked me to see if the project could send money so she could buy food for her children to have a real Thanksgiving. She had never been allowed to fix a turkey dinner. She also asked for winter coats so her children wouldn't be cold. Those children had not had new coats in two years, and she had never had a new coat since her marriage to Jake. Jake, however, had nice clothes, but then, he worked. This entire interview was told in confidence, and I promised that I would figure out how to get these things without her husband knowing she had told anyone.

Her final comments were, "We really are all right. Jake does keep a roof over our head and it was Vietnam that made him this way." Sarah is uneducated, isolated, with no friends, and totally dependent on Jake. Their children all have disabilities. Sarah, of course, is "just fine."

Karen married Mike twenty years ago. She was sixteen and he had just come back from Vietnam. He taught her to drive. She remembers how young and naive she was when the man she loved was fighting a war. She wore a P.O.W. bracelet and she wanted to marry a soldier. She never expected what she got. After twenty years, she was so worried about her son. He had started acting just like Mike. She sent him to counseling. He came home and told her their family was dysfunctional. Those words made her blood boil. She had worked hard for twenty years to have a normal family. She had been judged by people, she had been the stable person. She had held the full-time jobs. She had kept the children and family together. She had paid all the bills. She realized after twenty years that she had never had a goal. She had devoted her entire adult life to this man and that stupid war. She was sick of Mike threatening her and of the physical abuse she had taken. She was tired of the control and tired of feeling guilty about not being good enough. She was tired of not being able to leave for fear of the safety of her children, and she was tired of the emotional roller coaster she was on. And to top it all off, other people thought they were dysfunctional. But Karen was "all right" because Mike had finally agreed to go for counseling.

Carla is a wife of twenty-one years to a Vietnam veteran. She married the boy next door at age twenty-one. She was young and naive and he was brave and strong. After all, he had just gotten back from war. Her future in-laws told her that he was somehow different since his return. He was not the same boy they sent to war, but they assured her he was good and loving and would take care of her. He had only a ninth-grade education but promised to get vocational training.

Carla loves Jess. Basically he is a good person. She is angry. One of her neighbors about a year ago told her to get out of that crazy situation because her family was already dysfunctional. She had worked for so long to make things right. Jess was getting counseling and the children seemed to be doing better. She was worn out and hearing "dysfunctional" sent her into depression. She had lived for twenty years with a perimeter around her house, and her husband was on constant guard duty. No one entered unless he checked them out. Of course, over the years people stopped wanting to be checked out. Carla and the children never went in their house unless Jess searched it first. He slept with weapons loaded and ready.

Carla feels cheated, robbed of her adult life, her one-time goals. She is emotionally dead and has built up a wall. She has been homebound for years out of fear for her children or what Jess might do to someone else while she was gone. She is tired of being the superglue. She has no self-esteem. She is tired of doing odd jobs that pay little. Jess doesn't trust her being in the work force. Carla also has seen the negative behaviors that Jess displays being mimicked by her teenage sons. Carla would never marry someone like this again. She would never ever marry a soldier and would discourage her children from doing so either. Carla would also do everything humanly possible to keep her sons from serving in the military. But she is "all right."

I have mentioned miracles. Tom and I are living, breathing proof. The things I have learned about Vietnam wives are shocking. Tom and I are lucky. There are unsung heroes out there. I cry for them. They are isolated in their mixed-up lives. They are left alone. They are living in remote areas. Some are not allowed to have friends or family ties. They feel like hostages in their own homes. They have learned to distance emotionally every bit as much as the veteran. They are so used to running interference for the veteran, it becomes a way of life.

They are victims of violence. They live daily under the threat of violence. They all rationalize this type of behavior, blaming it on 'Nam or themselves. They make excuses. They deny the abuse.

They feel humiliated, terrorized, degraded, threatened, and frightened, and they have a sense of being trapped with no way out. They feel cheated out of a real life.

They are angry. They are angry because of always being afraid. They are angry at the government, angry at Vietnam. They have low self-esteem. They are angry because they have become ambivalent and angry because they hide their anger, angry because they are not well educated and totally dependent on the veteran, even if they are the breadwinners. They are tired of being judged by people who do not know the true story. They have no personal goals. They are angry because no one talks to them about PTSD, hers or her husband's. And most of all they are angry at the fact that no one cares about them.

After hearing such heart-breaking stories, it was easy to realize that Tom and I were miracles. Not all women who are married to Vietnam veterans are struggling, but as I further researched what I see as a monumental issue, it became apparent to me that the majority of wives of veterans who are dealing with issues such as PTSD and disabled children are all in the same situation. The wives are not considered part of the veterans' services. There is very little money from Alaska to New York to fund support and counseling groups for the wives.

I work in health care. Every day of my life I see physicians treating diseases, heart-breaking ailments, but I never ever see them only treat part of the problem. You have to treat the entire body, not just one part, if you want the body to function properly. I see the wives of our veterans being cut off like some kind of infected part that no one wants to treat. The whole is not going to work without all of the parts.

The entire issue has had me troubled for four years. When the call for papers came out for the national symposium, I joked about submitting a paper from the wives' point of view. I never thought it would be accepted. I thought it would be viewed as the complaining, bitching wives. We didn't fight the infamous war, so how would we know anything and, after all, it was a majority of veterans that would be selecting the papers. I was stunned when the word came. I finally had an opportunity to have an impact and perhaps help wives all across this country.

I have a wonderful husband who has been through hell. He has come a long way from ten years ago when we first met. He is not a monster or—even more important—he is not crazy and neither am I. I am an all-right person. I've been through hell. I have come a long way from ten years ago when we met. He has become loving, kind, and supportive of me as a mother, as a professional, as a wife. We have become best friends and lovers again. But we are the exception. We are both educated and very lucky. We were plugged into AOCAP. It is never easy to maintain this balance we have fought so hard to achieve. There are still those days, but they are fewer and fewer now. I understand more. I helped myself, but not until my darkest hour and, thanks to miracles, my most handsome husband Tom has come full circle and so have I. He wants a life and I want a life together. We have worked through some incredibly tough times. But what about the thousands of others who haven't found a miracle or haven't been as lucky and as blessed? That is why I am here. That is why we all really do need to hear this. And somehow we all need to act.

I still am confronted about being the wife of a Vietnam veteran and I'm still accused of being crazy. I still wonder about that from time to time, and I have just as often taken time to investigate my feelings concerning that statement. I have come to some different conclusions. It is not crazy to be married to or stick with someone you love, even if he is a Vietnam veteran. It is not crazy to observe growth and success of hundreds of not-so-young men as they struggle for and begin to find their place in life. It is not crazy to sit back and watch an adult female trying to make sense out of twenty lost years of life, and it is not crazy to try to help and try to have an impact in some way. It is not crazy to enjoy in my own personal and proud way what my veteran and thousands like him did for me and a country I love. It is not crazy to feel defeat more than victory in a war I never went to but lives in my home every day. It is not crazy to feel a tinge of sadness and emptiness when one knows so much of life has been wasted and gone. It is crazy to think even for one minute that wives don't count. And it is crazy to think that they can't have an impact on what is going on in the home.

I am of the belief that the roles of the wife and mother in a family are more important than anything. Anyone would be hard-pressed to convince me that wives and mothers don't matter, that they aren't part of the veterans' services and the overall well-being of Vietnam veterans' families. Our nation is under extreme anxiety right now because of the violence in our neighborhoods and amongst our children. Everywhere you turn, people are asking for better homes. You want better homes, better glue? Well, turn to the wives and mothers and you will find it. Heal the wife and mother and you have a good start on healing the veteran and the family. I don't wonder as much as I used to. These wives are not all right. No human being can live daily for twenty or more years under these kinds of pressures and be all right.

It is not easy to tell such a personal story or to share such heart-rending stories that began so long ago and could have such a myriad of titles. It is even harder to know, after sharing one's innermost feelings and being an advocate for thousands of women, that there is no ending to these stories I have shared and no end to the countless others that haven't been told. As we go on, perhaps, we should remember that we may some day be able to write an ending and that miracles do happen.

PTSD and the Family: Secondary Traumatization

Lisa Cosgrove, Ph.D.; Mary E. Brady, Ph.D.; and Patricia Peck, M.A., M.Ed.
Shriver Center University Affiliated Program
Agent Orange Class Assistance Program
Waltham, MA

Abstract

Although researchers have only recently begun to study the psychological impacts of growing up in a home with a parent who is suffering from post-traumatic stress disorder (PTSD), they are rapidly documenting the long-term effects that such family environments have on the psychological development of children of Vietnam veterans. Some clinicians have coined the term "secondary traumatization" to describe the symptomatology presented by children who have been adversely affected by their parent's PTSD.

This paper describes the affective, behavioral, and interpersonal ramifications of combat-related PTSD in terms of how a veteran's symptomatology affects his or her children; psychotherapeutic strategies and educational interventions that may help service providers to work better with children who suffer from secondary trauma; and program models for integrating psychotherapeutic strategies and educational interventions.

The authors' review of the literature suggests that children who live with a severely traumatized parent or who observe traumatizing events may be affected similarly to those who directly experienced such an event. A comprehensive evaluation of programs is needed to determine what existing programs or program components enable children who have been so affected through secondary traumatization to become healthy, productive members of society.

Lisa Cosgrove, Ph.D., *is a psychologist at the Shriver Center and is also affiliated with the University of Massachusetts in Boston.* ***Mary E. Brady, Ph.D.***, *is an educational specialist with the Shriver Center. She holds a Ph.D. in special education and rehabilitation and M.B.A. in management from Boston College, and an M.S. in special education from the University of California, Los Angeles.* ***Patricia Peck, M.A., M.Ed.,*** *is an educational specialist at the Shriver Center. She earned an M.A. in English from Penn State University, and an M.Ed. in early childhood and a C.A.E.S. in special education from Boston College.*

Although there has long been an interest in the psychological sequelae of traumatic events, and there has been a growing interest in understanding the emotional aftermath of witnessing violence, far less is known about the psychosocial transmission of violence. The formal diagnosis of post-traumatic stress disorder (PTSD), which was included in the third edition of the *Diagnostic & Statistical Manual of Mental Disorders (DSM III)* in 1980, has primarily been used to describe individuals who have directly experienced a traumatic life event (e.g., combat veterans, sexual assault victims, children who have been physically abused, etc.). As a result, although a body of research literature and clinical case studies that describe how PTSD affects both abuse victims and combat veterans exists, far fewer studies of the psychological impact of growing up in a home with a caretaker who has PTSD have been undertaken.

Recently, however, a number of researchers and clinicians have focused their attention on the intergenerational impact of PTSD (Danieli, 1985; Krugman, 1987; Rosenheck and Nathan, 1985; Rosenheck, 1986; and van der Kolk, 1988) and on the effect of PTSD on the family system (Catherall, 1992; Figley, 1983, 1985, 1989; Harkness, 1989; Jordan et al., 1992; Solomon, 1988). Their research has shown that people who are instrumental in assisting victims frequently suffer from some of the same symptoms as primary victims, a finding that raises the question of the "psychic cost" to family members of trauma victims (Davis and Friedman, 1985, p. 111). Some clinicians now use the term *secondary traumatization* to describe the symptomatology of children who are adversely affected by their parent's PTSD (Harkness, 1989; Rosenheck and Nathan, 1985).

This paper briefly describes the affective, behavioral, and interpersonal ramifications of combat-related PTSD in terms of how the veteran's symptomatology affects his or her children, which allows for a conceptual framework for understanding secondary traumatization; identifies psychotherapeutic strategies and educational interventions that may be of help to service providers working with children who suffer from secondary trauma; and describes program models for integrating psychotherapeutic strategies and educational interventions—the focus on integration enables schools to develop less fragmented and, thus, more effective service delivery systems.

PTSD is a severe and debilitating emotional disorder. A person suffering from PTSD presents with the following criteria and symptoms: he or she has experienced an event that is outside the range of usual human experience and would be markedly distressing to almost anyone; has instances of intrusive reexperiencing of the trauma; experiences numbing of general responsiveness or avoids stimuli associated with the trauma; has persistent symptoms of increased arousal—e.g., exaggerated startle response, hypervigilance, sleep disturbance, irritability or outbursts of anger, and difficulty concentrating; and symptoms persist for more than one month (APA, 1987).

The aforementioned symptomatology demonstrates the continued psychological centrality of the trauma for the victim. That is, the aftermath of trauma is often experienced in such a way that the victim—consciously and unconsciously—restructures his or her life in an effort to both make sense of the event and to try and alleviate its negative psychological impact (Cosgrove, 1987). Longitudinal studies of the long-term effects of trauma have generally found that although victims engage in many coping behaviors and show a decrease in severe symptomatology, readjustment following trauma is often a long-term process. Moreover, these studies suggest that many victims continue to suffer from anxiety-based symptoms and other manifestations of PTSD months and even years after the traumatizing event occurred (Eth and Pynoos, 1985; Green et al., 1991; Kiser et al., 1988; and Terr, 1983, 1991).

In terms of the epidemiology of PTSD, a recent study found that approximately 1 percent of the population suffers from PTSD, with a higher incidence (3.5 percent) among civilians exposed to physical attack and nonwounded Vietnam veterans and the highest prevalence (20 percent) in veterans wounded in Vietnam (Helzer et al., 1987). In 1988, the National Vietnam Veterans Readjustment Study reported that 481,000 men and 716 women currently suffer from some degree of PTSD as a result of their experience in war, and overall, 40 percent of Vietnam veterans have suffered from PTSD at some time in their life (cited in Camach, Bowen, and Hunt, 1991). In addition, it has been estimated that 900,000 Vietnam spouses and partners and approximately 1,098,000 children are affected by their respective partner's and father's combat-related PTSD (Matsakis, 1988). These statistics highlight the need for better assessment and responses to how PTSD affects parenting abilities and the family system as a whole.

For example, PTSD impedes one's ability to respond appropriately and consistently to environmental or interpersonal stimuli. Therefore, one is less able to establish and maintain close, stable, and supportive relationships. As a result, when a husband suffers from PTSD his partner may try to assume full responsibility for both child care and for the general well-being of the family (Matsakis, 1988; Solomon, 1992; Williams and Williams, 1987). Inevitably, this places a severe strain on marital and familial relationships, and the children in these families may not be provided with the structure, nurturance, and consistency necessary for healthy psychological development. It has also been observed that child care responsibilities can affect the "veterans' working through the transition from the 'reflex' of combat aggressiveness to adaptive nondestructive aggression in their current lives. For example, the 'terrible two's' seem to reawaken the painful effects of combat aggression . . ." (Haley, 1983, cited in Harkness 1989, p. 37). Thus, although the veteran with PTSD often becomes the "identified patient," all family members are adversely affected, with children being particularly vulnerable to the emotional disruption evidenced in the family system. Solomon (1988, p. 325) describes the impact of PTSD on family functioning as follows:

> Of the host of PTSD symptoms those that have direct negative effects on social relations are particularly significant for veterans' families. These symptoms include numbing of responsiveness . . . diminished interest in significant activities, feelings of detachment or alienation, and constricted affect. . . . Conflicts between aggressive impulses and the attempt to control them may affect the veteran's functioning as both father and husband.

In addition to the previously described symptomatology, many veterans suffering from combat-related PTSD frequently manifest labile affect and low frustration tolerance. In fact, it has been noted that "cyclic outbursts of rage are characteristic of some war veterans" and that "one of the most painful and problematic features of Vietnam veterans' families is that the veteran often does not sympathize with the pain of family members, but rather becomes hostile and distant" (Williams and Williams, 1987, pp. 222-223) despite the love and empathy he may feel. As a result of their hypervigilant comportment and sensitivity to effectively toned stimuli, many individuals with PTSD have difficulty modulating or controlling their aggressive feelings (van der Kolk, 1988). The parent who has PTSD sometimes displays unpredictable and intense rage, and at other times avoids any emotional involvement with family members. Children have difficulty making sense of these inconsistent responses and even very young children will assume responsibility for their parent's behavior.

The veteran's difficulty connecting with his or her children can start a vicious cycle of guilt, self-recrimination, frustration, and further withdrawal. Communication invariably suffers and family members eventually find themselves feeling increasingly disconnected from each other. In addition, interpersonal conflicts tend to be impulsively and sometimes aggressively acted out rather than verbally resolved, a tendency that can have a negative effect on children's emotional and psychosocial development. A leading expert in the field of PTSD poignantly describes how children are impacted by a parent's PTSD (van der Kolk, 1987, p. 181):

> Children in such families [with a traumatized father] invariably grow up with distorted ideas about their roles in family conflicts: they are likely to blame themselves and carry around a core of self hatred that is difficult to undo later in life. These children often

> develop difficulties in emotional involvement with others; their object relations frequently are characterized by withdrawal and caution lest the wounds of emotional betrayal once again be opened, or by intense involvements and repeated disappointments as nobody is found who can compensate for the sense of loss and betrayal they have carried since childhood.

Not surprisingly, recent research has shown that violent behavior by veteran fathers placed children at higher risk for behavioral, academic, and interpersonal problems (Harkness, 1989). Although children manifest a range of responses to violence, some age-specific responses have been documented. For example, as a group, younger children tend to internalize their feelings, turning their "fear and pain inward often becoming hyperactive and/or depressed . . . other children, especially older ones, seem to externalize their behavior so as to emulate and identify with the aggressive father. This identification is used as a defense [against] fears of attack, humiliation and abandonment." (Harkness, 1989, pp. 171-172). Research and clinical evidence strongly supports the belief that even indirect exposure to anger (i.e., witnessing violent outbursts) "causes negative emotional reactions in children" (Emery, 1989, p. 325). In fact, children as young as twelve months old have been found to respond to episodes of anger not directed at them with signs of distress ranging from crying to increased aggression (Cummings, cited in Emery, 1989). Assessing the level of family violence is an important task for the clinician working with veterans' families; it has been reported that about half of all Vietnam veterans' wives seeking counseling have experienced at least one episode of battering (Matsakis, 1988). In addition, a recent study documented significantly more violence in families of Vietnam veterans with PTSD than in families of veterans without PTSD (Jordan et al., 1992).

Moreover, it has been suggested that the problematic child behaviors reported by veteran parents "resemble behaviors exhibited by the father [with PTSD], e.g., depression, anxiety, low frustration tolerance and outbursts of anger . . . [such] behavior may be an attempt to identify with the father or to understand the father's behavior and thereby feel close to him" (Harkness, 1989, p. 170). Clinicians have described the often intense or symbiotic involvement children sometimes have with their traumatized parent. The overidentification with the parent with PTSD impedes the child's ability to individuate and develop age-appropriate autonomous behaviors. For example, ego boundary problems, anxiety, aggression, and preoccupation with specific events that were traumatic for the parent are reported as typical symptoms of children with secondary trauma (Rosenheck, 1985). It is also believed that long-term exposure to "reliving" experiences of the traumatized parent (e.g., vivid memories, flashbacks, etc.) fosters an unhealthy bond with the parent; in his or her identification with the parent via this intense exposure, the child "experiences in fantasy the same kinds of events his/her parent actually lived through [thereby] internalizing a frightening reality" (Rosenheck and Nathan, 1985, p. 539).

In light of such chaotic family experiences and commitment or attachment complications, it is not surprising that children identified as having "secondary trauma" exhibit symptoms and behaviors that are very similar to (and at times identical with) children diagnosed with PTSD. For example, children adversely affected by their parent's PTSD manifest emotional lability, depression, withdrawal, hyperarousal or hyperactivity, physical aggression, anxiety, low self-esteem, or acting-out behaviors (Harkness, 1989; Jordan et al., 1992; cf. Rosenheck and Nathan, 1985; and Solomon, 1988). Also, although the DSM III-R includes a separate category for dissociative disorders, a body of theoretical and clinical literature supports the view that dissociation is a response to trauma (cf. Braun, 1989; Chu and Dill, 1990; Famularo et al., 1991; and Paley, 1988) and that a relationship exists "between the degree of dissociation and degree of childhood stress" (Sanders and Giolas, 1991, p. 53). In fact, many clinicians describe dissociative symptoms in clients with PTSD (Matz, 1992).

Again, it is not surprising to see dissociative symptoms in children suffering from secondary traumatization. Unfortunately, however, dissociation may be misdiagnosed or misunderstood in both clinical and school settings. Rather than appreciating the dissociative symptomatology as a (coping) response resulting from severe stressors, clinicians and teachers alike may see such children's behaviors only as evidence of attentional disorders (e.g., ADHD). Another diagnostic difficulty relevant to the identification of both PTSD and secondary trauma stems from the fact that until recently, most trauma research focused on adults. In an attempt to further clarify the post-traumatic responses of children, the American Psychiatric Association (1993) recently suggested adding diagnostic descriptions that are specific to children. It has been proposed that the symptomatology of PTSD in the DSM IV include the qualifying statement "in children [the post-trauma response] may be expressed . . . by disorganized or agitated behavior" (APA, 1993, p. k:8). Indeed, it has been well documented that "children are less likely than adults to speak directly about their problems . . . their stress related difficulties may instead emerge in their schoolwork, in their relations with their peers, and in their relations with family members" (Hobfoll et al., 1991, p. 853). It is important, therefore, for clinicians and teachers to consider the role that family stress and PTSD may play in the development of children's disorganized, anxious, or even dissociative behaviors.

Perhaps it is most accurate to understand the secondary traumatization of veterans' children as being on a continuum—children who suffer the most deleterious effects live in violent homes and overidentify with the parent with PTSD. Indeed, although a number of veterans' families with PTSD are coping adequately, "the children of veterans with PTSD are more likely to have behavioral problems than children of veterans without PTSD, and more than one third of male veterans with PTSD have a child with problems in the clinically significant range" (Jordan et al., 1992, pp. 923-924). As the conceptual and clinical understanding of secondary trauma continues to improve, it is imperative that psychodiagnostic, psychotherapeutic, and educational strategies that address the emotional, social, and cognitive needs of these children be developed. The following two sections describe general approaches and specific interventions that may help clinicians, teachers, and related service personnel in their work with children of veterans. The concluding section describes program models that allow service providers to plan and deliver those interventions collaboratively, rather than in discipline-specific, fragmented ways.

Psychotherapeutic Strategies

Most of the psychotherapeutic strategies used to help children with PTSD can also be used in the treatment of secondary trauma (e.g., behavioral, cognitive-behavioral, and insight-oriented treatment strategies). However, because the secondary trauma described in this paper is acquired through contagion (i.e., it develops in response to stress and dysfunction within the family system), the child's symptomatology must be understood within the context of family dynamics, communication patterns, and identification with the parent with PTSD. As Rosenheck and Nathan (1985, p. 539) note, "psychotherapeutic intervention helps these children disentangle their experiences from those being relived by their fathers, with significant benefit to them and their families." Harkness (1989, p. 174) echoes a similar view:

> Children of Vietnam veterans with PTSD, especially those whose fathers are violent, are identifiable as 'high risk' children. . . . Effective intervention and treatment begins with identifying these families as 'high risk' and identifying through an early comprehensive assessment, specific problem areas. This assessment needs to focus not only on how people feel but closely examine individual and family dynamics, including addressing the issue of violence, which always has a negative effect on family stability and emotional tone.

In developing comprehensive clinical interventions, individual and group therapy should be augmented with family therapy. Although individual psychotherapy can provide the child with a safe place to break the often implicit code of silence about family life and group therapy can help the child realize that he or she is not alone (and, therefore, offer a powerfully validating experience), the majority of children also need family therapy. If systematic changes within the family do not occur, it is very difficult for these children—especially latency age and younger—to sustain the emotional and behavioral benefits of individual or group therapy.

Figley's (1988) empowerment approach to family therapy, with its emphasis on building family social supportiveness and developing new roles and skills for improving family communication, is particularly relevant for veterans' families dealing with the effects of PTSD. Also, although the goals are more modest, a psychoeducational model can be an effective intervention for higher-functioning families (cf. Cosgrove et al., 1993).

In terms of more specific interventions, children need the opportunity to articulate and explore their thoughts and feelings about the effects of their father's PTSD on their lives. In other words, the attempt should be made to "tether more chaotic family experiences to an event that can be talked about" (Dan, personal communication, November 19, 1993). It is also critical to teach children and families more effective communication and conflict resolution skills. Before implementing any skill-building strategies, however, the clinician must first facilitate the development of age-appropriate autonomous behaviors. Harkness (1989, pp. 174-176) speaks directly to this issue:

> Strengthening of ego functions should be a major focus of treatment with these children, with an emphasis on reality testing, increasing frustration tolerance and encouragement of verbalization as an alternative to re-enactment. These children need to recognize their separateness from their fathers . . . they need to become aware that they are not responsible for their parents' behavior and pain and do not need to feel guilty about it.

In addition, it is very important that clinicians who work with conduct-disordered children and children suffering from attentional, anxiety, or mood disorders appreciate the role that a veteran's PTSD may be playing as a contributing etiological factor. Similarly, clinicians might want to consider the (albeit informal) comorbid diagnosis of secondary trauma. More specifically, understanding the conduct-disordered adolescent's behavior within the context of secondary trauma can allow for a more thorough understanding of the individual's behavior as well as more proactive and interdisciplinary interventions (rather than reactive and punitive ones).

As mentioned previously, this is not to suggest that all such attentional and behavior problems are part of the PTSD/secondary trauma symptomatology. Much work is needed to understand fully the symptomatic and possible etiological overlap between various childhood emotional disorders (e.g., PTSD) and learning or behavior problems such as ADHD, conduct disorders, and learning disabilities. Considering the role that family stress and parental PTSD may play in the development of a child's attentional or disruptive behavior disorders can only enhance therapeutic interventions. That is, at both a behavioral and dynamic level, clinicians can attend to the ways in which a child may be affected by his or her parent's PTSD. Play therapy, for example, can provide an excellent opportunity for children to experiment with expressing their feelings. Psychotherapeutic board games, especially those that specifically address family issues, can be a nonthreatening and fun activity that can help children sort out their feelings and develop more healthy coping responses.

Finally, it is important to appreciate that no matter how many "dysfunctional" patterns are evidenced in the family with a traumatized parent, or how problematic a child's behavior is, both the family as a whole and the individual child possess coping strengths and emotional resiliency. In order to fully respond to children suffering from secondary trauma (and indeed, all clients), we must recognize that competence and dysfunction always coexist (Davidson, personal communication, April 23, 1992). In other words, we must not succumb to the tendency to define these families and children in terms of pathologies and deficits. Rather, without romanticizing their suffering, we should place their limitations and difficulties in context in a way that respects their integrity and maximizes their resources.

Educational Interventions

Most of the literature that addresses intervention strategies for traumatized children focuses on clinical rather than educational issues. In light of the previously described symptomatology, however, it is apparent that many children suffering from primary (i.e., PTSD) and secondary trauma manifest significant attention and behavior problems. For example, Yule and Williams (1990) provide a compelling description of classroom behaviors exhibited by a child who has experienced trauma. "[H]e is constantly on the move, snatching things, fiddling with things, not doing as he was asked, making noise, and generally being disruptive and defiant. At school, this child had great difficulty in concentrating, didn't listen to teachers, and couldn't answer questions" (Yule and Williams, 1990, p. 285).

Not surprisingly, children suffering from secondary trauma often have coexisting learning problems that frequently result from their trauma-based symptomatology. For example, many children exhibit decreased attention and memory, have difficulty concentrating, and present with inconsistent responses and poor organizational skills. There may also be a number of behavioral issues such as acting out self-injurious behaviors (cf. Harkness, 1989; Jordan et al., 1992; and Rosenheck and Nathan, 1985). Moreover, the children most adversely affected may present with dissociative behaviors in the classroom. Also, because of the numbing of affect or decreased responsiveness to external stimuli, traumatized children frequently have difficulty establishing and maintaining healthy peer relationships.

In this way, the teacher is challenged not only to identify children at risk for developing secondary trauma, but also to design classroom settings and specific assignments that maximize the traumatized child's learning potential. In addition, the classroom is the optimum setting to normalize the recovery process in part (Pynoos and Nadar, 1993) because the classroom environment minimizes fears by providing consistency and predictability. In fact, many children's fears are revealed through typical class activities and discussions. Pynoos and Nadar (1993) point out, however, that it is important that classroom interventions do not become a substitute for individual or family interventions. At the same time, teachers need to be aware that seemingly nonthreatening class assignments can trigger strong emotional reactions in these children. Thus, it is imperative that teachers maintain close contact with the school therapeutic staff or mental health agency counselors.

In terms of specific educational strategies, it is important to structure the classroom in such a way that the traumatized child feels safe and supported and is clearly aware of rules and expectations. For example, if classroom activities or demands become too overwhelming, the student and teacher could develop a plan whereby the student temporarily removes himself or herself from the situation, thereby retreating to a safer place. Similarly, it is most helpful to use positive reinforcement strategies rather than punitive or restraining measures. Indeed, the importance of the student's perception of safety and support inside the classroom cannot be overemphasized.

To achieve maximum success, intervention must be individualized; however, there are a number of general learning strategies that can be effective for many special-needs children, including those who have been traumatized. More specifically, learning strategies are techniques, principles, or rules that enable a student to solve problems and complete tasks independently. Learning strategies give the student an insight as to how he or she learns and how to effectively use what has been learned (Lenz et al., 1984). These strategies are particularly helpful for children suffering from PTSD or secondary trauma because many traumatized children underincorporate stimulus cues, making careless mistakes or reaching premature conclusions. The Learning Strategies Curriculum (Lenz et al., 1984) is an excellent example of a program designed not only to increase the students' organizational skills, but also to generalize their use in a variety of settings. Other learning strategies identified in the literature as being helpful for students with organizational or memory difficulties are also relevant for traumatized children. Graphic organizers, audio tapes of class lectures, books on tape, and organizational notebooks may be useful in planning educational interventions.

Another school intervention that may be helpful for students suffering from secondary trauma is the implementation of a mentor program. A mentor is a staff person within the school system who has been identified as someone who the student trusts and is a sounding board for the student to discuss concerns and problems with. A mentor, who meets with the student on a regular basis, ensures that the student remains current with both long- and short-range assignments. If necessary, a mentor could act as a go-between for the student and teacher. Insofar as a mentor program provides increased contact and connection, it can be a highly effective intervention for traumatized children.

Clearly, to respond fully to the educational needs of traumatized children, the classroom teacher needs to be aware of the behavioral manifestations of trauma. Only then can the teacher develop individualized strategies while simultaneously ensuring that the student makes a commitment to learn these strategies. Most importantly, however, the teacher must work together with mental health providers to design a classroom setting that is conducive to the traumatized child's recovery process and that facilitates his or her learning.

Toward an Integrated Service Delivery Approach

The mental health and learning needs exhibited by children who have been traumatized have been identified in the preceding sections of this paper. The interrelatedness of both those needs and the strategies necessary to foster success requires an expansion of services beyond those typically provided through schools. Children suffering from secondary trauma present with a range of emotional and academic problems. The next section of the paper will describe an integrated service delivery model and highlight examples of policy and practice initiatives at the national and state levels.

Traditionally, the educational and mental health service systems have been criticized for their lack of collaborative efforts on behalf of children with emotional needs (Forness, 1988; Kahn et al., 1992; Dolan, 1992). Recent developments in the field of service integration suggest movement away from the fragmented, discipline-specific approach to service delivery. As stated by Dolan (1992) in a report on models for integrating human services into the schools, an "emerging theme is that schools must be closely tied with other community agencies if they are to have any chance to remove the barriers to learning that result from health, economic, and family support factors" (p. 1).

The U.S. Departments of Education and of Health and Human Services, through a joint task force, have recently published a guide for "crafting a profamily system of education and human services" (Kahn and Kamerman, 1992). The Education and Human Services Consortium is a group of twenty-two national organizations advocating more cooperation and collaboration among schools and social service agencies. The National Center for Service Integration Information and Clearinghouse was established to compile and disseminate information regarding the growing number of groups interested in the concept and practice of service integration across a number of fields including education, public welfare, child welfare, mental health, public health, and employment. Revision to the federal Medicaid regulations has enabled funds to be used for case management at the school level for eligible students.

A number of states have enacted legislation, established cross-agency planning groups, and supported local program development. New Jersey, Iowa, Kentucky, and California are only a few of the states that have taken direct action to improve coordination among human service agencies. Each state, under Part H of Public Law 101-476, the comprehensive special-education bill, is mandated to provide such coordination for the services to families with children, age birth to three years, who have special needs. The same federal legislation requires each state to develop a plan for student-oriented, multiagency planning for students with special needs age fourteen through graduation.

At the local level, integrated services require an expansion of schools' accountability from learning outcomes to outcomes for the emotional, social, and learning dimensions of the child (Kahn, 1992; Forness, 1988; Dolan, 1992). Schools have responded to the multiple needs of students in varied ways with regard to actual services delivered, the financial arrangement required, and the overall administrative structures used to maintain the system. School based and school linked are two broad categories for discussing the wide range of models described in the service integration literature.

School-based programs are those physically housed with the school, as a multiservice center. The expanded service may be a part of the school structure, or a colocation arranged with other service agencies. A colocation usually includes shared space, a common referral system, and shared costs of running a service at a school (Dolan, 1992, p. 2).

In a role expansion mode, the school staff assume broader responsibilities such as case management or parent training. Schools might hire additional social workers, counselors, and health professionals, or paraprofessionals (Kahn and Kamerman, p. 24). School restructuring might bring a fundamental change in pupils' schedules, location and type of learning environments, and the process for planning programs of individual students. A high school might offer vocational training on the ground of a neighboring manufacturing site or technical trade school and incorporate counseling to develop appropriate psychosocial work skills as part of the daily schedules. New program-planning structures are especially important when multiple agencies share the site and programming responsibilities. The Success for All Program operating in more than thirty schools across the country combines school restructuring for academic support with colocation of human service agencies for a family support program (Slavin et al., 1992).

School-linked programs are those clusters of service agencies collaborating to meet the needs of the same client base. Kirst (1991) views such collaboration as "meshing" that goes beyond coordination. In addition to a common referral base, shared financial arrangement, and pupil planning processes, a lead agency is identified. This lead agency is most often the school, although other agencies could also service this function. School linkages enable schools to offer a wider range of services that are beyond what is normally viewed as within the expertise of school staff. The School Development Model (Comer, 1980; Comer, 1988) is used by an increasing number of schools across the country to expand the role of schools serving students who are disadvantaged. Although each school within the program might be linked with different types of community service agencies, frequently included might be housing agencies, a day care center, and links to a local hospital.

Mental health services, for students and other family members, whether by colocation or a school linkage, are considered to be at the more controversial end of the integrated service continuum (Dolan, 1992, p. 2), yet appear to be one of the most frequently used services, as in the New Jersey Youth Services Program (New Jersey Department of Human Services, 1990).

Comprehensive evaluation data from the various program models are not readily available because many programs are new, formative evaluation procedures were not initiated as the program began, and expected outcomes to be evaluated for each program vary. For example, improved attendance and a decrease in the drop-out rate might be tracked for one program, but sustained academic performance might be targeted for another (Slavin et al., 1992). The Center for Research on Effective Schooling for Disadvantaged Students (CDS) recently published a report reviewing existing data from a number of programs nationwide that have been in existence for a number of years and have shown positive outcomes. The Center has extrapolated the following components necessary for successful integration:

1. Collaborative planning;
2. Ownership by the school;
3. Principal's role as coordinator;
4. Case managers;
5. Shared resources;
6. Gradual phase-in; and
7. Training and staff development.

In summary, a review of the literature suggests that children who live with a severely traumatized parent or who observed traumatizing events may be affected similarly to those who directly experienced such an event. For example, children may be differently affected depending on the intensity of the event, the nature of the child and his or her relationship to those directly traumatized, and the follow-up support available. Mental health and educational interventions have been identified for use, depending on the age and specific needs of the child. Some program models used to integrate the mental health and educational services required for the child who has experienced trauma or secondary trauma have been described. The delivery of services to children who have been traumatized remains in need of a comprehensive evaluation to determine which program or program components enable the child to overcome barriers to learning and cope successfully in this complex world.

References

American Psychiatric Association. 1980. Diagnostic and statistical manual of mental disorders III. Washington, DC: American Psychiatric Association.

American Psychiatric Association. 1987. Diagnostic and statistical manual of mental disorders III-R. Washington, DC: American Psychiatric Association.

American Psychiatric Association. 1993. Diagnostic and statistical manual of mental disorders-IV draft criteria. Washington, DC: American Psychiatric Association.

Braun, B. 1989. Psychotherapy of the survivor of incest with a dissociative disorder. *Psychiatric Clinics of North America* 12(2):307-324.

Camach, P., K. Bowen, and D. Hunt. 1991. From a troubled past to an uncertain future: Vietnam veterans, a community at risk. Five-year follow-up report on the status of Vietnam veterans in the commonwealth of Massachusetts. Boston: The William Joiner Center for the Study of War and Social Consequence, University of Massachusetts at Boston.

Catherall, D. 1992. *Back from the brink: A family guide to overcoming traumatic stress*. New York: Bantam/Doubleday/Dell.

Chu, J., and D. Dill. 1990. Dissociative symptoms in relation to childhood physical and sexual abuse. *American Journal of Psychiatry* 147(7):887-892.

Comer, J. 1980. *School Power*. New York: Free Press.

Comer, J. 1988. Educating poor minority children. *Scientific American* 259(5): 42-48.

Cosgrove, L. 1987. The aftermath of sexual assault. Unpublished doctoral dissertation, Duquesne University, Pittsburgh.

Cosgrove, L., M. Brady, F. Scott, W. Holcomb, and P. Peck. 1993. Living together/learning together, post-traumatic stress disorder (PTSD). Unpublished manuscript.

Danieli, Y. 1985. The treatment and prevention of long-term effects and intergenerational transmission of victimization: A lesson from holocaust survivors and their children. In *Trauma and its wake*, ed. C.R. Figley, pp. 295-313. New York: Brunner/Mazel.

Davis, R., and L. Friedman. 1985. The emotional aftermath of crime and violence. In *Trauma and its wake*, ed. C. Figley, pp. 90-112. New York: Brunner/Mazel.

Dolan, L. 1992. *Models for integrating human services into the school*. Baltimore, MD: Center for Research on Effective Schooling for Disadvantaged Students, The Johns Hopkins University.

Emery, R. 1989. Family violence. *American Psychologist* 44(2):321-328.

Eth, S., and R. Pynoos. 1985. Children traumatized by witnessing acts of personal violence: Homicide, rape, or suicide behavior. In *Post-Traumatic Stress Disorder in Children*, ed. S. Eth and R. Pynoos, 17-44. Washington, DC: American Psychiatric Press, Inc.

Famularo, R., R. Kinscherff, and T. Fenton. 1991. Symptom differences in acute and chronic presentation of childhood post-traumatic stress disorder. *Child Abuse and Neglect* 14:439-444.

Figley, C. 1983. Catastrophes: An overview of family reactions. In *Stress and the family: Vol. 2. Coping with catastrophe* , ed. C. Figley and H. McCubbin, 3-20. New York: Brunner/Mazel.

Figley, C. 1985a. From victim to survivor: Social responsibility in the wake of catastrophe. In *Trauma and its wake*, ed. C. Figley, 398-415. New York: Brunner/Mazel.

Figley, C., ed. 1985b. *Trauma and its wake*. New York: Brunner/Mazel.

Figley, C. 1988. A five-phase treatment of post-traumatic stress disorder in families. *Journal of Traumatic Stress* 1(1):127-141.

Figley, C. 1989. *Helping traumatized families.* San Francisco: Jossey-Bass Publishers.

Forness, S. 1988. Planning for the needs of children with serious emotional disturbance: The national special education and mental health coalition. *Behavioral Disorders* 13(2):127-139.

Green, B., M. Korol, M. Grace, M. Vary, A. Leonard, G. Gleser, and S. Smitson-Cohen. 1991. Children and disaster: Age, gender, and parental effects on PTSD symptoms. *Journal of the American Academy of Child and Adolescent Psychiatry* 30(6):945-951.

Hardley, G., and B. Guerney. 1989. A psychoeducational approach. In *Treating Stress in Families*, ed. C. Figley, 158-181. New York: Brunner/Mazel.

Harkness, L. 1989. Children of war: A study of the offspring of Vietnam veterans with post-traumatic stress disorder. Unpublished doctoral dissertation, New York University.

Helzer, J., L. Robins, and L. McEvoy. 1987. Post-traumatic stress disorder in the general population. *The New England Journal of Medicine* 317:1630-1634.

Hobfoll, S., C. Spielberger, S. Breznitz, C. Figley, S. Folkman, B. Lepper-Green, D. Meichenbaum, N. Milgram, I. Sandler, I. Sarason, and B. van der Kolk. 1991. *American Psychologist* 46(8): 848-855.

Jordan, B., C. Marmar, J. Fairbank, W. Schlenger, R. Kulka, R. Hough, and D. Weiss. 1992. Problems in families of male Vietnam veterans with post-traumatic stress disorder. *Journal of Consulting and Clinical Psychology* 60(6):916-926.

Kahn, A., and S. Kamerman. 1992. Integrating service integration: An overview of initiatives, issues, and possibilities. New York: National Center for Children in Poverty, Columbia University School of Public Health.

Kirst, M. 1991. *Integrating children's services.* Menlo Park, CA: Education Sources.

Kirst, M. 1992. Supporting school-linked children's services. In *Rethinking school finance*, ed. A. Odden, 298-321. San Francisco: Jossey-Bass.

Kiser, L., B. Ackerman, E. Brown, N. Edwards, E. McColgan, R. Pugh, and D. Pruitt. 1988. Post-traumatic stress disorder in young children: A reaction to purported sexual abuse. *Journal of the American Academy of Child and Adolescent Psychiatry* 27(5):645-649.

Krugman, S. 1987. Trauma in the family: Perspectives on the intergenerational transmission of violence. In *Psychological Trauma*, ed. B. van der Kolk, 127-151. Washington, DC: American Psychiatric Press, Inc.

Lenz, K., J. Schumaker, D. Deshler, and V. Beals. 1984. *Learning strategies curriculum.* Lawrence, KS: University of Kansas.

Lovitt, T., S. Fisher, J. Freston, K. Kemp, R.C. Moore, B. Schroeder, and M. Baueernschmidt. 1990. Using precision teaching techniques: Translating research. *Teaching Exceptional Children* 22(3).

Matsakis, A. 1988. *Vietnam wives.* Kensington, MD: Woodbine House.

Matz, J. 1992. Needs of trauma survivors and their significant others. In-Service Training. Waltham, MA: Eunice Kennedy Shriver Center.

Melaville, A., and G. Asayesh. 1992. *Together we can: A guide to crafting community-based family-centered strategies for integrating education and human services.* U.S. Department of Education, Office of Education Research and Improvement, U.S. Department of Health and

Human Services, Office of the Assistant Secretary for Planning and Evaluation.

New Jersey Department of Human Services. 1990. The school-based youth services program. Trenton, NJ: Department of Human Services.

Paley, A. 1988. Growing up in chaos: The dissociative response. *The American Journal of Psychoanalysis* 48(1):72-83.

Pynoos, R., and K. Nader. 1993. Issues in the treatment of post-traumatic stress in children and adolescents. In *International Handbook of Traumatic Stress Syndromes*, ed. J. Wilson and B. Raphael, 535-549. New York: Plenum Press.

Rosenheck, R. 1986. Impact of post-traumatic stress disorder of World War II on the next generation. *Journal of Nervous Mental Disorders* 174(6):319-327.

Rosenheck, R., and P. Nathan. 1985. Secondary traumatization in children of Vietnam veterans. *Hospital and Community Psychiatry* 36(5):538-539.

Sanders, B., and M. Giolas. 1991. Dissociation and childhood trauma in psychologically disturbed adolescents. *American Journal of Psychiatry* 148(1):50-54.

Slavin, R., N. Madden, N. Karweit, L. Dolan, and B. Wasik. 1992. *Success for all: A relentless approach to prevention and early intervention in elementary schools*. Arlington, VA: Educational Research Services.

Solomon, Z. 1988. The effect of combat-related post-traumatic stress disorder on the family. *Psychiatry* 51:323-329.

Solomon, Z., M. Waysman, G. Levy, B. Fried, M. Mikulincer, R. Benbenishty, V. Florian, and A. Bleich. 1992. From front line to home front: A study of secondary traumatization. *Family Process* 31:289-302.

Terr, L. 1983. Chowchilla revisited: The effects of psychic trauma four years after a school-bus kidnapping. *American Journal of Psychiatry* 140:1543-1550.

Terr, L. 1991. Childhood traumas: An outline and overview. *American Journal of Psychiatry* 148(1):10-19.

van der Kolk, B., ed. 1984. *Post-traumatic stress disorder: psychological and biological sequelae*. Washington, DC: American Psychiatric Press, Inc.

van der Kolk, B. 1987. *Psychological trauma*. Washington, DC: American Psychiatric Press, Inc.

van der Kolk, B.A. 1988. Trauma in men: Effects on family life. In *Abuse and victimization: Across the life span*, ed. M. Straus, 170-186. Baltimore, MD: Johns Hopkins Press.

Williams, C., and T. Williams. 1987. Family therapy for Vietnam veterans. In *Post-traumatic stress disorders: A handbook for clinicians*, ed. T. Williams, 221-231. Cincinnati, OH: Disabled American Veterans.

Yule, W., and R. Williams, R. 1990. Post-traumatic stress reactions in children. *Journal of Traumatic Stress* 3(2):279-295.

Authors' Note

It is critical that mental health professionals and educators do not assume that because the veteran parent has PTSD his or her child's attentional problems result from parental PTSD. A thorough psychological, educational, and psychosocial evaluation must be conducted in order to assess the child's attentional and behavior problems and the impact those problems might have on learning.

Hidden Clients of Domestic Violence

Eileen Pencer, M.Ed., C.S.W., A.C.S.W.; and Jacqueline DeCarlo, C.S.W.
Lower Eastside Service Center, Inc.
Vietnam Veterans Family Services Center
New York, NY

Abstract

Violence within the family has received substantial attention in the past few years. Although little quantitative data exist concerning the incidence of violence within families of Vietnam veterans, the data that have been assembled indicate a need for clinical approaches that address this issue.

Traditionally, therapy for Vietnam veterans who physically abuse their spouses or children has focused on the abuser, rather than the whole family. Many now recognize that an inclusive mode of treatment is more effective. This paper evaluates the use of the Vietnam Veterans Family Services Center's (VVFSC) family-centered clinical approach in dealing with the problem of "domestic violence" among families of Vietnam veterans. A case study of Family A (comprising a Vietnam veteran, his wife, and two adolescent daughters) is used to contrast VVFSC's family-centered model, which combines goal-oriented behavioral therapy and Charles Figley's "empowerment approach," with the individual therapy-oriented model used at a Vet Center operated by the U.S. Department of Veterans Affairs.

The results of this study demonstrate the importance of family participation in the treatment of domestic violence.

Eileen Pencer, M.Ed., C.S.W., A.C.S.W., *is vice president and chief program officer of the Lower Eastside Service Center, where she oversees all treatment programs. She was responsible for the development of the Vietnam Veterans Family Services Center (VVFSC) at this site.* ***Jacqueline DeCarlo, C.S.W.***, *is the director of VVFSC at this site and oversees program operations; she served as a VVFSC family therapist and provided psychotherapy and case management services to families of Vietnam veterans before taking on this position.*

Although no formal national studies have been conducted on the prevalence of domestic violence among Vietnam veterans, records in a U.S. Department of Veterans Affairs Vet Center indicated that approximately "one-third of six hundred men" (Williams and Williams, 1985, p. 197) reported striking their partners. Candice Williams of the Disabled American Veterans' (DAV) Vietnam Veteran Outreach Program in Denver, Colorado, reported that half of the wives seen were victims of abuse (Matsakis, 1988, p. 140), and a Research Project at the Washington, D.C., U.S. Department of Veterans Affairs (VA) Medical Center found that one-fourth of the wives seen were victims of physical abuse (Matsakis, 1988, p. 140).

This paper evaluates the use of the Vietnam Veterans Family Services Center's (VVFSC) family-centered clinical approach to dealing with the problem of domestic violence. A case study of Family A is used to contrast VVFSC's family-centered model, which combines goal-oriented behavioral therapy and Charles Figley's "empowerment approach," with the model used at the Vet Center—which is oriented toward individual therapy. The VVFSC's experience with the Vet Center model stems from on-site work at Vet Center offices in Manhattan and Staten Island.

Domestic Violence and "Family Isolation"

One of the defining characteristics of couples and families experiencing domestic violence is that they "tend to be closed systems" (Krugman, 1986, p. 43). The couple relationship is frequently characterized by distorted communication and limited interaction with friends, relatives, and community and by "rigid expectations regarding loyalty, secrecy, privacy and control" (Tifft, 1993, p. 105). The family is often also organized around secrets and a distrust of nonfamily members (Krugman, 1986). Williams and Williams (1985) assert that in veterans' families, the tendency towards isolation is directly related to the veteran's individual experience of isolation and alienation.

Individual / Group Versus Family Treatment

Historically, veterans' treatment for domestic violence and violent behavior has focused on the individual (Figley, 1978, chap. 14). For example, a treatment strategy developed by Horowitz and Solomon (Figley, 1978, chap. 13) was designed to strengthen "violent impulse control" using an individual therapy approach. Traditionally, violent behavior treatment has been provided in "rap" groups comprised only of Vietnam veterans (Figley, 1978, chap. 10). The clinical experience of Williams and Williams (1985), however, shows that family treatment is preferable to individual or group treatment for family-related problems such as domestic violence. The authors state that "veterans often get symptom relief from individual or group therapy, but that unless planned interventions are done with family systems, the possibility of permanent change of behavior is reduced" (p. 195).

Figley (1978) points out that treatment that focuses on the individual only may have been an effective intervention for Vietnam veterans following military service, but that in the post-Vietnam era, he believes the "most presenting problems are enmeshed in the veteran's interpersonal network" (p. 283). Figley states further that because domestic violence occurs within the family network, inclusion of the family in the therapeutic context is essential and key to effective treatment.

Family A—Hidden Clients

Family A is comprised of Eric, a forty-two-year-old white Vietnam veteran, his forty-year-old wife, Christine, and their adolescent daughters, Barbara and Tina. In 1990, when Mr. A first sought individual therapy from the Vet Center for domestic violence, Mr. and Mrs. A had been married for more than twenty years. Mrs. A threatened to separate from Mr. A unless he sought treatment.

During his first individual counseling session, Mr. A disclosed that his marital relationship was fraught with difficulties and admitted to abusing his wife regularly. Mr. and Mrs. A were subsequently referred to a Vet Center counselor for couples counseling. They terminated treatment at the end of three months during a period when the abuse had apparently ceased. Following couples counseling and throughout the six-month duration of individual therapy, Mr. A disclosed no further incidents of domestic violence and insisted that it was no longer a problem. With treatment oriented toward the individual only—without family members present to confront his denial—Mr. A could perpetuate the illusion of family harmony.

Mr. A's Family of Origin

In individual therapy, Mr. A described his father as a bitter and sadistic Holocaust survivor with severe post-traumatic stress disorder (PTSD) who regularly abused his three sons by tying them up and whipping them. Mr. A said he was relieved when his father died suddenly of a heart attack at age forty-nine.

Mr. A described his seventy-year-old mother as a mild-mannered woman whose relationships with the A family were cordial, but superficial. Mr. A's mother was the only member in his family of origin with whom he maintained any contact. She lived in an apartment nearby and visited Family A's home several times each week.

Mr. A's reservoir of painful childhood memories also included difficult relationships with his two elder brothers. He described them as extremely rejecting of him and provided graphic examples to demonstrate the extent to which they had publicly humiliated him. Following his return from Vietnam, Mr. A severed all contact with them. Ten years later, he learned from his mother that both brothers also abused their wives.

Mr. A's experiences in his family of origin were strong indicators of a propensity for domestic violence. The sex-role socialization passed on by his father and two brothers left Mr. A with "no patterns to follow except ones of violence and power" (Browne, 1987, p. 34). Having been victimized as a child and having also witnessed his brothers' abuse, Mr. A anticipated threat and risk in all family relationships and believed that intimate relationships, in general, were unpredictable and to be controlled. This was the apparent genesis of his use of violence as a "personal style of relating in adult life" (Browne, 1987, p. 33) and of a cycle of domestic violence that would define Mr. A's marital and family life.

Mr. and Mrs. A's Relationship History

Before leaving for Vietnam, Mr. A became romantically involved with a young woman with whom he later corresponded. This correspondence abruptly ceased, leaving Mr. A confused and rejected and in need of support. Mr. A confided in another New Yorker (Mrs. A's brother) who encouraged him to replace the former correspondent with another and connected him with his sister (the future Mrs. A).

Mrs. A's brother is eight years older than she, and the family favorite. Their mother suffered from chronic cardiac problems and died of a heart attack at age forty-two. She refused to undergo an operation that might have saved her life. Within one year, Mrs. A's father, a weak and passive man, remarried a possessive and domineering woman who actively disliked Mrs. A and forced her out of the family home. Frightened and traumatized, with all of her belongings in three small boxes, she set out to start a new life. Shortly after her move, she received Mr. A's letter from Vietnam and gladly began to correspond with this potential suitor. When Mr. A returned from Vietnam, he met and fell in love with the young woman to whom he had confided the details of his wartime experience. One year later, the couple married in a civil ceremony and set out to see their fantasy of family life realized.

Following their wedding, Mr. A attended college while Mrs. A worked as a nurse's aide. During Mr. A's second semester of college, Mrs. A became pregnant and informed Mr. A of her plan to resign in six months. Mr. A grudgingly enrolled in part-time evening courses and returned to his former job as a sanitation worker. For the first time (in what was to become a chronic pattern), following a charged confrontation, Mr. A struck his wife in her belly, causing her to miscarry.

Children of the Family

Three years later, Mrs. A became pregnant again. To guard against the risk of miscarrying, she spent extended periods in Mr. A's mother's home at a safe distance from Mr. A. For the first time, Mrs. A confided about Mr. A's violent behavior and her fears of miscarriage to her mother-in-law. Mrs. A's reliance on family fits the first-time victim's pattern of relief-seeking: "Like the wife of an 'alcoholic' or 'mentally ill' husband, the woman who is battered tries to handle these recurring episodes through existing family arrangements and through her prior affective feelings" (Tifft, 1993, p. 62).

When their first child, Barbara, was born, Mr. and Mrs. A were not on speaking terms. Mr. A had recently completed his studies and was now employed as an engineer. From the beginning of his new position, Mr. A settled into a pattern of returning home preoccupied and anxious about his work performance. At least weekly, he provoked an argument with Mrs. A after which he would physically abuse her, saying that she had deliberately provoked him. At age three, Barbara attempted to intervene and protect her mother and was hit by her father—this was the only time Mr. A hit his daughter in this way. Barbara's birth was the watershed in a chronic pattern of abuse that corroded the marital relationship and shattered the idyllic family fantasy.

Tina, Mr. and Mrs. A's second daughter, was born four years later. She was an affectionate, easygoing child who immediately won the affection of her father. Mr. A directed all of his positive attention towards Tina, which fueled a rivalry between the two children.

In the years that followed, the frequency of abuse increased until in 1991, Mrs. A threatened separation unless Mr. A sought counseling for his violent behavior.

Domestic Violence from a "Family-Oriented" Perspective

Following an intake interview, Mr. A was again assigned to a Vet Center counselor for individual therapy and proceeded to reexplore the roots of his violent behavior within his family of origin, his angry feelings towards Mrs. A., and the frequency of abuse. This time, however, Mr. and Mrs. A were also assigned to an on-site VVFSC family therapist and were introduced to VVFSC's family-oriented behavioral approach, which had included strict prohibitions against violent behavior and emphasized family safety.

The first step in the modification of violent behavior is setting ground rules and consequences with clear "prohibitions against further abuse" (Taylor, 1984, p. 14). Paradoxically, sometimes this activates the couple to challenge the therapist's authority and test the boundaries of the treatment structure. According to Taylor, abusive behavior may represent an "extreme attempt to affect change within the relationship and often within the life patterns of the individuals" (p. 13). Viewed from this perspective, it is a cry for help.

In the third meeting with the family therapist, Mrs. A reported an escalation of spouse abuse and expressed fear for her and her children's safety. To coordinate a plan of action, the family therapist scheduled an emergency meeting with the individual counselor. To the family therapist's surprise, the counselor prescribed continuing individual treatment, but ending family treatment immediately, claiming that this plan would ensure family safety and avert abuse escalation. The VVFSC family therapist countered, arguing that this plan would place the family in further jeopardy, and requested a case conference with the VOC treatment team to advocate on behalf of the family. She was unable to gain support for her position.

The following day, the family therapist met with the VVFSC supervisor to determine a course of action. Both agreed that family treatment intervention was necessary and implemented a plan for continuing couples/family treatment. The supervisor contacted the counselor and informed him of VVFSC's responsibility as family therapists and advocates and outlined the risks inherent in the counselor's plan. She informed the counselor of the VVFSC's plan to continue couples and family treatment at the program's main office. The plan to shift clinical responsibility to the VVFSC was accepted. VVFSC's family-oriented treatment plan was now set to begin.

VVFSC's Behaviorally Oriented Treatment Approach

The "No-Violence" Contract

VVFSC's behaviorally oriented treatment approach for domestic violence teaches "communication, problem-solving and conflict-resolution skills" (Figley, 1989, p. 36). This approach is based on the premise that "battering is learned and triggered in the context of a deficit of alternative conflict resolution skills" (Tifft, 1993, p. 107). The success of this approach is contingent on identifying "battering patterns" (p. 108) and introducing alternative responses via learned skills.

As a first step in enforcing the "no-violence contract," Bograd (1984, p. 564) stresses the importance of and anticipates difficulties the family therapist can expect in establishing a therapeutic alliance with the battered wife and abusive husband:

> [But] abusive men usually attend treatment to placate their wives or to monitor the information discussed in sessions. A therapeutic alliance cannot be established with a man who isn't committed to addressing his violence or who seeks to control the therapy. The therapeutic alliance will be further compromised as the battered woman risks retaliation from her husband for what she discloses to the therapist.

Beginning with Mr. A, the family therapist seized the opportunity to establish a therapeutic alliance by outlining the contract conditions. The family therapist set firm prohibitions against violent behavior, rationalizations, and shifting responsibility to Mrs. A (Bograd, 1986) and established termination of conjoint treatment as a "negative consequence for rule-violation" (Tifft, 1993, p. 111). Another condition of the "no-violence contract" was that Mr. A attend a men's battering group at the Victims Services Center every week.

The family therapist followed Bograd's (1986, p. 45) model to enlist Mr. A's help "to identify the physical, emotional, and behavioral cues that preceded [sic] his violence, and the situations that commonly triggered his fights." Mr. A proposed a plan to "signal the escalation of conflict" (Tifft, 1993, p. 117) and to cue Mrs. A about his need for a "temporary time-out(s) from the relationship" (p. 117). Then, with input from Mrs. A, Mr. A identified "button-pushing patterns" (Taylor, 1984, p. 12) as a preventive strategy to avert conflict escalation.

Next, the family therapist helped Mrs. A construct a safety plan to protect herself by assessing potential danger, locating emergency housing, and, if necessary, securing an Order of Protection from the courts. This strategy represented the first step in Mrs. A's efforts to declare that she deserved "safety and protection" (Bograd, 1986, p. 47) and was capable of establishing autonomy.

Once the family therapist determined that the treatment alliance was on firmer footing, she devised a collaborative plan that integrated the work each had done separately. This process required that Mr. and Mrs. A review, evaluate, and objectively discuss angry exchanges that had transpired during the past week. Each described his or her own behavior and checked it out with the other's impressions to determine if impression matched experience. This was the first step in the development of self-awareness training (Taylor, 1984).

At this point, Mrs. A recommended a technique that would enable them to more accurately report their experiences and impressions of conflict situations. She suggested keeping an "anger/stress diary" (Taylor, 1984, p. 14), which appealed to Mr. A who inferred that this would ensure more accurate reporting on Mrs. A's part. The family therapist welcomed this plan and added that the diary would also provide opportunities to report on "problem-solving procedures" (p. 14) such as time-outs.

During ensuing sessions, Mr. and Mrs. A identified the need for a feedback mechanism to aid in "anger recognition" (Taylor, 1984, p. 15). This time, Mr. A recommended a "buddy system . . . to aid in anger build-up awareness" (p. 15) and ensure immediate feedback. Mrs. A pointed out that there was danger inherent in this plan because negative feedback might trigger a violent episode. To prevent this, Mr. A appealed to the family therapist to teach them, through role playing, the art of communicating positive, anger-reducing messages (p. 15).

Expanding Treatment Boundaries

Therapy progressed with the couple reporting improved communication and no further incidents of domestic violence. It was agreed that this would be an opportune time to invite family members to participate in the treatment work.

According to Figley (1989, p. 39), traumatized families are attempting to cope with an "extraordinary stressor which has disrupted their lives, their routine, sense of well-being, and confidence in the safety and predictability of daily life." Figley's approach to helping families withstand or recover from trauma such as domestic violence and restore self-esteem is "to empower the family to deal more effectively with past and future stressors" (p. 65).

The family therapist applied Figley's "empowerment approach" to help Family A take control of their lives and commit to the family-centered treatment goal. This began with Barbara and Tina telling the story, "from their own perspective without editing" (p. 79), of how domestic violence was a significant life-stressor for their family. The goal was to frame the problem and "purge these feelings" (p. 83) before shifting the focus to the family's work of recovery. The therapist stressed that recovery did not imply that the problem was over but that the process would equip the family with "powerful tools for managing future stressors" (p. 102).

Barbara's report began with a childhood memory of her father's brutal attack on her mother and her own futile effort to intervene. She stated that following this incident, she emotionally disengaged from her father and shifted her allegiance entirely to her mother (Tifft, 1993, p. 76). According to Barbara, Mr. A deliberately set up a rivalry between Tina and herself to recruit an ally to his side. Barbara attributed her own failing grades to a persistent preoccupation with her mother's safety and the stressful home environment. Barbara also expressed concern about the deteriorating family situation and its effect on all of Family A.

When it was her turn to report, Tina had the family's full attention. As Mr. A's favorite daughter and the family's seemingly best-adjusted member, Tina seemed to be immune from emotional pain and trauma. For this reason, all were struck by Tina's moving account of the burdensome responsibilities she carried as the favorite child and the guilt she suffered both for being unable to prevent the abuse and for loving the abuser. She stated that the cumulative effect of observing her mother being abused was to erode all positive feelings she had held for her father.

"Domestic Violence Fact Sheets" produced by the National Woman Abuse Prevention Project report that whether or not children are abused in households where domestic violence occurs, "the emotional effects of witnessing the abuse are similar to the psychological trauma associated with being a victim of child abuse." According to Domestic Violence Fact Sheets, Barbara and Tina suffered at least two of the emotional effects of domestic violence on children: recurrent anxiety that abuse is forthcoming and guilt for being unable to stop the abuse.

To improve communication exchange, the family therapist used Figley's (1989, p. 41) "family enrichment skills training approach." For example, to introduce the concept of "role flexibility" (p. 28), the family therapist used nonthreatening behavioral strategies, beginning with Mr. and Mrs. A. Responsibility for one week's grocery shopping was Mr. A's homework assignment; maintaining the family car was assigned to Mrs. A. In the course of these exercises, the family therapist noted that more productive methods of communication would positively alter family dynamics.

The boundaries of family-oriented treatment work were further expanded when Mrs. A, Barbara, and Tina asked to be seen in individual therapy by VVFSC family therapists. Another intriguing VVFSC treatment option was also used when Barbara invited her boyfriend to attend her individual sessions to explore, for the first time, long-standing relationship difficulties related to domestic violence.

Breaching the Contract

After three months of family therapy, following a battering incident, the family therapist received an urgent call from Mrs. A requesting a couples therapy session. During the session Mrs. A, who had by this time gained considerable self-confidence, actively resisted Mr. A's efforts to dominate her again through physical force and refused to believe his "pledge of nonviolence" (Herman, 1992, p. 168). She ordered Mr. A to leave the family home and steadfastly held to this position throughout the course of the session. Herman recommends that as long as the couple's goals are in conflict and the threat of violence persists, "The victim cannot speak freely in couple sessions, and conflictual issues in the relationship cannot possibly be discussed, without increasing the likelihood of a violent incident" (p. 168). Conjoint treatment is no longer an option.

In the course of individual therapy sessions, Mrs. A described the couple's special attachment and emotional bond. Herman (1992, p. 92) refers to this as "traumatic bonding":

> The victim may live in terror of his wrath, but she may also view him as the source of strength, guidance and life itself. The relationship may take on an extraordinary quality of specialness. Some battered women speak of entering a kind of exclusive, almost delusional world, embracing the grandiose belief system of their mates and voluntarily suppressing their own doubts as a proof of loyalty and submission.

Two weeks later, Mr. A campaigned to return home by reawakening the former courtshiplike quality of their relationship. At first, Mrs. A remained clearsighted and stood her ground, but Mr. A's "promises to reform" were convincing (Herman, 1992, p. 79), and she gradually softened her resistance. Within one month of the battering incident, Mr. A returned home and settled into former behaviors. Three weeks later, however, reality set in again, this time with greater force and cruelty than ever before. That battering incident would be the last.

Immediately following the incident, Mrs. A resolved to end the violence and the relationship. She requested a family session to inform her daughters, certain that they would support her decision to separate from Mr. A. Browne (1987, pp. 115-116) states that:

> The point of, or even the discussion of separation is one of the most dangerous times for partners in a violent relationship. Abusive men threatened with the loss of their mates may be severely depressed, angry, agitated, homicidal, or suicidal. Even attempts to discuss a separation can set off an angry attack.

Although the following morning Mr. A acceded to her request to leave, Mrs. A intended to take precautionary steps to ensure her own and the children's safety.

According to Bograd (1986), treatment is successful even though the family therapist is unable to keep the family together or help the husband contain and control his violence. In the case of Mr. and Mrs. A, "keeping them together and ending the violence turned out to be mutually exclusive goals" (p. 47). Bograd contends that in cases such as this, "the best outcome for a relationship characterized by repeated violence can be helping to end it" (p. 47).

In the months that followed, Mrs. A, Barbara, and Tina met weekly with the family therapist to obtain emotional support and direction in seeking legal and financial assistance. On occasion, Mr. A's mother also attended family sessions to provide encouragement and family support. Within six months, in accordance with Figley's "empowerment approach," Mrs. A, Barbara, and Tina's functioning level had increased and all were sharing in the restorative work of recovery.

Conclusion

The case study of Family A demonstrates the effectiveness of family-centered treatment and the importance of family participation. The entire family's participation in the resolution and restorative process is critical; responsibility for affecting and maintaining change cannot rest with the veteran alone. Currently, the VVFSC's family focus complements the Vet Center's veteran focus. This partnership and collaboration significantly enriches the Vet Center's service menu for clients and contributes to staff development.

The success of the VVFSC's treatment model for domestic violence argues for expanding the treatment focus (as with Family A) to include the family and elevate these services to primary status. The VVFSC's commitment to this community and the recovery of its families has further enhanced recognition of this intervention's success. Veterans' families have long deserved to have places to heal from domestic violence. It is critical that family-centered intervention be consistently provided, now and beyond the life of the VVFSC program.

References

Bograd, M. 1984. Family systems approach: A feminist critique. *American Journal of Orthopsychiatry* 54(4):558-568.

Bograd, M. 1986. Holding the line: Confronting the abusive partner. *Networker,* 44-47.

Browne, A. 1987. *When battered women kill*. New York: The Free Press, A Division of Macmillan, Inc.

Figley, C.R. 1989. *Helping traumatized families*. San Francisco: Jossey-Bass, Inc.

Herman, J.L. 1992. *Trauma and recovery: The aftermath of violence—from domestic abuse to political terror.* New York: A Division of Harper Collins Publishers, Inc.

Horowitz, M.J., and G.F. Solomon. 1975. Delayed stress response syndromes in Vietnam veterans. In *Stress disorders among Vietnam veterans: Theory, research and treatment,* ed. C.R. Figley, 268-280. New York: Brunner/Mazel, Inc.

Krugman, S. 1986. Challenging the tradition: In some families, violence is a way of life. *Networker,* 41-43.

Lifton, R.J. 1976. Advocacy and corruption in the healing profession. In *Stress disorders among Vietnam veterans: Theory, research and treatment,* ed. C.R. Figley, 209-230. New York: Brunner/Mazel, Inc.

Matsakis, A. 1988. *Vietnam wives: Women and children surviving life with veterans suffering Post-Traumatic Stress Disorder.* Washington, DC: Woodbine House, Inc.

National Woman Abuse Prevention Project. *Domestic violence fact sheets: Effects of domestic violence on children.*

Stanton, M.D., and C.R. Figley. 1978. Treating the Vietnam veteran within the family system. In *Stress disorders among Vietnam veterans: Theory, research and treatment,* ed. C.R. Figley, 281-289. New York: Brunner/Mazel, Inc.

Taylor, J.W. 1984. Structured conjoint therapy for spouse abuse cases. *Social Casework: The Journal of Contemporary Social Work* 65:11-18.

Tifft, L.L. 1993. *Battering of women: The failure of intervention and the case for prevention*. Boulder, CO: Westview Press, Inc.

Williams, C., and T. Williams. 1985. Family therapy for Vietnam veterans. In *The trauma of war: Stress and recovery in Viet Nam veterans*, ed. S. Sonnenberg, A. Blank, and J. Talbott, 195-209. Washington, DC: American Psychiatric Press.

Children of Vietnam:
A Third Generation

Mary A. Moyer, M.S.
The Next Step, Inc.
Albany, NY

Abstract

The effects of post-traumatic stress disorder (PTSD) can be transgenerational. Vietnam veterans sometimes pass the symptomatic behaviors and symptoms of PTSD to their children, many of whom were born before PTSD and its long-term effects on human behavior were recognized and before their veteran-parent had the benefit of treatment for the disorder. Still ignored as a population in need of care, as adults some of these children continue the pattern of PTSD-related negative behaviors in their child-rearing practices.

This paper focuses on veterans suffering from the dual disorders of alcoholism/substance abuse and PTSD, their significant others, and most especially, their children. It is based on nine years' experience with an outpatient substance abuse treatment program undertaken through a contract with the U.S. Department of Veterans Affairs (VA) Veterans Readjustment Counseling Program, a Veterans Outreach Center, and personal clinical experience with hundreds of veterans and their families suffering the consequences of PTSD and substance abuse. It concludes that the need remains for the Agent Orange Class Assistance Program (AOCAP), Veterans Outreach Centers, and clinicians who work with veterans to establish full-family programs that address the needs of the adult children of veterans, many of whom suffer their own traumas resulting from their exposure to apparent PTSD and concomitant substance abuse disorders.

Mary Moyer, M.S., *is executive director of The Next Step, Inc., a fourteen-bed recovery home for women suffering from alcoholism. She earned her M.S. in rehabilitation counseling from Virginia Commonwealth University, and is herself a Vietnam-era veteran and the widow of a Vietnam veteran.*

First recognized in the seventeenth century and later studied among war veterans, post-traumatic stress disorder (PTSD) was officially recognized by the American Psychiatric Association in 1980 (DSM-IIIR, pp. 247, 309.89). PTSD is defined as a cluster of symptoms experienced by individuals who have been exposed to a severe stressful event outside the range of normal human experience. Symptoms of the disorder may include nightmares, flashbacks, intrusive thoughts, emotional numbing, avoidance, and marked personality changes. Depression and substance abuse are common factors that result in dysfunctional behavior and reduction in the quality of life, not only for veterans but for their partners, spouses, children, and significant others.

Since 1980, in an effort to promote effective treatment for the veteran, a wealth of information and training opportunities has been made available to clinicians through the U.S. Department of Veterans Affairs, the Society for Traumatic Stress Studies, and local workshops. Until recently, clinicians and policy makers, particularly within the VA system and local substance abuse programs, believed that if a veteran's problems were resolved, the family system would be stabilized: this notion was largely dismissed with the advent of spouses' groups. When they first began, spouse groups focused on educating spouses and partners of veterans on the dynamics of PTSD and ways to help the veteran. They have evolved into groups that focus on personal conflicts related to spouses and partners. The substance abuse community also has developed specific programs for children—AlaTeen, AlaPreteen, and Adult Children of Alcoholics, for instance—but has done little to address the children's issues that result from growing up in a dysfunctional home where the father or mother is suffering from PTSD, substance abuse, or PTSD/codependency.

All persons who drink do not become alcoholics, nor do all persons who serve in a war zone suffer from PTSD. This paper focuses on persons who suffer from the dual disorders of alcoholism/substance abuse and PTSD, their significant others, and most especially, their children. It is based on nine years' experience with an outpatient substance abuse treatment program undertaken through a contract with the VA Veterans Readjustment Counseling Program, a Veterans Outreach Center, and personal clinical experience with hundreds of veterans and their families suffering the consequences of PTSD and substance abuse.

A veteran suffering from coexisting PTSD and addiction creates an environment of gross unpredictability. Spouses or partners walk on eggshells, never knowing what to expect. They attempt to cope with the confusion by making extra efforts to pacify the veteran. Thus, all of their energy is expended on trying to understand the behavior of the veteran and putting some stability into their relationships. Children are often left to fend for themselves; they develop their own system of survival by assuming certain roles in the family. Consequently, rather than being an integrated system that supports all family members, the family may become a fragmented system where personal survival is the primary goal of each family member. Low self-esteem, fear, anxiety, strong abandonment issues, and emotional shutdown often become a part of the psychological makeup of family members. Basic combat survival rules appear to apply to each family member: They are often carried into adult relationships and affect the adult children's interaction with their own offspring.

Case History

The case history below illustrates the effects that coexisting PTSD and addiction can have on a family. (Names have been changed to ensure confidentiality)

John was an "old soldier" when he went to Vietnam to serve as an infantry "grunt" with the 4th Infantry Division. Married for seven years, father of four children, and a career Army soldier, he and his family enjoyed the challenges the Army offered. John and his wife had a marriage "made in heaven." Pattie, John's wife, concurred with his perception of life before Vietnam. During his tour, he was seriously wounded during a mortar attack. Ultimately, John was discharged from the Army as a result of his injuries and received a 100 percent disability rating from the VA.

On returning home, John began to experience symptoms of PTSD and, although he drank socially before going to Vietnam, he began to drink heavily. Because of his disturbed sleep and violent dreams, Pattie was soon forced to sleep on the couch. The household became a pseudo Army camp with John behaving as a drill sergeant. Emotional intimacy between John and Pattie and John and his children disappeared. Conversation lessened and before long, John withdrew to his study and refused to become involved in family activities.

Pattie also began to change. In response to John's vacillating behavior from drill sergeant-like determination to isolation from the family, Pattie's behavior ranged from deep depression and withdrawal on John's bad days to happy and carefree on John's good days. During the happy and carefree periods, Pattie acted like she was on a honeymoon, giving all of her attention to John. The children, although present, were largely ignored. During her periods of withdrawal, she said virtually nothing to anyone and spent her time doing household chores. As her energy drained, she simply reclined on the couch and watched television, oblivious to her surroundings.

At one point, Pattie consulted a physician at the VA hospital but was told that John's problem was his nerves and that her role was to understand and overlook his behavior. The disguised suggestion was that Pattie may have contributed to John's problems by her "attitude," mood, and behavior.

Well-meaning friends suggested that Pattie see her physician. He was sympathetic, but his approach was to offer tranquilizers and sleeping pills. Another friend suggested AlAnon. Pattie willingly accepted the offer and found support from other women who were living with active alcoholism. Pattie had some difficulty accepting John's alcoholism, arguing that he only drank in the evenings so he could sleep. She attempted to talk with John about his drinking and to ask him to stop drinking. John responded by flying into a rage and telling her not to attend any more meetings.

Pattie was now convinced that John's problems were her fault, and she set about developing a strategy that would bring John back to the man she knew and loved before Vietnam. Her energies became totally focused on John.

The children were growing older. Throughout the post-Vietnam years, they witnessed and were subjected to the same physical violence and emotional abuse placed on their mother. They were forbidden from speaking to anyone about "family business." Friends were not permitted to visit because there were too many chores to do as well as homework. With no parent to turn to, they gradually began to develop their own survival skills.

Andrew, the oldest, became the surrogate father, valiantly trying to keep the younger children together, encouraging school achievement, making decisions that would not incur the wrath of either parent, and seeing that the general rules of the household were obeyed. He was generally a good student and gave his parents no trouble.

Liza was the second child. A bright and lovely young girl, she had heard far too often her parents' warning about boys and what she would become if she didn't heed their words. She resented Andrew's directions. Gradually, she began hanging out with the "wrong crowd," became promiscuous, and eventually left home to live with a boy in another city. Although she contacted her mother occasionally, she refused to return home. She married her boyfriend and remained estranged from her family.

Lori, the third child, coped with the family situation by staying "out of the way." She was an average student, did her required chores, but stayed mostly to herself—usually in her room. She was quiet and withdrawn, had few friends, and seemed to live in a world of her own making.

Josh, the youngest child, was the family clown. His impish behavior provided comic relief for the family. Josh was well liked in school, but his grades were poor, largely due to his inability to pay attention in class and complete assignments. In spite of Josh's shortcomings, he seemed to be John's favorite. Josh grew up believing his humor would get him out of any kind of trouble.

Tragically, John was killed in an automobile accident while drunk when Josh turned eighteen. Pattie was relieved that life with John was finally over, but the anger, frustration, and bitterness that had plagued her through the years seemed to intensify with each passing day.

Andrew, after leaving home, found himself establishing relationships with troubled young girls, striving to help them straighten out their lives. Always one to "do the right thing," he married a girl who became pregnant while living with him.

Andrew made a point of learning all he could about Vietnam and the effects on the men who served in combat. As he learned more, he began to see his mother as the culprit, blaming her for the problems in the family. He came to believe that his mother contributed to his father's death and chose to have contact with her only on rare occasions.

Although Andrew drank occasionally, he did not seem to be an alcoholic. With the constant concerns about his wife's emotional problems, he sought to make his home happy and focus on his baby. Because he worked all day and assumed the household responsibilities, Andrew had little time to worry about his mother.

By the time of her father's death Liza had been twice divorced. The mother of three children, she was involved in her third relationship and planned to marry soon. Her relationship with her mother remained estranged, although at times, she found herself acting like her mother and managing her family in the same manner as her father.

Lori remained at home and continued to stay to herself. She finished high school and began working at a local factory. She developed a close friendship with a girl she met at work, but seemed to have no interest in anything other than going to work and coming home to watch television.

Josh discovered the world of drugs, was convicted for possession and distribution, and was now serving time in a state prison.

This case demonstrates the need for treatment of children of Vietnam veterans as well as whole-family treatment for those children who are now adults, married, and raising children of their own.

Children exposed to a lifetime of dysfunction in an untreated family system develop their own PTSD symptoms. The VA and AOCAP have made strides in improving treatment delivery to family members by not only focusing on the veteran but also recognizing the unique treatment needs of spouses and partners who have suffered their own PTSD and codependency symptoms. An earnest attempt is being made to view alcoholism and drug addiction as bona fide independent diseases rather than mere symptoms of underlying problems or attempts at self-medication. But the need for programs that specifically address the treatment needs of children affected by exposure to these codisorders and suffering from their own symptomatology remains. In recent years, the VA has begun to address lack of self-esteem, anxiety, and fear in family members separately from the veteran's symptoms. The single-minded focus on educating families about the Vietnam War and ways to help the veteran has been replaced with the effective healing that comes from recognizing the trauma suffered by individual family members.

What we hope to accomplish here is to raise the level of awareness and generate effective treatment programs for children who have grown up in dysfunctional environments, left home, and have carried their scars with them to their current family units. Such children, left untreated, will perpetuate the dysfunction they experienced through their own child-rearing practices.

Woititz (1983) and Kritsberg (1984) describe the etiology of adult children of dysfunctional homes as follows:

- They guess at what normal is. Normal is defined according to what the family decides. Because of the isolation factor, children know no comparisons.
- They have difficulty following through on projects from beginning to end. Lack of confidence leads to insecurity and a fear of making mistakes. There is an eternal sense of doom.
- They lie because they believe that the truth will result in punishment, abandonment, or disapproval.
- They judge themselves without mercy because that is how their parents judged them.
- They have difficulty having fun because they never learned how to play.
- They take themselves too seriously.
- They have difficulty establishing intimate relationships.
- They overreact to change of any kind.
- They constantly seek approval and affirmation, and their emotions are limited to anger and sadness—happiness is measured only as an absence of pain.
- They feel different from others.
- They are overly responsible or irresponsible.
- They are extremely loyal even when the loyalty is undeserved and harmful to them.
- They are impulsive, seldom think things through, and have overwhelming feelings of hopelessness and helplessness.

By understanding these traits, it is easy to see how they impact on the adult children's own child-rearing practices. Early intervention is the key and can best be accomplished when appropriate programs exist in AOCAP and Vet Centers.

Treatment Approaches

Diagnostic Assessment

Children of dysfunction harbor an intense denial system. The need to feel normal creates the delusion that they have not been affected by their parents' behavior, and having little knowledge of normalcy, they may believe that their life was quite normal. Having been totally schooled in the need to protect family secrets, they are often embarrassed and ashamed, enabling further denial. Because of this, clinicians must approach the interview slowly, taking great care to maintain the dignity of the client while extracting information. Thus, making a diagnostic assessment may take several visits.

Assessment information should include any history of substance abuse history and psychiatric illness; memories of the veteran before he or she went to Vietnam; a description of behaviors after returning from Vietnam; and the children's perception of the mother's interaction with the family. In addition, the clinician should explore the adult child's relationship with his or her spouse or partner and his or her own interaction with any children in the family.

As the clinician interviews young children in the family, he or she should not be surprised to see a pattern of identical perceptions from parents and the children from both generations.

Developing Treatment Strategies

Group therapy is the preferred method of treatment. In the company of others with similar experiences, the adult children can safely describe their life experiences without fear of reprisal. Isolation is eradicated and normalcy begins to develop based on the knowledge that they are not alone. The goal of the group is to provide the basis for catharsis and reframing, to reinforce the tenacity and courage inherent in survival, and to develop the self-esteem of each member of the group. As old behaviors are unlearned, they are replaced with new, healthy behaviors learned through instruction and sharing.

As the parents are striving to learn these new skills, the young children benefit from specialized children's groups. Through art and play therapy, general group discussions, and audiovisual aids, children learn to communicate their feelings and develop healthy coping skills.

Family counseling is an important adjunct to group therapy. With the help of a skilled clinician, the children and parents have the opportunity to explore new skills and to begin to implement them within the family system. Feelings are communicated openly, and new issues are addressed as they emerge.

Bibliotherapy—which involves reading selected books and articles—and parenting skills training are helpful supports throughout therapy as are community support groups such as AlAnon, AlaTeen, Parents Anonymous, Families Anonymous, and church groups.

In summary, the third generation of Vietnam veterans, with the proper care, can end the intergenerational transmission of the effects of war trauma. Perhaps then, the veterans and their family members will truly be able to pass on the freedoms and enjoy the peace for which each in their own way fought so valiantly.

References

The Addiction Letter. 1993. Mapping your stages of healing from childhood abuse, 247, 309.89. Providence, RI: Manisses Communications.

American Psychiatric Association. 1980. *Diagnostic and Statistical Manual of Mental Disorders* 3d ed. Washington, DC: American Psychiatric Association.

Black, C. 1982. *It will never happen to me.* MAC Publishing.

Kritsberg, W. Nov./Dec. 1984. Chronic shock and emotional numbness in adult children of alcoholics. *Focus on Family,* 24(24):40.

Treanor, V., and T. Brinson. 1986. *Post-traumatic stress disorder and the alcoholic family system.* Paper presented at the 42nd NCA Forum, San Francisco, CA.

Woititz, J.G., Ed.D. 1983. *Adult children of alcoholics.* Health Communications.

Acknowledgment

I would like to thank the hundreds of adult children of Vietnam veterans who have shared their stories with me and who have allowed me the privilege of participating in their healing process.

A Clinical View of Children of Veterans with Post-Traumatic Stress Disorder

Mary C. James, B.A., M.Ed.; and Adrian H. Stilson
Community Outreach to Vietnam Era Returnees

Abstract

The clinical issues involving Vietnam veterans and their children require careful scrutiny and discernment. This paper looks at combat veterans as parents and how their issues impact their children. The clinical findings described are derived from thirteen years of work with Vietnam veteran families. First the impact of combat-related post-traumatic stress disorder (PTSD) is explored. The term "primary PTSD" is employed to describe this group. The behavior pattern and mode of interaction of veterans with primary PTSD is by definition directly connected to their combat experience. Various parenting issues unique to this group are detailed. The interesting and unexpected finding that the children of veterans with primary PTSD are largely intact and free of major psychopathology is discussed. In addition, various categories of veterans with "confounded PTSD," PTSD with other powerful clinical issues, are defined and discussed. Many of the children of veterans with confounded PTSD manifest behavior problems and psychological distress. It is suggested that many clinicians have inaccurately identified PTSD as the root of these children's difficulties, when in fact it has been our clinical finding that other confounding issues are the principle culprit.

This paper challenges the accepted notion that PTSD is negatively transmitted to children of Vietnam veterans (the term secondary PTSD is often used to describe this process) in favor of a more comprehensive look at the issues facing Vietnam veterans and their children. This comprehensive approach describes both the positive and negative influences Vietnam veterans have on their children as well as provides a more accurate and complete understanding of the veteran as parent. Implications of these findings for clinical treatment as well as for educational and social service settings are discussed.

***Mary C. James, B.A., M.Ed.,** is the cofounder and director of COVER, a counseling agency for Vietnam veterans and their families established in 1980. She received her B.A. and M.Ed. from the University of Virginia and is a licensed professional counselor in that state. **Adrian H. Stilson** has been working with Vietnam veterans and their children at COVER for the past five years. He attended Ohio State University and the University of Virginia and is a Vietnam veteran.*

Post-traumatic stress disorder (PTSD) as a result of the combat experience is no longer a debatable phenomenon. The nature, scope, and treatment of this disorder with regard to Vietnam veterans has received extensive attention. During the past twenty years, the understanding of the emotional and psychological effects of many other types of trauma has been enhanced as the field of the study of trauma has broadened its focus. Therapeutic approaches to trauma survivors have been refined. The concept that trauma can be transmitted to the next generation has been introduced. Most of this growth has been positive, and evolutionary. Regrettably though, the current field of trauma seems to have forgotten its birthplace. Even more regrettably, it appears that the nature of the combat veteran's response to trauma has been often forgotten or ignored to more easily fit the current paradigm of those involved in the treatment and study of PTSD.

This paper examines and seeks to clarify the effect of combat experience and PTSD on the veteran as parent and the resulting effect on his children. Initially the PTSD-affected veteran appears to have a profoundly negative impact on his family. The misperceived extent and nature of that negative impact has led to the currently popular notion of secondary PTSD. We would suggest that what initially appears so negative, merits more careful scrutiny. For the purposes of this paper, other issues often incorrectly included in the combat veteran persona are detailed under the heading "confounded PTSD." This paper presents conclusions drawn from the experiences of a veteran's counseling agency with a thirteen-year history of treatment and interactions with Vietnam veterans and their families.

A very important point to be emphasized in this paper is that an agency whose primary mandate is that of counseling Vietnam veteran families, like any agency with a large client population, will encounter a broad array of problems and issues. At Community Outreach to Vietnam Era Returnees (COVER) we have found it helpful to distinguish between veterans whose symptoms reflect what we have come to call primary PTSD, and those whose symptoms are the result of a combination of PTSD and other emotional problems, such as major mental illness, premorbid personality issues, substance abuse, and traumatic brain injury.

Veterans with primary PTSD, the main focus of this paper, are those veterans whose patterns of behavior and interaction reflect primarily their combat experience. The array of symptoms that are most relevant to the veteran as parent and that impact most on his children include isolation, anger, anxiety, depression, emotional numbing, and lack of emotional availability. In addition there are certain emotional attitudes that derive from the Vietnam experience and have powerful influences on the veteran as parent: such attitudes include the view of the world as a dangerous place and the child as a very vulnerable being.

In the course of our discussion of these symptoms and emotional attitudes, we will refer to various interventions that we believe can positively influence the veteran's parenting style and the emotional experience for his children. Foremost among them is the treatment by individual and group therapy of the veteran's PTSD. The veteran's symptoms are frequently a response to unprocessed and encapsulated traumatic events. When in the course of therapy an event is discovered (mindful that combat veterans usually have multiple traumatic events), verbalized, explored, and appropriate emotions of horror, fear, loss, and grief are acknowledged and ultimately experienced, the power of the event is defused, allowing the veteran to be available and more appropriately responsive to his children and others. A second major component in the treatment of parenting issues is that of work with the partner, often in a couples format. (It is worth noting that it has been our experience that most veteran parents have a partner.) We have found this to be extremely helpful both as an educational forum whereby the partner can come to understand the complex issues that the veteran may bring to parenting, and sometimes as an intervention whereby the partner can help the veteran to modify his parenting behaviors.

Primary PTSD

In our parenting work with Vietnam veterans, we have found that one of the most significant issues coloring a veteran's response to his children is his view of the world as an extremely hazardous and dangerous place. The combat veteran usually views his children as vulnerable and ill equipped for survival. His sense of responsibility for their preparation is great and immediate. He does not have the luxury of a view of childhood as a relatively long period of preparation for the adult world. The veteran's view of his children is similar to his view of replacements for his unit in Vietnam. Unfortunately the veteran often finds himself reenacting the arrival of "new guys" throughout his children's lives.

To look at the world from the veteran's perspective it is important to recognize that combat is a serious endeavor. The inexperienced learn from the experienced quickly if they are to survive. Little or no time is available for discussion, explanations, or compromise. Sensitivity to the feelings of others is of insignificant import. Anger, shame, and fear are employed because they achieve the quickest results. It is because the veteran takes so seriously the role of parent that he employs the methods acquired in Vietnam. His approach is authoritarian and his manner is frequently brusque and lacking in patience. It is difficult for the veteran to view mistakes as learning experiences. The veteran has learned that mistakes are often fatal. The loss of a comrade usually involved a real or perceived mistake. It has been our experience that the more combat a veteran experienced the more central this world view becomes and the more all-encompassing it is in every part of his life, especially parenting.

Emotional numbing as a symptom of primary PTSD can exert a very powerful effect on the veteran's parenting capabilities. The severing of emotional reactiveness as a result of combat trauma often results in a long-term condition in which the veteran's emotions are not accessible either to himself or to others, including family members. Often the veteran's emotional numbing is such that he may not be able to understand or identify the capacity he lacks. At the same time Vietnam veterans are full of paradoxes. It is not uncommon for veterans to disclose sitting with children after they are asleep and telling them how much they love them, what great kids they are, etc. One former doorgunner intimated that he believes children hear and internalize these messages. While the veteran remains fully responsible regarding the physical and financial needs of his family, he may have great difficulty responding to their daily emotional needs. For example, many partners and veterans themselves report the veteran's difficulty responding to, or even being around, a crying child. This appears to represent a generalized effect of PTSD rather than stemming from a specific event involving a child in Vietnam as many mental health professionals assume. The veteran may experience an intense sense of frustration due to his inability to meet his child's need and his concern may be expressed through anger rather than comforting behaviors. While it would be easy to view this phenomenon from strictly gender role lines, it has been our experience that this is not the case. The veterans do not view the world, much less their parenting role, along strict gender lines; rather the driving force behind their difficulty responding to emotional cues appears to be their war experience.

The impact of a parent's emotional unavailability upon a child may be significant. The child may receive the powerful message that it is better not to express emotion. Parental loyalty may induce the child to attempt to contain his emotions. The children may appear emotionally overcontrolled. At the other end of the continuum are those children we have seen whose behavior and emotional style reveals under- rather than oversocialization. They may be undercontrolled, demanding, and disruptive. We see these children attempting to elicit an emotional response from the parent, even if the only response they elicit is anger. Frequently, the mothers of children who manifest this behavior pattern have significant difficulty parenting as well. Across the range of children's responses to the veteran parent's emotional unavailability, there may be very similar underlying unmet needs. The child's sense of self-worth is established from the emotional connection with the parent; when this emotional connection is unavailable the child's sense of worth and value may become eroded.

It should be noted that in many cases, the partners of emotionally numbed veterans make significant strides to be sensitive parents, to recognize and attend to the emotional needs of their children. We have seen any number of children, particularly but not exclusively in these households, whose behavior and emotional style is developmentally appropriate and whose sense of self-worth appears to be quite intact.

To help the emotionally numbed veteran parent to better experience and attend to his child's emotional needs, he needs to be better able to experience and attend to his own emotional needs. We believe PTSD-focused counseling is critical to the process. The veteran can be fully responsible in regard to the physical and financial needs of the family. The veteran can develop techniques to manage his anger. The veteran can avoid exposing his children to his anxiety and depression. But, without treatment for his PTSD, the traumatized veteran usually does not have access to the emotional side of his personality.

A more behavioral component of treatment in some cases is that of instructing and training the veteran through sessions (either individual, couples, or parenting group) focused upon recognizing the child's emotional signals and learning appropriate responses to them.

Depression as a symptom of PTSD is very similar to emotional numbing in its effect upon the veteran's parenting behavior. With depression the veteran may be immobilized by protracted grieving or by a sense of profound alienation. Solvable problems may seem hopeless and the veteran may withdraw from involvement. Similar to emotional numbing, the veteran may be unable to identify the child's need for comfort and support, and he may be unable to act in a comforting manner. The depressed veteran, however, may not be as aware of his own liabilities and thus may be less consciously frustrated by them. Like emotional numbing, the goal of treatment is to help the veteran to resolve his depression through processing of the original losses, to recover a sense of competence and agency, and in some cases through specific parent training to learn to recognize and attend more appropriately to the child's emotional needs.

Isolation from the outside community is frequently a powerful component of the PTSD-affected veteran's array of issues. A sense of betrayal and mistrust, survival guilt, damaged self-esteem, depression, the erosion of interactive social skills, as well as the psychic weight of the encapsulated traumatic experience contribute to the veteran's isolation, which may be consciously self-imposed or be the result of a sense of rejection by the community. Isolation by the veteran may mean isolation for the entire family. Some children of Vietnam veterans have little exposure outside of school to other adults and children. As a result they have fewer alternative role models, fewer opportunities to witness adults with a wider emotional repertoire, fewer experiences in which they are attended to with a variety of responses. Isolation from the community also affects the children of Vietnam veterans in that they often miss out on parental involvement in the school or other activities. A seemingly paradoxical effect of isolation can occur regarding education. Vietnam veterans in many cases are acutely aware of the value of education and strenuously promote their children's academic endeavors, yet it is not uncommon that the veteran will never meet with the teachers or attend school functions. It is very important to note that if and when veterans do become involved, in school or other settings, that previous lack of involvement is not misperceived as lack of interest and that the veteran's impact is not minimized. While, as previously mentioned, it is often very difficult for veterans to be available and engaged, particularly on a continuing basis, their perceptiveness and insight are frequently uncanny. The same war experience that makes it difficult or impossible for veterans to be emotionally available often provides them with an ability to view situations quickly and with amazing clarity. Veterans often arrive at "the bottom line," or the root of the problem much more rapidly than most individuals. It is everyone's loss if the veteran's perceptions are not invited and valued in educational and other settings.

Anger

Vietnam veterans are notorious for their anger. The exact nature of their responses and the damage it generates has been largely exaggerated, from our clinical experience. It has been our experience that combat veterans are almost never physically abusive. If abuse is involved, it needs to be addressed as such and it is safe to predict that issues other than PTSD are involved, such as addiction, characterological problems, etc. Most veterans with primary PTSD are overcontrolled with their emotions, as discussed earlier. Anger is the emotion that is most frequently expressed by veterans; often it is the only emotion they express. We have found it helpful to support the veteran in understanding that his anger has a functional basis. Anger is often essential to his capacity for containing other emotions. Fear, pain, grief, loss, sadness, joy, and compassion were all life-threatening liabilities in Vietnam: Anger was a life-serving asset. The veteran with PTSD carries an overwhelming degree of fear, pain, grief, and sadness; anger functions as the emotional glue to maintain the containment. Parenting often involves the very emotions that the veteran can only comfortably express through anger. Anger is frequently what brings the veteran with a family into counseling. It is always better when working with veterans to work from the position increasing their parenting repertoire rather than taking something away. Telling a veteran his anger is not okay will only alienate him. It is important to acknowledge that anger may be very effective in motivating a child, but has the potential to be damaging, thus, whenever possible it is best to employ anger only in more extreme situations. At the same time it is often very helpful for the veteran, for the mother, and even counselors to learn to see the veteran's anger as a possible resource. Veteran anger can have a very functional basis within the family setting; it can be a very valuable indicator that something is amiss and needs to be addressed. Oftentimes the veteran is unaware of what the problem is, he just knows there is a problem. For example, the child may be experiencing some undiagnosed learning problems, he or she may be being bullied and unable to tell the parents, the child may have an undiagnosed health problem, there may be a problem within the school, etc.. If the veteran feels his concern is being taken seriously and addressed oftentimes the level of anger reduces or diminishes. It is no longer necessary.

It certainly would be everyone's preference that anger be extinguished, and oftentimes it needs to be modified, but it is unrealistic to expect that it can be eradicated entirely. Under the best of conditions, angry outbursts and harsh reprimands are likely to take place. Many times secondary problems emerge in an attempt to manage the anger, and these secondary problems can become quite consequential. A common scenario is a veteran parent reprimanding a child. The partner watches this and begins to feel the veteran is "being too hard" on the child. It is quite natural for the parent to disagree, and to take issue with a veteran husband who is reprimanding a child with anger that seems electrifying, but it is ineffective at best for the partner to get in the middle of such a reprimand. Trying to intervene may fuel the fire, and trigger an angry exchange between the veteran and partner which can be frightening for the child. It is even more likely to be more subtly destructive to intervene in that it serves to undermine the father's authority and demonstrates to the child that mom and dad have some serious differences on child raising. The child is then in the very unhealthy position of gaining too much power in the family. This type of situation is ripe for all kinds of power struggles, all of which are not healthy for children. Veteran anger which could be described as electrifying can feel awful and many people make the error of misnaming this anger abuse. Battering, name calling, pushing, shoving, are indeed abuse and should be dealt with as such. Simple anger is clearly unpleasant, any time one is the recipient, and veterans' anger can have an intensity that is particularly unpleasant to receive. Without ever using a curse word, making a threat, much less raising a hand, veterans' anger can cut to the quick. It can be very hard on the self-esteem of a child. It is sometimes helpful to inform the veteran parent that parental anger is potentially damaging to a child. Depending on its intensity and the means by which it is displayed and communicated, parental anger may terrify a child, undermine his or her sense of security, damage his or her self-esteem, and predispose him or her to an increased level of acting out and aggressive behavior. Ironically, the best person to come in and mend the bumps is the veteran. He can apologize for losing his temper (although from his view he never lost control), let the child know that his anger was motivated by concern for the child, and then discuss with the child what specifically his concerns are. Ideally the veteran position is supported by the partner. If the partner disagrees, it is best if she disagrees in private, out of earshot of the child. If the veteran changes his position after discussing it with the partner, the veteran can reapproach the child, informing the child "Your mother and I have decided . . ." The partner can come from the same position "Your father and I have decided. . . ," or "have changed our mind and want you to . . . ," or whatever. The most destructive circumstances involve anger that is undermined by a parent.

A couple of final points need to be emphasized on this topic. The first is that it is critical for professionals working with veterans to be very cognizant of their own behavior and attitudes with regard to veterans and anger and children. Judging or giving shame or guilt messages to veterans is to be strictly avoided. The combat veteran's perceptiveness and sensitivity will be working overtime. They can detect a shame message before the professional is even aware of having transmitted one. This development would at best stall a constructive therapeutic alliance, but it is also likely to be injurious. Combat veterans with primary PTSD tend to be extremely self-critical and they are likely to be crushed by the prospect of having in any way injured their children.

Finally, veterans with primary PTSD are coming from a position of deep concern for their children. Their style of parenting may appear atypical, unconventional, even archaic, but their goal is to be effective with their children. We have found veterans to be very open to suggestions and trying new methods to reach their goal of effectively raising their children if they feel the professional is genuinely coming from a position of concern for their child.

Divorce and Blended Families

During a counseling session a therapist asked a child "What's the worst thing in the world you can imagine that might happen?" A little girl replied, "It already happened. Mom kicked Dad out." (Hemfelt and Warren, p. 61). Divorce and separation are so commonplace in our society that we as adults can easily underestimate the loss involved, particularly for a child. In veteran families, divorce has been estimated to be at twice the rate of the nonveteran population. Looking at families and divorce from a slightly different perspective, it has been estimated that more veterans are living in families with stepchildren than are living in homes with their biological children. In summary, the loss involved with divorce has affected many, many veterans' households. Veterans, because of their war experience, often have some unique experiences with loss. Many have experienced enormous amounts of loss. Veterans characteristically have two opposite reactions to divorce involving their biological children; they are either very involved with their children and sometimes have custody or obtain custody—or they vanish. One axiom of trauma counseling is that opposites are the same. It could not be better illustrated than in veterans' response to their children during divorce.

Although they do not express or easily demonstrate it, veterans are particularly sensitive to pain and loss experienced by children. Veterans are acutely aware of the emotional turmoil their children face during divorce. When dealing with the experience of divorce, veterans characteristically assume one of two opposite positions in regards to their children.

If the veterans do not obtain custody they vigorously exercise their visitation rights, maintain close connections, and are vigilant regarding their children's well-being.

Veterans will allow themselves to be the object of their children's anger after divorce without reacting, believing their children need this emotion to cope with the divorce and their current situation. Sometimes the child withdraws from the veteran and opts to stay exclusively with the mother; that often happens in cases when the mother holds a great deal of hostility toward the veteran. Veterans frequently will patiently wait for their children to reenter their lives, placing few demands on the child and carrying little bitterness because of their understanding of their children's method of coping with loss.

Veterans' responses to their children after divorce can be in an opposite direction, as well. This approach also stems from their experience with war. All personal items were quickly removed after the loss of a comrade in Vietnam. It was not unusual to never speak of an individual after his death. Veterans will impose this method of coping on their children by quickly disconnecting, believing their children's pain will be less and their recovery will be quicker. One former partner of a Vietnam veteran expressed dismay at how "easily" her former Vietnam veteran husband signed papers giving up his daughter for adoption by the partner's new spouse. This action is reasonable from a combatant's perspective, and could be viewed as the ultimate act of selflessness and love, although this perspective is certainly not customary. From the veteran's perspective, he gave her up believing she could be better cared for in a two-parent home. This was done in spite of the tremendous personal cost to the veteran.

A significant number of veterans are stepparents in blended families. The family dynamic in the blended family often involves the combination of those PTSD issues the veteran brings and the existing issues of the family prior to the veteran's presence. Because of the difficulty and strain of single parenting it is not unusual for those existing issues to not be addressed or identified. The single mother has frequently been surviving with her children without the luxury of examining many issues. The veteran responds to the existing distress by assuming a "squad leader's" role. His PTSD propels immediate actions and limits his emotional understanding. Naturally, because the veteran's partner has been single-handedly holding the family together distress increases. As the children gain a sense of security with an added parent it becomes "safer" to express their unaddressed issues. The veteran's issues of betrayal, loss, isolation, and difficulty with frustration management are aroused. When the PTSD veteran's only available emotion is anger, the situation can become explosive. It is the norm that, when a blended family approaches COVER, the initial presenting problem in the family is the veteran. A family system approach with a team of therapists is promoted to address the layer of issues within the family underneath the veteran's PTSD.

Clinical Interventions

Most of our clinical interventions with children are in the form of individual counseling sessions. We suggest these session are qualitatively different from individual sessions offered by a private practitioner or mental health clinic due to the depth of the counselor's understanding of the impact of war. We believe that understanding lends itself to greater objectivity and ultimately better services for the child.

Individual sessions at COVER could be described as client centered. For young children, play therapy is employed, using the principles employed by Drs. Byron and Carol Norton (1990, 1992). For children and adolescents nine or ten years and older individual sessions are mostly verbal, with some use of art to help facilitate expression and provide a more metaphoric and less didactic form of communication. Two group formats are employed and are described below. To date, we have not used a more-traditional group counseling format. Our reasoning is both cultural and practical. We service a rural area that makes weekly group counseling logistically difficult. Secondly there is strong cultural taboo to disclosing in rural communities that can sometimes be overridden in an individual setting, but is virtually impossible to override in a group setting, *particularly* with children.

Clinical Interventions with Veterans

Most of the clinical interventions with veterans are in the form of individual and group work that is focused on PTSD issues. Sometimes individual and couples sessions are focused upon children and parenting issues, as mentioned earlier. The Parenting Group—a new intervention used at COVER (originated by Adrian Stilson)—is described below.

It has been our experience that issues confronting veteran parents can be effectively addressed in the group setting. Criteria for entrance into the Parenting Group by the veteran include substantial resolution (but not necessarily completion) of Vietnam-related issues, prior experience with the dynamics of the group process (usually realized during standard therapy for PTSD), and specific preparation for the group in individual counseling. This preparation would include but not be limited to issues and concepts such as 1) parenting is an improveable skill; 2) the perception of one's children as "new guys"; 3) the connection between the veteran's Vietnam experience and authoritarian styles of parenting; and 4) anger as an expression of concern (to include its ineffectiveness or inappropriateness). In the words of some veterans this is a graduate-level course and there are prerequisites for admission.

Members benefit from the reflection of their selves in their peers, the support gained during the many difficult periods of parenting, the introduction of different perceptions of situations (as well as validating confirmations of perceptions), the exposure to new ideas while strategizing solutions for specific problems, and the opportunity for healthy ventilation of the frustrations of parenting. The exclusively veteran composition of the Parenting Group allows members to address parenting issues prior to complete resolution of PTSD issues of trust and isolation that would prevent participation in a standard, open parenting group. It provides a safe place for veterans to explore parenting issues, without the uneasiness many veterans feel about exposing their unusual world view.

Play Group

Play groups can be a useful approach for children of veterans. Identifying the group as therapeutic can place a perceived stigma on children. The play group utilized at COVER is titled the Saturday Activity Club. Trips to museums, roller-skating outings, hikes, campouts, and other activities provide the motivation for involvement. The therapeutic issues addressed by a play group include:

Isolation is frequently a powerful component of a traumatized veteran's array of issues. In the veteran this issue is addressed in conjunction with the therapeutic process employed.

Many families reflect the symptomatic isolation of the veteran parent. This isolation is unwittingly imposed and does not represent an internal clinical issue for the veteran's children. Exposure to a variety of activities and the other group members addresses this issue. As the group dynamic evolves the members find they are able to give and receive support and acquire a sense of belonging. Appropriate methods of conflict resolution are acquired.

The group addresses the children's symptomatic subdued emotional affect. Similarly to isolation, this is not necessarily a deep-rooted clinical issue for the child. It is more likely representative of a learned behavior acquired to prevent "upsetting dad." The group provides and tacitly gives permission for emotional expression. Simply stated, the group provides the opportunity for children to behave as children.

Diffusing the mystery and taboo of Vietnam: the use of a veteran group moderator allows the members to inquire about Vietnam. This in turn removes its frightening power. It is not unusual for Vietnam to be a taboo subject in veteran families. Children learn that the veteran parent is not to be questioned or reminded of Vietnam. In this way Vietnam becomes a powerful, dangerous mystery. The group serves to neutralize its power.

Educational Workshops

Another form of intervention that has been very successful, possibly because it requires so little time commitment from busy families and also does not require participants' children to self-disclose, is our informational workshops. One extremely positive effect we have seen from this intervention is that if participants are properly screened before being invited to the workshop the session usually serves as a springboard for increased dialogue and communication between the veteran and his children. We are careful to invite participants from families who are not currently undergoing a crisis and in which the veteran is far enough along in his own treatment to be ready to begin a dialogue with his children about Vietnam. Good assessment and timing are essential to the success of this intervention, but it is time and energy well spent. The comments after these workshops, often from partners and veterans who could be described as taciturn, are very rewarding to hear, and what is even more rewarding is that even several years later, the workshop is often still looked upon as a positive influence and even a turning point in veteran parent-child communication.

The program is based on educational input and peer support and its goals are to:

1. Facilitate some understanding and empathy for the fathers' difficulties; in short to offer the children a comprehensible explanation of the war and of post-traumatic stress;
2. Acquaint them with peers who have experienced similar difficulties, thereby moderating their sense of isolation;
3. Help them understand the limits of their responsibility in the family; and
4. Provide them with some strategies for coping with family problems and with their own feelings.

The format for the intervention has been a workshop to which small groups of children, ages eight to sixteen, are invited. The workshop is co-led by a veteran and a mental health person experienced in working with children. We take care to explain the purpose and format of the workshop to the veterans, and to invite them to be the parent who transports the child to and from, so as to encourage closeness and possible discussion. Because we know the particular families well, we are able to tailor the presentation in part to cover particular issues or needs.

During the first part of the workshop the veteran talks about the war making use of maps, photos, etc. He offers specific vignettes of his own experiences. The emphasis of the discussion is upon the feelings of the veteran as a young recruit (virtually a teenager) far from home in a hostile country, the loneliness, the terrible fear of an unseen enemy, the physical discomforts and misery, the attachment to comrades, the anguish of loss, the cutting off of feelings at times, etc. Gory or horrifying incidents are not included. The children are encouraged to ask questions and to tell, if they know anything, about their dads' experiences.

In the second part of the workshop the mental health professional explains PTSD and other sequelae of the war in language that the children can understand. Specifically, the following symptoms of PTSD are described: depression (sadness, withdrawal, inability to have a good time); anger (irritability, unpredictable rage, quarrelsomeness); anxiety (nervousness, shaking, bad dreams, avoidance of certain situations, excessive security checks); emotional isolation (inhibition of affection); and unpredictability (rapid change of plans, inability to commit to definite plans). Specific behavioral problems such as substance abuse, fighting, flashbacks, or emotional problems warranting hospitalization are also briefly described. In most cases, explanations for the problems are related to possible war experiences, e.g., "Perhaps when he is sad, he is remembering a friend who was killed." When appropriate, reassurance is offered, e.g., "Even though veteran fathers sometimes find it hard to express affection, they do love their children very much." Throughout, the children are encouraged to relate observations about their own fathers, and insofar as possible, their observations are reflected in a generalizing way so as to convey that there are other fathers and other children who share these problems.

The workshop leaders also explain that often the mothers in veteran families are stressed and may at times behave in ways that are distressing to the children. The point is made that both the parents are doing the best that they can, but that they have not yet been able to get over all of the problems that the war has caused for them.

The feelings, perceptions, and misunderstandings that children in veteran families may have are described. The specific issues include: that children often feel that their dads' reactions are their fault, that they have not been good enough or have failed in some way; that children sometimes feel that they have to take sides when their parents fight; and that it is their responsibility to make things better. They are reminded that these problems are left over from the war and have nothing to do with the children. They are reassured that their fathers (and mothers) are adults, that they (the parents) are the ones who have to work on the problems, and that they are getting help from the COVER organization. If the workshop leaders feel that some children are concerned about possible family dissolution, they are reassured that their parents love them and will be there for them even if they do not remain together.

Finally the children are encouraged to think of ways to help themselves cope with these problems. Among the ideas offered reminding themselves that it is not their fault are: talking it over with others, e.g., parents, siblings, or a COVER staff member; engaging in pleasant activities, e.g., reading, playing with a friend or pet, playing a musical instrument, or even writing in a journal for some children. The general message that the workshop leaders try to convey is that it is okay for the children to focus upon their own lives and activities and leave the problems to the adults.

Confounded PTSD

We have seen five major categories of veterans with confounded PTSD:

1. Dual Diagnosis: PTSD Plus a Major Mental Illness Such as Bipolar Disorder or Paranoid Schizophrenia. The children in these families often are suffering from what isn't happening in the home as much as from what is. The person with the major mental illness often is ill equipped to provide a nurturing environment for children. We have found play groups to be beneficial to these children because it provides an opportunity to socialize with other children, and to help them learn how to behave "normally." Educational groups or workshops focused on a PTSD parent are *contraindicated;* educational workshops focused on major mental illness can be pertinent if the parents will consent. In every dual-diagnosed veteran we have treated the major mental illness had the dominant impact. These veterans did not behave like combat veterans. They behaved like medicated paranoid schizophrenics and persons suffering from bipolar disorder. It is not truthful or helpful to inform children about PTSD symptomatology or lead them to believe that "Vietnam made my father or stepfather this way." If these children ever have the experience of spending time in a home with a veteran with primary PTSD they will find themselves in unfamiliar territory. Ultimately it does not serve the children to misinform them. It has been our experience that the veteran and the family usually have much invested in a PTSD explanation of the veteran's behavior and are very resistant to the notion that the major mental illness is the primary problem. This resistance can make for a very delicate situation. Oftentimes these children are best served by counseling provided at a conventional mental health agency or by a private practitioner.

2. Dual Diagnosis: PTSD and Addiction. The horrendous damage of alcoholism and drug addiction on the individual and the family far exceeds the impact of PTSD. The nature of chemical dependency also prohibits useful therapeutic approaches to PTSD. That the addiction may have originated in a self-medicating attempt to manage PTSD does not preclude the necessity to clinically address the addiction independent of and prior to the PTSD.

Sadly, chemically dependent veterans often include those that are the product of inadequate, or improperly utilized treatment. Many of the veterans in this category are addicted to prescription drugs often prescribed by VA and other mental health professionals, but this situation is quite different from the veteran suffering from a major mental illness. These homes are typically very chaotic and the mother or significant other is frequently suffering from significant codependent issues. (This combination of factors means that these children usually have two very ill parents.) These children are best served through current treatment modalities for children of alcoholics, often including involvement in Alateen. While the veteran is actively using and not in recovery, some education work involving PTSD is helpful, but the main thrust of counseling work should focus on substance abuse and children of alcoholics issues. It is these issues that will be affecting the child (and veteran) principally. If and when the veteran stops drinking and actively using and enters recovery, PTSD focus can be increased. Following six to twelve months of sobriety (depending on the circumstances) PTSD issues can be emphasized, and the veteran and his PTSD issues can be introduced to the family treatment process.

Heavy substance abuse and addiction skew the pattern of PTSD, so that where child abuse is unlikely to occur in a home with primary PTSD, homes with active and heavy substance abuse and addiction are more likely to involve child abuse. Abuse can be committed by an outsider because the children are unprotected by the parents and are vulnerable because the family energy is focused on the substance abuse, and not on protecting the children. Abuse may be committed by the addicted veteran and sometimes by the codependent spouse. The observation of legal strictures regarding the reporting of child abuse is essential. Although the initial reaction is that of anger, addressing such issues directly, using legal guidelines when appropriate, is better for the veteran, and certainly better for the child. Obviously the manner in which treatment is executed in these families is critical. It is imperative that the counselor be very clear, very caring, and resolute. The family system is badly out of control; the counselor must impose control and limits. Frequently children in these families are withdrawn from treatment in a passive manner by one of the parents. Often the situation falls legally just short of abuse, and the counselor doesn't have leverage to reengage the child in the process. It is often very difficult for counselors involved. Counselors can take solace in that the family will probably resurface later, and the foundation will be in place for more progress the next time. Even if the family does not resurface, it is our belief that children receive the message and the caring even though they may not be aware of it for many years to come.

Therefore children in these homes may be suffering from issues relating to being the child of an alcoholic, PTSD issues, and abuse, and would need services tailored accordingly. Most likely the PTSD issues would be, at least initially, the least prominent.

3. PTSD and Significant Premorbid Issues. We have observed an interesting characteristic regarding these dual-issue veterans. Veterans who went to Vietnam with significant childhood abuse issues and served in a rear area experiencing little to no combat (Low PTSD with Abuse), have children with a higher number of abuse indicators (and we would postulate are more likely to abuse their children) than average. Serving in Vietnam in a rear area seems to have an amplifying effect with regard to the likelihood to abuse. Conversely, veterans who experienced heavy combat and who were abused (Heavy PTSD with Abuse) have children who do not exhibit abuse indicators. We believe these veterans are *less* likely to abuse their children than individuals with the same level of premorbid issues who did not go to Vietnam and certainly less likely than veterans who served in a rear area. We believe the defining variable is combat. For veterans who were abused as children and who were later in moderate to heavy combat, the effect of combat seems to dominate the effect of child abuse. The role of the combatants seems to define their behavior much more so than the earlier abuse. It could be argued that combat can serve an empowering role for the individual. Heavy combat is so horrific that it seems to draw compassion out of individuals, tremendous respect for pain, and a sense of protectiveness for those less able (particularly children).

In addition, serving in rear areas amidst those often wild and, from an observer's perspective, rough "real" soldiers can be very disempowering. It is our opinion that disempowered individuals who were abused are more likely to take on a perpetrators role with an individual of lesser status (such as a child). Interestingly, this group will often advertise their role as Vietnam veteran, wear a lot of paraphernalia, and use Vietnam as an excuse for any maladaptive behaviors. This explanation is inaccurate and prevents the individual from addressing the critical issue of his own abuse. The children of high-combat veterans with premorbid issues are usually free of major psychopathology and would benefit from services as described in the section Primary PTSD. The children of veterans with little or no combat experience who also have significant premorbid issues are some of the most damaged children we have encountered. Many of these children need a higher level of clinical care than we are able to offer and need to be referred. Those that are able to benefit from our services need individual therapy.

Educational workshops focusing on a parent with PTSD are contraindicated with these children. Probably the most frustrating (and telling) part of our efforts with these children is that as we begin to identify and address the abuse, the family seems to be instinctively prescient of this change of focus and disengages from treatment. It is very difficult to provide the treatment these children need.

4. Children of Veterans with PTSD and Traumatic Head Injury. Many children of Vietnam veterans with PTSD fall into this category because any soldier who was exposed to heavy combat was also quite likely to have received a head injury. Because of explosive concussions alone, there are few places as likely for head injuries as a combat zone. Veterans will frequently acknowledge, if asked, having had blood or fluid drain from their ears, which alone is a symptom of mild to moderate traumatic head injury. In addition many veterans have had injuries in car and motorcycle accidents since returning from Vietnam that could be attributed to a PTSD lifestyle. Therefore, it is our belief and experience that many Vietnam veterans have previously undiagnosed head injuries. Most of these injuries are probably not diagnosable at this point with a simple neurological examination, but may nonetheless have current impact on the veteran and his family. We have found it extremely helpful to refer veterans with a history suggestive of head injury to the University of Virginia Neuropsychology Lab for a neuropsychological assessment. These exams can detect head injury sequelae even in the absence of a positive neurological exam.

We believe head injuries and PTSD work together to exacerbate each other and at times work synergistically. An example might be a crowded shopping mall. For the survivors of a traumatic head injury, a crowded shopping mall is a sensory overload. There is simply too much information to process. They become overwhelmed, exhausted, and begin to have increasing difficulty keeping up with the flood of information. They may become slightly confused, forgetful, and irritable. For veterans with PTSD, a crowded shopping mall is a minefield of potential dangers. They often become anxious and hypervigilant trying to stay aware of the potential dangers. They continually mentally rehearse outcomes to various potentially hazardous situations. For example, they will have taken mental inventory of the location of fire escapes and extinguishers in the event of a fire and will have devised a couple of contingency plans in the event of a fight, random shooting, etc. If this same veteran has his children with him, his level of hypervigilance and anxiety will increase exponentially even though these symptoms may or may not be visible to an observer. Now the veteran is trying to manage himself as well as children who, from his perspective, have no concept of danger much less any ability to handle a situation should one develop. He feels an intense sense of responsibility for their welfare. He will often become dictatorial in an attempt to manage his unruly "squad." Put the same veteran in the same mall with his children and add in a head injury and one can begin to imagine the increasing stress for everyone.

For the purpose of clarifying the implications regarding parenting and the effects on children, there are several significant symptoms to note:

1. The most pronounced condition the traumatic brain injury (TBI) veteran deals with is fatigue. This veteran has too much to manage and he is tired most of the time. It has been suggested that the normal individual would need to have spent five hours at work to feel the way this veteran feels at the beginning of his day.

2. Often these veterans have difficulty with forgetfulness, which is a common symptom of TBI. Forgetting is inexcusable to a combat veteran—it is life threatening. The normal activity of a house, particularly with small children, can be so taxing to a veteran with PTSD and a head injury that a vicious cycle can easily be established. The more forgetful the veteran gets the more taxed and tired he becomes. The core feeling is shame—"I can't keep up," "I'm not fulfilling my responsibilities," but the shame is usually expressed through irritability or withdrawal.

3. Veterans often want everything in its place. For a veteran with a head injury this desire takes on even greater importance. The PTSD propels the safety issues with orderliness.

Head injury introduces memory problems that are best managed with orderliness. The coexistence of PTSD and head injury elevates the need to have "everything in its place" to new levels of significance. It is not uncommon for these veterans to report having lost (and found) their keys several times over the course of a morning.

We have formulated the following recommendations from the information we have received from veterans as well as civilian head injury survivors:

1. Veterans with head injuries often do best fulfilling parenting responsibilities in the morning when they are fresher and less fatigued. One veteran with a significant head injury routinely gets his children breakfast and off to school in the morning and his wife assumes evening responsibilities after work and school. If one of his children has a problem with homework or needs help with a school project the veteran is able to assist in the evening but is often more irritable, less efficient, and more easily frustrated with the task and with the child than he might be earlier in the day.

2. Pacing and routine are terribly important to the functioning and sense of well-being of head injury survivors. Short, frequent breaks are not luxurious or an attempt to be lazy, but rather essential to the head-injured veteran's functioning.

The best antidote for all the above is education—for the entire family. If the veteran learns and understands the effects of head injury, he will be validated, feel less shame, and be empowered to manage better. It is imperative to elicit the understanding and cooperation of the partner or mother. Head injuries are invisible and the partners often believe the veteran is forgetting on purpose or just doesn't care. The parents can become polarized and a battle can ensue between the parents that can be far more damaging to the children than the effects of the head injury and PTSD. Finally, informing the children at their developmental level is imperative also, and can be done by a counselor, or by an informed parent. The unspoken is far more powerful and potentially destructive for children than things that can be discussed openly. Children will often respond to information with a nod and an expression meaning "Yeah I already know that"—in the way children know things about their parents—but the act of an adult providing the information helps defuse the negative power the information may have and helps provide a sense of safety for the child. Many children may have concerns and questions that must be addressed. Some may try to "take care of daddy." Taking responsibility for a parent is something to be addressed swiftly by the counselor and by the parents if possible. It is never a child's responsibility to take care of a parent. Information about a parent's disability is provided to help children understand what they have inevitably already noticed—but responsibility and authority remains with the parents.

5. Physical Disability and PTSD. Physical disability does not confound the nature of PTSD, nor preclude a focused therapeutic approach to PTSD. It is included in this section to identify a powerful dynamic affecting the family in addition to the issues of primary PTSD.

In the words of one veteran who was severely disabled after stepping on a booby trap: "Most disabled people can do anything anyone else can do, they just can't do as much of it." The issues here are very similar to veterans with head injuries in that fatigue is a very real problem. Veterans who were wounded almost always also cope with chronic physical pain. It is one more thing they have to manage in their day along with any physical limitation. For spouses and children, the treatment is very similar to treatment of families with PTSD and head injuries—education and information sharing are the top priority with counseling as needed.

Conclusion

With all of the above categories we have emphasized some differences in treatment approaches, based upon differences in assessment of the veteran. We are aware that confidentiality is often an issue. Many times the veteran has not or will not sign a release of information, and oftentimes even if he has, it is not in the best interest of all parties to share information. The clinical staff may have a hunch about previous abuse, but it may not be sound judgment to share that hunch, even if releases are signed. Some of our agency's most frustrating cases have involved treatment of children and family members who have been quite damaged by the behavior of the veteran who claims his behavior "can't be helped because of Vietnam," when in fact war stress is not the problem at all, and has been grossly misrepresented. Interestingly when working with the child exclusively it is often possible to assess the veteran with accuracy based upon the issues presented by and demonstrated by the child.

Working within the categories specified above has nonetheless helped us provide better treatment. There appears to be a general tendency in the field to treat all children of Vietnam veterans similarly, and obviously we do not concur. Careful scrutiny of this broad class of individuals reveals some qualitative differences and distinctions which have been described in detail above. There are many issues within this broad class of individuals, and we believe treatment should be tailored accordingly.

As the reader can see, confounded PTSD is often not PTSD. The mistaken diagnosis of PTSD often serves to take the focus off the veteran's primary problem, be it a major mental illness or serious premorbid issues, making it unlikely that the veteran or the family gets appropriate treatment. Alcoholism, however, often coexists with PTSD. In terms of treatment sequence, it is almost always in the child's and the veteran's best interest to address the issues surrounding addiction first. If the veteran moves into recovery, work focused on PTSD becomes very important for the child as well as the veteran. (We have found it to be essential for relapse prevention to address PTSD in the veteran once recovery is fairly stable even if the veteran and family are doing well.) Head injury and physical disability resulting from wounding are included in the section Confounded PTSD but could possibly be better termed extensions of primary PTSD. Proper assessment can be a long, but we believe, essential process. It is only through thirteen years of work with this population that we have been able to arrive at the level of refinement in assessment that we have. Often we arrived there by learning from our mistakes in assessment. It is in everyone's best interest: the child, the veteran, the partner, to address issues as accurately as possible.

In carefully studying this population for an extended time a very prominent and unexpected pattern emerged. Veterans who were affected by their war experience can indeed have some negative effects on their children but their children as a group are intact and free of major psychopathology. Many are excelling in school and other areas. We have even wondered if the group may be candidates for an "at risk" study. In randomly pulling the veterans with primary PTSD we were struck with how well many of their children were doing in spite of the existence of many factors that would predispose their children to misfortune.

Children of veterans with confounded PTSD often demonstrate a very different profile, however. Many of these children have serious psychological issues. We might even postulate that certain combinations, such as substance abuse and PTSD, in the veteran parent can work synergistically to produce some very psychologically needy children. We have found many of these children have behavioral problems and are frequently in trouble at school and with the law.

We would theorize that the clinical finding that children of veterans with primary PTSD are doing so well may be a function of two qualities. The first is that because of the veterans' acute sense of the world as a dangerous place they protect their children from the outside influences better than the average parents. They are aware of danger and instinctively move their children away from it. Therefore their children are not likely to be damaged by outside influences such as pedophiles, bullies, etc. Secondly, although veterans with PTSD are infamous for their inability to demonstrate emotions (except for anger) they nonetheless have deep feelings about their children and instill this deep caring in their children. The child's connection with the veteran parent can be profound, and can last a lifetime.

Many clinicians who work with abused and disturbed children will relate that the common denominator with the parents of these children is the parents' level of self-interest; these parents do what is best for themselves, even though appearances are often otherwise. These parents will often go to great lengths to display how much they care and do for their children; but when one sifts through the many props and illusions, it is all designed to meet the parents' needs. Vietnam veterans with primary PTSD are usually the antithesis of these parents. They have little but disdain for appearances. They often appear indifferent, harsh, or callous. When their motivation is carefully examined, we have found them to be doing what they believe is best for the child, regardless of the personal consequences.

They employ skills they acquired under the harshest conditions, in situations that resulted in the most extreme consequences. Their parenting reflects their heightened sense of responsibility and the seriousness with which they approach this obligation. They characteristically give their children what they believe they need, not what merely appears appropriate. Their children seem to reflect this. They are characteristically self-reliant and fully engaged in life.

References

Hamfelt, R., and P. Warren. 1990. *Kids Who Carry Our Pain*. Nashville, TN: Thomas Nelson, Inc.

Norton, B., and C. Norton. 1990. *Meeting Children Through Play Therapy*. Conference, Richmond, VA, May 18–19.

Norton, B. 1992. *Play Therapy with Children*. Presentation, Charlottesville, VA, June 1.

Piaget, J. 1965. *The Child's Conception of the World*. Tortowa, NJ: Littlefield, Adams.

Rosenheck, R., and J. Thomson. 1986. Detoxification of Vietnam War trauma: A combined family individual approach. *Family Process* 25:559-569.

Schaefer, C.E., ed. 1976. *Therapeutic Use of Child's Play*. New York: Jason Aronson, Inc.

Williams, C. 1980. The veteran system with a focus on women partners. In *Post-Traumatic Stress Disorders of the Vietnam Veteran*, ed. T. Williams. Cincinnati, OH: Disabled American Veterans.

Acknowledgments

The information cited in the section on traumatic brain injury was obtained from inservices, presentations, and private conversations with each Dr. Jeffrey Barth, University of Virginia, Dr. Gregory O'Sharnick, Medical College of Virginia, and the late Dr. Jean Gauer.

Christine Reppucci has provided family services to Vietnam veterans' family members at COVER since 1982. It is on the foundation of her work that this paper is written.

Many thanks to Jennifer Saylor, a member of the COVER staff, for her many hours of editing and restructuring of this paper, not to mention her steady encouragement.

Authors' Note

The observations and conclusions presented are derived from the therapeutic experience with more than 2,000 Vietnam veterans. Two of those veterans are women. The understanding of PTSD gained from male veterans contributed to the meaningful treatment of these women veterans. Nevertheless, our experience does not permit us to generalize our conclusions concerning male veterans to female veterans. Therefore, we have chosen to eschew the use of "he/she," "his/her," or "father/mother" in favor of "he," "his," or "father." This usage should not be misinterpreted as a minimizing or discounting of women veterans and the impact of their Vietnam experience.

Part II

Meeting the Needs: The Agent Orange Class Assistance Program and the Development of New Service Systems

The scope and complexity of unmet human service needs described in papers found in Part I provide ample justification for the redesign of programs and service systems for Vietnam veterans and their families. Undoubtedly, veterans of other wars and other hostilities and their families would also benefit from new service approaches. Part II examines this subject.

Not only do the needs of family members adversely affected by war merit a response, but there is also growing recognition that the extent to which the veterans' service system succeeds in meeting a veteran's needs is often profoundly affected by the extent to which family needs are addressed. Likewise, because of the array of benefits and services for which veterans' families may be eligible, the lives of children with disabilities and medical conditions may be dramatically enhanced when public disability programs examine the veteran status of those seeking services for family members. And the unique counseling and other needs of such families can often be addressed more effectively when veterans' military experiences are taken into account.

Papers in Part II examine new service approaches, programs and systems, and their policy implications. An underlying theme of many of the papers is that human service professionals can best meet the needs of a family member by examining those needs and potential resources to meet them within the context of the family unit.

For Those Who Bore the Battle: Family-Centered Veterans' Services

Charles R. Figley, Ph.D.
Florida State University

Abstract

Families do not volunteer their sons or daughters for war, and they suffer greatly when a veteran son or daughter suffers. Family members provide each other with advice and guidance, emotional support and love, tangible aid, companionship, and a source of professional treatment compliance (e.g., getting other members to take their medicine). To view the veteran's family, rather than exclusively the veteran, as a legitimate recipient of service, will require a considerable change in orientation. For veterans' service providers and benefit systems to become family friendly, it will be necessary for them to become flexible and creative enough to help meet veterans' needs.

Family-centered medical care can use the Agent Orange Class Assistance Program (AOCAP), which has promoted a focus on veterans' families, as a model for service delivery. The concept should be incorporated in health care reform initiatives.

***Charles R. Figley, Ph.D.**, is director of the Psychosocial Stress Research Program and director of the Marriage and Family Therapy Center at Florida State University in Tallahassee, FL. He earned a Ph.D. in human development from Pennsylvania State University.*

Participants in the Agent Orange Class Assistance Program (AOCAP) symposium were personally escorted to the Vietnam Veterans Memorial Sunday morning by its founder, Jan Scruggs. "The Wall" is a remarkable memorial. Perhaps for the first time in the history of our country, through this memorial, Americans have more fully recognized the debt owed the men and women who died in battle. Everyone who visits the memorial will notice the names; will read the names, will think about the men and women who died, will recognize that war exacts a fee of life, and will confirm the debt owed to the memory of these people.

The Wall also marks the debt owed to the hundreds of thousands of spouses, children, parents, grandparents, and siblings who survived those lost to the Vietnam War. They must live with the emptiness created by the loss of their veteran every day for the rest of their lives. Where is the wall of names of living relatives and close friends of the men and women who died in Vietnam? They deserve to be honored, too, in recognition of the debt unpaid for those young lives.

This is what Lincoln had in mind when he said that we owe a debt of care for the brave soul "who shall have borne the battle, and for his widow, and his orphan." The warrior and family deserve attention today as much as in 1865, when these words were first spoken.

Thus, Lincoln and other American policy makers throughout American history have recognized the link between the sacrifices of soldiers and those of their families. This paper will discuss the psychosocial consequences of war and military service on family functioning and identify a series of policy and social service program options that address these consequences.

I want to share what we family social scientists have learned about how families function. And for the special purposes of this paper, I will focus on *veterans' families.*

The Burden of War on Veterans' Families and Children

The burdens imposed by war are carried not only by the veteran who actually fought, but also by those who bore his battle. This paper is about the importance of the family* to the veteran, to the community, and to the nation. In part, men and women join the military and risk their lives in war to benefit their community and country. Yet, according to a large body of evidence, soldiers' most immediate concerns are for those they love and who care for them.

Just as the nation owes a debt to its warriors, it also has an obligation to the families of the warriors. A warrior's family is capable of doing much more for the veteran than any institution, no matter how committed. However, there is another, equally important reason for attending to veterans' families: the war's effects are felt strongly by family members in their daily lives.

Systemic traumatic stress frequently infects and affects the families of war veterans. It will be noted later that the families of war veterans are affected directly and indirectly by the veterans' negative military and war experiences. They are affected directly by the disabilities—either physical or mental—of their war veteran family member. These disabilities may include, for example, ineffective wage-earning capacity, poor communication, inability to control anger and other impulsive behavior, as well as physical disabilities that may be a burden not only physically, but also financially and emotionally. Family members are also affected indirectly. This may be in the form of various disabilities arising from substance abuse or depression.

*The concept of the family has been defined elsewhere. Here, I propose that *family* refer to those people with whom one lives, and include household pets.

These direct and indirect effects of war service frequently lead to divorce or abandonment. The following section reviews the social science literature in an effort to account for these direct and indirect effects of war on the family.

The Family System

Scholars who study the family are impressed by its power to inspire, depress, protect, hide, influence, hurt, preoccupy, and obsess its members. The family is a system. Family members are connected to each other like the strands of a giant spider web. When one family member is affected by a major stressor, it sends shock waves throughout the web and affects everyone. A family functions well or not so well by virtue of its members. In functional families, members can prosper; the opposite is true in "dysfunctional families" (Figley and McCubbin, 1983).

One of the most important studies of the family is a study of veterans' families by Reuben Hill, a sociologist from the University of Minnesota. He discovered that war-related stress was clearly manifested in the lives of the families of war veterans (Hill, 1949). Most observers consider Hill to have originated the concept of family stress. He was the first to suggest that the system of the family is greatly affected by crisis events such as war and postwar reunion. This sociological orientation emerged into what was later to be called the ABCX model of family crisis (Hill, 1949) and has evolved into the Double ABCX model and subsequent models (e.g., McCubbin and Patterson, 1983), to the most recent model, the Topology Model of Family Adjustment and Adaptation (McCubbin and McCubbin, 1989). These models are discussed elsewhere (Figley, 1989a), but simply illustrate the fact that we know a great deal about how families function when confronted with stressors from outside the family system, such as the war experiences of one of its members. And in most cases, families cope well in spite of these extraordinary stressors.

McCubbin and McCubbin (1989), for example, suggest that resilient families can be characterized by high bonding and high flexibility. Resilient families are able to talk among themselves about what they want, when they want; everyone is involved in major decisions and shaping rules and practices in the family. They are able to compromise, willing to experiment with new ways of solving problems and issues. They recognize and demonstrate internal unity (e.g., the ability to work as a team and feel good about themselves and each other). They are comfortable engaging in various family activities together. Therefore, in spite of the external stressors imposed upon the family, including participating in and suffering from fighting in a war, resilient families overcome adversity in most cases.

McCubbin and McCubbin (1989) and other family scholars note, however, that a large portion of families are missing the key ingredients of high flexibility and high bonding that enable families to be resilient to a wide variety of stressors. Yet, when either—or especially if both—of these elements are missing or restricted, families cannot cope effectively. Moreover, in the case of war veterans' families, war-related stressors so incapacitate the veteran's ability to function, and so negatively affect other family members, that flexibility and bonding are severely affected (Figley and Kleber, in press).

Studies of Vietnam Veterans' Families

Although the causal relationship between war experiences and family dysfunction is not clear, research focusing on the families of Vietnam veterans shows a pattern. Among other things, the war reverberates within these systems long after the war is over. Those families with veterans suffering from post-traumatic stress disorder (PTSD) face experiences that differ fundamentally from those of families without a veteran member or with a veteran who is not suffering from PTSD (Figley and Kleber, in press; Figley, in press).

Figley (1986a) observed that the families of Vietnam combat veterans with PTSD were fundamentally different from other families. War veterans' families with PTSD had more marital problems, in terms of self-disclosure and expressiveness, hostility and aggression toward partners, and global marital maladjustment. These findings are consistent with Verbosky and Ryan (1988) and Maloney (1988).

The most important study of families of war veterans was actually mandated by the U.S. Congress in 1983, through Section 102 of Public Law 980-160. It called for the study of Vietnam veterans to include "an evaluation of the long-term effects of postwar psychological problems among Vietnam veterans on the families of such veterans (and on persons in other primary social relationships with such veterans)" (Kulka et al., 1990).

To follow this directive, the research team selected to conduct the study from the Research Triangle Institute, North Carolina, organized the National Vietnam Veterans Readjustment Study (NVVRS). Both scientists and policy makers viewed this study as the most comprehensive and definitive (Cranston, 1990). The team, following the most rigorous of epidemiological methodology, conducted 3,016 interviews with Vietnam war theater veterans matched by race, age, and gender with nontheater veterans and nonveterans. Among the findings:

- Approximately 30.6 percent of all male Vietnam theater veterans have or had PTSD at some time in their lives. This represents about 960,000 of the 3.14 million men who served in the war theater.
- Approximately 26.0 percent of all women Vietnam theater veterans have or had PTSD at some time in their lives. This represents about 1,900 of the 7,200 women who served in the war theater.
- Approximately 15.2 percent (479,000) of all male Vietnam theater veterans had PTSD at the time of the study. However, only 8.5 percent of all female Vietnam veterans had PTSD at the time of the study.
- Only 2.5 percent of all male and 1.1 percent of all female Vietnam-era veterans have PTSD; in comparison, 1.2 percent of all male and 0.3 percent of all female nonveterans have PTSD.
- Ethnicity among war theater veterans plays a major role in the current PTSD prevalence rates: 27.9 percent among Hispanics and 20.6 percent among African Americans, compared with 13.7 percent among whites and others.

The research team also interviewed 474 of the spouses/partners of Vietnam veterans. They were asked to "describe their own problems, as well as the problems of the veterans' children living at home" (Kulka et al., 1990, p. 236). The research team admitted in the report of their findings that they had not definitively resolved the cause-effect issue:

> Our data, of course, cannot definitely address the issue of the extent to which PTSD symptoms bring about family problems, or, alternatively, whether PTSD victims attract equally troubled wives and husbands, resulting in very disturbed and unstable family environments. However, the similarities between spouses of veterans with and without PTSD suggest that the source of marital and family discord may well be PTSD and its associated problems (p. 237).

The study found that families of Vietnam veterans who were diagnosed with war-related PTSD, when contrasted with those without such a diagnosis, have the following characteristics: (1) the veteran is remarried more often, (2) the veteran is married fewer years, (3) there is a higher estimate of PTSD in the spouse/partner, (4) higher rate of readjustment problems, (5) lower rate of life functioning, (6) higher rate of marital problems, (7) higher and more dangerous rate of family violence, (8) higher rate of childhood behavioral problems, (9) lower rate of subjective well-being among the spouse/partner, (10) higher rate of demoralization, and (11) a higher rate of vulnerability to a nervous breakdown (Kulka et al., 1990). These disturbing findings are not only consistent with other research that has focused on Vietnam veterans' families, they parallel the findings of Israeli war veterans' families.

Israeli War Veterans' Families

Solomon, Mikulincer, Freid, and Wosner (1987) looked at family characteristics and PTSD in a follow-up of Israeli combat stress reaction casualties. The study investigated the role of family status and family relationships in the course of combat-related PTSD. The data sources were medical records and questionnaires and scale data for a sample of 382 Israeli soldiers who suffered a combat stress reaction episode during the 1982 Lebanon war. One year after the war, married soldiers had higher rates of PTSD than did unmarried soldiers.

It is revealing to note that Solomon et al. (1987) also found higher rates of PTSD to be associated with low expressiveness, low cohesiveness, and high conflict in the families. This lends support to the notion of the deleterious impact of war-related PTSD on families and challenges the simplistic notion that the availability of a family does not automatically ameliorate the symptoms of PTSD. Without information about how the family functioned prior to the war, however, it is not possible to conclude that PTSD caused the dysfunction found among these families.

Solomon (1988) has noted the effect of combat-related PTSD on the family. Acknowledging that the literature on the detrimental effects of combat-related PTSD indicates a presence of guilt feelings, emotional withdrawal, and elevated levels of aggression in the returning veteran, Solomon predicted and found in her series of studies that the veterans with PTSD have a greater negative effect on their families than veterans without PTSD.

Thus, a war veteran with PTSD found it difficult, perhaps even impossible, fully to resume or undertake his formal roles of father, husband, and breadwinner upon his return. Therefore, it was not surprising that Solomon (1988) found that the wives and children of these veterans show psychiatric symptoms themselves to a much greater degree than individuals in families with veterans who do not have PTSD. Subsequent research by Solomon and her colleagues (Solomon et al., 1990), for example, found that wives of soldiers with PTSD are much more likely to suffer from higher levels of psychopathology and social dysfunction than those married to soldiers without PTSD.

Also, Solomon et al. (1992) found that, over time, the marital relations of Israeli combat veterans who suffered from PTSD were more conflictual, less intimate, less consensual, less cohesive, and were marked by less reported marital satisfaction than in marriages of combat veterans without PTSD. Most recently, Solomon (1993) reported that wives of veterans with PTSD, in contrast to wives of veterans without PTSD, had impaired social relations in a broad range of contexts, from inner feelings of loneliness attributable to impaired marital and family relations, to problems entering the wider social network.

The Power of Family Support

Despite hardship, families of veterans with PTSD are generally reluctant to seek professional help (Figley, 1989a). Perhaps the reason for this reluctance is the fact that families are expert at handling personal and interpersonal problems. It is obvious from the above review that families with war veteran members who have PTSD find it difficult to endure. Yet, the vast majority of war veteran families somehow prevailed. As indicated earlier, although approximately 30 percent of the male Vietnam veterans and 27 percent of the female Vietnam veterans had PTSD, only about 15 percent of the males and 8 percent of the females *currently* have PTSD. Therefore, although war stress exacts an enormous toll, the vast majority of the men (70 percent) and of the women (73 percent) were able, somehow, to avoid developing PTSD at all. And, somehow, half of the male Vietnam veterans (from 30 percent down to 15 percent) and nearly a third of the female Vietnam veterans (27 percent down to 8 percent) recovered from PTSD by the time of the study. It is reasonable to conclude, based on our understanding of the power of interpersonal relationships to provide social support and the role of social support in mitigating and even preventing stress reactions and disorders, that support from the families of Vietnam veterans enabled them to recover from the stress of war (Stanton and Figley, 1978;

Figley and Sprenkle, 1978; Hogancamp and Figley, 1983; Figley and Leventman, 1980, 1990; Figley, 1989a; Figley, 1989b).

How Families Help Traumatized Members

Families are affected by their war veteran members because they care so much. This caring, at the same time, goes a long way toward helping these war veterans recover. Exactly how they do it has been the focus of my research for two decades. It is clear that families play a vital role in the recovery process (Figley, 1983; 1988). As an intimate social support system, family members promote recovery in at least four separate and related ways: (1) detecting traumatic stress, (2) confronting the trauma, (3) urging the recapitulation of the catastrophe, and (4) facilitating resolution of the trauma-inducing conflicts.

Detecting Traumatic Stress

The concept of the family is derived from the Latin term *familia*, the root word of familiar, which means "household," and includes everyone who lives there (e.g., family members, housekeeper, boarders, live-in relatives, friends). Anyone bound by a household—whether tied by blood or law—becomes well aware of the habits, dispositions, and patterns of behavior of fellow inhabitants. Add to this the similarities of inherited and acquired traits of family members and what emerges in most families is a remarkable feel for the normal behavior of fellow members.

Thus, in a healthy family, when one family member is having a bad day, others know it immediately. When a family member has experienced a catastrophe, he or she is expected to behave differently. Even when a family member displays symptoms of post-traumatic stress disorder, for which the cause may yet be unknown, other family members detect the changed pattern of behavior almost immediately. In the case of a Vietnam veteran's family, his family knew how he was before the war and can immediately detect any changes in his behavior and attitudes. For example, a gentle, soft-spoken, optimistic young man might have returned as an aggressive, withdrawn pessimist. According to one Vietnam veteran's mother, "I could tell that the war had changed him when I looked into his eyes for the first time. And he knew that I knew, no matter what he said."

Confronting the Trauma

Once the traumatic or post-traumatic stress reactions are noticed, family members are also in a position to help the traumatized person. This may be done by simply linking his behavior to the war. The method of confrontation selected by loved ones is most often tailored to the veteran's needs and style. For some, the direct approach is used. A second, more subtle method of confronting the veteran has proven more effective over the years. This is not unlike confrontational methods taught to mental health practitioners. Yet, for the supporters of Vietnam veterans, their years of experience provide an important source of guidance for selecting just the right time and place to point out what they see. As a spouse noted to the author:

> When John started having problems related to the war he became depressed and withdrawn. My first instincts were to let him find his own space, but what finally worked was telling him how me and the kids were becoming scared of him. That got his attention.

Urging Recapitulation of the Traumatic Event

A third way that families provide social support and facilitate recovery from trauma is assisting the traumatized member to reconsider the traumatic events: to recapitulate what happened. This is very important to recovery. The process of recapitulation involves helping the traumatized person answer at least five fundamental questions:

- What happened to me that was so traumatic?
- Why did it happen to me?
- Why did I and others in the same situation act as we did?
- Why have I acted as I have since then?
- If something like this happens again, will I be able to cope more effectively?

During the process of recapitulation, family members help the victim to recall facets of the traumatic event and answer the questions noted above. Many Vietnam veterans do not really know the answers fully. They have tried to figure them out themselves from their own memory and the memories of other veterans. Sometimes the new-found information is painful and makes things worse. Most often, however, it brings relief. Often veterans believe that family members do not want to know, or they worry that, when informed, loved ones will react by criticizing, abandoning, or fearing the veteran (Figley and Sprenkle, 1978; Figley, 1983; Figley, 1989a).

Facilitating Resolution of Conflicts

Finally, the family can be extremely useful in helping the trauma victim work through traumatic memories and accompanying conflicts. Most important, families help victims by "reframing," or offering alternative ways of viewing the highly stressful event and the event-related consequences in a more positive or optimistic way. For example, the traumatic event was "God's test of our faith" or "it made us more aware of how other victims feel." Reframing helps the victim formulate a "healing theory" (Figley, 1989a). All five of the victim questions must be answered to the satisfaction of the victim. Most important, the family member serves as an effective facilitator in developing a healing theory.

This process requires considerable knowledge about the traumatized (veteran) family member: information that is well known to fellow family members, but acquired very slowly by therapists or others attempting to assist the victim. Family members, for example, may choose to be either active or passive, use mutual self-disclosure or not, be confrontive or not.

As noted elsewhere (Figley, 1983; 1989a), at least three separate activities within families with highly developed skills of social supportiveness can facilitate healing: clarifying insights, correcting distortions (placing blame and credit more objectively), and offering or supporting new and more "generous" or accurate perspectives on the catastrophe.

- **Clarifying Insights**. In studies of families who were effective in helping a traumatized family member (i.e., war veteran) recover from his memories of trauma, family members tended to be very effective in listening closely for insights from the traumatized person in a nonjudgmental and caring manner. Negative insights were ignored or accepted, positive insights were noticed and encouraged. Moreover, supportive family members would frequently remind the traumatized member of his insightfulness during subsequent attempts to answer the five fundamental questions in an effort to construct a healing theory, or to reframe some aspect of his experiences. In the case of effective Vietnam veteran families, spouses tended to listen carefully to what the veteran said and felt about his war experiences—in a wide variety of contexts (e.g., overhearing discussions with other war veterans)—inserting the information into later conversations, when the war veteran struggled to make sense out of it all.

- **Correcting Distortions**. Families successful in therapy tend to place blame and give credit more objectively than less successful families. Based on their years of experience living with family members, they are able to gently guide a fellow family member to view various situations from a different perspective. This is a part of what could be called basic family relations skills. An example of these skills is parents' extraordinary capacity to help their children sort out blame and credit for their actions. This may be due in part to some parents' spending more time with the children, knowing them better, and attaching more importance to having good communication skills and thus working at it more diligently. As noted earlier, recovering from traumatic stress entails developing more effective "memory management," and family involvement is key: it enables fellow members to manage memories more effectively by correcting distorted views or conclusions in a way that will lead to effective recovery.

- **Supporting Reframes**. Similarly, effective families are able to offer or support new and more "generous" or accurate perspectives on the catastrophe, the traumatic and post-traumatic stress, and stress reactions. This involves, for example, adding a positive connotation to what is currently viewed as negative. A Vietnam veteran's daughter once noted to the author that, when she was sixteen and was visiting the Vietnam War Memorial (The Wall), her father told her that he felt responsible for the death of Doug, a private in his squad who was killed in an ambush on a patrol.

> My dad kept saying that it was his fault because Doug was killed "on my watch." I simply asked dad, "Didn't you say some years ago that he was a screw-up? Wouldn't he have died if *anyone else* had been leading the patrol?" Dad got real quiet. Tears came to his eyes. He sighed and said, "You're right, honey," and never mentioned it again.

The ability to present new perspectives is the cornerstone of the healing process, and a skill critical to helping family members effectively work through traumatic experiences. These naturally occurring actions within the family system, or any other social support system, are the basis for our approach to helping families: Identify methods found to be effective in other families and teach them to families who are impaired in some way. But, at the same time a cost is associated with caring. These costs are reflected in the problems noted earlier among families living with a Vietnam War veteran with PTSD. Perhaps these families simply tried and failed to help their war veteran family member recover emotionally, and, in the process, were traumatized themselves (Catherall, 1992; Figley, 1995).

Family as a Mitigator of Stress

It is not surprising that veterans in their forties prize their families. Social science research has shown that social support is a critical human resource. Some argue (e.g., Caplan, 1974) that social support is the essence of friendship and marital commitment, and the glue of interpersonal relationships. It is connected to the human quest for lifelong companionship because it is connected to a sense of well-being and avoidance of stress. Hirsch (1980) noted from his research, for example, that the by-products of interpersonal interaction are five critical factors. These elements emerged from a comprehensive series of studies and a succession of factor analyses. The five support factors are:

- **Advice/Guidance.** Family members provide advice on ways of coping with various life stressors. Sometimes this advice and guidance is needed and helpful. Sometimes it is needed but not helpful, or helpful but not really needed.
- **Emotional Support and Love.** This element is hard to find anywhere else, with some degree of certainty and continuity, than in family life. Most people cite family members, particularly parents, as the primary source of love and emotional support.
- **Tangible Aid.** Hirsch (1980) reasoned that tangible aid, those items that are loaned, given, or stolen from family members and other supporters, are extremely valuable and save enormous energy and resources for the recipient of this aid.
- **Companionship.** All some people need to endure a difficult time—or any time—is the presence of someone with whom they feel comfortable and safe. Little else is required of the supporter.
- **Guidance.** Leadership, direction, and advice characterize this type of support. It is the sense that the supporter will enable the supported to save time and energy through his or her directions. A form of guidance takes place when a supporter, in particular one's

spouse, facilitates treatment compliance. Thus, families serve a vital role in ensuring that ill family members take their medicine, do their exercise, or otherwise follow whatever prescription was given to bring on recovery.

Family as an Intensifier of Stress

At the same time, however, family members are sources of stress. It is well known among mental health professionals that abuse in families is commonplace. Families can intensify stress by not attending to recipients of abuse, overreacting or reacting to issues that are unimportant, or participating in the abuse (Figley, 1989b).

Other stressors are those connected with normative life transitions (McCubbin and Figley, 1983; McCubbin and McCubbin, 1989). The most common are birth, marriage, entering and leaving school, children leaving home, retirement, and death.

Veterans' Family-Centered Service Delivery System

Given the central role of families in the healing process, it is all the more surprising that families are so uniformly excluded from programs devoted to the treatment of military veterans.

Medical practitioners have known for some time that the most effective way to care for people is by and through the family (Doherty, 1989; Doherty and Baird, 1983; 1987). Assuming that the extraordinary power of the family in health promotion is known and programs are built to fully engage these natural healing powers, how can a service delivery system be devised to harness that same power?

It would be easier for the veteran service providers truly to recognize the veteran's family as their "customer" if the following three questions were kept in mind: (1) What are the needs of the family according to the spokesperson, who may or may not be the veteran? (2) What are the intended consequences of the family intervention for everyone in the family? (3) What may be the unintended consequences of the family intervention for everyone in the family?

As noted earlier, the family is the best place in which to help war veterans to recover and to correct adverse effects on the family stemming from their efforts to help. Problems not unique to, but perhaps exacerbated by, the war experience may be better addressed in the family. It is clear that thousands of families have members who have substance abuse problems that may have originated with a traumatic event. A majority of those with PTSD turn to alcohol and other drugs for help in managing or coping with their symptoms, and become addicted (Figley, 1989a). Similarly, family violence and other forms of abuse are the primary source of traumatic stress (Bolton and Bolton, 1987). Thus, there is a critical need for a war veteran service delivery system that is family friendly and family centered.

Family-Centered Service Delivery System

Having a family-centered service delivery system simply means shift the customer from being the war veteran alone to being the war veteran and his family. As noted earlier, medicine has recognized the value of family practitioners who are not only general practitioners, but see the entire family as their patient (Doherty and Baird, 1983). The family practitioner is familiar with the health history and needs of everyone in the family. When a child is treated for an infection, the physician takes into account how the infection may have spread or may spread throughout the family and takes steps to ensure this does not happen. The family physician knows everybody in the family by name and disposition.

Family-centered mental health services are structured in a similar way. Indeed, the family therapist would be in constant consultation with the family physician to ensure a coordination of care. Family dentistry has the same family-centered sensitivity and application. Each of these practitioners looks for strengths and attempts to help the family identify and correct problems.

In family therapy, for example, family sessions are especially important in times of transition such as the birth, death, or departure of a family member. Good family-centered family therapy services are marked by these principles:

- **Do No Harm.** A family-centered approach involves practitioners who are not only concerned about the client family's immediate environment, but other environments as well: work, play, education, extended kin, community, nation. They would, of course, operate under the first principle of intervention, which is to at least do no harm. Some families that are functioning adequately may wish to function at a higher level, but are uncertain how to do so. Programs that are not sensitive to the natural, ameliorative complexity of the family may inadvertently do more harm than good. For example, it is not always wise to insist that families tell each other exactly how they feel at all times. Sometimes family members are unable to handle such information effectively and may become violent or depressed or react in some other undesirable way. Family-centered practitioners may not be able to make certain that their interventions will help, but at least they can be sure not to make the situation worse.
- **Be Empowerment Oriented**. Practitioners should always attempt to increase the power and sense of control within the family by helping members to realize and solve their own problems, that is, they should be empowerment oriented (Figley, 1989a). The obverse is also true: "if it doesn't work, don't do it again; do something different."
- **Share Knowledge** ("if others are helping they are part of the solution"). Family-centered practitioners view their clients within a larger, community context and, with the family's permission, collaborate with other professionals with some responsibility for the welfare of the family (e.g., physicians, teachers). This extends to sharing insights and important clinical methods and innovations with one's fellow professionals at conferences and through professional publications. The recently proposed national network of veterans' family service providers is an example of collaboration on national and regional as well as community levels, and will be discussed later as one of many by-products of the Agent Orange Class Assistance Program.

Family-Based Services

Consistent with the family-centered approach to service delivery, a family-based services (FBS) model, proposed by Insoo Kim Berg this year (Berg, 1994), is a blueprint for all practitioners. The FBS is based on approaches called "family preservation," "home-based services," or "in-home treatment." The characteristics of this approach, in addition to those noted above, include:

- Aggressive, intense, immediate, and goal-oriented service delivery;
- Team model of service—more than one person is assigned early in the intervention and they take care of each other's emotional as well as professional needs to avoid burnout and compassion fatigue (Figley, 1995);
- A needs assessment and treatment plan that governs the delivered services;
- Client participation in the design of the program of treatment;
- A general orientation to treatment (e.g., empowerment) is combined with specialized services (e.g., treatment of family abuse, substance abuse);
- Tailoring programs specifically to the needs of the family; and
- Service focus is on *solutions,* not on problems.

The Agent Orange Class Assistance Program: A National System of Family-Centered Assistance

There is, at least, a successful model that incorporates the characteristics noted above: AOCAP. This grant-funded national network of independent programs was established to address the needs of Vietnam veterans' families. In large measure, its uniqueness lies in the fact that it was developed in response to the needs of veterans rather than as a means to finding ways to use the service delivery system. AOCAP has not been limited in its responses by traditional bureaucratic structures, layers of hierarchical managers, standardized policies and procedures, or intimidation. It was not organized around a traditional central administrative office and did not insist on traditional methods of operation.

What AOCAP asked of its network of members was commitment to meeting the needs of veterans in their communities, in whatever way possible. It did this by first drawing on the member organizations' own professional and personal experiences within their communities. There was support for creating new, nontraditional programs, specialized programs, broad-based programs, and networking capacity among programs. Administrative support for sharing information with other grantees has been demonstrated through the AOCAP national and regional conferences.

What has emerged from this novel approach is a national network of family- and children-focused programs. A glance at project names around the country reveals this: Portland, Indiana's Community and Family Services; Green Bay, Wisconsin's Family Service Association of Brown Co.; Anaheim, California's Team of Advocates for Special Kids; Hawaii's Learning Disabilities Association; Tallahassee, Florida's Vietnam Veterans' Families Project; and many others.

These individual projects have been designed for the communities and families within which veterans live. The projects are staffed with individuals who are familiar with the community, with the values of that community, with the area's resources, and with how to access those resources for their clients. Additionally, they are linked to a national network of AOCAP providers, which enables these case managers to seek and find resources beyond their geographic boundaries. In a sense, AOCAP programs have been the link between resources in the community and resources beyond the community.

AOCAP programs took the unique approach of responding to Vietnam veterans' families' needs by minimizing, as much as possible, bureaucratic procedures and structures. In many ways, this network mirrors the development of the VA's Vet Centers. Like the original (1979) Vet Center mode, AOCAP was determined to be "lean and mean." It wanted to identify and meet the needs of war veterans quickly and with minimal paperwork.

This flexibility has allowed variety in program focus and design, collaboration with local, state, and federal programs, and inclusion of community issues that affect service delivery and accessibility. It has also allowed for program design that reflects the needs of veterans and their families.

To be effective, AOCAP case managers have to know about (1) veteran-related concerns and needs; (2) family issues common to these families; (3) the Social Security system and other social services established to help families with children with disabilities; (4) what community resources are available, how to access them, and how to assist families in becoming eligible for these services; and (5) all state and national laws, regulations, and services that affect their clients. AOCAP case managers must be extremely adaptable and flexible if they are to be responsive to their clients. The AOCAP network structure makes this more possible.

AOCAP has supported an extraordinary variety of programs. It is a network that has allowed for enough diversity to respond to a variety of needs, enough autonomy for differentiation, enough support for creativity, enough unity for self-confidence, and enough structure to keep these multifaceted programs a part of the whole.

At the same time, there is an extraordinary degree of collaboration among AOCAP projects. This is due, in part, to the computer-based network called VETNET. This e-mail and bulletin board service enables any member of the AOCAP network who has telephone communication and a modest amount of computer equipment to send and receive messages and documents, or simply chat with individuals in any of the scores of projects throughout the system.

Changing Policies within the VA

The current policies of the U. S. Department of Veterans Affairs' Veteran Health Administration never discuss families. This omission arises not because the administration is mean spirited or poorly informed; it is because the Congress has not changed the law to permit the VA to do so. Despite minor changes following the Persian Gulf War, the system operates under regulations written in 1992 that state: (Department of Veterans Affairs, 1992, p. 4.1).

> Significant others are seen if necessary to provide adequate readjustment counseling services to the veteran. Client numbers and records are maintained in the name of the

veteran; however, counseling case notes/progress notes on visits by significant others should be maintained as discrete and separate from the veteran's notes for continuity of notation, and so they can be easily extracted if a request for the veteran's counseling records is made (p. 4.1).

Thus, the law does not permit the VA to treat anyone *other than* the veteran. However, various proposals would permit the Veteran Health Administration's VA medical centers to expand their services to family members, as directed by the secretary of Veterans Affairs. If enacted, this provision would give the VA a reasonable chance of surviving in an era of universal health care. To compete with more established, private sector health care providers, however, the VA must adopt the characteristics of the AOCAP approach noted above. The challenge will be enormous. In the meantime, it would be wise for the VA to establish an effective partnership with AOCAP, perhaps through contracting for services.

Closing Observations

Appreciation for the role of the family in the health of its members is a concept that has emerged rather slowly over the past forty years. Increasingly, research is showing that families play a major role in both adding to and reducing stress for their members (McCubbin and Figley, 1983; Figley and McCubbin, 1983). By incorporating family members in the treatment process of persons with schizophrenia, substance abuse problems, diabetes, cancer, and other diseases, professionals are seeing improved compliance with treatment, longer periods of remission, and decreases in the use of high-cost medical services (Doherty and Baird, 1987).

Relationships between patient or family and service providers also improve. In short, the individual, family, and therapeutic system all benefit with family-centered services. The changes required, on the part of our service providers, to shift from veteran-centered to veteran-family-centered services are significant, and may require significant amounts of time before old methods can be replaced with new ones that are more functional.

The AOCAP legacy is its existence as a working, breathing model of service delivery to families where they live, empowering families to choose for themselves what is best for them. There is the belief in this delivery system that families are best equipped to know what is needed to correct the emotional scars of battle. The concept of AOCAP is one of high-quality service for the lowest possible cost for the most people.

A debt arises from every war, no matter how just or unjust. The debt is owed not only to those who served in war, but also to those families who love and care for these returned warriors. Families do not volunteer their sons or daughters for war. Families, because of their emotional connections with the veteran, suffer greatly when the veteran suffers. We cannot do much for those who bore the battle and died. Those who bore the battle and live on, however, *are the ones who deserve our collective appreciation*, as do their families.

References

Berg, I.K. 1994. *Family Based Services: A Solution-Focused Approach.* New York: Norton.

Bolton, F.G., and S.R. Bolton. 1987. *Working with Violent Families: A Guide for Clinical and Legal Practitioners.* Newbury Park, CA: Sage.

Caplan, G. 1974. *Support Systems and Community Mental Health.* New York: Behavioral Publications.

Catherall, D. 1992. *Back from the Brink: A Family Guide to Overcoming Traumatic Stress.* New York: Bantam/Doubleday/Dell.

Cranston, S.A. 1990. Forward. In *Trauma and the Vietnam War Generations: Report of Findings from the National Vietnam Veterans Readjustment Study,* ed. R.A. Kulka, W.E. Schlenger, J.A. Fairbank, R.L. Hough, B.K. Jordan, C.R. Marmar, and D.S. Weiss, pp. v-vi. New York: Brunner/Mazel.

Department of Veterans Affairs. 1992. *Readjustment Counseling Service Vet Centers: Direct Service*

Operations. M-12, Part II, (Chapter 4). Washington, DC: Veterans Health Administration.

Department of Veterans Affairs, Office of Statistical Analysis. 1994. Statistical estimates of the number of families and family members, derived from the 1990 U.S. Bureau of the Census. Personal Communication.

Doherty, W.J. 1989. Challenges to integration: Research and clinical issues. In *Family Systems in Medicine,* ed. C. N. Ramsey, 571-582. New York: The Guilford Press.

Doherty, W.J., and M.A. Baird, eds. 1983. *Family Therapy and Family Medicine: Toward the Primary Care of Families.* New York: Guilford Press.

Doherty, W.J., and M.A. Baird, eds. 1987. *Family-Centered Medical Care: A Clinical Casebook.* New York: Guilford Press.

Figley, C.R., ed. 1978. *Stress Disorders Among Vietnam Veterans: Theory, Research, and Treatment.* New York: Brunner/Mazel.

Figley, C.R. 1983. Families of catastrophe. In *Stress and the Family: Coping with Catastrophe*, ed. C.R. Figley and H.I. McCubbin. New York: Brunner/Mazel.

Figley, C.R., ed. 1985. *Trauma and Its Wake: The Study and Treatment of Post-traumatic Stress Disorder*. New York: Brunner/Mazel.

Figley, C.R. 1986. *Trauma and Its Wake, Volume II: Traumatic Stress Theory, Research, and Intervention*. New York: Brunner/Mazel.

Figley, C.R. 1988. A five-phase treatment of post-traumatic stress disorder in families. *Journal of Traumatic Stress* 1(1):127-141.

Figley, C.R. 1989a. *Helping Traumatized Families*. San Francisco: Jossey-Bass.

Figley, C.R. 1989b. *Treating Stress in Families*. New York: Brunner/Mazel.

Figley, C.R. 1995. *Compassion Fatigue: Secondary Traumatic Stress From Treating the Traumatized.* New York: Brunner/Mazel.

Figley, C.R. In press. Systemic traumatic stress. In *Psychotraumatology,* ed. G. Everly and J. Lating. New York: Plenum.

Figley, C.R., and R. Kleber. In press. Secondary traumatic stress. In *Beyond Trauma*, ed. R. Kleber, C.R. Figley, and B. Gerson. New York: Plenum.

Figley, C.R., and S. Leventman, eds. 1980; 1990. *Strangers at Home: Vietnam Veterans Since the War*, 1st ed., New York: Praeger. 2d ed., New York: Brunner/Mazel.

Figley, C.R., and H.I. McCubbin. 1983. *Stress and the Family, Volume II: Coping with Normative Transitions.* New York: Brunner/Mazel.

Figley, C.R., and W.R. Southerly. 1980. Psychosocial adjustment of veterans. In *Strangers at Home: Vietnam Veterans Since the War*, ed. C.R. Figley and S. Leventman. 1st ed., New York: Praeger. 2d ed., New York: Brunner/Mazel.

Figley, C.R., and D.H. Sprenkle. 1978. Delayed stress response syndrome: Family therapy indications. *Journal of Marriage and Family Counseling* 4(1):53-60.

Fox, P.A. 1994. An effective multi-modal priority model for counseling Hispanic Vietnam veterans' families adversely impacted by Agent Orange. Paper prepared for the AOCAP Symposium, May.

Friedel, F. 1980; 1992. Forward. In *Strangers at Home: Vietnam Veteran Since the War,* ed. C.R. Figley and S. Leventman. New York: Preager.

Glenn, M.J. 1987. *Collaborative Health Care: A Family-Oriented Model.* New York: Praeger.

Hill, R. 1949. *Families Under Stress: Adjustment to the Crisis of War, Separation and Reunion.* New York: Harper.

Hirsch, B.J. 1980. Natural support systems and coping with major life changes. *American Journal of Community Psychology* 8:159-171.

Hogancamp, V., and C.R. Figley. 1983. War: Bringing the battle home. In *Stress and the Family, Volume II: Coping with Catastrophe*, ed. C.R. Figley and H.I. McCubbin, pp. 148-165. New York: Brunner/Mazel.

Jordan, B., C. Marmar, J. Fairbank, W. Schlenger, R. Kulka, R. Hough, and D. Weiss. 1992. Problems in families of male Vietnam veterans with PTSD. *Journal of Consulting and Clinical Psychology* 60(6):916-926.

Kulka, R.A., W.E. Schlenger, J.A. Fairbank, R.L. Hough, B.K. Jordon, C.R. Marmar, and D.S. Weiss (eds.) 1990. Trauma and the Vietnam War Generations: Report of Findings from the National Vietnam Veterans Readjustment Study. New York: Brunner/Mazel.

May, G. 1994. New lamps for old: How the AOCAP service delivery model charts new directions in veterans' services. Paper prepared for the AOCAP Symposium, May.

McCubbin, H.I., B.B. Dahl, P.J. Metres, Jr., E.J. Hunter, and J.A. Plag. 1975. *Family Separation and Reunion: Families of Prisoners of War and Servicemen Missing in Action*. San Diego, CA: Center for POW Studies, Naval Health Research Center.

McCubbin, H.I., and C.R. Figley, eds. 1983. *Stress and the Family, Volume I: Coping with Normative Transitions.* New York: Brunner/Mazel.

McCubbin, H.I., and M. McCubbin. 1989. Theoretical orientations to family stress and coping. In *Treating Stress in Families,* ed. C.R. Figley, 3-43. New York: Brunner/Mazel.

McCubbin, H.I., and Patterson. 1983. Family transitions: Adaption to stress. In *Stress and the Family, Volume I: Coping with Normative Transitions,* ed. H.I. McCubbin and C.R. Figley, 5-25. New York: Brunner/Mazel.

Mitchell, H.D. 1994. Specific cultural and/or ethnic sensitivity issues that service providers must address when dealing with families of Navajo Vietnam veterans. Paper prepared for the AOCAP Symposium, May.

Ramsey, C.N., Jr. 1989. Toward a theory of family medicine. In *Family Systems in Medicine,* ed. C.N. Ramsey, 583-600. New York: The Guilford Press.

Scott, F.D., D. Crane, Y.C. Simon-Alvarez, and J.A. DeResta. 1994. A consortium for services to Vietnam veterans and their families: An innovative model for serving the veteran community. Paper prepared for the AOCAP Symposium, May.

Scott, W.J. 1994. The evolution of veteran benefits and services: The contribution of AOCAP in historical perspective. Paper prepared for the AOCAP Symposium, May.

Solomon, Z. 1993. *Combat Stress Reactions: The Enduring Toll of War.* New York: Plenum.

Solomon, Z. 1988. The effect of combat-related post-traumatic stress disorder on the family. *Psychiatry* 51:323-329.

Solomon, Z., M. Waysman, R. Belkin, G. Levy, M. Mikulincer, and D. Enoch. 1992. Marital relations and combat stress reaction: The wives' perspective. *Journal of Marriage and the Family* 54:316-326.

Solomon, Z., M. Waysman, and M. Mikulincer. 1990. Family functioning, societal support and combat-related psychopathology: The moderating role of loneliness. *Journal of Social and Clinical Psychology* 9:456-472.

Solomon, Z., M. Mukulincer, B. Fried, and Y. Wosner. 1987. Family characteristics and PTSD—a follow-up of Israeli combat stress reaction casualties. *Family Process* 26:383-394.

Stanton, M.D., and C.R. Figley. 1978. Treating the Vietnam veteran within the family system. In *Stress Disorders Among Vietnam Veterans: Theory, Research, and Treatment*, ed. C.R. Figley. New York: Brunner/Mazel.

Summers, J.A., K. Horn, A. Lazar, and C. Ritter. 1994. Designing veterans' family assistance services to meet the needs and preferences of families of Vietnam veterans who have children with special needs. Paper prepared for the AOCAP Symposium, May.

Acknowledgments

The author wishes to express his appreciation to Gail Davies and Gary May for their contributions and critical reviews of this paper. Responsibility for the content of this paper, of course, rests solely with the author.

Who Are AOCAP's Clients?
An Analysis of AOCAP Client Demographics

Michael R. Leaveck
Agent Orange Class Assistance Program
Washington, DC

Abstract

A survey of all seventy-three programs funded in 1994 by the Agent Orange Class Assistance Program (AOCAP) extracted client data for a three-month period in that year. Survey findings indicate that AOCAP serves in excess of 50,000 clients annually in some 14,000 families. Moreover, AOCAP services reach most Vietnam veterans within the context of their families and those services focus on families with children who have disabilities or are chronically ill. This survey confirms that AOCAP is reaching the members of the Agent Orange plaintiff class whose needs the court settlement was designed to serve.

__Michael R. Leaveck__ has been deputy director of the Agent Orange Class Assistance Program since its inception in 1989. He served as the California State Assembly's staff specialist on veterans affairs in the early 1980s, and in 1984 became legislative director for Vietnam Veterans of America (VVA). In that role, and later as VVA public affairs director, he was instrumental in the enactment of legislation that allowed court review of VA claims, and in preserving the VA Vet Center program. A Vietnam veteran, he served in the U.S. Navy from 1964 to 1967.

A demographic survey of clients served by projects funded by the Agent Orange Class Assistance Program (AOCAP) operating in the national network in 1994 revealed important and useful data. The results of the survey confirmed that AOCAP was indeed reaching the members of the Agent Orange plaintiff class whose needs the settlement was designed to serve.

The demographic data presented here and the general demographics of Vietnam veterans and their families are not the same. Although many descriptive data about Vietnam veterans can be applied to clients of the AOCAP network, the reverse almost certainly is not true. Many clients of the AOCAP network have been self-selected from the larger Vietnam veteran population, largely based on their prior knowledge of and even involvement in the issue of Agent Orange or Vietnam veterans' issues. Much of the outreach done by AOCAP projects was based on names and addresses of claimants in the Agent Orange settlement. In addition, by the very fact that these clients have sought help from programs that were newly created, they can be regarded as among the most needy of the general population of Vietnam veterans and their family members.

Many studies have shown that, in general, Vietnam veterans have successfully readjusted (U.S. Veterans Administration, 1983) and become productive and even economically prosperous members of American society (Cohany, 1992). At the same time, however, several national studies have shown that a significant minority of these individuals continue to have problems ranging from a less-than-productive employment history (Egendorf, et al., 1981) to continued troubles with post-traumatic stress disorder (PTSD) (Kulka, et al., 1988). The results of this survey were drawn from those veterans and their families who reached out to the AOCAP network for help, so it would be safe to assume that a large number of these Vietnam veterans would fall into the latter category. Therefore, it must be emphasized that generalizations about Vietnam veterans and their families based on this survey would not in any way be valid.

As with many studies of limited scope, the findings of this survey must be considered in the context of data yielded by other research efforts in order to gain a more complete demographic picture of Vietnam veterans and their families and the clients served with AOCAP funding. Data periodically published by the U.S. Department of Veterans Affairs (VA), for instance, reveal that the average age of Vietnam veterans was approximately forty-eight at the time of this survey. Data continuously collected by the National Information System for Vietnam Veterans and their Families (NIS), an AOCAP-funded national support project at the University of South Carolina, Center for Developmental Disabilities, show that the average age of the children of Vietnam veterans seeking help from the AOCAP network was approximately sixteen during that time-frame. Other studies, especially those that focus on those Vietnam veterans who have had difficulty readjusting to or assimilating into American society, have found significantly higher rates of divorce and remarriage among Vietnam veterans than those found in the U.S. population as a whole (Laurence et al., 1989).

General Survey Considerations

This survey was undertaken to learn more about the demographic profile of the clients served by the AOCAP network. The survey's intent was to determine whether the AOCAP network of programs is:

- Reaching and serving those members of the Agent Orange plaintiff class most in need of services;

- Serving a clientele that is ethnically balanced, with minority representation at least equal to each minority group's participation in the U.S. Armed Forces in Vietnam;
- Focusing on the family as the primary service unit; and
- Fulfilling the mandate of the Court to give services to children with disabilities or chronic health conditions a high priority.

Survey Methods

This survey utilized a 100 percent sample of the network of seventy-three AOCAP-funded projects operating during the time period surveyed. The AOCAP network is so diverse in its service methodologies, and has such wide regional and service population differences among its projects, that a statistically representative sample of any less than 100 percent would be difficult to construct and would produce unreliable results. All but three AOCAP-funded community-based projects operating during the sample period responded - two had been discontinued by the time of the survey.

The survey was conducted during January and February of 1995 and the data extracted encompassed the three-month period August 1, 1994, through October 31, 1994. A three-month period was assumed to be adequate to obtain representative data for one-quarter of a program year if the three-month period was reasonably representative. The period chosen was believed to meet that criterion as it was comprised of one month of the family vacation season, and two of a normal school year without significant interruptions by holidays. A continuous three-month period also facilitated data extraction by AOCAP-funded project personnel.

The survey employed a one-page instrument with brief instructions and advice to call the AOCAP office if any questions arose. The survey questionnaire was generally filled out by the AOCAP-funded agency's project director or equivalent. Follow-up phone contact was initiated if data submitted were incomplete or if they did not seem to correspond to data previously submitted to AOCAP. Over 50 percent of the respondents were contacted by phone for these and other clarification purposes.

The survey instrument was designed and constructed by the author with assistance from Bryan Smith, Ph.D., NIS project director. The instrument was pilot tested with five grantees from the AOCAP network before dissemination to the entire network. The survey was conducted by members of the AOCAP Washington, D.C. administrative staff, including the author.

Results

Annual Service Data

During the sample period, 12,811 individual clients were provided services by the AOCAP network. Taking the three-month sample period to be a representative quarter, the current annual total of AOCAP clients served is certainly in excess of 50,000. To check the integrity of this figure, survey total client data were compared with annual client census data collected from every AOCAP grantee. Such annual census data collected for the period July 1, 1993, through June 30, 1994, revealed that the AOCAP network served more than 32,000 new clients. Allowing for a sizable ongoing caseload, which nearly all grantees report, the figure of 50,000 clients being served annually by the AOCAP network is reasonable on its face. In addition, as mentioned earlier, data reported in response to this survey by a number of individual grantees were checked against previously submitted quarterly reports.

The AOCAP network has not served as many clients per year in every year of its existence; in the early years there weren't as many AOCAP projects funded as in 1994, and many of them needed a year and a half or more to reach full operating capacity.

For the same period sampled, the total number of client families served by the AOCAP network was 3,470. Therefore, the current annual total number of families served can be assumed to be nearly 14,000.

Client Categories

The survey revealed that the AOCAP network does indeed serve more than the veteran. In fact, Vietnam veterans make up less than 40 percent of all clients served. The survey results showed that the types of clients served by AOCAP projects are:

Category	Percent of Total Number of Clients (%)
Veterans	38.5
Children	41.4
Spouses/partners	17.3
Other family members	2.8
Children with disabilities or health conditions (as a percentage of the total # of clients)	30.8

Family Service Data

The AOCAP network served a total of 3,470 families during the sample period. In the vast majority of cases, a child was the primary client, but in most cases services were provided to other family members as well. Services were directed for these families as follows:

Primary Client	Percent of Total Number of Families (%)
Veteran	19.6
Veteran's child	69.8
Spouse/partner	9.4
Other family member	1.3

Additional data were collected pertaining to family composition. These data, not reported here, were collected to gain a perspective on family size, proportion of families headed by one parent or less, proportion of families where the veteran was present, and the proportion of families with more than one child with a disability. Although the data here were less reliable because of the difficulty grantees had in extracting them, an estimate of 2.5 individuals as a mean family size for families served by the AOCAP network is surely a safe one based on these family composition data. If the total number of families (3,470) is compared with the total number of individuals (12,811), and an estimated mean family size of 2.5 is applied, it appears that the majority of individual AOCAP clients were served within the context of the family.

When taken together, the percentage of individuals served who were children with a disability or a health condition (30.8 percent of total clients), and the percentage of families where the primary client was the child (69.8 percent), point strongly to a conclusion that AOCAP has fulfilled the Court mandate that services to Vietnam veterans' children with disabilities or health problems be a top priority.

Family Composition & Other Characteristics

Although there are myriad combinations of individuals that could conceivably fit into an accepted definition of "family," this survey primarily examined groups of people usually classified as "nuclear families." Also, the survey did not examine whether or not the children in the families surveyed were all from the same marriage. Nevertheless, the patterns of family composition found were traditional.

- Fully 82 percent of the families were intact, consisting of a veteran and spouse who may or may not have children.
- More than 68 percent of the families consisted of a veteran, spouse, and one or more children.
- In 16.5 percent of the families the veteran was absent from the family unit.
- Of the families served during the sample period, 75 percent had a child with a disability or a health problem.

The relatively low percentage of families where the veteran was absent (16.5 percent) may be explained by the difficulty AOCAP projects have encountered in finding a veteran's children once he or she is no longer present. Most outreach efforts have targeted veteran-oriented sources of clients, and families in which the veteran is absent have been shown not to identify as strongly with veteran-oriented service resources. The data do reveal the strength of the AOCAP network as a national family service program in finding and serving so many intact families, however tenuous the bonds of the family may be or however economically unsound its footing.

Family Socioeconomic Data

The best-recognized standards for determination of levels of income are set by the U.S. Department of Labor, Bureau of Labor Statistics. They vary considerably by Metropolitan Statistical Area, a geographical unit used by the U.S. Bureau of the Census. Definitions of "low income" under this scheme vary from approximately $17,000 for a family of four in areas of the rural South to over $29,000 in Orange County, California and in New York City. For purposes of this study, low income was defined as $22,000 annually for a family of four, a conservative income figure for that category. Middle income was defined as between $22,000 and $75,000, and high income was set at more than $75,000. Families served by the AOCAP network fell into these categories.

Income Level	Percent of Total Number of Families (%)
Low income	68.6
Middle income	30.8
High income	0.6

The survey found that 73.3 percent of the families served during the sample period had no private health insurance. Medicaid and VA health coverage were excluded for purposes of this study, so it is unknown how many families had coverage under these programs.

With so many families with children with disabilities or health problems (75 percent), the combination of lack of financial means and no available private health insurance surely qualifies the AOCAP service population as extremely needy, under severe strain, and vulnerable under any set of standards or definition.

Ethnic Data

A significant proportion (36.9 percent) of AOCAP clients are members of ethnic minority communities—a figure significantly higher than minority representation in the Vietnam veteran community as a whole. U.S. census data show that 13 percent of the American population is African American and 10 percent is Hispanic/Latino. This latter group, the fastest growing ethnic category in the United States, represented a significantly lower percentage at the time of the Vietnam War (Baskir and Strauss, 1978).

Ethnic Breakdown of AOCAP Clients

Ethnic Affiliation	Percent of Survey Population (%)
African American	22.3
Native American/Alaskan	2.6
White/Anglo	63.1
Latino	10.5
Asian/Pacific Rim	1.1
Other	0.4

Conclusions

The AOCAP network is clearly operating as a Vietnam veteran family-oriented national services program that gives priority to families with a child with a disability or chronic health problem.

It is believed that these data accurately represent the clients served annually by the AOCAP network at its mature and fully developed stage. Furthermore, because many of the individuals and client families examined by this survey remain on project caseloads for some time, it can be stated with a high degree of confidence that these characteristics of the AOCAP network will hold true for the foreseeable future.

References

Baskir, L., and W. Strauss. 1978. *Chance and Circumstance.* New York: Random House.

Cohany, S.R. 1992. The Vietnam-era cohort: Employment and earnings. *Monthly Labor Review* 115(6):3-15.

Egendorf, A., C. Kadushin, R.S. Laufer, G. Rothbart, and L. Sloan. 1981. *Legacies of Vietnam: Comparative Adjustment of Vietnam Veterans and their Peers.* New York: Center for Policy Research.

Kulka, R., W.E. Schlenger, J.A. Fairbank, R.L. Hough, K. Jordan, C.R. Marman, and D.S. Weiss. 1988. *National Vietnam Veterans Readjustment Study.* Research Triangle Park. NC: Research Triangle Institute.

Laurence, J.H., P.F. Ramsberger, and M.A. Gribben. 1989. *Effects of Military Experience on the Post-Service Lives of Low-Aptitude Recruits: Project 100,000 and the ASVAB Misnorming.* Alexandria, VA: Human Resources Research Organization.

U.S. Veterans Administration. 1983. *Data on Vietnam Era Veterans.* Washington, DC: Veterans Administration.

New Directions in "Care Second to None"

Wilbur J. Scott, Ph.D.
University of Oklahoma

Abstract

The effects of war on its participants are poorly understood; veterans often exhibit illness and injuries that depart from standard notions of what is combat related. Illnesses and injuries among veterans—especially latent disorders—frequently stir controversy.

Under these circumstances, the Agent Orange Class Action Program (AOCAP) arose from efforts of veterans to seek assistance and services. AOCAP matches veterans and their families with available, specialized services; it gives preference in awarding grants to programs serving children with disabilities; and it started the National Information Service to identify the full range of programs and services available nationally.

Wilbur J. Scott, Ph.D., *is associate professor of sociology at the University of Oklahoma. He served in Vietnam in 1968–1969 as a platoon leader in the 4th Infantry Division. His most recent book is* The Politics of Readjustment: Vietnam Veterans Since the War.

Many elements are common in the collective experience of Vietnam veterans. One, we had immense difficulties sharing our war experiences with others, including the veterans of other wars. In fact, for a time, the generation gap may have been greatest between veterans of World War II and Vietnam veterans. Two, the tragedies and casualties did not end at the battlefield's edge. They continued after we returned home. Three, we encountered delays and rejection at the VA. This was true initially for those of us seeking help for traumatic war neurosis and later for those asking for help with diseases and conditions associated with exposure to Agent Orange.

I want to make some general and comparative observations about the Vietnam experience and to provide specific commentary on the legacy of the Agent Orange controversy and the Agent Orange Class Assistance Program (AOCAP).

General Observations

To begin with, it's a fact: A society cannot easily repay soldiers for their wartime service. Soldiers risk life and limb for a combination of reasons, but the starting point is they do so because they are willing to literally *serve* their country. We all know this. An alternate way of saying that someone is in the military is to say, "He (or she) is in the service." Compensation and other veterans' benefits recognize this altruism and stand as visible symbols of collective gratitude or even guilt.

Veterans are likely to be disappointed. After the war, their service remains "priceless" and they are, in a sense, infinitely deserving. Noncombatants tire of this after a while. Further, treatment, compensation, and other veterans' benefits carry specific price tags and resources are finite. Often, the altruistic service of a nation's veterans clashes with fiscal constraints and political realities. The result is bitterness and disillusionment.

A second general observation is this: the effects of war on its participants are poorly understood. Beyond the obvious injuries of war, veterans often exhibit illnesses and injuries that depart from standard notions of what is combat related. In part, this occurs because the military often uses new weaponry and other inventions that have unforeseen consequences. In World War II, for instance, scientists at first pooh-poohed claims from Hiroshima and Nagasaki that there were casualties suffering the effects of radiation. Manhattan Project scientists had anticipated many lethal effects of the atom bomb, but not illness and death due to radiation exposure.

Confusion of this sort is especially likely in the case of latent disorders—conditions in which there is a time lag between the precipitating event and the emergence of serious symptoms. The time lag between exposure and consequence make the determination of cause and effect very difficult. After World War I, for instance, many veterans complained of respiratory ailments they thought were attributable to mustard gas exposure. Because the VA is responsible only for illnesses that are service connected, it was difficult in these cases to separate the effects of exposure to gas from the effects of noncombat factors such as cigarette smoking.

A similar problem occurred in the Agent Orange controversy. A VA study found in 1987 that Marine Corps Vietnam veterans had higher rates of proportionate mortality due to lung cancer and non-Hodgkin's lymphoma. Dr. Lawrence Hobson of the VA explained the findings in this way (Hobson, 1989):

> If I were a Vietnam veteran, I wouldn't be the least bit disturbed. . . . It would only be fair to conclude that among the deaths of Marines who served in Vietnam in that time period . . .There were a higher percentage of them who died of non-Hodgkin's

> lymphoma than of some other disease. As far as the lung cancer is concerned, there is a well-established link between lung cancer and cigarette smoking.

The bottom line is that illnesses and injuries among veterans—especially latent disorders—frequently stir controversy. The process is worse for some wars than others. Psychologists Joel Brende and Erwin Parson, who specialize in the treatment of war neurosis, offer a distinction between "good wars" and "bad wars." The terms reflect the orientation by significant segments of the public about the necessity, justness, purpose, and conduct of a war. Good wars enjoy strong and near-unanimous support and sacrifice by segments of the public. Although good wars do not necessarily produce contented veterans, they do have the characteristics that ease a veteran's readjustment to civilian life: the clear sense of mission and purpose provide a compelling context for military service and, afterwards, for making sense of war experiences.

Bad wars, conversely, make readjustment by veterans difficult. Brende and Parson (1985) write:

> Bad wars are undeclared wars. They are wars no one wants to take responsibility for. . . . In good wars the soldier feels that his is a legitimate mission; what he does in the war is shared symbolically with the entire country. However, in bad wars, what the soldier does in the war falls squarely on his shoulders. He alone bears the burden for killing, for it is unshared, unshareable. . . .

Comparisons between World War II—a good war—and the Vietnam war—a bad one—are unfortunate because they mislead. Still, it is hard to resist the temptation to compare them. After all, those asked to serve in Vietnam were the sons and daughters of the World War II generation. Comparisons drawn solely between World War II and the Vietnam War may, however, overstate the uniqueness of the Vietnam experience. World War II, with its broad-based support, victorious conclusion, and largesse in veterans' benefits, is the exception rather than the rule among our nation's wars. In other words, the experiences of Vietnam veterans parallel that of the veterans of all our other wars *except* World War II.

For example, Brende and Parson (1985) wrote of World War I returnees:

> There are widespread accounts in 1919 of the bitterness of World War I veterans. . . . [They] were bitter toward those who did not serve, toward those employers who were indifferent, and those in government who didn't seem to care. Moreover, they were angry because they had given all they had and had received little, if anything, in return. . . . The angry veteran would have found it difficult to fight again: "They said, 'The next war, if they want me, they'll have to burn the woods and sift the ashes.'"

Remember, I'm speaking here of World War I veterans. In May 1932, in the midst of the Great Depression, some 40,000 World War I veterans marched on Washington, D.C., to demand a "bonus"—a cash subsidy to help unemployed veterans. Congress resisted. The veterans formed a picket line around the Capitol and slept there for three days. The police tried to remove them. The then newly formed VA claimed that only a few of the marchers actually were war veterans. After two veterans were shot and killed by the police, 600 army troops—including 200 mounted cavalry—were brought in under the command of General Douglas MacArthur to run the veterans out of town.

Similarly, descriptions of the Korean War indicate it, too, provides a significant benchmark for assessing the Vietnam experience. Korean War veterans, for example, fought in a limited war that ended in a stalemate. A skewed sample of draft-age males participated, and toward the end of the war, the military used a one-year rotation system. Psychologist and Vietnam veteran Robert Fleming (1985) wrote of the Korean veteran:

> The soldiers [themselves] called it a "half-ass" war—a war in which hills were taken and given back the same day, and men died in a deadly game called 'King of the Mountain.' . . . The American public, however, cared little about what was happening there. . . . Similarly, the public paid little attention to the Korean War veteran, and he called little attention to himself.

Fleming concludes: If any veteran in American history deserves the title of the forgotten veteran, it is the Korean War veteran.

These observations raise the question of exactly what it is that a nation owes its veterans. In 1956, President Dwight Eisenhower asked General Omar Bradley to come up with an answer to the question. The Bradley Commission suggested two principles. First, we should provide medical care for service-connected illnesses and injuries; in addition, there should be programs to ease reentry into civilian life and restore career advantages lost while in the service. The second principle clarifies the first: when there is a doubt about a claim, the veteran should be given the benefit of the doubt.

In other words, the nation does not owe a lifetime of benefits and care for conditions unrelated to military service. The obligation is to address the wrongs stemming specifically from military experience, and to do so in a manner that gives the veteran the benefit of the doubt when his or her claim falls within grey areas.

Agent Orange Controversy

The basics of the Agent Orange controversy are well known. In the late 1970s, a number of veterans complained of illnesses of unknown and, ultimately, disputed origin. Civilian medical authorities diagnosed cancers and other disabling or life-threatening conditions. Some veterans sought assistance from the VA to confirm suspicions that exposure to Agent Orange in Vietnam caused the diseases. The scenario seemed unlikely and costly to VA administrators. Hence, these inquiries had no effective representation in the hospital system in which service-connected illnesses of veterans are certified and treated.

Neither the VA, nor anyone else for that matter, knew at the time if exposure to Agent Orange caused the ailments of which the veterans spoke. Most parties involved knew that dioxin—Agent Orange's unintended contaminant—was extremely toxic. They knew how Agent Orange's active compounds—2,4,5-T and 2,4-D—killed plants. But the question of whether these ingredients caused cancer, other diseases, and birth defects in humans via environmental exposures was another matter altogether. Ironically, the VA chose not to apply its own standard of giving the veteran the benefit of the doubt. The VA position, developed in 1978 by its Committee on the Health-Related Effects of Herbicides, called for cause-and-effect evidence as a precondition for treatment and compensation. This was a departure from the usual practice of requiring correlational data, a less restrictive requirement.

Ironic, too, is the fact that the Secretary of Veterans Affairs is empowered in certain instances to extend a "presumption of service-connection" for ailments. By definition, a presumption of service connection means the evidence that a disease is service connected is spotty, but the VA is willing to presume veterans who contracted it did so while in the service. For instance, although the evidence is not definitive, the VA has assumed that heart and circulatory problems are automatically service connected among veterans who have suffered traumatic amputations. VA administrators during the decade of the 1980s did not see fit to extend similar presumptions for Agent Orange claimants.

Blocked in their attempts to find satisfaction within the VA, some veterans sought to shift the battlefield to another arena in hopes of finding relief. Veteran Paul Reutershan filed a personal injury suit in July of 1978 against the manufacturers of Agent Orange. Following his death from cancer in December, others refiled his complaint as a class action suit in behalf of all Vietnam veterans and their families who might have been harmed by the herbicide. The lead attorney, Victor Yannacone, estimated the potential damages at more than $4 billion.

The Agent Orange class action suit made legal history. Two points are relevant here. First, veterans are not permitted to sue the government for illnesses or injuries incurred in the military. And prior to 1988, a veteran could not sue the VA for its ruling on claims: hence the rationale for naming the chemical manufacturers as defendants. This strategy also meant that the veteran plaintiffs had to focus on misdeed by the chemical companies, not the government. If the plaintiffs were too critical of the government, it might let the chemical companies off the hook.

Second, the suit expanded the circle of those potentially injured by the war to include the children of Vietnam veterans. From the beginning, veterans with children who suffered from birth defects and congenital diseases were among those who claimed harm from Agent Orange. For example, Vietnam veterans Michael Ryan and John Woods both testified in June of 1979 before a House subcommittee. They feared that their own exposure to Agent Orange had produced birth defects in their children. After describing his family's ordeal, Ryan stated: "We were told the enemy was in the bush and he wore black sandals. We never suspected the enemy could be in the air around us" (Hornblower, 1979).

And Woods, a former Green Beret and father of two normal sons before going to Vietnam and two with congenital health problems after his return, stated: "We are not the veterans. Our children are the veterans."

This required a rethinking in the medical community of how birth defects occur. Medical people had pretty much assumed that chemical hazards produce birth defects only if the mother is exposed during pregnancy. The suit contended that fathers exposed to the herbicide as much as ten years earlier were now siring children with birth defects. This seemed implausible to many researchers. Subsequent research has indicated, however, this contention is at least theoretically possible.

The lawsuit wound its way through the legal process for more than five years. There were five major categories of harm among the some 30,000 claimants represented by the plaintiffs: chloracne, systemic dysfunctions, neurological dysfunctions, cancers, and birth defects. Under presiding U.S. District Judge Jack B. Weinstein, the central legal issue became the strength of the scientific evidence supporting the claims rather than any misdeeds on the part of the chemical companies. Judge Weinstein urged both sides to settle out-of-court and the posture of the case enhanced this possibility.

Emergence and Structure of AOCAP

The two sides did settle on May 7, 1984, and the chemical companies established an initial fund of $180 million from which the plaintiffs could be compensated. Three months later, Judge Weinstein held the first of a series of hearings to determine the fairest and most equitable way to distribute the funds to the plaintiffs. He sought advice from both veterans and veterans' organizations. The $180 million grew to $240 million by the time all the appeals were completed.

Two-thirds of the money—$170 million—went to totally disabled Vietnam veteran plaintiffs and to the families of deceased plaintiffs. The fund set aside $42 million for grants to service organizations under what has become AOCAP and $10 million for an indemnity fund. Finally, attorneys' fees absorbed $13 million, and veterans from Australia and New Zealand (who also had filed Agent Orange claims) received $5 million.

The court provided general guidelines for dispensing AOCAP money. The top priority, it said, should go to disabled children of Vietnam veterans, because they had formed a significant part of the lawsuit. Under Director Dennis Rhoades, AOCAP began soliciting proposals in 1988. But what kind of proposals to fund? Michael Leaveck (1993) of AOCAP explained their considerations as follows:

> It was clear to us that we had to address the central issues that brought the suit about, especially birth defects among children . . . and after about five or six months . . . , we found out that there were a lot of Vietnam veterans' families out there who, because of their alienation, and . . . misleading impressions . . . about the suit and about the VA . . . hadn't really pursued other avenues of addressing their children's needs. . . . There was a tremendous need to . . . bridge those gaps in services and . . . facilitate re-entry into the . . . human services world that we have in this country for kids with disabilities.

AOCAP settled on three official goals. The first aimed at matching Vietnam veterans and their families with available, specialized programs. No funding would be given to programs duplicating government-funded services. Significantly, this policy meant searching out and securing services from agencies outside the VA (known by this time as the Department of Veterans Affairs). The VA, after all, is not commissioned to provide services for the families of veterans. AOCAP identified this step as the signature or hallmark of its program: it would secure services for veterans within a family context.

A second goal, in keeping with the spirit of the lawsuit and the guidelines of the court, gave preference in awarding grants to those programs serving children with disabilities. AOCAP interpreted this task broadly to include a wide range of family dysfunctions and problems, including those associated with post-traumatic stress disorder (PTSD). Veterans seeking help for their children would not have to prove that they had been harmed by Agent Orange. They simply would have to demonstrate that they served in Vietnam during the years in which Agent Orange was sprayed. For all intents and purposes, this provision was all-inclusive: our military sprayed herbicides in one form or another from 1962 to 1971.

The third priority flowed logically from the first two. AOCAP wished to establish a national clearinghouse for identifying the full range of programs and services available nationally. This comprehensive listing, with the clearinghouse serving as a conduit between the families of veterans and the programs that might serve them, would bridge the gaps among the support, technical, and training programs—putting in place what early Vietnam veteran activists used to call the "circle of treatment."

AOCAP funded its first proposals and in the process learned about disabilities and how to address them. Program leaders began with the assumption that children with disabilities needed surgery or medical treatment to "cure" disabling conditions. While some conditions did require corrective surgery and treatment, AOCAP realized that most disabilities are not reparable, that is, cannot be "fixed" so that the problem no longer exists. The task, they found, consisted more of securing ongoing services so that the families might gain the wherewithal to cope with and manage their children's disabilities.

They discovered, for example, that families with disabled children needed a variety of services they had not anticipated: training in living skills to foster greater independence among the children, recreation outlets such as wheelchair basketball and outdoor events to boost confidence and self-esteem, and, finally, respite care to give the parents themselves breaks from demanding routines. They also found that the families in need often had more than one disabled child.

From the evolution of these experiences, AOCAP moved to fund a blend of programs. Four basic types of funding areas have emerged. First, the largest share goes to veterans' organizations extending assistance or holding events for the families of Vietnam veterans. In 1992, about 35 percent of AOCAP's funding went to such programs. An example is The American Legion Vietnam Veteran Family Assistance Program. The Legion set up the program in 1989. Its purpose is to use the Legion's service officers network in fifteen states across the country to place the families of Vietnam veterans in touch with health and social service programs.

Disability service agencies comprise the second largest funding area and accounted for about 33 percent of AOCAP's budget in 1992. Here we find organizations that specialize in the treatment and management of disabilities, such as United Cerebral Palsy Associations, the Spina Bifida Association of America's Project Independence, and the like. The number, specialization, and resources of such organizations have increased dramatically in the past two decades as part of the phenomenon of grass-roots, self-help movements in the United States. They provide a rich resource for the families of veterans who, like others in similar circumstances, may assume mistakenly that they must go it alone. In addition to direct services, these organizations offer personal and emotional support by putting families confronting the same disability in contact with each other.

Classic, community-based, multiservice agencies make up the third funding area and cover about 25 percent of AOCAP's expenditures. These organizations fill an important niche precisely because they do address a range of issues and have as their target populations identifiable neighborhoods and communities. Overburdened families with disabled children may face an entire gamut of problems: a family may simultaneously need readjustment counseling for the father, job re-training for the mother, orthopedic equipment for the children, assistance in finding adequate housing, and an allotment of food stamps until back on its feet again. Tackling this litany of problems requires contacts with at least half a dozen federal, state, and public service agencies. Multiservice agencies, such as the Community Health Center of Oklahoma City, have the expertise and staff to address these problems as a package.

Finally, about 7 percent of AOCAP funds go to national support projects such as the National Veterans Legal Services Project (NVLSP) and the National Information System for Veterans and Their Families (NIS). NVLSP, under the direction of David Addlestone and Bart Stichman, used the law to challenge VA decisions and laid the legal groundwork for constructive change for almost two decades. For example, it was NVLSP that challenged in court the VA's decision to require cause-and-effect evidence as a precondition for treating and compensating Agent Orange claimants. In 1989, VA Administrator Edward Derwinski elected not to appeal a court's ruling favoring NVLSP's position. This decision reaffirmed the benefit-of-the-doubt principle and opened the door for a presumption of service connection for veterans who were Agent Orange claimants. The VA now extends the presumption for medical conditions such as chloracne, non-Hodgkin's lymphoma, soft-tissue sarcoma, and some respiratory and other cancers.

NIS, meanwhile, began in 1989 and has established itself as a national, progressive, and fully computerized referral system. To date, it has processed almost 16,000 inquiries from the families of Vietnam veterans. Director Bryan Smith writes in a paper prepared for this symposium (Smith, Mayfield-Smith, and Sudduth, 1994):

> It really doesn't take much imagination to see the complexity of the problems. . . . The NIS caller is often in a family . . . that is struggling with the debilitating consequences of primary and secondary PTSD. In each family, there may two or three children with different types of disabilities who are medically underserved, emotionally overburdened, and living in an isolated rural or inner-city neighborhood beset with its own problems. . . . The data . . . indicate that the frequency, diversity, and complexity of the conditions of Vietnam veteran families who used NIS appear to make them a unique group that deserves closer scientific scrutiny.

Conclusion

What conclusions might be drawn from this review of the Agent Orange controversy and the subsequent Agent Orange Class Assistance Program? To begin with, we should recall our general observations about U.S. wars and their aftermaths. It is unfortunate that the Vietnam experience is so often compared with that of World War II. We Vietnam veterans have had a readjustment process more similar in content to that of veterans of our other wars except World War II, which was the exception, not the rule. This finding suggests we should not think of our experience as unique.

Second, again we see in our war's aftermath that the effects of war are not fully understood and that we used weaponry and technology whose effects were not fully anticipated. Had we simply followed the principles put forth by the Bradley Commission, we could have reduced the pain and limited the scope of the suffering. The veteran deserves the benefit of the doubt.

More important, however, we see the importance of assuming the initiative and working together toward self-help. This drive has been carried out on a number of different issues by Vietnam veterans: the effort by a handful of Vietnam veterans, especially Jack Smith, who worked with sympathetic professionals to place the PTSD diagnosis in the American Psychiatric Association's diagnostic and statistical manual; the campaign to build the National Vietnam Veterans Memorial directed by Jan Scruggs; and now the many avenues and legacies of the Agent Orange controversy, capped off by AOCAP.

The specific contributions of AOCAP, beyond the considerable relief and benefits provided to its clientele, are twofold. First, its focus on the families of veterans suggests a unit of treatment, if different from that ordinarily provided. Typically, agencies and organizations address the veteran himself (or herself) as the unit of treatment. Vet Centers provide counseling for veterans with PTSD; VA Medical Centers treat veterans with service-connected injuries and illnesses. But what of their families? Is it not possible that family members also have conditions that are a product of the war or, alternatively, that the successful treatment of the veteran or family member hinges upon the health, cooperation, and support of the family as a whole? AOCAP has opened this door and offers the family as the unit of treatment.

Second, AOCAP, in keeping with the guidelines provided it by the court, sought service networks outside of the VA. In so doing, they identified an array of agencies and organizations to address the needs of veterans' families. This approach raises some intriguing possibilities for the future. The act that created the Veterans' Bureau at the turn of the century promised to give those who had borne the brunt of battle services second to none. Since then, the VA has grown in size—it is the nation's single-largest health care system—and most people assume the care of veterans must take place within it. However, perhaps the mandate of caring for those who have borne the battle can be best accomplished outside the VA system. John Terzano (1991) of the Vietnam Veterans of America Foundation says of this possibility:

> [General] Bradley's philosophy was . . . to provide them with care second to none. Now, interestingly, that doesn't necessarily mean the VA hospital health care system. . . . It's always been our view that war-wounded veterans should be given the opportunity to go to the doctor of their choice where they think that they're going to get the best care. . . . Like, give them a [health-care] credit card.

Perhaps we could apply both lessons supplied by AOCAP: the VA could restructure its format to consider veterans' families as the unit of treatment, and the VA could be only one of a range of health care options available to veterans and their families.

References

Brende, J., and E.R. Parson. 1985. *Vietnam Veterans: The Road to Recovery*. New York: Signet. p. 86.

Fleming, R. 1985. Post Vietnam syndrome: Neurosis or sociosis. *Psychiatry* 48:126.

Hobson, L. (1989). Telephone interview with author. Washington, DC. March 22.

Hornblower, M. 1979. A sinister drama of Agent Orange opens in Congress. *Washington Post*, A3. June.

Michael Leaveck. 1993. Personal interview with Charles Clay. Washington, DC. December 30.

Smith, B., K. Mayfield-Smith, and D. Sudduth. 1994. Some lingering consequences of the Vietnam War on the lives of Vietnam veterans and their families. Paper prepared for the National Symposium: Vietnam Veterans and their Families, Washington, DC.

John Terzano. 1991. Telephone interview with author. Washington, DC. April 4.

The Potential for Systemic Change in the Delivery of Services to Vietnam Veterans' Families

Gary E. May, A.C.S.W., C.C.S.W.
University of Southern Indiana
Department of Social Work

Bryan C. Smith, Ed.D.
University of South Carolina
Department of Pediatrics
Center for Developmental Disabilities

Abstract

This paper addresses some special characteristics of Vietnam veterans' families, especially where a disability is a factor, and explores the viability of innovative service delivery models to address these needs. Included in this discussion is a general description of service delivery vehicles for people with disabilities with a special emphasis on children and veterans. The focal point in this paper is the generic and veterans' health care systems in general and the Agent Orange Class Assistance Program (AOCAP) in particular. Important policy and program implications are identified.

Gary E. May, A.C.S.W., C.C.S.W., *is an assistant professor of social work in the department of social work at the University of Southern Indiana in Evansville, IN.* ***Bryan C. Smith, Ed.D.,*** *is a research associate professor for the department of pediatrics of the University of South Carolina's School of Medicine in Columbia, SC. He is the project director of the National Information System for Vietnam Veterans and Their Families, which is part of the Center for Developmental Disabilities.*

In comparison with other National Information System (NIS) client populations, Vietnam veterans' families suffer a higher incidence of chronic health conditions (Smith, Mayfield-Smith, and Sudduth, 1994). These problems affect the families' psychological, social, and economic well-being and productivity. Until 1989, no health or social systems existed to focus on the whole family and the numerous problems with which they struggle. Existing systems were exclusionary and uncoordinated, often geographically distant from the family needing service.

This paper explores an innovative service delivery model designed to address some health care needs of Vietnam veterans' families and their children. The discussion compares existing generic (civilian) and U.S. Department of Veterans Affairs (VA) health care delivery models with the Agent Orange Class Assistance Program (AOCAP) model. AOCAP has changed perspectives and methods of service delivery to Vietnam veterans' families. It may serve as an example for some aspects of national health care reform.

Special Characteristics of Vietnam Veterans' Families

The Vietnam era, as officially designated by the U.S. Congress, extended from August 5, 1964, through May 7, 1975. During this time, approximately 3.14 million men and women served in the U.S. armed forces in Vietnam (Kulka et al., 1988). The experiences of these veterans and the consequences of their military service have been described psychologically (Blank, 1982; Wilson, 1989; Haley, 1978; Williams, 1987; May, 1987; Kovic, 1976; Hogancamp and Figley, 1983), economically (Angrist, 1989), politically (Halberstam, 1972), and metaphorically as a national experience (Edelman, 1985; Brandon, 1984). The experiences and problems of these veterans have been lucrative fare for Hollywood.

The impact of the Vietnam experience on veterans' families is quantified in the 1988 National Vietnam Veterans Readjustment Study (NVVRS) (Kulka et al., 1988). Vietnam theater respondents in this study reported divorce (40 percent; 10 percent with two or more divorces), marital problems not resulting in divorce (14.1 percent), parental problems (23.1 percent), unhappiness or dissatisfaction with their lives (8.3 percent), isolation from others (12.5 percent), and vagrancy or homelessness (10 percent) (Kulka et al., 1988). These problems are compounded when post-traumatic stress disorder (PTSD) is present. Vietnam veterans with PTSD tend to be married, or cohabiting as if married, for an average of six or fewer years and have many more marital and family problems than do veterans without PTSD (Kulka et al., 1988).

According to Smith, Mayfield-Smith, and Sudduth (1994,) the health status of the members of Vietnam veterans' families who used the NIS for Vietnam Veterans and Their Families appeared to be below an acceptable standard. Smith et al. profile the Vietnam veteran family as one experiencing economic problems that stem in part from the family's dysfunctionality. This family is likely to be disadvantaged and underserved. Many children in these families have multiple disabilities.

The families have reported more than 900 distinct and frequently perplexing medical or related conditions. The greatest numbers reported included those in the areas of learning disabilities, skin abnormalities, immune deficiencies, and birth defects. Identified problems included a pattern of disability and chronic conditions, social problems, and poverty that seem unparalleled in other populations served by NIS. Smith et al. describe an incidence of many serious conditions among this population, particularly in children—incidence that is well above those who used other information and referral services similar to the NIS. The veterans' own disabling conditions place additional strains on family structures and contribute to isolation and the lack of access to adequate services.

Veterans' children with disabilities face risks of secondary disability as well as higher risks of mental health problems and educational dysfunction, as do other children with chronic conditions (Newacheck, 1989; McManus, Newacheck, and Greaney, 1990). Multiple studies document that children with long-term conditions carry about twice the risk of significant behavioral or psychiatric problems compared with apparently healthy children (Cadman, Boyle, and Szatmari, 1987). Most studies find that children with chronic central nervous system conditions appear to have up to five times the risk of having significant behavioral or psychiatric problems as do children without apparent illnesses (Pless and Roghmann, 1971).

Chronic conditions also significantly affect a child's ability to participate in regular education activities (Walker and Jacobs, 1985). Many developmental disabilities affect a child's ability to learn and create the need for special education services. Most chronic conditions have no direct impact on learning ability, although fatigue and the effects of medication may affect a child's cognitive abilities (Weeks, 1985). More commonly, a child faces frequent school absences because of chronic conditions such as asthma or immune deficiencies. Years ago, when a severely disabled child's life span was perceived as short, schooling was considered somewhat unimportant. Today, most such children survive to adulthood. A great need exists to improve educational opportunities and to diminish the effects of chronic conditions or its treatment on the child's participation in school (American Academy of Pediatrics, 1990).

Vietnam veterans face the usual problems all families face in raising their children. Sometimes, they have the additional challenges of addressing the ongoing needs accompanying their child's disability. (For an excellent overview of these challenges see Eisenberg, Sutkin, and Jansen, 1984). Because of the possible presence of unresolved consequences of their Vietnam experience, "approximately one in four Vietnam theater veterans currently has at least one serious readjustment problem, and approximately six percent have four or more" (Kulka et al., 1988, p. 6). Additional complexity and frustration result from limitations of the veteran health care delivery system, in which families often must try to work with service providers who seem to build barriers to services instead of bridges to them.

Veterans' families with members who have disabilities and chronic conditions often face additional problems including social stigma, prohibitive cost of services, transportation and architectural barriers, psychological consequences of disability, and many others (Eisenberg, Griggins, and Duval, 1982; Nagler, 1993). This reality challenges the effectiveness of traditional, residentially oriented, one-dimensional, single-focus delivery systems. Veterans' families, as do families facing similar problems, need assistance from a variety of service providers. They need a service system that provides advocacy, specialized educational services, general health services, specialized nursing services, social services, and financial planning. In addition, many need specialized therapies, such as nutrition, respiratory, hearing and speech, occupational and physical therapy. Because of the variety of services many veterans' families need, they also frequently need an advocate, and particularly, service coordination.

The Generic Health Care System

The civilian, or generic, health care system in the United States has been created using a medical hierarchical model. The physician and hospital are central to this system; all the ancillary professions and support services and facilities exist to improve the efficiency and effectiveness of these two central resources. Collectively, this amorphous assortment of health care providers and sites constitutes the generic health care delivery system.

The U.S. health care system provides the best care in the world for those who have access to it and who can afford it. The system is not available to all persons who need it because of cost and the unequal distribution of personnel and facilities. It provides coordinated care, but generally lacks an agreed-upon package of available services or benefits, including preventive, ambulatory, inpatient, and restorative care. Different levels of services are not linked, and there are no incentives for use of less resource-intensive services. There is a fee for service without single-source financing.

The generic system tries to balance the often antagonistic interests of consumers, health care providers, and the health care system. The consumer is the most variable of these components; some consumers choose minimal involvement and others opting to participate fully in the health care process. Full participation might include maintenance of wellness, prevention and health maintenance in the traditional sense; acute illness care; and restorative or rehabilitative care. The consumer in this arrangement may assume multiple roles, such as collector of data; decision maker based on the collected data; implementer of the decisions made by the consumer (or made by the health care provider with the active involvement of the consumer); and auditor of the care provided. It is through dynamic interaction between a well-trained, accessible health care provider and a well-informed consumer that a benefit usually accrues through improved health or higher social and economic productivity.

All the health care interventions that have been used for the past century in the United States are based upon the continuum of health and illness shown in Figure 1. The primary purpose of medical intervention is to reverse, prevent, or limit a movement away from a personal state of health. An intervention at some point along this continuum can stop or alter the process to keep it from progressing to the unfavorable outcomes of chronic conditions or death. The consumer's role as an active participant or a passive recipient becomes critical to his or her quality of life.

Figure 1. Continuum of Health and Illness in the United States

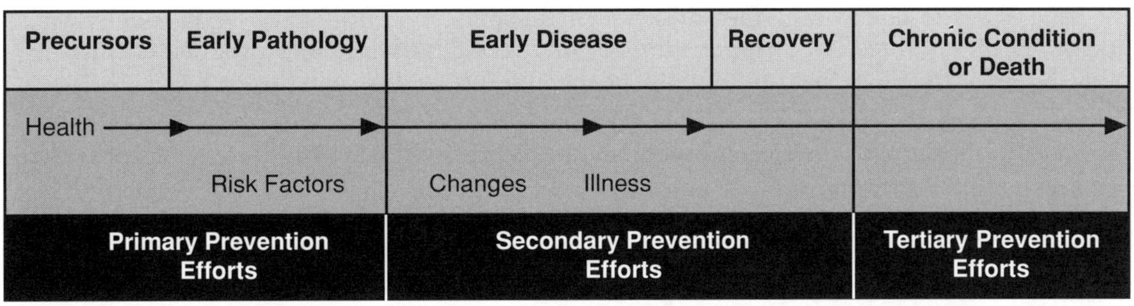

Figure 1 illustrates how most people start with an undefined condition of health. A person's life style and genetic endowments are functions that largely determine the risk factors. Risk factors accumulate to affect vulnerability that moves the person to the right on the continuum. When asymptomatic pathologic changes occur, the movement away from a positive state of health is usually still unknown to the individual. Up to this point, all actions taken to prevent disease or disability are called primary prevention. When the condition moves to acute early illness, intervention can occur to prevent its progression and assist in restoration. When these interventions fail, the early illness becomes classic disease; tertiary prevention measures can maintain the person's highest functional level and reduce progressive deterioration. Rehabilitation efforts are focused at this level.

If the consumer plays the principal role at the beginning of this continuum, the health care delivery system plays a very limited one. Primary prevention requires effort from the consumer, and an increasing investment of resources from society as a whole. In secondary prevention, there is a little less effort from the consumer and a little more from the system. Moving down the continuum, the consumer role becomes much smaller and the system role much greater. In contrast to his or her highly participatory role at the beginning of the continuum, the consumer at this point is often a noncompliant or unresponsive patient.

An example of the success of this continuum of care is the longevity of persons with developmental disabilities and chronic conditions. Survival rates for persons with these conditions represent a dramatic change within the past quarter-century; the changes result from major improvements in medical and surgical technologies and in the distribution and availability of care. Current estimates of mortality suggest that at least 90 percent of children, even those with very severe long-term conditions, survive to adulthood (Gortmaker and Sappenfield, 1984). With this success, the focus of care givers is now on improving the quality of life for chronically ill persons.

In recent years, many children with severe conditions, including those dependent on technology such as respirators or intravenous or tube feedings, have received care at home despite the fact that many of these children require nursing care, monitoring, and the aid of complicated equipment. This move toward increased home care is the result of several factors: the need of most families to take more responsibility for the care of their severely ill children and to have these children at home with the family, and the growth of technologies and efforts at cost containment that encourage home care as a less expensive alternative to in-hospital care (Perrin et al., 1992).

Veterans' Medical Care System

The delivery system for health care to eligible veterans consists principally of 172 medical centers and 231 outpatient clinics located throughout the United States. Additional access points set up to address the readjustment needs of Vietnam veterans are the 189 Vet Centers located throughout the country. With more than 225,000 employees, this health care system operates the largest hospital system in the world (Rhoades, 1985).

Because many VA health care facilities are affiliated with medical schools, this system often resembles the institutionalized portion of the generic health care delivery system. As it is in the generic health care system, the physician and hospital are central to health care delivery and all the other professions, support services, and facilities exist to improve their effectiveness. It, too, is based on the continuum of health and illness shown in Figure 1.

The alliance of VA facilities with medical schools represents an important educational resource for the nation's physicians and other health professionals. The alliance has provided some of the finest care and state-of-the-art technology, much of which found its beginning in the VA system. Despite this vanguard technological position, the system generally maintains the archaic practice of assigning the consumer a passive and largely uninvolved role. Federal law mandates the VA's health care mission and the way the VA achieves it. The system is mandated to provide hospital care, and may provide nursing home care, to veterans with service-related disabilities and to some others, such as veterans who were prisoners of war. The VA must also provide hospital care to very poor veterans. All other veterans may be furnished needed hospital or nursing home care if it is available; they must pay a portion of the cost of care.

The system demands placed on VA health care professionals are driven by the hierarchical medical model, which according to Germain and Gittermann (1980) "tends to view people's problems and needs within the person, overlooking social processes in which the person is embedded."

Problems identified in the NVVRS that are partly or wholly a consequence of veterans' conditions (divorce, marital problems, parental problems, unhappiness or dissatisfaction with life, isolation from others, and vagrancy or homelessness (Kulka et al., 1988)) indicate a need to focus on social processes.

For the Vietnam veteran with a child with a developmental disability, perhaps one of the most limiting characteristics of the VA medical delivery system is that it operates without a family orientation. It generally fails to recognize that the quality of treatment outcomes is influenced by the support and stability of the social systems with which the veteran is primarily involved (Cook et al., 1992).

The VA health care and services delivery system has been described in public forums by many Vietnam veterans as inaccessible to them because of an institutionalized paternalistic structure and attitude (May, 1993; U.S. Congress, 1994; C. Wilson, personal communication,

1989). The Vet Center program, more than any other service within the VA, has attempted to focus on treating the veteran in the family context. Clinical services have been offered to the spouses of Vietnam veterans in treatment in some Centers. Services for children and entire families of Vietnam veterans remain nonexistent or rare, focusing on a strict clinical rather than a case management approach.

Although the VA health care system still largely operates from a "come and get it" perspective, there have been occasional efforts to locate services more accessibly (Friedman, West, and Clark, 1987). Even the Vet Center program views family members of veterans as entitled to services only because of the veteran's eligibility status (National Veterans Legal Services Project, 1992).

The AOCAP System

Judge Jack B. Weinstein of the United States District Court for the Eastern District of New York defined the population to be helped by AOCAP as persons who served in the U.S. armed forces from 1961 to 1972 and were stationed in or near Vietnam. Certain spouses, parents, and children of these veterans are also eligible for funds and services available through the settlement.

AOCAP accepted the broad mandate to issue grants to organizations to provide services that address the needs and concerns of Vietnam veterans and their families. Since 1989, the Washington-based staff and grant development consultants have awarded more than 300 grants to a wide variety of organizations. The strength of this network has been enhanced by its ability to marshal or access resources beyond its immediate program boundaries. Comments from the field have resulted in many positive training, management, and resource-leveraging recommendations that have been instrumental in developing the network. It was apparent from the outset that the range of human services required to meet the needs of Vietnam veteran families must come from communities where the service providers have had only minimal contact with veterans. Until AOCAP was initiated, there had been an absence of contact and collaboration between and among organizations providing services primarily to veterans and organizations providing services primarily to children.

The goals and objectives of AOCAP have been:

- Services to families—provide service coordination and counseling to Vietnam veterans and their families, focusing on the veteran's war experiences as a major contributor to family dysfunction;
- Services to children with disabilities—build necessary linkages between the Vietnam veteran's family and the developmental disability and other social services provider communities; and
- National support programs—establish a national support network, including a veterans' law center, to provide technical assistance, training, and service linkages for the network of family services programs funded through AOCAP grants (Agent Orange Class Assistance Program, 1993).

The AOCAP network more closely resembles a social services model than a medical model in that AOCAP has allied itself with other organizations that are part of the disability service delivery system within the broader human services delivery system. The original AOCAP program developers were influenced by this system, and as a result they adopted a philosophy that closely resembled the disability system's values. They viewed persons with disabilities as persons who often had health problems that would be treated by providing medical care, and who often experience conditions that stem from physiological, psychological, and social factors affecting a person's development. They believed that all persons, including those with disabilities, have basic human rights and the potential for continuous growth and development. Consequently, they funded projects that would increase the adaptive behaviors of people with disabilities, enhancing their growth and development, and projects that engaged in systems change behavior, thereby improving general conditions for all citizens. (For a detailed description of the disability service system's philosophical base, see Koziowski, Hitzing, and Helsel, 1983.)

AOCAP promoted the attitude of personal empowerment through assertive service coordination by community-based grantees. A defining characteristic of the network has been the recognition that families are the primary decision makers for themselves and their children, making the family the focus for this newly formed service network. The services supported by AOCAP funding, unlike many large publicly funded programs, were based on the premise that flexibility and creative solutions were best suited to the diverse needs of the clients. Standardized responses to clients and uniformity within services offered were never conditions for awarding grants; insistence on and monitoring of quality of service and responsiveness to clients were primary in funding decisions (Agent Orange Class Assistance Program, 1993).

The challenges for the network were helping to meet the variety of service needs of Vietnam veterans' families, including family members with disabilities. AOCAP's goal was not to provide a cure, but rather to advocate, empower, and ensure access to resources supporting consumer efforts to solve problems. Families that include someone with a disability are confronted with ongoing, static needs in addition to those that change as the individual ages. This dynamic process places a considerable responsibility on family members to assume an important and active role in obtaining and managing services that may be offered through a variety of resources (Eisenberg et al., 1984).

For these families, the ability to interact effectively with a variety of service providers is particularly critical. To create an entry point for many veterans' families and one that could provide information and referral services on a national level, AOCAP funded the NIS as the central information clearinghouse for grantees and the clients they serve. The NIS helps coordinate the AOCAP network's activities by serving as an information clearinghouse for the network. Through its staff of information specialists, NIS becomes involved in relatively mundane but important tasks such as referring a family to a disability-related support group and in very complex case management and care coordination extending over several weeks.

Service coordination services are an essential component of the AOCAP network. The service coordination process begins with outreach to consumers and ends with the satisfactory resolution of the problem, in the process encouraging family empowerment and the capacity for self-advocacy and service coordination. Each AOCAP grantee has at least one staff member trained in service coordination to help Vietnam veterans' families.

A Case Study

The following description illustrates the activities and philosophy of the Agent Orange Class Assistance Program's network of grantees, including national support components. It points to the need for service coordination and gives an institutional perspective.

> The Buffalo, New York, office of the U.S. Department of Veterans Affairs Medical Center (VAMC) routinely contracts with C.O.P.I.N. House, a community-based private therapeutic community to provide intensive residential treatment for Vietnam veterans with PTSD. However, the VA regional office refused to approve the facility as a hospital for purposes of the temporary total disability compensation given to veterans whose service-connected disability requires treatment at a VA or VA-approved hospital for more than twenty-one days. The result was that veterans who received appropriate care at C.O.P.I.N. House of a quality at least equal to that provided by the VAMC and whose care was sanctioned and paid by the VA were denied the benefit of compensation during lengthy treatment simply because of the source of treatment.
>
> With the assistance of the National Veterans Legal Services Project, an AOCAP grantee, C.O.P.I.N., also a grantee, was able to get this incongruent financing policy rescinded by

the Board of Veterans' Appeals. The result of this action is that veterans now have another option for care that they can use without the additional worry about the financial consequences for themselves and their families.

This example shows, as do others, the need for and efficacy of advocacy, coordination, consumerism, and client-centeredness in the delivery of services to members of the class identified by the court.

Conclusions and Recommendations

AOCAP was created to meet the service needs of AOCAP class members that were not being met by existing bureaucratic units. Many Vietnam veterans perceive the management style and size of veterans' service institutions as unfriendly (C. Wilson, personal communication, 1989). The method of delivery of health services by the VA tends to be impersonal and disjointed, and veterans generally perceive it as inferior. This condition has been attributed, in part at least, to the type of veterans served—most of whom "possess the chief features that define our nation's high risk, medically indigent population" (Steward, 1992). Steward cites the frequent changes of primary care providers (changes dictated by academic schedule protocols of the medical schools rather than case status), confusing and fluid eligibility categories, and VA staff demoralization as contributors to the quality of care.

Many organizations in the human services communities who have infrequent contact with veterans operate under the incorrect assumption that the VA system is taking care of veterans. As a result, these organizations often fail to include consideration of veterans' issues or to address their problems. Steward (1992) states, "only 19 percent of veterans have used a VA hospital sometime during their lives." Obviously, veterans are receiving services elsewhere, or not at all.

The use of the medical model for service delivery contrasts sharply with the ecological, interactionist perspective widely accepted among professionals, most notably social workers, involved in providing a wide range of human services to diverse client groups (Simons and Aigner, 1985). It is this perspective that represents the most potential for meeting the needs of Vietnam veterans in the family context.

Data clearly support the sense that many professionals have that numerous veterans who need and could benefit from services are not receiving them. The NVVRS reveals that "7.5 percent of male Vietnam theater veterans reported having used VA services for a mental health problem" which represents "about one-fourth of their total . . . use of mental health services" (Kulka et al., 1988). Of the total number of veterans who used VA services, close to one-third made use of Vet Centers for their mental health problems (Kulka et al., 1988). The group with one of the most potentially debilitating major psychiatric disorders, PTSD, is underserved. The overwhelming majority (78 percent) of males and a near-majority (45 percent) of females with PTSD in the NVVRS had not sought treatment for their PTSD within the year before the survey (Kulka et al., 1988).

The reasons for not seeking treatment cited by likely PTSD case respondents in the NVVRS suggest a need for aggressive outreach and a psychoeducation intervention. Barriers to treatment included a desire to solve one's own problems; an assumption that the problem would get better by itself; the thought that treatment probably would not help; concern about what others might think; and a concern that others might find out about their problem (Kulka et al., 1988). A sizable minority (27 percent) cited concern about cost as a barrier to getting help (Kulka et al., 1988). Dichotomous explanations of these data are:

- Blame the victim—"The services are here, they just have to come and get them"; or
- Blame the system— "Important government institutions have violated the implicit social contract to demonstrate collective appreciation to veterans by providing needed support."

The AOCAP has demonstrated a decentralized, family-focused, community-based, consumer-driven, comprehensive model of service delivery to Vietnam veterans' families. The lasting success this network achieves will be contingent upon accomplishing the paradigm shift summarized in Table 1. Instead of recognizing the veteran as the only eligible service recipient and the family as involved only because of the veteran's primary eligibility, the AOCAP network accepted the family as the primary unit for service and the systems with which it interacts as targets for change. It approached this orientation from a perspective of consumer involvement and empowerment.

Table 1. Summary of the Three Systems Described

Characteristic	Generic Health Care	VA-Supported Care	AOCAP
Philosophical model	Medical	Medical	Social
Service limits	Set by provider	Congressionally mandated	Court order
Economy	Free enterprise	Congressionally mandated	Grant funded
Structure	Independent	Federal bureaucratic	Collaborative network
System entry	Fee for service	Qualifications	Class members
Focus	Patient	Veteran patient	Family
Consumer role	Variable—none to total	Little	Total involvement
Providers	Decentralized	Centralized	Community based
Level of prevention	All three levels with emphasis on 2 and 3	Late secondary and tertiary	All three levels
Outreach	None	Newsletter announcements, personal contacts	Direct mail, media, networking, personal contacts
Facilities	Community or proprietary	Government owned	Host agency owned

One result of this innovation has been the creation of linkages between disparate service delivery components that had no prior history of sustained, effective collaboration. The result has been the establishment of a durable commitment and competence to address previously unattended needs. Service providers were willing to participate in the exchange of old assumptions and methods for new ones. For many consumers, this approach has identified new sources for assistance and allies in a larger change process.

The AOCAP network represents a viable model of service coordination, advocacy, and organizational capacity-building that should be recognized in the ongoing effort toward health care reform. The efficiency this program has achieved is seen in the low administrative costs and the leveraging of substantial resources from other sources (Agent Orange Class Assistance Program Annual Report, 1993). The model could be applied to other combat or peacetime veterans currently served by the VA. Similarly, the systems change, service coordination techniques, and case-finding strategies could be used in other large, differentiated public and private programs.

The AOCAP experience has helped to identify several general veterans' public policy recommendations including integration of systems and services; inclusion of families in service systems; development of community-based resources; and training for providers of veterans' services (May, 1993).

The current system of fragmented, disjointed, institution-driven, and frequently antagonistic services to veterans should be better coordinated among the various agencies with relevant responsibilities. Linkages that foster predictably high-quality and coordinated services to veterans, as called for nearly forty years ago (President's Commission on Veterans' Pensions, 1956), should be mandated. Service relationships and formal interagency agreements between large, federally supported programs and appropriate state, local, and community-based public and private human services resources should be instituted and operationalized effectively.

Congress should mandate the Department of Veterans Affairs in particular to consider and fit the needs of the veteran within the context of his or her family. This would change the VA's focus from a strict veteran-driven service system to a family-oriented one, an orientation widely used in modern human services organizations.

Community-based organizations such as Base Camp in Nashville, Tennessee; Lower Eastside Service Center in New York; Swords to Plowshares in San Francisco; and the Universal Family Connection, Inc. in Chicago, have established a long and impressive history of providing quality services to veteran and nonveteran families. There is ample precedent for contracting with these types of organizations by the Departments of Veterans Affairs, Labor, Health and Human Services, and others. These contractual arrangements should be widened and extended. The obvious benefits include increased cost-effectiveness, efficacy, and easier access by veterans' families. As AOCAP began its work, feedback and suggestions from field staff identified the importance of inculcating the mission and methods into all levels of staff.

It was clear that there was a staff training need among AOCAP grantees. Even successful, well-managed organizations needed training in counseling methods, systems change, service coordination, the veterans' benefits system, and the role of unique background characteristics of veterans and persons with disabilities. The nature of the training conducted through AOCAP successfully capitalized on existing positive sentiment and skills to serve the unfamiliar populations organizations were serving. The training included not only information but also sensitization to the philosophy and values that drive the activities of AOCAP. These components, according to Peterson and Bickman (1988), play an

> important role in determining staff behavior. Etzioni (1975) suggests that the commitment of staff members to the organization is higher in organizations that are able to develop moral involvement by their members. Committed personnel are more likely to work hard to make the program function. Commitment thus relates to the degree to which personnel identify with program goals and see them as worthy causes.

Perhaps the most powerful, immeasurable quality of the success of this effort is captured in the words of the wife of a Vietnam veteran whose child has a developmental disability:

> Thank You
>
> I would like to express my sincere gratitude for all your assistance. Through your organization, my son Steven had the opportunity to regain his respiratory capacity. Through enabling us to return home to the environment he is less reactive to, he is able to resume a more personal lifestyle. You helped when all the other resources were expired. Through your efforts, Steven was able to get this far—and has hope and another chance. (Agent Orange Class Assistance Program Annual Report, 1992).

References

Agent Orange Class Assistance Program. 1992. *Fourth Annual Report*. Washington, DC: AOCAP.

Agent Orange Class Assistance Program. 1993. *Fifth Annual Report*. Washington, DC: AOCAP.

American Academy of Pediatrics, Committees on Children with Disabilities and School Health. 1990. Children with health impairments in schools. *Pediatrics* 86:636-638.

Angrist, J.D. 1989. Econometric analysis of the Vietnam era draft lottery. Ann Arbor, MI: UMI Dissertation Services.

Blank, A.S. 1982. Stresses of war: The example of Vietnam. *Handbook of Stress: Theoretical and Clinical Aspects.* New York: Free Press.

Brandon, H. 1984. *Casualties.* New York: St. Martin's Press.

Cadman, D., M. Boyle, and P. Szatmari. 1987. Chronic illness, disability, and mental and social well-being. *Pediatrics* 79:805-813.

Cook, C.A., L. Chadiha, B. Schmidt, J. Holloway, and J.L Satterwhite. 1992. High-risk screening mechanisms: Patient characteristics as predictors of social work utilization in the VA. *Social Work in Health Care* 16(4):101-117.

Edelman, B. 1985. *Dear America: Letters Home From Vietnam.* New York: Pocket Books.

Eisenberg, M.G., C. Griggins, and R.J. Duval. 1982. *Disabled People as Second Class Citizens.* New York: Springer.

Eisenberg, M.G., L.C. Sutkin, and M.A. Jansen. 1984. *Chronic Illness and Disability Through the Life Span: Effects on Self and Family.* New York: Springer.

Friedman, M.J., A.N. West, and A. Clark. 1987. Integration of VA and CMHC care: Utilization and long-term outcome. *Hospital and Community Psychiatry* 38(7):735-740.

Germain, C.B., and A. Gittermann. 1980. *The Life Model of Social Work Practice.* New York: Columbia University Press.

Gortmaker, S.L., and W. Sappenfield. 1984. Chronic childhood disorders: Prevalence and impact. *Pediatric Clinics of North America* 31:3-18.

Halberstam, D. 1972. *The Best and the Brightest.* New York: Random House.

Haley, S. 1978. Treatment implications of post-combat stress response syndromes for mental health professionals. *Stress Disorders Among Vietnam Veterans.* New York: Brunner/Mazel.

Hogancamp, V.E., and C.R. Figley. 1983. War: Bringing the battle home. *Stress and the Family: Volume II Coping with Catastrophe.* New York: Brunner/Mazel.

Kovic, R. 1976. *Born on the Fourth of July.* New York: McGraw-Hill.

Koziowski, R.E., W. Hitzing, and E. Helsel. 1983. Future directions in adult services. Position paper number 3. Columbus, OH: Ohio Developmental Disabilities Council.

Kulka, R.A., W.E. Schlenger, J.A. Fairbank, R.L. Hough, B.K. Jordan, C.R. Marmar, and D.S. Weiss. 1988. *Contractual Report of Findings from the National Vietnam Veterans Readjustment Study,* Vol. 1. Research Triangle Park, NC: Research Triangle Institute.

May, G.E. 1987. Counseling considerations in working with disabled Vietnam veterans. *Post-Traumatic Stress Disorders: A Handbook for Clinicians.* Cincinnati, OH: Disabled American Veterans.

May, G.E. 1993. Statement before the Subcommittee on Oversight and Investigations of the House Veterans Affairs Committee. *Health Care, Economic Opportunities and Social Services for Veterans and Their Dependents—A Community Perspective.* Serial No. 103-110, 16-18, and 86-93.

McManus, M.A., and P.W. Newacheck. 1989. Rural maternal, child and adolescent health. *Health Services Research* 23:807-848.

McManus, M.A., P.W. Newacheck, and A.M. Greaney. 1990. Young adults with special health care needs. *Pediatrics* 86:67-82.

Nagler, M. 1993. *Perspectives on Disability.* Palo Alto, CA: Health Markets Research.

National Veterans Legal Services Project. 1992. *Self-Help Guide on Veterans Family Benefits.* Washington, DC.

Newacheck, P.W. 1989. Adolescents with special health needs: Prevalence, severity, and access to health services. *Pediatrics* 84:872-881.

Perrin, J.M., B. Guyer, and J.M. Lawrence. 1992. Health care services for children and adolescents. *The Future of Children* 2:58-77.

Peterson, K.A., and L. Bickman. 1988. Program personnel: The missing ingredient in describing the program environment. *Evaluating Program Environments.* San Francisco: Jossey-Bass.

Pless, I.B., and K.J Roghmann. 1971. Chronic illness and its consequences: Observations based on three epidemiologic surveys. *Journal of Pediatrics* 79:51-59.

President's Commission on Veterans' Pensions, Omar N. Bradley, Chairman, 1956. *Findings and Recommendations: Veterans' Benefits in the United States.*

Rhoades, D., The Veterans Administration. 1985. In *The Viet Vet Survival Guide* by C. Kubey, D.F. Addlestone, R.E. O'Dell, K.D. Snyder, and B.F. Stichman. New York: Ballantine Books.

Simons, R.L., and S.M. Aigner. 1985. *Practice Principles: A Problem-Solving Approach to Social Work.* New York: Macmillan Publishing.

Smith, B.C., K.L. Mayfield-Smith, and D. Sudduth. 1994. Some lingering consequences of the Vietnam War on the lives of veterans and their families. Paper prepared for the Agent Orange Class Assistance Program Symposium.

Steward, C.A. 1992. *Investigating the Motivation of Veterans with Discretionary Eligibility Status to Use Veterans Hospitals.* Ann Arbor, MI: UMI Dissertation Services.

U.S. Congress. 1994. House Veterans Affairs Committee, Subcommittee on Oversight and Investigation. Hearing on the Department of Veterans Affairs response to post-traumatic stress disorder, Huntington, IN.

Walker, D.K., and F.H. Jacobs. 1985. Public school programs for chronically ill children. In *Issues in the Care of Children with Chronic Illness,* ed. N. Hobbs and J.M. Perrin, 615-655. San Francisco: Jossey-Bass.

Weeks, K.H. 1985. Private health insurance and chronically ill children. Issues in the care of children with chronic illness. In *Issues in the Care of Children with Chronic Illness,* ed. N. Hobbs and J.M. Perrin, 880-911. San Francisco: Jossey-Bass.

Williams, T. 1987. *Post-Traumatic Stress Disorders: A Handbook for Clinicians.* Cincinnati, OH: Disabled American Veterans.

Wilson, C. 1989. Personal communication.

Wilson, J.P. 1989. *Trauma Transformation and Healing: An Integrative Approach to Theory, Research, and Post-Traumatic Therapy.* New York: Brunner/Mazel.

Authors' Note

The authors thank the Social Work Department faculty at the University of Southern Indiana for their insight and helpful comments, and Julie, who provided invaluable research assistance.

Impact Analysis of the AOCAP Network of Services

Bryan C. Smith, Ed.D.; Kathy L. Mayfield-Smith, M.A., M.B.A.; and Dawn Sudduth, M.Ed.

National Information System for Vietnam Veterans and Their Families
Center for Developmental Disabilities, Department of Pediatrics
School of Medicine
The University of South Carolina
Columbia, SC

Abstract

The purpose of this study was to provide an indicator of the success or failure of the Agent Orange Class Assistance Program (AOCAP) network of services by measuring the success grantees had in bridging the separate arenas of veterans' and children's services. It was the hypothesis of the study that the network had accomplished cost-effective leveraging of resources to help Vietnam veterans and their families.

The study was conducted in two phases. The first phase involved data collection, survey development, and pilot testing of the survey. The second phase involved two groups: one group was composed of 150 class members who were selected randomly from the 4,380 client records of class members who called the National Information System for Vietnam Veterans and Their Families during the 1992 to 1993 fiscal year; the other group was composed of class members identified by grantees that could provide a measure of validity and represent an estimate of the minimum known leveraging of the network.

There was a slightly positive relationship between costs expended and benefits received before calling the NIS and a stronger positive relationship after involving the network. The network had a positive effect, which was indicated by an impact ratio of .036, where a ratio of less than 1.00 shows the impact was greater than the monetary costs accrued. For every AOCAP dollar spent, there was approximately a $27 return in outcomes, either through leveraged financial assistance or services received. The obtained difference was statistically significant; that is, there is little likelihood—less than 1 percent probability—that a difference could have resulted from a chance variation between the counterfactual and post-intervention.

The issue of why veterans' families need financial support was briefly explored to put the need for leveraging activities by grantees into perspective. Recommendations for additional analyses were also made.

Bryan C. Smith, Ed.D., *is a research associate professor for the Department of Pediatrics of the University of South Carolina's School of Medicine, Columbia, SC.* ***Kathy L. Mayfield-Smith, M.A., M.B.A.,*** *is a research assistant professor and the project director of the National Clearinghouse for Infants and Children with Disabilities and Life Threatening Conditions. These authors and* ***Dawn Sudduth, M.Ed.,*** *are the administrative team that leads the National Information System for Vietnam Veterans and Their Families, which is part of the department's Center for Developmental Disabilities.*

The Agent Orange product liability litigation is the class action lawsuit brought by Vietnam veterans and their families against the chemical companies that manufactured the herbicide commonly referred to as Agent Orange. The final settlement, which had appreciated to $240 million, was divided as follows: $170 million was designated to be paid directly to totally disabled veterans or to their survivors; $13 million went to plaintiffs' attorneys; $10 million went to an indemnity fund (and later was released for use by the Agent Orange Class Assistance program (AOCAP)); $5 million went to Australia and New Zealand; and $42 million was to be used to fund programs to benefit Vietnam veterans and their families. This last portion of the settlement carried the mandate to help the veterans' children, which became the charge and challenge of the newly created Agent Orange Class Assistance Program.

The AOCAP has operated under the direction and supervision of Judge Jack B. Weinstein of the United States District Court for the Eastern District of New York. The class it serves comprises persons who were in the U.S. armed forces from 1961 to 1972 and were stationed in or near Vietnam; certain spouses, parents, and children of Vietnam veterans are also class members. Broadly, AOCAP's charge was to award grants to support organizations and services that address the needs and concerns of Vietnam veterans and their families. Program goals were:

- Services for families—provide service coordination and counseling to Vietnam veterans and their families, focusing on the veterans' war experience as a major contributor to family dysfunction;
- Services to children with disabilities—build necessary linkages between the Vietnam veteran and the developmental disability and other social services communities; and
- National support programs—establish a national support network, including a veterans' law center, to provide technical assistance, training, and service linkages for the network of family service programs funded through AOCAP grants.

In the past grant year, seventy-three organizations with various missions and service areas constituted the AOCAP network of grantees. Because some states had more than one grantee and other programs served more than one state, an AOCAP-funded project could provide services to class members in every state and district as well as Puerto Rico. The grantees fell into four distinct organizational categories: twenty-four veterans' organizations; twenty-four disability service agencies; twenty family service agencies; and five national support projects.

The National Information System for Vietnam Veterans and Their Families (NIS) was one of the five national support projects. The primary function of this program was to conduct outreach activities and act as a central information and referral service for Vietnam veterans' families. Examples of its services ranged from the relatively simple task of referring a family to a disability-related support group for more information on a condition such as cerebral palsy to explaining to parents the rights guaranteed by the Individuals with Disabilities Education Act (IDEA) and assisting them in getting appropriate educational services for their child. Frequently, NIS faced even more complex challenges. For example, a family may have needed the coordination of a full range of services for an infant daughter who, hospitalized since birth, faced a 600-mile trip to another state to receive a liver transplant. The NIS worked with the family and AOCAP grantees to coordinate air transportation for the child and family, investigated Medicaid reciprocity between states, worked with programs such as the Ronald McDonald House to arrange housing, and enlisted various veterans' and philanthropic organizations to provide financial support for expenses not covered through insurance, Medicaid, or other family resources.

The NIS provided this assistance through a staff of information specialists who were trained to understand and untangle the intricacies of the disability, health, and social service delivery systems. They helped families sort out problems, identified available benefits and services, and often provided insight into issues related to their children's development. Most importantly, the information specialists helped families to understand how service agencies and processes work and how families can best navigate through bureaucracies to access the services to which they are entitled. The information specialists used a comprehensive database of more than 114,000 services that included Medicaid, Title V programs of the Social Security Act, special education programs, early-intervention services, and private resources such as parent support groups, disability-related organizations, and pharmaceutical foundations.

The NIS was a central part of the AOCAP network of service providers. Each network member was connected to all other grantees by electronic mail, which facilitated transmission of casenotes, or family intake records that listed referral resources recommended by the NIS. Referrals to grantees were made and casenotes transmitted when the grantee was able to provide some of the needed services, particularly service coordination. The effectiveness of this network was sustained by the collaboration between the NIS and the local AOCAP grantees.

Because of its links to other grantees and to class members entering the network, the NIS could provide quarterly needs-assessment data to the AOCAP administration for planning and development. Throughout the history of this activity, the dominant service need of veterans' families was for financial assistance services (79.7 percent of callers needed financial help), primarily to help pay medical bills, including outstanding and future ones. Because grantees and other service providers had limited budgets, they helped veterans' families locate entitlement programs for assistance. But complex eligibility criteria and other barriers often blocked them from doing so. Many grantees served as effective advocates and helped veterans' families overcome these hurdles. The scope and quantity of their advocacy and how successful it was, however, remain unknown.

In the fall of 1993, a study was conducted to determine what impact this newly formed network had had on the lives of Vietnam veterans' families. Specifically, the study measured costs to the network against some of the benefits received by these families; these measures were taken as an indicator of the success or failure of the AOCAP network in helping Vietnam veterans, their families, and their children with disabilities. This study assumes that part of the value of the network could be measured by the success grantees had in bridging the separate arenas of veterans' and children's services. The hypothesis of the study was that the network cost-effectively leveraged other resources to help Vietnam veterans and their families. Leveraging refers to the financially quantifiable outcomes of grantees' efforts to obtain services or funds from another resource through advocacy on behalf of a veteran or veteran's family.

Study Approach and Design

The study was conducted in two phases. The first phase involved a literature review, survey development, interviewer training, pilot testing of the survey and the method of data collection, and revision of the survey and process. The survey design began with a search to locate previous studies and data collection tools used in similar studies. After a review of existing materials and consultation with experts in the design and conduct of cost-benefit studies, researchers developed an interview protocol and survey.

The pilot study involved twenty-five class members drawn from the study population. Three trained interviewers working independently, conducted telephone interviews at various hours and days over several weeks to collect data and determine the best time to contact study participants. The pilot study revealed that: (1) only one in ten participants could be contacted during the work day; (2) study participants were reluctant to discuss financial benefits with a stranger; (3) the data collection method should provide advance contact with interviewees to establish credibility and rapport; and (4) the survey had to be reduced and simplified.

The second phase involved data collection from two groups of class members using the revised survey form and interview protocol. The first group included 150 individuals drawn randomly from the 4,380 client records of class members who had called the NIS during the 1992 to 1993 fiscal year. This timeframe was chosen because it was a period in which the network had stabilized and it was the earliest time that allowed an assessment of long-term follow-up (one year) to measure impact. An oversampling of 20 percent compensated for individuals whose address had changed or who had died. The second survey group was composed of class members identified by grantees and the NIS staff as examples of their program's "successes." The term "success" was not strictly defined, but grantees were encouraged to identify cases that they considered significant because of either financial or nonfinancial benefit, or both. Data collected on this group provided a measure of validity and an estimate of the minimum documented leveraging accomplished by the network.

The second phase began with computer-generated random NIS client record numbers. The records that were drawn represented individuals, not families, and the information requested in the study related only to the person represented by the selected record, even if the family's initial call to the NIS had also involved other family members. A personalized cover letter, a questionnaire customized for each sample member, and a postage-paid return envelope were mailed to each caller. The letter encouraged response to the survey in one of two ways: either call the toll-free NIS number to discuss the questionnaire, or mail the completed questionnaire back in the postage-paid envelope. Regardless of which option was chosen, trained interviewers spoke with each participant to reassure him or her of confidentiality and to gather some of the more sensitive financial data.

The respondents from the random sample were tracked from their contact with the NIS to determine the outcomes of their entry into the service delivery systems. All respondents were called to: (1) verify the resources to which the NIS had referred them and to identify all the programs within and outside the AOCAP network that they accessed; (2) specify the outcomes of the resources to which referrals had been made for the sample member; (3) assess the accrued monetary and nonmonetary outcomes; and (4) determine the individual's status after involvement with the AOCAP network. The service resources that respondents identified as having been helpful were asked to verify services and provide actual or estimated dollar values of the services delivered. Where the sample member had chosen not to follow through with referral resources or had made contact but had no identifiable outcome, the costs of the NIS effort were still assessed for the individual. When there was an outcome, it was assigned to a specific program or programs and reported as part of what was obtained for the client. When actual dollar amounts were available, they were used; when they were not, an estimate was made and verified by the service provider.

Costs included both out-of-pocket expenses paid by the family and costs accrued by the AOCAP-funded programs providing services. For example, if a veteran contacted the NIS and was referred to the University Affiliated Program of the University of Mississippi and to the Access Group, and both of these programs were able to assist the caller, the per-unit costs of all three programs (including the NIS) were used.

Actual or estimated costs of providing services were calculated per unit of service. If an organization helped 200 clients in the study year, the cost estimate was 1/200th of the costs of total program operation for that year. In this way, all noncapital outlay costs were factored into the estimate. Start-up and AOCAP administrative costs were not included. Personnel resources were a principal and costly ingredient of the system. By using total program costs by unit of service, the total personnel costs were included, rather than just the cost of the personnel involved in direct delivery of services.

If an outcome occurred without grantee intervention, it was not counted as a program outcome. Outcomes were either immediate (within a month from the time of initial contact with the AOCAP network of services) or long range (within a year). For example, a child with a disability may have needed an educational assessment to qualify for special education services. The cost of the initial evaluation, paid by the school district, was an immediate outcome, although it may have taken three months to obtain. When the child received the needed services determined by the evaluation, the costs of those services, also borne by the school, were counted as part of the long-range outcomes.

The study measured only the success of AOCAP grantees in leveraging resources to help Vietnam veterans and their families. Thus, AOCAP grantee services were not counted among the outcomes. For example, some grantees provided valuable direct services such as counseling, diagnosis and evaluation, advocacy, service coordination, and information referral, paid for by funding from AOCAP. The costs of these services were not included.

Some funds secured on behalf of class members were ongoing. For example, a class member entitled to Supplemental Security Income (SSI) may have been due a back payment of $15,000 and a monthly allotment of $300 until eighteen years of age and possibly continuing into adulthood. For study purposes, the outcome was the amount initially obtained, if it had been received, plus monthly payments received for that year. Future benefits were not counted because they would be based on speculation. A family's income status could change, for example, and entitlement regulations could be changed to reduce or eliminate future SSI or Medicaid benefits. Such changes are unpredictable and projections based on them are essentially speculative.

Any quantifiable outcomes that could be converted into dollar values were considered to be monetary outcomes. An example of a monetary outcome was money received from an insurance company for a veteran's child. Nonmonetary outcomes involved changes that could not be measured in dollars, such as an increase in family morale, gains in self-determination, or enabling a child to experience the joy of a personal accomplishment. Nonmonetary outcomes were described but were not expressed in any common unit of measure, such as a percentage of satisfaction with services provided. Although these outcomes cannot be included in impact calculations, they are important and were considered in drawing conclusions.

Analysis

A regression-discontinuity (RD) design was used to interpret the data from the random sample. From a methodological point of view, inferences drawn from this design are comparable in internal validity with conclusions from experimental designs (Trochim, 1990). Internal validity refers to whether or not the intervention being examined (entering the AOCAP system) caused a change in the outcome indicators (the benefits obtained). Internal validity is not concerned with the ability to generalize but instead focuses on whether a causal relationship exists.

In experimental or other quasi-experimental designs, researchers try to ensure that the experimental and control groups were equivalent prior to the intervention so that, post-intervention, differences can be attributed to the intervention (Campbell, 1986). The RD design involves no such assumption. Instead, the RD design assumes that the relationship between the variables being measured would be equivalent before and after the intervention. Thus, the strength of the RD design is dependent on the assumption that there is no spurious discontinuity in the relationship that coincided with the time of the intervention (time of entering the AOCAP network).

The investigators want to show that the intervention alone, rather than an influence by a threat to internal validity, caused any measured change. History, in its various forms, is the primary threat to RD internal validity. If the design had used a comparison (control) group for which the same sort of data were available, the threat of history would seem to be dispelled altogether. However, this was not done because, according to Mohr (1992), it would introduce other threats to internal validity. These threats may have been severe enough to make it questionable where there would have been much gained by introducing additional data from another group.

The RD design uses a frequency line graph that shows data and regression lines before and after the intervention. Figure 1 shows two possible outcomes, with each having the same regression lines but representing different results. The dashed line indicates the regression line that would be expected if the intervention had no effect. Figure 1A depicts a negative effect, where the costs exceeded the amount of the benefits obtained. Figure 1B shows a positive effect because the regression line has risen relative to what had been expected if the intervention had generated no effect. The discontinuity in the regression lines at the intervention implies the intervention had an effect. If the discontinuity shows a change in level vertically, it suggests that the intervention had a direct (main) effect; changes in slope show an interaction effect, or both. If discontinuity is clear at the intervention, then analytic results that indicate no intervention effect should not be accepted as plausible.

Figure 1. Two Hypothetical RD Designs

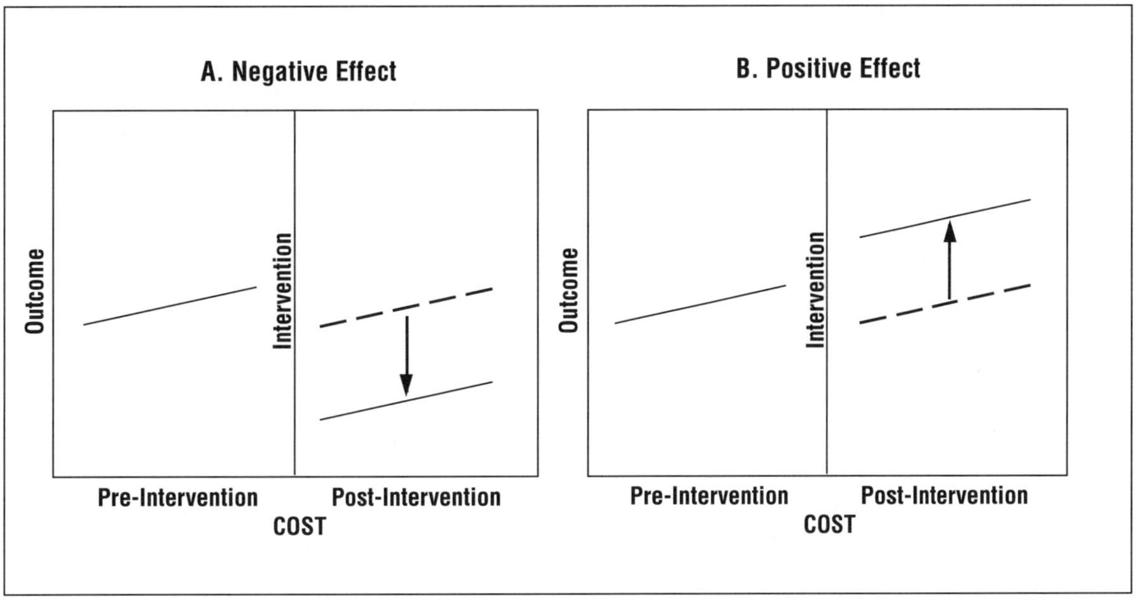

The impact is indicated by the difference between the observed result and the counterfactual. The counterfactual is a projection of the data into the time period occurring after the intervention point. If, for example, the line were straight and upwardly sloping, the counterfactual would simply be a copy of the pre-intervention line repeated after the intervention point, as shown by the dashed line in Figure 1.

Mohr (1992) states that significance tests may be quite a minor matter; in the econometric-modeling function of significance testing, the model must be specified without the omission of important external events or other forms of history. This means that a significance test on the intervention coefficient may be pointless by itself. Mohr explains that statistical significance does not tell whether the intervention caused a subsequent change and that it should be of relatively small concern. He emphasizes the confidence, which comes from examining the relationship graphically and from statistics, that whatever change did occur was attributable to the intervention and not to something else. Trochim (1990) suggests that the significance of the difference between the observed result of the intervention and the counterfactual be calculated using a standard t-test with the standard error of the coefficient. The t-test was used for measuring the significance of the difference between means where the variances are unequal, as described by Cochran and Cox (1957). However, a t-test is not a very robust measure, and its use may result in a Type I error, that is, in declaring that a change took place when it had not. Consequently, an analysis of variance was also conducted.

Results

Group One

Data were collected from fifty-two persons in the random sample who responded to the survey. This group consisted of parents of forty-four children of Vietnam veterans, seven veterans, and one veteran's spouse. For these individuals, the NIS had made a total of 152 referrals, based on the clients' service needs at the time they initially called. From the 152 referrals, thirty-six sample members had contacted seventy-four resources. Nine indicated that none of the referral resources they contacted could help them, and seven did not contact any resources.

NIS staff had made referrals for a wide variety of services, including support (including advocacy and respite), financial assistance, medical diagnosis and evaluation, education, and counseling. Of the total respondent group, a little more than half (n=27) indicated that they currently had service needs in addition to those identified in their initial call to the NIS. Families contacted referral organizations most frequently when the referral was for financial assistance, and they were more likely to follow through if a local AOCAP grantee was involved as a resource. Slightly more than half (53.5 percent) of the referral resources contacted were connected to entitlement programs. Each member of the sample was assessed the per-unit costs of all AOCAP grantees that helped that sample member. For example, when study participants contacted a grantee but did not pursue any resources, the per-unit costs of the grantee and the NIS were still assessed to them. Consequently, the minimum cost of any sample member was the per-unit cost of the NIS.

Thirty-three of the fifty-two study participants (63.5 percent) had a positive result, meaning their outcomes exceeded their related costs. The range of leveraged outcomes was from $395 to $109,580. The arithmetic mean, or average, was $13,787.

Nineteen study participants had a negative outcome, meaning the costs exceeded the outcomes. They included the nine sample members whom none of the referral resources could help and another seven who did not contact any of the resources. The remaining three had pursued the resources and received help, but the costs still exceeded the outcomes received.

Table 1 shows the callers' responses to the question of whether, in their opinion, the sample member's life had gotten "better," "worse," or "remained the same" after making contact with the AOCAP network: the majority of the respondents indicated that life had "remained the same," 31 percent indicated that life had gotten "better," and 29 percent indicated "worse." All of the participants who either found no help from the referral resources or did not contact any resource reported that life had gotten worse.

Table 1. Responses to the Survey Question: "How has <name>'s life changed in the past year?" (n=52)

Status	Child (n=44)	Veteran (n=7)	Significant Other (n=1)	Total (n=52)
No change	18 41%	2 29%	0 0	20 38%
Better	12 27%	3 43%	1 100%	16 31%
Worse	14 32%	1 14%	0 0	15 29%
No response	0 0	1 14%	0 0	1 2%

Thirty-four of the children in the study were between the ages of five and twenty-one, making them eligible in most states to receive educational services. Twenty-two respondents indicated that school services had changed in a positive manner for them since entering the network. The value of each school service, such as special education, homebound instruction, physical therapy, and speech and language therapy, was calculated from the frequency of the service multiplied by the estimated cost per hour of each service. When a child was in a regular class and was moved to a special education class, the cost difference between the two programs was used as the estimate of the school's cost and resulting benefit to the family. When schools did not provide an actual or estimated cost, the average of all the other schools' costs for providing the same service was used.

Figure 2 illustrates the number of persons receiving benefits and the amount of those benefits from each source. All resources, except education and Medicaid, are consumer self-reported as the amount of money received by the consumer. The dollar value of education services was estimated, as described earlier, and the Medicaid amount was the amount reported to the consumer by the state agency.

Figure 2. Sources of Leveraged Support for Class Members (n=52)

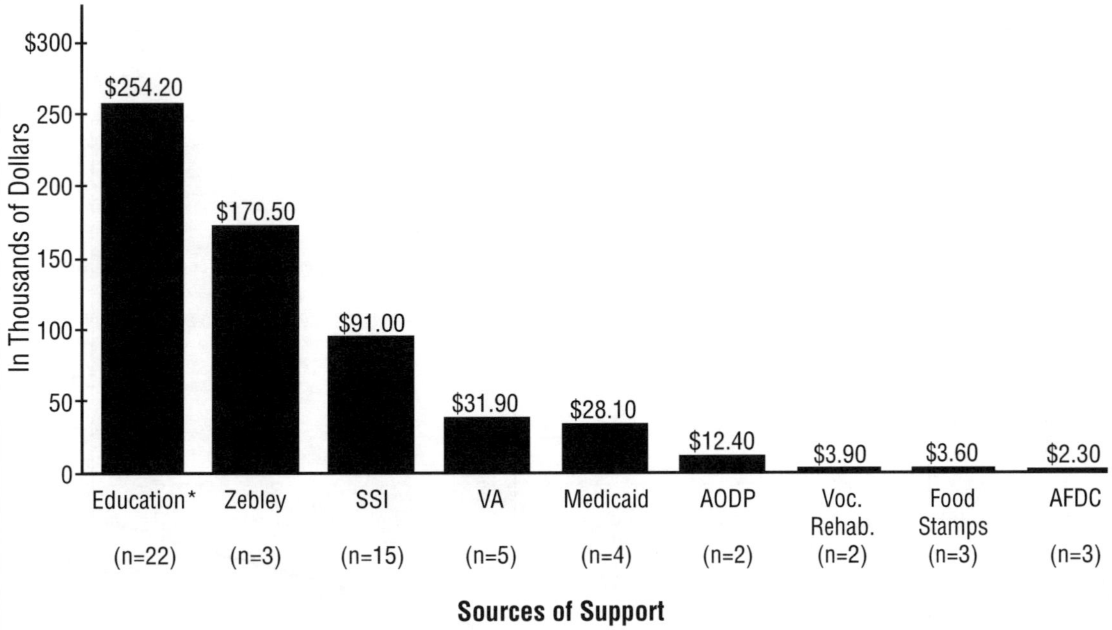

* Costs of services are estimated.

There were three children who were awarded *Zebley** back payments from SSI in the amounts of $3,500, $80,000, and $87,000. Two study participants needed assistive technology: one received a communication device ($395) obtained by a grantee, and the other, a motorized chair ($2,095) acquired through a community resource identified by a grantee.

**Sullivan* v. *Zebley*, 493 U.S. 521 (1990) was a class action lawsuit brought on behalf of all children denied SSI because the Social Security Administration found them "not disabled." In 1990, the U.S. Supreme Court decided that if children had been improperly denied benefits and were found disabled under the new rules, they could receive retroactive payments for all years since 1980. Claimants—often referred to as "Zebley children"—are eligible for Medicaid coverage in thirty-one states and in the District of Columbia.

Figure 3 shows the regression lines of pre- and post-intervention costs and benefits. The criterion line is the point at which members of the sample entered the AOCAP network by calling the NIS. A correlation between costs and benefits, calculated before entry into the network, was +.098; calculated after entry, the correlation was +.309. These correlations can be interpreted as showing a slight positive relationship between costs expended and benefits received before the intervention and a stronger positive relationship after the intervention.

In describing the intervention effect, the slope and position of the regression line are critical. To determine the change in the regression, it is necessary first to model both the time and possible sources of threats to internal validity; then, to characterize the change, the slopes and intercepts are described. The regression analysis produced a pre-intervention slope of 0.246 and a *y* intercept of 1,563. The post-intervention slope was 1.89 with a *y* intercept of 10,857.

The discontinuity in the regression lines in Figure 3 implies that the AOCAP program had a positive effect. The fact that the change was vertical suggests a main effect; the change in slope shows an interaction effect. The magnitude of the effect can be obtained from an impact ratio, which is the ratio of the costs incurred to the monetary outcomes associated with network efforts.

Figure 3. Regression Lines Pre- and Post-Intervention

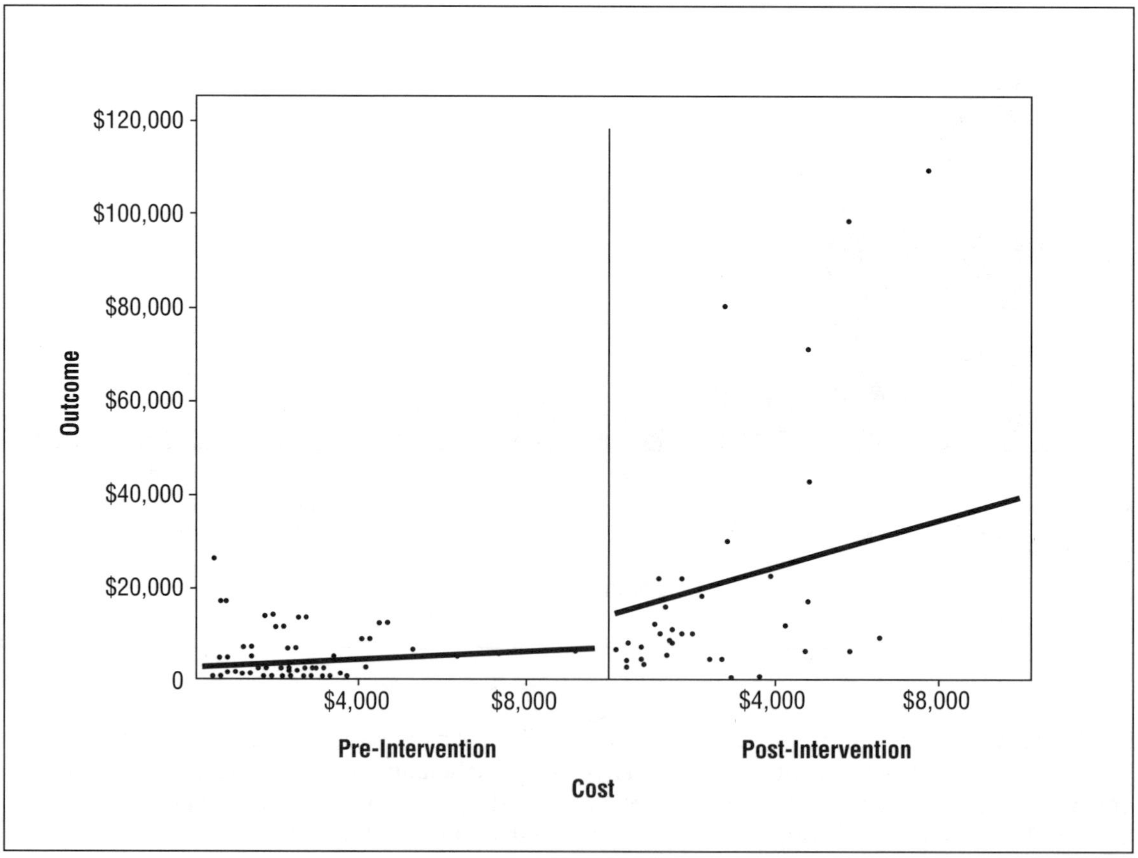

The impact ratio was calculated by subtracting the total pre-intervention costs ($54,765) from the post-intervention costs ($75,605), then dividing the difference by the result obtained by subtracting the pre-intervention outcomes ($93,440) from the post-intervention outcomes ($668,234). The impact ratio (20,839/574,794) was .036. A ratio of 1.00 means that cost and impact are equal; a ratio greater than 1.00 signals that the costs outweighed the impact. A ratio of less than 1.00 suggests that the impact is greater than the monetary costs accrued. By taking the net outcomes and dividing them by the net costs, a benefit-cost ratio showed that for every AOCAP dollar spent on services and equipment for this study group, there was a $27.58 return in outcomes, leveraged through either financial assistance or services received.

Individuals with zero pre- and post-intervention scores were dropped from the calculation of the standard t-test, resulting in a sample size of thirty-six. The difference between the post-intervention and the counterfactual produced a value of 3.698. The obtained difference was statistically significant; that is, there is little likelihood—less than 1 percent probability—that a difference could have resulted from a chance variation between the counterfactual and post-intervention (2.457 tabled t-value for a one-tailed test, from Table III in Fisher and Yates, 1963). An analysis of variance was also conducted; it produced an F-ratio that was statistically significant at the same level of confidence.

Group Two

To test the validity of the study findings and capture a minimum measure of network accomplishments, data were collected from a sampling of AOCAP grantees regarding their successful outcomes. Responses from twenty-three grantees provided monetary and nonmonetary data on seventy-eight class members they had served. Grantees reported a diversity of resources tapped to obtain the needed services or assistance and described the nonmonetary impact of the network. The amount of leveraged money per client ranged from a low of $121 for food to $122,000 from the U.S. Department of Veterans Affairs (VA). Table 2 identifies the amounts obtained from various sources of financial assistance by seventeen grantees for fifty-one clients. The data in this table are from twelve veterans' organizations, two disability service agencies, two family service agencies, and one national support project. Six grantees provided descriptions of successful outcomes that were examples of nonmonetary benefits.

Table 2. Sources of Financial Support Identified by Grantees

Source	Number of Grantees (n=17)	Number of Class Members (n=51)	Amount ($)
VA	5	18	460,818
SSI/SSDI	8	23	277,636
SSI Zebley	5	6	94,800
Workers' compensation	2	2	79,600
Parent support organization	2	12	34,752
Education	1	1	30,000
Tuition waiver	1	1	20,000
Miscellaneous	4	4	18,412
Medicaid	3	3	11,970
Corporate giving	2	2	11,700
Other grantee	2	2	2,700
Sunshine Foundation	1	1	1,300
Community fundraising	1	1	1,000
Total	37*	76*	1,044,688

* Totals do not equal the number of grantees or class members due to multiple resources accessed for individuals.

Discussion and Conclusions

Cost-benefit, cost-effectiveness, and impact studies are not synonymous. The first two compare costs of alternatives, usually to assist in making administrative decisions. An impact analysis determines the relationship between the costs of an initiative and its effect. It is a systematic approach to evaluating the relative outcomes of a project, and it examines the costs, benefits, and uncertainties to determine if the initiative was a beneficial means of meeting its objective. In this study, alternatives were not assessed because they involved systems that historically have not been fully functional in meeting the needs of Vietnam veterans' families, especially those having children with disabilities.

Because impact analyses, like cost-effectiveness or cost-benefit studies, are estimates, the conclusions drawn from them are subject to the level of accuracy of the data used. This study measured the degree to which the network had leveraged resources to help Vietnam veterans and their families. Self-reporting by families is subject to some degree of inaccuracy, such as underreporting Medicaid benefits. Because Medicaid is not a monthly amount received by the veteran's family, and it is paid directly to the service provider, the family may not know the exact dollar amount involved.

Despite efforts to reduce bias and provide accurate data in conducting this study, some significant limitations attend the design of this study. First, the design does not allow an evaluation of the impact of the whole system as a package of services. It quantifies the costs of and benefits obtained only by those programs and services that randomly selected clients had used. Secondly, it is restricted to a sample of individuals whose search for help had started with the NIS. It fails to capture those who went directly to a local grantee.

When expressed mathematically in the context of the RD design, various outcomes are examples of what are called transfer functions. The label is neutral in that it refers only to the empirical change in the regression after the intervention. The cause of the change, whether it be intervention or history or both, is an issue that must be considered once the transfer function has been adequately characterized.

The use of this type of RD design requires an exploration of any transfer function, particularly related to the internal validity factor of history. Transfer function would be strongly influenced by geographical location and timing. The fifty-two respondents came from twenty-two states, with the largest number (n=4) from North Carolina. The times of the initial calls by the respondents to the NIS spanned a seven-month period. Any external influence that would threaten internal validity must have been national and of a duration long enough to affect the time span. No such influence was known. It is more likely that the changes that occurred are attributable to the intervention than to some threat to internal validity because the interventions occurred independently and were temporally unrelated to each other.

Collecting data from this population was difficult because most of the questions on the survey and in the interviews related to money, either received by the clients or spent on their behalf. The study on barriers by Smith, Mayfield-Smith, and Sudduth (1994a) shows that one of the greatest reasons for apprehension of Vietnam veterans in disclosing financial information to individuals with an organization is fear of loss of entitlements.

A threat to external validity may have been introduced by the volunteerism that resulted in 34.7 percent of the random sample participating in this study. This small response limits the ability to make an inference of the findings from the sample to the population from which it was drawn. This raises the question of how these results would have changed if there had been a 100 percent response. Four scenarios are possible:

1. If the nonparticipant portion of the sample had costs that were the same as the participants and had received the same level of benefits, then the yield would have been the same—$27.58 for every AOCAP dollar spent;
2. If the nonparticipant portion of the sample had either lower costs or higher benefits, the yield would have exceeded the $27.58;

3. If the nonparticipant portion of the sample had either higher costs or lower benefits, the yield would have been below the $27.58; and

4. If the nonparticipant portion of the sample had costs that were the same as the participants and had zero benefits, the yield for every AOCAP dollar spent would be $7.59.

The inference that can be drawn from these possibilities is that the exact amount is not known and the best estimate of the amount of the benefits is between $7.59 and $27.58 for every dollar of AOCAP funds spent. Because this range of benefits is so great, the lower amount becomes the more reliable figure to use inferentially. The investigators tried to determine how close the actual yield was to $27.58. Ten nonrespondents were telephoned to determine why they chose not to participate and to see how their costs and benefits differed from the data collected from other members of the random sample. The ten interviews were all with male veteran callers and were conducted by a male veteran interviewer. Explanations for nonparticipation covered a range of reasons, two of which seemed most relevant to this study: (1) because their service needs had been met, they wanted to be left alone and desired no further involvement with any organization; and (2) they believed that the amount of money a family gets and how they spend it are private matters. Based on interviews with these ten nonrespondents, it appeared that the benefits received by the nonrespondents were greater than zero, and their involvement with the network, indicating costs to the network, was similar to that of the respondents. Some of the nonrespondents were satisfied with the help they received; and while most of them had new or additional needs, they felt they could manage on their own. From these ten follow-up interviews, it appeared that nonrespondents probably introduced bias that underestimated, not overestimated, the acquisition of benefits, and that $27.58 is a realistic, and probably conservative, result.

The question of why veterans' families need financial support is relevant to placing the need for leveraging activities by grantees in perspective. Financial assistance has primarily helped veterans' families meet their past and current indebtedness, consisting largely of health care costs. Like many parents of children with chronic illnesses, most veterans calling the NIS do not have insurance coverage for their children's medical, ancillary therapeutic, or hospital care. If they have insurance, they usually lack coverage for needed comprehensive and long-term care services. The Supreme Court ruling in *Sullivan* v. *Zebley* has led to expanded childhood eligibility for SSI and its often-associated Medicaid coverage. Veterans' children with disabilities who enter the AOCAP network have found that grantees can help them advocate to gain access to entitlements from SSI. Even for the veterans' children insured through traditional, employer-based family health insurance programs, many of the needed services have been unavailable or previously not covered. For many families who may be covered, the deductible and copayment provisions present a major hardship. Insurance contracts often exclude chronic conditions as preexisting conditions, and specialized long-term care may not be included in the coverage (Perrin and Stein, 1990).

Because persons with disabilities generally have their conditions, or effects of the conditions, throughout their lives, their need for services continues; as they get older, their service needs change. This dynamic state places a considerable responsibility on family members to assume an important and active role in obtaining services. Faced with what appears to be a complex web of agencies and professionals with vastly differing roles and missions, veterans' families were frequently unable to navigate the generic service system successfully on their own. Even sophisticated family members and experienced professionals have difficulty determining which agency has the responsibility or expertise to respond to a particular family need. In this study, an AOCAP grantee that was a central service coordinator made a critical difference in helping the veterans' families to obtain the services needed. This critical component of the services within the AOCAP network made the necessary linkages with community-based services and centralized specialty services and improved the delivery of comprehensive care to children with chronic illnesses and disabilities.

Children's health depends on a complex array of factors, with medical care being one element of the matrix. Family, home, and community environments play major roles in determining children's health. Adequate nutrition, safe surroundings, and healthy lifestyles may be as important to children's health as timely access to appropriate medical care. Even during childhood, health status may depend more on parental and community factors than on health care. Parents' responsibilities include encouraging healthy lifestyles, ensuring a safe home, and seeking necessary medical services. Parental behavior has an important impact not only on the physical health and development of children, but—for parents with post-traumatic stress disorder (PTSD), for example—on their mental and emotional health as well.

According to Smith, Mayfield-Smith, and Sudduth in a paper on the lingering consequences of the Vietnam War (1994b), the health status of the members of Vietnam veterans' families who used the NIS appears to be below an acceptable standard. These families' identified problems included a pattern of disability and chronic illness as well as social problems and poverty that seem unparalleled in comparison with other families, including those of other-era veterans. The incidence of many serious conditions among this population, particularly in children, appeared to be well above those who used other information and referral services similar to the NIS. In addition, the veterans' own disabling conditions have placed strains on family structures. The veteran's family faces additional disadvantages in the form of isolation, economic deprivation, and the lack of access to adequate services, such as transportation.

According to Hobbs (1985) and Cadman, Boyle, and Szatmari (1987), between 10 percent and 30 percent of all children in this country have some chronic health impairment, the most frequent being asthma and less severe forms of congenital heart disease. Other conditions are rare, which is contrary to what has been observed in veterans' families by Mekdeci (1993). Immune deficiencies and secondary PTSD create challenges for veterans' families similar to those from other chronic illnesses, with an important distinction: because other members of veterans' families are likely to have these or other disabling conditions, they may be unable to care for their children with disabilities or chronic illness.

When a veteran's family member needed help, lived where a local grantee was available, and was helped by that grantee, the family was more likely to follow through and contact recommended service providers than was a veteran family not linked to a local grantee. Many grantees seemed to increase follow-through by aggressive service coordination. When a grantee, after receiving casenotes from the NIS about a family, initiated contact with the veteran's family, there was a high likelihood of follow-through by the family. If, however, the grantee waited for the family to call and the family did not call, the family's effort to obtain services from the AOCAP network collapsed.

This study showed a spectrum of possible outcomes from entering the AOCAP network of services. At one end was a negative monetary benefit, when the veteran spent or lost wages to reach services only to learn that he or she was ineligible or unable to receive them. When the family member did not pursue possible solutions, the related costs of the AOCAP may have exceeded the benefits to the individual or family. At the other end of the spectrum was the leveraging of one-time and ongoing support and services. For example, for a veteran's child with a hearing deficit, a local grantee may have procured needed diagnostic services and assistive equipment. In this scenario, the outcome would be a one-time monetary benefit for an evaluation, assistive devices, and transportation costs to get the services. Ongoing monetary benefits might include speech and language therapy, remedial education, and possibly Medicaid or other financial support for which the veteran or child might be eligible. However, only the dollar amounts of received services or equipment were included in the analysis of this study.

Two study results seem contradictory to the AOCAP's overall successful record of networking to secure benefits for veterans' families. Slightly more than half of the study participants indicated that they currently had service needs in addition to what they had when they made the initial call to the NIS. Also, a relatively high percentage of study participants reported that their life had remained the same or gotten worse in the past year. Yet, both of these findings were not completely unexpected. To some extent, these observations indicate the ongoing and dynamic service needs and effects of chronicity that characterize the progressive and incurable nature of many disabilities, particularly developmental disabilities.

The existing system of non-AOCAP services, including veteran, child, and disability-related services, offers no guarantees that the requirements of each veteran's child with special health needs will be met appropriately. It is a fragmented system of care, one that predictably allows children to fall through the cracks created by the restrictive eligibility criteria of the very system intended to help them. The AOCAP approach appears to be a viable alternative, demonstrating that service networks can effectively make the necessary linkages between the community-based services and the centralized, specialty services needed to provide comprehensive care to veterans and their children with chronic illnesses and disabilities.

When veterans entered the AOCAP network, they faced a wide range of possible outcomes for their families. In this sample, some class members (17.3 percent) had problems that remained unresolved, and others (13.0 percent) chose not to pursue referrals that might have offered solutions. For some class members, in short, the AOCAP system did not work. For those whose service needs matched the available service options, however, the system did work; it worked more effectively when a local grantee was available to advocate for and support the family.

Referrals to service resources had been made to meet the class members' total service needs, not just financial support. No grantee had as its only mission the task of leveraging financial support. As effective providers of services such as counseling, diagnosis and evaluation, advocacy, information and referral, and service coordination, helping the family to obtain entitlements and services from other providers was a part of the grantee's function. The fact that grantees had considerable success in leveraging may be for a variety of reasons. It may have been due to their unique skills in advocating and interpreting how various agencies and processes work and their knowledge of how to best navigate through various bureaucracies to access resources and services to which family members are entitled. It may also be an indicator of the underserved nature of this population, inferred by the apparent failure of the traditional system to champion the issues to obtain entitlements for veterans or their family members.

Grantees' responses to the request for examples of program "success" describe a wide range of nonmonetary, qualitative impacts. The purpose of this request was to examine the potential of the system for bridging the service delivery systems in support of Vietnam veterans' families. As many of these outcomes would be extremely difficult to quantify, especially in terms of the value to the families, this study did not attempt to assign a value to them. They must be included, even descriptively, in the examination of the leveraging capacity and impact of this service system.

Grantees reported how they teamed up with families who were not self-advocating and helped them establish or reestablish this attribute. The partnership between grantee and family helped to replace frustration and anger with constructive planning and action and helped the family focus its energies on solving problems, instead of fighting them. The one quality that all grantees seemed to impart was the support that enabled the family to know that its situation, however daunting, was not the family's fault. Through this support, families were able to shelve the blame and start to build skills and plans for the future. It is impossible to assign a dollar value to the relief expressed by the wife of a veteran who, after an hour of talking, says, "You're the first person in twenty-five years who would just listen to our story."

Many veterans' families have experienced financial and emotional depression. If they had had to pay out-of-pocket for needed services, or dig deeper for the energy to pursue help, some would have done without the needed help instead. This study has shown that the network of grantees has succeeded, at least in part, in bridging veterans' and children's needs and services, making it possible for many veterans' families to obtain the services they have needed for so long. Through the dedication, creativity, and ingenuity of many grantees, the network accomplished a cost-effective leveraging of resources to help Vietnam veterans and their families.

Recommendations

This impact analysis was limited to an estimate of the ability of the AOCAP network to leverage resources to help Vietnam veterans and their families. Other factors should be examined to measure the total impact of the network. These factors need to be identified and appraised systematically.

One such factor is value of grantee-provided services. For example, one grantee indicated that it had provided detailed intervention in developing approximately sixty individualized education programs (IEPs). This intervention represented personnel costs estimated at $84,000. The value of such services was not included in this study; however, it represented significant benefit to the families affected. Grantees provided a variety of other services with measurable market values, such as service coordination, information and referral, counseling, support, diagnosis and evaluation, and assistive technology.

Another factor that deserves investigation is the effectiveness and accomplishments of the network in accessing existing systems. The study touched on the contribution of educational services, but the AOCAP network was able to effectively link families with many other public and private agencies. Some of these included local representative programs of agencies such as the Department of Veterans Affairs, Department of Labor, Administration on Developmental Disabilities, National Institute on Child Health and Development, Bureau of Maternal and Child Health, Administration for Children, Youth and Families, American Legion, Easter Seal Society, and United Cerebral Palsy Associations. Questions remain as to how these services have helped class members and to what extent the AOCAP's systems-change strategies have improved access to these services and affected methods of service delivery (family-centered care, for example).

Finally, it would be useful to measure the effectiveness of the AOCAP consumer-shaped and consumer-directed service system on increasing the self-help capacity of Vietnam veterans' families. To what degree have the grantees succeeded in enabling Vietnam veterans' families to achieve their maximum potential through increased independence, self-sufficiency, and productivity?

In most cases, the grantees were employing a true "family systems approach" in the provision of services to Vietnam veterans and their families. The use of this service protocol is certainly new, and perhaps even radical, in its application to this population. For many veterans, the family unit has been the foundation of their strength, and the AOCAP service system built on it and empowered them.

References

Cadman, D., M. Boyle, and P. Szatmari. 1987. Chronic illness, disability, and mental and social well-being. *Pediatrics* 79:805-813.

Campbell, D.T. 1986. Relabeling internal and external validity for applied social scientists. In *Advances in Quasi-experimental Designs and Analysis*. Special issue of *New Directions for Program Evaluation*, ed. W.M.K. Trochim, 31:67-77.

Cochran, W.G., and G.M. Cox. 1957. *Experimental Designs*. 2d ed. New York: John Wiley and Sons.

Fisher, R.A., and F. Yates. 1963. *Statistical Tables for Biological, Agricultural, and Medical Research*. 6th ed. New York: Hafner.

Hobbs, N., J.M. Perrin, and H.T. Ireys. 1985. *Chronically Ill Children and Their Families*. San Francisco: Jossey-Bass.

Mekdeci, B. 1993. Testimony to the House Veterans Affairs Committee on Aug. 4, 1993. Orlando, FL: Association for Birth Defect Children.

Mohr, L.B. 1992. *Impact Analysis for Program Evaluation.* Newbury Park, CA: Sage Publications.

Perrin, J.M., B. Guyer, and J.M. Lawrence. 1992. Health care services for children and adolescents. *The Future of Children* 2:58-77.

Perrin, J.M., and R.E.K. Stein. 1991. Reinterpreting disability: Changes in SSI for children. *Pediatrics* 88:1047-1051.

Smith, B.C., K.L. Mayfield-Smith, and D. Sudduth. 1994a. Barriers to service for many Vietnam veteran families. Unpublished paper prepared for the AOCAP Symposium.

Smith, B.C., K.L. Mayfield-Smith, and D. Sudduth. 1994b. Lingering consequences of the Vietnam War: Veterans' families with children with disabilities or chronic illness. Unpublished paper prepared for the AOCAP Symposium.

Trochim, W.M.K. 1990. The regression-discontinuity design. In *Research Methodology: Strengthening Causal Interpretations of Nonexperimental Data,* ed. L. Sechrest, E. Perrin, and J. Bunker. AHCPR Conference Proceedings. U.S. Department of Health and Human Services.

A Report from the Front

Dawn Sudduth, M.Ed.
Center for Developmental Disabilities
Department of Pediatrics
School of Medicine
The University of South Carolina
Columbia, SC

Abstract

The Agent Orange Class Assistance Program (AOCAP) created a network of diverse local social service organizations to provide family-centered programs to reach Vietnam veterans' families. This paper looks at the issues surrounding the delivery of services to veterans' families from the perspectives of fourteen professionals who have delivered a variety of social, therapeutic, advocacy, and educational services to Vietnam veterans and their families living within diverse geographical and cultural settings.

The perspectives of the service providers are presented as responses to twelve questions that relate to the social and health characteristics of the target population, the role of the veteran in the family dynamic, types of services these families need most frequently, the challenges that the service delivery system confronts in offering assistance, the impact of a family-centered approach, and the relative success of the AOCAP effort. Offered in a conversational style, the comments indicate support for the direction in which the AOCAP project was launched.

The author concludes that AOCAP has had a positive impact on local and state service providers and that traditional service delivery methods have had limited effectiveness for families of Vietnam veterans.

Dawn Sudduth, M.Ed., *is the assistant project director of the National Information System of Vietnam Veterans and Their Families, a project that is located at the University of South Carolina School of Medicine, Department of Pediatrics, and is part of the Center for Developmental Disabilities.*

The Agent Orange Class Assistance Program (AOCAP) was created as a result of the settlement of class action litigation brought by a group of approximately 248,000 Vietnam veterans or family members against the chemical companies that manufactured the herbicide commonly referred to as Agent Orange. Used as a defoliant during the Vietnam War, many believe that Agent Orange has left a tragic legacy of health problems for both the veterans exposed to the chemical and children born to the veterans after their return from the war. Although the largest portion of the settlement was designated to provide financial compensation to the most severely disabled veterans or their survivors, settlement money was also earmarked for AOCAP.

The money designated for AOCAP initially amounted to about $42 million, or 17.5 percent of the total settlement fund. The decision to create AOCAP was based on the belief that funds used to augment, and in many cases create, services for veterans' families would generate benefits that would exceed and outlast what could have been accomplished through the direct distribution of funds among such a large number of class members. AOCAP has funded approximately one hundred programs, over five-years, through a competitive grant process. Most awards went to local service organizations, including child- and family-focused programs at universities, traditional veteran service organizations, and community service providers.

In essence, AOCAP created an unusual marriage—a union of diverse organizations with little in common except the expertise and commitment to provide comprehensive services to veteran families. The linking of diverse programs into an effective network was as innovative as it was ambitious. The work accomplished through AOCAP is the first national-level initiative that has attempted to coordinate the full range of services needed by Vietnam veterans' families.

The staffs of individual programs had much to learn before they could implement coordinated services. Organizations whose prior focus was veterans' issues had to develop new areas of expertise concerning services and benefits for children with disabilities and special-health needs, while child-focused organizations needed to learn about existing services for veterans. This blurring of boundaries within the network soon came to symbolize the important changes needed within the human service delivery system overall.

This report offers a snapshot of how the front line viewed this endeavor. It was built on comments from fourteen individuals in the AOCAP network whose work placed them in direct contact with veterans' families. These individuals represent the diversity of organizations and backgrounds and the geographic scope of the network. Because of their roles as service coordinator, therapist, advocate, and sometimes a combination of these, those who contributed to this report saw both how the endeavor was accomplished—close up—and the impacts their respective AOCAP programs had on individual families. Their contributions to this report are in the form of responses to twelve fundamental questions about the delivery of services to Vietnam veterans' families. All of the contributors submitted their reactions without knowing how their colleagues at other programs had responded. Although their comments may sometimes seem repetitive, the fact that they arrived at similar conclusions independently is significant. Despite differences in their locales and backgrounds, they have identified problems that cross geographical and organizational boundaries.

Owing to the diversity of the population being served, the comments of those who contributed to this report do not necessarily describe all Vietnam veterans' families. It is also important to take this report on its own merits, recognizing its limitations. The information contributed by the individuals who have been working with veterans' families was not intended to be taken as the product of a research activity with its inherent controls and ability to infer. Rather, this report is intended to provide a means for looking at how the AOCAP mission unfolded at the family level, as reported subjectively by some of those who were closest to the various programs. Just as someone looks through a lens and chooses the image to capture with a camera, there are surely as many different views of what AOCAP has been able to accomplish as there are individuals involved. Despite its subjectivity, this report is a valuable, current look at commonly occurring scenarios among the Vietnam veterans' families who are turning to the various service delivery organizations to find resources needed to meet a full range of human service needs.

The fourteen individuals who contributed material to this report, including their affiliation within the AOCAP network, were:

- **Patrick Cork**—the AOCAP program director at the Family Service Association of Green Bay, Wisconsin—has fourteen years experience in clinical social work practice. He holds a master's degree in social work from the University of Milwaukee.
- **Ron DeChant**—family case manager at the Missouri Veterans Leadership Project in St. Louis, Missouri—has an extensive background in VA and Social Security claims representation. He earned a degree in organizational development and is a Vietnam-era veteran.
- **Bill Elmore**—executive director at the Missouri Veterans Leadership Project in St. Louis, Missouri—has an accomplished record of promoting veterans' issues at both the state and federal levels. He is a Vietnam veteran.
- **Larry Helm**—program manager at the Missouri Veterans Leadership Project in St. Louis, Missouri—is a former administrative chair of the National Veterans Task Force on Agent Orange and a Marine Corps Vietnam veteran.
- **Bill Greaver**—program coordinator of the AOCAP program at Universal Family Connection Inc., Chicago, Illinois—is currently pursuing a master's of divinity degree from the Lutheran School of Theology.
- **Marcia Cloutier**—employment and veterans counselor of the AOCAP program at Universal Family Connection Inc., Chicago, Illinois—is an employment/veterans counselor with an M.A. in counseling and development from Roosevelt University.
- **Peter LaCount**—project coordinator in the Department for Individual and Family Resources of the Kennedy-Krieger Institute in Baltimore, Maryland—has a background in special education and is pursuing a second master's degree in the health sciences program at Johns Hopkins University.
- **Suzanne Lindgren**—former case manager specialist with the AOCAP-funded program of the American Red Cross in Albuquerque, New Mexico—has a background in child and adolescent issues and is currently completing a doctorate in counseling psychology.
- **Mike McKelroy**—project coordinator for the AOCAP component of the Team of Advocates for Special Kids (TASK) in Anaheim, California—is a retired Marine who served three tours of duty in Vietnam and has three children with learning disabilities.
- **Anita McKelroy**—administrative assistant for the AOCAP component of TASK—is the mother of three children with learning disabilities.
- **Pat Power**—advocate for the AOCAP component of TASK—is the mother of a child with disabilities.
- **Kathy Norris**—project director of an AOCAP program that is administered jointly by the Arkansas University Affiliated Program in Little Rock and the Vietnam Veteran Leadership Project in Pine Bluff, Arkansas—was an early-intervention case management coordinator and a nursing instructor at the University of Arkansas.
- **Steve Pederson**—state coordinator of the American Legion's Vietnam Veteran Family Assistance Program in Sioux Falls, South Dakota, and coordinator for their AOCAP program—has a background in VA medical administration. He is a Marine Corps Vietnam veteran.
- **Kris Retlin**—program coordinator of Vietnam Veterans' Children's Services at the Occupational Center in Orange, New Jersey—has a background in education. She has a sibling and two children with disabilities.

Question One: Are there common characteristics of Vietnam veterans' families and if so, what are they?

- **Ron:** An overriding common characteristic is that before we can "help" any veteran or veteran's family, a level of trust must be established between us and the veteran. The general political character of our generation is one of mistrust in governmental affairs. How can these veterans' families be expected to trust institutions after their government led troops into battle with no armor? When the veterans did come home, their own society often rejected them for what they'd done with labels like "babykiller" or "loser."

- **Patrick:** In our program, we've frequently found that families of Vietnam veterans are "enmeshed"—the relationships between family members are overly dependent and close, and it is difficult for members to act independently of each other. Family interactions are often conflictual and communication skills are poor. Anger is a difficult emotion for these families, and it's usually expressed inappropriately through violence or demeaning verbal exchanges.

  The marital relationship in the Vietnam veteran's family is often hostile and dependent. Although the nonveteran spouse may have a great deal of authority in managing family affairs, the power imbalance is often resented by the veteran, who may be reluctant to assume any responsibility for family affairs. Communication with and the care of children is often handled by the nonveteran spouse, which adds to the emotional distance between the veteran and his or her children. It is common for the veteran to resent the attachment between the children and the nonveteran spouse, who in turn tends to become overly involved with the children, which furthers the enmeshment.

- **Peter:** In my opinion, there are both common characteristics among families of Vietnam veterans and similarities with other populations. In my experience, many of the families of Vietnam veterans seem very cautious of having outsiders involved with their families. They often have a history of being denied help or believe that their vocational, medical, and mental health needs have not been met previously. As a result, they are less trusting of individuals offering help now. It takes some time and effort to develop a level of trust, and consequently, a working relationship with families of Vietnam veterans. In my work with them, I've seen two opposite dynamics—families that are either enmeshed or disconnected.

  As I touched on earlier, the enmeshed families, in particular, seem to view most outsiders as a threat. They tend to distrust outsiders, particularly those who appear to them to want to take control away from the family. Typically, the family unit stays together despite intra-family conflicts and tends to change residences frequently. In contrast, the disconnected families seem to react passively, if at all, to stressful situations. The turmoil they feel remains inside of them and appears to have no escape.

  Overall, the families of Vietnam veterans that I have worked with appear to have many mental health needs. For married parents, discord is commonplace. The veterans often appear to be dealing with "ghosts" from the past that may involve unresolved issues from Vietnam, issues with family members, interpersonal problems at home, school, or in the workplace. Many of the veterans, I suspect, have undiagnosed cases of post-traumatic stress disorder (PTSD). In addition, the children of Vietnam veterans are frequently coping with cases of secondary PTSD.

- **Steve:** A common characteristic I have noticed is the unwillingness to seek assistance from state or federal government-affiliated facilities. The families tend to be more isolated in their lifestyles and thinking, which ultimately affects their ability to access the resources that could address their problems. Lack of knowledge about available services or a reluctance to participate in society is a detriment to the family as a whole, particularly when the parents are faced with the challenges of raising a child with disabilities. It appears the veteran would much rather go it alone than ask for help.

- **Anita:** A distinguishing characteristic of veterans' families is time that they lost together because of the veteran's tour of duty in Vietnam, and subsequent tours. What we have seen as a common link is the government's denial of connection between the veteran's exposure to Agent Orange and the presence of disabilities in the children. Living with the questions and the lack of accountability has been a common experience among many of the families.
- **Kris:** The Vietnam veterans' families who contact our agency are generally stressed out and looking for funds. Many believe the government is responsible for their circumstances. After we have listened to them with interest and empathy—for even ten minutes—it's hard to distinguish the parents in these families from any other parents who are striving for a higher quality of life for a child with a disability.
- **Kathy:** I would say that the common characteristics of Vietnam veterans' families are distrust of systems, isolationism, and a fierce sense of independence. Vietnam veterans' families differ from other families in our network both because of the length of time of the child's disability—veterans' children are not being newly diagnosed—and the families' previous, generally negative exposure to social systems in the past.
- **Bill E.:** For me, the one common denominator in Vietnam veterans' families is that *if* the veteran has unresolved issues relating to service in Vietnam, the family has had to bear the brunt of his or her reactions because federal, state, local, and even the veterans organizations have helped little or not at all, and usually long after the fact. In the case of homeless Vietnam veterans, a common trait seems to be that the veteran is disconnected from the family unit. Often when a homeless veteran makes the effort to change his situation, reuniting or reconciling with the family is a major motivating factor.
- **Pat:** I have found a common, but not exclusive, characteristic among Vietnam veterans: their families are diverse in their priorities concerning their children's educational needs. In addition, helping them to focus on issues concerning educational needs is one of the biggest challenges I've faced in working with these families.
- **Larry:** The length of time it has taken to resolve, or even begin to address, some of the issues surrounding the veteran's service in Vietnam is common to veterans' families. In part, this is both because the veteran is reluctant to approach traditional service delivery systems and because of the number of years it has taken the service delivery system to acknowledge a connection between the problems occurring and the veteran's service.
- **Suzanne:** The common thread that I have noticed among Vietnam veterans' families is their overprotectiveness of their children, which is part of the "enmeshment" dynamic. Frequently, parents are unable to let go of their children and allow them to individuate from the family. This "over-involvement" manifests itself in teenagers acting out and rebelling against the family. These children often appear immature and typically lack self-confidence.

Question Two: In what ways are Vietnam veterans' families different from or similar to any other diverse populations with whom you have had experience?

- **Peter:** Families of Vietnam veterans want the same things for their children as other families. They all want to have positive futures for their children and themselves. Families of Vietnam veterans mirror the needs of all families in economic, social, and emotional areas. I believe that many of the differences between families of Vietnam veterans and other families stem from the Vietnam experience. The veteran parent often has myriad unresolved issues and conscious anger around those issues.
- **Kris:** Every family we've seen has come to our agency with a unique set of circumstances. Even when families have similar needs, they live in different parts of the state and, consequently, deal with different service providers. We have noticed, however, that the veterans' children, who have what are sometimes considered less severe disabilities—emotional problems or learning disabilities—are truly among those that have, as the common expression goes, "fallen through the cracks" and have very limited supports and resources available to them.

- **Patrick:** We have found that Vietnam veterans' families will generally continue in therapy longer than other families. Once a level of trust has been established, the families display a high level of commitment toward change and will work to preserve their family. Families form bonds with one another around issues related to PTSD and are successful in creating more open family systems once a general understanding of PTSD is shared. We've also noticed that the families we work with seem to experience more physical health problems and appear to be more affected by existential issues manifested as midlife crises, questioning the meaning of life, and so forth.
- **Suzanne:** I believe that the veterans' families I have worked with comprise a unique group of individuals. These families are dealing with a multitude of issues—the diagnosis of PTSD after twenty plus years, the effects that PTSD has had on the family because the condition remained untreated for such a long time, substance abuse, rage, isolation, etc. I believe that the children who have lived with a veteran with untreated PTSD constitute a unique population in and of themselves.

Question Three: If you have worked with Vietnam veterans' families for more than five years, what changes, if any, have you seen in the types of problems these families are facing?

- **Larry:** We've seen an increase in the financial instability and health problems of veterans. I would say that in recent years, understanding of the issues surrounding Vietnam service has improved.
- **Steve:** I have not worked specifically with veterans' families for more than five years, but I have worked with the veterans for more than five years. From my experience, I have seen veterans getting more complacent and more resigned to their situations. They are often unwilling to really correct the problems that can be, or are already, major stressors in their lives.
- **Mike:** We've seen an increasing concern that there will be no AOCAP program or similar services for them to turn to in the future. From our experience, we've seen that most veterans' families have no medical insurance, no knowledge of the education laws, and in many cases, the veteran has no job, no money, or understanding of how the veteran systems work. When you add all of these elements together, a veteran's fear becomes a fear of the unknown. I really believe that without the AOCAP programs, the veterans' families won't make it.

Question Four: If your professional experience has been more oriented toward working with families that have a child with a disability, does a family's "veteran status" impact the strategies used to address the needs of the child and the needs of the family in any significant way ?

- **Bill G.:** Our program has always focused on the family. Because we use a holistic treatment modality, all of the various inputs of a family's structure are considered. Whether the input is positive or negative doesn't matter. We always look at the veteran's status, but this doesn't necessarily mean our strategy changes. It simply means that the family may have unique needs or benefits.
- **Ron**: Governmental accountability, or the lack thereof, plagues Vietnam veterans and their families. Our society has been duped into believing that the U.S. Department of Veterans Affairs (VA) takes care of its own. The general public's impression is that the VA cares not only for the veteran but provides care for his or her family and children. Not only is this not the case, but little has been done, in terms of regulations, to force the issue to be addressed.
- **Kathy:** Veteran status affects the issues facing a family that has a child with a disability because it makes the child or family eligible to receive assistance from some of the veteran organizations. The service- or nonservice-connected disability benefits that the father may receive makes some children ineligible for state services because of family

income. The families don't make enough money to provide what the child needs, but they make too much to qualify for assistance.

- **Peter:** I believe that veteran status impacts the way that strategies are developed to address the needs of the child and the needs of the family because of the prerequisite need to develop trust with the family. Many of the families we have encountered have had negative experiences with veteran services, the media, and so on, or have not had the needs of their family met, which has created a general sense of distrust for professionals. Often, the family's decision to isolate themselves from others contributes to a lack of knowledge about the developmental disabilities systems and resources available to the family.

  Another factor for these families is that the professionals they sometimes encounter in getting services for a child with a disability, because they are unfamiliar with veteran family issues, misinterpret a Vietnam veteran's anger and do not understand the link with PTSD. In addition, many of these families tend to operate in crisis mode, asking for assistance at the eleventh hour, when an earlier intervention might have proven more effective.

  Other issues common to these families are certain to have an impact where they occur, including children's own mental health needs due to secondary PTSD, which goes largely undiagnosed. Many of the children live in single-parent households or reside with parents who have marital difficulties or who are abusing alcohol and other substances.

- **Patrick:** What we have discovered with families that have a child with a disability is a need for more advocacy efforts to help them overcome their hostility and distrust of outside agencies.

- **Pat:** The veteran status of the parent changes how I approach working with the family because the veteran parent, usually the father, is difficult to reach. He is either extremely reserved or exactly the opposite. Developing a strategy for working with a veteran's family is, for me, more involved than for a nonveteran family.

- **Steve:** When veteran status is recognized or identified and the child of the veteran has a disability, we look at possibilities of the veteran obtaining additional benefits through entitlements such as service-connected compensation. It's not that the single veteran or the veteran without children is looked at with any less concern, but when a child with a disability is involved, more work goes into trying to obtain and identify the resources for which the veteran may qualify.

- **Mike:** With the veterans' families, there is not only a prerequisite need to establish trust, but frequently, the veteran or the family, must be given the opportunity to vent their anger before they can begin to focus on their child's needs. Only then can you move to empowering them and informing them about the services they need. They need to know that they are not alone and that someone cares. As a parent of children with disabilities, I have also been able to say to them, "I've been where you are." I've seen complete changes in families once they became knowledgeable and have someone walk them through the system.

Question Five: What have you seen as the most often needed interventions or services within the veteran family population?

- **Peter:** Service coordination is the most needed intervention. In general, families are frequently unaware of the services they qualify for, including services from both veteran and disabilities organizations in their communities. Frequently, mental health intervention is also needed. Families often request supportive counseling services for both adults and children. Through our project, we have also seen the children's needs for other specialist services such as speech and language pathology, occupational therapy, and physical therapy. Funds are also often needed for such things as copayments of insurance bills, emergency housing funds, and medical equipment. We have also seen a need for information about Agent Orange, substance abuse, and even where to get food.

- **Kathy:** The need for information has been a prevalent issue for these families. They not only need information about services but frequently need assistance in developing the skills that can make them effective advocates for their children. Information in itself is useless unless the family can be empowered to access existing services.
- **Bill E.:** Veterans and their families need real and expert assistance on how to interact with the VA to address compensation and other issues.
- **Larry:** Assistance in securing VA compensation, which in many cases offers a degree of financial stability, is often needed. After alleviating some of the family's financial problems and concurrently establishing trust, we can move on to dealing with the whole family.
- **Bill G.:** Our families often have children with disabilities, a father with disabilities whose earnings are limited to odd jobs, and a mother who is working part time. Money is what these families primarily need—money for therapy, and food, clothing, medicine, and other amenities. The interventions vary. We may assist the family members by steering them to resources that provide free food. Then, we may direct them to Public Aid, Social Security, and VA benefits. Dealing with all of the appointments and programs available to them is often overwhelming, which makes service coordination essential because it keeps them focused. This strategy allows us to assess the services previously received by the child and to evaluate whether we can improve on them.
- **Marcia:** Special education advocacy is often needed. These families are unaware of the many services that should be provided as part of an individual educational plan (IEP) if their child has a disability. We advocate by accompanying the family to meetings and helping to develop this plan.
- **Pat:** The most often needed service is placement of the child with a disability into an appropriate school with appropriate services. We have seen this, coupled with some sort of counseling or support, as a real stress reliever for these families.
- **Suzanne:** I've seen a frequent need for family therapy that openly addresses the issues of the Vietnam War and the problems that resulted for the veteran. Also, individual therapy seems to be critical for children who have been living in a family with a veteran suffering from PTSD and, consequently, have been exposed to substance abuse, angry outbursts, or violence. I have seen children who have lived for years in an atmosphere that requires that they "walk on eggshells." The family systems theory approach along with the individual therapy seem to be the most effective combination of treatment.
- **Patrick:** We find in our program that these families frequently need therapy. That therapy can require any combination of marital, family, or group treatment. All family members need basic education on PTSD. Marital and family therapy is sometimes resisted by veteran families but it is a primary intervention. When we cannot convince family members to become involved in therapy, we are less successful in our efforts. If we had to choose between marital and family therapy or group treatment, we would choose marital and family therapy.
- **Kris:** Sympathetic listening, filtering counseling, and trying to connect families with low-cost services in their communities are the interventions we most often use. Our parent education series, which has been well attended, has also been a significant part of what we've done. The series has given many parents the psychological supports they need but have had trouble finding. They often find it helpful to simply learn that many other families are dealing with similar problems. The workshops have also attracted professionals and parents who work with children challenged by a variety of disabilities: it fills a gap in training for families and staff that school districts have not been able to address because they lack the needed resources. As a side benefit, the workshops have opened another route for Vietnam veterans to find out about our program.

- **Steve:** Intervention needs vary, of course, but it seems that education about existing services and advocacy assistance are primary. It seems that overall, Vietnam veterans do not seek out resources the way that nonveteran individuals will, either because they lack knowledge or are reluctant to deal with anything associated with the state or federal government. Finding immediate, short-term cash resources has been another issue for most of the families I've dealt with, as have been resources to help pay for past medical bills and post-hospitalization counseling for children of Vietnam veterans. In general, financial assistance programs have probably made the greatest difference for most families because they give them breathing space from medical bills by relieving financial pressures, which ultimately affects the entire family in a positive way. In sum, the assistance from programs that provide medical cash resources and money for basic needs was the most often needed and most effective intervention.
- **Mike:** The most often needed interventions involve family needs. You can identify specific problems, like a veteran's PTSD, but unless the whole family is treated, the problems will not be solved. This is where the AOCAP network has really played a crucial role. Because we have been able to use the different organizations within the network, we have been able to assist entire families without going outside the AOCAP family. There is nothing within our state organizations that matches this network.

Question Six: In your work with Vietnam veterans' families, what issues have been the most difficult to resolve and why?

- **Larry:** The most difficult issue to resolve is the question of "What is going to happen to me, my husband, my kids, and my kids' kids because of Agent Orange?" No magic test can determine if a family has a problem. Thankfully, the AOCAP network has at least offered veterans' families somewhere to turn if problems occur. Before AOCAP, we just shook our heads and said, "We don't know."
- **Bill E.:** The most difficult issue is isolation and distrust of the federal system's willingness and ability to be of real assistance. The service delivery system has failed to meet the needs of veterans and their families for too many years.
- **Kathy:** The needs of the family are often connected in some way to a battle between the family and the VA service system. Dealing with this has been the most frustrating part of our work.
- **Patrick:** Building a sense of trust with Vietnam veterans' families can be a difficult process, but it is pivotal to success. Creating change in the role structure within a family is often resisted by all family members. The challenge is to decrease the enmeshment and redefine responsibility for family members.
- **Peter:** I think the most difficult problems to solve when working with families of Vietnam veterans involve the family's mental health. Because so many families of Vietnam veterans "cocoon" themselves and don't share their family's needs with appropriate persons or agencies, their mental health needs often go untreated for years or even decades. In addition, the families sometimes develop a coping style that allows them to function adequately in the school or work environment but doesn't address the family dynamics that generate a great deal of stress.

  Even under the best of circumstances, mental health needs are difficult to address. They are even more difficult to address with families of Vietnam veterans because the families are more cautious in seeking appropriate help. When and if families do seek help, the issues they face are often long term and far reaching.
- **Bill G.:** At times it appears that the family has been so overwhelmed for so long that they get discouraged. This discouragement is expressed by not keeping appointments or not following through with assignments. Sometimes they get only a portion of what they're entitled to because they simply don't follow through.
- **Marcia:** Often these families are discouraged by the fact that they must access several programs to meet one need. For example, to secure needed medical services for a child

with a disability that is not covered by Social Security, a family might access Public Aid and CHAMPVA and still have unpaid hospital bills. Understanding the requirements of and services offered by these programs and completing all of the required paperwork can be too difficult for a veteran with a disability to handle.

- **Steve:** The most difficult issues to resolve involve past medical bills, financial pressures, and the apathy veteran families have toward the "helping" resources. Getting assistive devices for children has also been difficult. Many of the families I've worked with would probably fall under the category referred to as the working poor. Although they sometimes have insurance coverage that covers most or part of the medical expenses incurred, invariably they cannot get themselves caught up financially. Often they have extreme debts because of a rider or exclusion of some sort that their coverage has on their children with disabilities. This strain affects the entire family in various ways that, although difficult to quantify or document, are nevertheless very real. Often it seems that the families are trying their best to deal with the pressures, but they're doing so without seeking assistance from outside sources which typically cost money that they can ill afford.
- **Pat:** The most difficult issue we have faced with veterans' families is trying to explain why their school districts do not help their children, when they are fully aware of the appropriate options that are not only available, but mandated by law.
- **Suzanne:** A particularly difficult issue for the children involves the emotional or physical absence of a parent, which often leads to poor self-esteem and feelings of responsibility and self-blame by the child. The children seem to feel extremely responsible for the veteran's behavior and believe that they can somehow control it. When they fail, they become depressed and self-blaming. Without an overt change in the veteran's behavior, children are unable to give up the illusion of control over the situation or their feelings of responsibility for the veteran's recovery. By the time intervention occurs, these patterns seem fairly well ingrained in the children. Because long periods of time have usually elapsed prior to any initial intervention, the issues are very difficult to resolve.
- **Mike:** My reaction to this question comes from my experience working in an AOCAP program and my having lived the same nightmare that many of our families have lived. From my experience, I know that some of the most difficult issues involve working through the anxieties and emotions that make counseling such a prevalent need for these families. These are people who have told themselves, or have been told, that if they were better parents this wouldn't be happening to their children. They know the frustration of feeling powerless—not knowing what to do for their children. These feelings are tough to work through. But, because of the assistance we received, my boys are going to make it, and my hope is that many of the families our program has helped will be able to say the same.

Question Seven: What changes, if any, have you seen in the delivery of human services to veterans and their families? Have you seen any movement toward a more family-centered philosophy in the delivery of services to veterans and their families?

- **Larry:** We see the family-centered approach within AOCAP, but we need much more time to have an impact on the myriad state and local service providers.
- **Kathy:** Family-centered services are becoming more prevalent in private and volunteer organizations, but the governmental bureaucracy has changed little. It does at least seem that more and more individuals within the agencies are recognizing the philosophy.
- **Kris:** As a community-based organization, we are peripheral to the veteran service community. New Jersey has Veteran's Service Officers in every county, four Vet Centers, two VA Hospitals, a statewide Vietnam Veterans of America Service Officer, and the only State Agent Orange Commission. Although we are not a part of the official

service system, our program is known to all of the listed offices. We refer veterans' issues to the appropriate office, and veterans' families who have a child with a disability are referred to us. At least at a state level, things are looking more hopeful for some form of a family-centered philosophy. A New Jersey Vietnam veteran memorial and education center are now under construction and the existing system is active and concerned with family issues. Family support officers were provided during Desert Storm and the following year through the New Jersey Department of Veterans Affairs: there has been a movement to continue the service.

- **Steve:** Fewer services are available and local, state, and county resources have dried up when compared with what was available when AOCAP began. At the same time, the workload of many service providers has increased. I have not seen a move toward a family-centered philosophy except in the AOCAP network, which does deal with the family as a whole and attempts to deliver information and services in a comprehensive way.
- **Peter:** I haven't seen a great movement toward a family-centered philosophy in working with families of Vietnam or other veterans. Although I don't have a long history of working with veteran's issues, I see little other than a medical model being used with these families. Usually, this only helps veterans—not their family members—cope with the veterans' medical problems. Aside from AOCAP programs that employ a family-centered modality, I see few programs attempting to meet the needs of veterans' families.
- **Suzanne:** I have seen very little focus on family therapy with veterans' families in New Mexico. The PTSD program at the VA only recently began to include some type of family component, and the Vet Centers I have dealt with seem to focus more on the veteran than his or her spouse or children. Although I've seen minimal movement locally, I have seen movement nationally, and believe it can't arrive too soon.

Question Eight: In what ways has the creation of the AOCAP network of programs contributed to changes at a local or state level or within the delivery systems overall? How would your community or service area be impacted if your program were to close at the conclusion of the AOCAP funding?

- **Anita:** The loss of AOCAP-funded programs would be significant in a number of ways. I fear that new issues will arise as future generations are born into these families. If there is no AOCAP or similar program to provide information with compassion and understanding, the situation will be terrible. I can't foresee any agency that will provide all of these services to veterans' families—at no cost—the way our program has. When parents call us, no one is turned away. AOCAP has in large part made that possible.
- **Kris:** The AOCAP network is exemplary because it has no boundaries. Most agencies deal with geographic catchment areas, a single disability, or a population defined by age—either children or adults. AOCAP crosses all borders, requiring only that one parent is a Vietnam veteran. A similar system for all individuals would be a real systems change.

  The resources gathered for the information and referral section of our program have become an important service that we will be able to continue to offer. AOCAP is one of several programs that has helped us grow from an agency that served a single county to one with a presence throughout New Jersey. The parent workshop series I mentioned earlier continues to draw participants from New York, New Jersey, and Pennsylvania and would leave a void if discontinued.
- **Kathy:** We are recognized as a resource for families at least in part because we encourage them to become their own service coordinators. Without our program, no resource would be available to address the issues that are unique to the families of Vietnam

veterans who have a child with a disability. If the program were to close, I think little would prevent services from again becoming fragmented and difficult for these families to obtain.

- **Steve:** The local and state resources I've dealt with are now identifying veterans and referring them to our program in an attempt to obtain better advocacy and to explore service areas that are unfamiliar to them. Our program, by linking Vietnam veterans with local service providers, gives them things they have not been able to get through conventional means. Closing the program in South Dakota, and likely in other places, would impact both veterans' families and local service providers because it would reduce the number available for their use. Conventional service providers have simply not provided families with the complete range of services our program has offered in addressing financial resources, advocacy, and education about available services.
- **Bill G.:** In the state of Illinois, we have seen very little in the area of change. In Cook County, if our AOCAP program ended, there would be a significant gap in services. Various agencies could provide some services that we offer, but few could offer case management at our level. For example, there will still be people assisting with VA benefits, but the emphasis will be on the veteran, not the family or other services. There will be people assisting children with disabilities, but only children who can afford the services.
- **Ron:** AOCAP and its affiliate programs have been a godsend for veterans and their families because they help them to function independently and become self-educated about the services available to them in their respective communities.
- **Patrick:** AOCAP has built the foundation for the growth of our Vietnam veterans program. Because of AOCAP, we have been able to increase our service level overall and have become known in the community as a provider for veterans and as a program that is allowed to engage in advocacy efforts for veterans. Although our program will continue after the AOCAP funding is expended, the scope of our service delivery may be reduced, especially with regard to family members of the veteran.
- **Suzanne:** I believe that the AOCAP-funded program in New Mexico has filled a definite need with regard to services for children and families. Our program focused primarily on veterans and their families living outside of the Albuquerque area. Because of this, I believe we did not reach many local veterans' families who were also in need of services. Our program encompassed a large geographical region that was covered by a small staff. I don't believe that changes occurred at the local or state level, but we acted as a large referral resource for the VA Hospital, Vet Centers, and other organizations affiliated with veterans. Ending AOCAP will impact services, especially to the veterans who are living in the rural areas of the state.
- **Peter:** If AOCAP closed tomorrow, I don't think that many of the programs that deal with family issues would be available to veterans. Veterans and their families would have to look for services within the existing social, disability, and veterans' services. Instead of having one family-centered program that links the unique problems of veterans and their families with the services they need, the family would have to have its needs met in a piecemeal fashion.

Question Nine: What changes, yet unmade, would you like to see in the delivery of human services to Vietnam veterans' families? What family needs do you still see unmet or inadequately met among Vietnam veterans' families?

- **Kris:** Human services is the key phrase. Our agency has always believed that the issues confronting Vietnam veterans with children who have disabilities are universal issues. The AOCAP network could easily serve many people who are in need of broad-based information, encouragement, and empowerment. Although this program has been important to many Vietnam veterans' families, there are millions of stressed-out families that could use a similar network. In New Jersey, the real barrier to the provision of family services is inadequate communication about existing services.

- **Bill E.:** This question would take volumes to answer. Suffice it to say, our nation's historical avoidance of the real issues that arose in the aftermath of the Vietnam War continues today. Unless, or until, we correct this, as a nation we will continue to avoid the societal issues that tear at the fabric of our nation.

- **Ron:** I would like to see the VA take a more active role in educating fellow agencies. Almost all federal agencies have a provision in their respective program goals that covers services for veterans and their families, yet almost all agencies defer to the VA, assuming that the VA is providing services to family members.

- **Bill G.:** I wish there would be greater coverage of the AOCAP network. In the state of Illinois, there are more than 360,000 Vietnam veterans—more than 150,000 of which live in Cook County alone. We are contracted to provide services to seventy-five families per year, but we usually double that number. Even so, thousands of veterans, spouses, and children remain in need of the type of quality services the AOCAP network provides.

  The national AOCAP philosophy is to merge veterans' groups, social service agencies, and disability agencies for children into a network that gives Vietnam veterans and their families access to the most services. Our agency tries to do this at a community level, but wide gaps exist in the service area. Directly east of us, in Northwest Indiana, there are 11,000 Vietnam veterans. We have finally told them if they can get to us, we will try to help. But thousands more could use our type of direct services. I personally fear for the day when the funding stops and the men and women with disabilities in our communities are again left to the mercies of the system.

- **Larry:** With few exceptions, the VA is mandated to treat only the veteran. The VA, the largest health care provider in the country, is prohibited from using a family-centered approach. This is similar to trying to improve the performance of a quarterback but training him separately from the team. The service delivery system needs must take the veteran's experiences into consideration, both in terms of how they have affected his relationships with family members and how they may impact the provision of services to the family.

- **Anita:** We've seen a definite need for affordable insurance. Many of the families we serve currently have no insurance. More information about existing services might at least keep them from going without some services—such as those available through the school systems—that they are entitled to receive regardless of whether they're insured.

- **Kathy:** I think a major issue is that parents need to be given credit for being the best judges of their needs and the needs of their children. Parents must be given the opportunity to be responsible for direct negotiation of services and payments. Many service organizations think that the VA is responsible for meeting the health needs of all family members. The spouses of veterans have a very difficult time getting any health care.

- **Patrick:** More attention must be paid to the medical needs of families that may have resulted from the veterans' exposure to Agent Orange. More outreach efforts are needed to find families of veterans and offer services to them. More is also needed to educate the general population about PTSD and Vietnam veterans' families.

- **Suzanne:** I would like to see family therapy (systems) implemented in the VA's PTSD program and in the Vet Centers whose primary clientele is veterans. Veterans' children are being overlooked and are developing secondary symptoms as a result of living with a veteran with PTSD. Even when community agencies treat these children, they are often not recognized as the children of Vietnam veterans. Although this information is critical for appropriate treatment, often it is not even considered.

- **Steve:** Service providers must be made aware of the benefits that can be obtained through service organizations and programs such as AOCAP. We are doing our best to educate local, state, and federal organizations about the additional resources that can be tapped when all else has failed. Frequently, however, these resource providers do not provide outreach or education for the families who need assistance. They assume that the population they serve already knows about them and where to turn, when in fact that population knows nothing about them. Social Security, for example, safeguards information about benefits and eligibility. They put up roadblocks and will almost bury anyone seeking assistance in paperwork to the point that they get frustrated and completely give up. Social Security and Supplemental Security Income (SSI) should be required to provide outreach to families of children with disabilities, as should the school systems. Making families fight for every inch of ground they get within the system is unfair to the children, and it reinforces the parents' apathy toward a system that seemingly reinforces failure.

Question Ten: In your work, have you seen geographical or cultural issues that impact the provision of, or lack of, adequate family services? If so, please elaborate.

- **Bill E.:** Absolutely. Ethnic, cultural, and geographic differences greatly impact our, and the families', abilities to secure effective assistance for real change in their circumstances.
- **Patrick:** In Wisconsin, the geographic issue is relevant to rural areas. We have veterans who travel more than two hours one way to receive services. Few providers are located in rural Wisconsin, and most are not trained regarding veterans and PTSD. We understand that veteran families may seek out rural sections of the country that allow greater isolation, but that complicates service delivery.
- **Ron:** Although typically the rural community lacks the services available in urban areas, it is interesting to note that the services that do exist are often housed in a joint structure—some type of health care center. This type of setting allows for comprehensive services to the family.
- **Larry:** As someone new to serving the rural community, I find the availability of services to be abysmal. I've also noted that public or any alternative transportation to and from those meager resources is nonexistent.
- **Bill G.:** We work with families from a diverse range of cultural, racial, and geographical areas. A trend we have found is that the farther away from Chicago the families live, the more out of touch they are with regard to available services. We also believe that a disproportionate number of families in the African American community have been turned down one or more times for certain services. Because of this, they don't reapply. For example, when the VA turns down an increase for service-connected benefits, the family seemingly doesn't even consider appealing the decision. If they do, they rarely seem to know the procedures that must be followed. Many also have difficulty distinguishing between state public aid, Social Security, and VA benefits, and thus, get them mixed up. A frequent misconception is that denial for one means a denial for all of these. So, when you suggest they apply for benefits for the child, they figure that they've already been denied.
- **Kathy:** In the South, people are very polite and respectful of authority. Consequently, they accept "no" much too readily. If the veteran service officer or the person down in the department of human services has told them "You're not eligible, so don't even apply," or "We've never heard of this," twenty years may pass before the family decides to try again. These families are very proud, and it is difficult for them to ask for help,

particularly in families who live in smaller communities. If you don't believe it's an issue, just look at how long these problems have been going on.

- **Suzanne:** Geographical issues are definitely a large barrier to veterans and their families receiving services. New Mexico is largely a rural state with many different Native American populations. Because the rural areas are often difficult to access, services in those areas are minimal at best. Satellite offices are needed around the state if the veterans living in outlying areas are to be properly serviced.
- **Anita:** In Southern California, where parents are often Spanish-speaking, many parents have a hard time just requesting records from the school districts, despite federal regulations that govern those requests. The fact that our staff and advocates are bilingual has been a big help to us and to the families we serve. Unfortunately, the state agencies funded to provide services in a culturally competent manner often do not have Spanish-speaking personnel. Agencies must be held to a greater level of accountability regarding this issue.
- **Peter:** I believe geographic differences play a great part in defining the problems facing families of Vietnam veterans. The differences may be as varied as the defining qualities of urban and rural life. Families living in an urban environment have different educational, vocational, economic, housing, nutritional, and mental health needs than families in a rural area. To say that all families' needs, regardless of geographic location, could be met with one set of guidelines would be terribly naive and equally ineffective.
- **Kris:** Our catchment area is six counties in northern New Jersey, and we have restricted our outreach to those counties. We do, however, have clients in every county in New Jersey. Word travels if an agency is sincerely making an effort to meet a need. In New Jersey, there is a real need for accessible information on what services exist for individuals with disabilities. Most parents are capable of seeking ways to help their children, but often simply don't know where to start. Gathering information from agencies is frustrating for parents because the agencies are overburdened and sometimes slow to return calls. Municipality lines sometimes are geographical barriers. Little information sharing goes on among towns, counties, and catchment areas, but because of AOCAP's broad base, we have been able to get beyond some of these barriers.
- **Steve:** In a state such as ours, which has a diverse population of Native Americans living on seven reservations, services available to cultural populations differ largely according to the willingness of the Native Americans to allow Anglo Americans to integrate within their culture and the willingness of the Anglo population to do so. I have had to work hard to gain their trust and find out what is specifically available through the tribes. Although the tribes are to a great extent self-sufficient, we have been asked to provide resources that are not available to them. The number of sparsely populated areas do create geographical problems for us. Most of the services are, of course, located in the more populated areas, so providing services to the more remote parts of the state is quite difficult because of the distance involved.

Question Eleven: What, if any, misconceptions did you have regarding Vietnam veterans' families that have been clarified through your work within an AOCAP-funded program? What misconceptions, if any, do you think exist among the general public and perhaps more specifically among policy makers concerning Vietnam veterans' families and their need for human services?

- **Ron:** Vietnam veterans and their families are still being stereotyped as crazy. Moreover, politicians still assume this population is being taken care of by the VA. Perhaps more collaboration by agencies within the AOCAP network could further educate the public about the plight of the Vietnam veteran and his or her family.
- **Anita:** I can't tell you how many times I have heard that Vietnam veterans are crazy. As the wife of a veteran, I can say that this just isn't true. People need to understand

that Vietnam veterans' families are like other families, with an important exception. Someone in these families saw the death of others at what we now recognize as having been a rather young age, or they came very close to experiencing it themselves. I don't know if anyone who hasn't experienced that can really understand how the veterans feel, but we all can at least assure these families that we know they aren't crazy and they aren't alone.

- **Bill E.:** The biggest, and most overriding misconception, which undermines all that we do, is that the VA "fixes those guys." In other words, veterans are a federal problem! The entire federal, state, and local service delivery system runs on this premise, which promotes an alienating and questioning attitude when any Vietnam veteran or veteran's family seeks assistance or guidance in a veteran-centered way. This pervasive, institutionalized response only drives the veteran and his or her family away and reinforces their perception that no one gives a damn.
- **Kathy:** I expected to be met with hostility by the families. Instead, they have been very receptive to the assistance we have been able to offer. Veterans' families definitely have unique problems related to the stress of their era and the stress of not having been given appropriate outlets for coping with changes.
- **Peter:** Some of the misconceptions that I had regarding families of Vietnam veterans were that: the needs of families of Vietnam veterans with children with disabilities were the same as all other families of children with disabilities; the mental health needs of Vietnam veterans and their families were no different from those of any other family of children with disabilities; the needs of families of Vietnam veterans are being met by the VA; secondary PTSD is not an important issue in families of Vietnam veterans; and families of Vietnam veterans use the same methods for coping as other families who have children with disabilities.
- **Larry:** The greatest misconception I had was that the VA takes care of all veterans' needs. Regarding the cause-and-effect issue of Agent Orange, or dioxin, on the children of veterans, there has been a credibility problem resulting from the Environmental Protection Agency's confusing, vacillating, and contradictory statements regarding the toxicity of dioxin. The general public, and yes, even service providers, still have doubts about whether exposure to Agent Orange by a veteran has resulted in birth defects, and, thus, is the reason why children of Vietnam veterans have so many special needs.
- **Bill G.:** I think Vietnam veterans' families are no different than other families who are in need. The Vietnam veteran family is "us." They are no different than we are. They experience the same joys and pain, and I think the American public in general sometimes forgets this very basic fact. Although families of Vietnam veterans may have a higher potential for internal problems, such as a father with PTSD or a child with a birth defect, they are still "us." I also believe that policy makers have only looked at the veteran in isolation from his family. I hope that AOCAP will, at the national level, be able to make inroads into correcting this flawed perspective.
- **Patrick:** The greatest misconception is the general public's belief that the symptoms of PTSD will disappear over time. Some professionals display frustration with veterans because they maintain symptoms and continue to have problems. We've found that many veterans have through the years become quite skillful at hiding PTSD issues, only to have them surface at mid-life or other life stages. There continues to be the thinking that Vietnam and all the problems veterans, or their families, have related to the war should be swept under the rug.
- **Kris:** The Vietnam War impacted everyone in the 1960s. Some young men were exposed to unbelievable brutality; others made career and marriage choices because of the war. Yet, Americans never realistically confronted the issues associated with the war. Because of this, it's still a shadow in our past that often reaches out and darkens lives. On a superficial level, the general public and lawmakers think the war is over and life has proceeded. In reality, the mixed emotions have never been resolved.

- **Steve:** I am a Vietnam combat veteran, and I have no misconceptions of the Vietnam veteran and his or her family problems. I know how to deal with the families, and I understand their frustrations. I believe that the general public wants to forget Vietnam veterans and pretend they never existed because their problems are often more complex and unfamiliar than what most people are prepared to encounter. Few Vietnam veterans have been elected to the Congress, so why would policy makers pursue something they don't understand themselves? I also believe that veterans are sometimes seen as being the same, and that the real variety of life experiences that veterans' families have had are disregarded.
- **Suzanne:** Before I began to work with Vietnam veterans and their families, I knew next to nothing about their issues and concerns. What I did know came from movies like *The Deer Hunter*. I have considered it a great privilege to work with veterans and their families. I have been extremely impressed with the veterans' concern for their children. Most of the veterans I work with are individuals who have been diagnosed with PTSD by the VA. Despite the seriousness and debilitating nature of their own problems, they actively seek help for their children.

  I believe that the general public, especially people in their mid-thirties and younger, are just as ignorant as I was of the veterans' plight and their issues. Policy makers, or at least the VA hospital, obviously didn't consider the ramifications the Vietnam War would have on veterans' spouses and children. A huge misconception was that the effect would be not as great on the spouse and the children. In actuality, the effect is almost as great on significant others as it is on the veteran.

Question Twelve: What do you consider to be the most significant accomplishment of your AOCAP-funded program? On a personal level, what have been your most memorable moments in your work with families in your AOCAP-funded program?

- **Ron:** The ability to help a family by assisting the veteran in presenting his or her claim for earned benefits has been rewarding for me personally. At one time, we had an AOCAP-funded transitional housing program. It was always nice to watch someone come into the program, sometimes nearly at the end of their rope, and literally see their appearance begin to change within a few short weeks. I've seen men come in underweight, with clothes and dreams in shreds, and leave the program four to six months later with a full belly, a new set of clothes, and most importantly, a restored sense of hope.
- **Larry:** A significant accomplishment of our program was the move from being primarily a veteran-centered program to a family-centered philosophy. Specifically, my most memorable moments involve a saved mortgage, a successful IEP, and collaboration with the Spina Bifida Home Accessibility Program on behalf of a veteran's child. No, I think that an even more memorable time was the afternoon that I spent four hours listening to the wife of a veteran who could not or would not speak to anyone else about her troubled husband and her kids. She had all of the resources identified and in place. She really didn't need a service from us. She was simply desperate for someone to listen to her.
- **Peter:** The most memorable moments that I've had working with the families of Vietnam veterans are the times when I was able to help a family negotiate a disabilities system or solve a problem. I believe that in doing so, I have helped families develop skills in self-advocacy. When AOCAP is no more, hopefully those families will have the skills they need to continue to advocate for themselves in a knowledgeable, proactive manner.
- **Patrick:** At our program, we focus on small changes veterans make for themselves and their families. These small and seemingly insignificant efforts build on one another toward healthier ways of being a family. We see veterans' families learning to trust each other and outside agencies, building support systems, and strengthening their

families. We sometimes work for more than a year with a family. The value of the work is seen in the faces of the family members when they say good-bye to us.

- **Kathy:** I believe that the most significant accomplishment of our program has been the establishment of a statewide service coordination system that is family-centered and community-based and will continue after AOCAP funding is gone.
- **Suzanne:** I believe that working with the children of veterans' families has been our most significant accomplishment. Services for these children are extremely limited. There is very little recognition of the unique issues they face. No particular moment has been memorable. Instead, I view the whole experience as memorable. On a personal level, my most important accomplishment has been having a veteran trust me enough to allow me to work with his family. Although I am a female in my thirties and obviously not a veteran, I was able to gain the trust of these individuals, which gave me a real sense of importance.
- **Steve:** Overall, serving as an advocate for the children is my most significant accomplishment. Seeing the system get beaten simply because of my persistence and willingness to go an extra mile or two for a family has been very satisfying because the results are tangible. I have not had this same fulfillment in other positions. As for a specific family, I had a family approach me as a last resort for their teenage son. They had no insurance on him because of his severe diabetes, which he could not control through conventional means. He was having to give himself six insulin shots per day, and he really needed an insulin pump implanted. It took some really time-intensive contacts and negotiations, but I was able to put together a complete package for the family. I was able to get the pump donated, the costs of the initial procedure covered, and the needed follow-up treatment. Costs for the pump, the implant procedure, and follow-up care totaled about $10,000. I would not have been able to do this type of work, and this young man likely would not have his insulin pump today, if I hadn't been part of an AOCAP-funded program.
- **Kris:** AOCAP has enabled our agency to make significant accomplishments: we became the first program to have clients in every county of the state; our agency broadened its focus to children and family issues; and, our program was a driving force behind our agency building a database of statewide information on services in New Jersey for individuals with disabilities. I would have to say that the parent education series has been the most significant accomplishment because it has been so well received and attended. It has touched thousands of lives and will continue as a valuable public service.

  Many families have called and poured out their troubles, concerns, and frustrations, and ended their conversations with, "Thank you so much for listening." I am always amazed that so many people have found comfort in such a simple counseling technique. Apparently, before us no one had taken the time to listen.

  If I had to single out a favorite moment, it was my interaction with a veteran who participated in a Wilderness Inquiry trip with two of his sons. Although he had camped extensively in his youth, he had not gone camping since Vietnam. The trip brought back good memories, opened up channels for communication with his sons, and gave the veteran a renewed sense of self-worth and accomplishment. He uses a wheelchair because of his peripheral neuropathy but paddled a canoe during the entire trip and made coffee for everyone "the way we did it in 'Nam."
- **Bill G.:** In looking back at specific families, one that comes to mind is a veteran that I worked with to get Social Security benefits for his son who was hospitalized in California. We were trying to do a number of things for him: finding him a way to get to California to see his son, trying to get his VA benefits increased and an Agent Orange claim approved, and getting him into a PTSD treatment program. All of these came through. This particular veteran is an African American, a Marine, and to be honest, when I first met him, I called in my supervisor because he kind of scared me.

> One day when he was in my office to work on some of his paperwork, I handed him a medal to look at. He said, "What's this?" I said, "It's a Bronze Star." He said, "It's real nice. Where'd you get it?" I said, "In the mail." He handed it back across the desk and I said, "That medal is yours." It took the next ten minutes to prove to him that I had ordered it, that it was his, and that it had been issued to him twenty plus years ago! He said, "I never knew I got one." He excused himself from my office with tears in his eyes.
>
> Over the past four years, I've had a lot of things happen that will remain memorable to me; but through all of them, what stands out is that the families we've worked with for any amount of time are not there for handouts or freebies; they want what they have rightfully deserved for so long—some help and some hope.

Summary

Step back from the details that these individuals have reported and a picture emerges—families struggling to survive, some with seemingly no reprieve in sight and some moving ahead. The picture brings out characteristics that distinguish Vietnam veterans' families from other family populations and similarities that unite them with many groups. It reveals the rough edges in existing means of delivering services and the difficulties that Vietnam veterans' families have had, and continue to have, in obtaining services from the existing systems. The picture provides an honest view of the progress made in the effort to initiate, if not accomplish, some fundamental changes in how organizations serve these families. What they have reported is both a gauge of what has been happening at the state and community levels and an important reminder of how much is yet to be done.

Vietnam veterans' families, as depicted in this report, are clearly distinguished from other families by the emotions that color their view of the institutions that are supposed to, and sometimes do, offer the help that they need. Every type of service organization represented has identified trust as the key issue that affects the interactions of many Vietnam veterans' families with human service providers. The issue is seemingly much worse if the organizations bear any affiliation, or even the appearance of affiliation, with the government. It is important to note that what they have brought up in their discussion of the issue of trust, or rather the common lack of it, is not a discussion of a handful of stereotypically paranoid Vietnam veterans.

They are instead speaking of a much more subtle, pervasive sentiment that, in different degrees, affects a wide spectrum of the families and is described by the terms isolated, enmeshed, and reluctant. In large part, they are describing families who have turned inward and turned away from most traditional human service organizations and away from the self-advocating behaviors that are often needed to successfully access available programs and benefits. Given societal attitudes toward the Vietnam War and the lack of proper attention and action given to the needs of the veterans and their families in the years since, a sense of alienation and distrust of anything governmental or institutional is an understandable, regrettable consequence of families having lived with something that most of the country filed away or forgot years ago. It is a consequence that has to be, and deserves to be, recognized in planning and delivering services to this population.

Another powerful factor that affects Vietnam veterans' families that the contributors to this report have observed independently is the undeniable presence of PTSD. A discussion of the effects of PTSD on Vietnam veterans' families is not about media images of the most severe cases, but is instead about a portion of our population that has lived with the disorder in varying degrees for too many years and that is still bearing the lasting effects of the events that caused it. Its effects have, in many cases, become part of a generation raised in homes where the disorder was undiagnosed, untreated, or inadequately treated. Like the trust factor, it is an enduring reality that has to be considered in working with Vietnam veterans' families.

The fact that traditional human service delivery methods have had limited effectiveness for these families is clearly spelled out in this report. The families of veterans are frequently isolated emotionally from outsiders and geographically from service providers. Typically, these families lack the health insurance and financial resources to purchase the services they need from the health care marketplace. Most service providers and policy makers assumed, incorrectly, that the needs of the veterans' families have been, and continue to be, adequately met through the mandated services of the VA. When the veterans and their family members have turned to public sources of assistance with health and counseling needs, they have frequently been met with limited programs burdened with application procedures that would frustrate even the most determined. Their need to find a wide variety of health care and other services has been multiplied by the fact that like many families, Vietnam veterans' families frequently face the challenges of raising children with disabilities and special-health needs.

The work accomplished through the AOCAP network has made a difference in the lives of hundreds of Vietnam veterans' families. It has also made a modest, but significant, beginning in changing how services are delivered to this population. The beginning lies in the service providers and service coordinators who have comprised the network, a small portion of whom are represented in this report. They comprise a small army of professionals who have had their own perspectives of serving Vietnam veterans' families shaped by their role in an AOCAP-funded program. At the outset, many of them had much to learn: the indications are that they did so quite well. As they work with families in the future and help shape policies at their respective organizations, their expertise will continue to be a subtle force for larger, lasting change.

There is a history involving these families that cannot be erased. It makes the effective delivery of services in the future challenging, but certainly not hopeless. The successes of AOCAP-funded programs have provided a credible demonstration of the effective coordination and provision of a wide range of services to the Vietnam veteran family population. Lessons learned from the AOCAP experience should be put into practice on a wider scale. It is clear that service providers cannot compartmentalize the needs of the family into needs of the veteran and those of the rest of the family and expect any real or lasting progress. The reality of the current service delivery system is that a dichotomy exists that separates one family member, the veteran, from the rest of the family and isolates the treatment and approach to the problems of the veteran from those of the family unit. An equally compelling reality is that this practice is no more effective with veteran families than we could possibly expect it to be with any other population of families. There must be a willingness and expertise to confront the fact that PTSD is still a factor that it is affecting entire families, and that it is a problem that requires a commitment of time and resources. The bureaucratic barriers that have frustrated anyone who has ever tried to obtain services from state, federal, and perhaps even some local public programs present a particularly burdensome problem for veterans' families. Until application procedures and program policies become less cryptic and restrictive, there will continue to be a significant need for service coordination and advocacy to help these families get the variety of services that they need.

What these individuals on the front line have reported, at the very least, suggests that fundamental issues on how services are provided to the Vietnam veteran family population need to be addressed. These veterans fought twenty plus years ago in Vietnam and have had to continue to fight for what they and their families are entitled to in the years since. It is time for peace and progress for these families and it is long overdue.

Building on the Experiences of the Agent Orange Class Assistance Program as a Catalyst to Achieve Systems Change

William E. Jones, Ph.D.; and Barbara J. Spoor, M.P.A.
American Association of University Affiliated Programs
Silver Spring, MD

Abstract

Systems change can be defined as carefully planned and managed change of policy and program development to meet identified and emerging or evolving needs of a targeted group of people. One such targeted group is Vietnam War veterans and their families. The traditional veterans' system focuses on service to the veteran, not the family; typically, there has also not been coordination between the veterans' and human services systems. In this paper, Agent Orange Class Assistance Program (AOCAP) grantees were asked to describe their service delivery experience.

That experience pinpoints the need for changes, particularly for increased collaboration, between and among several service systems that impact on the lives of Vietnam veterans and their families. AOCAP can serve as a model for successful change to a system that emphasizes coordination and collaboration at the local, state, and national levels and is tailored to meet the needs of veterans and their families.

William Jones, Ph.D., *is executive director of the American Association of University Affiliated Programs for Persons with Developmental Disabilities (AAUAP).* ***Barbara Spoor, M.P.A.,*** *is project coordinator of an AOCAP systems change grant at AAUAP.*

The process of service systems change is best understood in the context of evolving social values. Social values provide the impetus for the development of laws and policies and are reflected in those laws and policies. Because social values are fluid, rather than static, laws and policies are regularly revised, discarded, or reinterpreted and the programs and services they support are modified to reflect these changes. The process is a cyclical one, moving constantly between social values, policy and law, and program development and implementation.

In Western society, the origins of systems change as a necessary ongoing process can be traced in large part to the Industrial Revolution, which resulted in a more complex life that moved away from a home- and family-centered base. Persons who came to be perceived as "nonviable" or noncontributing participants in the community created a perceived need for special systems of support or care, such as welfare, prisons, and long-term hospitals or institutions. At the same time, the demands on other systems, such as education, became more pronounced and sophisticated, requiring new policies, practices, and outcomes to accommodate the changes in expectations and roles that were occurring in society.

Importantly, it was another group of veterans—especially those from World War II—who provided significant impetus for movement away from isolation and toward integration within the community. The qualifications and attributes they brought back from military service to a job and the community in general often required accommodations for various disabilities. Ensuing models in the areas of rehabilitation and education—such as the GI Bill—reflected a different acceptance level of a person's capabilities. The changes in societal attitudes and service reform that evolved from the veterans' experiences, successes, and contributions have continued to influence all services to people with disabilities ever since.

Recent landmark legislative initiatives affecting services to persons with disabilities include the Individuals with Disabilities Education Act (IDEA), which deals with educational services and focuses on collaborative efforts among service agencies dealing with children of ages birth through twenty-one, and the Americans with Disabilities Act (ADA), which ensures equal access and accommodation for persons of all ages with disabilities in employment, state and local government, public accommodations, telecommunications, and transportation. Additionally, the recently reauthorized Assistive Technology Act addresses systems change in laws, regulations, policies, and practices that promote consumer-responsive programs. Each of these policy, legislative, and service reforms mandates supports to people with disabilities so that they can live productive, independent lives in socially integrated settings.

Background

Lippitt, Watson, and Wesley (1958) identified seven phases of planned change that they use in a broad systemic context. The phases provide a framework for describing how a service (or "client") system can be successfully influenced, as well as for measuring how much change has occurred. Even when planned change is not succeeding, it is helpful to identify where the process may be stymied. In each of the pages described, a lead role may be played by either the system or the change agent, however, mutual agreement on major areas of concern is paramount to the process. The seven phases are:

- **Phase 1.** A client system discovers the need for help, sometimes with stimulation by a change agent;
- **Phase 2.** The helping relationship (client and change agent) is established and defined;

- **Phase 3.** The issues requiring change are identified and clarified by both the client and change agent;
- **Phase 4.** Alternative possibilities for change are examined; change goals or intentions are established by both entities;
- **Phase 5.** Changes in the reality situation are attempted;
- **Phase 6.** Change is generalized and stabilized; and
- **Phase 7.** The helping relationship ends or a different type of continuing relationship is defined.

Planned or systems change begins with theory; a practical application, such as the Agent Orange Class Assistance Program (AOCAP), can provide a concrete example of how the evolution of change can work. The AOCAP experience provides the example for analyzing the planned change process used in this paper. Lippitt, Watson, and Wesley's seven phases will be addressed individually, using AOCAP as a model for analysis.

A Client System Discovers the Need for Help

This paper defines the client system as the human services system (on local, state, and federal levels). The change agent is the Vietnam veteran class that formed the core of the AOCAP lawsuit against the government and the chemical companies that used the herbicide Agent Orange during the Vietnam War. The veterans who brought this suit believed that health and disability issues faced by a large number of veterans and their children could be traced to the use of Agent Orange.

The voluminous document that detailed the Agent Orange lawsuit settlement in 1984 provides an insight into the court's intent regarding long-term resolution of issues facing Vietnam veterans and their families. One passage unequivocally identifies a public responsibility for meeting their needs:

> In considering the fairness of the settlement, the court has looked to other sources of aid either presently available to the class or of potential benefit in the future. The government must be considered the source of ultimate protection whether or not there be a satisfactory demonstration of causal relationship to Agent Orange as a result of ongoing or future scientific studies. Government sources of aid exist and should continue to grow. Payment out of public funds is appropriate since many of the problems faced by Agent Orange exposed veterans are due to Vietnam War-related factors other than the effects of combat as well as the disappointing reception Vietnam veterans received from the American public and inadequate help from their own government (as compared, for example, to that received by World War II veterans) has caused much emotional stress and physical pain.
>
> Whether or not that pain was caused by Agent Orange, it is shared by a disproportionately large number of Vietnam veterans. They and their families should receive recognition, medical treatment and financial support. Many lives have been broken by the Vietnam experience. The suffering ones deserve succor. Their children are also tormented, perhaps because of Agent Orange, but certainly as a secondary result of the family tensions directly traceable to the Vietnam conflict. The negative ripple effects on other family members, the work place and other arenas of Vietnam veterans' lives have spread to all parts of our society and cannot be ignored. The injustices these brave men and women suffer poison the lives of all Americans whether or not they served in Vietnam. . . . Our country is rich in public and private resources of every kind. Those resources should be made available to members of the class as often as needed, close to their homes, and with as little bureaucratic red tape as possible. . . . The public received the benefit of combat service and should help defray the cost.

The lawsuit settlement clearly delineates where responsibility rests for long-term resolution to the problems facing Vietnam veterans and their families. Additionally, it provides the impetus for needed pressure on systems through creation of a change agent.

The Helping Relationship Is Established

The Agent Orange Class Assistance Program was established as a result of the class action lawsuit settlement by Vietnam veterans and their families against the chemical companies that supplied herbicides used in the U.S. war effort in Vietnam. AOCAP provides funding through grants to nonprofit organizations for programs and services of benefit to Vietnam veterans and their families. More than $50 million plus interest will be invested in the development of service supports and reform under AOCAP over its time-limited (seven- to eight-year) program life.

AOCAP operates under the direction and supervision of [now Senior] United States District Court Judge Jack B. Weinstein, who supervises the Agent Orange settlement. The Assistance Program gives priority to the concerns that led to the original lawsuit—providing services that are not currently available and bringing services to Vietnam veterans and their families who, for a variety of reasons, are not receiving needed assistance. The plaintiff class is treated as all persons who served in the armed forces in or near Vietnam between 1961 and 1972 and their spouses, children, and parents.

The three primary goals of AOCAP are:

- **Services for Families.** To provide case management and counseling to Vietnam veterans in the context of their families that takes into account the veteran's war experience as a major contributing factor to the challenges that families face.
- **Services for Children with Disabilities.** To build necessary links between the veteran, developmental disability, and other social service, public health, and education communities.
- **National Support Program**. To establish a national support network to provide technical assistance, training, and service linkages for the network of family services programs funded through AOCAP grants.

Since AOCAP has established Vietnam veteran family services, with an emphasis on those families with disabled children as its primary program thrust, the projects funded represent a mix of agencies with wide-ranging missions. Essentially, agencies fall into four categories: veterans' organizations, agencies serving persons with disabilities, community and family assistance programs, and national support projects.

As of 1994, seventy-four AOCAP grantees were operating across the country. Tables 1, 2, and 3 summarize descriptive and demographic information about projects, based on a survey in the fall of 1993, in which sixty grantees participated. (One national project with several state and local components is represented in aggregate in Tables 1–3, but is broken down by individual activities in Tables 4 and 5.)

Table 1. AOCAP Project Grantees by Type of Agency

Type of Agency	Number of Agencies	Percent of Agencies (%)
Private/community-based organization	38	63
Educational institution	6	10
Other	13	20
Combination of above	4	7
Total	**61**	**100**

Table 2. Primary Populations Served by AOCAP Project Grantees

Primary Population Served	Number of Agencies	Percent of Agencies (%)
Families	9	15
Veterans	2	3
Children with developmental disabilities	5	8
Other	4	7
Combination of above	40	67
Total	**60**	**100**

Most projects (66 percent) served a combination of client groups, reflecting the interrelatedness and complexity of problems and needs. It should be noted that AOCAP funding was primarily awarded to existing local, state, or national agencies to expand their base of operations, rather than to create new entities funded solely from this grant program.

Table 3. AOCAP Project Grantees by Geographic Service Area

Geographic Area Served	Number of Agencies	Percent of Agencies (%)
Urban	18	30
Suburban	1	2
Rural	6	10
Combination of above	35	58
Total	**60**	**100**

As with the population served, most projects serve a combination of urban and rural. Several grants focused specifically on either an urban or rural area because of the unique challenges presented in those locations.

The Issues Requiring Change Are Identified

Service providers have noted several factors regarding Vietnam veterans' families, particularly those with needs related to children with developmental or other disabilities. Many families are not accessing even the most basic social services such as Supplemental Security Income (SSI), Medicaid, and Aid to Families with Dependent Children (AFDC). Many of these families display instability traceable in many instances to post-traumatic stress disorder (PTSD). Finally, those families often experience a complex array of problems that involve the need for intervention through systems that historically have had little interface, such as systems for veterans and for persons with developmental disabilities. These systems often have conflicting regulations, eligibility guidelines, and service protocols. It is apparent to AOCAP projects that, to provide needed and effective services to these families through comprehensive service coordination, it is necessary to integrate service elements from a diversity of agencies and systems. These projects face lack of coordination, communication, and shared priorities among agencies created by public law to serve these families.

The veterans system has traditionally focused service delivery specifically and solely on the veteran. The system is also hospital based (for health and social services) and does not generally provide funding to state or local entities to deliver these services. Within the developmental disabilities field, only recently has service planning broadened to encompass families as well as individuals. These factors, coupled with the need for potential involvement by Vietnam veterans and their families with other systems (e.g., health, social services, education, alcohol and substance abuse, and mental health), point to a critical need for improved communications and collaboration among the systems.

Alternatives for Change Are Examined

By virtue of the multiple, complex needs of the populations served, all AOCAP projects were required to have a strong focus, if not primary involvement, in either service coordination or some form of service coordination, i.e., through the provision of information, referrals, outreach, and advocacy. By necessity, projects became involved with other service providers on the local and state levels. Although contact initially focused on individual and family needs, it became apparent that service system issues would need to be addressed. These experiences and results have built, and continue to build, the foundation for a successful transition from AOCAP-stimulated activities to a focus for ensuring service coordination collaboration in the future.

Tables 4 and 5 provide an overview of current contacts reported by AOCAP grantee projects.

To complement the "quantitative" picture of interagency involvement represented in these tables, project grantees were asked to describe their contacts with other service agencies (both state and local) in terms of: frequency of their contact with the agencies (weekly, monthly, or infrequently); and the nature of the dialogue with these entities. The latter question called for open-ended responses. Responses ranged from succinct to detailed and provide perhaps the best indicators that systems change is indeed occurring as people work together to meet other people's needs. Solutions created for one person often applied to the next person or family in need—and systems change was in operation.

The survey also addressed planning, and AOCAP project grantees were asked to identify resources they have looked at to continue services. A second related question asked how grantees would use those resources, including "transition of client service to other agencies" as one choice. In analyzing the responses, it was evident that systems change is in process or anticipated. A majority of respondents indicated that they anticipate that systems change will occur. Those who anticipate continuing to provide the services with other funding, however, also saw the necessity of systems change.

Changes in the Reality Situation Are Attempted

AOCAP was developed to enhance and ensure delivery of appropriate services to Vietnam veterans and their families. Problems with access to services reflect both individual and systemic limitations, and occur for a variety of reasons. The initial emphasis of AOCAP projects was on assisting families in identifying issues such as employment, housing, counseling, etc. It quickly became apparent that the most timely and effective intervention would be service coordination among the many systems with which a family may have to deal. While it is impractical to assume that any one system has responsibility to provide a comprehensive range of services to veterans and their families, it is conceivable and realistic, based on the AOCAP experience, to expect that awareness, coordination, and collaboration among systems can achieve that result.

The dynamics of the AOCAP network, in both enhancing services to families through service coordination and increasing awareness within other service systems of the needs of Vietnam veterans and their families, serve as a valuable model of intervention strategies. Veterans in the AOCAP network, like other special populations struggling to cross both obvious and invisible systemic barriers to secure needed services, require responsive and articulated policies and programs to meet identified needs.

Many AOCAP grantees have sought to increase public awareness about the needs of Vietnam veterans and their families and to develop coordinated services to meet those needs. Some examples are:

- A joint statewide conference (with follow-up regional workshops), held by a state veterans' agency, mental retardation and developmental disabilities office, and develop-

Table 4. AOCAP Grantee Involvement with Local Agencies

State or Territory	Veterans	Disabilities	Developmental Mental Health	Social Services	Education	Health
Alabama	■	■	■	■	■	■
Alaska	■	■	■	■	■	■
Arizona*						
Arkansas	■	■	■	■	■	■
California	■	■	■	■	■	■
Colorado	■	■	■	■	■	■
Connecticut	■	■	■	■	■	■
Delaware*						
District of Columbia	■			■	■	
Florida	■	■	■	■	■	■
Georgia	■	■			■	
Hawaii*						
Idaho*						
Illinois	■	■	■	■	■	■
Indiana	■	■	■	■	■	■
Iowa		■		■		
Kansas*						
Kentucky*						
Louisiana	■	■	■	■	■	■
Maine	■	■	■	■	■	■
Maryland	■	■	■	■	■	■
Massachusetts	■	■	■	■	■	■
Michigan	■	■	■	■	■	■
Minnesota	■	■	■	■	■	■
Mississippi	■	■	■	■	■	■
Missouri	■	■	■	■	■	■
Montana	■	■		■		■
Nebraska	■			■		■
Nevada*						
New Hampshire*						
New Jersey	■	■	■	■	■	■
New Mexico	■	■	■	■	■	■
New York	■	■	■	■	■	■
North Carolina	■	■		■		■
North Dakota*						
Ohio	■					
Oklahoma	■	■	■	■	■	■
Oregon*						
Pennsylvania	■	■	■	■	■	■
Puerto Rico	■	■	■	■	■	■
Rhode Island	■		■	■	■	
South Carolina*						
South Dakota	■	■	■	■	■	■
Tennessee			■			■
Texas	■	■	■	■	■	■
Utah	■	■	■	■	■	■
Vermont*						
Virginia		■	■	■	■	■
Washington*						
West Virginia	■	■	■	■	■	■
Wisconsin	■		■	■	■	■
Wyoming		■				

* States with no designation of involvement either did not have an AOCAP grant or did not participate in the grantee survey.

Table 5. AOCAP Grantee Involvement with State Agencies

State or Territory	Veterans	Disabilities	Developmental Mental Health	Social Services	Education	Health
Alabama	■	■		■		
Alaska	■	■	■	■	■	■
Arizona*						
Arkansas	■	■	■	■	■	■
California	■	■	■	■	■	■
Colorado	■		■			
Connecticut	■	■	■	■	■	■
Delaware*						
District of Columbia	■			■		
Florida	■	■	■	■	■	■
Georgia	■	■	■	■	■	■
Hawaii*	■	■	■	■	■	■
Idaho*						
Illinois	■	■	■	■	■	■
Indiana	■	■	■	■	■	■
Iowa		■		■		
Kansas*						
Kentucky*						
Louisiana	■	■	■	■	■	■
Maine	■	■	■	■	■	■
Maryland	■	■	■	■	■	■
Massachusetts	■	■	■	■	■	■
Michigan	■	■	■	■	■	■
Minnesota	■	■	■	■	■	■
Mississippi	■	■	■	■	■	■
Missouri	■	■	■	■	■	■
Montana	■			■		
Nebraska	■	■		■	■	
Nevada*						
New Hampshire*						
New Jersey	■	■		■	■	■
New Mexico	■	■	■	■	■	■
New York	■	■	■	■	■	■
North Carolina	■	■	■	■	■	■
North Dakota*						
Ohio	■	■	■	■	■	■
Oklahoma	■	■	■	■	■	■
Oregon*	■					
Pennsylvania	■	■	■	■	■	■
Puerto Rico	■	■	■	■	■	■
Rhode Island	■	■	■	■	■	
South Carolina*						
South Dakota	■	■	■	■	■	■
Tennessee	■	■	■			
Texas	■	■	■	■		■
Utah	■	■	■	■	■	■
Vermont*						
Virginia	■	■	■	■	■	■
Washington*						
West Virginia	■	■	■	■	■	■
Wisconsin	■		■	■		
Wyoming	■	■				

* States with no designation of involvement either did not have an AOCAP grant or did not participate in the grantee survey.

mental disabilities planning council (DDPC), explored Vietnam veterans' family issues and AOCAP projects.

- A full-day meeting, sponsored by an AOCAP grantee with assistance from a local University Affiliated Program, brought together service providers from the local and state levels as well as the public and private sectors to discuss mutual concerns.
- An AOCAP project grantee made a presentation to a state DDPC and followed up with provider agencies and consumers, based on DDPC member recommendations.
- A national AOCAP project developed a brochure dealing with Vietnam veteran and family issues which is targeted for distribution to hospital social work departments.
- Several pilot training projects were developed collaboratively with Special Education Training Resource Centers and U.S. Department of Veterans Affairs (VA) hospital and Vet Center staff.
- A working agreement was developed between an AOCAP project grantee and a local mental health service provider to share counseling and service coordination referrals.

Change Is Stabilized

In the process of managed systems change, once a problem has been identified, those parts of the solution that are already in place and workable are used as a foundation to achieve the desired outcomes in policy changes and subsequent program development. The activities described above are examples of how AOCAP project grantees identified workable components in existing services, began to bridge gaps in services, and supported the coordination of various service systems.

Several AOCAP project grantees have noted an initial reticence on the part of large (i.e., state) service systems to begin a dialogue with their program because of the perception that the AOCAP grantee represented a large unserved population that would impose additional stress on limited financial resources. As the dialogue continued, however, it became evident that the families were typically receiving services from several systems and that collaborative efforts could ameliorate many problems faced by providers.

After several years of concentrating on the development of high-quality, coordinated intervention services, it has become important both to chronicle the lessons learned and begin to ensure continuity of services to Vietnam veterans and their families.

The successes of the AOCAP service coordination focus include:

- Crystallization and understanding of problems facing Vietnam veterans and their families;
- Increased understanding of service needs;
- Increased number of persons served; and
- Development and demonstration of effective case management intervention strategies.

At the same time, AOCAP project grantees have met with consistent problems with various service systems, including:

- Lack of coordinated and integrated services, leading to an isolated approach to dealing with problems;
- Fragmentation and lack of continuity across service systems;
- People "falling between the cracks" and not receiving services; and
- Lack of appropriate use of resources (not necessarily lack of resources in general, although that may be a reality in some instances).

As Surles et al. (1992) have noted:

> If service coordination programs operate in isolation from policy and decision-making structures, the existence of larger social barriers to successful treatment can be a source of tremendous frustration for case managers. However, if channels of communication are open, policy issues quickly become more focused, and public discussion broadens to include coordination of natural supports, formal entitlement, and provision of equal access to other health services and opportunities. Public policy makers gain a new perspective on problems and potential solutions, and case managers gain the satisfaction of having played a part in sparking a dialogue that could potentially affect their clients' success.

Summary and Recommendations

The Helping Relationship Ends: A Different Type of Relationship Is Defined

Analysis of future needs of the AOCAP projects and feedback on their experiences indicates that three things must be at the top of the agenda if the needs of families are to be adequately met and sustained:

- An enhanced understanding on the part of traditional human services and veterans services systems of the needs of Vietnam veterans' families—particularly those with children with disabilities—and a more effective use and coordination of the resources available to address those needs.
- An increased awareness and use of AOCAP as a resource by local and state service providers who have public mandates to provide services needed by Vietnam veterans and their families.
- The integration and maintenance of the service coordination model that AOCAP has developed within the veterans' services and the existing human services network (including public and private developmental disabilities, health, social services, and education providers).

In addition to replication of the activities outlined earlier, which have been successfully used as initial steps toward planned change by AOCAP project grantees, the following specific recommendations address these three priority areas:

1. Use proceedings of the May 1994 national symposium on the lessons learned through AOCAP as a blueprint for future policy and program development within the veterans and human services systems.
2. Identify ways to bridge barriers between systems by identifying mutual goals and collaborative efforts to achieve them.
3. Maximize existing systems, processes, and resources to reflect and incorporate the unique needs of Vietnam veterans and their families. Specific systems that currently have responsibility for services in this area include the VA; the Administration on Developmental Disabilities and the Maternal and Child Health Bureau within the Department of Health and Human Services; the Department of Defense; and the Department of Education.
4. Develop individually and jointly funded initiatives at the federal, state, and local levels that exemplify innovative ways to address areas of need, such as increased public awareness, enhanced service coordination, and collaborative efforts in planning and service delivery.
5. Initiate a federal interagency work group, consisting of representatives from the agencies listed above, to develop recommendations for addressing issues identified by the

systems change process within and among each agency. This group could also provide direction and technical assistance to state and local governments in developing similar initiatives.

6. Implement a process to assist AOCAP project grantees in accessing creative funding sources such as public-private partnerships as a means for ensuring continuity of services.

Over the past five years, the AOCAP network has managed to adapt and respond effectively to changes in society and in service systems. The network has helped to design model intervention strategies tailored to the needs of Vietnam veterans and their families. Sustained implementation of these outcomes can have a long-term positive impact on both veterans' families and the systems that serve them.

To succeed with these challenges and opportunities, coordinated leadership initiatives must evolve on local, state, and national levels to maximize the potential for success (Masnick and Bane, 1980):

> What is the appropriate public response to these patterns of family needs? To juggle our institutions—education, health care, taxation, housing, work, social security, the law and so on—to accommodate the changing needs of families is seen by some as supporting the very forces that have thrown the family into a tailspin. But to defend current institutional arrangements in these areas or to implement new policies in the hopes of reversing trends in family and household structure that are viewed as undesirable would be to risk swimming against the tide of social change and thereby to ignore the emerging future needs of the American people.

Conclusion

In an address to an AOCAP conference in November 1991, Judge Weinstein observed:

> We have no illusions about the ability of this limited Settlement Fund to create a whole new and fully comprehensive system of services for Vietnam veterans and their families. Nor can we hope that the programs we fund through the Agent Orange Class Assistance Program will reach all of those who are in need of help. We can, however, continue to break down the barriers between the often isolated community of Vietnam veterans and the modern world of human services.
>
> The human services systems in this country have evolved into a complex of myriad independent agencies, complicated and widely varying eligibility requirements, confusing geographic catchment areas and overly bureaucratic processes. This is especially frustrating for veterans' families with needs relating to children with disabilities.

Similar sentiments were expressed by Vietnam veteran and AOCAP Advisory Board member Gary May during the same conference:

> This is, indeed, a unique opportunity for us all. It's an opportunity for us, individually and collectively, to make a difference. For those of us who are Vietnam veterans it's an important, perhaps once in a lifetime opportunity, for us to be a part of creating a positive legacy out of our very confusing and confused experiences in Vietnam. For those who are also in the social service delivery system and have historically dealt with people with developmental disabilities, it's a golden opportunity for us to recognize legitimate reasonable linkages between our efforts and the efforts of many others that have been occurring simultaneously and parallel for too many years.
>
> The challenge for us all is to understand the individuality of the veteran, the person with the developmental disability, and to arrange for a service delivery plan which recognizes those unique features of the groups. We need to challenge ourselves to

continue to press the frontier by making new contacts and insuring that we're always out there looking for new recruits and new allies to assist us in our efforts. We must be willing to take calculated and reasonable risks to expand the frontier of service delivery to insure that we reach the maximum number of people that we need to be reaching. And each of us needs to be unabashed in our willingness to make a commitment to make a difference.

If the challenges are many, the lessons to be learned from the growing successes of the AOCAP experience are equally abundant. With sustained collaborative efforts at the local, state, and national levels, an integrated service model is evolving that can better serve families of Vietnam veterans who need assistance from multiple systems. AOCAP projects have demonstrated in representative settings across this nation that service systems can collaborate and provide needed, integrated services to families. The principal challenge is to move the responsibility and mandate for this coordination and these outcomes to publicly supported service systems at the local, state, and federal levels. Systems change is the means by which the AOCAP network can collaborate with service systems to plan and manage this transition and achieve desired and sustained services and supports for Vietnam veterans and their families.

References

"Agent Orange" Product Liability Litigation. MDL No. 381. United States District Court, E.D. New York. Sept. 25, 1984, as modified.

Bennis, W. 1966. *Beyond Bureaucracy*. New York: McGraw-Hill.

Bennis, W., K. Benne, and R. Chin. 1985. *The Planning of Change*, 4th ed. New York: Holt, Rinehart & Winston.

Hagen, E.E. 1962. *On the Theory of Social Change.* The Dorsey Press.

LePierre, R.T. 1965. *Social Change.* New York: McGraw-Hill.

Lippitt, R., J. Watson, and B. Wesley. 1958. *The Dynamics of Planned Change.* New York: Harcourt Brace & Co.

Masnick, G., and M.J. Bane. 1980. *The Nations Families 1960-1990.* Boston: Auburn House Publishing Co.

May, G. 1991. Presentation to the AOCAP National Training Conference.

Surles, R.C., A.K. Blanch, D.L. Shern, and S.A. Donahue. 1992. Service Coordination as a Strategy for Systems Change. *Health Affairs* II(1).

Weinstein, Hon. J.B. 1991. Presentation to the AOCAP National Training Conference.

Acknowledgments

The authors gratefully acknowledge the contributions of Dr. Judith Holt of the University of Arkansas UAP, James Hudson, AOCAP project officer of Denver, CO, and Elaine Eklund, associate director of AOCAP.

AOCAP Service Coordination: Conceptual Framework, Outcomes, and Policy Implications

**Judith M. Holt, Ph.D.; Kathy Norris, B.S.N.;
Cathy Liles, M.S.E.; and Mark E. Swanson, M.D.
University of Arkansas University Affiliated Program
Little Rock, AR**

Abstract

A major component of the Agent Orange Class Assistance Program (AOCAP) is provision of service coordination to families of Vietnam veterans. Service coordination aims to address the concerns and priorities of families as well as individual family members, to support families' access to formal and informal resources, and to enable families to use resources in a way that enhances their competencies and skills. This value base of service coordination provides the framework for various implementation strategies used by AOCAP grantees. Outcomes of service coordination can be identified in both quantitative and qualitative terms.

The theoretical perspectives form a foundation for a more intensive examination of these principles as applied by the AOCAP grantees. Based on these findings, the authors offer recommendations for policy planners in examining the efficacy and viability of proactive, family-guided service coordination. Implications for structuring service initiatives from the federal and state level and strategies to more effectively use service coordination are identified.

Judith M. Holt, Ph.D., *is assistant professor at the University of Arkansas for Medical Sciences, Department of Pediatrics. She is also the interdisciplinary training director of the University of Arkansas University Affiliated Program.* ***Kathy Norris, B.S.N.,*** *is director of Project Access for the program.* ***Cathy Liles, M.S.E.,*** *serves as outreach training director of the program.* ***Mark E. Swanson, M.D.,*** *is an associate professor at the University of Arkansas for Medical Sciences, Department of Pediatrics, and the director of the program.*

The Agent Orange Class Assistance Program (AOCAP) was established with funds from the settlement of the class action suit brought by veterans and their families against the chemical companies that produced herbicides used by the United States military in Vietnam. The focus of AOCAP is to address the needs and concerns of Vietnam veterans and their families. AOCAP has currently awarded grants to seventy-four veterans' organizations, disability agencies, family service agencies, and national support projects throughout the United States. Interwoven throughout the broad AOCAP goals and the more specific grantee program objectives are the concepts of increased access, coordination, and integration of systems and services through effective service coordination principles. Based on national and regional training and ongoing technical assistance activities, all AOCAP grantees incorporated principles of service coordination not only into the workscope of each of their programs but on a daily basis with the Vietnam veterans and their families that they serve. The outcomes of these extensive service coordination activities have had an impact on families and service systems and have set the stage for future directions for AOCAP. This paper examines service coordination from a theoretical perspective and the benefits of its application within the AOCAP network and suggests implications for structuring future service initiatives.

Origin of Service Coordination

In 1863, the Commonwealth of Massachusetts, through its Board of Charities, initiated "an effort to coordinate public human services and to conserve public funds used in the care of the poor and the sick" (Weil et al., 1985, p. 4). From these attempts to assist vulnerable populations, the roots of case management emerged as did the tension between the ethic of aid to persons in need and the requirement to judiciously utilize and conserve public resources. Through settlement houses and charity organization societies, the concepts of service coordination and accountability were implemented in the early 1900s. Weil (1985) noted that the growth and role of case management were a reflection of the increasingly industrial and urban nature of the United States and the complexity of social, health, and human service systems. During the 1960s and early 1970s, when there was a rapid growth in categorical social programs, fragmented social service delivery systems, deinstitutionalization of persons with mental illness and mental retardation, and escalating numbers of demonstration projects, case management was introduced into the mainstream of the social service delivery systems. Medicaid and Medicare initiated federal reimbursement for these services and by the 1980s, case management was widely utilized across multiple state programs (Vourlekis, 1992).

Although case management's process and functions have been described and implemented in various ways, it may be defined as "a set of logical steps and a process of interaction within a service network which assure that a client receives needed services in a supportive, effective, efficient, and cost-effective manner" (Weil et al., 1985, p. 2).

The philosophical context of case management is described by Levine and Fleming (1984), Weil and Karb (1985), and Dunst and Trivette (1987), as follows:

1. The needs of families are unique, wide ranging, and vary over time; therefore, the system must be flexible.
2. Families can function in the community when provided with varying degrees of support and should be encouraged to function as independently as possible.
3. Families should be encouraged to assume an active, rather than passive, role in the case management process.

4. Case management is not a time-limited service but rather is ongoing and provides families with what they need, when they need it, and when they want it, for as long as necessary.

Though the concepts of self-determination, dignity, and independence of the families were clearly articulated throughout casework literature, the nature of the vulnerable populations served (e.g., elderly, economically and socially disadvantaged, persons with mental or physical disabilities, young children), unwieldy case loads, increasing paperwork requirements, and an undervalued role within the social service system often resulted in case managers who had a lack of time, skills, and authority, and a perceived lack of concern (McDonald, 1989). With a narrow focus on resource procurement and the steadily mounting demands of system mandates and billing requirements, case managers inadvertently contributed to long-term dependency and learned helplessness by not emphasizing and promoting the family's capacities and competencies (Dunst and Trivette, 1989).

New perspectives emerged in the late 1980s when professionals reexamined the ways in which services and supports were routinely provided to disadvantaged populations and to persons with disabilities. Traditional practices had targeted remediating the specific deficits of an individual with professionally constructed and implemented interventions. These models are slowly being replaced with a more holistic, consumer-driven, community-based approach that looks at the child in the context of the family and the family in the context of its environment. Interagency coordination and collaboration received an increasing emphasis as it became clear that a single agency could not address the multiple services and supports required by a family.

Weick (1989) suggested that policy makers and providers need to keep in mind that *all* people (regardless of disadvantage or disability) need to:

- Be seen, first of all, as people;
- Experience love and friendship;
- Experience continuity in their lives, especially in relation to the people who are important to them;
- Be respected and treated with dignity;
- Have access to opportunities and information, to make choices and to exercise their rights;
- Have a decent and appropriate place to live;
- Have meaningful employment and contribute to the community; and
- Have opportunities to continue to learn throughout their lives.

Out of this philosophy and context of systemic change, assumptions regarding case management also underwent significant alteration. The term "service coordination" was introduced as a more proactive, family-friendly term than the somewhat impersonal and clinical "case management." The areas of emphasis within service coordination were congruent with the emerging perspectives of how services and supports should be designed and provided. The following principles are representative of current practices in service coordination.

1. The empowerment model serves as the basis for service coordination. It encompasses the belief that all individuals and families have strengths and that the family should determine its own priorities, concerns, and choice of solutions. This is a significant shift from the older medical model that focused on diseases and deficits and accorded the family only a passive role with professionals often determining both the needs and solutions. Empowerment is defined "as family identification and recognition of needs, the ability to deploy competencies to obtain resources to meet needs, and self-attributions about the role family members played in accessing resources and meeting needs" (Dunst and Trivette, 1989, p. 94).

2. Service coordination is an ongoing process with varying functions and levels of intensity. Effective service coordination takes place in families' homes and in the communities where they live rather than in professional offices. Sensitivity to cultural diversity is central to this process and honors families' beliefs, values, and traditions.
3. Because members of families may have multiple concerns and challenges varying from appropriate housing for the family, speech therapy for a child, mental health services for an adolescent, etc., the service coordinator must be able to assist the family in addressing the issues that they have identified as most important and in acquiring services and support from multiple systems. A service coordinator must represent the interests of the family and not be limited by what his or her employing agency may offer.
4. Service coordinators need to assist families in identifying solutions that are available locally, are not stigmatizing, and do not involve extraordinary, extended bureaucratic procedures with limited return for the family. Solutions need to be tailored to fit the family.
5. From a systems perspective a service coordinator must be able to identify gaps in services and resources and develop collaborative coalitions to address these needs.
6. In the process of proactive service coordination, the service coordinator assists the traditional institutional-driven systems to become client-centered systems (Kingsley, 1991).

Vietnam Veterans and Families

These "best practice" principles in service coordination are applied within the AOCAP network with each grantee building on its own unique strengths. This process of incorporation was challenging because the veterans, families, and children present complex issues that include the health, emotional, and educational concerns of each member.

Many Vietnam veterans suspect that their wartime exposure to Agent Orange and other chemicals has caused them and their children to develop serious health problems (NIS, 1993). The uncertainty of the connection between health problems and the exposure to Agent Orange creates ambivalence for families. At this time only five diseases are recognized as being attributed to exposure to Agent Orange. Chloracne (a dermatological disorder), non-Hodgkin's lymphoma, and soft tissue sarcomas were the first three diseases found eligible for government compensation. The National Academy of Sciences (NAS) (NIS, 1993) announced conclusive evidence linking Agent Orange exposure to two additional diseases: a metabolic disorder called porphyria cutanea tarda; and Hodgkin's disease. Further investigation into the suspected linkage of Agent Orange to cancers of the respiratory system, prostate cancer, and multiple myeloma has been encouraged by the NAS (NIS, 1993). While this is progress, the reality of compensation is extremely slow and frustrating for families. Of 69,000 claims filed citing chloracne, non-Hodgkin's lymphoma, or soft tissue sarcomas, 553 claims have been approved and 29,000 are pending (*Arkansas Democrat-Gazette*, 1993).

The connection between the chronic diseases and disabilities of the children of veterans has not been determined. In their review of scientific literature, the NAS concluded the scientific data are inadequate or insufficient as evidence that there is an association between birth defects, childhood cancer in offspring, infertility, testicle cancer, and female reproductive cancer (NIS, 1993). Families remain deeply concerned over unanswered questions and overwhelmed by multiple health problems in their midst. For many families there are health concerns in several members (e.g., a father with post-traumatic stress disorder (PTSD) or Agent Orange–related cancer, a child with dermatological and learning problems, another child with behavioral problems, and a mother without health care resources or supports responsive to the complexity of the family's concerns) (Norris, 1994).

To provide a perspective on the complex problems, it is imperative to recognize the multiplicity of risk factors for these families. Schorr (1988), in a review of innovative programs that had succeeded in changing outcomes for disadvantaged populations, noted that those populations identified as the most vulnerable and at greatest risk of long-term damage were children growing up:

- In persistent poverty;
- In neighborhoods of concentrated poverty and social dislocation;
- In families that are homeless;
- With a parent who is mentally ill, alcoholic, or drug addicted; and
- With an isolated parent.

After reviewing demographic descriptors, fiscal resources, and major concerns of veterans and families receiving AOCAP services in Arkansas and Mississippi, planners found that 50 percent of the families had children who would be included in one or more of these categories, and 17 percent of the families had children who had more than one risk descriptor (Norris, 1994). Scott et al. (1994) report that a survey of 60,000 Vietnam veterans, conducted by the William Joiner Center for the Study of War and Social Consequences, found that 23.5 percent reported some degree of PTSD and 19.7 percent had a child with birth defects. In view of the multiple risk factors that challenge Vietnam veterans and their families, it is evident that the AOCAP grantees faced complicated, long-standing issues in providing appropriate supports and services.

The grantees had an additional responsibility that was integral to effectively addressing veterans' and families' needs. They had to master the intricacies of multiple local, state, and federal agencies that provide services, supports, and fiscal resources. Some of these agencies included the U.S. Department of Veterans Affairs (VA), Social Security Administration, Medicaid, special education services, rehabilitative services, health departments, developmental disabilities services, housing, post-secondary education, and community action programs.

System Change

In designing and implementing the AOCAP programs, agencies applied "best practice" principles of service coordination in the context of the families' interwoven, often emotionally charged, concerns and priorities. This served as the impetus for grantees to innovate, reassess, collaborate, and continually seek creative means of strengthening and supporting the families. Within this process, the AOCAP grantees became change agents. Acting as a catalyst, assisting the process, finding solutions, linking resources, and stabilizing and internalizing changes, the grantees have provided rich and varied experiences that help us understand how effective services and supports can be designed and delivered and how future services might be implemented and funded.

Schorr (1988), in describing programs that successfully addressed issues of poverty, health care, and social disadvantage, suggested that if such programs are to be widely implemented there are several challenges that must be addressed including:

- Knowing what works;
- Proving we can afford it;
- Attracting and training enough skilled and committed personnel; and
- Devising a variety of replication strategies.

Each of these challenges will be discussed in the context of the experiences and recommendations from four AOCAP grantees: the New England Consortium of eleven AOCAP grantees in Massachusetts, Maine, Rhode Island, and Connecticut (Scott et al., 1994); the Missouri

Vietnam Veterans Education and Resource System (MOVVERS), which provides services in the Ozark Mountain region of south central Missouri and Kansas City (Summers, Horn, Lazar, and Ritter, 1994); the Montana Vietnam Veterans Children's Assistance Program (VVCAP), which provided statewide services (Hollingshead, Harlow, and Belish, E., 1994); and Arkansas' statewide service coordination program, Project Access (Norris, 1994).

Knowing What Works

Although each of the projects had unique catchment areas, funding streams, and agency orientations, it is evident that common successful practices emerged across the projects. The "things that worked" that were common across projects centered on several themes: value base, service coordination, recruitment and intake procedures, access to resources, and inter-agency collaboration.

Value Base

In order to effectively support Vietnam veterans and their families, programs must have a strong value base that is sensitive to veteran, family, and disability issues. The impact of Vietnam has left many veterans cynical, distrustful of "the system," and often socially isolated. A successful AOCAP program must acknowledge these factors and treat both the veteran and family members with respect and dignity. Summers (1994, p. 5) suggests "that service program staff should scrupulously follow standards of best practice with these families: tact, empathy, support, nonjudgmentalness, sensitivity to 'touchy' subjects, and strict attention to confidentiality. It also implies total honesty and total integrity: making no promises one is unable to keep, following through without fail, and taking some immediate action that responds to the family's *expressed* or *perceived* needs rather than the service provider's perception of the family needs."

From the initial contact with the family and throughout the service coordination process, it must be clear that the agenda is the family's. The service coordinator responds to and supports the family's identified issues and pays careful attention to evidence of family members' strengths, skills, and competencies. This value-based approach builds on strengths, is respectful of and acknowledges unique challenges faced by the veterans and their families, and develops services and supports that are family-friendly, nonstigmatizing, culturally sensitive, and designed to enhance independence and self-sufficiency.

Service Coordination Recruitment and Intake

Each project identified the recruitment and intake component of the service coordination process as crucial to a successful program. Veterans who have avoided or deliberately limited contact with state and federal agencies are not likely, at this point, to spontaneously seek new programs or services. Among the eleven grantees in the New England Consortium, efforts to coordinate outreach activities and develop a mechanism for a single point of entry were priorities. A brochure outlining available services with contact names and telephone numbers (as well as a toll-free telephone number) streamlined the referral process. The Vietnam Veterans Children's Assistance Program in Montana and the New England Consortium initiated aggressive outreach efforts. In Montana, program staff "routinely travel to remote regions of their catchment areas and work with local resources, including meeting job service staff, Veterans of Foreign Wars and American Legion members, and public school staff. They set up tables wherever space might be available to sit down with veterans in those communities and discuss their needs for services" (Hollingshead et al., 1994). A public service video featuring Senator John Kerry was used to inform veterans and their families in the northeastern United States. Outreach efforts occurred within numerous communities, including veterans' organizations, family service organizations, and school systems. Both general outreach efforts (media, radio, newspapers) and targeted outreach efforts (meeting with local veterans' groups, educating professionals) ensure that eligible families will become aware of the service. The system must continue to use formal and informal networks on an ongoing basis.

The intake process itself should be informal with an emphasis on listening to each family member. Within this process, establishing a one-to-one relationship and building trust with the veteran and family members is imperative. An informal, friendly discussion is more useful than formal intake evaluations. During the intake and assessment phase, it was evident among all the programs that the concerns and needs identified by the families were wide ranging and crossed almost every service system boundary. Many families identified multiple areas of concern, some of which were long standing. Other families were in perpetual crisis for so many years that they appeared either numb or indifferent to proposed support. To address this problem the programs used referral techniques judiciously. "These participants wanted their informational needs met by someone who could 'cut to the chase' and simply provide the answer. As one veteran put it, 'Yeah, I know there is the VA, there are vet reps, there are 800 numbers, but I want help and answers. Who can I call to get that and not more bureaucratic crap?' " (Summers et al., 1994, pp. 12–13). Instead of over-reliance on information and referral activities, successful programs walked through the process with the participant family. That is, the service coordinator may have accompanied the family to complete an application for Supplemental Security Income (SSI) for their child or to an individualized education program (IEP) meeting at the school. Service coordinators worked at a pace that the families were comfortable with and did not impose an artificial sense of urgency on them.

Providing Access to Resources

One of the most difficult and challenging areas of developing programs that work was in accessing resources. Hollingshead et al. (1994, pp. 12-13) emphasized the following principles in providing access to resources:

1. Sensitivity to the family's circumstances, concerns, social structure, culture, biases, and reluctance to appeal for aid (welfare in their perspective) or to struggle with organizations such as the VA or the Social Security Administration.

2. Active pursuit of goods or services at reduced rates whenever the family's circumstances warrant. Emphasis is placed on assuring quality goods or services at minimum cost, using funding from other sources whenever possible.

3. Securing the funding arrangements such as SSI, Medicaid, VA disability monies, etc. which will provide families with far-reaching, long-term solutions to their concerns as opposed to simply purchasing an item and not addressing broader problems.

AOCAP programs crossed agency lines, using multiple funding streams and nontraditional resources when providing services. Examples of nontraditional resources utilized by the AOCAP grantee in Arkansas included:

- University of Tennessee School of Dentistry providing free examinations and discounting services for veterans and their children from Arkansas;
- College student in Magnolia acting as tutor for a child with spina bifida during the summer months to help him catch up with class;
- Fire Department helping build a wheelchair ramp;
- Ministerial Alliance paying for a room so that parents can stay close to hospitalized child;
- Arkansas Power and Light's "Project Deserve," administered by local Red Cross, paying up to $100 on delinquent electric bills for families with children with disabilities;
- Southwestern Bell "Reach Out Arkansas" Program discounting phone hook-up and prorating payments for rural family with daughter who has epilepsy and sleep apnea;
- Local women's service groups helping with transportation, birthday presents, and food; and
- Churches and Sunday school classes donating time and money.

Interagency Collaboration

During the process of providing access to services it became evident to the AOCAP grantees that for many families, innovative solutions had to be developed. In numerous circumstances no single funding source or agency could adequately address the identified need and only through collaboration could successful solutions be identified. Scott et al. (1994) describes an unemployed veteran who needed to obtain specially processed infant food for his daughter, who was on a highly restrictive diet. The family had already incurred significant costs in obtaining medical services for their daughter. Initially, the family contacted a family service agency, a New England Consortium member. This agency contacted corporate producers of infant food as well as food banks. A second consortium member, a veteran services agency, arranged transportation, and a third consortium agency coordinated the process for getting the food to the family. This illustrates a collaborative response to a singular need; anecdotal records indicate numerous other creative solutions with the AOCAP grantee serving as the catalyst to initiate change.

At the system level, the identification of gaps in services served as the mechanism for collaborating agencies to develop new procedures and strategies for addressing needs that had been previously unmet. The New England Consortium, cognizant of and in response to the concerns of veterans and their families, made significant steps toward systemic change. These eleven grantees in collaborative enterprise moved from agenda-setting to developing both fiscal and service strategies and assessing and reassessing their activities and outcomes on a family and system basis (Scott et al., 1994).

As these steps were implemented, consortium members revised their intake procedures to ensure that class members were identified and collected information was relevant to a number of potential service needs. These relatively straightforward procedures were implemented throughout agencies and resulted, for example, in encouraging staff of developmental disability programs to inquire of all new referrals whether a family member was a Vietnam veteran. These collaborative efforts pushed each agency to become not only more responsive to individual needs but also to move beyond their traditional boundaries. Disability program staff, for instance, learned about PTSD and its impact on a family, how to work with the VA, and where mental health services could be obtained. Veterans' organizations began to understand family systems, IEPs, and SSI for children; family service agencies became knowledgeable about disability services, the effect of secondary PTSD, and veterans' benefits. This process of intensive collaboration shifted the programs and procedures as well as the capacity of the systems to provide more sensitive and articulate responses to the needs of Vietnam veterans and their families.

Attracting and Training Enough Skilled and Committed Personnel

A program cannot be successful without personnel who are both competent and caring. Within the AOCAP grantees, the personnel employed included veterans, spouses and children of veterans, parents of children with disabilities, nurses, community liaisons, clinical psychologists, social workers, and special educators. The diversity of their backgrounds, training, and experiences invigorated and stimulated the network. Several relevant issues emerged from the mixture of personnel and perspectives. The need for a veteran's presence is significant. For Vietnam veterans, often estranged from the social service system and suspicious and hostile toward the government and the VA, someone who can "walk the walk and talk the talk" must be a member of the team. Initially, Vietnam veterans were often most comfortable with other veterans. Grantee personnel who were veterans provided valuable insight and strategies on VA programs and benefits. Nevertheless, the veteran perspective was not the single focus. Expertise from clinical specialists, special educators, or community liaisons trained as service coordinators was needed to effectively address the "whole" family as well as the intricate interagency concerns. Grantees met this need through direct employment of staff as well as collaborative staffing between and among agencies.

Within the New England Consortium, initial staff training focused on informing all staff of the programs available within each agency and the procedures for working with them. Emphasis was placed on ensuring confidentiality, responsiveness, and sensitivity. In-service presentations and site visits added to staff competencies. Quarterly consortium meetings provided an ongoing forum for identification of barriers, solutions, and training opportunities (Scott et al., 1994).

Summers et al. (1994) examined this issue from another perspective, suggesting that the primary characteristics of peer-directed programs are evident in many AOCAP grantees. The strength of veterans and their family members is acknowledged in all aspects of the organization's functions. However, to address all of the concerns of the families, it is often useful to involve staff representing several perspectives.

Project Access, the AOCAP grantee in Arkansas, has a staff composed of veterans, family members, and professionals (e.g., nurse, social worker, two Vietnam veterans, spouse of veteran, and child of veteran). All staff have been through extensive training in service coordination and ongoing training in communication with families and resource development. The project director acts as a regional service coordinator and makes home visits as part of on-the-job training and monitoring with the service coordinators. Communication between service coordinators in the field is encouraged to develop a shared experience and knowledge base. This staff composition with the strengths and varying perspectives of the staff members provides the basis for meeting diverse and multilevel needs of the veterans and their families.

Proving We Can Afford It

Perhaps the determination of whether we can afford these programs and services is to ask, "Can we afford not to provide them?" Based on the results of four years of AOCAP programs, it is clear that the challenges and concerns faced by veterans and their families cannot be readily resolved. With the passage of time, the concerns have become more embedded and less easily extricated and addressed. The age of the children served is indicative of the problem. The majority of the children are in their teens or early twenties. The frequent absence of consistent adequate health care, the compounding of emotional, learning, and behavioral problems, and the reality that even tenuous supports and services are often nonexistent for young adults brings the question of cost into sharp focus. The cost of supporting an adult on public assistance for a number of years is certainly less than aggressively trying to meet his needs now. For instance, in a family support and social service program, the cost was $2,600 per family (1985) compared with $3,600 per capita for foster care, $19,500 for group care, and up to $67,500 for institutional care (Schorr, 1988). These figures provide an example of the savings to the system if families can be supported in their communities.

Effective AOCAP service coordination has assisted families in receiving additional services and supports, including state and federal entitlement programs. For many of these entitlements, the families may have been eligible for extended periods but lacked knowledge of the programs or had been unable to surmount the difficulties in gaining entry. With AOCAP funding used for service coordination, additional resources were leveraged to meet the families' needs.

Devising a Variety of Replication Strategies

AOCAP has not yet completed its mission. As catalysts for systemic change in the provision of services to veterans and their families, agencies have taken significant steps, but several major obstacles remain. Many of the eligible class members and their families, particularly the children, still have significant needs that will require ongoing support and intervention. The veterans and the disability and family service systems are not yet consistently knowledgeable and responsive to the health, education, and social issues of these families. Of paramount importance is the question of how to continue and expand the support needed by veterans and their families and to further address system issues.

The AOCAP grantees have identified what works. But the principles of what works are applied within each program in a manner that is appropriate for the staff, the community, the veterans, and the families. Within each program, there are unique aspects that serve to meet the needs of veterans and families. Principles can be extracted and embedded in other programs, but attempts to replicate an AOCAP program exactly at other sites will not be successful. "Every program successfully serving high-risk populations has some attributes that are fragile, involve complex human relationships, and do not lend themselves to mass production" (Schorr, 1988). An AOCAP program in Massachusetts should not look exactly like a program in Arkansas. In any replication effort, the guiding principles should be adopted, rather than establishing arbitrary guidelines for staff qualifications, funding sources, or supporting agencies.

One of the factors that has contributed to the successes of AOCAP grantees was the minimal paperwork required by AOCAP. Paperwork, to a limited extent, is needed for documentation and continuity. However, the onerous paperwork that often accompanies programs of national scope generally serves to stagnate, not facilitate, the very components that are so critical for success: flexibility, creativity, responsiveness to multiple concerns, and "person centeredness."

With these cautionary notes in mind and based on the recommendations emerging from dialogue with members of the AOCAP network, several options suggest more in-depth exploration:

1. Given its capacity and visibility, the VA could, through its social services units or Vet Centers, provide the community-based outreach needed. In conjunction with the AOCAP grantees, the families currently being served could be brought within the VA system (Hollingshead et al., 1994). The VA has the fiscal and human resources to accomplish this, but a comprehensive reevaluation and expansion of its mission, intensive staff training, and overall procedural realignment would be required to ensure responsiveness, a holistic view, and sensitivity to the full range of veteran, family, and children's issues. AOCAP should collaborate with the VA to test this model in at least two sites and evaluate both the process and outcomes using significant input from the veterans and families served.

2. Geographically linked consortia (e.g., New England Consortium) could seek broad-based public funding, increased contractual support, and state and federal grants by leveraging their collective expertise and seeking resources with multiple funding components (Scott et al., 1994). Each agency would need to determine its essential fiscal needs and, with AOCAP technical assistance, design strategies to locate funding from multiple sources. AOCAP could add its credibility and expertise to the process through assistance with grant development and by targeting emerging federal initiatives.

3. A regional alliance of programs (across states) could provide assistance and training to local programs, serve as a funding advocate, and perhaps provide central administrative support (Summers et al., 1994). With no overlapping catchment areas, similar missions, and a commitment to the concept, this potential configuration should be further explored with attention paid to identifying possible funding sources for the central administrative functions.

4. AOCAP could design with relevant federal agencies a funding stream that could be used by individual grantees. This may require interagency dedication of funds, although the possibility of a single agency source should also be explored.

5. Grantees need to explore potential funding within each state to support their service coordination activities. The following are possible resources:

   - Medicaid (Title XIX of the Social Security Act) provides health care benefits to income-eligible individuals. Service coordination (defined as case management by

Medicaid) can be obtained through several programs such as targeted case management, waiver programs, and early periodic screening diagnosis and treatment.

- Title XX of the Social Security Act is the largest, most flexible block grant available to the states to support human service activities. These activities must be nonmedical in nature and delivered in the community. Allowable services include training and direct services and are usually targeted to vulnerable populations (e.g., elders, persons with developmental disabilities, children in foster care and protective services).
- Title V of the Social Security Act, the Maternal and Child Health (MCH) Block Grant, is a federal program of grants to states to provide family-centered, community-based, and coordinated care to children and mothers. A portion of the fund is targeted toward children with special health needs. Coordinated care includes the basic principles of service coordination.
- The Administration on Developmental Disabilities provides funds to each state to support a Developmental Disabilities Planning Council. This consumer-driven council provides funds for innovative programs to support children and adults with developmental disabilities and their families.

AOCAP could assist in this process by providing technical assistance and support to AOCAP grantees interested in exploring specific funding possibilities in their states.

Conclusion

What AOCAP grantees have learned should be applied across the range of human service programs and should significantly revise policies and procedures to ensure that:

- A strong value base of respect for the integrity of the family is established;
- An emphasis is placed on people, not paper;
- Collaborative partnerships with families, built on family strengths and capabilities, are developed and maintained;
- Creativity, flexibility, and a focus on the whole are emphasized; and
- Traditional agency boundaries are redesigned so that services can be accessed for veterans and their families in an effective and timely manner.

The legacy of AOCAP, and the Vietnam veterans and families that they serve, should provide a catalyst for change by expanding and enhancing the capacity of agencies to become partners in the long healing process.

References

Dunst, E., and C. Trivette. 1987. Enabling and empowering families: Conceptual and intervention issues. *School Psychology Review* 16:443-456.

Dunst, E., and C. Trivette. 1989. An enablement and empowerment perspective of case management. *Topics in Early Childhood Special Education* 8(4):87-100.

Hollingshead, G., M. Harlow, and E. Belish. 1994. A family-focused resource coordination model for the U.S. Department of Veterans Affairs. Unpublished manuscript.

Kingsley, C. 1991. *A Guide to Case Management for At-Risk Youth.* Boston, MA: Center for Human Resources at Brandeis University.

Levine, I., and M. Fleming. 1984. *Human Resource Development: Issues in Case Management.* Baltimore, MD: Center of Rehabilitation and Manpower Services.

McDonald, R. 1989. The search for one-stop shopping. In *Case Management: Historical, Current, and Future Directions*, ed. M. Ling, P. McAnnally, and C. Weick. Cambridge, MA: Brookline Books.

National Information System for Vietnam Veterans and Their Families. 1993. *NIS Information Sheet: Health Effects of Agent Orange.* Columbia, SC: Center for Developmental Disabilities.

Norris, K. 1994. Project Access: The Arkansas experience. Unpublished manuscript.

Schorr, L. 1988. *Within Our Reach: Breaking the Cycle of Disadvantage.* New York: Doubleday.

Scott, F., D. Crane, Y. Simon-Alvarez, and J. DeResta. 1994. A consortium for services to Vietnam veterans and their families: An innovative model for serving the veterans' community. Unpublished manuscript.

Summers, J., K. Horn, A. Lazar, and C. Ritter. 1994. Designing veteran family assistance services to meet the needs and preferences of Vietnam veterans who have children with special needs. Unpublished manuscript.

Arkansas Democrat-Gazette. July 1993. Two more diseases linked to Agent Orange.

Vourlekis, B. 1992. The policy and professional context of case management practice. In *Social Work Case Management*, ed. B. Vourlekis and R. Greene. New York: Aldine De Gruyter.

Weil, M., J. Karls, and Associates. 1985. *Case Management in Human Service Practice.* San Francisco: Jossey-Bass.

Wieck, C. 1989. A new way of thinking for case managers. In *Case Management: Historical, Current, and Future Directions,* ed. M. Linz, P. McAnnally, and C. Wieck. Cambridge, MA: Brookline Books.

Acknowledgment

This paper was supported by the University of Arkansas University Affiliated Program, 1120 Marshall Street, Suite 306, Little Rock, Arkansas 72202.

The Outcomes of a Services Evaluation for Families of Vietnam Veterans with Children with Disabilities in the Baltimore Metropolitan Area

Peter La Count, M.Ed.; Richard Iams, B.S.;
Jim Thomas, M.Ed., Major, United States Air Force (ret.); and Carolyn Mosher, B.A.

The Vietnam Veterans Family Support Project (VVFSP)
The Kennedy Krieger Institute
Baltimore, MD

Abstract

The Vietnam Veterans Family Support Project (VVFSP), located at the Kennedy Krieger Institute in Baltimore, MD, has been providing family-centered support services to families of Vietnam veterans who have children with disabilities since July 1990. The purpose of the VVFSP study was to: demographically describe the families associated with VVFSP; gain insight as to the quality and quantity of services offered by VVFSP; provide families with a method to rate their satisfaction with the services provided by VVFSP; and have the therapists involved with VVFSP families add insight concerning their working relationships with families of Vietnam veterans who have children with disabilities.

Demographic information was gathered on thirty-seven VVFSP families who were active during the period of September 1992 through August 1993. Thirty-one of these families were interviewed for the study. Researchers found that more than half the families associated with the project had at least one child with a mental health-related diagnosis. The family-centered service approach received an approval rating of more than 80 percent for all questions asked of clients. The project appears to be providing significant benefits to its target population. Because the inquiry covered a small population, more research is needed to determine if these mental health needs in children are typical of all families of Vietnam veterans.

***Peter La Count, M.Ed.**, is the project coordinator for the Vietnam Veterans Family Support Project (VVFSP) at the Kennedy Krieger Institute's Community Resources. **Richard Iams, B.S.**, is a data analyst at the Kennedy Krieger Institute's Family Center; **Jim Thomas, M.Ed., USAF (ret.)**, is a VVFSP volunteer and served as editor for this paper; and **Carolyn Mosher, B.A.**, works for the Kennedy Krieger Institute's Community Resources and assisted with the family interviews for this paper.*

The purposes of the Vietnam Veterans Family Support Project (VVFSP) service evaluation are fourfold:

- To describe the population studied;
- To determine the quantity and quality of services offered;
- To provide a method for families to rate their satisfaction with services; and
- To describe the families who receive support services from the perspectives of therapists.

The paper begins with a brief description of VVFSP, its criteria for services, and the services it offers to families. A demographic outline of the families who are receiving services from VVFSP—both for mental health and physiologically based diagnoses of VVFSP children—and the number of family contacts by VVFSP staff follows. The paper then describes the services offered by VVFSP, the numbers of families and individuals in the family who are making use of those services, and services received from other agencies.

A compilation of the qualitative and quantitative information gathered from the family interviews follows the description of services. (Thirty-seven families received services during the year studied (September 1992 to August 1993). Of these thirty-seven families, thirty-one were interviewed by telephone.)

The final section of the paper consists of interviews with six therapists (two educational specialists, two speech and language pathologists, one social worker, and one occupational therapist). These therapists were interviewed to determine if children with disabilities who were born into or live in a family where one parent is a Vietnam veteran differ from a cohort of 260 other children with disabilities with whom the therapists work.

The Vietnam Veterans Family Support Project

The Vietnam Veterans Family Support Project offers family-centered support services to families of Baltimore-area Vietnam veterans who have children with disabilities. It has operated under the direction of the Department for Individual and Family Resources of the Kennedy Krieger Institute since July 1990. The project employs two full-time staff persons—a project coordinator who oversees the day-to-day program operations and a planning coordinator who coordinates services offered to the families—and a team of occupational therapists, physical therapists, social workers, speech and language pathologists, and special educators. These therapists work with families on an ongoing basis.

Use of the family-centered concept is the key to the success of VVFSP's home-based support program. According to Roberts (1988), the basic tenet of the family-centered concept is that parents are the most able caregivers for their children. Families are the "experts" on their children, thus, service coordinators work most effectively when they act as consultants to families. When provided with accurate information, parents are the most qualified decision makers for their children (see Table 1) (Roberts, 1988).

Criteria for Receiving Services

VVFSP provides services to families based on the following criteria:

- A birth parent must have served in Southeast Asia between the years 1961 and 1972;
- At least one child born to the identified veteran parent must have a disability;
- Families must live in the Baltimore metropolitan area; and
- Participation in VVFSP is completely voluntary.

Table 1. Basic Tenets of the Family-Centered Concept

■ Families are generally composed of able caregivers.
■ The goal of the support program is to ensure stability and preserve the family unit.
■ Families are best able to make decisions about which outside services can and should be brought into the home to support their family.
■ Decisions about families should be guided by the family's strengths, needs, and desires.
■ Support programs should be designed to help families reach their potential.
■ Cultural sensitivity should be observed at all times.
■ Support systems should be built around existing community services.
■ Support services should be grounded in solid research and program development from which families and staff continue to build.

Description of Services

VVFSP provides a number of family-centered, home-based services for families. Families decide which services to receive and when and how frequently to receive them. Services offered by VVFSP include:

1. **Service Coordination**—to help families find and coordinate community resources to meet their needs. VVFSP bridges the gap between veterans and developmental disabilities service providers in the community to provide these services.
2. **Home-Based Professional Services**—to provide an occupational therapist, physical therapist, social worker, or speech and language pathologist. These specialists meet with families on a weekly or bi-weekly basis and provide parents with hands-on training to help their children to overcome barriers.
3. **Educational Advocacy—**to help parents through the special education process. Educators can assist teachers and parents with developing behavior plans for children in the school and the home. They can also advocate for families at annual review and dismissal (ARD) meetings and in the development of the individual education plan (IEP).
4. **Financial Assistance**—to help families purchase items or services that would not be affordable or available to them otherwise. This may include help to build ramps, obtain respite care, see a medical specialist, pay utility bills, or buy special equipment for the child with disabilities.
5. **Support Groups for Parents**—to help families make contact with other families who have children with disabilities. Parents can gather together once a month to exchange information and gain mutual support from one another.
6. **Educational Workshops for Parents**—to help families with a variety of topics including self-advocacy and behavior management skills, planning for the child's future, and understanding educational placements.
7. **Book, Toy, and Equipment Lending Library**—to help families learn more about their child's disability and available resources.

VVFSP Demographics

One of the purposes of this study was to document the diagnoses of the children of the Vietnam veterans participating in our program and compare the numbers of children with mental health and physiologically based diagnoses. Another goal was to determine which VVFSP

Table 2. Diagnoses of Children

Diagnosis	Number of Occurrences
Mental Health Diagnoses (26 or 32% of total diagnoses)	
Attention deficit hyperactivity disorder	13
Depression	8
Schizophreniform disorder	1
Secondary PTSD	2
Oppositional defiant disorder	1
Anxiety disorder	1
Physiologically Based Diagnoses (53 or 68% of total diagnoses)	
Mental retardation	4
Learning disabled	10
Pervasive developmental disorder	2
Physical birth defects	2
Cerebral palsy	4
Speech/language delay	8
Hearing impairment	2
Blindness, low vision	4
Hydrocephalus	1
Thyroid dysfunction	1
Erb palsy	1
Asthma	1
Seizure disorder	2
Wernicke's aphasia	1
Traumatic brain injury	1
Russel-Silver syndrome	1
Degenerative central nervous disorder	1
Endocrine disease	1
Minimal brain dysfunction	1
Stroke	1
Hypotonia	1
Femur focal disorder	1
Williams Syndrome	1
Allergies	1
No. of Families with Children with a Mental Health vs. Physiologically Based Diagnosis	
Mental health diagnoses	19
Physiologically based diagnoses	18

services were used most often and which Vietnam veteran family members used them most often. The numbers of home visits to families who have a child with a mental health diagnosis and those with a physiologically based diagnosis were also tallied.

Families become associated with VVFSP by choice. Although they come into the project through a number of channels, the Kennedy Krieger Institute, U.S. Department of Veterans Affairs (VA) Vet Centers, public service announcements, and self-referrals are the most frequent means by which families reach VVFSP. During their first contact with VVFSP, families are asked to provide background on their family history. VVFSP staff record family participation in VVFSP services and outside services. The number and type of contacts with each family is recorded in contact notes on an ongoing basis.

The diagnostic and service-related information obtained from the thirty-seven families who received services through VVFSP from September 1992 to August 1993 is shown in Tables 2 through 4.

This demographic synopsis of families associated with VVFSP is not an attempt to generalize the characteristics of all families of Vietnam veterans. It is only to describe the families with whom VVFSP works. As stated before, all information gathered by VVFSP is self-reported from the families.

The diagnoses of the children (see Table 2) cover a wide range of disabilities. VVFSP worked with fifty-one children with disabilities during the period of the study. Twenty-eight children were diagnosed with a physiologically related disability, and twenty-three children were diagnosed with a mental health disorder. (Twenty-three children had multiple diagnoses and one child died during the period of the study as a result of his disability.)

When dividing diagnoses into mental health and physiologically based, we found that 32 percent of all diagnoses derived from mental health problems, while 68 percent could be considered physiologically based. We also found that the ratio between families who have at least one child with some mental health diagnosis (nineteen) and families who have at least one child with a physiologically based diagnosis (eighteen) was nearly one-to-one. Of the twenty-six mental health diagnoses, thirteen were for attention deficit hyperactivity disorder (ADHD), eight were for depression, and two were secondary post-traumatic stress disorder (PTSD); one was for oppositional defiant disorder and one was for anxiety disorder. Fifty-three diagnoses were for physiologically related disorders. Of these diagnoses, the most numerous were: ten diagnoses of a learning disability, eight for speech or language delay, four for mental retardation, and four for blindness or low vision.

Table 3. Average Monthly Contacts

Total Average Contacts per Month (All Staff)	Number of Families
Less than 1.0	5
1.0-1.9	11
2.0-2.9	6
3.0-3.9	6
4.0-4.9	1
5.0-5.9	4
6.0-6.9	2
7.0-7.9	1
8.0-8.9	1
Average Monthly Contacts for All Families of Children with:	**Monthly Average**
Mental health diagnosis	4.59
Physiologically based diagnosis	1.78

When measuring the intensity of family needs, the average number of monthly contacts by any staff member is used (see Table 3). In VVFSP's family-centered model, contact is most often decided by family need. Thus, families who have the most needs are usually in contact with some staff member more frequently than families with fewer needs. Contacts are measured by telephone consultations, home visits, and agency visits (visit to VVFSP or another site, but not the home). These contacts were recorded in the form of contact notes, which are logged by staff after each contact with a family. Families with the mental health diagnosis averaged 4.59 contacts per month while families whose child had a physiological need averaged 1.78 contacts per month. It is from these data that we determined that families with at least one child with a mental health diagnosis have the greatest needs.

When measuring the frequency of services from VVFSP, families of veterans who reported receiving services from outside agencies were included in the sample (see Table 4). From this information, the evaluators were able to identify which VVFSP and non-VVFSP services were used by mothers, fathers, and children.

Of the thirty-seven families provided services during the year of the study, all received resource assistance from VVFSP for the parents. Thirty-two mothers received resource assistance, while eighteen fathers received this service. In thirteen families both the mother and father received resource assistance. Some of the more frequently used VVFSP services included: twenty-two individuals (nine mothers, one father, and eleven children) received support funds, twenty children received educational advocacy, nine individuals (five mothers, three children, and one father) received counseling, and six children received speech and language therapy.

Thirty-three of the thirty-seven families in the study received services from sources other than VVFSP (see Table 4). Of these thirty-three families, thirty-two children received special-education services. Other frequent outside sources used by families included: fourteen individuals (two fathers and twelve children) received counseling, thirteen families received some form of financial assistance, and five individuals (three mothers, two fathers, and one child) attended support groups. (Despite the prevalence of mental health needs in the children of the Vietnam veterans, only three received counseling from a VVFSP counselor. Families may have sought mental health services from sources other than the VVFSP for a number of reasons, including: the children were already linked with a mental health provider before coming to VVFSP; the distance to the family's home was too far for a VVFSP counselor to make the appropriate number of home visits; the family preferred going to an already familiar clinic; or the family preferred another provider for insurance reasons.)

Table 4. Services Used by Families

In-Program Services Offered by VVFSP to Families	Mother	Father	Children
Educational advocacy	0	0	20
Tutoring	0	0	4
Counseling	5	1	3
Support groups	0	0	0
Behavioral intervention	0	0	4
Speech therapy	N/A	N/A	6
Occupational therapy	N/A	N/A	3
Physical therapy	N/A	N/A	2
Physical modification of home	1	0	0
Resource assistance for parents	32	18	N/A
Referrals to other agencies	3	1	8
Literature information	3	0	1
Financial assistance			
≤$670	7	1	11
≥$671	2	0	0

Out-of-Program Services Received by Families	Mother	Father	Children
Tutoring	0	0	4
Family therapy	1	0	2
Group therapy	0	0	1
Individual therapy	0	2	12
Support groups	2	2	1
Financial assistance	3	2	8
Veterans' services	0	2	2
Supplemental Security Income (SSI)	0	0	4
Special education services	0	0	32
Home teaching	0	0	1
Occupational therapy	0	0	1
Speech therapy	0	0	2
Physical therapy	0	0	3
Educational advocacy	0	0	2
Long-term home medical care	0	0	4
Legal services	2	0	1
Hospitalization	1	1	1
Vocational training	0	0	1

Responses to VVFSP Family Satisfaction Surveys

Another major purpose of this research was to provide families with the opportunity to give the evaluators feedback regarding their level of satisfaction with VVFSP services. For this purpose the project coordinator developed a standardized family satisfaction interview form that allowed parents to rate the services provided to them by VVFSP staff.

Two university students and one employee of the Kennedy Krieger Institute used the survey to conduct telephone interviews with thirty-one of the thirty-seven families (one parent in each of the thirty-one households) over a three-week period. Families were called or written approximately two weeks before the surveys were administered to obtain their permission to be interviewed. The university students and the employee were not associated with VVFSP beforehand so family members had no previous knowledge of them. To strengthen the internal validity of the study, all three interviewers were given concurrent six-hour in-service training on how the interviews should be conducted. The interviewers read from a previously written script. As reported by the interviewers, the interviews took an average of ten to fifteen minutes to complete.

Six families were not interviewed: three had moved from the area and left no forwarding address or telephone number; and one family declined to be interviewed. Three families did not have telephones and responded to an equivalent mailed written survey; two families without telephones did not.

Because the answers to the free-response questions varied greatly and were determined by specific need, the responses for questions 3, 4, 5, 6, 8, 10, and 13 were divided into five categories: (1) financial support (VVFSP purchase of services); (2) coordination of services; (3) family support (emotional); (4) specialist support; and (5) any combinations. Answers to the survey were as follows.

1. ***Are you satisfied with the services your family receives from Peter/Patricia?***

n = 29		
Yes	27	93%
Somewhat	2	7%
No	0	0%
No response	2	

2. ***Do you understand the program and Peter's/Patricia's role?***

n = 29		
Yes	25	86%
Somewhat	3	10%
No	1	4%
No response	2	

3. ***What areas would you like to see made more clear? (If No or Somewhat to #2)***

n = 4		
Clarification about VVFSP purchase of service	2	50%
Clarification about a coordination issue	2	50%

4. ***What kinds of things does Peter/Patricia do for your family?***

n = 26		
VVFSP provides financial support	2	8%
VVFSP provides coordination of services	5	19%
VVFSP provides family support	5	19%
Provides financial and coordination support	4	15%
Provides financial and family support	1	4%
Provides financial and specialist support	1	4%
Provides coordination and family support	2	8%
Provides family support and specialist support	3	11%
Provides financial, coordination, and family support	2	8%
Provides coordination, family, and specialist support	1	4%
No response	4	

5. ***What does Peter/Patricia do the best?***

n = 24		
Provides coordination support	7	29%
Provides family support	12	50%
Provides other kinds of supports	3	13%
Provides coordination and family supports	2	8%
No response	6	

6. *What would you like to see Peter/Patricia do differently, if anything?*

n = 29		
Provide coordination support in a different manner	1	3%
Provide family support in a different manner	6	21%
Provide other supports in a different manner	1	3%
Coordination and other supports in another manner	1	3%
Family supports/other supports in other manner	2	7%
Nothing differently	18	62%
No response	2	

7. *Do you feel that the supports and services that you requested for all family members have been addressed?*

n = 25		
Yes	21	84%
Somewhat	4	16%
No	0	0%
No response	6	

8. *What areas would you like to see better addressed? (If No or Somewhat to #7)*

n = 8		
Provide more financial assistance	3	37.5%
Coordination issues need to be addressed	2	25%
Family support issues need to be addressed	2	25%
Coordination and family support addressed	1	12.5%

9. *Is Peter/Patricia supportive in stressful or crisis situations?*

n = 21		
Yes	16	76%
Somewhat	2	10%
No	3	14%
No response	10	

10. *How would you like to see Peter/Patricia work differently with your family in a crisis situation? (If No or Somewhat to #9)*

n = 7		
Provide more financial support	2	29%
Provide more family support	4	57%
Provide other supports	1	14%

11. *Has Peter/Patricia made a positive difference in your life?*

n = 25		
Yes	19	76%
Somewhat	3	12%
No	3	12%
No response	6	

12. *How happy are you with the overall services provided by VVFSP staff?*

n = 29		
Very happy	19	66%
Somewhat happy	9	31%
Somewhat unhappy	0	0%
Unhappy	1	3%
No response	2	

13. *What would you recommend to improve the overall services provided by VVFSP staff? (If Somewhat unhappy/Unhappy to #12)*

n = 9		
Provide more purchase of service money	4	44%
Provide more family support	4	44%
Have Vietnam veterans on staff	1	12%

14. ***Please rate the following services provided by VVFSP staff as:***

Very Good Good Fair Poor N/A

Service	Rating	Count	Percent
Finding outside resources for family	Very Good	15	60%
	Good	7	28%
n = 25	Fair	3	12%
	Poor	0	0%
	N/A	6	
Counseling for a family member	Very Good	9	69%
	Good	3	23%
n = 13	Fair	1	8%
	Poor	0	0%
	N/A	18	
Helping solve school/IEP issues	Very Good	10	47%
	Good	9	43%
n = 21	Fair	1	5%
	Poor	1	5%
	N/A	10	
Provide financial assistance for family	Very Good	11	44%
	Good	9	36%
n = 25	Fair	3	12%
	Poor	2	8%
	N/A	6	
Occupational therapy in your home	Very Good	4	100%
	Good	0	0%
n = 4	Fair	0	0%
	Poor	0	0%
	N/A	27	
Physical therapy in your home	Very Good	3	100%
	Good	0	0%
n = 3	Fair	0	0%
	Poor	0	0%
	N/A	28	
Speech/Language pathology in home	Very Good	4	75%
	Good	1	25%
n = 5	Fair	0	0%
	Poor	0	0%
	N/A	26	
Participation in support groups	Very Good	2	50%
	Good	1	25%

n = 4	Fair	1	25%
	Poor	0	0%
	N/A	27	
Book lending library	Very Good	3	43%
	Good	3	43%
n = 7	Fair	1	14%
	Poor	0	0%
	N/A	24	

15. Were you aware that all these services were available through VVFSP?

Yes	14	56%
No	11	44%

16. Are there any services that you were not aware of that you would be interested in receiving?

Yes	11	39%
No	15	54%
No response	2	7%

17. How long have you been receiving services from VVFSP?

Less than 1 year	5	16%
About 1 year	5	16%
About 2 years	21	68%

18. In your opinion, what changes would make the VVFSP program better for you and your family?

Change in purchase of service	2	7%
Change in coordination of services	7	25%
Change in family support	6	21%
Other changes	2	7%
Change purchase of service/coordination services	1	4%
No changes needed	10	36%

Project staff concluded that the results of this survey showed that the needs of families of Vietnam veterans were being met. Families were satisfied with VVFSP's services (93 percent), they understand the planning coordinator's roles (86 percent), and they are happy or somewhat happy with the overall services provided by VVFSP (97 percent). Families also rated as very good or good, the training, support, or counseling from the program (service coordination, i.e., finding outside resources, 88 percent, counseling 92 percent, educational advocacy 90 percent, financial assistance 80 percent, occupational therapy 100 percent, physical therapy 100 percent, speech/language pathology 100 percent, support groups 75 percent, and book lending library 86 percent). This would lead us to conclude that families are satisfied with VVFSP services and that the services are meeting their personal and family needs.

Interviews with VVFSP Specialists

Six therapists who provide home-based services were interviewed to gain insight into the differences between the children with disabilities whose parent is a Vietnam veteran and a cohort of 260 children who have disabilities. The therapists were asked nine free-response questions. To quantify the response on eight of the queries, the free-response inquiry was followed by a Likert Scale question. Therapists interviewed included: two special educators (SE), two speech and language pathologists (SL), one occupational therapist (OT), and one social worker (SW). These therapists have worked with no fewer than three and as many as six families of Vietnam veterans who have children with disabilities. They have collectively worked with hundreds of other families of children with disabilities.

The therapists were interviewed using a format created by the project coordinator, who also conducted all six in-person interviews. The interview questions and an analysis of the therapists' responses follows.

Question 1. What are the common characteristics and needs of families of Vietnam veterans who have children with disabilities and other families who have children with disabilities with whom you have worked?

Common Themes: All of the therapists noted that the families were in need of service coordination. The families with whom they work were all very interested in finding out what services were available in the community to help their children. All of the therapists believed that the family-centered model was effective in working with all types of families. Some of the therapists stated that the family-centered model worked somewhat effectively with families of Vietnam veterans noted as having a sense of "hopelessness" in the family. They believed that the few visits they had each month with the families only touched the surface of the families' issues.

The methods that you use when working with families of Vietnam veterans are:

Very effective	2 (SW, SE)
Somewhat effective	4 (SE, SL, SL, OT)
Somewhat ineffective	0
Very ineffective	0

Question 2. In what ways are families of Vietnam veterans similar or different from other families with children with disabilities with whom you have worked? Do you see their needs as being any different?

Common Themes: Five of the six therapists said that an emotional or mental health component was present in all the families of Vietnam veterans with whom they worked. Many specialists noted that there seemed to be more family stressors than in other families. The social worker noted that the children of Vietnam veterans behaved similarly to children from other families where a trauma had occurred or family violence was present. Other therapists noted that families of Vietnam veterans appear to experience more financial, family, and job stressors than other families. The therapists also noted that the children of Vietnam veterans tended to be older than the other children with whom they had worked. They noted that often these children had not received intervention as early as other children with disabilities.

Are families of Vietnam veterans as compared to other families with whom you work:

Very similar	1 (ES)
Somewhat similar	4 (OT, SL, SW, ES)
Somewhat different	1 (SL)
Very different	0

Question 3. What are some of the most difficult problems that you have faced when working with families of Vietnam veterans who have children with disabilities? With other families who have children with disabilities?

Common Themes: One common theme the therapists observed when working with all families with children with disabilities is dealing with the grief and feelings of loss of having a child with a disability. Some differences noted by the specialists included: the feeling with families of Vietnam veterans was that more services necessarily translates into better services, which the specialist did not feel was always true; the families of Vietnam veterans had a great many other emotional or mental health issues that prevented the specialist from doing his or her job; low family income was an issue that prevented some services from being implemented.

Are the problems that you faced with families of Vietnam veterans as compared to other families with whom you work:

Very difficult	0
Somewhat difficult	4 (ES, SL, SW, ES)
Somewhat easy	2 (OT, SL)
Very easy	0

Question 4. What are the positive aspects of the "family-centered" approach when working with families of children with disabilities? Does the family-centered approach work effectively with Vietnam veteran families with children with disabilities?

Common Themes: Despite some of the differences in families (particularly in areas of mental health) all of the therapists said that the family-centered model worked well with both sets of families. They felt that empowering the family to choose the type and duration of services worked in the family's best interests.

Does the family-centered approach when working with families of Vietnam veterans as opposed to other families with whom you work:

Work very well	5 (ES, SL, SL, SW, ES)
Somewhat well	1 (OT)
Somewhat poorly	0
Very poorly	0

Question 5. Do the Vietnam veterans that you work with speak about Vietnam and how it has impacted on their lives and their relationships with their children?

Common Themes: Only one therapist reported having ongoing conversations about the veteran's Vietnam experience. As a social worker, however, talking about this subject may have been closer to her expected or desired "role" for the family. All other therapists said they had never spoken to the veteran about the Vietnam experience. The therapists noted that when working with the child they almost exclusively worked with the mother, even when the father was living in the home.

Do these veterans speak out on this issue:

Every conversation	1 (SW)
Every other conversation	0
Once or twice	0
Never	5 (OT, ES, ES, SL, SL)

Question 6. Do you find that you have to present information to families of Vietnam veterans who have children with disabilities any differently than you do with other families who have children with disabilities?

Common Theme: When using the family-centered model, all the therapists believed they presented information to families in a similar manner. They made little or no distinction in this area.

Do you have to present information to families of Vietnam veterans as opposed to other families with whom you work:

Very differently	0
Somewhat differently	0
Somewhat the same	1 (SL)
The same	5 (ES, ES, SL, OT, SW)

Question 7. Do you note any differences in the children of Vietnam veterans with whom you work? Do you feel that these differences, if any, can be attributed to their parent's Vietnam experience?

Common Themes: Five of the six therapists said they observed more children with learning disabilities and emotional problems than in the other group of children with disabilities. They noted that the children of Vietnam veterans had more difficulty making friends, had problems with self-esteem, and had behavior similar to children who have been through significant trauma or abuse. The therapist who observed the children of Vietnam veterans as "somewhat the same" still observed an "emotional component" that did not usually exist in other families of children with disabilities. Two of the therapists felt confident in saying that they thought the father's Vietnam experience had something to do with the children's emotional problems. Three felt that they could not make this conclusion. One therapist said that the children of Vietnam veterans fell into the same continuum as other children with disabilities.

Do you note the children of families of Vietnam veterans as opposed to other children with whom you work as:

Very different	0
Somewhat different	4 (SL, SW, OT, SL)
Somewhat the same	1 (ES)
The same	1 (ES)

Question 8. From your observations, how do Vietnam veterans and their spouses cope with marital discord?

Common Themes: Three therapists noted communication problems between parents in families that were still intact. The social worker stated that none of the Vietnam veteran families who she had recommended for couples therapy or family therapy followed through with the recommendation. The three other therapists felt they did not know enough about the parents' relationship to make such a judgment.

Do Vietnam veterans and their spouses cope with this issue:

Very positively	0
Somewhat positively	0
Somewhat negatively	3 (SW, ES, SL)
Very negatively	0
Unsure	3 (ES, SL, OT)

Question 9. Briefly, what would you say are the most valuable lessons you have learned about working with families of Vietnam veterans?

Common Themes: One therapist noted the dangers of sending people off to war and the effects it has on children and families. Another therapist said that he had learned a great deal about children's school issues, because of the number of children of Vietnam veterans who had problems in school. Another noted the emotional trauma of families of Vietnam veterans during Operation Desert Storm. Two other therapists felt working with families of Vietnam veterans reinforced how important it is to work within the family-centered model.

The therapists working with VVFSP are in the unique position of being able to observe the similarities and differences of families of Vietnam veterans who have children with disabilities and other families of children with disabilities. The comparison group used in this study comprised a cohort of 260 children ages two months to twenty-one years. Forty-one percent of the children were between the ages of five and twenty-one. Some 63.5 percent of the children were male. Fifty percent of the children were African American, 45 percent white, and 5 percent were of other races. In addition, 15 percent of the children were diagnosed as having multiple disabilities; 19 percent were diagnosed with mental retardation, cerebral palsy, or both; approximately 14 percent were diagnosed with a speech and language delay; 13.8 percent with Down Syndrome; and 13.1 percent with autism.

The therapists interviewed viewed the similarities between the two groups as:

- Families in both groups were in need of service coordination;
- The family-centered approach works well with both groups;
- The families of the two groups were viewed as somewhat similar; and
- Information was presented in a similar fashion to both groups.

The therapists interviewed viewed the families of Vietnam veterans as different from other families in the following respects:

- Having a prevailing sense of hopelessness;
- The children having an underlying emotional/mental health component;
- The emotional/mental health component interfered with their lives; and
- Many of the children exhibited symptoms similar to children who experience abuse or violence in their family.

Conclusions

The purpose of this service evaluation was not to generalize a set of qualities for families of Vietnam veterans who have children with disabilities to the same general population. The purpose of this study was to describe demographically the families associated with VVFSP; determine the quality and quantity of services offered by VVFSP; provide a method for families to rate their satisfaction with the services provided by VVFSP; and have the therapists, who are in a unique position to observe many kinds of families, add insight concerning their working relationships with families of Vietnam veterans who have children with disabilities.

From the VVFSP service evaluation, we found that more than 50 percent of the families associated with VVFSP had at least one child with a mental health-related diagnosis. Families with a child with a mental health diagnosis appeared to have the greatest needs as measured by average monthly contacts. Families also appeared satisfied with the overall services provided by VVFSP's family-centered model. Thirty-one of thirty-seven provided services from September 1992 to August 1993 reflected at least an 80 percent approval rating for virtually all questions asked during a telephone interview. Six specialists who work with families of Vietnam veterans with children with disabilities and other children with disabilities found that both groups were reasonably similar in their family needs. One underlying theme noted by virtually all specialists, however, was that the children of Vietnam veterans seemed to have mental health needs that were not observed as often in other families who had children with disabilities.

From the data in this study, one major finding was the large number of children of Vietnam veterans in this project who have mental health needs. It would also seem that the children of Vietnam veterans have benefited from the services received from VVFSP. From the interviews with the therapists, it appears that addressing the mental health needs of the children results in reduced stress. More research needs to be done to determine if these mental health needs in children are typical of all families of Vietnam veterans.

References

Harkness, L.L. 1993. Transgenerational transmission of war-related trauma. In *International Handbook of Traumatic Stress Syndromes*, 643-653. New York: Plenum Press.

Roberts, R.N., Ph.D. 1988. Family support in the home: Home visiting programs and P.L. 990457. *Association for the Care of Children's Health*, 3-5.

Systems Development on Behalf of Children with Special Health Care Needs: Opportunities for Collaboration Between AOCAP and State Title V CSHCN Programs

John Reiss, Ph.D.
Associate Director, Institute for Child Health Policy
Assistant Professor of Pediatrics
University of Florida College of Medicine
Gainesville, FL

Abstract

Many Agent Orange Class Assistance Program (AOCAP)-funded projects and state Title V Program for Children with Special Health Care Needs (CSHCN) projects share several similarities. They seek to serve children and families with special needs; support the provision of family-centered, coordinated, community-based services; and are staffed by dedicated professionals with expertise in outreach, counseling, referral, and care coordination.

Nevertheless, AOCAP and CSHCN programs also have unique roles and responsibilities. AOCAP project staff have special expertise and experience in recognizing and understanding the specific, unique problems of Vietnam veterans and their families. The AOCAP projects are also supported through private, but time-limited funding, which gives them flexibility, but imposes a need to institutionalize their activities through long-term projects. Title V CSHCN programs, on the other hand, are supported through federal and state funds and are legislatively mandated to facilitate the development of a family-centered, community-based, culturally competent, coordinated system of care for children with special health care needs and their families. Thus, the children of Vietnam veterans are one of many "special populations" for which Title V has a responsibility.

Future cooperation and coordination between AOCAP and state Title V programs on behalf of Vietnam veterans' children with special needs are highly desirable. Information provided in this paper includes a review of the issues related to AOCAP/CSHCN program collaboration; an overview of Title V CSHCN roles, responsibilities, and activities on behalf of CSHCN; and alternative strategies for ensuring that children with special needs from families of Vietnam veterans have access to a full range of needed health and related services.

***John Reiss, Ph.D.**, serves as the associate director of the Institute for Child Health Policy (ICHP) and an assistant professor of pediatrics at the University of Florida. He received his Ph.D. in counseling psychology from the University of Florida in 1984.*

Many Agent Orange Class Assistance Program (AOCAP)-funded projects and state Title V Program for Children with Special Health Care Needs (CSHCN) projects share several important similarities. First, they seek to serve children and families with special needs. Second, each seeks to expand the availability of family-centered, coordinated, multidisciplinary, community-based services, in the face of limited resources. Finally, each program is staffed by dedicated individuals with expertise in providing outreach, counseling, care coordination, and assistance or referral for medical, mental health, and social services, in addition to nutritional, educational, and vocational aid to children with special health care needs and their families.

AOCAP and CSHCN programs also have unique roles and responsibilities related to children with special needs whose parent is a Vietnam veteran. AOCAP project staff have special expertise and experience in recognizing and understanding the specific, unique problems of Vietnam veterans and their families that resulted from the veteran's war experiences. The AOCAP projects are also supported through private, but time-limited funding, giving them flexibility, but also imposing the need to institutionalize their activities through state agencies or longer-term projects. Title V CSHCN programs, on the other hand, are legislatively mandated and are supported through federal and state funds. Part of their mission is to facilitate the development of a family-centered, community-based, culturally competent, coordinated system of care for all children with special health care needs. Thus, the children of Vietnam veterans are one of many "special populations" for which Title V has a responsibility.

Despite the ongoing efforts of both AOCAP and Title V program grantees, children with disabilities or chronic illnesses and their families often do not receive all the program services and assistance they need. In an effort to address this problem, representatives of the United States Public Health Service (USPHS) Maternal and Child Health Bureau, of the Agent Orange Class Assistance Program (AOCAP), of AOCAP grantees, and of state Title V CSHCN programs met in December 1992 (a list of the participants is included in Appendix 1). The National Center for Policy Coordination in Maternal and Child Health at the Institute for Child Health Policy, University of Florida, hosted the meeting. This national center is funded by MCHB to, in part, support and coordinate work group activities on behalf of CSHCN and their families. Through this working meeting, AOCAP and Title V representatives identified goals, objectives, and strategies for working together to increase access by CSHCN and their families to critically needed services and resources and to improve services. A draft working document was then reviewed and revised in January 1993 by representatives of American Legion projects funded by AOCAP.

The purpose of this paper is to describe and support the collaboration between AOCAP and state Title V CSHCN programs. The paper covers these areas:

- Overview of MCHB and Title V CSHCN roles, responsibilities, and activities on behalf of children with special health care needs and a review of barriers to AOCAP and CSHCN collaboration;
- Issues identified by the work group that are related to AOCAP and CSHCN program cooperation; and
- Summary of the goals, objectives, and strategies recommended by the work group for improving services of CSHCN for families of Vietnam veterans.

Mission, Roles, and Responsibilities of MCHB

At the federal level, the USPHS Maternal and Child Health Bureau (the Bureau or MCHB) is authorized under Title V of the Social Security Act (SSA) and has responsibility for assuring that the health and related needs of women, children, and families are appropriately addressed. The mission of MCHB, as articulated in the Bureau's vision statement, is to enhance the health of America's children and families by providing leadership in reshaping the system of care so that this system is comprehensive, family-centered, community-based, coordinated, and culturally competent, so that all the nation's mothers, children, and families have access to and receive the highest-quality care. As part of this commitment, the Bureau is working to reshape the system of care by integrating prevention and health promotion strategies, building the capacity of the state programs, strengthening private and public partnerships, and supporting program development, research, and training to ensure the integration of current scientific knowledge into the service delivery system.

The Bureau carries out its work through two major funding categories. MCH Block Grants to States are awarded to state health agencies on the basis of a specific formula and represent approximately 85 percent of Title V funds. Discretionary Grants, referred to as Special Projects of Regional and National Significance (SPRANS), constitute the other 15 percent of the annual appropriation and are awarded to a variety of applicant organizations on a competitive basis to support activities related to the health of mothers and children. The National Center for Policy Coordination is funded by the Bureau through a SPRANS grant.

State health agencies have great flexibility in using the resources they receive through the MCH block grants to improve the health of all mothers and children, consistent with the health status goals and national health objectives specified in *Healthy People 2000* (U.S. Public Health Service, 1990). States must provide a three-dollar match for every four federal dollars allocated and must use at least 30 percent of these funds for preventive and primary care services for children and at least another 30 percent for services for children with special health care needs. More specifically, these block grants funds are used to enable each state to:

1. Provide and assure mothers and children (especially those with low income or limited availability to services) access to quality maternal and child health services;
2. Reduce infant mortality and the incidence of preventable diseases and disabling conditions among children; reduce the need for in-patient and long-term services; promote the health of children by providing preventive and primary care services for low-income children;
3. Provide rehabilitative services for blind and disabled individuals under the age of sixteen years receiving Supplemental Security Income (SSI) benefits to the extent medical assistance for such services is not provided under Medicaid; and
4. Provide and promote family-centered, community-based, coordinated care for children with special health care needs and facilitate the development of community-based systems of services for such children and their families.

In 1993–1994, through its State Systems Development Initiative, MCHB is providing special small grants to assist state Maternal and Child Health (MCH) and CSHCN programs in the development and implementation of an infrastructure that shows results in establishing community-based service systems that:

- Meet the health and health-related needs of all children and their families;
- Address the physical, psychological, and social aspects of health care;
- Provide individualized attention for their special health care and related needs; and
- Link health care and services with other needed services and programs including, but not limited to, early intervention, educational, vocational, and mental health services.

As specified in the MCH Block Grant Guidance, state MCH and CSHCN grantees are expected to use State Systems Development Initiative (SSDI) funds to promote community service systems that reflect the following characteristics (U.S. Public Health Service, 1993):

- **Collaborative.** At the state level, the systems are characterized by collaboration between state MCH and CSHCN programs, other relevant state health and nonhealth agencies, and provider and consumer groups to facilitate the development of service systems at the community level. Such collaboration promotes the institutionalization of family-centered, culturally competent, and coordinated care at the community level. At the community level, the systems are characterized by public-private partnerships that link health-related and other community resources to form an organized network.

  In addition, these collaborations promote the participation of a broad range of families in the systems development process in order to ensure that their needs are addressed.

- **Family-Centered.** These systems recognize the importance of the family and reflect this in the way services are planned and delivered. Systems facilitate parent/professional collaboration, respond to family needs, recognize and build on individual and family strengths, and respect the diversity of families.

- **Community-Based.** These systems respond to needs identified by the community and draw from the community to address needs. Services are provided in or near the home community to the extent possible. The area encompassed by a community depends on a number of factors including population density, political subdivisions, existing arrangements for provision of services, and availability of resources.

- **Culturally Competent.** Systems are organized so as to be sensitive to culture and competent to serve culturally diverse groups. Cultural competence refers to a program's ability to honor and respect culturally related beliefs, values, interpersonal styles, attitudes, and behaviors of families including the multicultural staff who are providing services. It incorporates these values at the policy, administration, and practice level. Multilanguage materials and translation services are made available as needed.

- **Care-Coordinated.** Within these systems, the array of services is coordinated to ensure timeliness, appropriateness, continuity, and completeness of care.

- **Comprehensive.** Such systems encompass primary (including prevention), secondary, and tertiary health care, and address physical health, mental health, oral health, nutrition, health promotion, monitoring of development, parent and patient guidance, early intervention, and family planning. The systems also address needs for emergency medical, substance use and abuse, specialized mental health, educational, vocational, social, recreational, and family support services.

- **Universal.** Service systems are concerned with all children, adolescents, and their families in the community, whether served by private providers or public programs. This population includes children and adolescents with, or at risk for, disabilities, chronic conditions, health-related educational problems, and health-related behavioral or emotional problems.

- **Accessible.** The systems address the issue of physical access by assuring that services are located conveniently and are augmented, as appropriate, by home visiting, mobile services, school-based health services centers, satellite services, and other means to bring care closer to consumers. Such systems address the issue of temporal access by ensuring that a wide choice of service hours is made available. These systems also address the issue of financial access by ensuring that arrangements are made for financing mechanisms that bring needed services within the reach of all.

- **Developmentally Oriented.** Systems take into account the different kinds of needs that children, adolescents, and their families have at different stages of development by, for example:

- Helping expectant parents, new parents, and those who will provide care and services to understand the development of infants and young children;
- Addressing health-related behaviors with school-age children and youth; and
- Providing adolescent services in an atmosphere of trust and honoring wishes for confidentiality in all appropriate circumstances.

- **Accountable.** Such systems provide information concerning the performance and utilization of the community-based system of services.

MCHB and state CSHCN programs have been working for some time on the development of such systems. Currently, some states or communities within states have made great strides in implementing these systems, while others are still in the needs assessment and planning phase. The Bureau and state MCH and CSHCN programs also recognize that the development of these systems of care must be a cooperative effort, involving other initiatives, such as AOCAP grantees.

Mission, Roles, and Responsibilities of State Title V CSHCN Programs

As noted above, state Title V CSHCN programs have great flexibility in the way in which MCH block grant funds are used. These programs are state, not federal, programs. They are governed by state-specific legislation that specifies the program's eligibility policies (both medical and financial) and the scope of services offered. In addition, these programs are housed within different governmental units, are organized differently, and are known by different names in different states. For example, in Florida, the Title V CSHCN program is known as Children's Medical Services and is a program in the Department of Health and Rehabilitative Services; in Tennessee it is known as Children's Special Services and is part of the Maternal and Child Division of the Department of Health and Environment; in Kentucky the program is a free-standing entity known as the Commission for Handicapped Children. Some Title V CSHCN programs hire their own physicians and nurses, who provide direct services to children. Some states contract with hospitals and private pediatricians for services, while other programs provide no direct health care, but do provide diagnostic and care coordination services. These differences among Title V CSHCN programs can be confusing to families and other agencies. In an effort to address this problem, the National Center for Policy Coordination in Maternal and Child Health has recently compiled a directory that provides the name, address, phone numbers, eligibility criteria, and scope of services of most of the state Title V CSHCN programs.

Barriers to Coordinated and Comprehensive Care

The work group identified a number of barriers that impede children's and families' access to needed services. Interorganizational collaboration is difficult to achieve and requires a significant level of planning and ongoing effort. Specific organizational factors can act as barriers and some are particularly relevant to AOCAP projects, some to Title V programs.

Specific factors associated with AOCAP projects included AOCAP staff's limited:

- Knowledge of pediatric health care needs and standards;
- Experience with child health care systems, including state Title V Children with Special Health Care Needs (CSHCN) Programs; and
- Awareness about alternative funding sources.

Title V program factors include:

- Title V and MCHB's staffs' limited:

1. Experience with Vietnam veterans' families;
2. Knowledge of post-traumatic stress disorder (PTSD) and the extent to which this syndrome affects services and resources needed; and
3. Awareness of AOCAP and its grantees.

The work group also recognized that differences across state Title V programs, in terms of program name, eligibility criteria, and services, pose a barrier to AOCAP grantees' understanding of and access to these programs.

A number of family factors will also serve as barriers. Some factors are particularly relevant to families of Vietnam veterans. General family factors included their:

- Lack of awareness of available resources and services;
- Failure to identify their child's problems and needs; and
- Reluctance to accept and/or report their child's problems.

Issues related to the Vietnam veteran's war experiences were:

- Veteran's distrust of governmental agencies and programs;
- Impact of PTSD on the family's ability to address a child with special needs; and
- The psychological impact of worrying that exposure to Agent Orange may have caused the child's health or developmental problems.

To address these barriers, it was agreed that AOCAP grantees, Title V CSHCN programs, and MCHB-SPRANS grantees need to:

- Understand each program's mission, roles, and responsibilities;
- Understand the special health and social problems of Vietnam veterans and their families;
- Know about the broad range of services and resources available to address these problems through collaborative program efforts; and
- Develop and implement methods for effectively utilizing these resources through appropriate referrals.

Recommended Goals for AOCAP and Title V Cooperation

In order to overcome these barriers, AOCAP and Title V work group members agreed to achieve the following three goals:

- **Goal 1: Increase the awareness and understanding of health and social service organizations, professionals, and veteran services groups about the special health and social services needs of Vietnam veterans' families.** Increasing awareness involves both documenting the special needs of children from Vietnam veterans' families and increasing the awareness of professionals and organizations at the federal, state, and local levels about these special needs.

  The work group recommended that data from the AOCAP-supported National Information System be analyzed to determine the incidence and prevalence of special problems and needs of Vietnam veterans' families, compared with similar populations (as served by Title V CSHCN programs). The work group also urged that data on services provided to veteran families served by CSHCN through AOCAP and other health and social services agencies be collected and analyzed.

  In order to provide this information to AOCAP grantees, state Title V CSHCN programs, and other public and private programs that serve children with special needs, the group recommended a variety of strategies. Recommended strategies include developing a series of fact sheets and a more formal training curriculum to assist health professionals and veteran services groups in identifying and recognizing the special health and social services needs of Vietnam veterans' families. The fact sheets and the curriculum would then be made available to a broad range of professionals and organizations including veterans' organizations, state veterans affairs commissions, university veterans' advocates, University Affiliated Program (UAP) faculty and students, Title V CSHCN leadership and staff, and MCHB-SPRANS grantees. Informational articles could be published in magazines and journals that reach the veteran, health, and social service communities.

- **Goal 2: Ensure that Vietnam veterans' children who have special needs access and maximize all health and social service program benefits available to them, including insurance and entitlement programs.** Ensuring access to care involves both outreach to families and the provision of information and referral services.

  The recommended strategies for implementing a joint Title V and AOCAP outreach effort involve:

  a. Selecting one or two states in which to develop a demonstration outreach program and identifying the current outreach activities of Title V, AOCAP, and other veterans' organizations in these states;

  b. Jointly identifying where outreach coordination is possible and developing guidelines for implementing a coordinated outreach program;

  c. Developing a joint prototype intake or application form that includes questions regarding Vietnam veteran status, training intake staff on implementing the form, and conducting a needs assessment of identified AOCAP-eligible families; and

  d. Disseminating the guidelines at meetings and conferences of the organizations involved.

  The work group recommended that some AOCAP grantees work with selected Title V CSHCN-affiliated clinics and serve as an on-site resource for veterans' families that are being served. Implementing this effort would involve identifying one or two Title V CSHCN clinics with large patient loads (urban and rural) and assigning a veterans' advocate who would assist veterans' families in meeting their basic needs. Developing and implementing compatible (AOCAP and Title V) protocols for referrals would be the next step. The protocols for referrals would include service coordination and follow-up with AOCAP grantees, Title V CSHCN programs, the Supplemental Security Income (SSI) Program, special education, mental health, and vocational rehabilitation programs. The work group recommended that training for AOCAP grantees and other veteran groups then be implemented to ensure their awareness of all health and social service resources that may be available to veterans in their respective states. Such training could be carried out in collaboration with state Title V programs, University Affiliated Programs, state veteran services officers, and others with expertise in health and social service resources in their states.

  AOCAP projects should be listed as part of the state 1-800 information and referral services that are administered by each state Title V and Part H programs for infants and toddlers.

- **Goal 3: Ensure that services for Vietnam veterans' children with disabilities are family-centered, comprehensive, and coordinated, and provided in a manner that promotes the increased independence, productivity, and empowerment of the child and family.** MCHB and Title V CSHCN programs are significant resources in ensuring family-centered care. A primary mission of MCHB and Title V CSHCN programs is to promote the development of such care.

The work group recommended that AOCAP grantees learn about information and training resources developed through Title V Block Grant SPRANS funding to support the development of family-centered, community-based, coordinated, culturally competent systems of care. Information about the various federal, state, and local initiatives for children with special needs, including Healthy Start, Part H of the Education of the Handicapped Act Amendments of 1986 (Individuals with Disabilities Education Act), and the Americans with Disabilities Act of 1990 (ADA) is also available.

Special emphasis should be placed on improving veteran families' access to quality primary and preventive care, including dental, vision, hearing, and immunizations services. Such efforts could include the development or dissemination of:

a. A protocol for AOCAP intake screening that includes preventive issues (e.g., questions regarding children's immunizations and dental and eye examinations);

b. Parenting education and peer counseling materials to increase families' understanding of the need for primary and preventive care;

c. A process of referrals to ensure that primary care providers to whom agencies refer are competent and knowledgeable about PTSD and other problems unique to Vietnam veterans and their families; and

d. A protocol for Title V programs to assist AOCAP grantees with identifying strategically located, competent health providers.

AOCAP grantees could be provided with information about the activities of MCHB and state Title V programs to promote two activities. The first is the formation of self-help support groups of families to empower the families to deal with their own problems and facilitate access to the system. The second is the participation of families in the design, monitoring, and evaluation of services provided through AOCAP grantees.

Summary and Conclusions

Current systems of services for children are often characterized by duplication and fragmentation, and often do not make optimal use of available personnel and financial resources. Developing coordinated, family-centered systems is a complex, problematic process that involves addressing complex inter- and intra-agency program and policy issues. The primary problems encountered in systems change are to:

- Reach consensus among the organizations and agencies responsible for addressing problems concerning the nature and extent of the common issues that they are facing and how they should be addressed;
- Overcome organizational concerns about protecting their own identities, ideologies, roles, and resources; and
- Address problems jointly by combining agency personnel and resources.

The findings and recommendations of the AOCAP and Title V work group constitute a draft statement of consensus regarding the problems of Vietnam veterans' families and their children with special needs and the ways in which AOCAP and Title V can work together to address these problems. Leadership at the federal level has supported the development of a blueprint. The challenge now is for the staff of Title V programs and AOCAP projects to focus a measure of their limited financial and personnel resources on setting priorities and taking collaborative actions at the state and local levels.

Appendix 1. Work Group Participants

The American Legion
John Hanson, Director
Division of National Veterans Affairs and Rehabilitation
The American Legion
1608 K Street, N.W.
Washington, DC 20006

Max Tenberg, Director
American Legion Vietnam Veterans Family Assistance Program (VVFAP)
1608 K Street, N.W.
Washington, DC 20006

Andy Aelmore, State Coordinator
VVFAP, C/O Vet Center
413 S. Patti
Wichita, KS 67211

Steve Pederson, State Coordinator
VVFAP, South Dakota Division of Veterans Affairs
C/O VARO
2501 W. 22nd St.
P.O. Box 5046
Sioux Falls, SD 57117

Fred Smith, State Coordinator
VVFAP, C/O VA 19-27
North Main Street
Wilkes-Barre, PA 18701

Agent Orange Class Assistance Program (AOCAP)
Dennis Rhoades, Executive Director
Agent Orange Class Assistance Program (AOCAP)
P.O. Box 27413
Washington, DC 20038-7413

Deborah Crane, Director
Federation for Children with Special Needs
P.O. Box 992
Westfield, MA 01086

Mac Rattan, Program Developmental Specialist
Training and Technical Assistance Program
American GI Forum
1017 N. Main, Suite 200
San Antonio, TX 78212

Tom Goonan, Associate Program Director
Veterans/Children with Disabilities
Utah State University
Logan, UT 84322

Bryan Smith, Ed.D., Director
National Information System for Vietnam Veterans and Their Families
University of South Carolina
Columbia, SC 29208

James Stuart, Grant Representative
Agent Orange Class Assistance Program (AOCAP)
P.O. Box 27413
Washington, DC 20038-7413

Maternal and Child Health Bureau (MCHB)
John Shwab, Chief
Habilitative Services Branch
Division of Children with Special Health Needs
Maternal and Child Health Bureau
Parklawn Building, Room 18A27
5600 Fishers Lane
Rockville, MD 20857

State Title V CSHCN Programs
Cassie Lauver, ACSW, Director
Services for Children with Special Health Care Needs
Kansas Dept. of Health and Environment
900 S.W. Jackson, Room 1005N
Topeka, KS 66612-1290

Jerry Wiley, MD, Medical Consultant
Children and Youth Section
North Carolina Dept. of Environment, Health, and Natural Resources
P.O. Box 27687
Raleigh, NC 27611-7687

Sandra Durick, Director
MCH—Children's Special Health Services Programs
South Dakota Department of Health
118 W. Capitol
Pierre, SD 57501

Consultant
Billy M. Sandlin, MSPH
Senior Project Manager
The Circle, Inc.
8201 Greensboro Drive, Suite 600
McLean, VA 22102

Work Group Facilitator
John Reiss, PhD, Director
National Center for Policy Coordination in Maternal and Child Health
5700 S.W. 34th Street, Suite 323
Gainesville, FL 32608-5367

References

U.S. Public Health Service. 1990. *Healthy people 2000: National health promotion and disease prevention objectives.* DHHS Publication No. (PHS) 91-50213. Washington, DC: U.S. Government Printing Office.

U.S. Public Health Service. 1993. Grant application guidance for establishment of a state infrastructure to support the implementation of community-based systems of services to meet the primary and special health care and service needs of children and their families. Rockville, MD: Maternal and Child Health Bureau.

A Consortium for Services to Vietnam Veterans and Their Families: An Innovative Model for Serving the Veteran Community

Frank D. Scott, Ph.D., Eunice Kennedy Shriver Center for Mental Retardation
Deborah Crane, Federation for Children with Special Needs
Ynes C. Simon-Alvarez, Veterans Benefits Clearinghouse, Inc.
Joseph A. DeResta, Vietnam Era Veterans Association

Abstract

The Agent Orange Class Assistance Program (AOCAP) funded eleven projects in New England to provide Vietnam veterans and their families a single-point entry system for a comprehensive package of services. The New England Consortium for Services to Vietnam Veterans and Their Families was established. It developed a published charter and mission statement. As a result of sharing limited resources, the Vietnam veteran community benefited through the coordination of efforts and improved effectiveness of individual agencies. Specific activities included coordinated outreach efforts publicizing a toll-free telephone number that provided access to services from any of the member organizations. There are a number of examples of cooperative efforts to fill gaps in service needs from existing public and private systems, including the consortium network.

Membership in the consortium increased the prominence and credibility of individual agencies. National and regional impacts of consortium activities included increased collaboration between U.S. Department of Veterans Affairs (VA) personnel and other professionals serving the Vietnam veteran community and expansion of family-oriented services in VA facilities. The benefits of establishing formal partnerships with other agencies serving similar client groups can be clearly demonstrated.

Frank D. Scott, Ph.D., *is a school psychologist at the Eunice Kennedy Shriver Center for Mental Retardation in Waltham, MA, where he has served for fifteen years. He earned his doctorate in school psychology from the University of Rhode Island and has extensive experience in the assessment of developmental disabilities, and advocacy for education services.* ***Deborah Crane*** *is project director of the Agent Orange Parent Network, Federation for Children with Special needs in Boston, MA. She has been providing information and training to parents of children with disabilities since 1978, is married to a disabled Vietnam veteran, and lost a brother in the Vietnam War.* ***Ynes C. Simon-Alvarez*** *is director of AOCAP's Project Hope at the Veterans' Benefits Clearinghouse, Inc. in Roxbury, MA, where she also provides translator/interpreter services to clients. Her husband is a Vietnam combat veteran.* ***Joseph A. Resta*** *is program coordinator of counseling services for the AOCAP's Vietnam Era Veterans Association of Rhode Island in Providence. He was a combat medic with the 25th Infantry Division in Vietnam in 1968 and 1969. He was wounded in an ambush near Dau Tieng and is a recipient of the Purple Heart.*

This presentation describes the initiative of eleven Agent Orange Class Assistance Program (AOCAP)-funded projects to provide Vietnam veterans and their families in the New England region a coordinated and comprehensive service delivery system. The initiative is a collaborative process marked by a commitment to deliver maximum benefit to the Vietnam veteran community as a result of AOCAP funds and to seek ways to serve the community in the future. Development of the New England Consortium for Services to Vietnam Veterans and Their Families also involved an evolutionary process that began with informal meetings among individuals from a few service agencies and developed into a formal organization with a stated mission and a charter detailing issues of membership, governance, goals, objectives, and operating mechanisms.

Why should time and effort be expended in forming collaborative relationships, particularly in a situation where the funds provided by AOCAP are available for only a limited period of time? In a study of various metropolitan collaborations at the Institute for Educational Leadership, Blank (1986) provides an explanation from an agency perspective:

> Many motivations combine to stimulate cross-sector cooperative activities. They reflect needs, expectations, and perceived self-interest. People and institutions are moved to collaborate by a *common view* of an important *perceived need*. It is when major participants have a common interest or goal and are struggling hard to overcome barriers to achieving the goal that collaboration is most likely to bring progress toward durable consensus for action. (p. viii)

The National Assembly of National Voluntary Health and Social Welfare Organizations in a manual on collaboration (1991) specified numerous ways in which communities could benefit. Advantages that were particularly relevant among AOCAP agencies included goals to:

- Identify gaps in current services and cooperate to fill the gaps;
- Provide better services to clients through interagency communication about client needs, referral programs, and client case management;
- Develop a greater understanding of client and community needs by seeing the whole picture;
- Improve communication with organizations within the community and, through those organizations, to larger segments of the community;
- Mobilize action to effect needed changes through collective advocacy;
- Achieve greater visibility with decision makers, the media, and the community; and
- Enhance staff skill levels by sharing information and organizing joint training programs.

AOCAP-funded agencies in the New England region shared the perceived need to quickly reach veterans' families who required their services while also leveraging limited resources. Considerable evidence was available that veteran and family needs were significant and required urgent attention.

A comprehensive survey of 170,000 Vietnam-era veterans who live in Massachusetts, approximately 60,000 of whom served in Vietnam, was conducted in 1988 by The William Joiner Center for the Study of War and Social Consequences. These self-reported data (Camacho, Bowen, and Hunt, 1991) indicated that 19.7 percent of Vietnam veterans' families with children had at least one child with one or more birth defects and that 23.5 percent of all Vietnam veterans reported suffering from some degree of post-traumatic stress disorder (PTSD). Such statistics, extrapolated across the New England region, suggested that the number of Vietnam veterans and family members who could potentially benefit from AOCAP services numbered in the tens of thousands.

Forming the Consortium

A series of informal meetings of agency representatives occurred as successive organizations in the region were awarded AOCAP funding. Initial meetings consisted of sharing information regarding services each agency had to offer and discussing ideas for outreach strategies.

As the number of AOCAP agencies in New England grew, and as informal meetings led to fruitful discussions of obstacles to overcome and of achievements to accomplish, agencies recognized that they collectively possessed invaluable assets that could be exploited for mutual benefit: expertise in a variety of disciplines and diversity in backgrounds that fostered a broad perspective.

In addition, they recognized that duplication of agency services was wasteful and should be avoided. Perhaps the most compelling reasons for forming an association of service agencies is a credo developed by Donna Stark from the Maryland Children and Families Reform Initiative (Blank and Lombardi, 1991). In "What Families Want from Human Services," she states:

> First they want support for what their priorities are, not for what we want their priorities to be. They want one person—not several persons helping them negotiate difficult situations and difficult systems; they want a user-friendly system that doesn't give them the run-around from one agency to another with millions of forms to fill out to get some basic responses; they want services that are comprehensive enough to respond to their entire family's needs and respond to the causes rather than the symptoms of the issues that they bring before us. . . . And they want us to appreciate the diversity of their lifestyles and their values. (p. 7)

The spirit of this philosophy was repeatedly stated at meetings and private discussions among agency members. AOCAP provided reinforcement in the form of mandates and regional training conferences that emphasized service coordination as an essential responsibility.

These factors met the conditions described by the Center for the Study of Social Policy (CSSP) in determining the usefulness of a new, collaborative enterprise. Further, CSSP advised that such new entities should engage in the following functions (Ooms and Owen, 1992):

1. Agenda setting and strategy development;
2. Developing new service strategies;
3. Coordinating fiscal strategies; and
4. Monitoring, supporting, and reassessing these activities and maintaining accountability for child and family outcomes.

These topics were frequently the focus of early, informal meetings, and it was therefore a natural step to formalize relationships through the creation of the New England Consortium for Services to Vietnam Veterans and Their Families in the spring of 1991.

Initial Outreach Efforts

In addition to strengthening ties among member agencies, an immediate priority was to develop a coordinated outreach effort and a single-point client entry mechanism to gain access to any member agency.

These goals were realized first through the development and dissemination of a brochure that outlined available services and provided the name and telephone number of a contact person for each consortium agency. The brochure (as well as other promotional materials) prominently featured a toll-free telephone number through which callers could obtain information and referral to any of the services offered within the consortium. Agencies developed interagency referral procedures that were flexible enough to allow for improvements after implementation. The groups also developed a coordinated and multifaceted outreach plan. Distribution of consortium brochures occurred through a comprehensive canvassing of schools, public welfare offices, and veteran outreach centers, particularly in the Commonwealth of Massachusetts where six of the eleven consortium agencies are located.

Other outreach efforts began. Agencies recruited leaders of veterans' service organizations as associate and ex-officio members; they provided guidance and assistance in the distribution of brochures at veteran rallies and published announcements in their newsletters. Senator John Kerry, a prominent advocate for Vietnam veteran issues, recorded audio and video public service announcements. Consortium members contacted and monitored broadcast stations in order to ensure that the public service announcements would be aired. In addition, consortium members appeared on local radio stations that aired programs on veterans' issues and described AOCAP-funded services that were available.

These coordinated efforts were the first tangible products of the consortium, and they resulted in publicizing available services to large segments of the Vietnam veteran community.

A Vehicle for Systems Change

In awarding grants, AOCAP executed a strategy that attempted to recruit the efforts of diverse human service agencies to serve the needs of Vietnam veterans and their families. Local groups throughout the country received a total of sixty-six grants. In addition, eight national support projects were established as resources for local agencies to develop more comprehensive services (National Agent Orange Training and Technical Assistance Project, 1992). In New England, eleven agencies received funds to provide a variety of discrete services, documented in a statement of work for each agency. Although there previously was some overlap in clientele, these agencies traditionally served different populations within the three human service sectors presented in Table 1. Ongoing dialogue between each agency's project director and an AOCAP grant representative further refined the objectives that each project sought to accomplish. This process had an immediate impact on each host agency, particularly those that provided multifaceted services to their clientele.

In attempting to illustrate levels of impacts, it is necessary to view each agency as operating within a systems perspective. A number of disciplines (e.g., organizational psychology, community psychology) have arisen studying aspects of organizational behavior. Authors (Bryson, 1988; Heller and Monahan, 1977; Murrell, 1973) describe human service agencies as systems that are interconnected to other systems that vary in size and complexity. Figure 1 depicts the relationships between AOCAP and the human service sectors through its funded projects. Relationships are depicted via bidirectional arrows to reflect that a dynamic process is occurring and that each organization is influenced by these relationships. Because the AOCAP grants to local agencies were awarded over a period of time, limits in the services that could be provided by early grantees undoubtedly affected AOCAP's later choices for awards. Such limitations could include geographical and programmatic factors as well as the skills and competencies within each agency.

Improved Systems

Agencies receiving AOCAP grants recognized that their effectiveness was often related to their specialized services as well as their newly inaugurated ability to provide information and referral in areas that they had not served previously. For example, developmental disability

Table 1. AOCAP-Funded Agencies in the New England Region

Type	Agencies Funded
Veteran service agencies	■ Veterans Benefits Clearinghouse (Roxbury, MA) ■ Vietnam Era Veterans Association (Providence, RI) ■ Vietnam Veterans Mobile Family Services Program (Pittsfield, MA) ■ Veterans' Support Services, Inc. (Portland, ME) ■ New England Shelter for Homeless Veterans (Boston, MA)
Developmental disability service agencies	■ Agent Orange Parent Network (Westfield, MA) ■ Vietnam Veterans Family Services Project (Waltham, MA) ■ Spina Bifida Association of America-AOCAP (Yarmouth, ME)
Family assistance service agencies	■ Family Services Association of Central Connecticut, Inc. (Meriden, CT) ■ Vietnam Veterans Agent Orange Victims, Inc. (Darien, CT) ■ Vietnam Veteran Family Project (Belmont, MA)

service agencies, although competent in identifying the educational and therapeutic needs of disabled children, did not have the skills to address veterans' benefit issues nor did they have frequent experience in addressing the problems of a family with a veteran parent suffering from PTSD. Conversely, veteran service agencies often were not aware that veterans had children with disabilities or whether there were other social service needs within the family.

As a result, AOCAP agencies in the New England region reported (New England Consortium memorandum, October 1993) that they devised new client intake procedures to specifically identify class members and to collect introductory information that would enable staff to determine their service needs. For many agencies, these intake procedures were implemented

Figure 1. Establishment of Relationships by AOCAP with Service Agencies in the New England Region

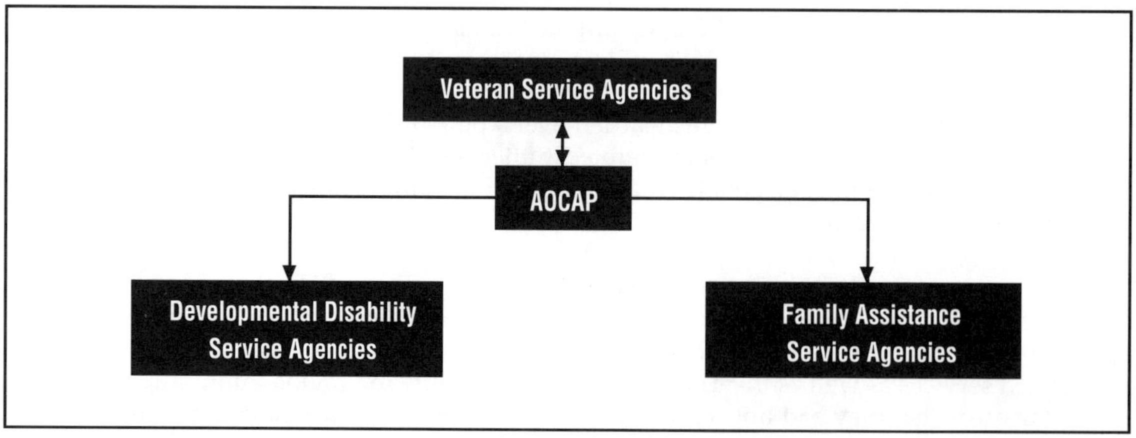

not only by the staff assigned to the AOCAP project but by all the staff with intake responsibilities *throughout the agency*.

Intake staff within developmental disability agencies now routinely inquired whether the caller was a member of a Vietnam veteran family. Data collection instruments were revised to record the information and to direct the caller to program staff who could provide assistance. New England INDEX, an independent project of one of the consortium agencies, developed and maintains a computerized information and referral system for individuals with developmental disabilities, and also revised its questionnaires to service providers in the community. In questions directed toward therapeutic counselors, entries have been added to identify those who describe themselves as competent in veterans' issues, particularly PTSD and its effects on families.

AOCAP awards also influenced agencies in recognizing a need to develop greater expertise outside their traditional area of service provision. This need encompassed a wide range of issues, such as the known effects of dioxin exposure, the application process for Supplemental Security Income benefits, and understanding the effects of PTSD on the veteran and his or her family. Such knowledge and skill development was necessary not only to devise effective programs and procedures but also to work with each family in a sensitive manner; the aim was to minimize bureaucratic obstacles. In addition, each agency needed to expand locally based information and referral networks that could offer access to more specialized services than could be provided by its staff. Finally, it was clear that each AOCAP-funded agency would need to develop aggressive outreach strategies, particularly in their nontraditional service areas.

The mandates and forces described above initiated the collaborative process that led to the establishment of the New England Consortium for Services to Vietnam Veterans and Their Families (hereafter referred to as The New England Consortium). The relationships formed by the consortium are depicted in Figure 2. A commitment was made to strengthen relationships by drafting a formal charter and mission statement and by an agreement to meet on a quarterly basis to address ongoing issues of mutual concern.

Figure 2. Establishment of the New England Consortium for Services to Vietnam Veterans and Their Families

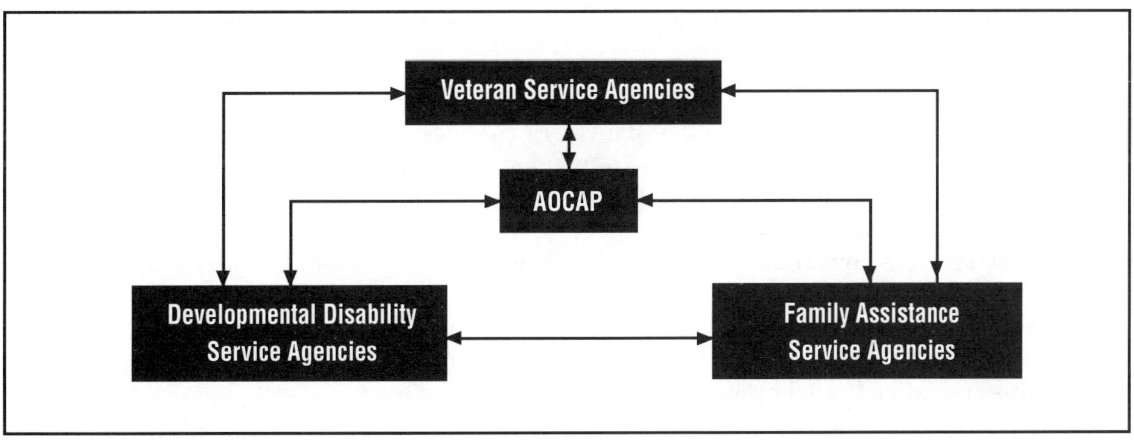

Each agency experienced system changes as a result of these new relationships. Several agencies reported that the meetings leading to the formation of the consortium were the first opportunities to share information with other agencies outside their typical service area.

Program Changes

In addition to committing resources for a coordinated outreach effort and to sharing information on services each agency could offer, the design of programmatic services was also affected. A developmental disability agency reported it had implemented a model involving individual assistance and short-term counseling on educational advocacy issues. The impetus for the change began when staff learned of the extreme social isolation experienced by many Vietnam veteran families. This information led agency staff to conclude that the typical format of offering group workshops would often not be effective. In another example, staff in one urban veteran service agency, serving minority communities, indicated to staff in a developmental disability agency located in a nearby suburb that access to services would be impossible for many urban families because they rely on public transportation. As a result, the suburban developmental disability agency was flexible in sending staff to alternative sites that were more accessible to the minority communities.

The most significant area of system change for each agency as a result of membership in the consortium was in staff development. During the consortium's initial phase, interagency communication informed fellow members of programs, procedures, and ways to reach programs within an agency. More importantly, each agency offered information on unique aspects of its clientele and made suggestions to ensure that interagency referrals were handled in a responsive and sensitive manner. In-service presentations that were open to all staff of consortium agencies provided an opportunity to share this information. Staff who made site visits also presented and received firsthand knowledge of a particular agency's operations. Several agencies reported increases in serving clients from minority communities as a result of the coordinated outreach efforts undertaken by the consortium and interagency referrals. Because individuals from minority communities often face more obstacles in obtaining services, agencies paid particular attention to competently meeting their needs.

Consortium meetings, held on a quarterly schedule, provided ongoing opportunities for staff development of member agencies. A portion of most meetings was set aside to discuss obstacles encountered in service delivery. Agencies shared their difficulties; one such difficulty was the determination of eligibility for Supplemental Security Income and Medicaid benefits. Following up on information provided during AOCAP's regional training conferences, agencies would provide additional information to members regarding differences among state policies and practices within the New England region. An agency in one service area sought advice from agencies that had greater expertise. Nonveteran service agencies were particularly interested in receiving accurate and appropriate referral information concerning veterans' benefit issues.

Another type of discussion focused on unusual or complex client needs that required specialized expertise. One staff member of a veteran service agency reported (New England Consortium memorandum, 1993) that the knowledge and support of other veteran service staff was valuable in such situations and that discussions helped him to identify new local resources and develop effective advocacy strategies. In another example, the three developmental disability agencies consulted each other in assisting a veteran's family who required van modifications for a child with severe physical disabilities. Consultation involved determination of the most appropriate type of modifications, locating a supplier who could perform the work at a reasonable cost, and assisting with advocacy for the procurement of the necessary funds. This specialized collaboration is illustrated in Figure 3.

Similar diagrams would be appropriate for illustrating specialized supportive relationships within the veteran service and family assistance service areas. Agencies that were proximate geographically, such as the pair of agencies located in Connecticut and the four programs located in the Boston metropolitan area, developed strong bonds. Proximity was a natural advantage for interagency referrals and for establishing partnerships in the provision of ongoing technical assistance.

Figure 3. Technical Assistance Relationships among Developmental Disability Service Agencies within the New England Consortium for Services to Vietnam Veterans and Their Families

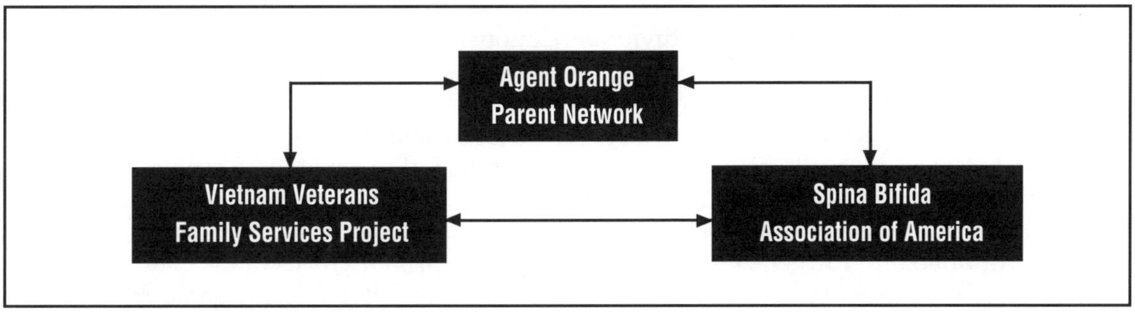

Identifying Service Gaps

The most important function of the consortium, however, was in identifying gaps in service delivery to Vietnam veterans' families. This identification led to collaborative efforts among agencies from different service areas to eliminate the gaps. At times, such efforts were prompted by the unique needs of a particular family. One example involved an unemployed veteran's daughter who was on a highly restricted diet that limited her to processed infant food. A family assistance service agency was the initial point of contact. The parents sought help with the extraordinary medical costs incurred in the care of their daughter. The family health counselor from this agency recruited donations from corporate producers of infant food and from food banks; a veteran service agency transported the donated food to a third consortium agency that coordinated the transfer of the food to the family in need.

Collaborative efforts also involved other AOCAP agencies outside the New England region in attempting to reduce service delivery gaps. An invitation from Wilderness Inquiry in Minneapolis to provide one of their trips exclusively for AOCAP families led to a consortium initiative to provide a structured recreational experience for adolescent children of Vietnam veterans. Experience suggested that many Vietnam veterans' families were socially isolated, which created adverse emotional impacts on their children. The wilderness trip was an opportunity for adolescent children with mild social difficulties to establish new relationships and to gain confidence in their own abilities. Four consortium agencies participated in the recruitment and screening of eligible adolescents. A veteran service agency provided a van and drivers for round-trip transportation of the adolescents between Massachusetts and northern Maine, and another agency provided a supervising chaperon for the duration of the trip.

A final example of a collaborative effort to reduce a service delivery gap was the creation of an innovative treatment model that is designed specifically for families with a Vietnam veteran father diagnosed with post-traumatic stress disorder. A half-day psychoeducational workshop helped family members appreciate the dynamics of their relationships, provided an environment for improved communication, and helped identify goals of mutual benefit to all family members. A complete description of this treatment model is being presented in an address at this AOCAP symposium (Cosgrove, Holcomb, and Peck, 1994). Services for members of families with a veteran who has PTSD were virtually nonexistent; the treatment and workshop model recognized that fact.

To date, the workshop has been presented at two different consortium sites and at two nonconsortium sites. Preparations are in progress for offering the workshop at additional sites. Consortium members have actively recruited families that would benefit from this service. In addition, staff have provided perceptive feedback on the effects of the workshop on participating families.

Expansion of the Service Delivery Network

Further evidence of systems change is apparent in the increased personal contacts and professional resources that are utilized by each member of the New England Consortium. These resources became available through individual relationships developed by agencies prior to the formation of the New England Consortium. Relationships to the broader community that were introduced to the consortium through its members are depicted in Figure 4. As in previous figures, relationships are illustrated with bidirectional arrows to reflect that they are nonhierarchical and mutually beneficial. Examples of the links provided by each of the three service areas are presented in Table 2. A coordinated outreach plan tapped these resources immediately. Relationships that were developed with the broader community during outreach planning continued for further consultation, although the primary focus of the consortium shifted toward implementation of programs and addressed service delivery gaps. Several of these relationships attained formal recognition; for example, associate and ex-officio memberships were created for key advisors. Often, associate members demonstrated further commitment by attending and participating in quarterly consortium meetings.

Figure 4. Resources Introduced Through Agencies within Each of Three Service Areas of the New England Consortium

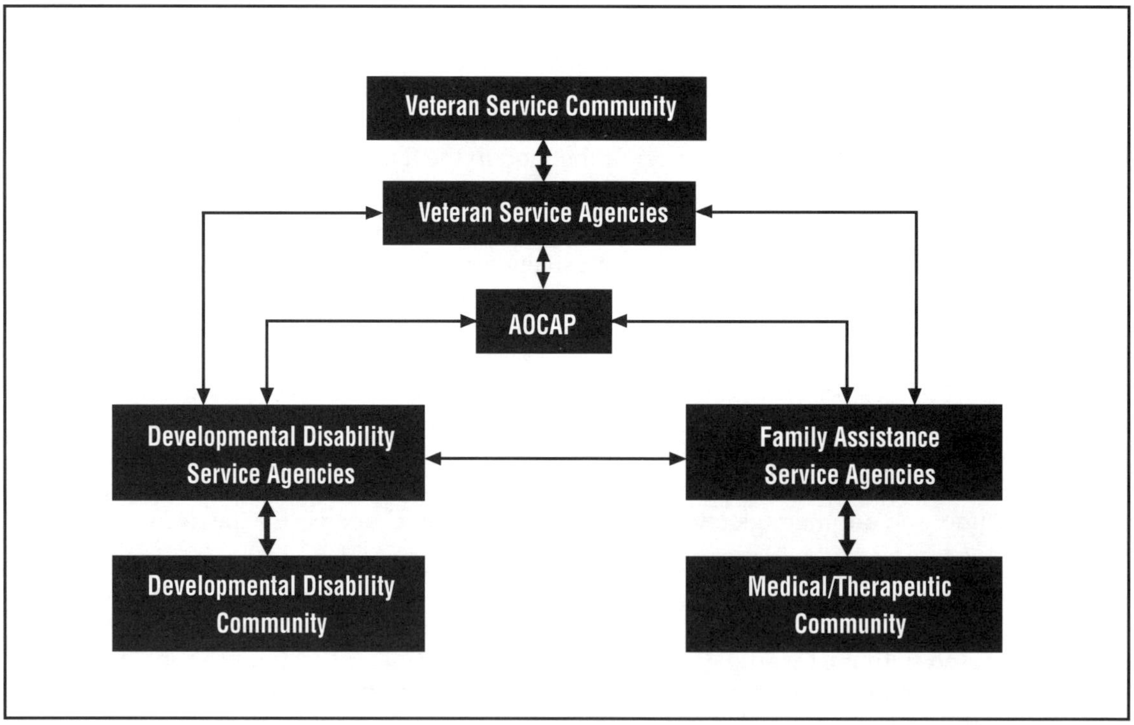

Moreover, agency contacts in the general community provided a steady source of family referrals to consortium agencies. As a result of this process, new and durable relationships were formed across service areas and are highlighted in Figure 5. For example, developmental disability and family assistance service agencies within the consortium established ties with numerous veteran outreach centers, particularly those within close geographical proximity. In another example, a veteran service agency in the consortium donated mobile transportation services to the Massachusetts Special Olympics. The agency's increased visibility in the community is being rewarded by greater success in fundraising efforts.

Table 2. Specialized Links to the General Community Provided by Each Service Area to the New England Consortium

Links from:	Links to:
Veteran service agencies	■ U.S. Department of Veteran Affairs (VA) (Federal) — VA medical centers — VA regional offices — VA veteran readjustment counseling centers ■ State Departments of Veteran Affairs ■ Veteran service organizations; examples include: — Vietnam Veterans of America — Disabled American Veterans — Veterans of Foreign Wars — The American Legion
Developmental disability service agencies	■ State developmental disability councils ■ Public school systems ■ Allied health professional organizations/ Therapeutic providers ■ Universities
Family assistance service agencies	■ Medical services/suppliers ■ Mental health providers ■ Hospitals

Consortium members, through various initiatives, are influential in creating systems change in other agencies. One veteran service agency arranged quarterly meetings with clinical staff at a U.S. Department of Veterans Affairs (VA) Hospital National PTSD Center in Boston to review the status of veteran referrals and to coordinate outpatient follow-up procedures. The aforementioned psychoeducational workshops offered to families with a veteran father with PTSD also featured clinical staff from the National PTSD Center at the West Haven (Connecticut) VA Hospital. In addition, VA and outreach center clinicians have participated as trainees in workshops presented at last year's Vietnam Veterans of America national conference and at the Brockton (Massachusetts) VA Hospital. The latter experience was particularly successful; staff at that facility subsequently expanded available family services by providing ongoing counseling groups for adolescents with family members who have service-connected PTSD. Finally, consortium members are participating in a separate coalition of mental health providers that includes plans to sponsor a two-day conference focusing on the impact of PTSD on veterans' family members. Such efforts are gradually influencing a broad network of service providers to develop more comprehensive treatment models for families with these issues.

Systems Change and Implications for the Future

At this time, with AOCAP settlement funds nearly exhausted, it is clear that the relationships developed through the New England Consortium and the increased effectiveness that has been attained in serving the veteran population are worth preserving. There are efforts to seek alternative funding sources to maintain existing programs and to develop new initiatives for identified unmet service needs. One veteran service agency reported (New England Consortium memorandum, 1993) that membership in the consortium has already assisted in fundraising efforts by emphasizing client access to a total package of available services rather

Figure 5. New Links Established Through Introduction of Community Resources to the New England Consortium

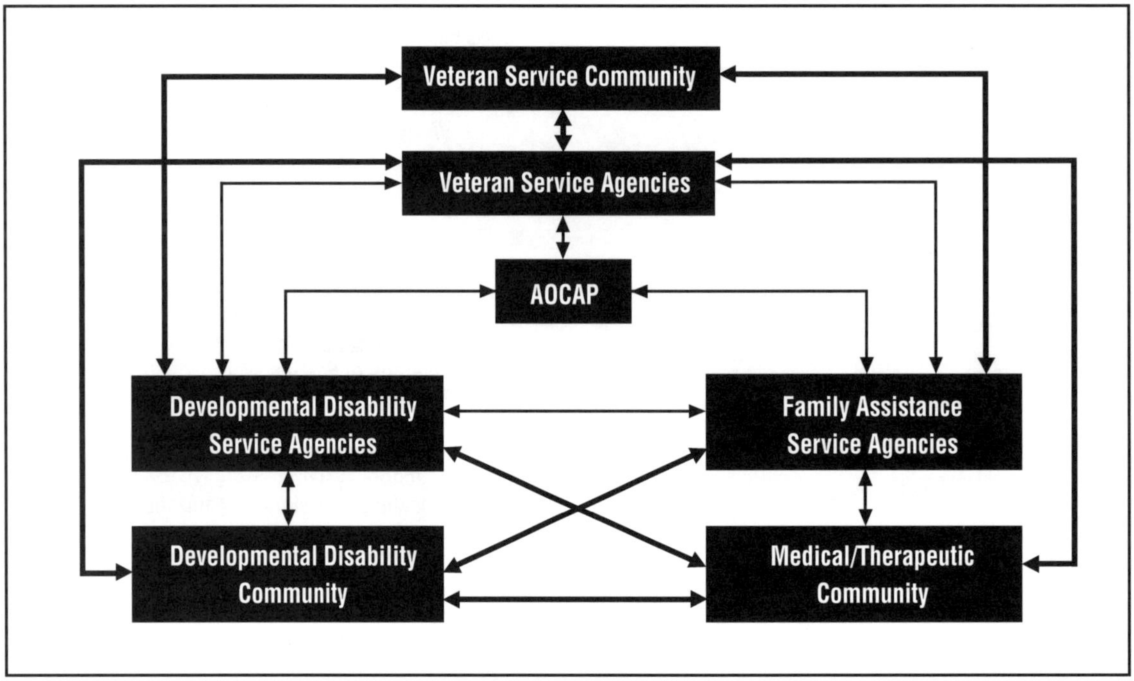

than to the more limited resources of a single agency. A family assistance service agency also indicated that the broadened network they had achieved through the consortium resulted in obtaining contracts to provide specified services.

Collaborative efforts among consortium members are also occurring in the development of grant proposals to federal agencies. Without an infusion of new sources of funds that recognize and dedicate a portion of funding for collaborative efforts, it is inevitable that the present organizational structure of the New England Consortium will be increasingly difficult to maintain. Agency staff will be reallocated to serve alternative populations reflecting funding sources with other priorities. Commitments to meet on a regular basis will eventually become impossible for many staff members. Current efforts, if they are successful, will avoid this outcome. But even if such events should occur, enduring system changes will have been accomplished in the form of each agency's awareness of the needs of Vietnam veterans and their families, of staff skills developed during the life of the consortium, and of the personal contacts and knowledge of resources that each staff member will continue to possess regardless of their individual responsibilities. These resources will also continue to be more readily accessible because of information provided to computerized information and referral systems such as New England INDEX. Finally, activities consortium members will continue to have ripple effects through the systemic changes that have taken place in the broad service network serving Vietnam veterans and their families.

References

Blank, M.J. 1986. *Metrolink-A study of eight different metropolitan communities.* Washington, DC: Institute for Educational Leadership.

Blank, M.J., and J. Lombardi. 1991. *Toward improved services for children and families: Forging new relationships through collaboration.* Washington, DC: Institute for Educational Leadership.

Bryson, J.M. 1988. *Strategic planning for public and nonprofit organizations: A guide to strengthening and sustaining organizational achievement.* San Francisco: Jossey-Bass Publishers.

Camacho, P.R., K.J. Bowen, and D. Hunt. 1991. *From a troubled past to an uncertain future: Vietnam veterans, a community at risk.* Boston: The William Joiner Center for the Study of War and Social Consequences.

Cosgrove, L., W.L. Holcomb, and P. Peck. 1994. Helping families understand post-traumatic stress disorder: A psychoeducational workshop model. Symposium of the Agent Orange Class Assistance Program, Washington, DC.

Heller, K., and J. Monahan. 1977. *Psychology and community change.* Homewood, IL: Dorsey Press.

Murrell, S.A. 1973. *Community psychology and social systems: A conceptual framework and intervention guide.* New York: Behavioral Publications.

National Agent Orange Training and Technical Assistance Project. 1992. *New alliances for Vietnam veterans and their families: Resource guide.* Washington, DC: Agent Orange Class Assistance Program.

National Assembly of National Voluntary Health and Social Welfare Organizations. 1991. *The community collaboration manual.* Washington, DC.

Ooms, T., and T. Owen. 1992. *Coordination, collaboration, integration: Strategies for serving families more effectively.* Washington, DC: The AAMFT Research and Education Foundation.

Part III

Tailoring Services to the Client: Cultural and Community Sensitivity in the AOCAP System

Human service program managers across the nation continue to struggle with fundamental questions of how to provide services that truly meet the individual needs of the members of a highly diverse population. These program personnel strive to do so equitably and with sensitivity to racial, ethnic, disability, age, sex, and other differences of those they serve. Offering services to a diverse clientele is far easier than ensuring the equitable delivery of services. Issues of trust, language, culture, and geography render substantial subpopulations of veterans and their families even more severely underserved and unserved than Vietnam veterans as a whole.

Although rural communities are undergoing unprecedented economic, environmental, and social stress, veterans and their families living in those areas typically have far fewer options with respect to veterans' and public disability service systems. Even when special efforts are made to extend programs to traditionally underserved communities, attitudinal and other nongeographic barriers may limit their scope and effectiveness. Papers in Part III explore and illuminate these issues.

Sea Worms, Northern Lights, and Vietnam: The Other Forgotten Warriors Project in Alaska

Tima Priess, M.A.
The Other Forgotten Warrior Project
College of Liberal Arts
University of Alaska Fairbanks

Abstract

The Other Forgotten Warriors Project (TOFWP), housed at the Fairbanks Vet Center and administered by the College of Liberal Arts of the University of Alaska Fairbanks, expanded counseling and outreach services available to Alaska's Vietnam veterans and their families. The project set up a service partnership between the Agent Orange Class Assistance Program (AOCAP), which funded the project, and the Readjustment Counseling Service of the U.S. Department of Veterans Affairs. The alliance has created new networks and working relationships, integrating individuals and community and social networks, as well as state, federal, and private agencies. The project is challenged by many unique cultures, vast rural geography, severe climatic conditions, and communication logistics. In conjunction with local systems and networks, the project developed outreach efforts and a training course on the effects of trauma for caregivers at all levels. The cultures of the region required project creativity and innovation in reaching veterans and veterans' families, the use of existing spiritual belief systems and ceremonies, and the encouragement of individual empowerment as important aspects of the program.

Tima Priess *is a program coordinator/therapist at the Fairbanks Vet Center, Fairbanks, AK. She holds an M.A. in community psychology from the University of Alaska Fairbanks.*

He sat at the kitchen table with binoculars, staring out the window across the frozen beach. The morning's pancakes and sticky syrup lay spilled and scattered over the table. While he searched the Bering Sea for the telltale blow of a whale, he spoke quietly about hanging out the door of a chopper with a machine gun, searching the jungle for snipers while wounded teenagers were dragged to his medevac in Vietnam.

From this isolated village of 140 people on the Seward Peninsula, eight men went to war in Vietnam. As in other Alaska Native villages I've traveled to, the issues related to Vietnam are interwined with alcohol, domestic violence, the loss of culture, and suicide. There are no simple answers. There is nothing straightforward or simple up here except the wind, the water, and the land. This is a place of extremes, of blazing sun and dark cold. It is a place where collision between humans and nature means disaster. The only way to survive is to dance with the elements.

There is a wisdom in these places of isolation where people gather together for sustenance, support, and survival. This wisdom infuses the soul and nurtures the spirit. It includes using resources well, maintaining connections with family, respecting the elders and the knowledge they carry, and sharing what there is. This pattern of community and relationship, of interconnection and communication with resources, has a parallel in service delivery to Vietnam veterans and their families in rural Alaska.

Outreach to Rural Alaska: Project Origin

When I finished my graduate internship in community psychology at the Fairbanks Vet Center, I realized that my commitment to veterans and their families living in rural Alaska had just begun. During those eight months, I helped create the Vet Center's first group for female partners of Vietnam veterans. And, I learned that there was virtually no outreach program to rural Bush Alaska because of the Vet Center's staffing and budgetary limitations. With the support and encouragement of team leader, Dr. Ken Green of the Vet Center, I wrote The Other Forgotten Warriors Project (TOFWP, the Project) proposal to respond to those needs.

There are 586,412 square miles in Alaska and the capital city of Anchorage is home to half of the state's 500,000 inhabitants. The population density is approximately one person per square mile. One hundred sixty villages scattered from the arctic North to the rain forests of Southeast Alaska are the homes of Athapascan, Tsimshian, Haida, Gwichin Athapascan, Tanaina Athapascan, and Tlingit Indians; Aleuts; and Yupik, Siberian Yupik, and Inupiat Eskimos. Alaska Natives make up 20 percent of the population of Alaska, with the majority of non-Natives living in Anchorage and Fairbanks. Of the approximately 68,000 veterans in Alaska, about 28,600 are Vietnam-era veterans.

"Availability of services" has a totally different meaning in Alaska than in any other state in the nation; here, it often means reliance on long-distance service delivery. The vast majority of the villages in Alaska are accessible only by plane, riverboat, and snow machine. In addition to the tendency to isolate and distrust government, which is common to Vietnam veterans, cultural bias, extreme weather conditions, distance, and the cost of intrastate travel make contact difficult.

The Project was initially designed to expand the range and availability of counseling and outreach services for Vietnam veterans and families living in Interior Alaska, a vast rural area with unique cultural and geographic issues, problems, and needs. The Project has expanded in scope to include many remote areas outside this service area. The town closest to Fairbanks is an hour and a half away by car, which in winter can seem as far as an hour's plane ride to a remote village. Although there are sixteen villages in the interior region around Fairbanks, so far, there has been a greater response to Project outreach efforts in locations beyond the interior.

Addressing the multiplicity of veterans' needs in Alaska requires integrating a multitude of individual, community, and social networks as well as state, federal, and private agencies. TOFWP was set up through the College of Rural Alaska of the University of Alaska Fairbanks to use the college's extensive rural network. The university trains health and mental health paraprofessionals and teachers in villages; it has considerable experience and expertise in providing educational outreach services to the largely rural population of the entire state.

In addition to the involvement of the University of Alaska Fairbanks as grant administrator, the Fairbanks Vet Center provides the operating base for the entire program. In a precedent-setting agreement, the Agent Orange Class Assistance Program (AOCAP) set up a service partnership with the Readjustment Counseling Service (RCS) to provide office space, telephones, and clinical expertise. This agreement has allowed the Vet Center to expand its outreach and its services to women and children and has provided an invaluable opportunity for the AOCAP Project to use the Department of Veterans Affairs (VA) network and services. Instead of red tape and frustration, an alliance is forming to allow the creation of new networks and working relationships between the VA and Alaska's state and local agencies.

Family Involvement Crucial to Program

There are four Vet Centers in Alaska—in Fairbanks, Kenai, Anchorage, and Wasilla (an hour from Anchorage)—but necessary funds have not been allocated to serve veterans outside these urban areas. And although RCS has begun to open its doors to veterans' families, its priority has always been the veteran, not the family.

Native corporations, such as the Tanana Chiefs Conference (TCC) in Fairbanks, provide social services to their constituents in outlying areas. Local and statewide organizations also provide mental health and case management services. But awareness of the impact of Vietnam service on individuals and communities is limited or nonexistent within most agencies.

Because such a large percentage of the service area is outside city limits in extremely remote areas, communication and public education are of utmost importance. Vietnam veterans and their families living in these remote areas are not easily identified and have very limited access to service.

> *Dorothy moved to a small village from a distant village when she married. For seven years, she lived with a veteran who drank constantly. When he drank, he became violent. At twenty-six years old, she is missing most of her front teeth because of poor nutrition and battering. When he got angry, she often had no place to go. With no immediate family in the village, she became something of an outcast, ashamed to return to the same neighbors for help and unable to go home to her parents because she had no money to fly there. She begins to shake when she talks about hiding in an unheated storage shed in the middle of a winter blizzard.*
>
> *Although his drinking has stopped, her fear remains. She says she's still afraid to speak. When his frustration builds, the whole family grows quiet. He is racked with guilt over his anger, and suffers unresolved pain over his service in Vietnam. She feels she is dying inside. A paraprofessional counselor flies in occasionally, but she feels ashamed to talk with a man. She is bright, but with young children and little money to get to town, she has lost hope for a future for herself.*

TOFWP has demonstrated through its outreach activities that treating individuals without involvement of families and communities is self-defeating. Working on issues of communication, trust, and isolation with a veteran who has no support network is self-defeating, if not damaging. Most agencies in Alaska never inquire about military service and overlook combat post-traumatic stress disorder (PTSD) as a contributing factor when dealing with dysfunctional families. Social and community involvement are keys to effective treatment, but one must also juggle a number of agencies and communication systems to raise awareness of veterans' issues and overcome cultural barriers to effective treatment modalities.

Amanda was referred to the Project through an Indian Child Welfare Agency (ICWA) worker. The thirteen-year-old child of an Alaska Native veteran, she had a history of alcohol abuse and running away from home. Her parents, Richard and Eleanor, were both alcoholics living on the streets in Fairbanks when their daughter was raped by a man from their home village. When the parents came in to talk, Richard was ready to take the perpetrator out. Eleanor spoke privately of her inability to stop drinking when she was coerced by her partner to party. She was afraid he would carry out his suicide threats if she left him.

Richard, a combat veteran, was in Vietnam and eighteen years old when he received an emergency leave to attend his father's funeral. He returned home alone on a fourteen-hour flight, the only breathing passenger on a plane filled with caskets. He agreed to begin talking with a readjustment counselor at the Vet Center. This began the family's two-year process involving the Vet Center, TOFWP, and various child welfare workers.

Initially, Richard refused to consider alcohol treatment for fear of being locked up inside a treatment facility. Through networking with the Fairbanks Native Association, the whole family, including their nine-year-old son, entered a Native-run alcohol treatment center structured like the fish camps that many Natives live in during the summer.

Through a combination of individual, couple, group, and family counseling, TOFWP and the Vet Center staff have developed many successful interventions with families. For example, Richard's family was given a new opportunity to rebuild their lives because of the Vet Center's involvement with Richard, TOFWP's involvement with the family, contact with the Native treatment center, and myriad other social agencies.

During the first two years of this AOCAP grant, TOFWP engaged a child therapist to work with children under eighteen. This past year, the University of Alaska Fairbanks contracted with the Fairbanks Resource Agency (FRA) to provide counseling services for children. FRA's primary focus is working with developmentally disabled children and adults, which has expanded TOFWP's access to that statewide network of resources. For the purposes of this grant, the agency also works with children who don't fit the category of developmentally disabled.

By developing ties with the Project and the Vet Center, FRA has become aware of Vietnam veterans in its program who have parenting or other issues related to Vietnam and to PTSD. FRA has expanded an educational outreach program in the school system that was initiated by a former child therapist with TOFWP. FRA has also started a successful series of art therapy groups at the Fairbanks Youth Correctional Facility, which houses a number of male children of Vietnam veterans.

Often, a veteran's initial decision to contact the Vet Center results from relationship problems. While he continues in individual counseling with a Vet Center counselor, his partner will begin counseling with TOFWP. The couple and the two therapists may agree to meet for conjoint sessions. The children may work with staff at FRA, and the whole family may meet together with all three counselors. The parents may also be individually involved in the combat PTSD group and with the Significant Others group, which are cofacilitated by TOFWP and the Vet Center. Although this intensive involvement is not appropriate for all, it has worked very well with many families.

Sometimes, the engagement of other family members happens in unusual ways. The veteran population in Alaska includes many veterans who moved up here to get away from everywhere else—the end-of-the-road scenario. Many of these veterans live isolated lives in

Bush cabins, sometimes alone and sometimes with family. Sometimes they get found by accident.

> *Thomas, recently separated from the Army, asked to talk with me after having been referred by the American Legion service officer at the Vet Center who was helping him process a disability claim. The twenty-five-year-old son of a Marine, he said he'd been straight and sober for a year before he went on a binge and ended up with a felony conviction. While on parole, he had been fired by his boss, who had read Thomas' name in the Anchorage paper in an article describing a robbery. Thomas denied responsibility but was fired anyway—only to learn that it was his father, who has the same name, who had been arrested. Thomas hadn't seen his father in twenty-four years and was devastated that the man who had abandoned him was now apparently the cause of his firing and a threat to his regained sobriety.*
>
> *Some time later, when I pulled Thomas' file, I noticed a second file with the same name. His father had been sent to prison in Fairbanks and had been court-ordered to the Vet Center for PTSD counseling. A successful reconciliation between the two was arranged, and, almost two years later, both are straight and sober and celebrated their Narcotics Anonymous birthdays together. After a year of group and individual counseling with both TOFWP and the Vet Center, the father, a highly motivated individual, reconciled with his other two children and his ex-wife, landed a responsible job, and entered an inpatient PTSD center to continue to heal his Vietnam traumas. He will be returning soon to start his own business with the help of the Division of Vocational Rehabilitation.*

Trauma Training Package Developed for Care Providers

When the Project was conceived, it was recognized that AOCAP's definition of "direct services" would have to bend to accommodate the special needs of clients beyond the reach of the Vet Center. An integral part of the Project has been the development of a training package, "Effects of Trauma on Families of Vietnam Vets," for primary care providers involved in the care or potential care of Vietnam veterans' families. In rural Alaska, this includes village health aides, who are responsible for initial first aid, emergency care, and referral. For the most part, these health aids have only basic medical training and no counseling training beyond on-the-job experience.

I had initially assumed that if anyone knew who all the veterans were, or had been (the suicide rate is very high), it would be the health aides and paraprofessional counselors in the villages. By providing them with basic knowledge of the effects and symptoms of PTSD and sensitizing them to the Vietnam experience, I had hoped that they would in turn be able to help veterans and families directly. However, they often don't know who all the vets are. Nor have most of them any understanding of what difference it might make if they did know. In fact, no one asks. TOFWP's needs assessment of care providers in the interior region made it pretty clear that in the villages or in the city, no one really knows how many veterans are out there because no one has bothered to find out.

There are no accurate figures on how many Vietnam veterans live in the villages or how many families have been directly affected by Vietnam. In small villages of a couple of hundred people or less, "family" is a relative term. Children are often raised by extended family members, adopted according to tribal law, or fostered out. The lines between who is an AOCAP class member and who is not are very fuzzy when alcohol, domestic violence, and broken families are taken into account. "Father" can mean "blood father" or the "one who raised me."

Using the audio-conference capabilities of the university, the first "Effects of Trauma" class was set up with fifteen students from three villages located in the interior, on the eastern border with Canada, and on the northwest coast of the Seward Peninsula. Two-hour classes were held by telephone twice a week for three weeks, earning the students one college credit toward a degree in human services technology.

Although the training goal was certainly accomplished, it was not without some crucial lessons about the training methods given the subject matter presented, geography encountered, the composition of the class, and Alaskana. The telephone site in one village was under water when the Yukon River flooded during ice breakup, so they had to cancel at the last minute. Students in another village had to crowd into the back office of the gas station because the telephone transformer in their school building was blown up by someone with a rifle.

Health aides, National Guard soldiers, substance abuse counselors, and clergy were among those who took the class. All were class members. Five were veterans. All had suffered trauma from war, family suicides, violence, or rape. It became apparent, from the feedback received at on-site follow-up visits, that talking about trauma by telephone with traumatized individuals who were strangers to each other had its limits. For example, one veteran who had trouble with the communication logistics and delays had been a radio operator in Nam; his PTSD was triggered every time the phone cut off and left someone hanging.

Later classes were reformatted in response to the students' feedback and the telephone problems. Instead of an audio-conference, the classes were held as two-day workshops on site in hub villages. This change led to deeper understanding of the challenges facing both veterans and village care providers and afforded a glimmer of understanding of possible solutions.

Health aides are almost always women who have been born in or near the village in which they work. They are, in effect, medicine women for their villages. They provide prenatal care and deliver babies, medicate sore throats, give shots for allergies and diabetes, care for the dying, patch up battered women, and administer tests for venereal disease. They are often first on the scene of shootings, teen suicides, deaths by freezing, drownings, and snowmobile accidents. Often, they discover that the victim is their own relative. When someone survives, they're heroines; when someone dies, they're overcome by their limitations. They know secrets. And they are usually related to half the village.

What I also discovered on my visits was that in many cases the care providers are themselves suffering from PTSD. Many of them have a Vietnam veteran in their family. The boundaries fade. Being bombarded with a series of traumatic accidents and deaths in a tiny village takes its toll. Talking about rape with your niece when the perpetrator is your brother-in-law may be impossible. Helping your aunt prepare her husband for burial is painful when you've just lost your father. Treating an alcoholic combat veteran who's just been in a three-wheeler accident when you know nothing about PTSD can be frightening.

> *They sat in a circle around the table, some taking notes, some looking shell-shocked. Ida told of being alone in her clinic when a veteran covered with blood from an accident was brought in for treatment. When she bent over him, he jumped up, screamed for her to keep her head down, and pinned her on the floor to protect her from sappers. She still has nightmares.*
>
> *Karen said that when she was seventeen, a veteran in her village got drunk, strapped on bandoliers, and shot her sister as she walked to her aunt's house. Karen was pulled to safety and prevented from getting shot when she tried to go to the aid of her sister, who kept calling for her as she died. Sixteen years later, married to a veteran, she has never cried for her sister or related her marriage troubles to her trauma or to his military service.*
>
> *Doris said she stopped getting close to people after she was unable to save her nephew who was shot in a hunting accident. She says she feels guilty that she has no patience with her grandchildren. She resents them coming over to her house even though she knows they often have no choice when both their parents are drinking. Her son-in-law is a Vietnam veteran.*

Putting the Pieces Together

So what sense to make of all this? How to balance the needs of veterans with the needs of the villages in general? How to combine solutions for both Native and non-Native veterans and their families? How to approach a staggering panoply of social problems and issues? In a time of declining revenue and shrinking resources, where are the answers going to come from?

What is missing and what is simply hidden? How to approach the vast range of problems and challenges without becoming overwhelmed and overcome?

> *It goes back to the dance . . . and the worms.*
>
> *On my last trip, I stayed with a veteran and his family in a small village. After talking with another veteran across the road, I stumbled back in the dark and bumped into a large bucket in the arctic entryway of my host's home. Peering in the half-light, I was surprised to see what I thought were carrots, amazed that they would grow on this icy coast. When I went into the kitchen, the kids were playing with a bucket of them. In the light, they looked . . . different.*
>
> *"Oh, they're Swedish potatoes," I said.*
>
> *"No!" the kids yelled, laughing, "They're worms!"*
>
> *I looked at their mother with disbelief.*
>
> *"Worms," she said.*
>
> *"Really? How do you cook them?"*
>
> *"You don't," she said.*
>
> *With a sense of foreboding, I watched them hoist a huge bowl of these 2" x 6" beauties onto the table and prepare to eat them. This was done first by pinching off the end, or . . . uh . . . the head. Like squeezing toothpaste out of a tube, they squished a varied array of guts into a bowl that remained on the table, rapidly filling up with offal while the skins were dipped in seal oil and devoured with obvious relish.*
>
> *I thought I saw one move in the bowl. . .*
>
> *"They're all dead, aren't they?" I said tentatively.*
>
> *"Most," he said, chewing.*
>
> *(I admit to taking a dare and eating a tiny piece. What did it taste like? A callus dipped in Wesson oil.)*

So what on earth does this have to do with anything? What it taught me is that the food, the answers, and the resources are there, but not in the form to which I am accustomed. Life in Alaska demands flexibility and resourcefulness: finding solutions for the problems facing veterans' families requires the same creativity and innovation. Solutions cannot be imposed from the outside. Alaskan villages and their inhabitants have been studied and preached to and band-aided and despaired over. Solutions must come from the people themselves.

One of the most important tasks for a healer is the acknowledgment of one's own humanness. The role of the service provider, like that of a good healer or therapist, is to help access, acknowledge, and develop what is already there—both in self and in others. The task is to recognize that we hold our own power, our own potential, our own healing, and our own choices. By walking with clients in this way, we empower them to become involved in their own process of healing, and they empower us to resist the imposition of fixing and changing them.

This is not to deny that there are innocent victims and responsible perpetrators. This is not to say that some are denied access to power by those in power. I am referring to the process of empowerment, of marshaling resources from within to match those that are offered. These inner resources reside in individuals, in communities, in the land, in cultures, and in patterns of belief.

> *We had shared two days of tears, laughs, and secrets. The people in the room, who came from many different places in and around Nome, had built a certain level of trust with each other. I asked if there was anything in their culture that created the same kind of opportunity for dialogue and sharing. Linda, Anna, and Jules remembered going to the "kazigi," the community*

house. They said that hunters would share their experiences of sealing or whaling and would sometimes depict the hunt with ivory and wood figurines of boats and animals and whales. Hunters and warriors were held in high esteem in the villages and the kazigi was a place where they could debrief from their dangerous adventures.

When we discussed the importance of talking about traumatic events, Rose and Joanna remembered their grandmothers telling them that if you saw a bad thing, you had to tell someone. Otherwise you could go crazy or have trouble with your eyes, with seeing. Sam told of an elder who had gotten lost on the ice. When he was found, he wouldn't tell anyone what he had seen out there. He went crazy and died.

The wisdom is still held by the people.

Harold Napoleon, a Yupik Eskimo writer, has written a very influential monograph, *Yuuyaraq: The Way of the Human Being* (Napoleon, 1991), which proposes that the current problems in the Alaska Native community stem from intergenerational PTSD. He relates that at the turn of the century, a major flu epidemic was introduced into the Native population by traders, trappers, and others. This "Great Death" killed thousands of Native people in Alaska; up to 60 percent of the Eskimo and Athapaskan people died. The survivors suffered terribly, often witnessing their entire family or village being wiped out by disease.

When the missionaries arrived, according to Napoleon, they found a passive and compliant people, not because it was their nature, but because they were traumatized. Not only had a whole generation been wiped out virtually overnight, but the culture and traditional knowledge of healing that had sustained the people for generations was turned upside down. They had believed illness to be the result of evil or a broken taboo. Faced with catastrophic illness beyond their ability to cope, their respect for the traditional shamans and healers waned. It was replaced with self-blame and guilt for events over which they had no control.

The breakdown in social structure continued with the introduction of church boarding schools, which removed young children from families that were already overwhelmed with loss. The children were indoctrinated into a White culture that punished them severely for speaking their own language, then dumped them back into villages where their new ways were alien even to their parents.

The villages continued to experience social upheavals during the 1960s and 1970s. By the time Alaska Native men went off to Vietnam, their roles as hunters and providers were at risk. Those who made it through culture shock and war often came back with their young identities as Native males shattered. These oppressed men had gone to war where they were given new identities and trained to become the oppressor. When they returned to their villages, they came home to families who had been only on the receiving end of oppression and had little understanding for these young warriors. As a result, power conflicts between generations, the sexes, and clans were exacerbated.

Several generations later, most elders have still not spoken of the Great Death. Their children and grandchildren, having survived subsequent famines and upheaval, are now drowning in alcohol and physical, emotional, and familial abuse. Napoleon calls for the healing to begin with talking circles and heartfelt communication with the elders. He asks that the silence be broken.

Alaska Natives, like other Native American, Hispanic, and Black Vietnam veterans, are at high risk of developing PTSD because of a combination of factors, including disproportionately high participation in combat units, racism, culturally defined masculine roles, and identification with the Vietnamese. The term "Alaska Native" refers to a group of many distinct villages, tribes, and language groups that see themselves as separate from Native American tribes in the lower forty-eight states. In Vietnam, many Natives, Asian Americans, and Hispanics were lumped together, further eroding their individual and cultural sense of self and adding to their sense of alienation after the war.

Ceremony and Healing

Warriors are created by culture to protect and to kill and to do battle with the enemies of the community. On return, the warrior is either cleansed, honored, and reintegrated, or else maligned and relegated to the edges of society and awareness. How the community views and treats its symbols of violence and rage has a direct impact on how it heals from violence and rage.

All of us, whatever our cultural backgrounds, have come from aboriginal tribal ancestors. And most indigenous cultures, at some time, all over the world, have had honoring ceremonies for returning warriors. Warriors took responsibility for going to war and protecting their villages; the villages took responsibility for accepting and reintegrating warriors back into the community. Ceremonies to honor and cleanse them of the killing were in the nature and spirit of things.

It was understood that the warriors and all that created them—their parents, their teachers, their power animals, their environment—are all part of a unified whole. To bring the community and the warriors back into balance, ceremonies were performed to heal mind, body, and spirit and to put the pieces back together again. Without these ceremonies, the warrior and the community remain disintegrated within themselves and between one another, both missing integral parts. Community involvement is, therefore, a necessary part of the healing process.

To augment individual and group therapy and address these needs for community, TOFWP has included ceremonies as part of the healing journey. Sometimes they have involved veterans and families who are already being served by TOFWP and the Vet Center. Sometimes the ceremonies have been public events that include veterans and family members who had no previous contact with the Vet Center.

> *A group of veterans, seven men and one woman, spanning three wars, stood in silence around a tub of earth on Memorial Day. In the center of the tub, planted in the earth, a single white candle flickered. As each member of the group bent forward to light his or her own white candle from this one, all spoke their intention of commitment to the next twelve weeks of intense work. Some of them spoke of fallen friends on this Memorial Day and planted their candles, watered by tears, in the tub with the others.*
>
> *For the next twelve weeks, while the work of healing went on, this tub of earth containing the melted candles stood in a corner of the group meeting room of the Vet Center. On the last day of the group, we carried this bucket of tears, of hopes, of losses, of pain, and of dreams, out to the Chena River. Once again, the group stood in a circle, and once again, this time silently, they spoke their intentions and commitment to letting go of what they could. We poured the tub's contents into the river and watched in silence as the earth was carried away. Some of it circled back, some of it stayed on the surface a long time, and some of it simply disappeared.*

Two years ago, in Anchorage, TOFWP and a handful of Native veterans and friends held a Veterans Day honoring and homecoming ceremony that was attended by more than 400 people. The event may have been one of the first in the state. It was attended by veterans, families, Natives, and non-Natives and included honoring dances, pipe ceremonies, a special warrior's honoring ceremony, and a women's talking circle.

> *In a quiet room away from the drums and noise, fourteen women from different cultures and different countries sat in a circle. We shared a common bond of being a daughter, or partner, or sister, or friend of a warrior. In the center of our circle were feathers and stones, special jewelry, and other such things of meaning. A medicine woman from New Mexico passed around a shell of smoldering sage. As each woman let the sweet sacred smoke wash over her, she focused on cleansing and purifying herself and the room in which we sat.*
>
> *When the sage had completed the circle, a carved ebony figure of a wounded warrior was passed around. As the figure passed from woman to woman, each in turn held it and spoke from her*

heart about her journey, her pain, her joy, her hopes and fears. No one spoke but the one holding the carving, and her story was received by the others with compassion, nods of acknowledgment, smiles of agreement, laughter, and tears. When all who wanted to had spoken, fourteen voices came together as one song and the circle ended.

This year, a group of veterans and families and friends from the community held a week-long Veterans Day program in Fairbanks. It was highlighted by a five-day event involving more than 220 people reading a chronological list of the names on The Wall. The week also included a Vietnam veteran talking about his healing process through work in Russia with Afghan veterans. And, on another evening, veterans of World War II, Korea, Vietnam, and the Persian Gulf talked about their personal sacrifices in a living history program. The week ended with a pipe ceremony honoring warriors and their families.

Last August, the Spiritual Unity of the Tribes Gathering was held for five days in the Athapascan village of Tanacross. Eight hundred people came from villages all over Alaska, cities all over the country, and countries all over the world, including Siberia. One day was dedicated to honoring veterans.

It began with a Lakota medicine man performing a special warrior's pipe ceremony for fifteen veterans and three female supporters. A very powerful talking circle followed. After dinner, a dance honoring the veterans was held in the Athapascan way. The dance involved an inner circle of veterans and an outer circle moving in the opposite direction. As the two groups passed by each other, they shook hands and the veterans were thanked and welcomed home.

The veterans were then asked to continue to stand in the center of the circle around the drum. A Navajo grandmother blessed specially beaded combat service ribbons with corn meal and then blessed each veteran, offering them each a ribbon. A Shoshone fancy dancer did a grass dance around the veterans, and when he finished, everyone cheered, clapped, and yelled, welcoming the veterans home. Many veterans underwent very powerful healing experiences.

For years, Manuel kept at a distance from his partner and his emotions. With tears running down his face, he said he finally was forced to look into the eyes of "them," those who had shamed him and called him "baby-killer." He felt his anger and rage had melted and that he might finally be able to see and accept love.

Lorraine, a nurse, said she still felt her heart was locked but she would never again be able to say that love was not there if she opened to it. She said she had decided to make a pilgrimage to Washington, D.C., for the dedication of the Vietnam Women's Memorial.

A week after the ceremony, Steven appeared almost to have physically changed. His voice was softer, he moved more slowly, his eyes were steady and clear. He said he had never felt so much love in his life and had finally realized that the hole he'd felt for twenty-five years was the place he'd never come home to. And, he said, "I came home that night."

Hal had been hesitant about participating at all. He wasn't sure about ceremonies and such but was curious. The next day he sat quietly and said that he had seen an eagle drape a cloak around his shoulders during the ceremony. He said he was filled with a sense of peace and that it was the first time he had felt any honor over what he had done in Vietnam.

Ben, who had been a corpsman at the siege of Khe Sanh, said that when he smoked the pipe he had flashed back to a scene from the siege that he thought he'd hallucinated at the time. After working without a break for fifty-three hours, he had stepped out of the operating room and seen one pale white body with red hair lying among the body bags. When he inhaled the smoke from the ceremonial pipe, he instantly recognized the body as his own. He realized that he had died there with the others he couldn't save at Khe Sanh, and it was time to bring that part of himself home.

Healing the Soul

The word "trauma" comes from the Greek word for wound. A traumatic event is a wounding of the soul, whether the trauma be due to war, or due to rape. The black emptiness created when the world turns upside down and inside out is a tear in the expected warp and weave of the universe. Trauma is a wound of alienation, of having one's connection to people and to the world ripped and shredded. The path back to healing includes being able to regain a sense of connection and to shed the cloak of helplessness and loss.

If trauma is a wound to the soul, then the healing process must involve spiritual healing, in some form, to bring people home to themselves. Ceremonies performed in a respectful, sacred manner can reach across all boundaries of race and color. The image of an original Unity or Wholeness is at the core of the concept of holistic health, which defines health as a balance between body, mind, and spirit. When that sense of balance is disrupted and integrity or sense of Unity is ruptured, traumatization can occur.

For the healing to be achieved, the individual's or community's nightmare of pain, grief, and anger has to be validated, listened to, and supported. Distrust must be supplanted by discernment, isolation by community, powerlessness by empowerment, shame by honor. All who are identified as part of the community, be they family or friend, seen or unseen, alive or in the spirit world, all have a part to play and a wisdom to be listened to.

As healing from trauma involves validation of emotions, making intellectual sense of the event, putting one's life and environment back together again, and binding one's wounds, so it also includes acknowledgment of the connection to a collective sense of Unity, the source of healing. Reconnecting the warrior through acknowledging the relationship to community, family, and the web of life is an integral part of the journey to Wholeness.

It is said that if you stand under the Northern Lights on a cold, clear night in winter, quietly watching and listening, you can hear the Lights whoosh and crackle. Some say they are the souls of children who have died, dancing across the sky. Others say they are torches held by the ancestors to guide hunters at night. Some invest them with wisdom, because they have always been there and have always watched and listened. Some say that to gain wisdom and know what to do, you must learn how to watch and how to listen.

References

Napoleon, H. 1991. *Yuuyaraq: The Way of the Human Being,* ed. E. Madsen. Fairbanks: Center for Cross-Cultural Studies, University of Alaska Fairbanks, College of Rural Alaska.

Cultural and Ethnic-Sensitive Issues That Service Providers Must Address When Dealing with Families of Navajo Vietnam Veterans

Helen D. Mitchell, Ph.D.
Center for Persons with Disabilities
Utah State University
Logan, UT

Lee Bitsui
Navajo Agent Orange Family Assistance Program
Ft. Defiance, AZ

Abstract

The families of Navajo Vietnam veterans live in two different worlds—one is that of modern society as lived on the reservation, the other is the more traditional "Navajo Way." In addition, members of the Navajo tribe have different views of wealth, politics, and cultural change from those of non-Indians.

The many patriotic, loyal Navajo Vietnam veterans seeking help for their families are caught between these two worlds. The cultural or ethnic-sensitive issues that service providers must address when working with families of Native American veterans present a unique concern.

This paper discusses these issues and the modern and traditional approaches used on the Navajo reservation when working with Vietnam veterans and their families.

Helen Mitchell, Ph.D., *has worked primarily with preschool programs for the past twenty years. She was a staff member of the National Diffusion Network/MAPPS Project, a home-community-based intervention program for at-risk and handicapped children in rural and remote areas. Ms. Mitchell holds an M.S. degree in counseling and child development and a Ph.D. in developmental psychology with a minor in special education.* ***Lee Bitsui*** *is a case manager, coordinator, and supervisor for the Navajo Agent Orange Family Assistance Program.*

Within the boundaries of the United States is another nation. It extends for hundreds of miles and encompasses landscape that for many typifies the American West—vast open spaces that can be described as dramatic and compelling, yet underdeveloped and harsh. Despite its seeming emptiness, this part of the United States is populated by one of the largest single Native American tribes—the Navajos. They share proximity with other groups, primarily the Hopi and Zuni (Mather, 1990). The land expands across 25,000 square miles in Arizona, New Mexico, and Utah (an area approximately the size of New England) and has more than 2,000 miles of shoreline, fifteen national monuments such as Monument Valley and Canyon de Chelley, tribal parks, and historical sites (Stan, 1989). Linguistically, the Navajo's origins lie north among Athapaskan speakers, suggesting that the Navajo people came to the Southwest long after their neighbors, the Pueblo Indians, who were primarily agriculturally dependent. These nomadic people are now settled on the largest sovereign reservation in the United States. They also have the greatest number of members living on a reservation and reflect a story of endurance and adaptability.

The story of the Navajos includes a change from nomadic and semiagrarian lifestyle to forced settlement. This period of transition was marked by armed conflict, forced migrations, starvation, and disease. When referring to themselves in their native tongue, Navajo translates into Dineh or The People. Through Navajo legend and anthropological studies, the Dineh have been described as related to the Athabascans of Alaska and the Sarells of Canada (Roessell).

As of 1990, the five largest American Indian tribes in the United States were:

Tribe	Population
1. Cherokee	308,132
2. Navajo	219,198
3. Chypewa	103,826
4. Sioux	103,255
5. Choctaw	81,299

That same year, the five reservations with the largest American Indian population were:

1. Navajo Nation (Arizona, New Mexico, Utah)	146,001
2. Pine Ridge Sioux (Nebraska, South Dakota)	11,182
3. Fort Apache (Arizona)	9,825
4. Arla River (Arizona)	9,116
5. Tohono O'Oodham (Arizona)	8,480

The Tribal Government

The Navajo tribal government was established in 1923 to meet the needs of American oil companies that wanted to lease Navajo land for oil exploration. The tribal government consists of the tribal chairman, vice chairman, and eighty-eight council delegates who represent 109 regions (known as chapters) from throughout the Navajo Reservation. Council delegates meet at least four times each year in Window Rock, Arizona, the Navajo Nation's capital. The Navajo tribal government is believed to be the largest and most sophisticated form of American Indian government.

The Navajo tribal council is the heart of the government. All other functions, people, agencies, and officials receive their authority and guidelines from the tribal council. The chairman represents the tribe's interest only at the will of the law makers. Tribal council members are concerned with order and stability, justice, protection of cultural values, efficiency, and the balancing of written and unwritten law. They act as representatives of all Navajo people and function as decision makers regarding tribal requests. Their primary responsibility is to make law (Eck, 1976).

The People

The Dineh believe there are two classes of people—the Earth People and the Holy People. The Earth people are ordinary mortals: the Holy People have the power to aid or harm Earth People. The Holy People taught the Dineh to live in harmony with Mother Earth, Father Sky, and other elements such as man, animals, plants, and insects.

The number four permeates traditional Navajo philosophy. In the Navajo culture, there are four directions, four seasons, the first four clans, and four colors that are associated with four sacred mountains: Mount Blanca, the eastern mountain in New Mexico (white); Mount Tailor, the southern mountain near Grants, New Mexico (turquoise); San Francisco Peaks, which represents the western mountain near Flagstaff, Arizona (yellow, abalone, coral); and Mount Hesperus, which represents the north near Durango, Colorado (black, jet).

The Earth People are part of the universe and must do everything they can to maintain harmony or balance on Mother Earth. Generations of Navajos have called Dinetah, "the Land of the People," the Navajo's sacred land within their four sacred mountains. Tradition holds that life and happiness is possible for anyone who lives within the boundaries of the four sacred mountains and abides by the laws of the Holy Ones (Leighton and Kluckhom, 1974) .

The Medicine Man

If disharmony occurs in an individual's life, medicine men, prayers, songs, herbs, and ceremonies are used to help cure or restore harmony and balance. The medicine man is an individual uniquely qualified to diagnose a person's problem. A disorder comes in the form of an illness, which usually is the result of the violation of a taboo, the mistreatment of animals, reptiles, or an attack by one of the Holy People. A violation may result in cancer, respiratory problems, blindness, deafness, disfigurement, seizures, mental disorders, diarrhea, or vomiting. Many Navajos believe that everything that occurs in a person's life happens for a reason. Nothing is coincidence. Anything a Navajo thinks, says, or does may affect him or her.

There are more than fifty different kinds of ceremonies in the Navajo culture. They are performed at specific times, for specific reasons, and may last from several hours up to nine days (Prerelia, 1979).

Healing Costs

The fees of a medicine man vary according to circumstances. A diagnostician, one who diagnoses an illness and recommends a ceremony, often charges about $30. A medicine man may also charge $30 for a prayer to protect a patient against illness. A one-night Blessing Way ceremony for a girl's rite of puberty may cost $20 plus the largest piece of the ceremonial cake baked for the girl. Expenses for the girl's family could reach into the hundreds of dollars.

Medicine men often charge up to $500 for a Night Way ceremony, a rite to cure people of physical handicaps. But the patient's family may have a $1,500 to $2,000 bill. This covers food, dancers' fees, a helper's fee, and ceremonial items such as buckskins, baskets, blankets, and fabrics.

Negative Thoughts

Many Navajos believe that to anticipate problems is to cause them. For instance:

- Taking a healthy child to a doctor is like putting a curse on the boy or girl.
- Wearing a seat belt is like willing an accident to occur.
- Having a negative thought might cause it to come true.
- Asking a parent to write a will is an attempt to get rid of the parent.

Navajo president Peterson Zah said traditional Navajos regard using a seat belt as an invitation for bad things to happen. "It's like you are wishing for those things to happen to you," he said. Navajo culture stresses positive thinking. Words are powerful.

Religion

There is a great deal of flexibility among the Navajos. They are a pragmatic people and tend to seek spiritual power wherever they can find it. Navajos are allowed to change. It is thought "as long as you know your path" and "that belief is healthy for you," it is acceptable to change.

Christians entered Navajo country in the late 1880s; since then Christianity has touched the life of most Navajos. The spread of Christianity likely marked the end of old-time traditional religion (Roessell).

Elder medicine men talk of a blissful religious life predating the Christians, when life revolved around religious ceremonies. Medicine men observed the rites of the seasons, beginning with spring when thunder triggered Enemy Way ceremonies for warriors. These rites cleansed war veterans of foreign elements that caused nightmares. Other ceremonies throughout the year sustained the people as they tried to retain harmony with the environment and the Holy People. In its purest form, traditional Navajo religion, as practiced before the Treaty of 1868, has almost disappeared. Many Navajos have become Christians or have joined the Native American Church, whose theology is based on the beliefs of the Apache, Kiowa, Sioux, Cheyenne, and other tribes. They may mix the beliefs of two or three religions.

Numerous Christian denominations are active on the reservation. The Native American Church has approximately 20,000 members. Most Navajos are influenced by all three religions.

The key differences between traditional Navajo religion and the Native American Church are as follows:

- Traditional Navajos believe plants, animals, minerals, and mountains are endowed with power. Every part of the world is endowed with spirit. Man, nature, and the supernatural are inextricably interwoven.
- Members of the Native American Church believe that God rules man and nature; he is above all and contains all. God rules both man and nature.

The Navajo Youth

Most young Navajos learn what they should have, want, and look like from television, movies, and popular music. They aspire to be members of both the world at large and the tribe of their birth. Navajo youth dress in t-shirts, listen to rock music, and wear baseball caps in the fashionable manner—backwards. Teenagers everywhere feel themselves apart from the world of their grandparents. Some Navajo teenagers make fun of more traditional groups, but many of their grandparents speak no English, offer blessings to the Holy People, and find the world of the white man difficult to comprehend. But Navajo youth who become "too Anglo" can be criticized by their leaders. For instance, during the outbreak of the so-called mystery illness

(Hanta virus), whose earliest victims were young, athletic, robust Navajos, some medicine men placed blame on the youth saying they had strayed too far from the Navajo way. The general belief was that people who still followed the old ways were not being harmed. Navajo youth are sometimes placed between two different worlds, causing self-doubt. "We have to balance what we are taught with what is offered by modern society," said Navajo president Peterson Zah.

Many Navajos lack household conveniences that are considered standard necessities. Seventy-seven percent of occupied homes on the reservation do not have a telephone. Thirty percent of all homes lack a bedroom. Thirty percent lack complete plumbing facilities. Only about 30 percent are hooked up to a public sewer system. Wood is the most common heating fuel (only 6 percent use electricity).

Before the 1950s, few Navajos attended public schools. Now most children on the reservations do so. The language spoken at home is most frequently reported as the Navajo language.

Navajo Reservation: Total Navajo children ages 5 years and older—131,229	
Speak only English	22,855
Do not speak English well	18,658
Native American Language	107,665

(Source: the 1990 U.S. Census)

For many years Navajo parents saw little reason to send their children to the White man's schools. Formal education seemed irrelevant. World War II changed that belief and introduced Navajos to the American dream through the armed forces and war-related jobs. By 1990, college enrollment had risen to 5,552 in public colleges and 661 in private ones.

The Navajo Veteran

Navajos are renowned for their bravery and patriotism. During World War II, more than 3,000 Navajos served in the military. Among them, a select few were inducted and trained in the U.S. Marine Corps to become "code talkers" on the front line. The Navajo language, scrambled by the code talkers, proved to be the only code that could not be broken during that war. It was used in such a way that even an individual who understood Navajo could not decipher the military code. The Navajo people and their language greatly helped to win the war, but this information was kept secret for many years in case the language had to be used again (Paul, 1992).

Today, many young Navajos enlist in the armed forces every year. The military offers steady work, which is hard to find at home, and an honored place as a warrior for the Navajo people and land. More than 4,000 Navajo men and women served in Vietnam. Reasons for entering the service vary, but a large majority believed that duty, honor, and family and tribal traditions were important reasons for joining the armed forces. More than 60 percent went into the U.S. Army, 20 percent into the Marines: Most were between the ages of eighteen and twenty-one when they began their military service.

Problems associated with the Navajo Vietnam veterans' wartime experience include alcoholism, drug addiction, depression, sleep intrusion, flashbacks, anger or rage, survivor guilt, and the inability to maintain sound relationships with close friends and family members. A significant number of Navajo Vietnam veterans had combat exposure, and approximately 30 percent were wounded.

Navajo Vietnam veterans are very proud of, and concerned with, keeping tradition alive. They are respectful of their tribal elders, customs, and ceremonies. They also can be wary of standard American therapeutic methods. Many Vietnam veterans have a sickness the Navajos call "being tainted by the enemy." In the world outside the reservation, it is known as post-traumatic stress disorder (PTSD). Some Vietnam veterans are troubled by the ghosts of their wartime enemies. Traditional Navajos believe illnesses result from the violation of taboos. In one veteran's case, the violation occurred when he came in contact with dead enemy soldiers. His platoon sometimes dug up earthen mounds that the Vietnamese had made to look like graves to hide ammunition. He often had to help to rebury the corpses. He got through the war injury-free because of spiritual help from his father who repeatedly said Navajo protection prayers during his son's tour in Vietnam. After the war, he eventually participated in a ceremony to counteract his wartime experiences. His was called the Blackening Way ceremony, which restores the balance between harmony and peace. Many Navajos believe this is the only way to get rid of PTSD.

Agent Orange Family Assistance Program

Navajo Reservation

The Agent Orange Class Assistance Program (AOCAP) offers services to families of Vietnam veterans who have children with special needs.

Program Goals

The program has the following goals:

- Provide information to parents about their children's special conditions;
- Increase parents' knowledge of available resources and how to obtain the resources they need;
- Assist the Vietnam veterans' families in obtaining social and medical counseling and other rehabilitative services;
- Enable children to be mainstreamed into local educational programs and community activities; and
- Assist parents in becoming successful advocates for their children.

Services

To meet the needs of Vietnam veterans' families, the program:

- Provides information and referrals to eligible families;
- Provides comprehensive assessment and diagnostic services when needed;
- Helps families develop an individualized family service plan of their choice; and
- Provides direct and follow-up services and maintains contact with families to ensure service delivery.

Unique problems surface when attempting to deliver quality services for a person whose culture and racial origin place them in a highly disadvantaged position from the majority. Program deficiencies affecting persons of the mainstream culture surface more easily and solutions can be reached. Even when status differences exist between an Anglo case manager and an Anglo client, they share the same world in that they speak the same language, value education, have similar concepts of life success, and view the economic world in similar terms. The same cannot be said of the Navajos. They do not share the economic resources generally available to other Americans. Program plans must always be reviewed within the context of the individual's unique economic, religious, and social background. In our concern for cultural differences, we are aware that Navajos do not speak with a single voice. Most Anglos have little or no contact with the Navajo people, and it is easy to overlook differences and misjudge the complexity of rehabilitation problems. It is necessary to examine each individual or family in relation to the beliefs or characteristics of that unique individual or family when designing a program plan for the delivery of services. The professional caseworker must work from within the Native American cultural framework and values.

Examples

A typical client is Mr. Y., a Vietnam veteran from the Navajo reservation in Arizona. He enlisted in the war before he was eighteen years old, with his parents' consent. He chose a combat unit in the Marines and believed that being an Indian helped him secure a position in an elite group. He was spiritually counseled by his tribe before going to war and felt this protected him. On his return to the community, he was spiritually cleansed but never received counseling. He still suffers from night terrors, sleep disturbances, and anxiety. His family of ten children includes several foster children. Some have learning disabilities and health problems. AOCAP provided financial aid for eye problems (eye glasses) and coordinated with the school on special educational needs. The Vietnam veteran himself requested a healing ceremony with a medicine man, and partial funding was granted. He was also referred to a veterans' group for counseling.

Mr. T., a Vietnam veteran, reported the following health problems: headaches, sleeplessness, skin rashes, and kidney problems. Since his tour of duty in Vietnam, he cannot tolerate loud noises. He has been hospitalized for "skin sores and itches." He was not helped to his satisfaction by the Indian Health Services' doctors at the hospital. He states many of the same problems can be seen in his children. One son, sixteen years of age, has a hearing loss, poor vision, sleep disturbances, and a learning disability. He recently attempted suicide and was placed in a rehabilitation center in New Mexico for five weeks. The parents were unhappy with the treatment program and complained of racism and a lack of proper counseling. The parents requested a healing ceremony for the son. AOCAP also worked with school personnel for reinstatement in school or home teaching when he was ill. We made a referral for family counseling at the Indian Mental Health Center.

K.T. is a thirteen-year-old son of a Vietnam veteran who lives on the Navajo reservation with his divorced mother, two sisters, and two brothers. His mother works at the local school. K.T.'s mother reported that her son was having difficulties in mathematics: she was concerned about his graduation credits. K.T. likes to bike and skateboard with his friends and is also a very talented artist but lacks art materials and supplies. An educational assessment revealed he had average ability to learn. Assistance from AOCAP staff included partial payment for summer home tutoring in math to augment that provided by the school and art supplies that were purchased at Utah State University and mailed to K.T.

Summary

Case management on the Navajo reservation can include working with poverty, unemployment, dietary deficiencies, substandard housing, lack of sanitation, and education as well as apathy towards federal programs. Navajo veterans are proud of and very concerned with keeping tradition alive. They are respectful of tribal elders, customs, and ceremonies. They can also be critical of standard Anglo therapeutic methods. This means that case managers should have an understanding of and a basic respect for the Navajo culture if they are to be successful.

References

Dine Beiina. 1987. An analysis of the Navajo political system by David Wilkens. *A Journal of Navajo Life* 1(1).

Eck, N. 1976. *Contemporary Navajo Affairs*. Chinle, AZ: Navajo Curriculum Center, Rough Rock Demonstration School.

Hall, E.T. 1990. *The Silent Language*. New York: Doubleday.

Iverson, P. 1990. *The Navajos*. Chelsen House Publishers.

Leighton, D., and C. Kluckhom. 1974. *Children of the People*. New York: Octagon Books.

Mather, C. 1990. *Native America.* New York: Clarkson N. Potter, Inc.

McNitt, F. 1972. *Navajo Wars*. Lincoln, NE: The University of New Mexico Press.

Paul, D.A. 1992. *The Navajo Code Talkers*. Dorrance Publishing Co., Inc.

Prerelia, F.P. 1979. *The Churches and the Indian Schools*. Lincoln, NE: University of Nebraska Press.

Roessell, R.A. *Dinetah, Navajo History*. Vol. 1. Chinle, AZ.

Stan, S. 1989. *The Navajo: Indian Tribes of America*. Rourke Publications, Inc.

Yazzie, E. *Navajo History*. Vol. 1. Chinle, AZ.

An Effective Multimodal Priority Model for Counseling Hispanic Vietnam Veteran Families Adversely Impacted by Agent Orange

Patricia A. Fox-Whipple, M.F.C.C.
American GI Forum, National Veterans Outreach Program
Los Angeles, CA

Abstract

Research has already shown that attempts to provide counseling services for Hispanic families have been generally ineffective because the methods used to provide counseling services are fundamentally incompatible with the rules, roles, and rituals inherent in the Hispanic culture. This study reports a new multimodal priority model that was established to increase the use of family counseling services by Hispanic Vietnam veteran families who are Agent Orange class members.

These modalities of the priority model described include casework support that focuses on basic food, shelter, medical, employment, and financial needs; education advocacy and assistance, including training parents to intercede for their children's educational rights as well as furthering their own scholastic ambitions; and psychological counseling (individuals, couples, families) that focuses on crisis management, post-traumatic stress disorder (PTSD), anger management, depression, acculturation, parenting skill enhancement, behavior modification, assertiveness training, relaxation therapy, communication skills, and building self-esteem.

The research is based on a pilot study undertaken in Los Angeles County. Vietnam veterans and their spouses were surveyed to determine which treatment or treatment modalities produced the most successful outcomes in terms of meeting the basic needs of families of Hispanic Vietnam veterans.

Patricia A. Fox-Whipple, M.F.C.C., *holds a master's degree in psychology from Sierra University (UWW) in Costa Mesa, CA, and is currently pursuing a doctoral degree in psychology from Kensington University in Glendale, CA. She is the project coordinator for the American GI Forum, National Veterans Outreach Program, in Los Angeles, CA.*

During the past thirty years, numerous research studies have focused on why mental health services are underutilized by Hispanics, including Vietnam veterans and their families. Most of these studies have focused exclusively on Vietnam veterans' problems associated with Agent Orange, post-traumatic stress disorder (PTSD), and Hispanics' use of mental health and other available community services. Few have addressed Vietnam veterans and their families' use of counseling services.

Several theories regarding possible causes of this underutilization problem have been published. The majority of published studies have focused on one or more possible causes, often claiming a singular factor explains a complex interrelated system. Researchers from a variety of disciplines have found it unexpectedly difficult to coordinate their findings with their colleagues, and are commonly unable to synthesize discipline-specific data.

Recent literature suggests that there are several factors responsible for the lack of Hispanic families' participation in mental health and community services. In a recent review, Reeves (1986) reports several reasons for the previously mentioned underuse of mental health services by Hispanics.

Reeves indicated that a primary factor in the lack of use of mental health services is failure of the service agency to accommodate the needs of the Hispanic family. Other researchers (Acosta, 1979; Barrera, 1978; Becerra and Greenblatt, 1981, 1986; Curtis, 1990; Inclan, 1990; Lorenzo, 1989; Marcos, 1988; Reeves, 1986) found that factors that influence the underuse of services include: acculturation; ethnic and cultural variables; treatment costs; limited numbers of Hispanic professionals; agency locations; and transportation availability.

Similar results were reported by Woodward, Dwinell, and Arons (1992) in a literature review and discussion concerned with financial and cultural barriers to use of mental health services by Hispanics.

Becerra and Greenblatt (1981, 1986) found that among a sample of veterans surveyed, a higher percentage of Vietnam veterans were found to use U.S. Department of Veterans Affairs (VA) hospitals for mental health services. No significant differences were reported between Hispanics and non-Hispanics regarding behaviors associated with seeking mental health services. Overall, Hispanic veterans expressed dissatisfaction with the services available through the VA hospitals. Hispanic veterans who used the VA hospital for services tended to have limited, if any, financial resources.

One possible explanation for the heavy reliance on publicly funded treatments may lie in a recent review of the costs and uses of public mental health services among ethnic populations. Hu, Snowden, and Jerrell (1992) found that Hispanics personally incurred the lowest costs for mental health services.

After interviewing only forty-four Hispanic and forty-one white veterans with primary symptoms of schizophrenia, Escobar, Randolph, and Hill (1986) theorized that Hispanic veterans spent less time hospitalized than their white counterparts. In addition, the Hispanic interviewees reported higher incidents of somatization.

Vietnam veterans who presented with fears of Agent Orange toxicity reported significantly more medical and psychological disorders suggestive of PTSD, psychosomatic etiologies, and other mental and physical disorders (Blackburn, 1983; Korgeski and Leon, 1983).

Family members and spouses of Vietnam veterans who suffered from PTSD exhibited similar symptomatology and psychiatric disorders (Coughlan, 1987; Solomon, 1988). As Solomon (1988) indicates, these families are reluctant to seek mental health services.

A possible explanation for this reluctance may be the problems associated with mental illness, low income, high unemployment, poor education, and limited transportation (Acosta, 1979; Locke, 1992; McKinley, 1987; Perez and Salazar, 1993). Finally, education and income may limit the number of Hispanics entering the labor force, resulting in the lack of bilingual mental health professionals (Perez and Salazar, 1993; Reeves, 1986).

The purpose of this research was to determine if the use of counseling services by Hispanic Vietnam veterans and their families would increase if food, shelter, medical, employment, financial, education, and other basic needs were also provided for through the counseling center.

Method

Subjects

Bilingual-coded surveys and cover letters were sent to 200 Vietnam veterans and their spouses. Of the respondents contacted, 27.5 percent returned completed questionnaires. Fifty-five respondents (forty-three males and twelve females) answered the survey questions in English; none answered in Spanish.

The racial composition of the fifty-five persons sampled included: twenty-two Hispanics, four blacks, twenty-three whites, and five persons from other racial backgrounds. One male respondent refused to identify his ethnic affiliation. The most heavily populated age group ranged from forty-one to forty-five years for male Vietnam veterans and from thirty-five to forty years for female spouses. The average total yearly income for respondents' families ranged from $5,000 to $14,999.

Materials

All questions were presented both in Spanish and English. Participants were guided to respond according to a sample question as illustrated in the "Introduction" to the survey. All surveys were accompanied by a stamped, self-addressed envelope.

The Mental Health and Community Services Survey (MH&CSS) was divided into two sections. The first part included eleven questions concerning the demographic characteristics of the respondent. This section is labeled in the analyses of the data reported as "Biographical Information." The second part of the survey, labeled "Mental Health & Community Services," included two questions concerning family opinions and information on mental health and community services. The importance of all respondents—even those who had not used such services—answering these questions was emphasized.

All respondents were asked to estimate how likely they were to receive counseling services from an agency devoted to addressing their personal or family needs—e.g., food, shelter or housing, or transportation—using a seven-point Likert-type scale where one means "very likely," and seven means "very unlikely." A seven-point Likert-type scale (0 = "never," 6 = "6–7 days/week"), was also employed for questions where respondents were asked to estimate the extent to which their family used mental health and community services during the past year.

After each of the two sections of the survey was completed, all participants were asked to provide additional comments in the blank space provided. A surprising number of respondents (twenty) took advantage of this opportunity to provide comments.

Design and Procedure

This pilot study is based on a blind random selection of fifty-five Vietnam veterans and their spouses from an existing database of these veterans. A survey covering demographic characteristics as well as opinions and information on their use of mental health and community services was administered by mail.

Results

Demographic Characteristics

Table 1 provides a tabulation of the demographic characteristics of Vietnam veterans and their spouses as reported in the first part of the MH&CSS survey. Education-level information for the respondent's spouse was also requested. One male respondent did not include his age, race, marital status, citizenship, or religious preference, thus the tabulations for these categories only show fifty-four responses.

Mental Health and Community Services Survey

Vietnam veterans and their spouses were asked to respond to a question regarding the likelihood or unlikelihood of their using counseling services from an agency that might also assist them or their family members with the following services: food, shelter, employment, job training, transportation, veterans' benefits, Social Security benefits, school problems, readjustment counseling, and information and referrals to other community resources. These items were also presented on a seven-point Likert-type scale ranging from very likely (1) to very unlikely (7) (see Table 2).

No significant group difference between blacks, Hispanics, whites, and others was indicated in Table 2. For three items—shelter, transportation, and employment assistance—no significant group differences between unemployed and employed respondents emerged. On the singular item, veterans' benefits assistance, no significant group difference by income levels ($0 ≥ $45,000) was indicated.

As reported in Table 2, the analysis suggests that respondents who were unemployed—and had an income level of between $5,000 and $14,999—were very likely to use counseling services from an agency that provides food assistance. In addition, respondents who were unemployed with no income or with an income level range of from $5,000 to $14,999 were very likely to use counseling services from an agency devoted to addressing job training. Also, unemployed respondents were very likely to use counseling when the agency assisted with veterans' benefits. Finally, respondents who were unemployed and had an income level of between $5,000 and $14,999 were very likely to have an interest in using a counseling agency that provides assistance with employment.

Separate one-way analyses of variance were conducted for each of the ten statements. Eight statement indices using sex, race, and current employment status as independent variables are included (see Table 3). The areas where statistical differences arose dealt with race and current employment status.

Blacks (M=1.0), others (M=2.0), and Hispanics (M=2.7), more than whites (M=3.9), reported a greater likelihood of receiving counseling services from an agency that would assist with food. Respondents employed part-time reported they were less likely to use counseling services when the agency assisted with transportation.

Table 3 includes estimates of the previous year's use of mental health and community services reported by Vietnam veterans and their spouses. The following ten services were assessed: food bank, shelter, county or private hospital, VA hospital, counseling center, Vet Center, church, curanderos, educational meeting, other. These items were answered on a seven-point scale ranging from never (0) to daily (6).

Separate one-way analyses of variance were conducted for each of the ten statements. Six statement indices using sex, race, and current employment status as independent variables are included (see Table 4). The only statistical difference related to race and the extent to which respondents used county and private hospitals during the previous year. Hispanics reported using county or private hospitals more times within the past year than blacks, others, and whites.

Table 1. Demographic Characteristics of Survey Respondents (n = 55)

Demographic Characteristics	Number of Respondents	Percentage of Respondents
Sex		
Female	12	21.8
Male	43	78.2
Age		
30–34	1	1.9
35–40	7	13.0
41–45	24	44.4
46–50	17	31.5
Over 50	5	9.3
Citizen		
Yes	47	87.0
No	7	13.0
Race		
Black	4	7.4
Hispanic or Mexican American	22	40.7
White, not of Hispanic origin	23	42.6
Other	5	9.3
Marital status		
Never married	5	9.3
Currently married	27	50.0
No longer married	22	40.7
Job Status		
None	45	81.8
Yes, part-time	2	3.6
Yes, full-time	8	14.5

Demographic Characteristics	Number of Respondents	Percentage of Respondents
Religious preference		
Catholic	28	51.9
Lutheran	2	3.7
Protestant	8	14.8
Other religion	10	18.5
No religion	6	11.1
Church attendance		
Never	8	14.5
1–2 times per year	22	40.0
Less than 1 time/month	3	5.5
1–3 months	5	9.1
Once a week	10	18.2
Weekly plus	7	12.7
Income		
No income	16	29.1
Less than $5,000	4	7.3
$5,000–$14,999	18	32.7
$15,000–$24,999	7	12.7
$25,000–$34,999	4	7.3
$35,000–$44,999	5	9.1
$45,000 or more	1	1.8
Hours per week on job		
Under 10	45	81.8
10–39 (Actual hrs. 25, 28)	2	3.6
40 or more	8	14.5

Education Level	Veteran		Spouse (n=29)	
	Number	Percent (%)	Number	Percent (%)
No formal education	0	0.0	0	0.0
Less than high school	1	1.8	4	13.8
Some high school	7	12.7	3	10.3
High school graduate or GED	7	12.7	5	17.2
Technical school	4	7.3	2	6.9
Some college	28	50.9	13	44.8
College graduate or more	8	14.5	2	6.9

Received Financial Assistance	Yes Number	No Percent (%)	Number	Percent (%)
General relief/welfare/child support	12	21.8	43	78.2
Social Security Administration	13	23.6	42	76.4
VA benefits	4	7.3	51	92.7
Other	9	16.4	46	83.6

Table 2. Likelihood That Respondent Will Use Counseling Services from an Agency That Provides Assistance with Basic Social and Economic Needs Based on Employment Status, Race, and Income Level

Employment Status and Likelihood of Using Counseling for:	Unemployed (n=45)	Part-Time (n=2)	Full-Time (n=8)	x	p
Food					
Very likely	36.4	0.0	9.1	33.56	0.00
Moderately likely	9.1	0.0	1.8		
Slightly likely	12.7	0.0	0.0		
Neither	1.8	0.0	1.8		
Slightly unlikely	5.5	0.0	0.0		
Moderately unlikely	0.0	1.8	0.0		
Very unlikely	16.4	1.8	1.8		
Shelter					
Very likely	23.6	0.0	1.8	11.09	0.52
Moderately likely	10.9	0.0	5.5		
Slightly likely	7.3	0.0	0.0		
Neither	7.3	0.0	3.6		
Slightly unlikely	5.5	0.0	0.0		
Moderately unlikely	3.6	0.0	0.0		
Very unlikely	23.6	3.6	3.6		
Transportation					
Very likely	38.2	0.0	1.8	14.84	0.14
Moderately likely	7.3	0.0	5.5		
Slightly likely	12.7	0.0	3.6		
Neither	5.5	0.0	1.8		
Moderately unlikely	1.8	0.0	0.0		
Very unlikely	16.4	3.6	1.8		
Employment					
Very likely	47.3	1.8	5.5	5.51	0.85
Moderately likely	7.3	0.0	3.6		
Slightly likely	5.5	0.0	0.0		
Neither	3.6	0.0	1.8		
Slightly unlikely	3.6	0.0	0.0		
Very unlikely	14.5	1.8	3.6		
Job Training					
Very likely	45.5	1.8	3.6	53.59	0.03
Moderately likely	9.1	0.0	3.6		
Slightly likely	3.6	0.0	1.8		
Neither	3.6	0.0	1.8		
Very unlikely	1.8	0.0	0.0		
Moderately unlikely	1.8	0.0	0.0		
Very unlikely	18.2	1.8	1.8		
Veterans' Benefits					
Very likely	56.4	1.8	7.3	22.35	0.01
Moderately likely	0.0	0.0	5.5		
Slightly likely	3.6	0.0	1.8		
Neither	3.6	0.0	0.0		
Slightly unlikely	1.8	0.0	0.0		
Very unlikely	9.1	1.8	1.8		

Table 2. Continued

Race and Likelihood of Using Counseling for:	Black (n=4)	Hispanic (n=22)	White (n=23)	Other (n=5)	x	p
Food						
Very likely	7.4	20.4	13.0	3.7	16.71	0.54
Moderately likely	0.0	5.6	3.7	1.9		
Slightly likely	0.0	5.6	3.7	3.7		
Neither	0.0	0.0	3.7	0.0		
Slightly unlikely	0.0	1.9	3.7	0.0		
Moderately unlikely	0.0	0.0	1.9	0.0		
Very unlikely	0.0	7.4	13.0	0.0		
Shelter						
Very likely	1.9	11.1	9.3	3.7	18.53	0.42
Moderately likely	1.9	9.3	5.6	0.0		
Slightly likely	1.9	3.7	1.9	0.0		
Neither	0.0	5.6	1.9	1.9		
Slightly unlikely	1.9	0.0	3.7	0.0		
Moderately unlikely	0.0	0.0	1.9	1.9		
Very unlikely	0.0	11.1	18.5	1.9		
Transportation						
Very likely	3.7	16.7	14.8	5.6	13.00	0.60
Moderately likely	0.0	7.4	5.6	0.0		
Slightly likely	3.7	7.4	5.6	0.0		
Neither	0.0	1.9	1.9	1.9		
Moderately unlikely	0.0	1.9	0.0	0.0		
Very unlikely	0.0	5.6	14.8	1.9		
Employment						
Very likely	7.4	20.4	24.1	3.7	21.34	0.13
Moderately likely	0.0	5.6	3.7	1.9		
Slightly likely	0.0	3.7	1.9	0.0		
Neither	0.0	0.0	1.9	3.7		
Slightly unlikely	0.0	3.7	0.0	0.0		
Very unlikely	0.0	7.4	11.1	0.0		
Job Training						
Very likely	7.4	16.7	24.1	3.7	25.90	0.10
Moderately likely	0.0	5.6	3.7	3.7		
Slightly likely	0.0	5.6	0.0	0.0		
Neither	0.0	3.7	1.9	0.0		
Slightly unlikely	0.0	1.9	0.0	0.0		
Moderately unlikely	0.0	0.0	0.0	1.9		
Very unlikely	0.0	7.4	13.0	0.0		
Veterans' Benefits						
Very likely	5.6	27.8	25.9	5.6	18.5	0.24
Moderately likely	0.0	1.9	3.7	0.0		
Slightly likely	0.0	1.9	1.9	1.9		
Neither	1.9	5.6	1.9	0.0		
Slightly unlikely	0.0	0.0	0.0	1.9		
Very unlikely	0.0	3.7	9.3	0.0		

Table 2. Continued

Income and Likelihood of Using Counseling for:	0 (n=16)	<$5,000 (n=4)	$5-14,999 (n=18)	$15-24,999 (n=7)	$25-34,999 (n=4)	$35-44,999 (n=5)	≥$45,000 (n=1)	x	p
Food									
Very likely	10.9	7.3	14.5	9.1	1.8	1.8	0.0	76.35	0.00
Moderately likely	0.0	0.0	9.1	0.0	0.0	1.8	0.0		
Slightly likely	5.5	0.0	0.0	1.8	3.6	1.8	0.0		
Neither	1.8	0.0	0.0	0.0	0.0	0.0	1.8		
Slightly unlikely	5.5	0.0	0.0	0.0	0.0	0.0	0.0		
Moderately unlikely	0.0	0.0	0.0	1.8	0.0	0.0	0.0		
Very unlikely	5.5	0.0	9.1	0.0	1.8	3.6	0.0		
Employment									
Very likely	20.0	5.5	18.2	5.5	1.8	3.6	0.0	44.72	0.04
Moderately likely	1.8	0.0	0.0	5.5	1.8	1.8	0.0		
Slightly likely	1.8	0.0	3.6	0.0	0.0	0.0	0.0		
Neither	0.0	1.8	1.8	0.0	1.8	0.0	1.8		
Slightly unlikely	0.0	1.8	1.8	0.0	0.0	0.0	0.0		
Very unlikely	5.5	0.0	7.3	1.8	1.8	3.6	0.0		
Job Training									
Very likely	18.2	7.3	16.4	5.5	1.8	1.8	0.0	53.59	0.03
Moderately likely	1.8	0.0	0.0	3.6	3.6	3.6	0.0		
Slightly likely	3.6	0.0	0.0	1.8	0.0	0.0	0.0		
Neither	0.0	0.0	3.6	0.0	0.0	0.0	1.8		
Slightly unlikely	0.0	0.0	0.0	1.8	0.0	0.0	0.0		
Moderately unlikely	0.0	0.0	1.8	0.0	0.0	0.0	0.0		
Very unlikely	5.5	0.0	10.9	0.0	1.8	3.6	0.0		
Veterans' Benefits									
Very likely	16.4	7.3	23.6	9.1	5.5	3.6	0.0	41.98	0.07
Moderately likely	0.0	0.0	0.0	1.8	0.0	1.8	1.8		
Slightly likely	3.6	0.0	1.8	0.0	0.0	0.0	0.0		
Neither	5.5	0.0	3.6	0.0	0.0	0.0	0.0		
Slightly unlikely	0.0	0.0	0.0	1.8	0.0	0.0	0.0		
Very unlikely	3.6	0.0	3.6	0.0	1.8	3.6	0.0		

Table 3. Extent to Which Respondents Say They Are Likely to Receive Counseling Services from an Agency to Obtain Food, Shelter, Employment, Transportation, Job Training, Readjustment, Veterans' Benefits, and Social Security Benefits

		Food			Shelter			Employment			Transportation		
Characteristics	**n**	**M**	**SD**	**F**	**M**	**SD**	**F**	**M**	**SD**	**F**	**M**	**SD**	**F**
Sex													
Female	12	2.25	1.96	1.47	3.83	2.55	0.01	2.58	2.19	0.05	3.50	2.71	0.50
Male	43	3.19	2.46		3.91	2.48		2.77	2.47		2.95	2.67	
Race													
Black	4	1.00	0.00	2.73*	2.75	1.71	1.00	1.00	0.00	0.76	2.00	1.15	0.83
Hispanic	22	2.68	2.32	3.45		2.42		2.77	2.37		2.73	2.14	
White	23	3.91	2.54		4.52	2.59		2.87	2.62		3.61	2.66	
Other	5	2.00	1.00		3.80	2.77		2.40	1.52		2.80	2.68	
Employment													
None	45	2.96	2.34	2.74	3.80	2.48	1.71	2.60	2.33	0.45	2.91	2.30	3.12*
Part-time	2	6.50	0.71		7.00	0.00		4.00	4.24		7.00	0.00	
Full-time	8	2.25	2.19		3.63	2.33		3.13	2.59		3.00	1.85	

		Job Training			Readjustment			Veterans' Benefits			Social Security Benefits		
Characteristics	**n**	**M**	**SD**	**F**	**M**	**SD**	**F**	**M**	**SD**	**F**	**M**	**SD**	**F**
Sex													
Female	12	2.92	2.27	0.00	2.42	1.83	0.16	2.25	2.05	0.00	2.75	2.42	0.08
Male	43	2.86	2.53		2.70	2.26		2.28	2.14		2.98	2.47	
Race													
Black	4	1.00	0.00	0.89	2.75	2.87	0.11	1.75	1.50	0.32	2.75	2.87	0.18
Hispanic	22	2.95	2.28		2.45	1.79		2.09	1.93		2.59	2.13	
White	23	3.04	2.75		2.83	2.55		2.61	2.48		3.13	2.77	
Other	5	2.40	2.07		2.80	1.79		2.20	1.79		2.80	1.79	
Job Status													
None	45	2.78	2.49	0.28	2.56	2.07	0.43	2.22	2.05	0.70	2.80	2.42	0.54
Part-time	2	4.00	4.24		4.00	4.24		4.00	4.24		4.50	3.54	
Full-time	8	3.13	2.10		2.75	2.43		2.13	2.03		3.25	2.55	

*$p \leq .05$

Note: All four statements were assessed on a 7-point likely-unlikely dimension, scored +1 to +7.

Table 4. Extent to Which Respondents Used Mental Health and Community Services within the Past Year

Characteristics	n	Food Bank M	Food Bank SD	Food Bank F	Shelter M	Shelter SD	Shelter F	Hospital M	Hospital SD	Hospital F	VA Hospital M	VA Hospital SD	VA Hospital F
Sex													
Female	12	1.08	1.31	0.06	0.00	0.00	1.23	0.42	0.79	0.30	1.00	1.86	0.06
Male	43	0.95	1.65		0.49	1.52		0.60	1.12		1.14	1.66	
Race													
Black	4	0.25	0.50	1.81	0.00	0.00	0.58	0.50	0.58	3.58*	0.25	0.50	0.62
Hispanic	22	1.45	1.92		0.68	1.84		1.09	1.38		1.18	1.62	
White	23	0.57	1.31		0.22	1.04		0.22	0.60		1.09	1.90	
Other	5	1.60	0.89		0.20	0.45		0.00	0.00		1.80	1.64	
Job Status													
None	45	1.11	1.65	0.92	0.47	1.49	0.48	0.62	1.11	0.48	1.36	1.77	2.83
Part-time	2	0.00	0.00		0.00	0.00		0.00	0.00		0.00	0.00	
Full-time	8	0.50	1.07		0.00	0.00		0.38	0.74		0.00	0.00	

Characteristics	n	Counseling Center M	Counseling Center SD	Counseling Center F	Vet Center M	Vet Center SD	Vet Center F
Sex							
Female	12	1.67	1.78	0.74	1.00	1.76	0.17
Male	43	1.23	1.48		0.81	1.28	
Race							
Black	4	0.25	0.50	1.79	0.25	0.50	0.83
Hispanic	22	1.73	1.67		1.18	1.62	
White	23	1.04	1.49		0.65	0.98	
Other	5	2.00	1.22		1.00	2.24	
Job Status							
None	45	1.29	1.50	1.28	0.98	1.44	1.05
Part-time	2	0.00	0.00		0.00	0.00	
Full-time	8	1.88	1.81		0.38	1.06	

*$p \leq .05$

Note: Scale 0 = Never; 1 = Less than 1/month; 2 = 1/ month; 3 = 2–3 days/month; 4 = 1–2 days/week; 5 = 3–5 days/week; 6 = 6-7 days/week.

Discussion

To summarize, the data suggest and support the likelihood of increased use of counseling services by Hispanic or Latino Vietnam veterans and their families when food assistance is provided by the agency.

Many Hispanic Vietnam veterans and their families are plagued by problems associated with basic social, economic, physical, and psychological needs. Similar results were reported by the above-mentioned research studies addressing use of mental health services by Hispanics. This study does not, however, support Becerra and Greenblatt's (1981,1986) findings that Vietnam veterans used the VA hospital for mental health services, and no significant difference among ethnic groups was reported. One reason for the discrepancies may be that this study covered the family mental health–seeking behavior vs. the individual veteran's behavior.

Fundamental needs become paramount among individuals and families when a deficit exists. It is important to note whether a particular need has been satisfied recently and how strong other, more basic, needs may be. In priority order, casework support focusing on fundamental physiological needs must be satisfied; then other psychological areas can be addressed. Mental health workers must be sensitive to personal and family needs. Therefore, initial screening may be required to rule out "need deficits" before psychotherapy can be successfully employed.

As supported by this study, individual needs do not always follow a specific order. One possible explanation for respondents' expressing a strong interest in job training, employment assistance, and veterans' benefits may be related to their low income, socioeconomic status, and unemployment. These same fundamental needs are often routinely satisfied but may be adversely influenced by environmental variables such as high unemployment, high-crime communities, limited housing, poor health and education facilities, agency locations, and transportation availability.

It is clear from this pilot study that Hispanic Vietnam veterans and their families as well as other ethnic groups report a need for counseling services that emphasize providing assistance on everyday psychosocial stressors where "need deficits" are most often encountered.

Because of the specific problems associated with Vietnam veterans and their families, an effective comprehensive perspective encompassing the total realm of social, economic, physiological, and psychological needs may be indicated and therefore highly recommended in the delivery of counseling services to Hispanic Vietnam veterans and their families. More exhaustive research is needed to determine what the most effective service delivery program should include.

References

Acosta, F.X. 1979. Barriers between mental health services and Mexican American examination of a paradox. *American Journal of Community Psychology* 14(10):504-505.

Barrera, M., Jr. 1978. Mexican-American mental service utilization: A critical examination of some proposed variables. *Community Mental Health Journal* 14(1):43.

Becerra, R.M., and M. Greenblatt. 1981. The mental health-seeking behavior of Hispanic veterans. *Comprehensive Psychology* 22(1):124-133.

Becerra, R.M., and M. Greenblatt. 1981. The needs of Hispanic Vietnam veterans. In *Psychiatric Epidemiology and Prevention: The Possibilities* (Series No. 8), ed. R.L. Hough, P.A. Gongia, V.B. Brown, and S.E. Goldston, 273-284. Los Angeles, CA: Prevention Publications.

Blackburn, A.B. 1983. Review of the effects of Agent Orange: A psychiatric perspective on controversy. *Military Medicine* 148(4):333-340.

Coughlan, K. 1987. Women partners of Vietnam vets. *Journal of Psychosocial Nursing and Mental Health Services* 25(10):25-27.

Curtis, P.A. 1990. The consequences of acculturation of service delivery and research with Hispanic families. Special Issue: Culture and clinical social work. *Child and Adolescent Social Work Journal* 7(2):147-159.

Escobar, J.I., I. Javier, E.T. Randolph, and M. Hill. 1986. Symptoms of schizophrenia in Hispanic and Anglo veterans. *Culture, Medicine and Psychiatry* 10(3):259-276.

Hu, T., L.R. Snowden, and J.M. Jerrell. 1992. Costs and use of public mental health and substance abuse services. *Journal of Mental Health Administration* 19(3):278-287.

Inclan, J. 1990. Understanding Hispanic families: A curriculum outline. Special Issue: Working with the urban poor. *Journal of Strategic and Systemic Therapies* 9(3):64-82.

Korgeski, G.P., and G.R. Leon. 1983. Correlates of self-reported and objectively determined exposure to Agent Orange. *American Journal of Psychiatry* 140(11):1443-1449.

Locke, D.C. 1992. *Increasing Multicultural Understanding: A Comprehensive Model.* Newbury Park, CA: Sage Publications.

Lorenzo, G. 1989. Current issues in the assessment and treatment of ethnic minority populations. *Psychotherapy in Private Practice* 7(3):133-140.

Marcos, L.R. 1988. Understanding ethnicity in psychotherapy with Hispanic patients. *American Journal of Psychoanalysis* 48(1):35-42.

McKinley, V. 1987. Group therapy as a treatment of modality of special value for Hispanic patients. *International Journal of Group Psychotherapy* 37(2):255-268.

Perez, S.M., and D.D. Salazar. 1993. Economic, labor force, and social implications of Latino education and population trends. *Hispanic Journal of Behavioral Sciences* 15(2):188-229.

Reeves, K. 1986. Hispanic utilization of an ethnic mental health clinic. *Journal of Psychosocial Nursing and Mental Health Services* 24(2):23-26.

Solomon, Z. 1988. The effect of combat-related post traumatic stress disorder on the family. *Psychiatry* 51(3):323-329.

Woodward, A.M., A.D. Dwinell, and B.S. Arons. 1992. Barriers to mental health care for Hispanic Americans: A literature review and discussion. Special issue: Multicultural mental health and substance abuse services. *Journal of Mental Health Administration* 19(3):224-236.

Rural Veterans: Traumas and Transition

Wayne Price, L.C.S.W., M.P.A.
Grants Pass, OR, Vet Center

Abstract

Rural veterans and their families need specialized assistance during times of life crises. Many Vietnam veterans are experiencing traumatic events such as loss of employment or major health problems. These concerns, in addition to unresolved post-traumatic stress disorder (PTSD), can create significant difficulties for veterans and their family members which may result in a reevaluation of family values and dynamics.

Strategies for assisting rural veterans and their families during such times may pose a dilemma for the caregiver. A veteran may resist outside intervention and feel alienated from organizations that may be able to provide services or additional help. Strategies are required to approach and help an individual in this condition and frame of mind. Often there is a need to mobilize a variety of different agencies to provide what limited resources may exist and then encourage the veteran to accept their assistance.

***Wayne Price, L.C.S.W., M.P.A.**, is team leader of the Vet Center in Grants Pass, OR. He is a Vietnam veteran. He served as a social work specialist and medic.*

Rural veterans are an underserved population. Their wide diversity, in not only vast geographical areas but also in cultural and individual differences, makes them a difficult and more expensive group to service. Historically, they have had limited political power in pursuing services and have characteristics of isolationism and self-reliance, which have limited their pursuit of needed entitlements.

Caregivers have needed to rely on informal as well as formal resources in order to provide much needed services to rural veterans. Often it is necessary for other family members to take on the role of advocate to ensure the veteran's medical and psychological needs are met. It is vital for the rural service provider to identify sources within the family, as well as community, best to coordinate and mobilize resources. The large number of needs and limited resources creates a monumental challenge for the caregivers involved in this process.

The challenge for politicians and decision makers at the state and national levels is to develop a variety of service models that can meet the multitude of needs that rural veterans may experience as a result of psychological and medical problems and financial and geographical restraints. Meeting this challenge involves implementing a variety of models reflecting the most urgent needs of veterans and their families in specific rural areas, and with sensitivity to local cultures. This, in a time of governmental fiscal restraints, is the challenge that faces those concerned with providing adequate care to eligible veterans and their families.

Rural Environment

It is important to note that all rural areas are not alike and that they are not static. Although the U.S. Bureau of the Census defines rural as those individuals living in towns with a population of less than 2,500 or in open spaces (Cordes, 1987), perhaps a more useful way of defining what is rural is the one that is outlined by Ken Deavers (1992). He describes rural areas as having three characteristics: small-scale, low-density settlements; distance from large urban centers; and increasing specialization of rural economies. When rural economies are defined according to their economic nature, they include areas that are involved in farming; manufacturing; mining; specialized government counties, where specific government installations exist; persistent poverty counties; federal land counties, where at least a third of the areas are owned by the federal government; and destination retirement counties (Cordes, 1987).

Rural people tend to have more confidence in local institutions rather than larger, outside ones. There is a strong value in self-sufficiency and individualism, with a somewhat stronger religious involvement as a group than urban people (Bigbee, 1993).* Although there may be differences in how rural areas are defined, most people who live in them have a sense of identity to a rural life style. One-fourth of the U.S. population lives in rural areas (Bachrach, 1983). Depending upon how rural is defined, this involves between 40 million and 60 million people.

Many rural households remain patriarchal, family- and work-oriented. When the veteran is not able to find a job or continue working because of illness, often his or her spouse must take on added responsibilities on behalf of the family. The wife must help her husband identify and access resources. Without persistent, quick action, the family can become homeless as well, which commonly happens with single veterans. Unfortunately, some organiza-

*Combat veterans in rural areas who are involved in seeking services are, of course, usually male. Outreach to rural women veterans, although important, has historically been difficult to achieve in relation to similar efforts in more urban areas.

tions tend to eliminate the spouse from the helping process rather than incorporate them into the process as a key member of the treatment team.

Economic Realities

Rural economies tend to be specialized (Deavers, 1992). There has been a shift from rural economies based primarily on farming to economies based on a variety of sources including manufacturing, retirement, and mining and natural resources (Human and Wasem, 1991). The economies are greatly influenced by conditions and policy decisions made far from the local area. This has led to a boom and bust cycle in many rural economies. Median incomes of rural families are approximately 75 percent of that of urban families. One in six rural residents lives in poverty compared with one in ten in urban areas (Bigbee, 1993). Unemployment rates continue to be higher in rural areas. There are fewer higher paying occupations in rural areas compared with metropolitan areas, and there is a larger number of working poor. Underemployment is a significant factor in suppressing family incomes in rural communities.

In addition to these preexisting economic hardships, much of the 1980s was characterized by an economic downsizing (Human and Wasem, 1991). Although there may be brief periods of modest improvement, many rural areas are experiencing a decline, making it increasingly difficult for economically disadvantaged rural people to maintain their current standards of living. This results in fewer services being available because of a reduced tax base and limited political power. Catastrophes, such as loss of employment or major illness, create havoc for these families when they occur. There are limited job training opportunities and few jobs even for those with the training. Because affected families often do not have personal resources, the crisis is immediate and severe.

Rural Health Care Delivery

The geographic and economic characteristics of rural life have a significant impact on the delivery of health care services. The more isolated a community, the higher its poverty rate. Many authors describe the lack of availability of services, particularly mental health services, in rural areas (Human and Wasem, 1991; Manolis, 1987; and Meyer, 1990). Lack of adequately trained personnel creates difficulty in the delivery of services. High workloads and limited opportunity for continuing education as well as professional isolation tend to increase staff burnout for rural health caregivers. Service providers who come from more urban areas to live and work in rural settings must take time and effort to become accepted (Bachrach, 1983).

Access to services by individual clients is another common problem found in rural areas. Factors making access to services more difficult include long distances to providers, lack of public transportation, and the lack of outreach services. Although attempts (such as small outpatient clinics or mobile treatment units) have been made in various rural areas to address this problem, this circumstance continues to be a major impediment to obtaining care. Acceptability of services refers to those services being offered in a manner acceptable to potential clients. Local beliefs about the nature of specific problems and trust in the provider are elements of this problem. Many veterans complain of the red tape involved when they seek services at various U.S. Department of Veterans Affairs (VA) facilities. Long waits and discourteous treatment by staff are common complaints by veteran clientele.

These problems are aggravated when specialized care not available on the local level is required. Obtaining such care could involve traveling even longer distances to urban areas and being treated by large health care institutions that, historically, lack the personal touch more characteristic of services provided in a rural setting. This quality, along with mistrust of providers, will lead individuals to seek private medical care when it is financially feasible to do so. One study found that lack of the personal touch was the primary reason eligible veterans sought care through private practitioners (Licciardone, 1990). Other factors that could impact the care of health services in a rural environment include local mores that incorporate a sense of fatalism, which is particularly true within the veteran community. With many living in rural communities, there is a certain stigma in seeking mental health care. Barriers, such as county lines, mountain ranges, rivers, or other geographical features may add further psychological limitations to seeking care.

Outpatient travel costs are an impediment to providing care in rural settings. Bachrach (1983) reports that the cost of such travel is $0.59 per mile in rural areas compared with $0.08 in urban areas. When outreach is involved to more remote rural areas, staff travel to these outlying areas is the most significant cost item in the delivery of these services (Bachrach, 1983). The dispersed populations hinder the delivery of services because catchment areas tend to be much larger.

Veterans

Retirement-aged veterans tend to reflect the migration patterns that are reflective of the retirement age bracket (Cowper and Longino, 1992). There are a significant number of Vietnam veterans who led a transitory lifestyle during the 1970s and 1980s. These veterans, now in their forties and early fifties, tend to be more settled. For those who live in rural areas, many of their attitudes of isolation, self-sufficiency, and mistrust of larger, governmental institutions tend to reflect those of their community. Many veterans, however, seem often to demonstrate more pronounced beliefs in this regard.

Veterans tend to earn incomes equivalent to those of nonveterans with similar educational backgrounds. Veterans who served in combat areas, however, tend to earn approximately 10 percent less than veterans who were not in combat. As described earlier, unemployment and underemployment are problems for combat veterans in rural settings, particularly those who suffer from post-traumatic stress disorder (PTSD). Some of these veterans live very isolated lives and have major problems finding and maintaining adequate employment.

Veterans who have been able to maintain family relationships appear to be coping somewhat better economically than veterans who do not. But marital relationships of combat veterans are characterized by more conflict, less intimacy, less cohesion, less expressiveness and satisfaction than those of veterans who were not in combat (Solomon et al., 1992). Combat veterans are also likely to have trouble integrating past memories with present experiences, to have an impaired self-concept, and to use depersonalization in their interactions with others as well as to have difficulty with depression, shame, anger, and a general impairment of social relationships (Figley and Sprenkle, 1976).

Coming to grips with their past combat experiences has aggravated the problems of low self-esteem, isolation, financial instability, and marital discord. When a veteran is confronted with a serious life crisis, such as loss of employment and more particularly major medical illness, there often needs to be a reevaluation and shift of responsibilities within the family unit. Commonly, it is necessary for the spouse to become more assertive in decision making and helping to choreograph attempts to access care.

Veterans seem to be more effective in dealing with the many frustrations involved in obtaining care when assisted by their significant other. Spouses can play an important role in navigating the many barriers involved in obtaining treatment and providing encouragement to the veterans to stay involved in the process. When major traumas do occur, often there is a reemergence of PTSD symptoms, even though gains may have been made in prior treatment. It is important for the caregiver to involve all capable family members in the treatment process. It is also important to prioritize goals and to limit counseling objectives until a plan of action is set in motion for the treatment of medical problems, employment issues, or other basic needs issues.

Perceptions and Realities

One study on differences in perceptions of well-being between urban and rural populations in the United States indicated that the key factors determining one's perception of well-being are financial status, marital status, and education (Mookherjee, 1988). A study on psychological well-being by Amato and Zuo (1992) found that poverty and marital status have a major impact on a sense of well-being, but that these problems are more pronounced in rural areas. They concluded that there is a significant relationship between stress and chronic strains associated with poverty. There are fewer social supports and a more negative attitude toward reliance on public assistance in rural areas.

The economically disadvantaged veteran in a rural area is an underserved population. Reports by the Office of Rural Health Policy and the VA's Commission on Future Structure of Veterans Health Care have documented this condition. Most studies have detailed the lack of availability and a lack of accessibility to services for rural veterans. Both reports described approaches to dealing with these problems, but there are indications that Congress has been sidestepping them or not dealing with the key issues in a direct and timely manner. Many legislative recommendations involve amending tax codes, reducing regulatory barriers, and providing educational assistance to would-be caregivers. This effort is being undertaken at a time when existing service organizations, including rural hospitals, mental health agencies, social service organizations, and VA facilities, are inadequately funded to provide the same level of care that they had in previous years. In effect, the need for multiple services is increasing, and the limited resources available are actually decreasing. The result is a crisis in accessing care while the need is of critical proportions.

Procedures and Policies

Rural caregivers must develop both formal and informal networks to provide assistance to their clients with a multitude of problems. This involves coordinating efforts with other agencies within the community to meet objectives. Although rural health and mental health clinics as well as mobile medical vans help meet needs in some rural areas, the demands are overshadowed by the needs.

Rural mental health, medical, and social service providers must be able to identify developing problems within their area. They must form alliances, both formal and informal, to coordinate better their efforts to provide the best possible care to veterans and other clients. This is critical because of the limited resources, including personnel and financial limitations. Some willingness to experiment may be necessary because of the evolving needs of a community and the difference between one rural area and another.

There is often a need to refocus the delivery of services. Plans must be in place to ensure that clients are getting their basic needs met. Otherwise, attempts at therapy will be futile. This may require a therapist becoming actively involved helping the client meet social service needs. Manolis (1987) referred to a similar situation when he described it often being necessary for primary care physicians to act in the role of psychiatrists. There is often a need to become a generalist care provider to ensure that all the needs of a client are met.

In some locales, the use of mobile vans or satellite treatment units may not prove to be cost-effective or acceptable to local cultures. Many opportunities arise to organize efforts to meet the needs of clients, which does not necessarily have to be done by traditional organizations. One example of this is in Josephine County, Oregon, where a coalition of veterans' organizations formed to make up food boxes for homeless individuals and indigent families. They arranged for these boxes to be provided by existing organizations where veterans are likely to come for professional services. One veterans' organization worked in cooperation with a regional VA facility to obtain their own van. This van is used to provide transportation to medical appointments for veterans without private transportation. This effort has greatly enhanced the accessibility of care. The local Vet Center helps coordinate these efforts, even though the primary sponsors are the veterans' organizations.

Efforts may include collaboration with other agencies providing similar services to maximize efficient use of existing resources. Vet Centers in many rural areas cooperate with local community organizations, churches, or Indian tribes to conduct group therapy in locations far from their offices.

Some primary care efforts in certain areas have been arranged along similar lines. These coordinated efforts, based on local needs and resources, often would benefit from outside funding, but usually policy makers do not exhibit the flexibility to meet unique community circumstances.

Policy Making

Policy makers often have a better understanding of the current health crisis in rural America than many local communities give them credit for. The problem appears to be in how to develop plans that are equitable and cost-effective. Unfortunately, two difficulties often arise: policy decisions at the national level may not translate to the specific needs of local communities; and long delays occur in getting necessary legislation enacted and implemented. Even when legislation is enacted, it may not focus directly on the primary needs.

Oliver Meadows of the VA Commission on Veterans Health Care testified regarding rural service needs and solutions before the Committee on Veterans Affairs in the U.S. House of Representatives. He described the problems of availability and accessibility of care, and offered a number of possible solutions, including increased use of services on a contracting and fee basis. He also discussed the sharing of resources by the VA with other public agencies (Meadows, 1991).

Bachrach (1983) also talks about the failure of service planners to appreciate the unique cultural and socioeconomic features of rural areas. He implies that urban decision makers may not fully understand the diversity of rural cultures.

It may prove valuable for federal decision makers to review the grants made by private veterans' advocacy organizations to gain a better understanding of the accomplishments of these private grants. Providing grants to meet unique needs of specific localities could prove to be a viable approach to addressing problems in rural settings. Increased communication between federal decision makers and the local community would likely prove helpful.

Conclusions

As the rural veteran population ages, and because of lingering stress-related problems, psychological and medical difficulties will increase. There will be a growing demand for services by an already underserved population, which will add to strains on the veteran and his family. They may need to develop new roles and responsibilities within the family. Spouses may need to become better educated about how to access care delivery systems and become the primary advocate.

Local caregivers must be aware of this situation and be prepared to assist veterans and their families to meet these new challenges. At the same time, local caregivers must renew outreach efforts and cooperative efforts with other agencies and informal caregivers to meet these needs. There is no one solution to this array of difficulties. Therefore, strategies must be developed at the local level to meet the most pressing needs in their specific rural areas.

Policy makers at the national level must be made aware of the complexities of the problems and develop policies that can deliver services in an appropriate and timely manner. This outcome will require increased or reallocated funding and an openness to trying innovative approaches. Rural veterans, their families, and care providers will require the support of policy makers to ensure the adoption of legislation and other policies providing for concentrated efforts on a continuing basis.

References

Amato, P., and J. Zuo. 1992. Rural poverty, urban poverty, and psychological well-being. *The Sociological Quarterly* 33(2):229-240.

Bachrach, L., Ph.D. 1983. Psychiatric services in rural areas: A sociological overview. *Hospital and Community Psychiatry* 34(3):215-226.

Bigbee, J., R.N., Ph.D. 1993. The uniqueness of rural nursing. *Rural Nursing* 28(1):131-144.

Cohany, S. 1992. The Vietnam-era cohort: Employment and earnings. *Monthly Labor Review,* June 1992, 15.

Cordes, S. 1987. The changing rural environment and the relationship between health services and rural development. *Health Services Research* 23(6):757-784.

Cowper, D., M.A., and C. Longino, Jr., Ph.D. 1992. Veteran interstate migration and VA health service use. *The Gerontologist* 32(1):44-50.

Deavers, K. 1992. What is rural? *Policy Studies Journal* 20(2):184-189.

Decoufle, P., P. Holmgreen, C. Boyle, and N. Strope. 1992. Self-reported health status of Vietnam veterans in relation to perceived exposure to herbicides and combat. *American Journal of Epidemiology* 135(3):312-323.

DeLeon, P., M. Wakefield, A. Schultz, J. Williams, and G. VanderBos. 1989. Rural America. *American Psychologist* 44(10):1298-1306.

Figley, C.R., Ph.D., and D. Sprenkle, Ph.D. 1976. Delayed stress response syndrome: Family therapy indications. *Journal of Marriage and Family Counseling* 4(3):53-59.

Harris, R., and L. Leininger. 1992. Preventive care in rural primary care practice. *Cancer Weekly*, Nov. 23, 15(1).

Human, J., and C. Wasem. 1991. Rural mental health in America. *American Psychologist* 46(3):232-239.

Licciardone, J. 1990. Use of Veterans Administration outpatient facilities by older, rural veterans. *Journal of American Osteopath Association* 90(4):331-336.

Long, N., Ph.D., K. Chamberlain, M.A., and C. Vincent, M.A. 1992. The health and mental health of New Zealand Vietnam War veterans with post-traumatic stress disorder. *The New Zealand Medical Journal* 105(944):417-419.

Manolis, D., M.D. 1987. Diffusing the crisis in rural mental health care. *Minnesota Medicine* 70:14-15.

Meadows, O. 1991. VA Commission on the Future Structure of Veterans Health Care. Statement before Committees on Veterans' Affairs, U.S. Senate and House of Representatives. Oct. 23, 1991, 1-19.

Meyer, H. 1990. Rural America—Surmounting the obstacles to mental health care. *Minnesota Medicine* 73:24-31.

Mookherjee, H. 1988. Perceptions of well-being by metropolitan and nonmetropolitan populations in the United States. *The Journal of Social Psychology* 132(4):513-534.

Solomon, Z., M. Waysman, R. Belkin, G. Levy, M. Mikulincer, and D. Enoch. 1992. Marital relations and combat stress reaction: The wives' perspective. *Journal of Marriage and the Family* 54:316-326.

Geographic and Demographic Influences on Three University-Based AOCAP Projects in the Gulf-South Region

Melanie Deffendall, M.A.; and Bonnie M. Kelly, M.A., N.C.S.P.
Louisiana State University Medical Center

Gail Davies, R.N., M.S.W.; and Mary Janik Smith, A.C.S.W.
Florida State University

Susan Turner, M.S.W.; and Bruce L. Hoem, M.A.
University of Southern Mississippi

Abstract

In comparing three Agent Orange Class Assistance Program (AOCAP) projects in the Gulf South, this research has identified differing demographics among the population served, resource availability gaps, and differences in the service delivery process. Veterans and their families are the recipients of social, mental health, educational, and health services under these AOCAP projects. Projects in Florida, Louisiana, and Mississippi aim to provide comprehensive services but approach the task in different ways due to the types of available resources, client population, and urban or rural character of the regions the projects serve. The Florida project is asked to provide marital and family therapy most often while the Louisiana project focuses on service coordination and outreach. The Mississippi project delivers service coordination primarily to children of veterans.

Case studies representing each of the three areas are included in the paper. This comparison of the three projects points out the difficulty of delivering service in a rural area and to the need to examine holistically the needs of the population being served, wherever it is located. Contributing to the success of the projects are strong efforts in service coordination, collaboration, and communication with other agencies and groups.

***Melanie Deffendall** has a master's degree in sociology and is the service coordinator for the Vietnam Veterans Family Support Project, Louisiana State University Medical Center. **Bonnie M. Kelly, M.A., N.C.S.P.**, is the project coordinator for the Vietnam Veterans Family Support Project at the Louisiana State University Medical Center. **Gail Davies, R.N., M.S.W.**, is the associate director of the Vietnam Veterans Families Project at Florida State University. **Mary Janik Smith, A.C.S.W.**, is the project assistant, Vietnam Veterans Families Project, Florida State University. **Susan Turner, M.S.W.**, serves as the project coordinator for the Mississippi Vietnam Veterans' Family Support Network, University of Southern Mississippi. **Bruce L. Hoem, M.A.**, is service coordinator for the Mississippi Vietnam Veterans' Family Support Network, University of Southern Mississippi.*

Three Agent Orange Class Assistance Programs (AOCAP) located in the Gulf-South region are profiled in this paper. Although each project is both family oriented and designed to assist Vietnam veterans and their families with accessing services, the differences among the programs are notable.

This paper examines the commonalities and differences among the projects, with regard to the rural and urban nature of the geographic locale, the characteristics of the veteran population served by each project, the scope of resources available, and the key elements of the service delivery process. This project comparison reveals gaps in and among service systems for Vietnam veterans' families. Case histories provide insight into the function of each project.

Rural and Urban Density

The rural-urban nature of the geographic locale of an agency has an effect on the availability and accessibility of support services and resources (Martinez-Brawley, 1980; Krout, 1991). Table 1 provides a numerical description of the catchment areas, state populations, the Vietnam veteran populations, and the urbanization rate of each state.

Table 1. State Population Statistics

	Florida	Louisiana	Mississippi
Population 1992	13,413,000	4,150,000	2,564,000
Vietnam veteran population*	466,000	130,000	67,000
Percent urbanization	90.8	69.2	30.5
Population density/ square mile	217.8	87.6	53.2

*U.S. Department of Veterans Affairs, Management Science Services. Annual report of the Secretary of Veterans Affairs, Fiscal Year 1991.

Source: PC Globe, 1990

Florida Project

The Vietnam Veterans Families Project (VVFP)—a program of the Florida State University's Marriage and Family Therapy Center—is located in Tallahassee, Florida, but serves thirty-six counties in Florida, nineteen counties in Georgia, and seventeen counties in Alabama. Of these states, Florida is the most densely populated state, and large farm tracts and scattered small towns make up the majority of the geography for this seventy-two-county catchment area. Primarily rural in nature, the VVFP catchment area does include urban areas. The relatively larger urbanized populations are concentrated in the area's four largest cities: Jacksonville on the east coast, Tallahassee at the midpoint, Pensacola in the far-western panhandle, and Mobile in coastal Alabama. This represents a 500-mile total east-to-west spread: on average, project staff travel approximately 1,000 miles per quarter to deliver services to this large region.

If accessibility to the university clinic setting is not possible because of the family's circumstances, home-based services are available. In the most outlying catchment areas, where referrals tend to be more infrequent, service is provided primarily through telephone consultations and referrals.

Louisiana Project

The Vietnam Veteran Family Support Project (VVFSP), is located within the Human Development Center, (a University Affiliated Program) of the School of Allied Health Professions of Louisiana State University Medical Center in New Orleans, Louisiana. It serves the metropolitan area of New Orleans which is comprised of six parishes. The catchment area has a population of approximately 1,306,900 persons* with 37,003 Vietnam-era veterans (VA, 1990). In addition to the highly urbanized metropolitan area, services are also provided to surrounding rural parishes.

Mississippi Project

The Mississippi Vietnam Veterans' Family Support Network (MVVFSN) is located within the Institute for Disability Studies, (a University Affiliated Program) of the University of Southern Mississippi, Hattiesburg, Mississippi. The catchment area for the Mississippi project includes twenty-six counties in the southern portion of the state. The Vietnam veteran population served by the project resides primarily in rural areas. Mississippi's total population is a little more than 2.5 million people, and the urbanization rate for this highly rural state is 30.5 persons per square mile. Because of the rural nature of the state, many of the veterans have few or no services within 100 miles of their homes.

Client Profiles

To describe the caseload for each project, a number of client variables will be examined. These variables include: characteristics of the initial contact person, race or ethnicity, veteran's presence in the home, marital status, educational level, and employment status.

Florida Project

The characteristics of the veteran population served by VVFP does not mirror the demographics of the population at large in the catchment area. As shown in Table 2, the VVFP serves a predominately Caucasian clientele at a rate even higher than exists in the region at large with minorities being underrepresented.

Table 2. Vietnam Veterans' Families Project Population by Ethnicity/Race

Group/State	Percent Caucasian	Percent African American	Percent Other
VVFP clients	88	8	4
Florida	84	14	2
Georgia	72	27	1
Alabama	73	26	1

Source: Florida Project records, 1993.

In 34 percent of the client families, the veteran was living in the home. The veteran was not in the home in 29 percent of the cases, and his whereabouts were either unknown or not reported in 11 percent of the cases. For the remaining 26 percent, the veteran was not a member of the nuclear family, i.e., the client could be an emancipated adult child of a veteran.

*All population statistics for the three projects are from a computer data program produced by PC Globe, Inc., Tempe, AZ, 1990.

Initial contact with the project typically came from the veteran's nuclear family. The composite profile of the initial contact person is a married spouse or adult child of the veteran, who is currently a college student or a college graduate employed either on a full- or part-time basis.

Louisiana Project

A survey of the veteran families served by the Louisiana project found that the veteran was the family member who made the initial contact most often; the spouse made the initial contact slightly less frequently. Of the total number of families included in the sample, 46 percent were African American and 54 percent were Caucasian. The racial and ethnic makeup of the metropolitan New Orleans area is 34.7 percent African American and 62.2 percent Caucasian.

Although 56 percent of the veterans lived in the home with their family, 20 percent did not. In 6 percent of the sample, the veteran died during the time he was receiving help from the project. The majority of the veterans were married.

The majority of the veterans had completed high school, and the remaining percent had some college or graduate school education. Thirty-six percent of the sample were employed, 28 percent were unemployed, 24 percent were disabled, and 6 percent were deceased.

Mississippi Project

The Mississippi project survey found that initial contact with the project was most often made by the spouse of the veteran; the veteran made the initial contact slightly less frequently. Most of the clients served by the project were Caucasian. In 64 percent of the cases surveyed, the veteran was present in the home. Sixty-three percent of the veterans were married. The educational levels of veterans served by the project follow: 11 percent had some high school, 37 percent had a high school diploma, and 26 percent had completed some college. Only 33 percent of the veterans were employed, and 44 percent were either unemployed or disabled.

Resources

The number of available resources within a project's catchment area influences, the nature and scope of services provided. A description of services available within each project's catchment area illustrates how a project's context affects its functioning.

Florida Project

As part of the preliminary work in developing the structure for VVFP, a survey was designed and sent to approximately seventy-five social and mental health service agencies in the catchment area that were likely to come in contact with Vietnam veterans and families with disabilities. The agencies were asked about the major service needs of their clientele, as well as their perceptions of service gaps.

The major findings stressed the need to provide prompt services with a minimum of "red tape." Accommodation to clients' limited abilities to travel was also stressed. Home-based services were seen as more convenient for clients but costly or infeasible for service providers.

There are two U.S. Department of Veterans Affairs (VA) medical centers located within fifty miles of one another in north central Florida, and an outpatient clinic and a Vet Center in each of the three large Florida cities—Jacksonville, Pensacola, and Tallahassee. Within the Georgia counties serviced, there is one VA medical center, and there is one VA outpatient clinic in the Alabama area.

Data collected from case files indicated that 75 percent of client requests were for either individual, couple, or family therapy. Assistance with applying for other benefits, including veterans' benefits, constituted another 13.5 percent; remaining requests were for child or parenting assistance and basic information and referral services.

Table 3. Veteran Characteristics per Project by Percent

	Florida	Louisiana	Mississippi
Initial contact made by			
Veteran	17	50	46
Spouse	18	48	52
Child	37	0	2
Others	28	2	0
Race/ethnicity			
African American	8	46	12
Caucasian	88	54	86
Other	4	0	2
Veteran present in home			
Yes	34	56	64
No	29	20	36
Deceased	0	6	0
Unknown	11	18	0
Not applicable	26	0	0
Marital status			
Married	47	46	63
Never married	29	0	0
Separated/divorced	21	42	32
Widowed	0	2	5
Other/unknown	3	10	0
Educational level			
Some grade school	0	0	2
Completed grade school	0	0	
Some high school	0	26	11
High school diploma	21	42	37
Technical school	14	0	0
Some college	0	10	26
Completed college	34	8	4
Some graduate work	0	2	0
Graduate degree	26	0	0
Unknown	5	12	16
Employment status			
Employed	NA	36	33
Unemployed	NA	28	12
Disabled	NA	24	32
Retired	NA	0	2
Deceased	NA	6	6
Unknown	NA	6	14
Sample size	111	50	81

Source: Florida Project records, 1993.

Louisiana Project

Because the project is located in an urban area, many resources are available to veterans and their families. Within the catchment area, services are available to veterans through the VA Hospital, a Vet Center, a regional VA office (federal), and the Louisiana Department of Veteran Affairs (several local offices).

Veterans in the metropolitan area of New Orleans have access to help from a variety of sources. Numerous veterans' organizations have chapters in the metropolitan New Orleans area. In addition to VA services, a public hospital in New Orleans offers a full range of medical and psychiatric services.

Mississippi Project

A wide variety of social services exists within Hattiesburg. The nearest VA Medical Center is located in Gulfport, a distance of seventy miles from Hattiesburg, and a second VA Medical Center is located in Jackson, a distance of eighty-five miles. Vet Centers are located in Jackson and Biloxi. Because services for veterans and their children with disabilities are centralized in more urban areas, in predominately rural areas access to needed services is difficult. Data collected from case files indicated that families were seeking counseling, assistance with benefits, as well as assistance with formulating an individual education plan (IEP). In response to those requests, MVVFSN interfaced with social service agencies, veterans' organizations, school systems, parent groups, and protection and advocacy groups on a regular basis.

Project Description

The geographic location and the population characteristics of each project have an effect on their focus and structure. This section will discuss the focus, availability, and accessibility of resources, as well as the structure of each project.

Florida Project

The primary goals of the Florida project are to provide families with: marriage and family therapy; information, referral, and case management services—using a computer database and hard-copy resource directories for all of the counties in the catchment area; and developmental and diagnostic assessment of children of veterans. The VVFP maintains an extensive collection of relevant readings extracted from current professional and mainstream sources as well as videotapes that focus on issues relevant to Vietnam veterans and families with children with disabilities.

The project is staffed by family therapy interns who are doctoral students of the Interdivisional Program in Marriage and Family Therapy. Class members are represented on the staff, especially in key administrative positions.

Services are provided in the university clinic offices, in the client's home or other community setting, or by telephone. By far, the greatest amount of service activity for the project occurs within the 200-mile radius surrounding Tallahassee, where the clinic is located. Because there is a greater concentration of Agent Orange class members living in this area, the outpatient clinic delivery system was determined to be the most efficient.

In the most rural area, use of a satellite office model has allowed project staff to provide counseling and case management services to veterans' families in an efficient and economical manner. When accessibility to either the university clinic setting or the outstation setting is impossible because of the family's circumstances, home-based services are available. In the most outlying catchment areas, where referrals tend to be more infrequent, service is provided primarily through telephone consultations and referrals.

The screening portion of the intake process occurs both during the initial phone call and the first therapy session, when basic background information is obtained and a brief summary of the services requested is documented. Based on requests for services, clients are matched with an appropriate service provider.

During the initial interview, background information about the client or family, details concerning service requests, an assessment of the family system, and an evaluation of available and accessible area resources are obtained. A treatment plan is then developed in concert with the family.

Case management and family therapy are the two most frequently requested services. As described above, data from case files indicate that clients requested individual, couple, or family therapy 75 percent of the time. The therapeutic issues most frequently encountered include conflict resolution, parenting issues and skills building, substance abuse, communication breakdowns, stress management, readjustment or developmental issues, and PTSD-related issues.

Service provision is only part of VVFP. Consistent with the philosophy of the university community, and under its auspices, the project seeks to contribute to the body of knowledge concerning treatment practices and principles for working with traumatized clients. The project is committed to research and to the development of theory surrounding pivotal issues experienced by this population, e.g., PTSD, secondary PTSD, substance abuse, domestic violence, and so on. The project is engaged in ongoing efforts to refine diagnostic instruments for use with this population, to increase the dialogue among involved treatment professionals in the community, and to research and evaluate service mechanisms to ensure state-of-the-art treatment and intervention.

Louisiana Project

The project was designed to meet the needs of families of Vietnam veterans who may have concerns about the physical, emotional, developmental, or behavioral functioning of their children. The project also offers outreach, information and referral, education, advocacy, service coordination, and family support services. Consultation and training on veterans' issues are also provided to community service providers. The project maintains a library that houses a broad range of information on issues of interest to Vietnam veterans and their families, such as PTSD, disabilities, parenting, education, and other concerns. Referrals are made using a database of local providers in consultation with the National Information System.

Project staff consists of a project coordinator, who is also a school psychologist, two service coordinators, an administrative assistant, and a secretary. The staff assists veterans, their families, teachers, and professionals in providing technical assistance to schools and service providers. Service plans are developed in concert with the family to identify family goals. The plans outline services and activities to meet those goals, and families are empowered in self-advocacy to accomplish their goals (Dunst and Trivette 1989). VVFSP staff are available to provide as much support as needed on an ongoing basis. An advisory board, composed of veterans, family members, service providers, and representatives from the veteran community, meets quarterly to offer recommendations and lend support.

Mississippi Project

The MVVFSN project obtains referrals from various sources such as Vet Centers, VA hospitals, Veteran Service Office (VSO) officers, news releases, school systems, and National Information Systems. Once a family contacts the project, eligibility is established. The service coordinators record basic information over the telephone, and attempt to determine if there is a child in the home with a disability. Once the disability is documented, a history of the services the child has received, as well as problems the family may be having with the child or the service system, are obtained. A home visit is scheduled to spend time with the family and to identify family priorities including desired outcomes the family may have for themselves. At the first home visit an individual family service plan (IFSP) is formulated by the families and service coordinators. The IFSP helps the families better define their needs for services. The service coordinators work to keep the plan simple and not overwhelming. The main objective of the IFSP is to document prioritized needs of the families and to establish a plan to meet those needs. For families who have been unable to effectively negotiate service agencies it is imperative that the plan outline realistic and timely strategies to achieve positive outcomes.

After the IFSP is developed, the service coordinators and the families work together to implement the plan. Because families will often remain guarded until the service coordinators demonstrate they are trustworthy, it is imperative that the service coordinators fulfill their responsibilities on the IFSP.

Networking and linking with formal agencies is an integral part of the project, but more important is the development of informal support networks such as families, friends, and parent and advocacy organizations. Given the rural nature of the state and the lack of access to conventional services, service coordinators depend heavily on unconventional sources for support. Many communities in rural counties lack basic human service agencies. To make referrals work for families, service coordinators depend on imagination and creative sources to get the needed resources to the families.

Case Histories

The following case histories demonstrate how the unique functions and characteristics of each project are implemented when working with veteran client families. But these histories do not fully reflect the comprehensive nature of the services offered by the projects. Although these are actual case histories, names have been changed to protect client confidentiality.

Florida Project

This family consists of a married couple (a twenty-six-year-old female and a forty-year-old male) and a maternal son, Joey, who is five years old. Both Mr. and Mrs. Smith were married previously. Mr. Smith had two sons from his first marriage who live with their mother. Mrs. Smith has one child, Joey, from her first marriage. Joey's biological father is a Vietnam veteran.

The family came to the project because Joey was experiencing irritability, a lack of compliance in the home, occasional fits of anger that included throwing and breaking things, and disruptive behaviors that led to expulsion from a number of preschool and group-oriented social activities. Mrs. Smith believed that Joey's behavior was related to the mental and physical abuse she experienced from her first husband when they were living together. At the time of intake, Joey's father had expressed an increasing interest in visits with his son and a number of visits had taken place.

The treatment included twenty-one sessions, using cotherapists. The sessions focused primarily on marital- and parenting-related issues. Most of the sessions included Mr. and Mrs. Smith and twelve of the sessions included Joey. The treatment also included two field observations of Joey, standardized psychometric and educational assessment referral on behalf of Joey, and referral to a physician for medication evaluation. Joey was subsequently prescribed Ritalin. A consultation with a multidisciplinary advocacy program for children and families has led to in-home behavioral management, preschool services, and respite services.

Louisiana Project

Ms. Jane Doe is an articulate, strong woman in her mid-forties with five living children. She has been a widow for five years, receives food stamps, and currently resides with two teenage sons in subsidized housing in the New Orleans inner-city area.

Ms. Doe's husband was a highly decorated army veteran who served in Vietnam from 1968 to 1970. He received an honorable discharge and, on his return from service, was gainfully employed. Several years after his return from Vietnam, he suffered a massive stroke and became totally disabled. His stroke was not considered a service-connected disability even though he had suffered seizures during military service. Although claims were filed for service-connected disability due to PTSD, he was repeatedly denied because his alcoholism was not recognized as a common symptom of PTSD (Jelinek and Williams, 1984). Five years after the stroke he died as a result of gastrointestinal bleeding.

Several years after the death of her husband, Ms. Doe contacted the Louisiana project to request assistance in securing appropriate educational services for her two sons. The sixteen-year-old had previously been identified as having a mild mental disability. The fourteen-year-old, who had not yet been identified with a disability, was doing poorly in a regular education class. Ms. Doe had previously applied for Supplemental Social Security for her sixteen-year-old son, but was denied benefits.

A service consultant and the school psychologist, in conjunction with Ms. Doe and her family, developed a service plan to work toward meeting the family's needs. Project staff helped to secure an educational evaluation for her fourteen-year-old son and assisted Ms. Doe in applying for Zebley funds* for her sixteen-year-old mentally disabled son. An educational evaluation was completed with project staff assistance and $27,000 was awarded to the family from the Zebley Fund.

Although this family history reveals many successful events, Ms. Doe appears to suffer from possible secondary traumatization (Waysman et al., 1993) and has a history of inconsistent follow-through on recommendations. She has admitted to occasional illegal drug use. Ms. Doe moves frequently and consistently fails to keep scheduled appointments. Project staff were unable to successfully schedule IEP meetings with Ms. Doe and school personnel to plan her fourteen-year-old son's educational program and individual transition plan. She occasionally contacts the project for further assistance but fails to follow through on recommendations for herself and her family despite her obvious concern for her family.

Mississippi Project

Ms. Anderson contacted the project through a local post of the American Legion. The child designated in need of MVVFSN services was a son born with paraplegic cerebral palsy.

Ms. Anderson explained that her son had never done well in school because he had missed many classes. She was concerned because he was two grade levels behind his friends and seemed inappropriately placed through his IEP.

Ms. Anderson had communicated to the school that she believed her son could perform work appropriate to his age level and needed physical therapy. At the time of the home visit Ms. Anderson and the school had come to no agreements on these two issues.

Ms. Anderson stated that she had once applied for Supplemental Security Income (SSI) for her son, but had been denied, yet she had received a letter from the Social Security Administration saying that her son was a member of the Zebley class, and that she should apply again. She did but that application was also denied. In addition, Mr. Anderson had also been denied disability compensation from the VA for leg and back injuries he said were incurred in Vietnam, and he had been denied benefits through Social Security: he was unable to work.

An IFSP that prioritized the three major issues was developed as follows: first, the service coordinator and Ms. Anderson would arrange a face-to-face meeting with school officials; next, the service coordinator would link the Andersons with an SSI specialist from the AOCAP project; and third, the service coordinator would link the Andersons with Children's Medical Program. Another issue to be dealt with at a later date would involve Mr. Anderson's efforts to obtain disability compensation.

Following an IEP meeting, an appropriate placement was secured for Ms. Anderson's son and physical therapy was provided. After intervention by the SSI specialist Ms. Anderson's son was awarded SSI benefits, including retroactive payments for his Zebley classification.

Next, the service coordinator referred the family to the local health department where they applied to the Children's Medical Program. The Andersons' son was eventually accepted for

*"In a case called *Sullivan* v. *Zebley*, the United States Supreme Court ruled in February 1990 that, over the prior ten years, Social Security had illegally denied SSI payments to many children with disabilities. As a result, a child who was turned down after January 1, 1980, at any level of appeal, may really be eligible for SSI—and may also be entitled to benefits back to the date the child first applied. These children are called members of the Zebley class" (Mental Health Law Project, 1991).

participation in the program, and appointments were scheduled at a hospital where he would be examined and treated on a regular basis at no cost to the family.

The service coordinator has met with the Andersons nine times at their home, traveled more than 500 miles, and made more than thirty phone calls on their behalf. The Andersons are becoming adept at meeting challenges in a logical, systematic way, and less and less of the service coordinator's time is required to help this family meet its goals. In fact, Ms. Anderson has become active in community self-help organizations and is now showing other parents how to go about meeting the goals they have for their children with disabilities.

Conclusion

The three AOCAP projects discussed in this paper differ in many respects. When examined on a rural-urban dimension, distinct differences emerge. Although all three projects serve veterans and their families in both rural and urban settings, the project in Mississippi can be characterized as the most rural, and the Louisiana and Florida projects as primarily urban.

The proximity of available and accessible resources to families served by the projects is related to the rural-urban location of the family. Consequently, families living in rural areas are at a disadvantage with regard to availability and accessibility of veteran, health, and social services (Krout, 1991). Accessing services is more difficult for families with children who have disabilities and are located in rural areas than for families in urban areas. Families located in rural areas often have a scarcity of resources or environmental barriers, as well as value and belief conflicts that may interfere with their ability to access the service (Fiene and Taylor, 1991). In addition to this, families located in urban areas often have a much greater understanding of the services available to them and how to access those services than do families in rural areas.

The focus of the projects is similar in that all three were designed to provide services to the families of veterans. However, the individual service delivery systems for each project differ significantly. The Florida project focuses on family counseling and case management. The focus of the Louisiana project is on service coordination, outreach, and training. The Mississippi project focuses on service coordination for children with disabilities.

The case studies reflect the problems encountered when working with Vietnam veterans and their families who are attempting to access services. For veteran families there are many gaps in available social support services, particularly if the veteran has a disability or a child with a disability.

A number of service gaps have been identified. These gaps may be due in part to the relative degree of urbanization, lack of "user-friendly" policies, or a lack of public awareness. Regardless of the causes, the three AOCAP projects have identified several service categories that have not met the needs of this veteran population.

These gaps include: a lack of community-based services that strive to maintain family unity through services such as respite care, home nursing, advocacy, and transportation for people with disabilities; limited available and affordable medical care for the children of veterans and veteran organizations, both private and public, that serve and support the veteran in a family context; and bureaucratic processes, which create additional barriers and delays, as do rigid eligibility criteria. These gaps are even more pronounced in rural areas that lack proactive outreach programs.

When focusing on the individual veteran, clearly more services for homeless or indigent veterans are necessary. The continuum of employment-related services for veterans also contains gaps. Few private or public agencies focus on the family when working with veterans. Even when the family is targeted as the unit for assistance, the range of services is minimal. This is especially true when there is a child with a disability in the family.

Additional gaps include: a lack of cash grants to pay for past-due rent, utilities, medical services, and adaptive equipment; minimal available and affordable housing for veterans and their families; limited employment opportunities and training programs; and affordable family therapy.

Through the examination of a number of key features of a social services program, its relative strengths and weaknesses can be determined. Such an analysis can be useful in the ongoing evolution of a service agency. Also, vital to the construction or modification of a service system is the need to consider the context in which services will be provided and the unique characteristics of the population to be served. A successful program will thoughtfully consider both of these two main variables when determining what they will offer and how services can best be made available to the consumer.

The creation of AOCAP, a nationwide system of services to address the needs of a targeted population, was a novel contribution to both the social services and legal arenas. Future efforts to replicate such a service delivery system can be assisted by an examination of these three projects to determine what was successful.

Several factors have contributed to the successes of all three projects. The most significant is the collaborative relationships between key community leaders and veterans' organizations, which led to the development of an intervention network. This network, VETnet, is an avenue for mutual consultation and referral. On a larger scale, the availability of VETnet, as well as national and regional AOCAP conferences, allows for an even broader exchange of information and ideas.

Streamlined administrative processes, which provided for more prompt responses to client service requests, were an additional asset, and the degree of autonomy available through the projects' setting fostered the development of creative solutions to client problems. In-service training programs have contributed to increased staff effectiveness in meeting the unique, multifaceted needs of this population. Moreover, operating as an integrated project within a university setting ensured exposure to state-of-the-art intervention techniques, both on theoretical and direct practice application levels. The use of a toll-free number also helped to make services more accessible.

The establishment of VETnet and the regional conferences allowed for easy consultation with other projects for soliciting advice, offering suggestions and information, and networking. Service gaps have been, and are likely to continue to be, encountered in the delivery of social services. It is through the continual awareness of the successes and failures of a program within its larger context that effective service strategies evolve to best meet the needs of program clientele.

References

Department of Veterans Affairs. 1991. *Annual Report of the Secretary of Veterans Affairs* No. 553.

Department of Veterans Affairs. 1990. *1990 Census Data on Veterans.* Louisiana.

Dunst, C. J., and C. Trivette. 1989. An enablement and empowerment perspective of case management. *Topics in Early Childhood Special Education* 8(4):87-102.

Fiene, J., and P.A. Taylor. 1991. Serving rural families of developmentally disabled children: A case management model. *Social Work* 36(4):323-327.

Jelinek, J. M., and T. Williams. 1984. Post-traumatic stress disorder and substance abuse in Vietnam combat veterans: Treatment problems, strategies and recommendations. *Journal of Substance Abuse Treatment* 1:87-97.

Krout, J. A. 1991. Rural area agencies on aging: An overview of activities and policy issues. *Journal of Aging Studies* 5(4):409-424.

Martinez-Brawley, E. E. 1980. Identifying and describing the context of rural in social work. *Arete* 6(2): 21-32.

Mental Health Law Project. 1991. *SSI New Opportunities for Children with Disabilities.* Washington, DC.

PC Globe, Inc. 1990. Tempe, AZ. Computer data program.

Rothman, J. 1991. A model of case management: Toward empirically based practice. *Social Work* 36(6):520-528.

Schwartz , L.S. 1987. Image. *Journal of Nursing Scholarship* 19(4):168-173.

Waysman, M., M. Mikulincer, Z. Solomon, and M. Weisenburg. 1993. Secondary traumatization among wives of post-traumatic combat veterans: A family typology. *Journal of Family Psychology* 7(1):104-118.

Part IV

Multidimensional Service Challenges: Marshalling Resources Across Systems for Vietnam Veterans and Their Families

Among the challenges facing all AOCAP grantees was that of maximizing the impact of program dollars—employing scarce resources to leverage benefits and services resulting in substantive improvements in the lives of Vietnam veterans and their families. AOCAP grantees met this challenge, achieving superlative results with limited budgetary resources.

Many symposium papers focused on how grantees structured their initiatives to meet community needs. These papers demonstrate the extent to which grantees have succeeded in cutting across traditional service system boundaries and employing new service and treatment approaches to offer a human services delivery system that meets the needs of Vietnam veterans and their families economically and effectively.

The papers in Part IV detail but a few of the creative programs that have proved both cost-effective and responsive. Additionally, some programs focused on identifying resources to which the target population was entitled, but which were especially difficult to obtain. Initiatives designed to help class members realize the full range of benefits and services for which they were eligible, and to achieve their rightful status with respect to other government programs, are also described in Part IV.

The Triple-Stress Jeopardy of Agent Orange Class Members and a Collaborative Multidimensional Service Model

Lorraine Laurin, Duane Schielke, George Blatchley, and Walter Russell
United Cerebral Palsy Association of the North Country
Canton, NY

Abstract

A triple jeopardy of stress exists for some Vietnam veterans and their families. Among veterans experiencing negative effects of their service, a belief that the "establishment" is a major barrier to successful access to and satisfaction with service outcomes is common. As a result, these veterans seem highly susceptible to the debilitating effects of chronic stress. A second stress is associated with not knowing what the ultimate effects of exposure to Agent Orange might be. And a third is the stress of not knowing what effects of exposure to Agent Orange might be passed on to the veteran's children.

Because of the uniqueness of this constituency's needs, cooperation between the Vietnam veteran community and a resourceful organization that can provide reliable ongoing services is essential. The sponsoring agency developed a multidimensional, collaborative service model to identify Agent Orange Class Assistance Program (AOCAP) class members in the northern, rural counties of New York State, targeting families with children who are experiencing chronic health or disabling conditions and providing comprehensive case management and family support services to those families.

***Lorraine Laurin** has directed the North Country Division of the United Cerebral Palsy Associations of New York State, Inc., since its inception in 1975; she is a registered nurse. **Duane Schielke** is the associate executive director of UCPA of NYS, Inc., where he directs the Metropolitan New York Community Services Division which employs over 1,500 staff to provide direct services to individuals primarily experiencing developmental disabilities with an annual budget of over $57,000,000; he was an Army sergeant who served in Vietnam for fourteen months in combat duty. **George Blatchley** has been the coordinator of the project since 1990; he was a Marine Corps Sergeant who served one year of combat duty in Vietnam. **Walter Russell** has been a case manager in the program for two years; he served in Vietnam for two years as an Air Force pilot.*

Every war has inherent casualties, and its inordinate stress takes a toll. Nonetheless, the experience of Vietnam veterans remains unique. Understanding their experiences is a prerequisite to serving them successfully. First, other than the "DMZ" at the north-south border, there were no fronts or mass movements during the Vietnam War; it was a very mobile war. "Helicopters made the difference. Soldiers who would have died on battlefields in World War II and Korea were evacuated to hospitals, sometimes within minutes of being wounded. While the percentage of soldiers that *survived* in Vietnam was higher than in any other war, the injuries they suffered were far more traumatic because it was a guerrilla war. There were more amputations in Vietnam than in World War II and Korea combined. Three hundred thousand troops were injured, half of them severely. In Vietnam, a gunshot wound to the chest was a routine wound. Land mines, grenades, rockets and mortars mauled, maimed, and mutilated the youngest soldiers America ever sent into combat" (Palmer, 1993).

Second, although Vietnam-era technology of reporting remote occurrences is antiquated compared to CNN's "on location" images of live rocketry during Desert Storm, Vietnam brought war's current events to nightly TV news. We did not see briefings commanded by General Norman Swartzkopf, we saw anti-war demonstrations graphically reported alongside battlefield news clips of soldiers falling in the service of an unpopular cause. No victory parades or hero's accolades would cushion the return home and its harsh realities for Vietnam veterans.

John P. Wilson (1991), after conducting extensive studies of Vietnam-era veterans, reports that, "Upon returning home from military duty, the individual veteran frequently felt a disquieting sense of uncertainty, alienation, and estrangement from himself and society. While he was happy to be alive and 'back home,' something did not seem quite right or in its place. The men in our sample reported that they had trouble 'fitting in' and finding a niche in society. They often said that their sense of self-sameness and continuity with the past was changed in confusing ways. Future goals and commitments were unclear and intangible . . . [and the veteran was] grappling with questions central to his sense of identity and belief system. He struggled with ideological incongruities, moral dilemmas, and philosophical valuing."

Wilson (1991, p. 127) likens this questioning to Erik Erikson's "developmental task of identity versus role confusion which normally occurs in late adolescence." He asserts that in the normal development process "most cultures grant to youth at this time a 'psychosocial moratorium' in which to explore oneself . . . [and] . . . engage in many activities without necessarily making commitments to them or prematurely defining an adult set of roles and responsibilities. If all goes well, then childhood identifications get transformed into a more or less crystallized sense of identity and emotional stability" (Wilson, 1991, p.132). "Where the identity process is disrupted, delayed, or made extremely difficult due to personal, social, or cultural reasons, then a sense of role confusion or identity diffusion may predominate the individual's subjective sense of self-sameness and continuity in time and space" (Wilson, 1991, p. 132).

Wilson (1991, p. 133) believes that our culture typically affords an "extended period of time for the moratorium, ranging somewhere from late adolescence to the late twenties" and notes that "the soldier in Vietnam was typically between the ages seventeen and twenty-five, with the average being closer to 20." Wilson (1991, p. 134) allows that some military experiences and activities may result in "a more profound and complex understanding of cultural processes and prevailing technologies," but contends that "these things would be difficult for the soldier in Vietnam since there was reasonable doubt about the moral and political legitimacy of the war within the country." Concomitantly, "[The] . . . guerrilla nature in which it was difficult to discern friend from foe, led to a psychological situation that made it difficult for the soldier to maintain a healthy sense of control and predictability over the events occurring around him" (Wilson, 1991, pp. 134-35). In essence, Wilson (1991, p. 134) concludes that the manner in which the individual resolved this "existential quagmire" determined his or her success in achieving ego identification and personality integration, both positively and negatively. In turn, this success is likely to be related to the individual's capacity to effectively cope with stress and its outcomes.

Extreme stress may result in post-traumatic stress disorder (PTSD), which causes "reexperiencing the trauma through dreams or recurrent and intrusive thoughts; emotional numbing such as feeling detached from others, and symptoms of autonomic arousal such as irritability and exaggerated startle response" any time following the traumatic occurrence from which the behavior stems (Anderson and Black, 1991). Only recently have clinicians and other service providers recognized that field hospital nurses have been carrying the debilitating burden of their experiences for more than twenty years because they could not find effective treatment (Palmer, 1993). Unfortunately, PTSD gained its distinction when its manifestation was improperly typified by the media as a crazed Vietnam combat veteran experiencing menacing flashbacks, indiscriminately lashing out through the muzzle of an automatic assault weapon. This mass media image cast an unwarranted shroud of negativism on all Vietnam War participants. Nevertheless, the high incidence rates of PTSD from Vietnam service warrants its distinction as the first source of "Stress Jeopardy" (Goodwin, 1993).

The second source originates in the lingering uncertainty veterans have about how exposure to Agent Orange will ultimately affect them personally. Pending epidemiological studies that would provide better indicators, veterans are unable to resolve the stress associated with the "time-bomb" effect of exposure. From what is known, "there is a positive association between herbicides and (1) soft tissues sarcoma, (2) non-Hodgkin's lymphoma, (3) Hodgkin's disease, (4) chloracne, and (5) porphyria cutanea tarda (in genetically susceptible individuals) [and] . . . 'limited/suggestive evidence' of an association between exposure to herbicides used in Vietnam and three other types of cancer: respiratory cancers (including lung, larynx, and trachea), prostrate cancer, and multiple myeloma" (Department of Veterans Affairs, 1993).

Despite some inconclusive findings about exposure over a lifetime, some veterans are experiencing the births of children who have chronic health and disabling conditions. Whatever the cause, rearing a child with these chronic conditions is the third source of Stress Jeopardy that can significantly affect the daily lives of the entire family.

I. B. Pless clearly details the stress accompanying care of a child with chronic conditions through firsthand accounts from parents, characterized as those practical problems that can only be resolved with money or other resources and those that require "thought, imagination, time and effort" (Pless, 1980). Pless advises that, "It is not the magnitude of problems, but the unrelieved demands from hour to hour and day to day that dominates their lives. Even in the best of families, unless they can find some relief from the need for constant supervision, the drain can be stultifying." Pless succinctly cites the stresses:

A. Day-to-day stress

1. Constant attention
2. Reaction of others
3. Social relations
4. Effect on siblings
5. Marital relations

B. Life maintenance stress

1. Financial stress
2. Housing
3. Transportation
4. Clothing and appliances
5. Need for support

C. Worries about the future

1. Further children
2. Schooling and vocational training
3. Residential care

Lazarus and Folkman (1984) have conducted extensive studies on the debilitating effects of stress on families, documenting the dysfunctional outcomes that may occur if its effects are not managed, or dissipated. Naturally occurring or acquired stress management and coping skills may, however, not only prevent dysfunction, they may also build stronger family ties and improved support for all family members (Lazarus and Folkman, 1984).

The Project

In 1990, the United Cerebral Palsy Associations of New York State, Inc., North Country Division (UCPA, North Country) in Canton, New York, was awarded an Agent Orange Class Assistance Program (AOCAP) grant.* The project's primary purposes are to identify qualifying Vietnam veterans living in the rural northern New York counties of Essex, Clinton, Franklin, and St. Lawrence who have children who are experiencing chronic health or disabling conditions and provide information, referral, and follow-along services; ongoing, comprehensive case management; and family support services. The region is unique in that it encompasses two active armed-services bases: Fort Drum in Watertown and the Plattsburgh Air Force Base. This project has provided service to 112 Vietnam veterans and their families.

The Project Constituency

Fifty-one veterans required assistance from the AOCAP Direct Payment Program,* local veterans affairs counselors, or referral to local community services. The remaining sixty-one class members, their forty-seven spouses, and their eighty-five children who were experiencing chronic health or disabling conditions, received ongoing, comprehensive, home-based case management and family support services. Many veterans encountered were distrusting, reclusive, bitter about their Vietnam experience, and pessimistic that the "system" has anything credible to offer. From the citations above, it may be inferred that the group is typical. Eighteen percent of the veterans encountered were also more than 50 percent disabled—some from conditions that might be related to exposure to Agent Orange. Fourteen class members were single parents. It is notable that 52 percent of these Vietnam veterans had experienced multiple marriages: the children encountered were from the most recent marriage. Only one of the eighty-five children was over the age of twenty-one. The children from previous marriages typically did not live in the immediate area and maintained minimal contact with the class members.

The eighty-five children encountered who experience chronic health or disabling conditions present, in aggregate, 125 separately diagnosed conditions, as detailed in Table 1. The most prevalent conditions were developmental disabilities, with learning disabilities the most frequent, but including mental retardation, epilepsy, autism, cerebral palsy, and combinations thereof. Next in frequency were chronic health conditions, followed by emotional conditions and behavioral disorders, many of which were sufficiently severe to be classified as "PINS."** The outcomes of their conditions are startling. They experience social isolation, are often

---

*The grant monies distributed by the Assistance Program are a portion of the fund created by the settlement of the Agent Orange case. *In re: Agent Orange Product Liability Litigation,* MDL No. 381 (E.D.N.Y.). The Assistance Program has been created by and is administered under the authority of the United States District Court for the Eastern District of New York (the Court), and this grant has been awarded under the authority of and will be supervised by the Court, 1990.

**"Person in Need of Supervision" as defined in Section 371 (6) of the NYS Social Services Law: a male less than sixteen years of age and female less than eighteen years of age who is habitually truant or who is incorrigible, ungovernable or habitually disobedient and beyond the lawful control of parent or other lawful authority.

Table 1: Chronic Health and Disabling Conditions of Project Children

Disability	Number of Occurrences	Disability	Number of Occurrences
Developmental Disabilities		**Medical and health**	
Learning disabilities	22	Speech impairment	6
With medical condition	20	Eye surgery (by age 4)	4
With PINS petition	7	Asthma (biweekly shots)	3
With other disability	8	Congenital facial deformity	3
Mental retardation	5	Skin eruptions	2
Cerebral palsy	3	Aortic stenosis	2
Epilepsy	1	Hearing aids (by age 13)	2
Autism	1	Hypospadias	2
Aarskop Syndrome	1	Orthopedic impairment	2
Subtotal	**68**	A gamma globulin anemia	1
		Dysfunctional kidney	1
Mental health		Hemophilia	1
Severe emotional condition	12	Hemomangioma	1
With PINS petition	7	Kowaski disease	1
Other (including children in		Mitral valve prolapse	1
professional counseling)	5	Von Willibrand disease	1
Subtotal	**24**	**Subtotal**	**33**
Total of all occurrences			**125**

embarrassed about their family, perform poorly in school, and generally exhibit the typical wear and tear that comes with living in a dysfunctional family (Lazarus and Folkman, 1984). These families expressed concern about securing and affording adequate care and treatment for their children. The nagging distress about the future haunts their daily lives along with the concern that their exposure may have caused their children's conditions and potentially impact future generations. The extent of these conditions is remarkable and should prompt us to look beyond the symptoms to the cause.

Of equal interest is the fact that project participants who were divorced and subsequently remarried exhibited a strong commitment to their current relationship. These families seemed to experience mutual support among the members and usually became successful self-advocates once specific needs and resources are identified. This would appear to support Wilson's contention that "the struggle of identity versus role confusion will persist until some balance is reached that establishes a relative degree of self-sameness and continuity" (Wilson, 1991). These veterans seem to have achieved some manageable balance and have reduced their "Stress Jeopardy." One of the project's objectives was to use this success as a benchmark and replicate this phenomenon.

A Collaborative, Multidimensional Service Model: Outreach, Case Management, and Family Support

First, an advisory board was established to steer the project. Board membership included representatives from the local Vietnam veteran community and the sponsoring agency, which included as one of its members a Vietnam veteran class member. Second, hiring Vietnam veterans as case managers was critically important to the success of outreach efforts. UCPA, North Country provided ongoing case problem-solving support with its wealth of resources that are oriented to the needs of individuals experiencing chronic health and disabling conditions, and their families. When meshed with the special needs of the Vietnam veterans, a unique partnership and a multidimensional approach evolved. Six dimensions have been identified as critical elements to the project model.

The first is **Outreach and Case Finding.** The whereabouts of the veterans must be established in order to initiate personal contact with a peer—a Vietnam veteran case manager. Participating in locally organized Vietnam veteran groups enabled them to establish personal contact with the veterans and to build a relationship based on their Vietnam service camaraderie. Once rapport was established and the veterans believed that the program had credibility, they asked questions and enrolled in the services. The project case managers were then usually successful in establishing (or in many cases, reestablishing) productive linkages with the local veterans affairs counselor and other service providers.

Information about the project was publicly disseminated via newspaper, radio, television, distributed brochures, and myriad speaking engagements to every receptive social service provider, membership organization, and service club. This community awareness added to the legitimacy of the project, which specifically disclaimed any ties with the government or the U.S. Department of Veterans Affairs (VA). It was also surmised that some veterans would, in the normal course of events, approach their local department of social services (DSS) office to seek assistance. At this point, they were receptive to being referred to the project. Through successful marketing, the question: "Are you or your spouse a Vietnam veteran?" was added to application forms, and case workers willingly made successful referrals. It is noteworthy to reaffirm, however, that direct services are most often only accepted after an initial personal contact by another veteran with a common interest.

These grass-root endeavors enabled the project to reach class members in a sensitive manner. When the peer—the Vietnam veteran case managers—exhibited the qualities of being resourceful, independent, and nonclinical, with unending patience to listen, they then "got their foot in the door" to arrange a convenient time for a confidential home visit. This fact takes into account that most often the veterans were disposed to discuss service-related, confidential matters only in the privacy of their homes.

The second dimension is **Assessment and Goal Planning**. The purpose of the initial visit is to observe family interactions, assess home management skills, and share information. Subsequent visits are convened to develop a written family goal plan (FGP), which formulates a strategy to ensure family members' access to medical, nutritional, educational, rehabilitation, vocational, housing, social, financial, counseling, and crisis services as needed. The entire family is encouraged to participate and express their needs. Once a plan is developed, it provides a framework for the management of stress. Ongoing, home-based contacts provide a continuous means for the case managers to ensure that problem-solving strategies are adapted to the changing needs of each unique family unit.

The third dimension is **Assurance of Access to Direct Services.** Each FGP must provide five assurances that ensure the project's quality and the satisfaction of its consumers.

1. Assurance that family members receive appropriate routine and special medical care and health-related services. The case managers assist in arranging emergency care, diagnostic evaluations, treatment; rehabilitative intervention for any medical, psychiatric, motor, or cognitive problems; and the procurement of adaptive equipment, communication devices, technological adaptations, and home modifications. Because finances often present barriers to access, the project provides direct reimbursement for transportation expenses and direct funding of medical goods not reimbursed elsewhere.

2. Assurance that housing is adequate, as a precursor to creating a positive home environment. The case managers provide thorough information on eligibility criteria and provide referrals for accessible housing, rental assistance, and other housing support services. The case managers must ensure that the FGP addresses the entire home environment with goals to promote stability and stress reduction. Assistance with functional home-management skills is also often necessary.

3. Assurance that each child will receive appropriate services in concert with their developmental needs and the desires of the family. Depending on their age, most children with chronic health conditions and disabilities are eligible for federally entitled early

intervention; preschool or school-aged educational and related services as appropriate; and a written individualized education plan (*Individuals with Disabilities Education Act,* 20 U.S.C. Section 1400, 1401 (a)(20)). Although this guarantees certain rights, due process can be threatening and overwhelming to parents who are not prepared. The case managers must offer to attend meetings with parents to help ensure that they have the opportunity to verbalize their choices in the formulation of their child's individualized plan. The FGP must also include provisions for the continuation of liaison activities, i.e., attendance at teacher or program conferences or participation in counseling when appropriate. Planning must also address the transition from childhood services to adult services, i.e., employment or vocational or independent-living services, or in some cases, residential placement or supported housing.

4. Assurance that assistance is reliably available to mitigate conflict or crisis situations within the family unit is a crucial responsibility of the case managers. Families often must be referred to professional counseling programs to alleviate the effects of divorce, PTSD, drug and alcohol abuse, or domestic violence, but the consistent availability of the case manager provides a safety net. Additionally, siblings and the extended family often require assistance in understanding the needs of a family member who is experiencing a chronic health or disabling condition and need the opportunity to express issues constructively. Respite is also a necessary family support service to reduce the day-to-day burden of care. Many children encountered, particularly those experiencing emotional problems, did not have adequate social skills to be able to experience the benefits of inclusion in community activities. When these issues were properly addressed, the families were afforded the opportunity to participate in community social and recreational activities and share normalizing experiences.

5. Assurance of an adequate financial plan as a positive catalyst for family unity and stability. The dissemination of information on eligibility and availability of resources that offer financial assistance is a prime role of the case managers. The case managers help families in budgeting, preparing benefit applications, and ensure due process by arranging and participating in meetings and hearings with agencies such as the DSS, VA, and Social Security Administration. As a result, many families receive ongoing income assistance, such as Social Security and veterans' or home relief benefits. The case managers assist the family in securing financial coverage of medical expenses from third-party payers and access to the AOCAP Direct Payment Program.

In the course of fulfilling the assurances of the project, UCPA, North Country provided the following direct services: pediatric screening clinics; audiology assessments; counseling; dentistry; orthopedic assessments; optometry; occupational, physical, and speech/language therapy; pediatric medicine; respite; and transportation. Since many families experience complex problems and face various sources of stress, case managers must be proficient at identifying resources and providing continuous quality oversight. The project case managers received extensive training in advocacy and resource access, the nature and needs of individuals experiencing disabilities and their families, communication techniques, and record keeping as well as confidentiality and rights of consumers.

The fourth dimension is **Reliable Service Coordination**. Each FGP is unique and relies on a variety of services from many providers. The case managers facilitate communication and organize networking between the family, physicians, and other health care providers. Table 2 details the variety of contacts made by the project case managers. The extensiveness of these resources is remarkable, and it illustrates the clear need for ongoing coordination through the maze of bureaucracies. The primary categories of services are government agencies and services, health and medical services, legal services, private social services, fraternal organizations, and veterans' service organizations.

The fifth dimension is **Self-Advocacy**. The key to ensuring effective referral outcomes is the provision of consistent oversight while facilitating self-advocacy. Armed with an FGP and recognizing that they will progress through transitions, the families' knowledge of how to access and receive services is their link to self-reliance. The project case managers help parents in evaluating the appropriateness of programs and services so that informed choices can be exercised. Family members may be trained to self-advocate in matters of access, inclusion, integration, and assurance of rights through ongoing program visits, placement arrangements, and conferences with service providers. As an adjunct, the training of law enforcement and other community and public service personnel regarding the abilities and characteristics of people with disabilities also fosters their inclusion in the community at large.

The sixth dimension, **Record Keeping and Documentation,** ensures the integrity and quality of the project. Accurate records of case management activities are kept under strict confidential standards. The case managers initiate and maintain a case record that must minimally consist of an intake synopsis, permission to release or obtain consumer records, assessments and diagnostic evaluations, the written FGP, treatment interventions, ongoing casenotes, referral contacts, and outcomes. The case managers must also complete monthly, quarterly, and annual reports in a timely and conscientious manner. These data enable the measurement of efforts and outcomes to focus continuous quality improvement efforts.

Summary and Conclusion

The experience gained in the three years of this project offers insight into the unique needs of Vietnam veterans with children experiencing chronic health or disabling conditions. These families exhibit multiple, ongoing needs, and they are in serious jeopardy of experiencing the negative effects of stress. This report details the uniqueness of this constituency and outlines a successful service model that may be replicated. The primary purpose of the project is to locate AOCAP class members in the four northernmost rural counties in New York State that are in proximity of two active military bases. A dynamic outreach effort identified 112 Vietnam veterans. Fifty-one were made aware of AOCAP benefits and referred for generic services as necessary. Sixty-one of the class member families included eighty-five children with chronic health or disabling conditions. These families are the project's primary target group and receive comprehensive, home-based case management, family support, and direct services.

The sponsoring agency is a not-for-profit, health and social service organization that typically offers medical and health-related, rehabilitation, community living, and community support services to individuals with developmental disabilities and their families. To overcome the Vietnam veterans' typical wariness of government, and particularly VA assistance, the legitimacy of the project had to be established. A project advisory board was formed with its core membership from local Vietnam veteran organizations, which also facilitated essential collaboration. In addition, Vietnam veterans were hired as case managers, and case management services were provided in the privacy of the participants' homes.

Marketing efforts included public media and local workshops with civic and community service organizations to promote awareness of the group's unique needs as well as networking and referral. The comprehensiveness of the needs of the participating families with children experiencing chronic health or disabling conditions required contact with more than one hundred other service providers and organizations, as detailed in Table 2. Although many organizations that serve veterans provide family services or have programs for families with members experiencing chronic health or disabling conditions, none is likely to specifically provide these services in a manner with the comprehensiveness the participants in the project require. Again, collaboration is essential in the project model in order to pool resources.

The project model has six dimensions: outreach and case finding, assessment and goal planning, assurance of access to direct services, reliable service coordination, self-advocacy, and record keeping and documentation. The five assurances serve as quality benchmarks to ensure that each Family Goal Plan is adequate, comprehensive, and is satisfying the participants. The project model has several components that would enable replication by several organizations working in collaboration. Organizations providing direct services to families with children experiencing disabilities can likely better serve families of Vietnam veterans where they encounter them if they adapt their approaches to the unique needs of this group.

Table 2. Referral and Service Contacts

Government Agencies and Services

County Mental Health Departments
County Youth Services Bureau
Gouverneur Correctional Facility
NYS Police
NYS Veterans Affairs Adjudication Office
NYS Office of Mental Retardation and Developmental Disabilities
Plattsburgh Air Force Base
Sheriffs' Departments
Substance and Alcohol Abuse Council
County Social Services Departments
Dannamora Maximum Security Prison
NYS Department of Social Services
New Jersey Agent Orange Commission
NYS Division of Veteran Affairs
NYS Vocational and Education Services for Individuals with Disabilities
Ogdensburg Correctional Facility
Physically Handicapped Children's Program
Riverview Correctional Facility
Social Security Administration
United States Postal Service

Health and Medical Services

Affiliated University Hospitals
Boston Children's Hospital
A. Barton Hepbuern Hospital
Massena Memorial Hospital
UCP Affiliates/ Clinics
Upstate Medical Center, Syracuse
VA Hospital, Syracuse
Albany Medical Center
Canton-Potsdam Hospital
E. J. Noble Hospital
Hospital Detoxification Units
Medical Center Hospital of Vermont
University of Rochester Hospital
VA Hospital, Albany

Legal Services

Attorneys (private)
Bazelon Center for Mental Health Law
National Information System
North Country Legal Aid
Administrative Law Judges
Family Court
National Veterans' Legal Services Project

Private Social Services and Fraternal Organizations

The Access Group, UCPA
American Red Cross
Autism Research Institute
Boy Scouts/Girl Scouts
County Medical Societies
NYS Elks (BPOE)
Headstart
Inter-Agency Council of Family Planning
Kiwanis
National Austrian Institute
Rose Hill Adolescent Chemical Dependency Programs
Woodline House
Association of Retarded Citizens
Applied Humanistics
Big Brother/Big Sister
Catholic Charities
Crisis Hotlines
Evergreen Housing Project
Independent Living Centers
Joint Committee for Economic Opportunities
Literacy Volunteers
Planned Parenthood
United Way
YMCA/YWCA

Veterans' Service Organizations

The American Legion
Disabled American Veterans
Northern New York Vietnam Veterans
Vietnam Veterans of Northern New York
AMVETS
LZ Freedom
Veterans of Foreign Wars

United Cerebral Palsy Associations of New York State, Inc., North Country Division provided the following services: pediatric screening clinics; audiology assessments; counseling; dental care; orthopedic evaluations; pediatric medicine; podiatry; vision testing; occupational, physical, and speech therapy; respite; and transportation.

To that end, the sponsoring agency has conducted presentations in New York State and disseminated information to the national network of United Cerebral Palsy Association Affiliates to increase the recognition of the unique characteristics and needs of the Vietnam veteran community. Further outreach is clearly necessary to disseminate this information further. Biomarkers or other means of identifying the presence of exposure to Agent Orange and its relationship to health-related conditions in both the veterans and their children would also add an element of predictability that currently does not exist.

References

Anderson, N.C., M.D., Ph.D, and D.W. Black, M.D. 1991. *Introductory Textbook of Psychiatry,* 242-243. Washington, DC: American Psychiatric Press, Inc.

Goodwin, J., Ph.D. 1993. The etiology of combat-related post-traumatic stress disorders. *Readjustment Problems Among Vietnam Veterans.* Cincinnati, OH: Disabled American Veterans.

Lazarus, R.S., and S. Folkman. 1984. *Stress, Appraisal and Coping.* New York: Springer.

Palmer, L. 1993. The nurses of Vietnam, still wounded. *The New York Times Magazine,* p. 38. November 7.

Pless, I.B. 1980. *The Practical Management of the Developmentally Disabled Child,* 412-424. St. Louis, MO: The C. V. Mosby Company.

U. S. Department of Veterans Affairs. 1993. NAS issues report; Finds positive link between Agent Orange and five conditions; Others may be associated; Calls for Additional Research, *Agent Orange Review,* 1. September.

Wilson, J.P. 1991. Conflict, stress, and growth. In *Strangers at Home: Vietnam Veterans Since the War,* ed. C. R. Figley, Ph.D., and S. Leventman, 126, 127, 132-135. New York: Brunner/ Mazel.

Acknowledgments

The project advisory board performed an essential task in steering the program and in supporting its credibility. Their effort and commitment warrant special recognition: Randy Burke, Kim Halpin, Peter Havens, John Hill, Henry Matoes, and Lee Tessier. The authors also served on the project advisory board. Appreciation is also extended to Ron L. Smith, resource specialist at UCPA of NYS, for his assistance in preparing this manuscript.

A Family-Focused Resource Coordination Model for the U.S. Department of Veterans Affairs

Gordon Hollingshead, M.P.A.; Margaret Harlow, B.A.; and El Belish, M.A.
University of Montana
Montana University Affiliated Rural Institute on Disabilities

Abstract

Many families of veterans have been adversely affected by the veterans' experiences during the Vietnam War. This paper examines the physical and psychological consequences of the Vietnam experience—both for veterans and their families.

The need for family-focused resource coordination assistance is identified as central to addressing the mental health, physiologically based, and financial problems that Vietnam veterans' families face. The service delivery guidelines developed by Montana University's Vietnam Veterans Children's Assistance Program (VVCAP) are used to delineate the resource coordination system components that address the concerns of families. The rationale for each component is described, reinforcing an emphasis on a community-based, family-focused resource coordination effort for Vietnam veterans and their families. The federal government and particularly the U.S. Department of Veterans Affairs (VA) are urged to take the lead in coordinating resources to help these families cope with their problems.

Finally, this paper calls for a transformation of service systems for veterans, suggesting policy initiatives that Congress and the VA should undertake to establish a family-focused approach to services and enhance the quality of existing services.

Gordon Hollingshead, M.P.A., *currently serves as program director for Montana University's VVCAP, bringing thirteen years' experience in working with individuals with disabilities in a variety of roles including direct care, habilitation director, social worker, staff development, and community case management. He holds a master's in public administration from the University of Montana.* ***Margaret Harlow, B.A.,*** *served as a resource coordinator for the Montana Vietnam Veterans Children's Assistance Program. She is currently completing work on a master's degree in early childhood intervention while also working with children and families of Vietnam veterans.* ***El Belish, M.A.,*** *has served as program director for the AOCAP program based at LifeQuest in Sheridan, Wyoming. He is a Vietnam veteran and holds a master's degree in American studies from the University of Wyoming.*

The scientific community continues to show interest in health conditions in Vietnam veterans that have relationships to Agent Orange exposure. As a result of that interest, the U.S. Department of Veterans Affairs (VA) has extended health and medical assistance for those affected (VA, 1993). However, families of Vietnam veterans, like many other Americans, are struggling with thousands of dollars in medical bills related to the veterans' and children's ailments that are possibly related to the veterans' exposure to Agent Orange. In many cases, family structures have collapsed because of financial crises or the veterans' post-traumatic stress disorder (PTSD)-related problems. Many Vietnam veterans' children have been struggling all their lives with a multitude of unusual health problems. Too often, many of these children have been identified as displaying behavior problems when they in fact have learning disabilities or other learning disorders. As seen by the Montana Vietnam Veterans Children's Assistance Program (VVCAP), unless these children's conditions are accurately diagnosed and effectively treated, the children are at risk of entering into the justice system. Veterans with children having extraordinary needs have historically attempted resource coordination without a thorough understanding of the service delivery systems for children with special needs (Hollingshead, Dwyer, and Spas, 1993).

A clear pathway for addressing these families' troubling circumstances has been identified using state-of-the-art resource coordination methods, and projects funded by the Agent Orange Class Assistance Program (AOCAP) have begun to make headway in addressing this adversity. However, programs cannot overcome all the obstacles encountered without collaborative support from larger governmental systems such as the VA and the Department of Health and Human Services. The excessive medical costs and trauma, whether or not related to the exposure of the veteran to Agent Orange, must be identified and adequately addressed. Directly or indirectly, they are the legacy and responsibility of the citizenry that placed them in that precarious situation in the first place.

This paper serves as a call for a transformation in the service systems for veterans. It is time to move from an outdated medical model of facility-based treatment that focuses almost solely on the veteran, to a family-focused, community-based resource coordination model of service delivery. Such a model of resource coordination as established in each state by AOCAP serves as a demonstration of the proposed connection between the veteran and his family and the service systems for veterans and the disability and health care community.

Family-Focused, Community-Based Service Delivery

Addressing social, health-related, or emotional problems within the context of the family and community systems is not a new concept. Much of the literature regarding treatment modalities in the areas of disabilities (Simeonsson and Bailey, 1990; Winton and Turnbull, 1981; Dunst, Trivette, and Deal, 1988; Leviton, Mueller, and Kauffman, 1992), substance abuse and mental health (Friesen and Koroloff, 1990; Stroul and Goldman, 1990; Szapaczniki and Kurtines, 1989) emphasizes the value of addressing the individual as an important participant within a family unit. That unit is part of a broad network of social and interpersonal involvements that will also affect and be affected as an outcome of the treatment for that individual.

Family units as defined by the individual, the culture, and the members vary over time depending on birth, death, and marriage, and may include only the immediate members—husband, wife, and children—or extended family and close friends. Carter and McGoldrick (1989) contend that what a person calls family is the emotional subsystems reacting to past, present, and anticipated future relationships. The family is always a system; within this system each family member has a distinct role. That role does not necessarily reside within the individual, but reflects how that person has adapted and found a place within the family system (Yerbie, Buerkel-Rothfus, and Bochner, 1990).

According to Szapaczniki and Kurtines (1989), a basic tenet of family system theory maintains that the family must be looked at as a whole organism. The family is much more than the individuals of which it is composed. The influence of the family is quite powerful; it unknowingly exerts its power to keep a member from changing or causing a member to behave more appropriately. Individual behaviors, disabilities, and health problems, therefore, do not occur in isolation. They arise in the context of the system in which the individuals find themselves. Family and individual behavior are interactive and interdependent. A linkage referred to as the Principle of Complementarity implies that a change in one person will influence adjustments or changes in the rest of the family. Given the power the family has on its members' behaviors, logic would suggest an imperative to use the family system to influence its members' behaviors, encouraging the health of the member and the family as a whole (Szapaczniki and Kurtines, 1989).

Addressing the concerns within a family context has the potential of being a more cost-effective approach. Framo (1976) identified the cost benefits in his discussion regarding establishment of a family unit within a mental health center. He indicated that the family model deals with the real problems of people, rather than the symptomatic consequences of family disturbances. Moreover, the family approach offers the opportunity for secondary and tertiary prevention, helps avoid duplication of services, and delivers more efficient and rapid help at reduced cost. Referring to the experience of a family crisis unit in Colorado, Framo points out that by treating whole families in crisis they were able to avoid hospitalization of a member with a mental health problem more than 85 percent of the time, at one-sixth the cost of hospital treatment. Follow-up several years later showed that these patients were functioning far better than a control group of patients who had been admitted to the hospital.

Stroul and Goldman (1990), in a study of home-based psychiatric services for juveniles funded by the National Institute of Mental Health Child and Adolescent Service System Program (CASSP), came to two general conclusions regarding the cost of home-based services. First, the reported costs are incurred in serving an entire family. The investment is used to treat the entire family rather than to support the cost of one child in an out-of-home placement. Secondly, the cost per average episode of out-of-home placement in any setting is far greater than the cost per average episode of home-based services. Stroul and Goldman (1990) indicate that the most frequently used measure of the effectiveness of home-based services has been the prevention of out-of-home placements. Based on this citation, programs have been reporting success rates of between 70 and 90 percent (Hinckley and Ellis, 1985; Bryce and Lloyd, 1982).

With heightened attention to reform and financing of the national health care system, it is also time to attend to veterans in the broader sense of their health care and treatment as related to their role in family units. To assist an individual without attending to the related issues within the family system provides a less-than-genuinely effective, far-reaching, and long-lasting solution to the problem. Such an approach becomes an indulgence of treatment time and dollars in this era of fiscal austerity and cutbacks.

A Resource Coordination Model

Programs funded with AOCAP money, such as Montana's VVCAP, have been striving for three years or more to find medical and financial solutions for these children and their families. Staff in AOCAP programs have encountered the difficulties and seen the impact of these troubling circumstances, not just in the children but also in the entire family social structure. Central to the difficulties faced by veterans and their families is a health care resource coordination issue. Many within the veterans' services field are unfamiliar with the resources available to families within the disabilities field. Similarly, those within the disability service system are unaware that there may be services and assistance available for these families from the veterans' service system. In many cases, the resources may exist, but no one organization functions as a clearinghouse—one system of access to ensure that everyone is aware of all available resources within the veterans' services and the disability fields.

The VVCAP resource coordination model helps families acquire equipment, services, and funding from community resources, and functions as the cornerstone of this discussion. This system provides the specialized knowledge needed to help families systematically address their complex circumstances. This model, established to address the needs of these families, is formulated around the components discussed in the following sections.

1. Accurate, equitable identification of children and families most in need of resource coordination services

As a first step in this activity, considerable effort is applied to increasing awareness within the veteran community that services and assistance are available. A major component of the resource coordination model therefore is outreach—seeking out those most in need wherever they might be found. Program staff routinely travel to remote regions of their catchment areas to meet and work with local resources, including job service staff, VFW and American Legion members, and public school staff. They establish sites wherever space might be available to sit down with veterans in those communities and discuss their needs for services. Advertising on TV and radio and in newspapers is conducted prior to the visits, and posters are distributed to local businesses.

As a next step in this phase, a prioritization process is employed to assess the needs of the many individuals responding to the outreach. Those in need of more comprehensive resource coordination are identified. They are the families requiring more intensive assistance in addressing their concerns. Many contacting the program are in need of only information and referral (I&R), requesting assistance that is routinely provided by a specific service agency or provider to which they can be referred. While this effort may be regarded as merely I&R, to avoid duplication of services and effort it is critical to have a highly visible, nonthreatening contact agency available for this purpose. That agency must be well versed in the array of services and assistance to be accessed both within the disability and veterans' service communities.

2. Accurate, comprehensive identification of the child's and family's needs and strengths

Once it has been determined that the family is in need of full resource coordination services, program staff engage in a more in-depth analysis of the total family picture. This study includes identifying not only the problems and needs but also the families' strengths and resources, including the natural support systems that have always been available to them and can be brought to bear on the presenting problems. This phase lies at the heart of the resource coordination effort with the focus on the family as the source of strength for or frustration of any effort, to address the family's difficulties. Any staff or agencies facing a situation in which a veteran or other family member needs assistance must be fully cognizant of the broader dynamics of the family's functioning.

As an example, a child referred to VVCAP suffered from progressively severe abdominal pains, a strange rash that often covered much of her body, and extreme ongoing headaches. After a thorough medical workup, no specific physical basis could be identified as causing the health problems. However, her father displayed serious psychological symptoms of what appeared to be a PTSD condition, although the condition had never been diagnosed. He was unwilling to travel the hundreds of miles necessary for diagnosis and treatment at a distant VA facility. With the resource coordinator's help, the physician addressing the child's problems considered that information and inferred that the child's problems might be a response to her father's behaviors. The physician then recommended the child for therapy to help her more effectively cope with the father's problems. This approach decreased the physical problems she experienced. The father has since undertaken therapy himself to deal with his difficulties.

As a matter of course, therefore, identification of the family's presenting problem requires attention to a number of factors that influence the family system, creating imbalance and trauma to the stability of that unit. The three predominant domains addressed by the VVCAP are: (1) the veteran's PTSD and the havoc it can cause for all involved; (2) the impact experienced by the family unit as the veteran's health deteriorates; and (3) the effect on the family unit as the children's physical or mental health is found to be affected. Given the information from family systems theories, it is difficult to imagine effectively addressing any one of those aspects with hopes of success, and value for the dollars spent on the treatment, without addressing broader problems frequently found in troubled family systems.

3. Development of a service plan to meet needs

All too often, veterans have been severely disappointed regarding efforts on their behalf to address their needs, leaving a sense of betrayal. To assure recipients of VVCAP services that they will not be disappointed, the procedures to be followed in addressing the needs of the family members are summarized in a service plan. This plan of action ensures accountability in the identification, arrangement, and coordination of services. The resource coordinator and the family formulate the plan, shaping it into a few specifically worded, concise statements designed to guide resolution of the family's needs and concerns. The statements, formally drafted as objectives, are entered into a resource management plan (RMP) document. This RMP serves as an instrument for measuring progress in assisting a family.

Objectives are worded to reflect a program orientation based on empowerment of families. Families are to be encouraged to function as independently as possible, and to assume an active rather than passive role in their own case management. According to Dunst and Trivette (1989), empowerment approaches to case management assume that individuals have existing strengths as well as the capacity to become more competent. Families are expected to be actively involved in procuring needed resources and are given decision-making power in terms of defining their needs and deciding upon the particular resources and sources of support to obtain. Development of the RMP document and objectives takes on significance then as a tool for demonstrating that empowerment process in action.

4. Identifying, arranging, and coordinating services in the local area

Once the RMP has been agreed upon and signed, the activities identified in the objectives (e.g., evaluations, equipment, transportation, instruction, and counseling) are implemented. The family, with the resource coordinator, identifies sources for the services and goods specified in the RMP. Frequently, the family has been using a specific provider, doctor, or school service but needs advocacy or assistance with funding. Many organizations require prior notification and approval before they will fund a service or product. For instance, to have a school system pay for a second opinion evaluation the family must first obtain the school's participation in arranging the independent evaluation, or the school may not be obligated to fund it. Attention must therefore be directed to a provider's procedural steps to ensure that the best possible funding arrangements are made.

Guiding principles emphasized during this phase of activity with the family include:

- Sensitivity to the family's circumstances, concerns, social structure, culture, biases, and reluctance to appeal for aid (welfare, in their perspective) or struggle with bureaucratic organizations such as the VA or the Social Security Administration;
- Active pursuit of goods or services at reduced rates whenever the family's circumstances warrant; emphasis is placed on ensuring quality goods or services at minimum cost, using funding from other sources whenever possible; and
- Securing of funding arrangements such as Supplemental Security Income (SSI), Medicaid, VA disability payments, etc., which will provide families with far-reaching, long-

term solutions to their concerns as opposed simply to purchasing an item and not addressing broader problems.

5. Assist families in obtaining funding for needed services, equipment, etc., from a variety of other resources for which families might qualify

All too often, the tendency is to see one particular system as responsible for solving problems. Resolution of the funding dilemma lies at the heart of VVCAP resource coordination. VVCAP has funds only to "apply a bandaid" to the many, larger concerns identified by families. Whenever possible, more concrete solutions must be identified. Many funding sources are available, of which the family and the agencies they have been working with often seem to be unaware. Thus, the resource coordination role is now defined as investigating and following up on leads regarding potential sources that will address the particular concern.

Alternative funding for services or goods takes many forms, based on the family financial situation, conditions addressed by specific funding organizations, and the legal responsibilities of public schools, Vet Centers, and state-funded organizations. All potential sources of funding must be assessed. Examples include:

- Personal family health insurance;
- Medicaid;
- SSI, and Supplemental Security Disability Income (SSDI);
- VA-funded benefits, Vet Centers, and the Vet Center Fee Contractors in other cities, and civilian health programs of the VA such as CHAMPUS or CHAMPVA;
- Fraternal and service organizations: the Lions Club, Shriners Club, the American Legion, and the VFW;
- Public school or state educational agency funding;
- Indian Health Services; and
- Private foundations or agencies such as:
    - The American Kidney Fund;
    - The Access Group, funded by AOCAP;
    - Air LifeLine; and
    - Children's Special Health Services (CSHS), for a specific array of chronic health problems in children.

This list by no means constitutes an exhaustive review of all potential funding sources. As the pursuit for the answers to the funding puzzle continues, the list continues to grow as well.

As an advocate of the family and investigator of funding agencies, the resource coordinator also becomes an agent of change. In this capacity, staff help funding agencies identify gaps in services and families in need who don't fit a specific eligibility criteria. The resource coordinator assists the funding agency in broadening or redefining its criteria and approach to serving clients. Such assistance is most effective, not as a result of confrontation, but rather through a collaborative effort between VVCAP and the funding agency, with the ultimate goal of resolving issues of unmet needs for families.

6. Providing financial assistance to eligible families to purchase services or materials when other funding resources are exhausted

As discussed previously, the first step toward using VVCAP dollars involves exploring all other potential sources of funding. When no other funding sources are available, VVCAP funds are used up to a maximum ceiling dollar amount. VVCAP has only a small pool of funds available to families for specific health-related concerns when no other funding sources can be identified. For the Montana program, these funds became available following approval by the Resource Management Team (RMT). The RMT is a local advisory team composed of disability, veterans, and health care professionals and clients. Input from the advisory team ensures that other alternatives have been thoroughly exhausted and VVCAP funding is the last remaining option.

7. Advocacy, empowering families through information and support about disability laws, the legal rights of their children with disabilities, and how to interact assertively with schools and agencies

Frequently, individuals within this population are seen as victims of the sense of disenfranchisement that they have felt for many years. That response, of course, dates to when they were drafted or chose to enlist, felt they were misled and may have been exposed to possible toxins on the battlefield, and given a minimal if not negative welcome home. The outcome is a sense of passivity and helplessness, and the perspective that they and their children are continuing in a role as victims. Coupled with that view is an undercurrent of deep-seated anger, a fury at the government that inflicted this condition on them and then abandoned them.

This VVCAP resource coordination effort, employing the principles of empowerment, strives to convey to the individual and the family that they do have the existing strengths and capacity to become more able to manage their circumstances. They do have the ability to make a genuine difference in the systems that they are to deal with, making those systems far more responsive to the needs of the individuals. They are no longer victims but can be active agents of change. From writing objectives to securing assistance for families, empowerment and use of families' natural support systems is basic to a state-of-the-art resource coordination model for veterans and their families. To the maximum extent possible, this approach meets the needs of the families served by the VVCAP. It alleviates some concerns and difficulties of parenting children with extreme medical, developmental, or behaviorally challenging disabilities.

To ensure that resource coordination activities will be most effective, a basic philosophical orientation for coordinators emphasizes the empowerment of families by:

- Assuming a positive and proactive stance toward families;
- Emphasizing the families' responsibility for solving problems and meeting needs;
- Assuming that all families have the capacity to understand, learn, and manage events in their lives;
- Building on family strengths rather than correcting deficits;
- Proactively working with families in an anticipatory fashion rather than waiting for things to go wrong before intervening; and
- Promoting acquisition of competencies that permit families to become better able to negotiate their developmental course (Bandura, 1977, 1982).

Additionally, professionals skilled in enabling and empowering families:

- Place major emphasis upon helping families identify and prioritize their needs from their own and not a professional's point of view;
- Encourage active family participation as part of mobilizing resources to meet needs;
- Use partnerships and parent-professional collaboration as the foundation for creating opportunities for families to become more capable and competent;
- Provide families with the necessary information to make informed decisions about their needs and courses of action to meet needs; and
- Accept and support decisions made by families.

Collectively, these characteristics are the underpinnings of the VVCAP empowerment and enablement model of resource coordination. To the extent that VVCAP resource coordination practices embody all or most of these characteristics, help-giving efforts will not only have competency-producing influences, but will also more likely enable families to come away from VVCAP resource coordination exchanges with a greater sense of being able to manage life events effectively (Bandura, 1977, 1982).

An Acceptance of Responsibility

The children served by VVCAP are among the offspring of 2.4 million men and women who fought for the United States in Vietnam. They experienced conditions in Southeast Asia with minimal understanding of the possible meaning of those experiences for themselves and their children. Field and Kerr (1988) indicated that the majority of Vietnam veterans' children (60 percent) fell into the range of twelve to seventeen years old at the time of their study. A survey of 550 families with children having disabilities in Montana who were receiving services from seven child and family service providers revealed that resource coordination and advocacy for their children's needs were high priorities, and that they became increasingly important as their children reached this age range (Maloney, Bjorgen, and Hollingshead, 1989). Current VVCAP efforts in Montana have found that most of the children have been involved in the public school system for a number of years and have received services from various agencies and programs. Despite these services, they continue to have many unmet needs. Those needs include surgeries, psychological evaluations and counseling, comprehensive assistance with the transition from public schools to the post-secondary environment, diagnosis and treatment for learning disabilities and attention deficit disorder, jaw and facial reconstructive surgery, educational assistants and respite services, and medications for a variety of health problems.

The scientific data linking parental exposure to Agent Orange and offspring health problems are currently lacking. As a proud nation, it is tragic that the debates and deliberations could drag on for yet another twenty years. In the meantime, an entire generation of children is growing up requiring treatments and surgeries, and sometimes dying, enveloped in a cloud of doubts and questions about a relationship between their problems and Agent Orange. It is imperative that the U.S. government act expeditiously to address those doubts, questions, and enormous needs that are presented by those veterans and their families. As a most important outcome of the AOCAP effort, it is critical that the policy makers formally implement a family-focused, community-based resource coordination effort as initiated by the AOCAP programs.

The Future Department of Veterans Affairs—Model for National Health Care

With the eventual implementation of national health care reform, it appears that the VA will not be seriously affected. However, the VA is also in a position at this historic national crossroads to take bold action on its own to reform and enhance its own system of health care. Excellence, as defined by Thomas Peters and Robert Waterman, Jr. in their classic 1982 work, *In Search of Excellence*, is associated with those organizations that are continuously innovative, organizations that are especially adroit at continually responding to change of any sort in their environments. The VA takes pride in its many innovative contributions to medicine and rehabilitation. In that spirit of innovation and research into enhanced service delivery models, the VA has the potential to set state-of-the-art standards in this service delivery area.

The VA could enlarge on the role of its social services programs, incorporating a family-focused service delivery model as seen in AOCAP and other service programs. Such an approach could be established as a collaborative effort among the VA, AOCAP, state veterans' affairs programs, disability service systems, state developmental disabilities planning and advisory councils, and other agencies important to the overlap of these domains. Embarked on as a research effort, the VA could assess the impact of this proposed resource coordination model. An assessment could evaluate the overall quality and cost-effectiveness of treatment when arranged and provided within the family and community versus a treatment facility.

Using this holistic approach, the potential exists for identifying more productive means of addressing issues such as veterans' homelessness and involvement with the criminal justice system. It could be determined whether more comprehensive assistance in the family and community would favorably affect movement into those circumstances by veterans and their children. Such analysis could have major implications and form a bridge for possible collaborative efforts with states, most of which are struggling to house their current prison populations, a high percentage of whom are Vietnam veterans.

The efforts by VVCAP in provision of a family-focused, community-based resource coordination system has only scratched the surface of the greater need for this approach within the veteran community, not only for Vietnam veterans but also for veterans of the many other wars and their families. In many ways, in many VA centers throughout the country, the concepts identified within the VVCAP resource coordination model are undoubtedly in place and functioning well. As indicated throughout this discussion, however, the VA in a much broader sense could address the needs of the veteran as a family member with the array of disabling conditions, health problems, natural support systems, and strengths available within that family milieu.

In the next two years, AOCAP will be phased out of existence. This approach to addressing the veterans' and their families' broader needs will not have reached the many who are still in need of such assistance. The VA is in a position to address the needs of veterans as important participants within their family systems, employing the AOCAP model of resource coordination currently in place throughout the fifty states. This document urges policy initiatives by Congress and the VA to establish a family-focused approach to services, enhancing the quality of services, and taking the necessary strides toward excellence.

References

Bandura, A. 1977. Self-efficacy: Toward a unifying theory of behavioral change. *Psychological Review* 84:191-215.

Bandura, A. 1982. Self-efficacy mechanism in a human service agency. *American Psychologist* 37:122-147.

Bryce, M., and J. Lloyd. 1982. *Placement prevention and family reunification: A view from the child welfare sector.* Rev. ed. Iowa City: The University of Iowa School of Social Work, National Resource Center on Family Based Services.

Carter, B., M. McGoldrick. 1989. Overview: The changing family life cycle—A framework for family therapy. 2d ed. In *Changing Family Life-Cycle,* ed. E. Carter and M. McGoldrick, 3-28. Boston: Allyn & Bacon.

Dunst, C.J., and C.M. Trivette. 1989. An enablement and empowerment perspective of case management. *Topics in Early Childhood Special Education* 8(4): 87-102.

Dunst, C.J., C.M. Trivette, and D.A. Deal. 1988. *Enabling and empowering families: Principles and guidelines for practice.* Cambridge, MA: Brookline Books.

Field B., and C. Kerr. 1988. Reproductive behavior and consistent patterns of abnormality in offspring of Vietnam veterans. *Journal of Medical Genetics* 25:819-826.

Framo, J.L. 1976. Chronicle of a struggle to establish a family unit within a community mental health center. In *Family Therapy: Theory and Practice,* ed. P. J. Geurin, Jr., 23-40. New York: Gardner Press.

Friesen, B.J., and N.M. Koroloff. 1990. Family-centered services: Implications for mental health administration and research. *Journal of Mental Health Administration* 17(1):13-25.

Herring, G.C. 1986. *America's Longest War: The United States and Vietnam 1950-1975.* 2d ed. New York: Alfred A. Knopf.

Hinckley, E., and F. Ellis. 1985. An effective alternative to residential placement: Home-based services. *Journal of Clinical Psychology* 14(3):209-213.

Hollingshead, G., K. Dwyer, and D. Spas. 1993. *Vietnam veterans' children's assistance program: A response to the Agent Orange legacy.* Missoula, MT: Montana University Affiliated Program Satellite.

Leviton, A., M. Mueller, and C. Kauffman. 1992. The family-centered consultation model: Practical applications for professionals. *Infants and Young Children* 4(3):1-8.

Maloney, T., D. Bjorgen, and G. Hollingshead. 1989. *Consumer evaluation of Montana child and family training and support services.* Missoula, MT: Montana University Affiliated Program Satellite.

Peters, T., and R.H. Waterman, Jr. 1982. *In Search of Excellence.* New York: Harper & Row Publishers, Inc.

Simeonsson, R.J., and D.B. Bailey. 1990. Family dimensions in early intervention. In *Handbook of Early Childhood Intervention,* eds. S.J. Meisels and J.P. Shonkoff, 428-444. New York: Cambridge University Press.

Stroul B., and S. Goldman. 1990. Study of community based services for children and adolescents who are severely emotionally disturbed. *Journal of Mental Health Administration* 17(1):61-77.

Szapacniki, J., and W.M. Kurtines. 1989. Basic concepts in brief strategic family therapy. In *Breakthroughs in Family Therapy With Drug Abusing and Problem Youth,* eds. J. Szapacniki and W. M. Kurtines. New York: Springer.

U.S. Department of Veteran Affairs. 1993. *DVA to Award Additional Benefits for Agent Orange-related Illnesses.* Washington, DC: Office of Public Affairs News Service.

Winton, P., and A. Turnbull. 1981. Parent involvement as viewed by parents of preschool handicapped children. *Topics in Early Childhood Special Education* 1(3):11-19.

Yerbie, J., N. Buerkel-Rothfus, and A.P. Bochner. 1990. *Understanding family communication.* Scottsdale, AZ: Gorsuch Scarsbrick.

Acknowledgments

I thank Jim Hudson, AOCAP grant officer, and the Montana VVCAP staff (Debbie Murtagh, Margaret Harlow, Catherine Ward, and Gloria Brown) for their invaluable support in preparing this paper.

Vietnam Veteran Family Assistance Program: A Collaborative Private Agency–Public University Student Intern–Assisted Service and Education Delivery Model

Harry J. Macy, Ph.D.
Department of Social Work
Ball State University
Muncie, IN

Larry Braden
Community and Family Service, Incorporated
Portland, IN

Roger Lloyd
Vietnam Veterans Family Assistance Program
Muncie, IN

Abstract

The formalized partnership between a private not-for-profit social service agency and an academic department housed in a public university to provide student interns to supplement the staffing resources of a Vietnam Veteran Family Assistance Program (VVFAP) is described along with the theoretical basis for the family-based service model developed to address the national program goals of the Agent Orange Class Assistance Program (AOCAP). Evaluative results of the VVFAP service and partnership program provide a replicable model of care management for meeting the current and continuing long-term service needs of Vietnam veterans and their families.

***Harry J. Macy, Ph.D.**, is chairperson and professor of the department of social work, Ball State University. **Larry Braden** is executive director of Community and Family Service, Inc., and has a degree in social work. **Roger Lloyd** is director of the Vietnam Veterans Family Assistance Program in Muncie, IN. He has a science degree from Ball State University and is a Vietnam veteran.*

Since 1991, the Vietnam Veteran Family Assistance Program (VVFAP) has provided more than 400 veteran families with an array of family-oriented support, evaluation, and intervention services, including counseling, advocacy, household support, resource referral assistance, respite care, transportation, and social networking opportunities. A formalized service partnership between an Indiana-based, private not-for-profit corporation committed to serving at-risk veteran families, and a nationally accredited baccalaureate social work degree program housed at a public university, has resulted in the creation of a staffing resource arrangement that has enhanced the overall quality of both the social service and social work education programs.

This paper describes the rationale and structure of the service approaches developed by the VVFAP to achieve the goals of the Agent Orange Class Assistance Program (AOCAP) within east central Indiana. A description of the partnership between the Community and Family Service agency (CFS) and the Department of Social Work housed at Ball State University is then provided within the context of the family-focused service approaches developed. The staffing arrangements, program services developed, and the types of interventions used to serve veteran families can be replicated and serve as a viable means to address the continuing service needs of an at-risk national consumer population.

Service Management Model

The three major service priorities identified in the fourth annual report of the AOCAP served as the basic framework for the selection and design of the program's services provided by VVFAP (Rhoades, 1992). These three service priorities included:

1. **Services to families.** Provide case management and counseling that focuses on the veteran's war experiences as a major contributing factor to family dysfunction of Vietnam veterans and their families;
2. **Services for children with disabilities.** Build necessary links between the Vietnam veteran and developmental disability and other social services communities; and
3. **National support programs.** Establish a national support network, a veterans' law center to provide technical assistance, including training and service linkages for the network of family services programs funded through AOCAP grants.

To address these three national service priorities, VVFAP needed to create a range of service interventions designed to address simultaneously the immediate individualized service needs of specific veterans and their families, and the universal continuing needs of an underserved population common to all Vietnam veterans and their families. The resulting selection of service approaches was based on: the potential for achieving short-term improvements in immediate problem situations; and the need to provide continual assistance that would promote customer self-reliance in accessing and receiving sustaining assistance, entitlements, and opportunities from private and public service systems, and help customers take advantage of informal community-based social and personal support networks.

As a result of the dual focus on both the veteran family as a service consumer and the potential collective needs of all of the veteran families, several theoretical models were integrated and adapted to fulfill the project objectives. Each of these models is summarized to explain the theoretical basis for the interventions and the scope of services required to fulfill the objectives of the VVFAP.

An Ecological Service Approach

Human service providers often regard veterans and their family members as the locus of the problem. VVFAP avoided this assumption, establishing the person-in-environment configuration as a major premise of its service approaches. This configuration was used to simultaneously identify the quality of relationships among family members, as well as between the family and the sustaining service systems and the institutional-based educational, spiritual, political, social, and economic resources and opportunities required to provide long-term developmental supports. This internal-external reciprocal ecological relationship perspective recognizes the interrelationships between individuals and their social environments and the adaptive patterns used by both individuals and the families over time. It is a perspective that helps in planning interventions that address current, continuing, and projected service needs of individuals as well as their families.

In the problem assessment and definition service phases, for example, the person-in-environment perspective was applied to gain an understanding of individual and family behavioral patterns within the problem situation context. It also guided the exploration about the nature and quality of the transactions between these families and their social and support systems designed to meet their continuing economic, social, health, educational, and psychological needs. The ecological perspective identified by Germain and Gitterman (1980) helped staff to maintain a holistic service perspective and also promoted the recognition of personal and family strengths of the consumers individually and collectively.

All referrals to the VVFAP required the completion of a generic problem-solving process consisting of assessment, service planning, intervention, evaluation, termination, and follow-up. The problem assessment phases required the determination of underlying factors that had contributed to the current difficulty, and the identification of both personal and environmental issues that appeared to sustain the defined dysfunctioning. Many veterans have, during the years since the war, experienced periodic problems of adaptation and readjustment, including the delayed emergence of the impact of the Vietnam experience. Difficulty talking about the experience, withholding of emotions, and the psychological buffers needed to survive the combat experience all combined to produce difficulty with interpersonal familial relationships. Consequently, assessing the social and family environment is particularly relevant when children are involved because service planning should include developmental information about the people with whom, and circumstances in which, the dependent has lived. An assessment of the current transactions among the individuals in a veteran's family and among these families and their social and physical environments helps define both short- and long-term service goals.

The ecological-assessment perspective also has proven to be a useful approach to understanding the residual effects of the war experience on the veteran who manifests a variety of behaviors symptomatic of post-traumatic stress disorder (PTSD). In her work with Vietnam veterans, Brown (1984) identified a subtype of PTSD, a "delayed post-traumatic stress disorder," characterized by an onset of symptoms of anxiety at least six months after the trauma, whereby the veteran exhibits the following types of behavioral patterns:

- Intrusive thoughts and flashbacks of traumatic events provoked by otherwise innocuous stimuli, such as a helicopter overhead or the backfire of a car. Sights and sounds reminiscent of the war can serve to transport the veteran from the here-and-now back to the jungles of Vietnam.
- Sleep disturbances and vivid nightmares in which particular scenes are replayed and life events are reexperienced.
- Alienation and isolation from persons and social experiences. The veteran often has difficulty in forming and maintaining close interpersonal relationships because of a numbing of emotional response, a process that was essential for survival in combat.
- Depression associated with survival guilt, for having survived experiences in which others died, and moral guilt, for having participated in acts of war.

The ecological perspective on the long-term post-traumatic stress effects on family stability and the dynamics of the marital-dyad relationship was useful in assessing not only the service needs of the veteran but those of the entire family.

In planning service intervention, Brown (1984) notes:

> The emergency of a delayed stress response affects not only the veteran, but also the members of his family system, often posing a threat to the stability of the family unit and the viability of the marital-dyad relationship. When the veteran and his family seek assistance in dealing with problems they identify as directly related to or associated with the veteran's experiences in Vietnam, intervention for the family system as a unit can be difficult. This difficulty stems from the complexity of the veteran's war history, the way in which he has internalized his experiences since the war, and the manner in which the family has adapted and organized itself in relation to the veteran.

Client WT is illustrative of the delayed reaction syndrome.

> Mr. WT voluntarily walked into the office of the VVFAP because he had "heard" about the program and he was "having some trouble with himself, his family, and his work situation." He explained that some of his co-workers were teasing him about Vietnam and that he "felt that he was going to lose control and hurt someone." He had episodes of rage, and over the years his family learned to fear him and feel as though they had to "walk on glass" in order to not set him off.

The family-focused ecological approach used by the VVFAP staff required that the family be supported as it examined long-term relationship issues. This opening process helps the family examine its adaptive patterns, identify strengths, define common expectations, and join together in securing needed resources, as opposed to seeing the problems and needs as only veteran centered and psychological in nature. Assistance was given to Client WT to obtain personal psychiatric counseling. In addition, his wife became a member of a support group and both cooperated in informing their children about what was happening in their lives. From this family-centered orientation, resource needs extend beyond psychological ones and include a broad spectrum of social, educational, spiritual, and support services as efforts to improve communication among family members.

Dual Cultural Perspective

A conceptual model for examining the long-term developmental effects on children living in veterans' families, and the quality of the interrelationships between these families and their ability to access institutional-based resource systems required for their well-being, is the "dual perspective" (Norton et al., 1978). The dual perspective "posits that all people are simultaneously embedded in at least two basic interrelated social systems: (1) that of their immediate socioeconomic, cultural, or racial environments represented by their [biological] family and [social] community of residence" from which social and emotional support flows, and "(2) that of the economic, political, and educational systems of the wider society" from which survival entitlements are provided to maintain their safety, economic, spiritual, political, and education needs (Norton, 1993). For an individual to reach potential, the functioning of the two interrelated social systems must occur simultaneously and be relatively consistent in their respective expectations. The degree of mutuality and quality of beneficial supports from the two concurrent social systems in turn promotes harmony and interdependence between the individual and society.

Although the dual perspective was created to force practitioners to recognize the importance of ethnic diversity, it is also a useful perspective when selecting interventions designed to build on their strengths and link these families with sustained economic, social, educational, and health service networks located in their residential communities. Specifically, a "goal . . . of this . . . framework was to prevent the a priori assignment of pathology to behavior that was functional in the client's specific family and community system but that seemed incongruent and even dysfunctional from the perspective of the larger societal system" (Norton, 1993). The framework provided an assessment dimension to understanding the effects of long-term individual and family dysfunctioning, and to identifying services needed to begin to link family members with each other, and to families with the essential community and institutional support systems (Norton and Kivnick, 1993). The application of the perspective in working with veteran families required that VVFAP staff devise service approaches that individualized and valued social group differences.

The dual perspective provided the VVFAP staff with a method for examining the developmental needs of both the individual family members and the needs of the family as it fulfilled its responsibility to socialize and nurture family members. Assessment revealed that these families were generally isolated socially, had experienced long-term episodic periods of conflict and violence, and that family relationships were generally emotionally sterile. As a resource for nurturing and socialization of individual members, the family group generally was very limited. As a consequence, children raised in this type of family exhibited a variety of individual adjustment patterns, including poor educational performance, a sense of personal inadequacy, and uncertainty about personal goals and aspirations. In addition, many displayed genetically based physical difficulties.

The general alienation experienced by the veteran on his return from active duty often became a norm for the entire family, and, over time, the family had difficulty effectively accessing and receiving supports and services from community-based resource systems, including public education, economic supports, churches, and social supports. Client JB is illustrative of a common veteran family profile. The veteran contacted the VVFAP because of his concern that alcohol abuse was becoming a medical problem; there was a growing pattern of verbal and physical abuse within the family. Over the years, family members had adopted a pattern of codependence in their relationship, helped keep the abuse a "family secret," and as individuals and as a unit were unable to access community services because of feelings of guilt and embarrassment. The families were insulated socially, lacked information about alcohol abuse, and required supportive assistance in accessing the available community-based counseling and drug treatment services. Thus, creating bridges between family members and between the family and community resource systems became a primary service objective.

Case Management Services

A modified case management model was adapted to provide the universal social service needs of facilitating access to resource systems, providing helping or therapeutic assistance, and promoting the developmental and socialization resources of the families (Rothman, 1991). Case management service delivery consisted of helping the veteran, individual family members, and families make informed choices about securing entitlements, opportunities, and services; assisting with gaining timely access to resource systems; and providing individualized supportive encouragement and advocacy and facilitating the coordination of various specialized service systems in an integrated family-centered fashion.

Case management services were applied using a problem-solving approach that consisted of five sequential processes: assessment, planning, intervention, monitoring, and evaluation. In the spirit of the project, the value context of this rational problem-solving process included the value orientations of:

- Client-centered service delivery—creating and providing specialized family-focused services rather than providing existing agency services only;
- Empowerment—enabling services provided in a manner that promotes, to the fullest extent possible, client-based control, and determination to promote self-help, self-reliance, and strengthening of informal support networks to promote the continuity of care beyond the existence of the VVFAP project;
- Dignity and respect—focusing confidential service provision on strengths of client system to promote self-worth, competence, and affirmation;

- Community-based coordination—linking families into an array of social, emotional, and resource networks with other veteran families; and
- Adaptability—creating and delivering consistent and flexible client-centered services.

Because many of the families contained adult developmentally disabled children, case management services included a focus on client empowerment, examining the interface among individuals, family, and community, in both an urban and a rural context characterized by a scarcity of formal resource systems, long-term failure experiences in effectively accessing formal resource systems, environmental barriers, and sense of despair fostered by long-term family dysfunctioning (Fiene and Taylor, 1991).

Because many veterans and their families had severed contact with resource systems, thereby reducing or eliminating service utilization, the case-finding component of the case management model was an important continuing activity. The experience of the staff with direct identification and contact with veterans showed this approach to have very limited success. When contact was made, most veterans were very reluctant at best. Secondary and informal referrals were found to be much more effective and promoted the program goal of social networking among the families.

Project Service Structure

CFS, located in Portland, Indiana, was incorporated in December 1965 as a 501(c)(3) Indiana not-for-profit human service corporation providing an array of direct assistance services to at-risk individuals and families, including education, health, employment, transportation, nutrition, housing, and emergency financial services. It also engages in human resource development to improve the overall quality of community life within a ten-county region located in east central Indiana. In addition to the VVFAP program, the overall service mission of CFS (Braden 1990) "is to promote the well being and self-sufficiency of residents by providing a range of coordinated programs that include, but are not limited to, the following:

- Advocacy and outreach services;
- Case management;
- Elderly transportation service;
- Employment and training program;
- Energy assistance program;
- Food, medical and nutrition services;
- Housing preservation;
- Well child/prenatal clinic;
- Volunteer income tax assistance;
- Weatherization services; and
- Women, Infants, and Children Supplemental Feeding Program (WIC)."

CFS has substantial experience in providing a broad range of services, and has, over the years, established very solid service relationships with a broad array of private and public human services agencies. As a result, a targeted consumer population—the families of Vietnam veterans—benefited from being included as an at-risk population to be served by the organization.

The social work internship portion of the partnership was designed to fulfill a major program-accrediting standard which requires that each of the 420 accredited baccalaureate social work programs housed in institutions of higher education located throughout the United States provide every student with a structured field-based internship or field practicum. This internship requires that each student complete a minimum of 400 clock hours in an approved practicum site and demonstrate, under supervision, the basic professional competencies of an entry-level practitioner. Specifically, the performance objectives of the internship as defined by the 1992 Commission on Standards and Accreditation of the Council on Social Work Education requires that a senior-level student demonstrate entry-level professional competencies in an approved social service setting. These competencies require a demonstrated mastery of practice, social policy, and social research interventions designed to address the current identified needs of individual clients as well as the conditions that support the continuing vulnerability of the client population.

In addition to the professional competencies and the performance outcomes of the required field practicum, several curriculum content areas also focus on content related to the social service needs of veterans and their families. These curriculum areas include social and economic justice, populations at risk, social work practice interventions, and social welfare policy and services (Randolph, 1992).

The VVFAP represented a viable practicum placement opportunity that provided a rich diversity of learning opportunities commensurate with the standards of an accredited baccalaureate social work degree program.

Table 1 identifies the service blueprint that integrates the theoretical models, the problem-solving service process, and the interrelationship between the program staff and social work student interns.

The partnership between the baccalaureate social work program and the VVFAP provided a structure that resulted both in increased services to veterans' families, and in a significant field-based learning experience for students. The arrangement provided a means for the strengths of a social service organization and an academic program to be enhanced, and also provided an improved public service.

The placement process consisted of a series of planned steps. Each step occurred in a sequential manner as students completed their final semester on campus and prepared to enter the full-time off-campus practicum placement (Macy and Gildner, 1993). To promote replication by other service organizations and other social work academic programs, each of the major phases of the placement is summarized below.

During the sixteen-week period of their final campus semester, students are enrolled in senior-level elective courses and two social work practice classes that provide content on methods for working with individuals, families, groups, organizations, and communities. In these practice classes, students apply the practice method concepts to a client population of interest. The client population is then researched by the students and the basis for being vulnerable is reported. This academic practice study of a vulnerable population occurs at the same time that a student is completing the application for practicum, which requires investigation of available sites, refinement of career interests, defining learning strengths and needs, and collaboration with faculty advisors. The practice study for students interested in the VVFAP site focused on such areas as the history of chemical warfare, veteran services, identification and evaluation of national policies and programs for veterans, nature and etiology of combat-related PTSD, and the history of the Agent Orange Class Assistance Program. This academic study of issues provided a beginning orientation and understanding of fundamental information needed for successful entry into the VVFAP placement.

The placement selection process consisted of the following additional steps:

- A student would schedule a pre-placement interview with the director of VVFAP, who would receive the student's Application to Practicum file materials for the academic program.
- An evaluative review of file materials, assessment interview and description of potential learning and service assignments, nature of supervision, and identification of major program policies and procedures for student interns would be provided.

Table 1. VVFAP Field-Based Program Service Structure

Veteran Family Population and Service System Focus	I. VVFAP Services and Management System	Veteran Family Units and Focus Services
■ Participate in media events. ■ Design resource classification system. ■ Make public awareness presentations to secondary referral resources. ■ Community education series on needs of Vietnam veterans or families.	**A. Outreach and Information Programs.** ■ Community-wide public information, consumer education, and development of referral systems. Examples of service tasks: ■ Veterans information fairs; ■ Host secondary principals' quidance and school-based nurses; ■ Media releases and conducting talk/call-in radio/TV presentation; ■ Provision of Agent Orange information to medics, assessment staff; ■ Resource identification, contact, and development. **B. Family-based assessment, referral, and care management.** ■ Home-based contact and information services. ■ Intake information, planning, and supportive services.	■ Visit community-based agency and collect eligibility materials. ■ Prepare summary of medical-based information related to Agent Orange and conduct in-service to contracted medical services.
Population Resource Planning	**II. Service System Intake**	**Family Unit Resources Planning**
■ Complete referral for psychological testing and collaborate on findings. ■ Identification/resolution of common barriers to use of services (e.g., transportation, documentation, etc.)	Examples of service tasks: ■ Individual and family assessment; ■ Medical/physical; ■ Psychological; ■ Psychosocial; ■ Situational (financial, housing, transportation, etc.); ■ Service needs identification and care planning.	■ Complete psychosocial history. ■ Referral family units/members with agency resource systems. ■ Assistance in meeting eligibility requirements.
Population Services Collaboration	**III. Service Provision Planning and Implementation**	**Family Unit Service Coordination and Integration**
■ Assist with creating volunteer service group and identify common needs. ■ Conduct in-service for secondary and adult education personnel focused on identifying at-risk children.	■ Goal setting (long and short term). ■ Intervention (specialized and care management) planning based on outcome of individual and family assets. ■ Specialized and care management service coordination and integration initiated.	■ Complete home/office visits to monitor service provision. ■ Provide face-to-face or telephone follow-up family unit advocacy. ■ Cofacilitate spouse support groups.

Table 1. Continued.

Population Services Collaboration	III. Service Provision Planning and Implementation	Family Unit Service Coordination and Integration
	■ Linking client systems with formal and informal systems: **Formal**: Chemical dependency services; Psychiatric; Family therapy; Therapeutic groups **Informal**: Support groups for veteran, spouse, adult children; Weekend family retreats and sponsored outings.	
Population Service Monitoring	**IV. Coordinate Tailored Services**	**Family Unit Monitoring**
■ Contract fundamental service providers to improve clarification of policies/proceedings. ■ Complete analysis of service system gaps and identify risk factors to determine future needs.	■ Care coordination meeting service consultation/collaboration.	■ Provide support and follow-along to family unit. ■ Link families with support services (e.g., groups, respite care, etc.).
	V. Outcome Evaluation and Termination	**Family Unit Evaluation**
	■ Evaluate approaches defined.	■ Complete case evaluation (i.e., single subject).
	VI. Service System Formalization	**Family Unit Services Modification**
	■ Identify financial, socio-political factors. ■ Grant assistance.	■ Identify major gaps in interagency service delivery system and analyze causes. ■ Convene selected agency-based responsibilities; regulate changes to negotiate service policies and procedures.

Source: Adapted from J. Rothman. 1993. A Model of case management: Toward empirically based practice. *Social Work* 8:523.

- If the outcome of the placement evaluative conference was mutually satisfactory, the VVFAP director would receive practicum materials for use during the placement. This includes course syllabus and the student's midterm and final performance evaluation forms.

- During the fifteen-week placement, three agency-based conferences are held with the practicum supervisor, the student, and the faculty practicum instructor. The first conference, completed within two weeks of the beginning of the placement, consists of completing the Teaching-Learning Contract in which learning goals are identified and assignments are selected. Performance evaluations are completed at both the midpoint and final week of the placement. In addition, the faculty liaison provides consultation services to assist staff in addressing service gaps and needed policy changes.

During the actual placement, students complete assignments that address the service needs of veteran families and assist VVFAP staff in providing services to address the common needs of the veteran population. Assignments given to a practicum student include:

- Responsibility for ten to twelve families receiving care management services;
- Staffing the telephone and walk-in desk;
- Completing public presentations to explain program services;
- Participating in care and service coordination meetings with collateral service providers;
- Facilitating weekly spouse support groups; and
- Checking and updating files on community resources, changes in entitlements, etc.

Summary and Conclusion

The VVFAP represents the benefits of a collaborative partnership between a private social service organization and a baccalaureate social work program, located in a public university, which can result in improved service provision for veteran families. Evaluation of the project suggests that it has achieved its objectives and has developed a well-specified, replicable model of care management that can be used to serve veterans and their families both on a request-for-service, and also on a continuing maintenance basis. This project created a service delivery approach that fits the needs of an at-risk group of American citizens whose long-term needs must be addressed on a continuing basis by our national, state, and local resource systems.

References

Braden, L. 1990. *Vietnam Veteran Family Assistance Program Proposal*. Portland, IN: Community and Family Services, Inc.

Brown, P. 1984. Legacies of a war: Treatment considerations with Vietnam veterans and their families. *Social Work* 4:372-373.

Fiene, J., and P. Taylor. 1991. Serving rural families of developmentally disabled children: A case management model. *Social Work* 4:323-327.

Germain, C., and A. Gitterman. 1980. *The Life Model of Social Work Practice.* New York: Columbia University Press.

Macy, H., and J. Gildner. 1993. *Social Work Practicum Handbook.* Muncie, IN: Ball State University.

Norton, D. 1993. Diversity, early socialization, and temporal development: The dual perspective revisited. *Social Work* 1:83.

Norton, D., F. Brown, G. Brown, E. Francis, F. Mirase, and R. Valle. 1978. *The Dual Perspective: Inclusion of Ethnic Minority Content in Social Work Education.* New York: Council on Social Work Education.

Randolph, N. 1992. *Curriculum Policy Statement for Baccalaureate Degree Programs in Social Work Education.* Alexandria, VA: Council On Social Work Education, Inc.

Rhoades, D. 1992. *Fourth Annual Report*. Washington, DC: Agent Orange Class Assistance Program.

Rothman, J. 1991. A model of case management: Toward empirically based practice. *Social Work* 6:520-528.

Between the Courts and Congress: Leveraging VA Benefits for the Agent Orange Plaintiff Class

Barton F. Stichman, J.D., LL.M.
National Veterans Legal Services Project
Washington, DC

Abstract

The U.S. Department of Veterans Affairs (VA) routinely denied claims for disabilities associated with Agent Orange exposure until litigation was brought by Vietnam Veterans of America Legal Services, a predecessor of the National Veterans Legal Services Project (NVLSP), and others in 1986. The court ruled that the VA discriminated against disability claims of Vietnam veterans who believed they were affected by Agent Orange exposure. By seeking court action, involving the media, advocating in Congress, and working with other veterans' advocates, the litigants mobilized forces outside the veteran community on veterans' behalf.

The advocacy effort resulted in funds to assist Vietnam veterans, and veterans' families, who believed they had been injured by exposure to Agent Orange, and in changes in the way veterans' affairs policy making is conducted. NVLSP's activities, which included working with government agencies and the scientific community and on legislation to direct the VA to change its practices, can serve as a model for advocates of systemic change in government policy making and decision making.

Barton F. Stichman, J.D., LL.M., *is co-director of the National Veterans Legal Services Project (NVLSP), an AOCAP grantee. He also served as one of the attorneys representing the members of the plaintiff class in the* Nehmer *litigation discussed in this paper.*

Our nation has long recognized that it owes a great debt to those who served in the U.S. armed forces. This recognition supports federal law and regulations requiring the executive branch of the federal government, through the U.S. Department of Veterans Affairs (VA), to provide free medical care and tax-free monthly cash payments to veterans who suffer disabilities that are connected to their military service. The VA is also required to provide tax-free monthly cash payments and other benefits to certain surviving family members of veterans whose deaths are related to military service.

When the Agent Orange Class Assistance Program (AOCAP) was created, the federal government had stubbornly refused to honor this national policy for an important segment of the veteran population. During the past two decades, thousands of Vietnam veterans have contracted seriously disabling illnesses that have devastated their lives and the lives of their families. Vietnam veterans and their families have long believed that many of these diseases may be connected to their exposure during military service to the herbicide Agent Orange. Fidelity to national policy required the government to come to the aid of these veterans and their families. Instead, the government callously ignored their needs.

This paper describes the strategy developed by one AOCAP grantee to persuade the federal government to respond appropriately to these Vietnam veterans and their families. This strategy, developed by the National Veterans Legal Services Project (NVLSP), ultimately produced more than $450 million in tax-free cash payments to these Vietnam veterans. The amount of money NVLSP helped to generate is nearly three times the amount of the fund created by the manufacturers of Agent Orange in the settlement to the veterans' class action product liability suit.[1]

NVLSP's strategy can be used as a model by those who wish to persuade the government to respond appropriately to the needs of other groups of veterans. It is already clear that the success of NVLSP's strategy has caused the federal government to alter its decision-making process; other groups will not need to go to such extraordinary lengths to force the government to live up to its obligations.

The Problem: Systemic Government Disregard of the Needs of Vietnam Veterans

In the late 1970s, the media began to cover the allegations of Vietnam veterans that exposure to Agent Orange was connected to seriously disabling conditions that they were experiencing, such as cancer and birth defects in their offspring.

These veterans and their families sought redress from the two institutions they believed were responsible for their suffering: the chemical companies that manufactured the herbicide (which, many believed, had known of the dangers of their product) and the federal government (which had ordered the herbicide's production and spraying). Efforts at redress from the chemical companies focused on a single vehicle: federal lawsuits that ultimately were consolidated into a class action. Getting the federal government to honor its obligations proved much more complex.

The method used by the federal government to formulate a response to the veterans' allegations was a traditional one. The deeply embedded policy and decision-making apparatus in veterans' affairs involves three entities: the VA, the congressionally chartered veterans' service organizations (VSOs)—the largest of which are The American Legion, the Disabled American Veterans, and the Veterans of Foreign Wars—and the U.S. House and Senate committees on veterans' affairs.

For decades, policies were formulated and problems resolved by negotiations among staff members from these three groups—negotiations in which outside institutions or individuals were rarely allowed to participate. Within the executive branch, the president and his staff traditionally let the VA handle veterans' affairs on its own. The legislature had essentially delegated its role to the House and Senate veterans' affairs committees, which traditionally exercised exclusive control over veterans' issues; members of Congress not on these committees rarely had significant effect on veterans' affairs. The third branch of the federal government, the judiciary, had been excluded entirely by two statutes. One barred court review of VA benefit adjudications and one barred veterans from suing the government for compensation for injuries incurred during military service.

Accordingly, when the allegations concerning Agent Orange came to the fore, the response was formulated by the traditional policy-making apparatus. After a review of the scientific literature on Agent Orange conducted by VA scientists, the VA determined without further review that the only condition associated with exposure to Agent Orange was chloracne (a skin condition). Without conducting a formal rule-making proceeding and considering public comment, the VA issued an unpublished directive to its adjudicators to deny all Agent Orange claims unless the claimed condition was chloracne. Tens of thousands of Agent Orange death and disability claims were denied as a result.

Public hearings were held by the House and Senate veterans' affairs committees at which the VA defended its "nothing but chloracne" policy. The VSOs and the veterans' affairs committees essentially acquiesced; they settled for legislation that, one, directed the VA to conduct an epidemiologic study of Vietnam veterans exposed to Agent Orange and,[2] two, required the VA to provide health care for disabilities that the applying veteran believed were related to Agent Orange (unless the VA could point to a cause other than the herbicide).[3]

The government's response did not relieve the pressure exerted on it by Vietnam veterans and their allies. The media continued to highlight the plight of these veterans and their families. In the early 1980s, the public gradually began to accept the proposition that the nation as a whole had mistreated those it had sent to fight in Vietnam. Responding to these pressures, the House and Senate veterans' affairs committees in 1984 agreed to legislation requiring the VA to take a modest step to open the process to outside influences.

Under the provisions of the Veterans' Dioxin and Radiation Exposure Compensation Standards Act (Dioxin Act),[4] the VA was to create an advisory committee composed of knowledgeable non-VA scientists and, after considering the views of the advisory committee and the public, to promulgate formal rules to govern the adjudication of Agent Orange compensation claims.

The VA went through the motions of complying with the legislation. It created an advisory committee and it conducted a public rule-making proceeding. Despite an approach that appeared to be more open to comment, the VA influenced the process so that the results would confirm the position it had reached in isolation earlier.

First, the VA assembled a group of scientists who would be amenable to its viewpoint. No scientist who believed that exposure to dioxin (the toxic contaminant in Agent Orange) posed significant health risks was allowed to serve on the committee. The VA provided limited financial support to the committee for the conduct of its legislatively mandated work: an annual budget of $45,000. Finally, the VA manipulated the process by telling the scientists that, in order to warrant compensation, the scientific evidence must show that there is a strict cause-and-effect relationship between exposure to dioxin and disease—the strict standard used in tort litigation to determine liability.

In August 1985, the results of the inquiry required under the 1984 Dioxin Act were made public. The VA promulgated a formal rule to govern all VA disability and death claims based on exposure to Agent Orange: only veterans suffering from chloracne would receive compensation.[5] The other parts of the traditional policy-making apparatus (the VSOs and the veterans' affairs committees) accepted the results of the VA proceeding. Nothing had changed.

Making the Government Honor Its Obligations

Before AOCAP was created, attorneys for the National Veterans Legal Services Project[6] began to develop a strategy to combat the government's intransigence on Agent Orange. They had monitored the VA's 1985 rule-making proceeding and researched legal and scientific issues. From the information they gathered, they reached two major conclusions:

- The standard the VA had used to decide whether to service connect diseases associated with exposure to Agent Orange was a higher standard than the one the VA used to service connect diseases experienced by other groups of veterans; and
- The methodology used by the scientific community outside the VA to study Agent Orange was much more rigorous than the VA's process, and the conclusions reached by this community about the health risks associated with Agent Orange were far graver than the VA's conclusions.

The VA's longstanding failure to treat Vietnam veterans as it had other veterans appeared to NVLSP to be deliberate and driven by budgetary concerns. The problem was exacerbated by the failure of the traditional policy-making apparatus in the veterans' affairs arena to correct this discriminatory treatment. The VSOs and the Senate and House veterans' affairs committees had allowed the VA to act in isolation and to ignore its normal standards for deciding whether to designate specific diseases as service connected.

Thus, NVLSP concluded it had to reach beyond the normal veterans' affairs decision-making apparatus for help in addressing the Agent Orange problem. This decision proved to be critical.

Resort to the Judiciary

One important entity that had not played a role in the development of the government's Agent Orange policy was the judicial branch. NVLSP was well aware that Congress had prohibited judicial intervention since 1933. But NVLSP also knew that there was a potential loophole in the law. Some federal jurisdictions recognized a narrow exception to the bar on judicial intervention that allowed federal courts to review the legality of VA regulations.

NVLSP crafted a lawsuit to fit within this loophole. In 1986, it[7] filed suit in the Northern District of California, where judicial precedent recognized the loophole, challenging the VA's Agent Orange regulations. The lawsuit was instituted by Vietnam Veterans of America, several individual Vietnam veterans, and several widows of Vietnam veterans on behalf of a class defined similarly to the class served by AOCAP.[8] NVLSP charged that the VA had violated the 1984 Dioxin Act in developing its 1985 Agent Orange rules.

The VA responded immediately by trying to get the lawsuit transferred to the District of Columbia, which did not recognize the loophole on which NVLSP was relying. This effort failed and the litigation moved forward in California.

In 1989, after three years of intensive litigation, the United States District Court for the Northern District of California ruled in favor of the *Nehmer* class of Vietnam veterans and their families.[9] The court agreed with NVLSP that the VA had not traditionally required proof of a cause-and-effect relationship to service connect a disease. NVLSP had shown that in other circumstances the VA had granted disability and death compensation using a less stringent standard—an epidemiologically based significant statistical association between an event that happened during military service and later disease.

The court accepted NVLSP's argument that the VA had discriminated against Vietnam veterans by requiring a higher-than-normal standard of proof and thus had violated the 1984 Dioxin Act. The court also agreed with NVLSP that the VA had violated the law by refusing to give Vietnam veterans the benefit of the doubt in reviewing the scientific evidence.

To remedy these violations, the court struck down the VA's Agent Orange rules. It overturned thousands of decisions the VA had issued denying benefits to veterans exposed to Agent Orange.

The court ordered the VA advisory committee to reread the scientific literature on dioxin. The court also ordered the VA's hand-picked scientists to apply the more commonly used, less stringent standard of proof (that is, only a significant statistical association) and resolve any benefit of the doubt in a veteran's favor. The court directed the VA to create new Agent Orange rules to include all of the diseases that were found to be associated with Agent Orange after consideration of the advisory committee's views. Finally, the court told the VA to reopen the thousands of Agent Orange claims denied in the past and review them again under the newly developed rules.

At the time of the *Nehmer* decision, the leadership of the VA had changed. President Bush had appointed former U.S. Representative Edward Derwinski to head the agency. To the dismay of VA officials who had engineered the agency's policy on Agent Orange for the past decade, Secretary of Veterans Affairs Derwinski announced eight days after the *Nehmer* decision that the VA would not appeal.[10] The VA, he said, would comply with the law.

AOCAP Funds NVLSP

AOCAP believed that the *Nehmer* victory provided a significant opportunity to leverage a substantial amount of money for the benefit of the class it served. It funded NVLSP to take advantage of that opportunity. The funds were not to be used to pursue a primarily judicial remedy—that had already been won—nor to chart a legislative course. AOCAP wanted to foster NVLSP's strategy of involving forces outside the normal veterans' affairs policy-making mechanism to help ensure a just result for Vietnam veterans and their families.

The decision to fund NVLSP was not based only on the fact that this organization had litigated *Nehmer*. As a group serving veterans and their families on a national basis, NVLSP was well placed to maximize the opportunities created by the *Nehmer* decision. NVLSP had a number of other characteristics that made it suited to the purpose. It had already served for many years as a national clearinghouse and support center in veterans' law. It was an organization to which veterans' advocates around the country turned for information, advice, advocacy materials, and training. Because it was not a membership organization, it was not required to respond to conflicting political pressures generated within the organization.

To reap the full benefits of *Nehmer*, it was not only necessary to ensure that the VA properly implemented the court victory; it was also necessary to tell veterans and advocates around the country how to take advantage of the new rules. NVLSP's ability to reach out to the geographically scattered class and to respond to requests for assistance nationwide was important.

Finally, funding NVLSP to help AOCAP class members receive their due from the VA fulfilled a need identified during the fairness hearings held by United States District Judge Jack B. Weinstein before AOCAP was created. As Judge Weinstein stated in his opinion approving the creation of a class assistance foundation:[11]

> Witnesses at the Fairness Hearings, a number of distribution proposals submitted to the court, and suggestions received by the Special Master have called for the establishment of a national legal center to help veterans exposed to Agent Orange. . . . [I]t was felt that an additional need exists for a national legal center that will work for increased Vietnam veteran benefits . . .

Accordingly, a regionally based organization would be hard-pressed to serve the role AOCAP envisioned. As a respected, independent national advocacy and support center, NVLSP was well suited to it.

Adding Views from the Scientific Community

The *Nehmer* victory created an opportunity for justice for Vietnam veterans and their families. The court decision did not, however, prevent the VA from reaffirming its "nothing but chloracne" policy. The VA and its advisory committee could review the scientific literature again and determine that chloracne was the only disease with a significant statistical association with exposure to Agent Orange, and then reaffirm the thousands of claims denials that had been invalidated by the *Nehmer* decision.

The methodology the VA had used to evaluate the health effects of exposure to Agent Orange did not inspire confidence that Vietnam veterans would be treated fairly in the court-ordered re-review. Until 1985, the VA relied exclusively on scientists who were VA employees. Although mandated by the 1984 Dioxin Act to use non-VA scientists to evaluate the scientific literature, the VA had not sought a group with a balance of viewpoints.

The VA limited the advisory committee members by refusing to allocate sufficient funds to accomplish the committee's mission in a scientifically valid manner. There were other forms of interference as well; for example, the studies offered to the scientists for review were generally selected by the VA, rather than by the committee. This prevented an independent review. One of the VA officials controlling the literature selection was Lawrence Hobson, M.D., Ph.D., deputy director of the VA's Agent Orange Projects Office. Hobson, who felt Agent Orange posed no threat to humans, summarized his views on Agent Orange in a 1986 article[12] as follows:

> [I]n the late 1970's and early 1980's, the mysterious TCDD [dioxin] had assumed the properties of black magic —pervasive, unpredictable, and malevolent—in the minds of many people. Like such magic, to them TCDD must be the result of ill-intentioned witches or warlocks and these could only be the chemists and chemical companies who produced the noxious material. People who denounced the concept of such witchcraft by cautioning that the fearsome results attributed to TCDD and its carrier were unproved were in turn denounced as supporters of the witchcraft.
>
> There is no doubt that the fear engendered in the United States by TCDD spread quickly and widely. Who was responsible for disseminating this "black magic"? Unfortunately, the blame is widespread. It includes certainly the media, some Vietnam veterans, a fringe of scientists and doctors, a few public agencies and legislators who saw a chance to "protect" the veterans or the public. Somewhat later some lawyers assisted, especially when it seemed that enormous suits for damages could be engendered. Then too, the very caution that characterizes good scientists and physicians hampered their ability to stem the outcry and the witchhunt.
>
> More to the point is the matter of how such an event can be handled or better still avoided in the future. Witchhunts have been stopped in individual episodes when tempers cooled, discontented groups found peace, and the excesses of belief in the attendant black magic were seen for what they are. This seems to be happening now with the TCDD episode, largely as scientific evidence mounts that the compound really presents no threat from the exposure experienced by the veterans and the public at large.

There were additional reasons for Vietnam veterans and their families to be skeptical about the fairness of the VA's decision-making process. The VA's methodology for evaluating Agent Orange differed dramatically from the process used by other reputable scientists and institutions— "the fringe of scientists and doctors [and] a few public agencies" referred to by Dr. Hobson.

One of the unnamed public agencies Dr. Hobson meant was the U.S. Environmental Protection Agency, which had issued a twelve-volume document on polychlorinated dibenzo-p-dioxins in 1985.[13] The EPA's purpose in preparing the document, *Health Assessment Docu-*

ment for Polychlorinated Dibenzo-p-dioxins (EPA-HAD), was to have recognized medical or scientific authorities, in fields necessary for assessing the health effects of exposure to dioxin, review the pertinent scientific studies to determine adverse health effects in humans. The EPA-HAD project was directed by Dr. Debdas Mukerjee, a senior science advisor with the Environmental Criteria and Assessment Office of the EPA in Cincinnati, Ohio. A comprehensive literature search was conducted by Dr. Dibak K. Basu, Dr. Mukerjee, and Dr. Michael W. Neal of the Life and Environmental Sciences Division of the Syracuse Research Corporation in Syracuse, New York. This literature search found approximately 700 pertinent scientific studies. Drs. Basu, Mukerjee, and Neal reviewed each study and prepared a rough draft that described the studies' findings and made conclusions based on them.

The rough draft was then subjected to peer review. (Peer review is a commonly accepted and widely used practice in which independent scientists critically review, evaluate, and comment on a study or other scientific article.) The peer review panel for the EPA-HAD draft consisted of thirty-four recognized medical and scientific authorities familiar with the scientific studies of possible adverse health effects of exposure to dioxin in humans. The panel members were selected to reflect a cross-section of those concerned with dioxin and health issues, including authorities from chemical companies, academia, government, and environmental groups, and dioxin experts from countries other than the United States. All thirty-four members of the peer review panel reviewed all 700 studies listed in the EPA-HAD bibliography, even though some of them had read the cited studies in the past, to obtain a focused, rational, and intelligent evaluation of the literature.

When the EPA finally issued the document in 1985, it consisted of 608 pages of analysis, divided into 15 chapters. Among other things, the EPA-HAD concluded that "2, 3, 7, 8-TCDD [dioxin] should be regarded as a 'probable' human carcinogen."[14]

In comparison with the EPA's expert review of the literature, the limited methodology used by the VA advisory committee was clearly weak. For example, after four years of operation, the VA committee had reviewed only seventy-four dioxin studies. Even the VA committee appeared to recognize the deficiencies in its process, as is reflected in the following exchange during one of its meetings: [15]

> DR. COLTON [the head of the dioxin panel of the advisory committee]: "[O]ne of the problems that I have with our whole process is that we are looking always at individual studies and the validity of an individual study and yet very often, most often, we draw conclusions really by a synthesis of all the existing studies. I feel that any decision that we make about exposed or not exposed shouldn't really come from just our review of what we said about one study. It really should come somehow from even some small subcommittee doing a synthesis of all these studies that we've reviewed that deal with that issue."
>
> MR. CONWAY [the VA's Executive Secretary to the advisory committee]: "I agree with you, Dr. Colton, that what you need to do is not to just focus on one study and then make a determination based on that one study. What I thought we had agree[d] [to] previously was that when making your . . . recommendations to the Agency you would take into ac[count] all of the material that you were aware of, putting it into a perspective and, particularly in light of the additional materials which are made available to you at a current meeting and then making a recommendation one way or the other."
>
> DR. COLTON: "That is assuming an awful lot that many of us that are not in this [field] entirely or their whole profession[al] life do not have in our memory banks—what results were or what the outcomes were from all the studies that have been reviewed over the past several years. . . . I still feel hesitant about drawing any kind of conclusion based solely on an oral presentation here."
>
> MR. MEADOWS [the Chairman of the committee]: "I doubt that this Committee is going to be able to enjoy the luxury of being able to proceed in a somewhat orderly way through these questions that you are talking about."

It was clear that the VA was unwilling to allocate adequate resources, as the EPA had done in producing EPA-HAD. Derwinski's VA was also unwilling to change the membership of its advisory committee to reflect a diversity of views. The VSOs and the House and Senate veterans' affairs committees were unwilling to force the VA to change.

The judicial branch of government had proven helpful in breaking the status quo. But because of the judiciary's lack of expertise in scientific matters and its traditional reluctance to interpose its views in matters of science, NVLSP concluded that the judiciary alone would not give Vietnam veterans justice.

Nonetheless, the *Nehmer* decision had established rules that could lead to justice. NVLSP concluded that an essential ingredient to future decisions was unbiased information from the scientific community outside the VA. But in view of the VA's longstanding intransigence on Agent Orange, it was unlikely that this input alone would persuade the VA to change course. NVLSP concluded that it needed to enlist the support of other forces to break the logjam: the media and at least some of the powerful veterans' service organizations.

Accordingly, NVLSP obtained the backing of two veterans' organizations (The American Legion and Vietnam Veterans of America) and organized a group of scientists to produce a written analysis of the scientific literature on Agent Orange that the VA could not ignore. The executive summary of this document stated:[16]

> For over a decade, the opponents of disability and death compensation for Vietnam veterans exposed to Agent Orange in the U.S. Congress and the Department of Veterans Affairs have based their opposition on the assertion that there is not enough scientific evidence to show a link between Agent Orange exposure and any disease other than chloracne. The VA is currently conducting a rulemaking proceeding under mandate of a statute and a federal court order that focuses on this very issue.
>
> Because [NVLSP, The American Legion, and Vietnam Veterans of America] have been dissatisfied with the efforts of the VA and its Advisory Committee on Environmental Hazards in this rulemaking proceeding, we decided it was essential to a fair resolution of the Agent Orange issue for an independent group of scientists to address the issues currently under consideration by Congress and the VA. We therefore assembled the Agent Orange Scientific Task Force—a group of prominent, independent scientists who are knowledgeable about the scientific studies concerning the health effects of exposure to dioxin. We asked the Task Force to prepare a report that summarizes its review of the scientific literature related to potential human health effects associated with exposure to phenoxyacetic acid herbicides and/or their associated contaminants (chlorinated dioxins). In reviewing the scientific literature, we asked the Task Force to determine which adverse health effects, if any, are associated with exposure to dioxin, using the standard the VA and its Advisory Committee have adopted in the rulemaking proceeding.

NVLSP organized this effort. It canvassed the scientific community to identify reputable experts and persuaded seven scientists to serve on the task force[17] without charging a fee for their services. NVLSP then provided support and guidance to the task force by securing copies of studies selected for review, providing legal advice on the standard of proof to be applied, and helping the scientists draft the task force's report, especially in comparing the task force's work with that of the VA advisory committee.

The task force's methodology differed in important respects from that of the methodology the VA advisory committee had been using. First, the task force determined that many more dioxin studies were pertinent to its task than had the VA advisory committee. Thus, many more studies were reviewed and evaluated.

Second, the task force did not follow the VA advisory committee's method of classifying studies. The "[a]dvisory [c]ommittee simply classified studies as positive or negative and then tallied them, apparently under the theory that all studies are equal and can be viewed independently from all other knowledge on the subject."[18] The task force called this procedure "unprecedented."[19] "Individual studies show associations in varying degrees, but the ultimate conclusion about an association is the result of synthesizing all of the available data to determine their overall or aggregate meaning."[20]

While the task force went about its work, the VA advisory committee reconvened to follow the mandate of the court in *Nehmer*. It first considered non-Hodgkin's lymphoma (NHL), one of the types of cancer most frequently associated in the scientific literature with exposure to dioxin. In December 1989, the VA advisory committee concluded that, even under the lower standard mandated by the court (significant statistical association), NHL was not related to dioxin. Thus, the advisory committee recommended to Secretary Derwinski that NHL should not receive service-connected status.

The Agent Orange Scientific Task Force released its report four months later, in April 1990, before Secretary Derwinski acted on the NHL recommendation. The task force's conclusions were far different from the VA's long-standing position:[21]

> Following review of the scientific literature, the Task Force concluded there is a significant statistical association between exposure to phenoxyacetic acid herbicides and/or their associated contaminants (chlorinated dioxins) and the following adverse health effects: (1) non-Hodgkin's lymphoma, (2) soft tissue sarcoma, (3) skin disorders/chloracne, (4) subclinical hepatotoxic effects (including secondary coproporphyrinuria and chronic hepatic porphyria), and (5) porphyria cutanea tarda (most likely only in individuals with inherited uroporphyrinogen decarboxylase deficiency). The aggregate interpretation of several sound studies showing a statistically significant association for each of these conditions makes this conclusion inescapable.
>
> Further, the scientific evidence supporting the existence of a significant statistical association between exposure to phenoxyacetic acid herbicides and/or their associated contaminants (chlorinated dioxins) is at least as strong as the scientific evidence of a lack of the association for the following adverse health effects: (1) Hodgkin's disease, (2) neurologic effects, and (3) reproductive and development effects. For each of these health effects, there are sound scientific studies showing statistical significance and strong scientific evidence of an association between exposure and effect. However, a statistically significant association is not as consistently supported for these effects as for the first group of health effects.
>
> The above eight adverse effects satisfy the VA's test for an association which qualifies for disability compensation, i.e., where the scientific evidence shows that a significant statistical association is "at least as likely as not." 38 C.F.R. § 1.17(d)(1).
>
> The Task Force concluded [that] there are other adverse health effects for which there is sound scientific evidence of an association with exposure, but the evidence does not reach the level of formal statistical significance. Nevertheless, were the Task Force a policy-making body concerned with disability compensation for veterans, it might conclude that compensation was due. However, the Task Force was limited to determining the existence of a significant statistical association, and the limited data available at this time show an association, but not a significant statistical association, between exposure to phenoxyacetic acid herbicides and/or dioxin and the following diseases: leukemias, cancers of the kidney, testis, pancreas, stomach, prostate, colon, hepatobiliary tract, and brain, psychological effects, immunological abnormalities, gastrointestinal ulcer, and altered lipid metabolism. Further research should be directed at these associations, and policy-makers, cognizant of the limitations on finding significant statistical associations and of the obligation to give the veteran the benefit of the doubt, would be justified in viewing these disorders in a more conclusive light for the purpose of establishing entitlement to disability compensation.

NVLSP enlisted the media to publicize the task force's conclusions. Other important forces joined in. Leaders of the Vietnam Veterans in Congress Caucus held a press conference embracing the report and arguing that it provided the basis for changing the VA's "nothing but chloracne" compensation policy. The American Legion, VVA, and NVLSP then presented the report to Secretary Derwinski and his advisory committee.

One month later, another significant report was issued. The Centers for Disease Control (CDC) released the results of an epidemiologic study known as the Selected Cancers Study.[22] CDC had compared the incidence of seven types of cancer among veterans who had served in Vietnam with the incidence among veterans who had not served in Vietnam. Exposure to Agent Orange was not examined in this study. Nevertheless, the study found a significant statistical association between NHL and service in Vietnam: the rate of incidences of NHL among Vietnam veterans was nearly 50 percent higher than the incidence of NHL among non-Vietnam veterans.

With both the Agent Orange Scientific Task Force and the CDC pointing to a link with NHL, Secretary Derwinski then rejected the recommendations of his own advisory committee. He announced that death and disability compensation would be granted to any Vietnam veteran who developed NHL, no matter how long after discharge the cancer arose.[23]

Congress Requires Independent Review

The victory on NHL marked a watershed for Agent Orange policy. The *Nehmer* victory, the Agent Orange Scientific Task Force report, and Secretary Derwinski's rejection of the work of his own advisory committee combined to give Vietnam veteran leaders in Congress the ammunition to convince the House and Senate veterans' affairs committees that the VA had so bungled the assignment Congress had given it in 1984 that it could not be trusted now.

While this legislative effort was moving forward, the VA continued to implement the *Nehmer* court order. In its first meeting after release of the task force report, the VA advisory committee considered another cancer: soft tissue sarcomas (STS). The Agent Orange Scientific Task Force report had found a significant statistical association of exposure to Agent Orange with STS, as it had with NHL.

The task force report apparently had an effect: for the first time in five years of deliberations, the VA advisory committee made a positive recommendation on a disease other than chloracne. It found the evidence on STS sufficient to satisfy the standard of proof required by the court. Secretary Derwinski immediately announced that STS would join NHL on the list of diseases considered service connected when manifested by a Vietnam veteran.[24]

Significant amounts in compensation benefits began to flow to Vietnam veterans and their families. The Congressional Budget Office estimated that over the following two years, the VA would be required to pay $104 million in death and disability benefits for NHL and STS.[25]

To the dismay of the VA, however, this action did not diminish the momentum for remedial legislation. Vietnam veterans in Congress drafted legislation to transfer control of the scientific review process from the VA. The drafts focused on:

- Codifying the VA's decisions on NHL and STS (so that a subsequent VA secretary could not reverse the decision to provide benefits for these diseases);
- Removing from the VA the role of analyzing the scientific evidence by disbanding the VA advisory committee and transferring its function to a group independent of the government;
- Requiring the independent group to review the scientific literature on dioxin again;
- Giving the independent group enough financial resources to do the job in a professional manner; and
- Requiring the VA secretary to again promulgate Agent Orange compensation rules—after considering the findings of the independent group.

The proponents of the legislation contacted NVLSP for advice concerning identification of a trustworthy scientific and medical review body. The National Academy of Sciences (NAS) was ultimately named.

Another critical factor in the legislation was the standard of proof that should be applied. "Significant statistical association" was certainly more beneficial to Vietnam veterans than a strict cause-and-effect standard. But the Agent Orange Scientific Task Force report made clear that significant statistical association had its limits. "In order for epidemiologic studies to find statistically significant associations between exposure and health effects," the task force report had stated, "these studies must have sufficient power and sensitivity."[26] According to the task force, findings that have statistical significance are difficult to reach when it comes to dioxin: "A major problem with the various epidemiologic studies of people exposed to pheroxyacetic acid herbicides is that there have not been many large populations with known exposure available for study and follow-up over long periods, or where such populations exist, like Vietnam veterans and the Vietnamese, these have not been adequately studied."[27]

Accordingly, the legislation was drafted to require a "positive association" rather than a "significant statistical association."[28] The legislation also favored Vietnam veterans by specifically instructing the VA to apply the benefit of the doubt principle—which, NVLSP had successfully argued in *Nehmer,* the VA was required to apply. A positive association was defined to exist "if the credible evidence for the association is equal to or outweighs the credible evidence against the association."[29]

The legislation also responded to the task force's conclusion that "large populations with known exposure available for study . . . , like Vietnam veterans . . . , have not been adequately studied."[30] Shortly before the task force issued its report, the VA had concluded that an epidemiologic study of Vietnam veterans exposed to Agent Orange could not be conducted in a scientifically valid manner. The legislation asked for help in resolving this dispute between the task force and the VA by requesting NAS to "make any recommendations it has for additional scientific studies to resolve areas of continuing scientific uncertainty relating to herbicide exposure."[31]

Another issue Congress needed to address was whether to cancel the court-ordered rule-making proceeding the VA was then conducting. The VA and its advisory committee had already dealt with NHL and STS, but there were dozens of other diseases they had yet to analyze.

The VA argued that if the NAS was going to revisit the entire Agent Orange issue, there was no need for the VA to complete the court-ordered rule making. Congress rejected this argument. It required the VA to complete the *Nehmer* rule making and gave the VA six months from the date of enactment to finish.[32]

Thus, Vietnam veterans would be given two bites at the apple: additional diseases could join NHL and STS on the list of compensable diseases through either the *Nehmer* rule making or the NAS review.

On February 6, 1991, President Bush signed the Agent Orange Act of 1991 into law. Coincidentally, the VA had scheduled its next advisory committee meeting shortly afterward. As they settled into their seats, the scientists were informed by the VA that Congress had just ordered the NAS to replace the committee, that NAS would be assigned the tasks originally given to the committee, that NAS would be given $1 million to do the job, and that the committee was required to complete its analysis of the remaining diseases within six months, before its congressionally ordered death on August 7, 1991.

The scientists—selected by the VA six years earlier, consistently loyal to the VA, even testifying in support of the VA during the *Nehmer* litigation—broke ranks:[33]

> DR. COLTON [head of the dioxin panel on the committee]: "I think where the National Academy [of Sciences] might be really at an advantage is that I think we have been very limited in the staff work that [the VA has put] into this. In one sense, Fred [Conway, the VA's Executive Secretary to the committee] has really had to do [it] all . . . [t]he VA has r[e]ally exercised a lot of restraint in using their [sic] own resources to help with the staff work here. . . ."

DR. NEAL [another advisory committee member]: "I'd go further. I would say for the record that the lack of support for this Committee is a disgrace. . . . The VA now is a [cabinet-level] department and it has a committee of this stature, it seems to me it has the responsibility to learn how much support [is necessary]. The [National] Academy [of Sciences] wouldn't touch anything on these terms. . . . Given the gravity of the problem[,] the way it has been run [by the VA] out of the hip pocket, it doesn't reflect well on the VA. . . ."

MR. CONWAY: "Congress made available in FY '91 $1 million for the NAS to do its review and analysis. My budget last year [was] $45,000."

Legal Maneuvers

During and following the legislative battle, NVLSP engaged in a series of legal maneuvers designed to maximize the compensation that Vietnam veterans and their families would ultimately receive.

Notice to the Class

The initial *Nehmer* court order required the VA to reevaluate all Agent Orange claims that were filed after, or were pending on, September 25, 1985. Approximately 29,000 claimants fit within this category.[34] But these claimants were not the only ones affected by Agent Orange. Many veterans and their survivors did not file claims because they thought it would be fruitless, given the VA's "nothing but chloracne" policy.

Accordingly, NVLSP asked for a court order requiring the VA to notify potential Agent Orange claimants that the VA was reconsidering, and might ultimately change, its Agent Orange compensation rules. The maneuver was successful. The VA was required to mail notices to more than 200,000 veterans on its Agent Orange registry. The notice provided advice to those who had not yet filed claims.[35] More than 2,300 of these veterans contacted NVLSP for more information. They were sent personal responses, including NVLSP's "Self-Help Guide on Agent Orange," informing them how to maximize the benefits to which they might eventually become entitled.

Retroactive Benefits

The court required that claims be readjudicated under the rules the VA promulgated after the court-ordered re-review. Benefits were to be paid prospectively to any who won in such a readjudication. But the court's order did not address the right to retroactive benefits.

NVLSP went back to court to address this problem. Negotiations with the VA ensued. Although no law required it, NVLSP insisted that a veteran or survivor who won under the rules the VA adopted after *Nehmer* should be paid benefits retroactively to the date on which the claim had been initially filed or the date of disability or death, whichever was later.

NVLSP's provision could have cost the VA hundreds of millions of dollars. One year of benefits for a totally disabled veteran is approximately $20,000 tax free. If a totally disabled veteran had first filed a claim in 1983 and the VA granted the claim in the 1990s, the veteran would be entitled to more than $140,000 in tax-free retroactive benefits under NVLSP's proposal.

But when this was being negotiated, the VA had not yet been forced to provide any additional compensation. At the time, nothing required the VA to compensate any condition but chloracne. To settle the matter, the VA agreed to a consent order incorporating NVLSP's proposal[36]—apparently under the premise that no diseases would ultimately be added under the court-ordered review.

The VA's Attempted Escape

NVLSP's victory on the retroactivity issue was rewarded when the VA later decided to make NHL and STS service-connected conditions. The VA then compensated veterans who suffered from these cancers and survivors of those who had died from these diseases, retroactively to the date on which each claim had been filed. Tens of millions of dollars in retroactive benefits were paid. But the NVLSP retroactivity victory applied not only to these diseases but also to any other disease that the VA decided to service connect as a result of the court-ordered rule making.

The Agent Orange Act of 1991 heightened the importance of NVLSP's retroactivity victory in *Nehmer*. The Act did *not* authorize retroactive benefits for claimants who might succeed as a result of the NAS review.[37] But Agent Orange claims based on diseases other than NHL and STS would result in retroactive benefits as a result of *Nehmer* if the VA added additional diseases during the six-month wrap-up period authorized under the act.

To NVLSP's dismay, the first meeting of the VA advisory committee after passage of the Agent Orange Act revealed not only that the VA's scientists were unhappy with the agency's lack of support but also that the VA had no intention of completing the court-ordered rule making. To remedy this problem, NVLSP went back to court.

The court proceeding resulted in another settlement.[38] NVLSP agreed to drop its demand that the VA complete the court-ordered rule making (thereby eliminating one of the two bites at the apple). In exchange, the VA agreed to:

- Wait for another year—until the NAS issued its report and the VA decided whether additional diseases should be compensable—before adjudicating the 29,000 Agent Orange claims that the *Nehmer* court required the VA to re-decide;
- Decide these Agent Orange claims under the rules the VA would adopt after receiving the NAS report; and
- Apply NVLSP's victory on retroactivity to any granted claims.

In other words, NVLSP got the VA to agree to circumvent the provision in the Agent Orange Act of 1991 that did not authorize retroactive benefits for claimants who might succeed as a result of the NAS review. Depending on the NAS review, this agreement could finally result in millions of dollars in additional benefits being paid to Agent Orange victims.

Assume that the VA promulgated regulations in 1993 to service connect three additional diseases as a result of the NAS review. Without the NVLSP-VA agreement, a claimant with one of these diseases who had first filed a claim in 1983, would receive back benefits only to 1993 (when the regulations adding the diseases became effective). With the NVLSP-VA agreement, however, this same claimant would receive retroactive benefits back to 1983—ten additional years' worth of compensation.

Of course, when NVLSP and the VA reached their agreement, no one knew what the results of the NAS review would be. If no diseases were added, the agreement wouldn't help anyone, because no one would be entitled to any new benefits, either prospectively or retroactively.

Independent Review Pays Off

During the summer of 1993, the NAS announced the results of its work and released a 600-page report.[39] The NAS scientists had reviewed more than 6,000 abstracts of scientific and medical articles and conducted detailed analyses of 230 epidemiologic studies. The NAS disagreed with much that the VA had done over the years. They concluded that scientific studies show that many diseases are statistically associated with Agent Orange—not just NHL and STS. For example, NAS concluded that:

- Even though the VA had refused to recognize a connection with Hodgkin's disease (a malignant lymphoma characterized by progressive anemia and enlargement of the lymph nodes, spleen, and liver), "the pattern of results [in the studies] is strikingly consistent" and shows "a positive association" with exposure;[40]

- The studies relating to porphyria cutanea tarda (PCT, a liver dysfunction characterized by thinning and blistering of the skin in sun-exposed areas) also show "a positive association;"[41]
- With regard to prostate cancer, "there was a strong indication of a dose-response relationship in one study and a consistent positive association in a number of others;"[42]
- For multiple myeloma (a cancer of bone marrow cells), "a consistent pattern of elevated risks appears in the studies which have been conducted;"[43] and
- Respiratory cancers such as lung, larynx, and trachea cancer belong in a similar category with multiple myeloma and prostate cancer.[44]

For many other cancers and for birth defects, NAS concluded that there was "insufficient evidence to determine whether an association exists."[45] According to the NAS, more studies are needed on these problems.

On the same day the NAS report was released, Secretary of Veterans Affairs Jesse Brown announced that the VA would add Hodgkin's disease and PCT to the list of service-connected diseases based on exposure to Agent Orange.[46] These two diseases had the strongest evidence supporting service connection, according to the NAS report. The NAS report also provided strong evidence that diseases in addition to these two should be service connected under the "positive association" standard and benefit of the doubt principle embodied in the Agent Orange Act of 1991. Secretary Brown invited veterans' organizations to comment on whether others of these associated diseases should be service connected.

NVLSP was the only organization to respond formally, arguing that the VA had to service connect a number of additional diseases to comply with the 1991 Act. Although NVLSP did not threaten litigation, it was plain that NVLSP could seek court review of the VA's position. Secretary Brown then added multiple myeloma and respiratory cancers of the lungs, larynx, and trachea to the list of compensable diseases.

The NAS report also worked to the benefit of Vietnam veterans and their families when it came to the need for additional scientific studies. NAS recommended that the VA take a number of steps to develop models for herbicide exposure that would allow for a scientifically valid epidemiologic study of Vietnam veterans who were exposed to Agent Orange.[47] Secretary Brown responded favorably, asking NAS to assist the VA in developing and testing these models.[48]

Retroactivity Revisited

The VA has estimated that by service connecting four additional diseases (Hodgkin's disease, PCT, multiple myeloma, and respiratory cancers), the VA will have to pay $350 million in death and disability benefits over the next five years (1994 to 1998).[49] This figure does not include the retroactive benefits required by the NVLSP-VA agreement. The VA's willingness to abide by that agreement was called into question by a draft VA directive, given to NVLSP for comment, that ignored the agreement's retroactive benefits provisions. After negotiation, however, the VA agreed in February 1994 to amend its directive to provide benefits called for in the prior agreement.[50]

After a struggle lasting more than a decade, Vietnam veterans and their families finally began to receive the government benefits they deserved. And the need for additional scientific studies relating to their exposure to Agent Orange finally began to receive serious attention.

The Lessons Learned

NVLSP's investment in the activities discussed here has produced a remarkable dividend: less than $1 million has been used to help produce more than $450 million. This $450 million will be distributed based on degree of disability, and the beneficiaries will be those veterans and veterans' families whose injuries are the most likely to have resulted from Agent Orange.

The money is not all. NVLSP's activities have immutably altered the way veterans' affairs decisions are reached; NVLSP's use of the federal courts helped pave the way for a permanent role in veterans' affairs for the judicial branch of government. Congress repealed the long-standing bar to court review of VA decision making in 1988. It created a new court—the United States Court of Veterans Appeals—with authority to review the VA's decisions on individual claims for benefits, as well as its rule-making decisions.[51] Veterans of all eras and their families may now obtain court review of VA decisions that vitally affect their lives.

The veterans' affairs policy-making apparatus has also largely accepted the wisdom of requiring contributions from the scientific community at large on issues for which scientific judgment is needed. This approach is especially desirable with regard to VA compensation and health care policy for latent diseases, which may not become manifest until after military service is completed. Claims of latent diseases have been raised with the VA for decades; they come from veterans who participated in the U.S. atomic weapons testing program, veterans exposed to traumatic war stressors, Vietnam veterans exposed to Agent Orange, and Persian Gulf veterans. These groups have been among those least satisfied with the way the VA has served them.

The involvement of the scientific community outside the VA proved indispensable to the progress that has been made in resolving the Agent Orange controversy. General acceptance of this community's role in resolving questions related to latent diseases is currently evident in policy-makers' discussions of the claims of Persian Gulf veterans.

Another legacy of NVLSP is activities that relate to the standard of proof that should be applied to claims regarding latent diseases. The intense debate over the appropriate standard during the Agent Orange battle highlighted the importance of this issue, and its resolution has left an important precedent. The VA will never again be able to subject claims such as those now being advanced by Persian Gulf veterans to a required showing of cause and effect. Epidemiologically based association will be all that is required.

In summary, NVLSP's work made it possible to secure a large amount in compensation benefits for the most deserving members of the AOCAP class. This effort has also permanently changed the course of veterans' affairs in ways that will benefit veterans and veterans' families of all years, of past wars and of wars not yet fought.

Endnotes

1. *In re "Agent Orange" Product Liability Litigation,* 611 F. Supp. 1396, *aff'd in part, rev'd in part,* 818 F.2d 179 (2d Cir. 1987); *see also In re "Agent Orange" Product Liability Litigation,* 689 F. Supp. 1250 (E.D.N.Y. 1988) (memorandum and order on distribution on remand).
2. Pub. L. No. 96-151, further amended by Pub. L. No. 97-72.
3. Pub. L. No. 97-72.
4. Pub. L. No. 98-542. This legislation required the VA to take these same modest steps with regard to veterans exposed to ionizing radiation as a result of the U.S. atomic weapons testing program.
5. 38 C.F.R. § 3.311 (1985).
6. NVLSP is an independent nonprofit advocacy and policy organization. NVLSP is the successor to Vietnam Veterans of America Legal Services, the former legal component of Vietnam Veterans of America. When the attorneys now on staff at NVLSP were devising the strategy discussed in this paper for challenging the VA's 1985 Agent Orange rules, they were employed by Vietnam Veterans of America Legal Services. For ease of reference, this paper refers to NVLSP even during periods in which NVLSP's lawyers were employed by Vietnam Veterans of America Legal Services.
7. At the time this lawsuit was filed, NVLSP's lawyers were employed by Vietnam Veterans of America Legal Services. See note 6, *supra.*
8. The class served by AOCAP includes persons who were members of the U.S. armed forces

from 1961 to 1972 and who were exposed to Agent Orange or other phenoxy herbicides while in or near Vietnam. The class also includes spouses, parents, and children of such veterans born before Jan. 1, 1984. *In re Agent Orange Product Liability Litigation,* 100 F.R.D. 718 (E.D.N.Y. 1983), *mandamus denied,* 725 F.2d 858 (2d Cir.), *cert. denied,* 456 U.S. 1067 (1984).

9. *Nehmer* v. *Veterans Administration,* 712 F. Supp. 1404 (N.D. Cal. 1989).
10. Letter from Secretary of Veterans Affairs Edward J. Derwinski to Attorney General Richard L. Thornburgh (May 11, 1989).
11. *In re "Agent Orange" Product Liability Litigation,* 611 F. Supp. 1396, 1440-41 (E.D.N.Y. 1985), *aff'd in part, rev'd in part,* 818 F. 2d 179 (2d Cir. 1987).
12. Hobson, Lawrence B. 1986. Dioxin and Witchcraft. *Chemosphere* 15 (9-12), N23-N26.
13. Environmental Protection Agency. 1985. Health Assessment Document for Polychlorinated Dibenzo-p-dioxin. EPA 600/8-84/014F. Cincinnati, OH: Environmental Criteria and Assessment Office. (Hereafter, EPA-HAD.)
14. EPA-HAD at 2-8.
15. Transcript of VA Veterans' Advisory Committee on Environmental Hazards Meeting of Oct. 15, 1987, at 97-108.
16. Agent Orange Scientific Task Force, *Human Health Effects Associated with Exposure to Herbicides and/or their Associated Contaminants—Chlorinated Dioxins.* Washington, DC: April 1990, at i.
17. The members of the Agent Orange Scientific Task Force were: Richard W. Clapp, M.P.H., Sc.D., Director of Environmental Health Studies, JSI Research & Training Institute, Inc.; Barry Commoner, Ph.D., Center for the Biology of Natural Systems, Queens College, CUNY; John D. Constable, M.D., Associate Clinical Professor of Surgery, Harvard Medical School; Samuel S. Epstein, M.D., Professor of Occupational and Environmental Medicine, University of Illinois; Peter C. Kahn, Ph.D., Associate Professor of Biochemistry, Department of Biochemistry and Microbiology, Rutgers University; James R. Olson, Ph.D., Associate Professor, Department of Pharmacology and Therapeutics, School of Medicine and Biomedical Sciences, University of Buffalo; David M. Ozonoff, M.D., M.P.H., Professor and Chief, Environmental Health Section, Boston University of Public Health.
18. Task Force report at 3.
19. Id.
20. Id. at 3-4.
21. Task Force report at ii-iii.
22. Centers for Disease Control. *The Association of Selected Cancers with Service in the U.S. Military in Vietnam.* May 29, 1990.
23. *See* 55 *Federal Register* 43, 124 (Oct. 26, 1990) (to be codified at 38 C.F.R. § 3.313).
24. *See* 56 *Federal Register* 51, 663 (Oct. 15, 1991) (to be codified at 38 C.F.R. § 3.311).
25. Supplemental Declaration of Angela Franklin, filed Dec. 6, 1991, in *Nehmer* v. *Veterans Administration,* Civ. No. C-86-6160 (TEH) (N.D. Cal.).
26. Task Force report at 2.
27. Id. at 2.
28. Agent Orange Act of 1991, 38 U.S.C. § 316 (4) (b) (1), P.L. 102-4, 105 Stat. 10, 12 (Feb. 6, 1991) (Agent Orange Act of 1991).
29. Id. at § (4) (b) (3).
30. Task Force report at 2.
31. Agent Orange Act of 1991 at Section 3, part (e).
32. Id. at Section 10, part (e).

33. Transcript of VA Veterans' Advisory Committee on Environmental Hazards meeting on Jan. 29, 1991, at 131-32.
34. Attachment to letter from Secretary of Veterans Affairs Jesse Brown to Service Organization Officials, at para. 15 (Aug. 4, 1993).
35. Stipulation and Order, No. C-86-6160 (N.D. Cal. Jan. 10, 1990).
36. Stipulation and Order, No. C-86-6160 (N.D. Cal. Jan. 10, 1990).
37. 38 U.S.C. § 116(c)(2).
38 Stipulation and Order, No. CV-86-6160 (N.D.Cal. May 20, 1991).
39. Institute of Medicine. 1993. *Veterans and Agent Orange: Health Effects of Herbicides Used in Vietnam.* Washington, DC: National Academy Press.
40. NAS report at 1-6, 1-8.
41. Id. at 1-6.
42. Id. at 1-10.
43. Id.
44. Id. at 1-6.
45. Id.
46. *See* 59 *Federal Register* 5106 (Feb. 3, 1994).
47. NAS report at 1-14 to 1-19.
48. Department of Veterans Affairs, News Release: VA to Award Additional Benefits for Agent Orange-Related Illnesses (Sept. 27, 1993).
49. Id.
50. VBA Circular 21-94-1 (Feb. 15, 1994).
51. Veterans' Judicial Review Act, P.L. 100-687, 102 Stat. 4111 (Nov. 18, 1988).

A Shock to the System: Training Advocates under the Veterans' Judicial Review Act

Ronald B. Abrams, Esq.
National Veterans Legal Services Project
Washington, DC

Abstract

Many veterans served by the Agent Orange Class Assistance Program (AOCAP) have filed, or should file, claims for veterans' benefits with the U.S. Department of Veterans Affairs (VA). The VA's claims process was completely informal until the United States Court of Veterans Appeals, founded in 1988, began to review VA decisions.

This review pointed up the need for better information and training for veterans' advocates. To supply that need in a way consonant with AOCAP's overall goals, AOCAP has supported, among other efforts, the National Veterans Legal Services Project's publications and training programs.

The survey reported here indicates that veterans' advocates have found NVLSP materials consistently helpful in their daily work. Because the materials are deliberately designed to encourage an active approach to the VA benefits system, this perceived usefulness argues well for the hoped-for, long-term effect of increased empowerment of veterans and their families.

Ronald D. Abrams, Esq., *was a lawyer with the VA from 1975 to 1988, where he was legal consultant to the Compensation and Pension Service and was recognized as an expert in due process. He joined the staff of the National Veterans Legal Services Project in 1989.*

The benefits system administered by the U.S. Department of Veterans Affairs (VA) is unusual in its reliance on a network of lay advocates. Most claimants for VA benefits are represented, free, by a service representative (or service officer) hired by a state, a county, or a veterans' organization. The relative informality of VA proceedings, which characterizes the agency's administrative appeals process as well as its original claims work, has made this possible. However, many significant VA procedures and policies have changed notably since 1988, when Congress established the United States Court of Veterans Appeals and VA claims decisions first became subject to judicial review.*

This development occurred nearly contemporaneously with the founding of the Agent Orange Class Assistance Program (AOCAP) in January 1989. AOCAP's primary efforts include establishing or supporting four types of organization—veterans' organizations, disability services agencies, family services agencies, and national support projects. The veterans' organizations and the services agencies provide services directly to Vietnam veterans and their families; the national support projects provide consultation, technical assistance, training, and other services to the other members of the AOCAP network. One of these national support projects is the National Veterans Legal Services Project (NVLSP).

For veterans' advocates, the founding of the United States Court of Veterans Appeals has meant an increased need for information. For years, advocates' only real source of information about veterans' benefits and VA procedures was the VA itself; unsurprisingly, this information exclusively reflected agency interpretations and policies. The possibility of appeal outside the agency has opened not only individual decisions to correction, but also the VA's policies and interpretations of law. To make judicial review work, however, advocates first had to be convinced that the VA could be wrong and could be successfully challenged. Without materials that give some other point of view than the VA's, many advocates would find it difficult or impossible to make the best use of the new court's decisions and the changes that have followed—or should have followed—from them.

This lack of independent information represents a real problem, especially with respect to claims for disability benefits. Before judicial review, most veterans' advocates found that VA adjudicators refused to consider most private medical evidence, all medical opinion (the VA's own physicians were encouraged to provide only clinical evidence), and any type of legal analysis. They also often refused to respond to advocates' arguments. It was an unwritten VA policy that its rating boards, hearing officers, and Board of Veterans' Appeals members and staff had the exclusive right to draw medical and legal conclusions.

VA rating board members and members of the Board of Veterans' Appeals (BVA) became accustomed to making claims decisions based on their own unfounded medical conclusions. As a result, many veterans' advocates became convinced that it was fruitless to do more than help a veteran to fill out forms, depending entirely on the VA to develop and analyze veterans' claims.

It was for these reasons that AOCAP funded NVLSP to start a series of publications and training sessions. A newsletter for those representing claimants for VA benefits, called *The Veterans Advocate,* began publication in 1989; with support from AOCAP, it is made available below cost to veterans' service representatives, legal services representatives, and other veterans' advocates across the country. AOCAP has also supported NVLSP's series of self-help guides, which are widely distributed, and its compendium of veterans' law for lay advocates and attorneys, the *Veterans Benefits Manual.*

---

*38 U.S.C. §§ 7251-7298.

NVLSP staff have provided consulting and referral services to more than 8,500 Vietnam veterans, family members, or representatives. Formal training in veterans' law has been offered to lay advocates and attorneys to help them take advantage of the new court's decisions; more than 4,500 advocates have attended such sessions.

The publications and training efforts have had three main objectives. The first is to offer advocates a source of legal analysis keyed to the advocate's, not the VA's, point of view. The second is to demonstrate that the VA is not infallible. The third is to provide veterans' advocates with practical advice about how to use decisions of the Court of Veterans Appeals to help their clients.

NVLSP was not widely known among veterans' advocates in 1989. Most practitioners were used to getting advice from the VA or the service organization they worked for (if they did). Some had been involved in VA law for more than ten years. What help could a group of Washington attorneys be to advocates already inundated with information and managing huge caseloads? NVLSP's materials had to be relevant and interesting, and above all, they had to be credible.

The survey of the veterans' advocate community described here was undertaken to determine if the written materials and training session provided by NVLSP have had discernible effects. Do advocates themselves think that these materials and trainings have made a difference in their work?

Methods

NVLSP staff conducted a telephone survey of a national sample of a population comprising current subscribers to *The Veterans Advocate, Veterans Benefits Manual* buyers, and training-session attendees. The total population numbered approximately 4,000, from which a sample of approximately 240 was drawn. Every effort was made to include all the different types of veterans' advocates, including private attorneys, Legal Services Corporation attorneys, and county, state, and national service representatives, from a variety of locations.

There was about a three-to-one ratio of calls attempted to surveys completed. Some potential respondents were not available, some were not at the listed phone number, and some, despite their inclusion in NVLSP's lists, were not working in veterans' law. These included, for example, Legal Services Corporation attorneys who had bought NVLSP publications to complete their libraries.

Eighty persons completed the survey. More than half (53 percent) of those surveyed had worked in veterans' law for more than ten years; 30 percent had done so for more than six and less than ten years. Eighty percent were involved in direct representation of claimants for VA benefits; the other 20 percent were advocates for veterans in other ways—for example, as congressional caseworkers or managers of service organizations. Forty-nine percent were service officers who represent veterans before the VA; 10 percent were attorneys who represent veterans. Most of the remaining 41 percent were service officers whose work does not involve direct representation of veterans.

The survey included questions on ownership and use of NVLSP publications and, as a rough gauge of actual use, on lending practices.

Results

Of the eighty persons who finished the survey, 92 percent owned or had access to the *Veterans Benefits Manual*; 21 percent had purchased their own copy, 55 percent obtained the *Veterans Benefits Manual* through their organization, and 24 percent shared a copy with other people in their organization. No one borrowed another purchaser's copy. Eighty-five percent of those surveyed subscribed or had access to *The Veterans Advocate;* 16 percent had paid for it themselves, 53 percent subscribed through their organization, and 31 percent shared copies within their organization.

Fifty-seven percent of those who owned a copy of the *Veterans Benefits Manual* permitted others to borrow the manual. Most (84 percent) shared their copy of the *Veterans Benefits Manual* with five or fewer people. Most (75 percent) of those who controlled a subscription to *The Veterans Advocate* permitted others to share their copies (82 percent with five or fewer persons). Nineteen percent of those who controlled a *Veterans Benefits Manual* or subscription to *The Veterans Advocate* shared their copies with VA employees.

Publications

Sixty percent of those who had access to a *Veterans Benefits Manual* reported using it regularly and 24 percent reported using it occasionally. Forty-nine percent of those who have access to the *Veterans Benefits Manual* said they used it regularly to research specific cases; 29 percent said they regularly read sections of interest. Only 3 percent of those with access to a copy said they do not use the manual regularly. Sixty-two percent of those who have access to the *Veterans Benefits Manual* often use the information and advocacy tips the manual provides to do their jobs.

Twenty-nine percent of respondents with access to a copy of the *Veterans Benefits Manual* reported that the manual helped them obtain benefits for many claimants; 24 percent said the manual had helped them obtain benefits for some claimants, and 23 percent said the manual had helped them obtain benefits for a few claimants. Twenty-four percent stated that the *Veterans Benefits Manual* had not helped them obtain benefits for claimants.

Sixty-two percent of those who had access to *The Veterans Advocate* reported using it regularly and 28 percent reported using it occasionally. Sixty-five percent of those who have access to *The Veterans Advocate* reported that they read it thoroughly; 34 percent said they read only articles of specific interest. Sixty-seven percent of those with access to *The Veterans Advocate* often use its information and advocacy tips to do their jobs. All respondents who controlled a *Veterans Advocate* subscription said that they saved the newsletter to use as a research tool.

Thirty-four percent of those with access to *The Veterans Advocate* said that the newsletter had helped them obtain benefits for many claimants; 24 percent said that *The Veterans Advocate* had helped them obtain benefits for some claimants; and 19 percent said it had helped them win benefits for a few claimants. Twenty-three percent stated that *The Veterans Advocate* had not helped them obtain benefits for claimants.

Trainings

Sixty percent of those surveyed stated that they had attended an NVLSP training session. Eighty-three percent of those who had done so described the training session as having been very helpful to them in their representation of veterans; 88 percent said that the matters covered by the training had a practical application to their work. Nearly all (90 percent) said that they would attend another NVLSP training; all said that they would recommend these sessions to other veterans' advocates.

Of those who had attended an NVLSP training, 40 percent reported that it had helped them obtain benefits for many claimants, 19 percent said that the training had helped them obtain benefits for some claimants, and 19 percent said that the training had helped them obtain benefits for a few claimants. Twenty-three percent stated that the training had not helped them obtain benefits for claimants.

Keeping Up with Change

Forty-four percent of respondents with access to the *Veterans Benefits Manual* reported that the manual helped them very much in taking advantage of changes in VA law and Court of Veterans Appeals decisions. Thirty-six percent stated that the *Veterans Benefits Manual* helped somewhat; 20 percent said it helped a little.

Fifty-nine percent of respondents with access to *The Veterans Advocate* stated that the newsletter helped them very much in taking advantage of changes in law and Court of Veterans Appeals decisions. Thirty-one percent said that the newsletter helped somewhat; 10 percent said it helped them a little.

Sixty-one percent of those who had attended an NVLSP training stated that the training had helped them very much in taking advantage of changes in law and Court of Veterans Appeals decisions. Twenty-nine percent said the training had helped them somewhat; 10 percent stated that the training had helped them a little.

Discussion

The informal nature of the survey design limits the reach of the conclusions that can be drawn. For example, because the sample was drawn from NVLSP's own lists, the high proportion of respondents who said they regularly used *The Veterans Advocate*—a subscription newsletter—is not surprising. And, partly because the interviewers identified themselves as NVLSP staff, the survey results no doubt reflect a positive response bias.

Those who completed the survey were a highly experienced group of veterans' advocates. More than half of those with access to the *Veterans Benefits Manual* (79 percent) or *The Veterans Advocate* (84 percent) obtained the publication through the organization they worked for, which was most often a veterans' service organization. This suggests that national, state, and local service organizations have decided that independent advocacy tools, such as NVLSP's publications, are needed even by experienced employees who represent claimants seeking VA benefits. The relatively high figures reported for use suggest that advocates do find the publications to be credible and helpful.

The very positive evaluation of NVLSP trainings can be partly explained by the fact that most attendees are highly motivated to start with. For many, a day's training session is also a much more direct and memorable way of acquiring information than is paging through a legal manual or newsletter.

Some corroboration of these results comes from an informal survey of *pro bono* attorneys participating in The Veterans Consortium Pro Bono Program, a joint program of The American Legion, Disabled American Veterans, Paralyzed Veterans of America, and the National Veterans Legal Services Project. Thirty-eight attorneys of forty-one who had completed one or more cases through the program and returned the survey reported that the *Veterans Benefits Manual* was one of the two most valuable sources of information they were given (mean score of 3.72 on a scale of 1 (fair) to 4 (excellent)).*

Most respondents share their copies of NVLSP publications. Nineteen percent share their copies with VA employees, indicating at least some interest by VA employees in the interpretation of claims issues by those outside the VA.

Overall, the survey responses suggest that many veterans and veterans' advocates are taking an active approach to benefits claims before the VA, offering arguments and evidence as well as filled-in forms. This active approach fits well with AOCAP's thematic goal of nurturing empowerment among those it serves by increasing their independence, self-sufficiency, productivity, and understanding of the human services systems. Over time, this increased role for veterans and veterans' advocates will make a lasting difference to veterans and veterans' families, and through them, to the country as a whole.

---

* Data provided by Ronald W. Scholz, Esq., director of screening, The Veterans Consortium Pro Bono Program.

Ameliorating the Adverse Consequences of VA-Accrued Benefits Law for Survivors of Vietnam Veterans

Michael E. Wildhaber, Esq., with Jason R. Davitian, Esq.
Washington, DC

Abstract

Serious shortcomings exist in the current law that governs the payment of "due and unpaid" monetary benefits by the U.S. Department of Veterans Affairs (VA) to the surviving dependent family members of a deceased veteran. These benefits, called "accrued benefits," are compensation, pension, or other periodic monetary benefits that the veteran claimed from the VA during his or her lifetime and was otherwise entitled to, but never collected, because he or she died before the VA's final decision to award the benefits.

The amount of due and unpaid benefits at issue in a particular case can be significant to surviving family members because of the average length of time it takes for the VA to adjudicate a typical compensation or pension claim. Current accrued benefits law places formidable barriers in the path of survivors—including a policy not to inform many survivors of their potential entitlement—that limit the amount of these benefits that is recovered and often prevent any recovery at all.

The consequences of the current accrued benefits law on the class of Agent Orange veterans and their families is especially pronounced. Although the VA has recently softened its policy of resisting payment of compensation benefits based on Agent Orange exposure, many Vietnam veterans claiming these benefits have died in the past ten to fifteen years. The survivors of these veterans are unable to benefit from the retroactive payments their spouse, parents, or child would receive under the VA's new Agent Orange rules. Survivors of veterans who die in the future before the VA completes adjudication of their claims will only benefit to the meager extent that the accrued benefits law allows.

This paper describes the various rules governing the payment of accrued benefits to eligible surviving family members, and discusses the harsh toll exacted from family members by these rules. It concludes with several recommendations on initiatives that Congress and the VA should undertake to ameliorate these adverse effects.

Michael E. Wildhaber *is an attorney in private practice in the District of Columbia concentrating in veterans' benefits law and military records corrections issues. He worked as an attorney with the National Veterans Legal Services Project (NVLSP) from 1985 to 1994.* ***Jason R. Davitian*** *is currently an attorney with NVLSP. He conducted valuable legal research during the preparation of this paper.*

When a veteran dies while receiving monetary benefits from the U.S. Department of Veterans Affairs (VA), or while he or she has a pending claim for such benefits, the veteran's claim does not die with the veteran. That veteran's surviving spouse, dependent children, or dependent parents are potentially entitled to all or part of the benefits the veteran claimed and was owed while living but that remain unpaid at the time of death. Monetary benefits of this type are called "accrued benefits." Any monetary benefit paid by the VA on a periodic basis, except for service member's indemnity and other types of insurance benefits, can potentially result in accrued benefits.[1] Examples of such benefits include service-connected disability compensation, non-service-connected pension, education benefits, and even clothing allowance.

The accrued benefits the VA pays to a veteran's surviving family members are not as generous as it might seem. In fact, the family of a veteran who dies while a claim is pending—but not finally adjudicated by the VA—suffers more than the immediate and grievous personal loss of father, mother, spouse, or child. They stand to lose potentially significant amounts of the monetary benefits that the veteran would have received from the VA and that would have been available to support the family or to repay debts incurred as a result of the veteran's disability but for his or her untimely death.

This result appears as an obvious anomaly, emanating as it does from the federal agency especially charged "to care for him who shall have borne the battle, *and for his widow, and his orphan*."[2] Nonetheless, under current VA accrued benefits laws, a veteran's survivors forfeit all but one year's worth of the benefits that otherwise would have been payable to the veteran. This rule greatly reduces the amount a family recovers if the veteran's claim was pending for much longer than one year. Other rules governing the payment of accrued benefits stack the deck against the family even more, decreasing the likelihood of recovering any of the accrued benefits.[3]

The consequences of the accrued benefits law affect all veterans and veterans' families who claim VA benefits. Because of the large number of pending, and potentially new, Agent Orange claims, however, the consequences for the Agent Orange class of Vietnam veterans and their families are especially dramatic. This is true for the following two reasons:

- First, until recently, the VA's long-standing policy was to resist recognizing disabilities for compensation purposes if the claims were associated with exposure to dioxin. This policy has resulted in the protracted adjudication of Agent Orange claims and a begrudging, piecemeal application of the compensation system to the class of Agent Orange victims, and it has created a backlog of about 36,000 Agent Orange compensation claims that have accumulated over the past ten to fifteen years and are now pending before the VA in some form.[4]
- Second, efforts to change VA policies on Agent Orange compensation by the class reached a new peak when the VA recently decided to recognize at least six categories of disabilities as associated with exposure to dioxin.[5] This change, forced by the *Nehmer* litigation,[6] opened the door to the backlog of 36,000 existing Agent Orange claims as well as to thousands of potential new claims.[7]

Both of these factors will create a steady flow of Agent Orange claims for adjudication by the VA for many years to come.[8] Because many veterans suffering from the effects of Agent Orange exposure became sicker over the years and inevitably died and will continue to do so, the accrued benefits law will have an adverse effect on their surviving family members.

Creation of Accrued Benefits

The circumstance that most often leads to forced forfeiture of significant benefits by a veteran's survivors is the veteran's death while his or her claim for benefits is still pending final resolution by the VA.[9] These circumstances typically involve a sizable amount of due and unpaid benefits because of the length of time it takes for the VA to resolve a claim for monetary benefits. On average, it takes a VA regional office 226 days to adjudicate a compensation claim and 128 days for a pension claim.[10] In fiscal year 1993, however, the average time the Board of Veterans' Appeals (BVA) took to adjudicate an appeal was 466 days.[11]

Thus, if a veteran is forced to appeal to the BVA, the *average* time the VA takes to adjudicate the claim is roughly two years. Many claims remain pending for much longer periods. If the veteran's claim is granted, the VA is generally required to pay benefits from the date the claim was first submitted. Thus, it may owe the veteran many years of back benefits.

Basic Eligibility Requirements

Four requirements impact a survivor's eligibility to receive benefits from the VA after a veteran dies. First, before a survivor can recover a veteran's benefits, the VA must adjudicate the issue of whether the veteran was entitled to the benefits. This determination must either have already been made (but not yet announced or acted on prior to death) or be based on "evidence in the [veteran's VA claims] file at date of death."[12] The latter is obviously a more difficult requirement to meet. If the veteran did not succeed in obtaining sufficient evidence to win his or her claim in life, survivors attempting to recover those benefits must rely on what may be a relatively poor record.

Second, on the veteran's death, his or her claim does not automatically evolve into a survivor's accrued benefits claim. Survivors must submit a separate application for these benefits to the VA "within one year after the date of [the veteran's] death."[13] The VA does not have effective provisions to notify survivors that they need to file a timely application. For many survivors, the requirement that they submit a separate application can be a significant barrier to receiving these benefits.

Third, regardless of how many months or years of back benefits the veteran would have received if the claim were successful and the veteran were still alive, the survivor may receive only the amount "due and unpaid for a period not to exceed one year."[14] In other words, even if a veteran fought for compensation benefits for five years, only to die just prior to being awarded the benefits, the VA will not pay the veteran's survivors the five years' worth of back benefits that the veteran would have received. The benefits survivors will receive are limited to the amount that would have been received over one year.

Fourth, persons eligible to claim and receive accrued benefits must fit one of the following specific categories of survivors—presented here in descending order of priority. The veteran's spouse is first in order.[15] If there is no surviving spouse, benefits are paid to the veteran's dependent children (in equal shares to each child).[16] If the veteran is not survived by a spouse or dependent children, benefits are paid to the veteran's surviving dependent parents (also in equal shares).[17] Although a dependent child is generally one below the age of majority,[18] parents are deemed dependent if their income and that of those they support is below specified limits.[19] If no survivors fit these categories, by statute, reimbursement is paid to anyone who bore the expense of the veteran's "last sickness and burial."[20]

In dramatic contrast, the death of a Social Security Disability Insurance (SSDI) claimant during the course of such a claim does not result in the harsh effects described above. Although the Social Security Administration (SSA) must determine that the deceased claimant was entitled to the benefits and an eligible survivor must submit an application form to receive any payment owed, there is no time limit for applications and no limit on the amount of benefits to be paid.[21] All sums owed the SSDI claimant will be paid to his or her survivors, or if none exist, to the deceased's estate.[22]

Other Accrued Benefits Rules

Other Rules before the VA Regional Office and BVA

The VA has no specific published regulations governing its procedures for notifying surviving family members and others of their potential entitlement to accrued benefits and their right to apply for these benefits. Instead, the VA is guided by its unpublished *Adjudication Procedure Manual, M21-1.* According to *M21-1,* the VA must provide notice to possible claimants for accrued benefits only "if the name and address of a surviving spouse or child is on record and (1) the veteran died in service, or (2) there is any indication that the veteran's death might have been service-connected, or (3) the veteran ever received compensation or pension."[23]

The VA advises other known survivors of the need to file an application only if the it has already determined that an "accrued amount" is payable and "is of such size that the claimant's expense in procuring evidence would be justified."[24] In other words, only if the VA has first determined that the original service connection or rating increase claim of the veteran is meritorious and that it involves a sum of money the VA considers worthwhile does the agency inform the potential surviving beneficiary that an application must be filed.

VA statistics indicate that its failure to inform potential accrued benefits claimants of the need to file an application adversely affects the vast majority of such cases. In fiscal year 1993, the VA reported that only 1,392 accrued benefits claims were filed.[25] This represents roughly only 13 percent of all cases where the veteran died while his or her claim for compensation or pension benefits was pending.[26] In 87 percent of claims that are pending at the time the veteran-claimant dies, no survivor files a subsequent claim for accrued benefits.

Other Rules before the United States Court of Veterans Appeals

If the veteran dies while his or her claim is on appeal before the United States Court of Veterans Appeals (CVA), the situation for survivors or other beneficiaries potentially entitled to accrued benefits is even worse. With respect to informing these claimants of the requirement that an accrued benefits application must be filed within one year of the veteran's death, the VA Office of General Counsel, which represents the VA before the CVA, takes the position that the VA has no obligation to advise anyone of these requirements.[27]

In addition, the CVA has held that a veteran's original claim for service connection is a different claim altogether from the accrued benefits claim that arises when the veteran dies, even though both claims have the same factual basis (i.e., the disability at issue, which must be found to be service connected, is the same in each claim).[28] The significance of this holding is that the death of an appellant whose appeal is pending before the court causes that claim to expire with the veteran, freezing forever in place the final adverse decision of the BVA. The veteran's survivors are then forced to obtain and submit "new and material evidence" to initiate their accrued benefits claims. Thus, the only way that a claim that has been subject to a previous final denial can be "reopened" on the same factual basis, is if the claimant submits new and material evidence.[29]

Practical Consequences for Survivors

The accrued benefits statute and related VA policies and practices severely affect the survivors of veterans who have been prosecuting meritorious claims for benefits for many years. The VA is in a position to delay adjudication of such claims, especially the claims of seriously ill veterans, and thus avoid paying many years of back benefits if the delay is so long that the veteran dies. Indeed, the VA has no formal rules or procedures for expediting the adjudication of claims of seriously or terminally ill veterans.[30]

An example of such a result is the case of Albert A. Mokal, a World War II veteran who received a serious shell fragment wound to the brain.[31] In 1980, he sought a rating increase, effective back to 1948, for his wounds based on the allegation that the VA had committed a clear and unmistakable error by failing to award the increase at that time.[32] For the next twelve years the VA repeatedly denied Mr. Mokal's claim. In February 1992, however, he was vindicated when the CVA agreed with his allegation and reversed the VA.[33]

Unfortunately, Mr. Mokal never lived to realize his victory; he died before the CVA's decision was issued. If Mr. Mokal had lived, he would now be receiving retroactive benefits—effective from 1948 and totaling hundreds of thousands of dollars—from the VA. Although Mr. Mokal's daughter—who personally cared for the veteran for decades—was substituted by the CVA as the appellant in her father's case, she was denied his accrued benefits. Because of the accrued benefits rules, she did not meet the definition of an eligible survivor.[34] The most Mr. Mokal's daughter can hope to recover from her father's pyrrhic victory is reimbursement for the cost of his last sickness and burial.

With respect to Vietnam veterans and their survivors as a class, the adverse effect of the accrued benefits law has been intensified by the complexity of Agent Orange claims adjudication caused by the VA's long-standing resistance to recognizing and compensating disabilities related to Agent Orange exposure. Many veterans who could have benefited from the VA's recent or future recognition of such disabilities have died. In these cases, even if survivors get future benefits in the form of dependency or indemnity compensation (DIC), because the VA has recognized the veteran's cause of death was from a service-connected Agent Orange disability,[35] the family will not receive the retroactive benefits the veteran would have gotten if he or she had lived.[36]

In many cases, the family loses entitlement to even these meager benefits because the VA does not have an affirmative policy to inform families about them. Most survivors are either misinformed or uninformed about the need to apply for accrued benefits. Moreover, their risk of missing out on these benefits altogether is significant because of the one-year application deadline.

If the claim progresses as far as the CVA, the risk of the veteran's family not receiving accrued benefits is even higher. First, the delay in the final resolution of the case increases the odds that a seriously ill veteran will not live to see the claim resolved. Second, it is more likely that survivors will not receive proper notice of their potential entitlement to accrued benefits and the steps they must take to apply for them. Current VA procedures for notifying potential beneficiaries of the need and time limit to file an application when the claim is at the level of the court are worse than those in effect at the agency level. Thus, affected survivors cannot turn the case into a new, separate claim for accrued benefits as easily.

Third, if the veteran dies while his or her case is before the court, under current CVA caselaw, the existing BVA denial of the veteran's claim becomes final. Survivors who apply for accrued benefits within the applicable time period cannot proceed using the same record the veteran used to prosecute the original service connection claim. Instead, they must produce new and material evidence before the VA will reconsider the claim. This requirement places a considerable burden on the survivor, who will not have the benefit of the veteran's participation in the development of potentially crucial evidence.

Possible Solutions to the Harsh Impact of the Accrued Benefits Law

The current framework for handling and paying accrued benefits claims is principally a creation of Congress. Even if the VA had the desire and will to address its inequities, its authority to adjust the adverse impact of the accrued benefits law is limited. The most effective means for resolving the problems caused by the accrued benefits statute and by related VA policies and procedures is for Congress to enact new legislation.

Indeed, congressional action of this nature is the only means for achieving a truly effective solution. Repealing the one-year application deadline and the one-year limit on the amount of accrued benefits payable and requiring the VA to provide adequate notice to potential beneficiaries would essentially resolve the current unfairness for all accrued benefits claimants. If a means for rectifying the problem created by the death of the veteran whose claim was pending before the CVA were included (that is, creation of automatic standing in a deceased veteran's estate, for the benefit of eligible survivors, to continue the veteran's appeal to a final judicial resolution), the problem of the survivors being saddled with the existing BVA denial of the late veteran's claim would be resolved, and survivors would be relieved of the burden of automatically being required to produce new and material evidence if they wish to pursue the claim by reopening it at the VA regional office.

Short of a comprehensive legislative solution, Congress could make several intermediate adjustments that would help significantly. One would be to create an exception to the one-year limitation on the amount of back benefits payable when it can be shown that the VA's delay in adjudicating a claim was negligent, intentional, or otherwise egregious. Another would be to address cases in which the deceased veteran's family can demonstrate significant financial hardship, either because they made financial sacrifices to care for the veteran during his or her lifetime, or because the veteran's disability and subsequent death placed surviving family members in serious future financial jeopardy.

Many of the inequities in the current system would be resolved if Congress took the simple step of explicitly requiring that the VA provide adequate notice of the application requirements and deadlines to all potential accrued benefits claimants. Such a provision could state that the one-year application deadline would be tolled (that is, suspended), if the VA could not show that it provided the proper notice to a claimant.

At a minimum, because of the special harm the accrued benefits law causes the survivors of Agent Orange class members, remedial legislation of the types discussed above should be enacted to benefit this specific class of survivors. This group waited too many years for benefits they were entitled to because of VA inaction and erroneous decision making regarding Agent Orange-related disabilities.

With respect to the effect a veteran's death has on the accrued benefits claim of any survivor while the case is before the CVA, a simple legislative amendment that makes the accrued benefits statute inapplicable would solve this problem. Such an amendment would state that once a living veteran has prosecuted his or her claim by filing a notice of appeal to the CVA, the accrued benefits statute (that is, its various limitations) no longer applies. Any survivor, as an heir to the veteran's estate, would then automatically have an interest in the benefits the veteran might be awarded and thus standing to pursue those benefits as the appellant before the court. The fairness of such an amendment is easily recognized and sets affected claims apart: inherent in the fact that it was necessary for the veteran to appeal his or her claim to its final successful conclusion to the court is that the denial of the claim and the length of the delay was especially egregious.

A partial regulatory solution instituted by the VA itself, within the existing statutory framework, is not inconceivable. The VA on its own is probably without authority to adjust the statutory restriction on the one-year limitation on the amount of back benefits payable. It can, however, amend its policies on how potential claimants are informed about accrued benefits. For example, the VA could explicitly adopt a policy that it must inform all potential accrued benefits claimants of the application process and deadline. In spite of the one-year application deadline specified in the statute, the agency could create its own exceptions to the deadline where its efforts to notify all potential beneficiaries fell short. The source of legal authority for the VA to make these amendments comes from other statutory provisions governing the VA. The spirit of many VA statutes creates a nonadversarial adjudication process and requires that the VA assist claimants in the development of their claims.[37] These provisions should provide the VA with more-than-adequate legal authority to craft a lack-of-notice exception to the bare language of the accrued benefits statute.

Endnotes

1. 38 U.S.C.A. § 5121(a) (1991).

2. Source: Abraham Lincoln's 2nd Inaugural Address (1864) (emphasis added). This quote, engraved on the side of the granite walls of the U.S. Department of Veterans Affairs central office in Washington, D.C., is the unofficial motto of the VA.

3. The rules governing the payment of accrued benefits have not always been so harsh. Following World War I, Congress placed no limits on the amount of the payment of benefits that may have accrued prior to a veteran's death, or to which survivors, including the veteran's estate, the benefits could be paid. The only requirements were that the veteran was "entitled to receive the same," and if the veteran's estate had no heirs, the benefits could only escheat to the federal treasury. *See* World War Veterans' Act of 1924, Ch. 320 (Tit. I, § 26). By 1943, however, all the restrictions that exist in the current accrued benefits statute were in place, the last being the most significant: the amount of accrued benefits to be paid to an eligible survivor was limited to one year's worth of the unpaid benefits. Act of July 13, 1943, Pub. L. 144, Ch. 233 (§ 12), 57 Stat. 554.

4. *See The Veterans Advocate* 1(6):11 (Feb. 1990).

5. Non-Hodgkin's lymphoma, soft tissue sarcoma, and chloracne were given this status by Congress in 1991. Agent Orange Act of 1991, Pub. L. No. 102-4. The VA itself has issued final rules recognizing Hodgkin's disease and porphyria cutanea tarda (PCT) as being associated with Agent Orange exposure. 59 Fed. Reg. 5106 (1994). Multiple myeloma and respiratory cancers have been the subject of proposed rules acknowledging their association with Agent Orange exposure. 59 Fed. Reg. 5161 (1994) (proposed rules).

6. *Nehmer* v. *U.S. Veterans Administration*, No. CV-86-6160 (N.D.Cal. May 14, 1991) (Final Stipulation); B.F. Stichman. 1994. Between the Courts and Congress: Leveraging VA Benefits for the Agent Orange Plaintiff Class. Unpublished paper prepared for the Agent Orange Class Assistance Program Symposium.

7. At the time the VA's Agent Orange rules were held to be unlawful, the VA reported that more than 200,000 veterans were included in the VA's Agent Orange Registry. *See Nehmer* v. *U.S. Veterans Administration*, 712 F. Supp. 1404 (N.D.Cal. 1989).

8. Contributing to the awareness of Agent Orange class members and their families about VA compensation and accrued benefits claims for dioxin-related disabilities are the activities of the National Veterans Legal Services Project (NVLSP) and other service providers funded by the Agent Orange Class Assistance Program (AOCAP). *See* AOCAP Fifth Annual Report (November 1993). For example, to date, NVLSP has distributed more than 45,000 copies of its Agent Orange Self-Help Guide, which provides comprehensive, easy-to-follow instructions about how to prepare and submit a claim to the VA for Agent Orange compensation benefits. *Id.* at 10.

9. The other common scenario creating accrued benefits occurs when a veteran was already receiving ongoing monthly monetary benefits at the time of his or her death. The VA will immediately terminate the payment of any further amounts, effective the first day of the month in which the veteran died. 38 C.F.R. § 3.500(g)(1) (1992). Even if the veteran died at the end of the month, is owed the benefits to be paid for that month, and is survived by a spouse or other dependents, the VA withholds payment. *Id.* The spouse and other survivors are entitled to the benefits, but they must submit a separate claim for them as accrued benefits. Although these hurdles placed before a veteran's survivors are also unnecessarily bureaucratic and harsh, because these types of accrued benefits involve relatively small sums in comparison to those that are created when the veteran is seeking an original grant of service connection or an increase in the level of a rating going back many months or years, this paper focuses on the latter.

10. Department of Veterans Affairs FY 1995 Budget Submission, 4:2-43 (Feb. 1994).

11. Statement of Charles L. Cragin, Chairman, Board of Veterans' Appeals, before the Subcommittee on Compensation, Pension and Insurance, Committee on Veterans' Affairs, House of Representatives (Feb. 23, 1994).

12. 38 U.S.C.A. § 5121(a) (1991).

13. Id. § 5121(c).

14. Id. § 5121(a).

15. Id. § 5121(a)(2)(A).

16. Id. § 5121(a)(2)(B).

17. Id. § 5121(a)(2)(C).

18. 38 C.F.R. § 3.57(a) (1992).

19. Id. § 3.250 (1992).

20. 38 U.S.C.A. § 5121(a)(5) (1991).

21. 42 U.S.C.A. § 404(d) (1992).

22. Id.

23. *VA Adjudication Procedure Manual, M21-1*, Part II, ¶ 5.29(b)(1)-(3) (July 2, 1990).

24. *VA Adjudication Procedure Manual, M21-1*, Part III, ¶ 2.17 (Feb. 26, 1993).

25. Source: Field Operations Staff, VA Compensation and Pension Service.

26. The VA does not compile direct statistics on the number of veterans who die while they have a compensation claim pending. However, examination of other VA statistics provides these percentages. Out of the veteran population of 26 million, approximately 487,400, or 2 percent of the total, died in fiscal year 1993. Also in fiscal year 1993, the VA reported that 528,078 claims for compensation or pension were pending. Applying the 2 percent rate of death for the veteran population as a whole to the number of pending compensation and pension claims yields a total of 10,562 deaths in such cases. Source: Field Operations Staff, VA Compensation and Pension Service.

27. *See Oseo* v. *Brown*, U.S. Vet. App. No. 92-90 (The Secretary's Memorandum in Response to the Court's March 9, 1993 Order, at 21-22) (June 21, 1993).

28. *See Zevalkink* v. *Brown*, U.S. Vet. App. No. 91-1683, slip op. at 8 (Aug. 17, 1993), *recons'd pending* (Oct. 6, 1993) (per curiam order).

29. Id. Another means to reopen a previous final denial is to allege that the prior decision was the product of "clear and unmistakable error." *See* 38 C.F.R. § 3.105(a) (1992). Showing clear and unmistakable error in a previous final agency decision is generally a very difficult standard to meet and is a complex topic that is beyond the scope of this paper.

30. *See* letter of R.J. Vogel, VA Chief Benefits Director (June 29, 1989) (explaining the lack of a VA policy to expedite claims of terminally ill claimants), on file with the National Veterans Legal Services Project.

31. *See Mokal* v. *Brown*, 5 Vet. App. 146 (1993).

32. *See* note 27, *supra*.

33. *Mokal* v. *Brown*, *supra*.

34. Mr. Mokal's surviving daughter is not considered to be his "child" for the purpose of

payment of accrued benefits because she does not meet the definition of a "dependent" child. 38 U.S.C.A. §§ 101(4)(A), 5121(a)(2)(B) (1991).

35. The VA provides compensation benefits—prospectively—to the survivors of veterans who die from disability or injury that is service connected. 38 C.F.R. § 3.5 (1992). Generally, the condition must be shown to be either the "principal" or "contributory" cause of death. Id. § 3.312. Moreover, the amount of DIC benefits paid to survivors is much less than what a seriously disabled living veteran would receive. *Compare* 38 U.S.C. §1311 (DIC rates) and §1114 (rates of wartime disability compensation).

36. The situation of David Maier is a typical illustration of the length of time it may take for many Agent Orange class members and their families to have their individual cases resolved. Mr. Maier is a named individual plaintiff in the class action lawsuit that successfully challenged the VA's rules governing claims for compensation of Agent Orange–related disabilities. *See Nehmer* v. *U.S. Veterans Administration*, 712 F. Supp. 1404 (N.D.Cal. 1989).

A brown water Navy veteran in Vietnam in 1968, Mr. Maier developed soft tissue sarcoma (STS) in his left arm, which ultimately required the amputation of his arm and left shoulder. His original claim for service connection of STS based on exposure to Agent Orange was filed on September 23, 1982. The Cleveland VA Regional Office denied the claim, and Mr. Maier filed an appeal that remained unresolved for ten years, until the VA was forced through the *Nehmer* litigation to publish final Agent Orange regulations. Final regulations, published in October 1991, established presumptive service connection of STS in veterans exposed to Agent Orange. Mr. Maier was granted service connection for the residuals of this condition effective from 1985. As a result, he was awarded several hundred thousand dollars in retroactive benefits. Although he had to wait more than a decade to receive his benefits, he can be counted among the fortunate. If he had died prior to the promulgation of the new Agent Orange regulations or the post-regulation rating decision in his individual case, his family would only have received one year's worth of these benefits.

37. *See, e.g.*, 38 U.S.C.A. §§ 5107(a) (1991) (duty to assist in development of claim), 7104(a) (duty to consider all evidence and material of record and applicable provisions of law and regulation), 7722(c) (duty to inform claimants of entitlement to benefits). Another important source of such legal authority is 38 U.S.C.A. § 501 (1991), which authorizes the secretary of the VA to promulgate any lawful regulation "necessary or appropriate to carry out the laws administered by the Department and are consistent with those laws, including . . . the manner and form of adjudications and awards." Id. at § 501(a)(4).

Part V

Children of Vietnam Veterans and the Legacy of the War: Psychosociological Effects, Disabilities, and Appropriate Family Service Strategies

Most American combatants in Vietnam were teenagers or very young adults when drafted or enlisted. Some had married and started families before departing for Vietnam. Most would do so within a few years after their return home. A substantial number of these young persons suffered profoundly adverse psychological effects from their experiences in the Vietnam theater, as did earlier U.S. combatants returning from Europe, the Pacific, and Korea.

VA medical centers attempted to respond to Vietnam veterans' mental health needs by expanding mental health and drug and alcohol outpatient and inpatient treatment programs. Vet Centers were established to improve access to VA treatment. But most Vietnam veterans with psychological or psychiatric conditions never sought treatment. And treated or not, scant attention was given by the VA, the Department of Health, Education and Welfare (now the Department of Health and Human Services), and other government and nongovernmental institutions to the severely damaging effects that some veterans' war-related traumas were having on spouses. Even less notice was paid to effects on their children. Vietnam veterans' families with children with a disability or medical condition experienced another overlay of stressors.

The fact that many veterans believe their children acquired their disabilities as a result of the veteran's exposure to dioxin in Vietnam, and the distrust of and enmity toward institutions that many Vietnam veterans feel, challenge the best outreach and service coordination programs striving to help this population. The AOCAP Board of Advisors recognized the tragic oversight of the government regarding needs of children and families and designed a grantmaking program emphasizing services to family members, especially children with disabilities or medical conditions.

Papers in Part V report findings concerning the psychosocial effects of the Vietnam War on veterans' children and spouses, and describe strategies successfully addressing some of those needs.

Designing Veteran Family Assistance Services to Meet the Needs and Preferences of Families of Vietnam Veterans Who Have Children with Special Needs

Jean Ann Summers, Ph.D.; Karen Horn, B.A.; Amy Lazar, M.S.W., A.C.S.W.; and Charles Ritter, B.A.

Abstract

Wars affect whole families, not simply the individual who serves in uniform. The Agent Orange Class Assistance Program (AOCAP) has joined the new trend in health and social services for a veteran or child with special needs—support for the individual's whole family. The Missouri Vietnam Veterans Education and Resource System (MOVVERS), a member of the AOCAP network, provides comprehensive family service coordination, information, and educational services. MOVVERS drew on its experience and on a conference and symposium to develop recommendations for model veterans' family support services designed to meet special needs.

Research involved asking focus groups of veterans, spouses or widows, and children of veterans about their current needs and problems that result from experiences with the Vietnam War, and about their preferences for a service program that would be useful. Needs-assessment sections of family service plans were also analyzed.

A predominant emotion in focus group members was anger, with resultant perceptions and allegations of mistreatment and discrimination, which suggests that service program staff should scrupulously follow best practice standards with these families: tact, empathy, respect, and other elements of sensitivity. The value of whole-family or family-centered services was evident in findings that families expressed needs for a wide range of services. Some focus group participants expressed a need for opportunities to talk to, socialize with, or be served by other veterans' family members. Many also expressed needs for information on available resources and for job and other training.

A responsive service system is recommended in which veterans' family needs, such as the need for sensitivity and respect, are matched by service delivery implications, in this case, management values and staff skills that emphasize sensitivity, tact, and a "customer-oriented" attitude. A national network to support local veterans' family service programs could be tailored to meet the needs of the people MOVVERS intends to serve.

***Jean Ann Summers, Ph.D.,** is associate director for program development, Institute for Human Development, University Affiliated Program, University of Missouri–Kansas City. She has been involved in research on the impact of special needs on families and the development of effective family support models. **Karen Horn, B.A.,** is coordinator of urban services for the MOVVERS (Missouri Vietnam Veterans Education and Resource System) program. She has experience in working with troubled youth and their families. Her father was killed in Vietnam. She is a member of Sons and Daughters in Touch, a national support network of persons who lost a parent in Vietnam. **Amy Lazar, M.S.W., A.C.S.W.,** coordinator of MOVVERS, is responsible for inservice training for the project. She was a Red Cross social worker who served in Vietnam. **Charles Ritter, B.A.,** rural services coordinator of MOVVERS, is retired from the U.S. Navy. He served two tours in Vietnam as a medic.*

The Agent Orange Class Assistance Program (AOCAP) has joined a burgeoning new trend in the design of health and social service systems: that significant change for anyone—be it a veteran or a child with special needs—can be best achieved in the context of support to the individual's whole family. Recognition of the family rather than the individual as the "client" for whom the service system is responsible has become a hallmark of "best practice" in the fields of disability services (Biklen, 1991; Covert, 1992), early education (Dunst, Trivette, and Deal, 1988; Shelton, Jeppson, and Johnson, 1989; Turnbull and Summers, 1987), alcohol and drug treatment (Fossum and Mason, 1986), and welfare reform programs (Schorr, 1989), to name a few. Through the impetus of AOCAP projects, that same recognition is also gaining ground in veterans' service organizations.

The growing recognition of responsibility for serving whole families in veterans' service organizations has come about through the accumulating evidence of the pervasive impact of wars in general, and the Vietnam War in particular, on whole-family systems (Hogancamp and Figley, 1983). The impacts on spouses and children of separation and reunification (McCubbin, Hunter, and Metres, 1974), post-traumatic stress disorder (PTSD) (Soloman, 1988), and disability (Turnbull and Turnbull, 1990) have been well documented. All of these indirect impacts are, of course, in addition to the direct impacts on children with disabilities and spouses who have had miscarriages or other fertility problems. Understanding how best to serve these families requires a better understanding of the nature of the needs those direct and indirect impacts generate.

The Missouri Vietnam Veterans Education and Resource System (MOVVERS) is a member of the AOCAP network of programs. Like many of our sister programs, we have been providing comprehensive family service coordination, information, and educational services for two years now. The overall purposes of this paper are twofold. First, we want to describe some family needs and services as we documented them in our focus groups and in our formal and informal assessments of the families we are serving. Second, we want to propose recommendations for model veterans' family support services that are designed to meet those needs. These recommendations flow from the proceedings of a conference of veterans' families and service providers held in spring 1993, in our rural region, and a two-day symposium of Midwest Regional AOCAP programs, held in fall 1993.

Veteran Family Needs Assessment: Method

One objective of the MOVVERS project was to assess needs of families of Vietnam veterans living in our catchment areas. MOVVERS serves two very different areas in Missouri. Our rural services area is located in the south central part of Missouri and is a part of the Ozark mountain area. The economy is poor and much of the population is undereducated. A number of the families we are serving are people who either have lived in the area for generations, or whose veteran-fathers took their families and "went to the woods" as part of their reaction to the Vietnam War. In contrast, our urban services area encompasses the Kansas City metropolitan area. Our inner-city clientele includes some homeless veteran families as well as African American and other minority groups. Thus, we have two very different types of clientele in our catchment areas, who on the surface hold nothing in common except the fact that they are veteran families considered to be "underserved."

The methodology we chose for our needs assessment was the use of focus groups. We knew this particular population did not typically respond to such methods as mailed-in questionnaires or telephone surveys. We believed the focus group approach would allow us to establish more rapport, generate an atmosphere of trust, and get a more free-flowing and open discussion of needs. We convened focus groups consisting of veterans, spouses or widows, and sons and daughters of veterans. Five focus groups were convened in all, involving a total of twenty-five participants.

In each focus group, we asked the participants two basic questions: (1) What are some of the needs and problems you have now as a result of your experiences with the Vietnam War? (2) What are your preferences for a service program that you would find useful? Focus group sessions lasted approximately two hours, with the facilitator asking probe or follow-up questions to help the participants elaborate on their comments or build on one other's thoughts. Field notes were transcribed, coded, and sorted using a standard method for focus group data analysis (Krueger, 1988; Morgan, 1988).

In addition to the focus groups, we analyzed the needs-assessment sections of the family service plans we developed for each family we are serving. Conversations with these families included gathering information not only about their immediate needs requiring assistance, but also their preferences about the types of services they would use. These data, from about thirty-five families, were folded into the content analysis of the focus group field notes to provide a second data source for this assessment. This technique of collecting data from more than one source is commonly used in qualitative studies to corroborate or triangulate the validity of the information collected (Stainback and Stainback, 1984).

Not surprisingly, given our two basic questions, the focus group participants and client-families generated two broad types of responses. First, they suggested a number of specific or general types of service needs that, in their perception, were not currently being met by other service organizations. Second, they gave their preferences for *how* those services should be delivered, to maximize their usefulness to them. A discussion of the study results follows.

Veteran Family Needs and Services Preferences

Sensitivity and Respect

Need

One predominant emotion of our focus group participants was anger. There was a perception that the "system"—both military and civilian—had betrayed them, failed to meet their needs, treated them with disrespect, or just plain ignored them. These feelings were displayed through a litany of examples of perceptions and allegations of mistreatment and discrimination: claim denials, lost or mishandled paperwork, or incompetent treatment by the U.S. Department of Veterans Affairs (VA) and by military health and social services; rejections or snubs from veterans organizations; job discrimination; rough or insensitive treatment by law enforcement officials; and general rejection and negative stereotyping by the community at large.

Whether these perceived betrayals and discriminations are correct is beside the point. The family's *perceptions* and *interpretations* of their interactions with service agencies as harmful and deliberate have made many of them extremely cautious and distrustful of anyone proposing to provide them with services. Thus, one of the most often expressed sentiments when asked about service needs was for a service that "treats us like human beings."

Service Implications

The need for respect implied in that statement suggests that service program staff should scrupulously follow standards of best practice with these families: tact, empathy, support, nonjudgmentalness, sensitivity to "touchy" subjects, and strict attention to confidentiality. It also implies total honesty and total integrity: making no promises one is unable to keep, following through without fail, and taking some immediate action that responds to the family's *expressed* or *perceived* needs rather than the service provider's perception of the family's needs. Actions truly do speak louder than words.

The need for sensitivity has been emphasized by more general populations of families of children with disabilities (Summers et al., 1990). With Vietnam veterans' families, however, the need goes beyond the normal bounds for polite sensitivity. The mistrust and suspicion displayed by some of these families means that a new service provider is not just starting at "ground zero" in the attempt to establish a trusting relationship, but indeed is "in the hole," and must try to win back the trust that has been lost in previous contacts with one or more other service agencies. This means that a flexible, open timeframe in the initial phases of the service delivery process is a crucial part of the overall process. A family that has perceived itself as mistreated in the past will have little tolerance for a lengthy assessment or diagnostic process involving what they may see as meaningless questionnaires, bureaucratic paperwork, eligibility guidelines, and so on. In contrast, an initial meeting may involve no more than an open-ended chat, with no paperwork evident, between the service coordinator and veteran-parent. This initial contact should result in some sort of concrete action, such as a follow-up with requested information, that is immediately responsive to one or more of the issues broached by the veteran-parent. Finishing a complete "assessment" of the whole family's needs, strengths, and objectives becomes an evolving process that is filled in over time, as rapport is established.

Broad Spectrum, Multiple Needs

Needs

The specific needs expressed by the focus group participants and by the families we are serving range across a wide variety of financial, medical, mental health, social service, and educational assistance needs. The range and scope of needs among the families we are serving has led us to believe that the specific needs are less important to document than the fact that these families may often fall into the category we call "multiply challenged." That is, many of these families are experiencing a variety of problems all at once: the veteran-father may be unemployed and on partial disability for a physical or emotional problem related to PTSD; the wife may be showing effects of "secondary PTSD"; and one or more of the children may have physical, learning, or emotional disabilities.

The need to provide whole-family or family-centered services is recognized in many human services and disabilities-related service fields (e.g., Shelton, Jeppson, and Johnson, 1989). In many cases, however, the concept may be given lip service as an ideal yet to be implemented on a routine basis in a service program. The reality is that typical service programs in both the veteran system and the disability service system continue to focus on the targeted individual rather than the family. This is a particularly difficult situation for a veteran's family with multiple, whole-family needs. On the one hand, the VA medical model is focused primarily on the veteran and may not serve family members unless the veteran is involved (e.g., spouse support groups available only for spouses of veterans in treatment for PTSD). Many times, however, the veteran cannot or is not involved because of divorce, geographical separation, incarceration, or other factors. For their part, community services may not ask or take into account relevant factors relating to the family's military experience. Or, if they do discover the family member's veteran status, they may make an automatic (and sometimes inappropriate) referral to the VA system.

Whether or not service programs are family centered, a need remains for a coordinated approach to attacking the various multiple needs a family may have. Multiple problems in a family may mean that one problem serves as a barrier to solving another. For example, a father's aversion to authority and confrontation may be a barrier to effective advocacy for a child's special education program with the school system. Further, in families with multiple problems there is a "stress pile-up" (McCubbin and Patterson, 1983) that leaves little room for additional stressors, even small ones. This means that an event that would cause hardly a ripple in some families, such as a flat tire on a car, could trigger a major crisis in a family with multiple challenges (e.g., the flat tire can't be fixed because of lack of money, the lack of transportation results in loss of a job, and so on) (Kagan and Schlosberg, 1989).

Service Implications

For families with multiple challenges, the expressed needs were for "whatever it takes" to sort through the tangle of problems and access services. These families expressed frustration that, among the various service agencies with whom they had contact, no single agency had either the authority for, or the knowledge of, resources to address all their problems. This became the role of the MOVVERS program. For example, helping one family access alcohol treatment for the veteran-father required arranging assistance to pay the utility bills so that the father could feel comfortable leaving his family behind during the winter. Arranging transportation is another, more typical example.

As they considered the issues of multiple needs and needs that could not be neatly categorized as the responsibility of any particular service agency, the participants in our Spring Conference coined the term "one-stop shopping." This term was not seen so much as a single agency or entity with authority to provide all of the variety of services needed. Rather, it was seen as a single point of entry in which the staff could help the family put together a "package" of assistance from a variety of formal and informal sources, to meet these families' needs.

Social Support and Community

Needs

Some focus group participants expressed a need for either formal or informal opportunities to talk to, socialize with, or be served by, other veterans' family members. One widow of a Vietnam veteran who had died of cancer came to our project's attention because she placed an ad in a local paper seeking others like her. When asked what services would have been helpful during her husband's illness, she echoed this same theme of need for social contact: "It would have been nice to have somebody come over to the house just to talk and let me know I wasn't alone." One daughter of a Vietnam veteran who didn't come home summed up many feelings of veterans, spouses, and children when she said, "For twenty-five years I didn't talk about Vietnam. I felt alone and ashamed. To find out that there are others out there just like me, who have similar feelings and experiences, is a great strength and support. I know that when I talk they are listening and really do care and understand."

In addition to the need for support groups and general social support, focus group participants stressed the importance of having veterans or veterans' family members as part of the service staff. A common phrase was, "you have to walk the walk in order to talk the talk." This call for service providers who are veterans is part of the trust issue described above, but it is also part of the hunger we perceived among our participants to meet and talk with others who have had similar experiences. One focus group participant, asked about preferences for training or information, expressed a desire to receive job or vocational training from other Vietnam veterans. This particular focus group session ended with the participants brainstorming the development of their own construction company, run by themselves and hiring only Vietnam veterans, on the theory that "we need a place to work where we know we are accepted."

Service Implications

The need to have social contact with others who have similar experiences carries an obvious implication that one of the components of the "one-stop shopping" service program should be a mechanism to put people in touch with one another. Depending on needs and individual preferences, this may include organized support groups of veterans, spouses, sons and daughters, widows, and so on. It may also include a service in which veterans or family members have agreed to let the agency match them with another person who is experiencing some challenges, so that they can serve as a sympathetic ear on a more one-on-one basis. This service is modeled after Parent-to-Parent programs (Santelli, 1992), which have had great success among families of children with disabilities. Finally, facilitating social connections might mean simply providing referral information about veterans' social and service associations with which the service agency is affiliated, such as Vietnam Veterans of America, Gold Star Mothers, Sons and Daughters in Touch, and so on.

A more complex service implication is the issue of staffing service programs predominantly with veterans or veterans' family members. This point suggests that the primary service characteristic is that it is a self-help organization or peer-directed program. To be effective, a peer-directed program should incorporate veterans and family members at all levels of the organization, as advisory board members, administrators, service staff, and volunteer participants. A peer-directed program can enhance the sense of empowerment for service recipients, who perceive the program as being operated "*by* us, rather than *for* us."

At the same time that veterans and family members need to be highly visible and in more than token control of the organization, it is important to note a few lessons about peer-provider models that have been learned by programs serving other populations, such as disadvantaged families in Head Start (Zigler and Valentine, 1979). These programs have learned that the status of peer *alone* does not necessarily make a person a qualified peer counselor or service coordinator. In fact, some peer-staff persons have exhibited the opposite attitudes to the compassion and empathy that were the intended outcomes of using a peer model in the first place (e.g., "If I made it, why can't she?"). Even when the peer provider does have the requisite empathic response, it does not mean he or she has the skills to avoid overidentification or creating dependency, or that he or she can successfully intervene in a crisis. These are skills that come from training. Further, peer providers may also be vulnerable to setbacks or relapses of their own problems as a result of stressful interactions with the families they are trying to serve (Kagan and Schlosberg, 1989). Finally, if the ultimate goal is to foster inclusion of these families in the rest of the community, a peer-directed program potentially could actually increase the sense of isolation and "separateness" of the veteran family through unintentional extension of the concept that "nobody else can understand us."

We want to emphasize that none of these cautions is intended to suggest that we should not have peer-directed programs. On the contrary, we are strongly committed to the concept. We do, however, believe that peer professionals should be supported by intensive training and back-up support from other professionals. Perhaps the ideal model provides a mixed staff—some veterans' family members, some not—of professionals who are all seen as caring individuals. Further, fostering a sense of belonging in the community as a whole can be accomplished through a peer-directed, one-stop-shopping program (as described above) *if* that program sees its role as connecting its families to any and all potential resources in the community (e.g., veterans' programs, civilian social programs, church-directed private agencies). It also means that the organization should never lose sight of the ultimate goals for families being served: independence, inclusion or membership in the community at large, and empowerment to do for themselves rather than having others do for them. In other words, peer direction or self-help is a means, not an end.

Advocacy, Training, and General Information

Need

Many needs expressed by our families and by focus group participants related to the need for information and training. These ranged from relatively simple requests for information about the nature of particular disabilities or diseases, to more complex informational and educational needs, such as job training or education to facilitate their working with professionals serving their children with special needs. The way in which these veterans need that information to be provided may be more important than the actual types or content of the information needs expressed. That is, our families expressed little patience with the task of ferreting out information that resembles, as one participant put it, "circling like a vulture. You call this number and they give you another number, and that guy gives you another and another, until—if you're lucky, you finally zero in on the guy who can answer your question." These participants wanted their information needs met by someone who could "cut to the chase" and simply provide the answer. As one veteran put it, "Yeah, I know there is the VA, there are vet reps, there are 800 numbers, but I want help and answers. Who can I call to get that and not more bureaucratic crap?"

Related to information and training needs is the need for advocacy assistance. Families with multiple challenges and a long history of dependency may need active help in using the information they are given. They also may need someone to participate with them directly as they attempt to access some of the services they have perceived as previously inhospitable to them. As one wife stated, "you are kind of shy about asking for help when you have been slapped in the face so much." As another participant put it, "currently you have to stumble around the system. . . . There should be somebody to sit down with you and say: 'what are your problems?' and guide you on how and where to go . . . walk you through the system."

The need for information and advocacy assistance is illustrated by a case history from one of the families we serve. A crisis was precipitated in this family when their application for food stamps was denied because their income was $76 per month over the allowed guidelines. In conversation with our service coordinator, it was discovered that the family had overlooked several medical expenses and two dependents in making their application for food stamps. The veteran decided to ask for a hearing to present the additional information, and was subsequently successful. This example illustrates how simply providing the information and eligibility guidelines may not be sufficient; careful review and assistance in the entire process, from completing applications through filing appeals, may be required.

Service Implications

Information and referral is a common service offered by many agencies. The message from these focus group participants is that the information and referral service provided should be scrupulously up-to-date and accurate. The implications are, first, that the service provider needs to take the time to accurately pinpoint the exact nature of the information request being made. Taking calls for information is not a clerical function. It requires techniques of active listening and careful questioning to help the caller clarify the request well enough in his or her own mind to allow an accurate understanding of the information wanted. Second, the agency should have enough information about referral resources to ensure an appropriate match with the request. Finally, the program should have an active and rigorous mechanism to follow up, if not every referral, at least a large proportion of referrals made, to find out what happened, make sure the referral was appropriate, and if necessary update the information resource in the file.

Advocacy assistance involves providing active help and guidance about the family's rights and about procedures for accessing services and benefits. On a more personal level, it may involve knowing how to circumvent a more standard and impersonal intake procedure to directly access specific individuals in a service program who are more approachable, competent, or "can-do" than others. In many other cases, it may involve simply "being there" at the side of the veteran or family member, as a knowledgeable and supportive presence. We have found that the mere presence of an advocate provides moral support to the family member, and also tends to help the service provider be more accountable.

Conclusion: Recommendations for a Responsive Service System

Table 1 presents a summary of service needs and associated service implications, as expressed by our focus groups and needs profiles of the families we are serving. The needs and preferences reflected in Table 1 involve inductively derived principles drawn from accumulated comments, needs profiles, interview notes, and experiences of our staff. In the jargon of qualitative research, they represent a sort of "grounded theory" (Glaser and Strauss, 1967)

Table 1. Vietnam Veterans' Family Needs and Associated Service Implications

Service Needs	Service Delivery Implications
Sensitivity and Respect Families expressed a need to be treated with sensitivity and to have their concerns validated and respected.	■ Management values and staff skills should emphasize sensitivity and tact as well as a "customer-oriented" attitude. ■ Intake, assessment, and service delivery planning should be open-ended, informal, and ongoing with minimal paperwork. ■ Immediate follow-up should be provided with concrete demonstrations of direct relevance to family-stated concerns.
Broad Spectrum, Multiple Needs Many families experience multiple needs or challenges, resulting in: ■ Need to address whole-family, broad range of needs all at once; and ■ Need to address "small" stressors to prevent triggering larger family crises.	■ Open, flexible services with access to interagency, community-wide resources and a commitment to do "whatever it takes" to meet needs. ■ Broad and unlimited definition of role and scope of the service agency for whole-family, whole-person needs: "one-stop shopping."
Social Support and Community ■ Need for social and emotional support from peers. ■ Need to receive services from peers.	■ Organized support groups for veterans, spouses, sons and daughters, widows, etc. ■ Individual matches with peers who have experienced similar situations. ■ Peer-directed and peer-staffed services supported by intensive training and ongoing support.
Information, Advocacy, and Training ■ Need for accessible and accurate information. ■ Need for advocacy assistance in accessing services.	■ Information and referral services staffed by responsive listeners, utilizing detailed, accurate, and continuously updated information. ■ Advocacy assistance to provide knowledgeable guidance and moral support in accessing services.

of service practice principles that, in the opinion of our project participants, constitute characteristics of programs they would find useful and effective to meet their needs. The data are admittedly from a relatively small sample located in only two limited geographic areas. How valid are these "grass-roots-derived" principles? To answer that question, we reviewed two other more extensive qualitative studies intended to identify characteristics of programs that are successfully serving other human service populations, to compare our findings with theirs. Table 2 displays, in the first column, our veterans' family preferences for service characteristics; in the second column, characteristics of successful programs serving families who are disadvantaged (Schorr, 1989); and in the third column, characteristics of successful programs serving people with developmental disabilities (Taylor, Bogdan, and Racino, 1991).

The programs reviewed by these three studies cover a broad range of purposes. Beyond our MOVVERS project—serving Vietnam veterans' families—they represent teen pregnancy programs, prenatal care, child health and early education, and family support for disadvan-

Table 2. Comparison of Veteran Family Preferences for Service Program Characteristics with Other Reviews of Successful Programs

Veteran Family Preferences for Service Programs	Characteristics of Successful Programs Serving Disadvantaged Families (Schorr, 1989)	Characteristics of Successful Programs Serving People with Developmental Disabilities (Taylor et al., 1991)
■ Focus on response to family-perceived rather than professional-perceived needs. ■ Open-ended, informal process for intake, assessment, and service delivery. ■ Immediate follow-up and concrete response to needs. ■ Open, flexible services to provide "whatever it takes" to meet needs. ■ Available connections to support from peers. ■ Peer-directed and peer-staffed services. ■ Accurate, responsive information and referral. ■ Advocacy assistance and guidance to access services.	■ Broad spectrum services, with attention to family-perceived needs. ■ Willingness to cross traditional professional and bureaucratic boundaries. ■ View of the child in context of family and family in context of its surroundings. ■ Staffed by people who are seen as caring, respectful, and worthy of trust. ■ Able to creatively adapt or circumvent traditional professional and bureaucratic limitations when necessary. ■ Able to redefine professional roles to meet immediate needs.	■ Person-centered philosophy involving respect for person and family; people served are the focus of decisions. ■ Open, flexible, willing to change and try new ideas. ■ Participatory decision making involving clients, families, staff, and management. ■ More concerned with doing good than looking good. ■ Refusal to define themselves in terms of narrow service categories.

taged families (Schorr, 1989); they also represent family support and family service coordination, as well as supported living and community inclusion programs for people with developmental disabilities (Taylor, Bogdan, and Racino, 1991). Yet they echo common themes about successful programs: they are small, intimate programs that are community based; they are consumer focused and embrace "bureaucracy-averse" values; and they are flexible, open, committed to change, and able to do "whatever it takes" to meet needs.

Attempting to envision a national network of these small, peer-directed, and community-based programs boggles the mind. Certainly some sort of nurturing matrix (especially for funding!) seems necessary to encourage the development of these programs. Yet the requirements of creating a national system are in some ways antithetical to the best practice service characteristics we have defined. A national system must be accountable—therefore it must leave a "paper trail." A national system is by definition large—therefore there is a danger of impersonality and rigidity. And so on.

To ponder this dilemma as we consider prospects for survival after the demise of AOCAP, we at MOVVERS, along with several of our Midwestern sister AOCAP programs, have formed an Alliance. At our first meeting in October 1993, we first came to an agreement about the characteristics of "ideal" veteran family service organizations, which closely paralleled the findings of this report. To support those ideal services, we then envisioned an alliance or consortium of programs that would provide assistance and training to local programs, serve as an advocate for those programs, and (perhaps) provide a central administrative funding structure for them. Local programs would be autonomous and would derive the bulk of their funding from local or state public and private resources.

A national network to support local veteran family service programs would embrace exactly the same values and characteristics with respect to the local programs as local programs are expected to embrace with respect to the families they serve. A national network would view itself as facilitative advocates for local programs rather than authoritarian overseers. It would consider itself the servant rather than the boss, use the carrot rather than the stick, encourage creativity rather than conformity to specified procedures. And so on.

Perhaps this description seems to be a dream. But we think it is an achievable one. And, if the reader is as familiar with the Vietnam veterans' families as we are, we think you will agree: more than any other system one can envision, it is more truly tailored to meet the needs of the people we intend to serve.

References

Biklen, D. 1991. In support of families. In *Life in the community: Case studies of organizations supporting people with disabilities,* ed. S.J. Taylor, R. Bogdan, and J.A. Racino, 35-70. Baltimore, MD: Paul H. Brookes Publishing Co.

Covert, S.B. 1992. Supporting families. In *Natural supports in school, at work, and in the community for people with severe disabilities,* ed. J. Nisbet, 121-163. Baltimore, MD: Paul H. Brookes Publishing Co.

Dunst, C.J., C. Trivette, and A. Deal. 1988. *Enabling and empowering families.* Cambridge, MA: Brookline Books.

Fossum, M.A., and M.J. Mason. 1986. *Facing shame: Families in recovery.* New York: W.W. Norton & Co.

Glaser, B.G., and A.L. Strauss. 1967. *The discovery of grounded theory: Strategies for qualitative research.* New York: Aldine.

Hogancamp, V.E., and C.R. Figley. 1983. War: Bringing the battle home. In *Stress and the family: Vol. II: Coping with catastrophe,* ed. C.R. Figley and H.I. McCubbin, 148-165. New York: Brunner/Mazel.

Kagan, R., and S. Schlosberg. 1989. *Families in perpetual crisis.* New York: Norton.

Krueger, R.A. 1988. *Focus groups: A practical guide for applied research.* Newbury Park, CA: Sage.

McCubbin, H.I., E.J. Hunter, and P. Metres. 1974. Adaptation of the family to the prisoner of war and missing in action experience. In *Family separation and reunion,* ed. H.I. McCubbin, B.B. Dahl, P. Metres, E.J. Hunter, and J. Plag. Washington, DC: U.S. Government Printing Office.

McCubbin, H.I., and J.M. Patterson. 1983. The family stress process: The double ABCX model of adjustment and adaptation. In *Social stress and the family: Advances and developments in family stress theory and research,* ed. H.I. McCubbin, M.B. Sussman, and J.M. Patterson, 7-38. New York: The Haworth Press.

Morgan, D.L. 1988. *Focus groups as qualitative research.* Newbury Park, CA: Sage.

Santelli, E. 1992. *Parent to parent national survey project.* Lawrence, KS: University of Kansas, Beach Center on Families and Disability.

Schorr, L.B. 1989. *Within our reach: Breaking the cycle of disadvantage.* New York: Doubleday.

Shelton, T.L., E.S. Jeppson, and B.H. Johnson. 1989. *Family-centered care for children with special health care needs.* Washington, DC: Association for the Care of Children's Health.

Stainback, S., and W. Stainback. 1984. Methodological considerations in qualitative research. *The Journal of the Association for Persons with Severe Handicaps* 9: 296-303.

Soloman, Z. 1988. The effect of combat-related post-traumatic stress disorder on the family. *Psychiatry* 51:323-329.

Summers, J.A., C. Dell'Oliver, A.P. Turnbull, H.A. Benson, E. Santelli, M. Campbell, and E. Siegel-Causey. 1990. Examining the individualized family service plan process: What are family and practitioner preferences? *Topics In Early Childhood Special Education* 10:78-99.

Taylor, S.J., R. Bogdan, and J.A. Racino, eds. 1991. *Life in the community: Case studies of organizations supporting people with disabilities.* Baltimore, MD: Paul H. Brookes Publishing Co.

Turnbull, A.P., and J.A. Summers. 1987. From parent involvement to family support: Evolution to revolution. In *New perspectives on Down Syndrome,* ed. S.M. Pueschel, C. Tingey, J.E. Rynders, A.C. Crocker, and D.M. Crutcher, 289-306. Baltimore, MD: Paul H. Brookes Publishing Co.

Turnbull, A.P., and H.R. Turnbull III. 1990. *Families, professionals, and exceptionality: A special partnership.* Columbus, OH: Merrill Publishing Company.

Zigler, E., and J. Valentine, eds. 1979. *Project Head Start: A legacy of the war on poverty.* New York: Free Press.

Serving the Children of Vietnam Veterans

Susan Pincus, M.D.; Mary DeVivo, M.S.W.; and Marian Presberg, Ph.D.
Albert Einstein College of Medicine of Yeshiva University
Department of Pediatrics

Abstract

In 1990, the Children's Evaluation and Rehabilitation Center, a multidisciplinary child evaluation and rehabilitation center affiliated with Albert Einstein College of Medicine of Yeshiva University, began providing services to the Vietnam veteran community through a grant provided by the Agent Orange Class Assistance Program (AOCAP). Before this program was established, services in this population were felt to be inadequate, inaccessible, or nonexistent. AOCAP funding provided the resources the center needed to offer services to an underserved population that would not have been reached if outreach efforts had not been undertaken.

This paper discusses the advantages of linking services for Vietnam veterans and their families to agencies that serve children with developmental disabilities. Patient responses to a program satisfaction questionnaire, together with demographic data collected by the center, document the success of this program, as well as the need for similar linkages between the veteran and generic health care systems. Responses to the questionnaire also demonstrate that Vietnam veterans have children with special needs and that many veterans believe that their children's disabilities are related to their own Vietnam experience or to their exposure to substances such as Agent Orange.

Demographic data further support the idea that, without AOCAP funding, services provided at a center such as the Children's Evaluation and Rehabilitation Center would have otherwise been unavailable to or underutilized by the majority of families served. Findings from this study show a need for future alternative funding solutions to continue to serve veterans who have children with developmental disabilities.

Susan Pincus, M.D., *is an assistant clinical professor in the Department of Pediatrics and Family Practice at Albert Einstein College of Medicine, Yeshiva University, where she has also served as co-director of Services for Families and Children of Vietnam Veterans, an AOCAP program.* ***Mary DeVivo, M.S.W.,*** *also served as co-director of the AOCAP program at Albert Einstein College of Medicine. She also maintains a private practice in Westchester County, NY.* ***Marian Presberg, Ph.D.,*** *is a clinical instructor at the Kennedy Center, Albert Einstein College of Medicine; she works with high-risk infants and children, as well as families who have members who are HIV-positive, maintains a private practice, and is a psychology consultant in Westchester County, NY.*

The traditional system of veterans' benefits and services is veteran directed. Services and benefits are provided to the veteran directly. That system provides few services to members of the veteran's family. This paper describes the veteran and his or her family's experiences with generic health care services that have been linked to programs and personnel engaged in the provision of veterans' services. Services for children with developmental disabilities provided by the Children's Evaluation and Rehabilitation Center—a multidisciplinary child evaluation and rehabilitation center affiliated with Albert Einstein College of Medicine of Yeshiva University—are the specific focus of this study. The Agent Orange Class Assistance Program (AOCAP) Request for Proposal (AOCAP, 1991) described the attempt to link these two service providers as being the result of the Agent Orange litigation and settlement that led to the establishment of AOCAP. AOCAP funds programs and services that benefit Vietnam veterans and their families.

History

The AOCAP Request for Proposal stated that its mandate was to fund projects and organizations that addressed the needs and concerns expressed by Vietnam veterans and their families. Throughout the Agent Orange litigation, Vietnam veterans expressed concern about the health of their children. (The veterans were concerned about whether exposure to Agent Orange might have caused disabilities and special-health needs in their children.) The AOCAP distribution plan set aside a substantial fund to aid children of members of the class with birth defects.

Silbergeld and Mattison's (1987) review of studies on the reproductive effect of 2,3,7,8-tetrachloro-dibenzo-p-dioxin (dioxin) found the scientific literature on the paternally mediated effects of dioxin, the toxic ingredient in Agent Orange, to be inconclusive. Several epidemiological studies have been undertaken to determine the effect of dioxin on those with occupational or environmental exposure, but each has had significant limitations. Data on actual group or individual exposures are not available and exposure assessment was largely inferential. In addition, only a limited range of reproductive endpoints were assessed, in most cases fertility and incidence of overt morphological defects in newborn infants. Lathrop, Wolfe, Albanese, and Moynahan (1984) studied Vietnam veterans and found no differences between veterans who were likely to have had significant dioxin exposure from Agent Orange and control groups in terms of overall fertility, sperm count, or sperm morphology. They did, however, find differences in birth outcomes, noting an increase in reported incidents of minor birth defects, neonatal death, and learning disabilities in surviving children of veterans who had been exposed to Agent Orange. Erikson et al. (1984) conducted a study that relied on self-estimation of Agent Orange exposure among several hundred Vietnam veterans in the Atlanta area. Their study found small increases in the rates of certain birth defects, e.g., spina bifida and cleft palate in the children of Vietnam veterans.

In 1990, the Children's Evaluation and Rehabilitation Center, which is the largest diagnostic and treatment center for mentally retarded and developmentally disabled children in New York City, received funding from AOCAP to expand services to include the children of Vietnam veterans. The center uses an interdisciplinary team approach that emphasizes case management and continuity of care and focuses on working with families and other caretakers to help their children. It is comprised of a number of major clinical programs including five specialized interdisciplinary teams: a pediatric rehabilitation unit, an infant and preschool unit, a school-age unit, an adolescent unit, and a communications disorders group. At a minimum, each team or unit includes a pediatrician, a psychiatrist, a psychologist, a social worker, a speech-language pathologist, and a special educator. In addition, special consultation services are available including genetics, ophthalmology, ear, nose, and throat, neurology, and orthopedics. Clinics for the management of difficult-to-control behavioral disorders and for behavior management are also components of the center.

AOCAP funding provided for training on the unique needs of Vietnam veterans and their families to ensure that the center's staff were sensitized to the issues of this population. Staff were made aware of the need for taking a military history course and the importance of understanding the consequences of the war on the mental and physical health of the veterans and their families. Through this training staff learned about the problems and frustrations many veterans had faced since the war when attempting to secure health care and social services for themselves and their families.

The AOCAP grant enabled the center to identify thirty to fifty children each year who had developmental disabilities and whose parents may have been exposed to Agent Orange. Proof of exposure was not a prerequisite for services. To address some of the negative feelings veterans had about health facilities, the clinic altered its operating procedures to allow for more flexibility with this population. A veteran's very first call to the center was handled by someone with experience in veterans' issues. After the first call to the clinic, a case manager was assigned to the family. This case manager was available to assist families with current difficulties in their communities or at the center. We provided comprehensive multidisciplinary diagnostic services through an experienced existing program. Center staff were more flexible when appointments were missed and provided assistance with transportation when individuals lacked the means to get to the center. In addition, no one was refused diagnostic or treatment services because they were unable to pay. Services offered by the center included the diagnostic and treatment services listed above, tutoring, counseling, and camp scholarships.

A significant part of our project involved extensive outreach. We attempted to make class members in our area aware of the services that their children and families could obtain at the center through a public information campaign, including newspaper, television, and radio advertisements as well as an advertisement in the New York City subways. We worked closely with various veterans' organizations and other AOCAP-funded programs so that veterans might learn of our services. In an effort to increase referrals to our center, outreach was also directed at mental health clinics, schools, churches, and community recreation centers.

From the outset, center staff believed they would be able to reach a significant number of class members who had children with suspected developmental disabilities and unmet health care needs. We believed that these needs were unmet because other developmental disability service providers were either unaffordable or inaccessible. Because most developmental disability service providers were unaware of the special needs of Vietnam veterans and their families, we also believed that families would be attracted to the center and would experience greater satisfaction with the services offered within the facility. To determine if these initial assumptions were correct, three years after the center's AOCAP grant began, families who had received services through the project were sent a family satisfaction survey.

Demographic Information

Data accumulated over the three years of the AOCAP grant serve to describe the demographic characteristics of the population of veterans and veterans' families served by the center. The total number of veterans' families served was 120. The total number of individual children seen was 164—children ranged in age from twelve months to twenty-one years. The male-to-female ratio was four to three. The racial makeup of the children seen was as follows: 31.6 percent were African American; 37.5 percent were Hispanic; and 30.9 percent were Caucasian. Table 1 shows the results of the diagnostic assessment of these children. Children were seen even when the veteran was no longer residing in the household. (Over the three years of the grant, an average of 57 percent of the veterans were living in the household—43 percent were not.)

Table 1. Developmental Disability Diagnosis*

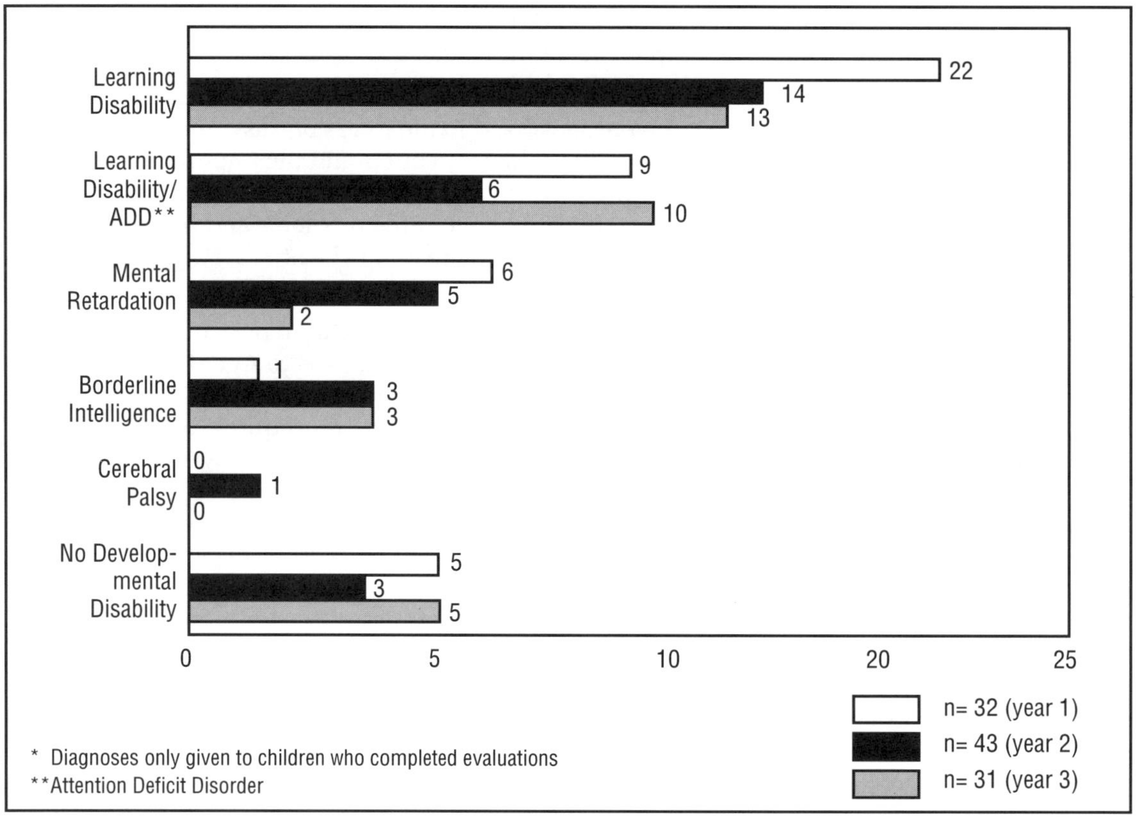

Initial referral sources are listed in Table 2. In terms of changes in the center's internal system, during every new intake telephone call, the caller was asked if a biological parent was a Vietnam veteran. This question was also asked during the first meeting with every child who came to the center's clinic. If a biological parent was a Vietnam veteran, the family was referred directly to the Agent Orange Project. (In Table 2, "Uniondale" refers to respondent letters sent out to original class members whose children are still in need of developmental services in our geographic area.)

In terms of payment, over the three years, an average of 30.8 percent of the families paid with Medicaid; 34 percent were partially insured; and 35.2 percent had no insurance coverage. As a result of the project, no family was charged out-of-pocket fees that they otherwise would have had to pay. (If the family had no insurance, they received free treatment; if they had co-payment responsibilities, those fees were waived.)

Program Evaluation

One hundred and fourteen questionnaires were mailed to all families who had completed a screening and partial evaluation at the center during the first three years of the AOCAP grant. Because many of those families had more than one child who received services from the center, the total number of children on whom the questionnaire was based was 147. The questionnaire was a program evaluation instrument designed to receive feedback on services provided, to assess needs that had not been met, and determine future program directions. Thirty-seven families (33 percent) responded, with the following results.

All (100 percent) of the families who responded to the questionnaire said that they were satisfied with the intake and screening process at the center. Eighty-four percent of the respon-

Table 2. Referral Network

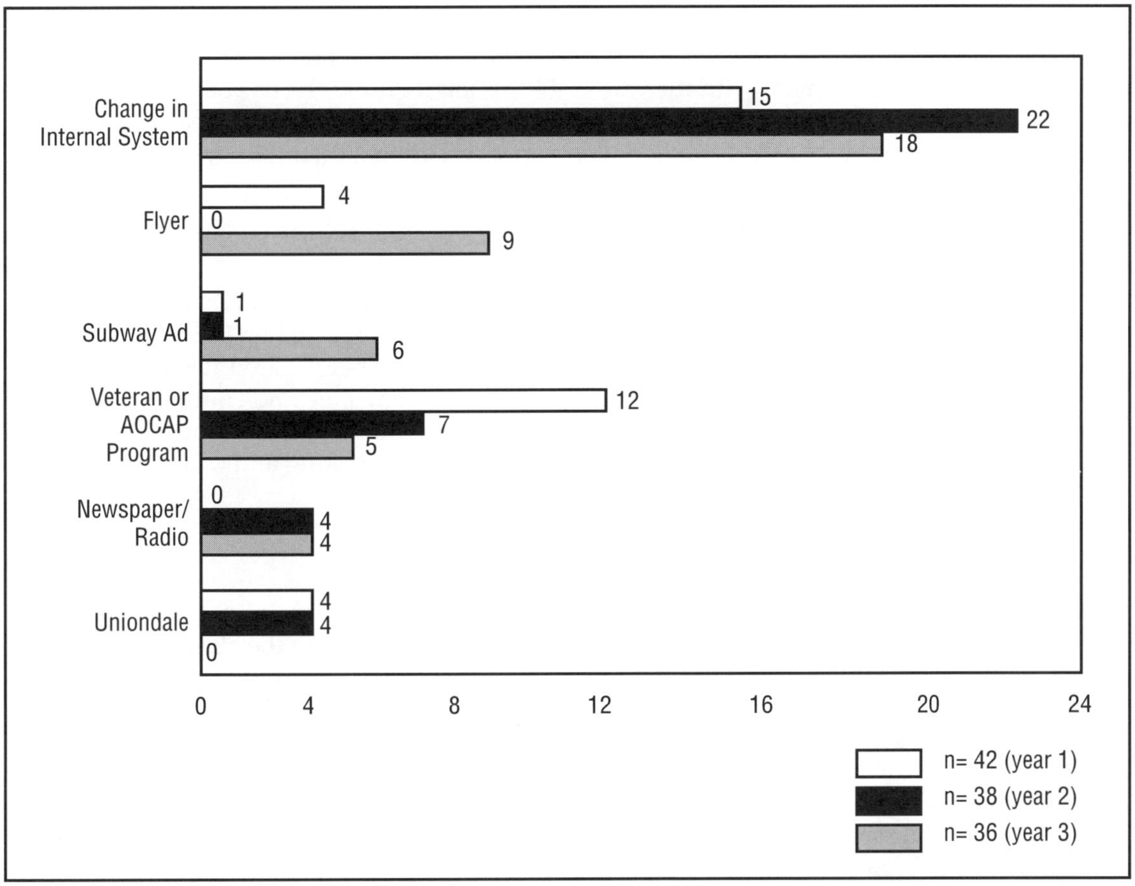

dents believed that their child had benefited from the results of their evaluation. Some of the respondents' comments were: "excellent thorough intake. . . ." "improved child's awareness of deficits. . . ." "I knew something was not right so being able to evaluate . . . was all I needed to put a title to his disorder." "After being diagnosed, I was able to inform the teachers at school so they could handle the situation with better understanding."

Most of the respondents (60 percent) had children who were receiving some type of treatment service, and many children were receiving multiple treatment services including tutoring, counseling, medication for behavior management, dental services, and physical therapy. Of the families whose children were in treatment, 82 percent felt satisfied with the services they received. Respondents commented that: "We were able to find out her weaknesses and we are now working on them through tutoring." "[H]er tutor has given her a lot of confidence in her school work." "[S]ince he received speech therapy he has become more outgoing and confident." Many of those who were not getting services at the center indicated that they couldn't come because they lived too far away. Families said things such as: "I wish you were closer," "What about us? We cannot get to . . . Who helps us?" The funding received by the center enabled many families to obtain services that they might not have had access to otherwise. Seventy-eight percent of the respondents said that they would not have been able to complete the evaluation or receive medical services without the added assistance provided by this program. Families noted, for example, that: "We were able to get the help that our child definitely needs and care which we otherwise would not be able to afford. . . ."

When asked if they believed that their child's problems resulted from their parents' possible exposure to Agent Orange, the majority (74 percent) of parents believed there was a direct link. Another question asked was whether families felt that their child's problems could be related to the Vietnam experience of their parent, other than possible exposure to Agent Orange. Half (50 percent) of the respondents attributed their child's difficulties to the Vietnam experience. Some of the families' comments were: "he is paranoid and he drinks which I feel is correlated to his involvement with the war. . . ," "his job required the use of toxic and caustic chemicals. . . ," "bizarre behavior by father and social rejection . . . ," "No financial support. . . ," and "permanently disabled father carries emotional distress. . . ."

When respondents were asked to compare services offered by the center with services offered by similar providers, 70 percent said that the center's services were better than those offered elsewhere.

Finally, veterans were asked about the impact that the center program had had on them as a veteran. Almost all (96 percent) of the veterans said that the program had benefited them. Veterans made comments such as: "Knowing that my child was being cared for properly, helped my peace of mind." "It's important to keep this program alive and continue to improve services offered to children of the 'Vietnam Experience Era.'" "It's comforting to know that there is a place where Vietnam vets can take their family for testing and counseling."

Discussion

Examined together, the demographic data collected by center staff, and the results of the mailed questionnaire indicate the Vietnam War is still having effects on the children of Vietnam veterans. Vietnam veterans have children with developmental disabilities and these children appear to have had health needs that have not been appropriately addressed. Linking generic health care services for children with developmental disabilities with those services primarily directed towards veterans has been effective. Veterans and their families have been satisfied with this type of service and many now feel that finally they are getting what should have been their "fair share" for the past two decades.

The center attained its initial goal of reaching thirty to fifty children with suspected developmental disabilities each year. Outreach efforts, especially those made through veterans' groups, were successful in attracting clients. The project's most successful outreach resource, however, was education center staff, who with the added knowledge of the special needs of children of Vietnam veterans, were able to refer many families to the center's program.

Once referred to the program, all (100 percent) of the veterans and their families who responded to the mailed survey were satisfied with the initial intake and screening process. Although the survey sample may have been biased—respondents may have been those who received the most services or were the most satisfied with the services—there was general satisfaction with the evaluation (84 percent of respondents), as well as with treatment services (81 percent of respondents). We believe this was a result of the extensive case management provided to the veteran families—an effort intended to offset previous experiences with more bureaucratic agencies that had been perceived as being less flexible in their dealings with veterans. In addition, center staff became sensitized to the problems of Vietnam veterans, which resulted in better-prepared and more appropriate social and medical histories. Stellman, Stellman, and Sommer (1988a) underscored this problem when during their study of Vietnam veterans they found that even when asking only about experience with VA health facilities, little attention was paid to questions about the veteran's service history.

The center's demographic data point to the fact that many children had developmental disabilities and were in need of diagnosis and treatment. The majority (70 percent) of the children who had evaluations at the center had learning disabilities, including attention deficit disorders, and 20 percent had a diagnosis of mental retardation or borderline intelligence. Although 60 percent of those evaluated and who responded to the questionnaire were receiving treatment at the center, some were able to secure proper services through their schools once a diagnosis was made. Many of those who were not receiving treatment through the center indicated that distance from the center's clinic was a major factor. Thus, there still appear to be children with additional needs with regard to their developmental disability.

In another study by Stellman, Stellman, and Sommer (1988b), a questionnaire was mailed to Vietnam veterans who belonged to the American Legion. The results of that study documented a high level of behavioral disturbance among veterans who returned from combat. These disturbances were still present even fifteen years after their combat experience. They included problems such as post-traumatic stress disorder (PTSD), depression, alcoholism, and drug abuse. Jordan et al. (1992), in their study of problems in families of male Vietnam veterans with PTSD, noted that individuals closest to a person with a major psychiatric disorder may suffer most, and that the effects of such problems can extend from one generation to the next. Results of the center's questionnaire pointed out that half of the respondents believed that their children's problems were related to the veteran-parent's Vietnam experience. Families of the veterans believed that the veterans' ongoing emotional distress related to their war experience had had a major impact on how their children functioned. In their comments, all noted things such as combat experience. Stellman et al. (1988b) observed that although herbicide exposure could not independently predict psychosocial outcomes among Vietnam veterans, it did significantly predict adverse outcomes when entered as a cross-product term with combat. Of the center's respondents, 74 percent believed that their children's problems were directly related to the veterans' Agent Orange exposure. The center, of course, has no way of verifying those beliefs.

One of the most important aspects of the center's program was its affordability. More than two-thirds of center patients had only partial or no insurance. For many of these families, diagnosis and treatment would have been unobtainable. In fact, 78 percent of the survey respondents stated that they would have been unable to complete the evaluation process or receive treatment services without the financial assistance AOCAP provided to the center.

In summary, AOCAP's use of community-based service providers is a unique and effective model. Vietnam veterans were able to secure necessary services for their children with developmental disabilities. Veterans and their families believed that many of these disabilities were directly linked to the veterans' service in Vietnam. Almost all (96 percent) of the veterans who returned the center's questionnaire believed that the center's program had benefited them as veterans. This is probably AOCAP's greatest legacy to Vietnam veterans—help for their children.

References

Agent Orange Class Assistance Program. 1991. Request for Proposal. Washington, DC: Agent Orange Class Assistance Program.

Erikson, J.D., J. Mulinare, and P.W. McClain. 1984. Vietnam veterans' risk for fathering babies with birth defects. *Journal of the American Medical Association* 252:903-912.

Jordan, B.K., C.R. Mamar, J.A. Fairbank, W.E. Schlenger, R.A. Kulka, R.L. Hough, and D.S. Weiss. 1992. Problems in families of male Vietnam veterans with post-traumatic stress disorder. *Journal of Consulting and Clinical Psychology* 60 (6):916-926.

Lathrop, G.D., W.H. Wolfe, R.A. Albanese, and P.M. Moynahan. 1984. *An Epidemiology Investigation of Health Effects in Air Force Personnel Following Exposure to Herbicides.* Brooks Air Force Base, TX: U.S. Air Force.

Silbergeld, E.K., and D.R. Mattison. 1987. Experimental and clinical studies on the reproductive toxicology of 2,3,7,8-tetrachloro-dibenzo-p-dioxin. *American Journal of Industrial Medicine* 11:131-144.

Stellman, J.M., S.D. Stellman, and J.F. Sommer. 1988a. Utilization, attitudes and experience of Vietnam era veterans with Veterans Administration health facilities: The American Legion experience. *Environmental Research* 47:193-209.

Stellman, J.M., S.D. Stellman, and J.F. Sommer. 1988b. Social and behavior consequences of the Vietnam experience among American Legionnaires. *Environmental Research* 47:129-149.

Helping Families Understand Post-Traumatic Stress Disorder: A Psychoeducational Workshop Model

Lisa Cosgrove, Ph.D.; William L. Holcomb; and Patricia Peck, M.A., M.Ed.
The Vietnam Veterans Family Services Project
Eunice Kennedy Shriver Center
Waltham, MA

Abstract

Clinicians have only recently begun to address how traumatic phenomena are transmitted psychosocially. Some clinicians use the term secondary traumatization *to describe the symptomatology of children who grow up in a home with a severely traumatized parent. One often-overlooked high-risk group are the children of Vietnam veterans suffering from combat-related post-traumatic stress disorder (PTSD).*

This paper describes a psychoeducational workshop model developed to meet the needs of families affected by a veteran's PTSD. The half-day family workshop employs both didactic and participatory components to address the behavioral, social, and emotional aspects of living with a family member who is suffering from PTSD. Its purpose is to help family members address how PTSD symptomatology affects the family functioning and develop some basic coping skills and strategies for improving communication and resolving conflicts more effectively. To that end, the workshop includes sessions for family members grouped by family role (i.e., spouse or partner, PTSD survivor, children, parents) and the family as a whole.

Lisa Cosgrove, Ph.D., *is a psychologist at the Shriver Center. She is also affiliated with the University of Massachusetts in Boston.* ***William L. Holcomb*** *is a behavioral psychologist at the Shriver Center.* ***Patricia Peck, M.A., M.Ed.,*** *is an educational specialist at the Shriver Center. She earned an M.A. in English from Penn State University, and an M.Ed. in early childhood and a C.A.E.S. in special education from Boston College.*

It is really impossible to properly address the [post-traumatic stress disorder] PTSD of veterans in isolation from their families. The husband's [PTSD] starts a vicious circle, creating disturbances in his wife and children, which in turn may augment his own illness. Such an intertwined complex of problems cannot be solved by intervention focused only on the PTSD casualty himself. What is needed is a series of activities, which include . . . help for his family. (Solomon, 1988, p. 327)

As our conceptual and clinical understanding of PTSD grows, it becomes increasingly apparent that, at both a psychodiagnostic and psychotherapeutic level, clinicians need to appreciate more fully the social and interpersonal effects of PTSD. Until recently, most clinical and empirical literature focused on the intrapsychic and behavioral implications of PTSD in terms of the individual's functioning and, concomitantly, the strategies relevant to individual (and to a lesser degree, group) psychotherapy. However, a leading expert in the field of PTSD has argued cogently for adopting a systems perspective when assessing and treating individuals suffering from PTSD: "a systems perspective always view[s] individuals within a social context, most often involving the family . . . [for] the trauma experienced by one family member may be experienced by the entire family system" (Figley, 1987, pp. 4-5). In fact, some clinicians use the term *secondary traumatization* to describe the often profound impact of growing up in a home with a veteran parent with PTSD (Rosenheck and Nathan, 1985; Harkness, 1989). The purpose of this paper is to discuss the familial effects of PTSD, focusing mainly on children's responses, and to describe a psychoeducational model as one time-limited intervention strategy that may be effective for helping some veterans' families.

The psychoeducational model outlined here differs in some important ways from other psychoeducational approaches to therapy. For example, some clinicians see the goals of a psychoeducational approach as completely compatible with "the goals of other family therapies [including] symptom removal and the resolution of presenting problems . . ." (Hardley and Guerney, 1989, p. 159). Although a discussion of the distinction between psychoeducational and psychotherapeutic strategies is beyond the scope of this paper, the goals of the proposed psychoeducational workshop model are modest, the format is time limited, and the overall focus is didactic rather than experiential. For example, although the tasks involved in the group activities are implemented in a psychologically informed manner, families are not expected to resolve long-standing emotional issues. Rather, it is hoped that this psychoeducational workshop will help participants develop a more explicit sense of their respective needs within the family, that they will learn a common language for expressing these needs, and that they will learn some basic coping skills and behavioral strategies for improving communications and resolving conflicts more effectively. It is critical, therefore, that family members understand that, although they are expected to participate fully in the various activities, their involvement in this workshop will be very different from any involvement they may have had in therapeutic modalities such as family, couples, group, or individual psychotherapy.

Thus, we envision our model as one that focuses primarily on teaching participants basic behavioral "tools" that can be used to identify and work on family problems.

Review of Literature on Secondary Trauma

Although the veteran with PTSD often becomes the identified patient, all family members are adversely affected, and children are particularly vulnerable to the emotional disruption evidenced in the family system. The term *secondary trauma* has been used to describe the psychological contagion that can occur in traumatized families (Rosenheck and Nathan, 1985; Harkness, 1989). Solomon (1988, p. 325) describes the impact of PTSD on family functioning as follows:

> Of the host of PTSD symptoms those that have direct negative effects on social relations are particularly significant for veterans' families. These symptoms include numbing of responsiveness . . . diminished interest in significant activities, feelings of detachment or alienation, and constricted affect. . . . Conflicts between aggressive impulses and the attempt to control them may affect the veteran's functioning as both father and husband.

Many veterans suffering from combat-related PTSD manifest labile affect and low frustration tolerance. For example, Williams and Williams (1987) describe the difficulties many veterans have controlling their anger or connecting with family members despite the love and empathy they feel. Thus, a parent with PTSD sometimes displays unpredictable and intense rage, and avoids any emotional involvement with family members at other times. Children have difficulty making sense of these inconsistent responses and even very young children will assume responsibility for their parent's behavior. The veteran's difficulty connecting with his or her children can start a vicious cycle of guilt, self-recrimination, frustration, and further withdrawal. Invariably, communication suffers and family members eventually find themselves feeling increasingly disconnected from each other. In addition, interpersonal conflicts tend to be impulsively and sometimes aggressively acted out rather than verbally resolved, a tendency that can have a negative effect on children's emotional and psychosocial development. Describing how children are impacted by a parent's PTSD, van der Kolk (1988, p.181) poignantly notes:

> Children in such families [with a traumatized father] invariably grow up with distorted ideas about their roles in family conflicts: they are likely to blame themselves and carry around a core of self-hatred that is difficult to undo later in life. These children often develop difficulties in emotional involvement with others; their object relations frequently are characterized by withdrawal and caution lest the wounds of emotional betrayal once again be opened, or by intense involvements and repeated disappointments as nobody is found who can compensate for the sense of loss and betrayal they have carried since childhood.

Not surprisingly, recent research has shown that violent behavior by veteran fathers places children at higher risk for behavioral, academic, and interpersonal problems (Harkness, 1989). Although children manifest a range of responses to violence, some age-specific responses have been documented. For example, as a group, younger children tend to internalize their feelings, turning their "fear and pain inward often becoming hyperactive and/or depressed . . . other children, especially older ones, seem to externalize their behavior so as to emulate and identify with the aggressive father. This identification is used as a defense [against] fears of attack, humiliation and abandonment" (Harkness, 1989, pp. 171-172). Research and clinical evidence strongly supports the belief that even indirect exposure to anger (i.e., witnessing violent outbursts) "causes negative emotional reactions in children" (Emery, 1989, p. 325). In fact, children as young as twelve months old have been found to respond to episodes of anger not directed at them with signs of distress ranging from crying to increased aggression (Cummings, cited in Emery, 1989). Unfortunately, many Vietnam veterans have problems with physical aggression; it has been reported that about half of all Vietnam veterans' wives seeking counseling have experienced at least one episode of battering (Matsakis, 1988). A recent study found that families of Vietnam veterans with PTSD are subjected to significantly more violence than families of veterans without PTSD (Jordan et al., 1992, p. 923).

Researchers suggest that the problematic child behaviors reported by veteran parents "resemble behaviors exhibited by the father [with PTSD] (e.g., depression, anxiety, low frustration tolerance and outburst of anger) . . . [such] behavior may be an attempt to identify with the father or to understand the father's behavior and thereby feel close to him" (Harkness, 1989, p. 170). Indeed, clinicians have described the often intense or symbiotic involvement children sometimes have with their traumatized parent. Overidentification with a parent with PTSD impedes the child's ability to individuate and develop age-appropriate autonomous behaviors. For example, ego boundary problems, anxiety, aggression, and preoccupation with specific events that were traumatic for the parent are reported as typical symptoms of children with secondary trauma (Rosenheck and Nathan, 1985). It is also believed that long-term exposure to "reliving" experiences of the traumatized parent (e.g., vivid memories, flashbacks, etc.) fosters an unhealthy bond with the parent; in his or her identification with the parent via this intense exposure, the child "experiences in fantasy the same kinds of events his/her parent actually lived through [thereby] internalizing a frightening reality" (Rosenheck and Nathan, 1985, p. 539).

In light of such chaotic family experiences and commitment or attachment complications, it is not surprising that children identified with "secondary trauma" exhibit symptoms and behaviors that are very similar to, and at times identical with, children diagnosed with PTSD. For example, children adversely affected by their parent's PTSD manifest emotional liability, depression, withdrawal, hyperarousal or hyperactivity, physical aggression, anxiety, low self-esteem, or acting-out behaviors (Rosenheck and Nathan, 1985; Harkness, 1989; Jordan et al., 1992; Solomon, 1988). Thus, it is perhaps most accurate to understand the secondary traumatization of veterans' children as being on a continuum; those children who live in violent homes and who overidentify with the parent with PTSD suffer the most deleterious effects. Indeed, although a number of veteran families with PTSD are coping adequately, it has been found that "the children of veterans with PTSD are more likely to have behavioral problems than children of veterans without PTSD, and more than one-third of male veterans with PTSD have a child with problems in the clinically significant range" (Jordan et al., 1992, pp. 923–924). As our conceptual and clinical understanding of secondary trauma improves, it is imperative that we develop psychodiagnostic, psychotherapeutic, and educational strategies that address the emotional, social, and cognitive needs of these children.

Workshop Design

This paper describes a time-limited psychoeducational workshop model that can be used for veteran families affected by PTSD. First, a brief explanation of the background of our agency and how we became involved in the development and implementation of the Living Together/ Learning Together Family Workshop model is provided. The remainder of the paper describes the goals, characteristics, and specific components of the model. The level of detail provided is not sufficient for the reader to replicate the workshop without additional information. Rather, an attempt has been made to communicate the key features needed to understand the principles involved in the design of the PTSD psychoeducational workshop.

The Shriver Center University Affiliated Program has been evaluating children, youth, and adults with disabilities for almost twenty-five years. In addition, the center's staff have provided technical assistance to schools and human services agencies, in-service training to professionals and parents involved in the lives of those with disabilities, and preservice training for students entering helping profession fields. In fall 1990, the Shriver Center received a grant from the Agent Orange Class Assistance Program (AOCAP) to target the unique needs of children of Vietnam veterans with known or suspected disabilities. During those early project days, we received a number of calls from parents, usually mothers, who were extremely concerned that their children were exhibiting behavior "just like their dad (who has PTSD)" and were doing poorly in school. For many the school problems were new, and for most their cognitive abilities suggested performance was below what could be expected. A surprising number were not yet receiving special-needs services, and the more typical special-needs diagnosis did not seem appropriate. We hired consultants, spoke with families, interviewed mental health providers and other AOCAP grantees, and came to the conclusion that PTSD within the home was a significant contributor to the children's problems. Most mothers, however, reported that the topic was never discussed within the home. Often parents attended group or individual therapy sessions related to PTSD, but supports had not been extended to their children.

The Vietnam Veterans Family Services Project set the development of a family workshop as a goal. We envisioned this half-day psychoeducational workshop as a place where families could develop a shared understanding of the impact PTSD might be having on them. More specifically, the PTSD Living Together/Learning Together Family workshop has two main goals: help participants understand how PTSD symptomatology affects the entire family; and help participants develop some basic coping skills and strategies for improving communication and resolving conflicts more effectively. It is hoped that each family will leave the workshop with a written agreement to resolve a specific area of conflict in a more constructive way.

With regard to the first workshop goal, it is important to remember that the emphasis is on family dynamics. That is, although the veteran comes to the workshop as the "identified patient" within the family system, every attempt is made to move beyond a "PTSD victim" focus. The staff must work hard to maintain a balance between acknowledging the (very real and often debilitating) effects of PTSD on the veteran while simultaneously encouraging a proactive (rather than reactive) stance on the part of *all* family members. Thus, in terms of the second goal, veterans and their families are encouraged to think about and use their respective competencies and coping skills. The belief that all families have the capacity to work together in more effective and rewarding ways is conveyed, and veterans and their families are encouraged to think about and use their respective competencies and coping skills. The workshop provides families with the opportunity to learn about specific "tools" that can enhance family functioning.

Selection of Families

The need for careful selection of the families who will participate cannot be overemphasized. The ability to effectively communicate with participants, and the benefit to the family, are directly linked to their ability to assimilate information in a psychoeducational format. The most important consideration in recruiting potential families is, perhaps, the level of pathology within the family system. In light of the psychoeducational focus and because the model is designed as a half-day workshop only, it is critical that participants be sufficiently emotionally stable to benefit from a didactic format. The symptomatology of PTSD is complex and the challenge of managing its anxiety-based symptoms is an everyday, long-term project. Veterans who are suffering from severe PTSD, or have active substance abuse problems, should be referred for more individually based psychotherapeutic treatment intervention. Similarly, families currently suffering from domestic violence problems would benefit more fully from individual and family psychotherapeutic treatment modalities.

Sometimes a particular family member (an older adolescent or a veteran who believes he or she will be made into the family scapegoat, for example) will be very reluctant to attend the workshop. Every attempt should be made, however, to encourage full-family involvement. If a family member refuses to participate but all other family members are willing to attend the workshop, it is strongly recommended that the family be "paired" (i.e., placed in the same family group) with another family whose parent or sibling is also not in attendance. In addition, the staff person providing the introductory remarks should make every attempt to recognize the difficulty in getting all family members to attend and commend those present for making the effort toward improving their family life by their attendance. Finally, because of the intensive nature of the workshop, it is also recommended that attendance be limited to a maximum of ten families.

Staffing the Workshop

Although the focus of the workshop is psychoeducational, it is important that some of the workshop staff have clinical expertise and that others have some familiarity with behavior management techniques. Because of the emphasis on family dynamics, it is also recommended that at least some of the clinical staff have family therapy experience. The various groups are designed to educate participants rather than help them work through emotional issues; however, it is inevitable that strong feelings or unresolved issues will arise at some point during the workshop. Thus, to attend to participants' needs and facilitate the goals of the workshop, the staff should be comfortable dealing with such issues when they arise.

Moreover, they should be competent and sensitive in terms of acknowledging long-standing psychological issues, while simultaneously reframing them in terms of the psychoeducational goals of the workshop. For example, the purpose of the parents' group is to provide parents with a working knowledge of some of the fundamental principles of behavior intervention techniques so that they can identify situations in their home where the techniques can be used. Sometimes, however, participants raise relationship issues that would be more appropriately dealt with in couples therapy. Concerns about the quality of the marital relationship are valid and important, but they are beyond the scope of this workshop and parenting group. Therefore, the staff leading this group must be able sensitively to refocus the discussion or, if possible, reframe the problem by identifying relevant parenting strategies.

Workshop Format and Group Activities

Once all family members are assembled, the half-day psychoeducational workshop begins with brief welcoming remarks. These opening remarks are followed by a series of group sessions, including three adult groups—one for veterans, one for spouses, and one for parents—two children's groups, and a multiple-family group. Each group session is approximately one hour in duration, with breaks scheduled between the sessions. (See Figure 1 for a flowchart of the workshop format.) All parents first attend a group session on parenting strategies to improve communication and resolve conflicts with their children. Simultaneously, the children attend the first children's group, which is designed to increase knowledge of the Vietnam experience and, in age-appropriate ways, address the intrafamilial effects of PTSD.

The next series of concurrent groups includes separate meetings for veterans, spouses, and children. The veterans' group focuses on how PTSD symptomatology affects spouses and children, and how veterans suffering from PTSD might communicate more effectively with their families. The spouses' group encourages participants to identify how their spouses' PTSD affects their lives and teaches techniques for communicating more effectively and resolving conflicts more productively. The second children's group gives children the opportunity to explore thoughts and feelings about their parents' PTSD. The next component of the workshop reunites the families into small groups (typically two families per group) and facilitates the application of previously learned behavioral concepts by asking families to identify and commit to one family-relevant goal. At the end of the workshop, all participants are assembled for closing remarks. Each of these components is described in further detail below.

Welcoming Remarks

Welcoming remarks are a brief (fifteen to twenty minutes) but critical component of the workshop. It is the first contact between participants and workshop staff. As such, opening remarks help set the tenor for the entire workshop. Effective welcoming remarks should include the following:

- First, and perhaps foremost, the staff person or guest speaker should begin by connecting emotionally with and involving the children. Although it is important to use this time to address the basic ways PTSD affects the family, it is equally important to provide a warm, down-to-earth introduction that invites participation and conveys clearly that the workshop format is interactional. One technique for accomplishing this goal is to have the children come to the front of the room and sit in a circle, and ask them specific, but nonthreatening, questions about their families. For example, it is helpful to ask children what they have in common or what they know about PTSD.
- Second, they should include an explicit description of the structure and intent of the half-day workshop. The speaker should reiterate that the workshop is psychoeducational rather than psychotherapeutic (this information should also have been made clear to prospective participants when their family was selected). It is helpful to discuss briefly and provide an example of the difference between a psychoeducational and psychotherapeutic format and to allay any fears that individual

Figure 1. Flowchart of Workshop Format

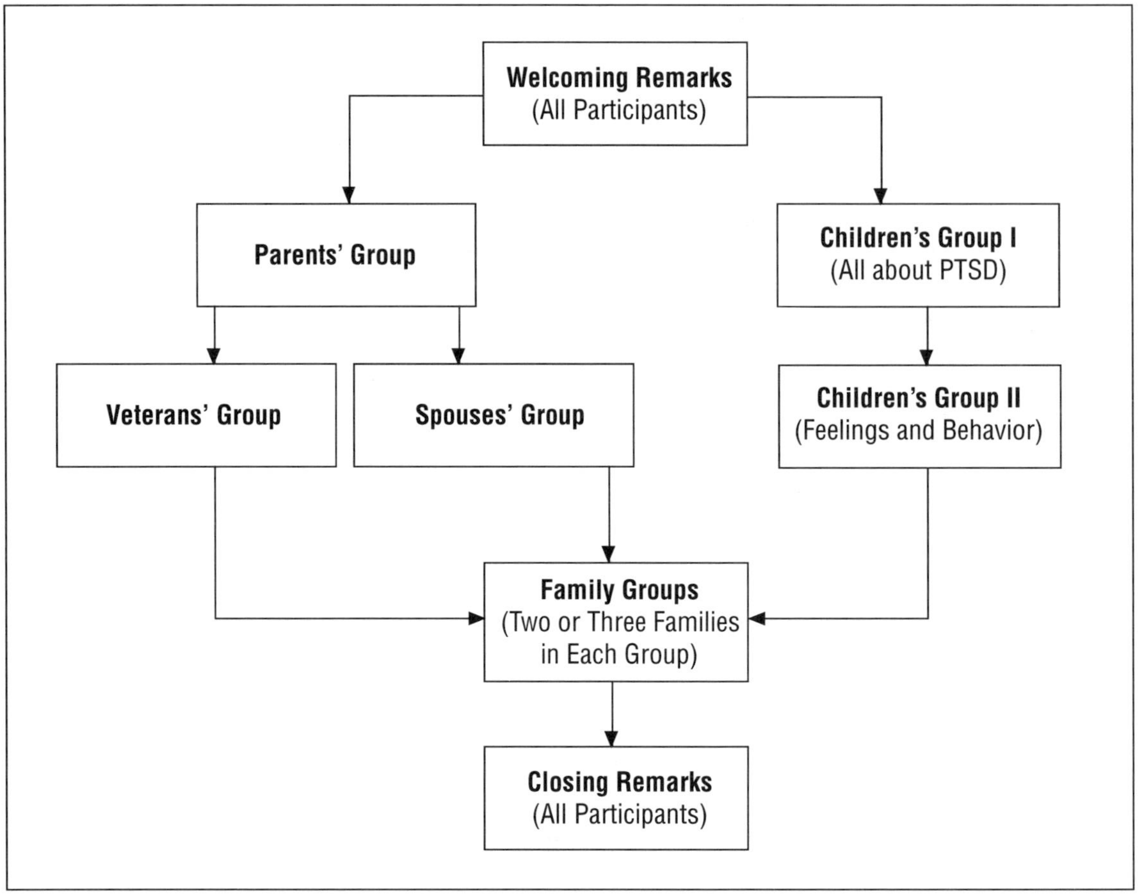

family members (i.e., the veterans) will be scapegoated. It is, therefore, particularly important to emphasize the *family* focus of the workshop.

Parents' Group

The Parents' Group provides parents with a working knowledge of some of the fundamental principles of behavior intervention techniques. Emphasis is placed on positive reinforcement strategies, and parents are introduced to the use of these techniques to help them understand that they can build appropriate behavior within the family to replace maladaptive patterns. Although many of these principles are relevant to all families, every attempt is made to focus the discussion on issues particularly relevant to veterans' families affected by PTSD. A particular focus of this group is on teaching parents how to identify situations where these techniques can be used to improve communication and resolve conflicts with their children. A "Family Plan" worksheet, which provides a format for identifying particular conflicts within a family, is used to provide examples whenever possible. A number of activities are used to encourage active participation and discussion by the parents.

Veterans' Group

The Veterans' Group is an hour-long session during which veterans are asked to examine ways that PTSD symptomatology affects spouses and children. Every attempt is made to help the veterans look at their symptomatology in terms of its interpersonal familial impact (vs. how it affects the veterans at an individual intrapsychic level). Group members are also encouraged to adopt a *proactive* (rather than *reactive)* comportment. That is, the group leader must work hard at conveying the fact that competency and PTSD can, and do, coexist. Although specific questions have been developed to help focus this discussion, it is critical for the group leader to set a tone that encourages veterans to think about their needs and behavior within the context of the family. This group also helps veterans to differentiate among assertive, aggressive, passive, and passive-aggressive responses so that they can learn how to communicate more effectively with their families and resolve conflicts in assertive rather than aggressive ways. During the final part of the session, veterans are asked to think about a specific problem or goal that they would like to work on in their families. Group facilitators then help participants focus on what they (the veterans) would be willing to do to resolve the identical problem or achieve the desired goal.

Spouses' Group

The Spouses' Group is an hour-long session that encourages participants to identify ways that their partners' PTSD affects their lives. Thus, one of the group leader's tasks is to ensure that participants understand the interpersonal effects of combat-related PTSD. Spouses are also encouraged to think about how they might take better care of themselves in light of the challenge of living with someone with PTSD. For example, it is quite common for a veteran's spouse to find herself in a "compassion trap, in which she sacrificed for many years her own needs for the rest of her family" (Solomon, 1988, p. 327). Also, in ways similar to the Veterans' Group, spouses are taught how to differentiate between aggressive, assertive, passive, and passive-aggressive responses so that they too can communicate more effectively and resolve conflicts more productively. Specific questions have also been developed to help guide this discussion. In addition, the group leader discusses the importance of gender roles and social expectations in the development of assertive behaviors and in the tendency for women to take responsibility for family functioning. Because of the lack of supports for spouses, networking and sharing of supports is strongly encouraged. At the end of the group, spouses are also asked to think about a specific problem or goal that they would be willing to work on in their families.

Children's Group

The two Children's Groups are designed to provide children with a general understanding of the social and political context in which the Vietnam War was fought and to define and discuss PTSD in age-appropriate language. Participants are also encouraged to explore thoughts and feelings about the effects of their fathers' PTSD in their lives. The groups should proceed in a step-wise fashion, with discussion about the Vietnam War preceding any exploration of thoughts and feelings. In this way, the discussion progresses from neutral issues to more affect-laden material. Ideally, groups should be composed of children no more than three years apart (e.g., seven- to ten-year-olds) so that the material can be discussed in a manner consonant with the developmental (vs. chronological) age of group participants.

Although the first group is often more informational or didactic in focus, it is recommended that the group leader encourage participation rather than simply present the material in a lecture format. Encouraging participation in the first group will both increase group cohesion and help the leaders to assess and monitor the children's perceptions, fantasies, and emotional issues. In terms of the actual content of the group, it is important to address briefly both the history of the Vietnam War and the tone of the 1960s (i.e., the anti-war movement and its effect on returning veterans). Also, using age-appropriate terms and language, the general concept of trauma should be addressed and, concomitantly, the main symptoms of PTSD should be discussed. In addition, because children and adolescents sometimes repeat expressions without a solid conceptual understanding of their meanings, it is important to explore jargonized responses (e.g., "my dad says he's working through his PTSD") in greater detail. Finally, group leaders should use this group to emphasize the fact that children are not responsible for their fathers' PTSD or their parents' behavior. The goal for this group is to foster a deeper understanding of what their veteran parent has lived through, while simultaneously eliminating the guilt or sense of responsibility they may feel for their parents' difficulties.

Although the two Children's Groups overlap both in terms of format and content, the second group is more open-ended with regard to discussion. Also, at least implicitly, the group leader encourages participants to focus on relevant personal and family-related problems. Thus, the group leader's task is twofold: he or she should focus the discussion on how a parent's PTSD has an impact on all family members, while also normalizing family conflict and encouraging the development of problem-solving ideas and behaviors. Several themes arise frequently and merit careful attention by the group leader. Children often bring up a number of similar fears, concerns, or questions; thus, the leader should listen attentively for such similarities and identify them for the group so that participants can better appreciate that they are not alone and that many families struggle with common problems. Important differences often exist in coping styles; it is, therefore, equally important for children to recognize that people cope in a variety of ways; and children will often describe their veteran parents' behavior without fully recognizing the relationship between the stated behavior and PTSD. All too often, children will assume responsibility for their parents' symptomatology. The second children's group provides an important opportunity to help children realize that they are not responsible for their parents' behavior or problems.

Family Groups

The primary purpose of the Family Group is to review the goals of the workshop and give families the opportunity to practice the skills they learned in previous groups. This portion of the workshop is typically conducted by dividing participants into groups of two or three families with two facilitators from the workshop staff in each group. Including more than one family in each group provides the opportunity for coping strategies as well as modeling of the techniques learned earlier in the workshop. The group facilitators foster discussion among all family members by encouraging the use of problem-solving approaches learned in the previous component groups. Points stressed include: getting along better means different things to different families, but all families have to work at communicating with each other and resolving conflicts that arise in daily life; and learning how to identify and talk honestly about one's feelings and concerns, trying to see another person's point of view, and being willing to compromise are all necessary tools in communicating more effectively and resolving conflicts productively. The Family Plan worksheet is used as a guide to prompt families into selecting an appropriate, realistic, and shared goal. The primary function of the facilitators in the Family Group is to ensure selection of a reasonable short-term goal and to encourage the use of previously learned behavioral concepts and techniques.

Closing Remarks

Following the Family Groups, a staff guest speaker should provide brief (ten to fifteen minutes) closing remarks to facilitate closure and encourage follow-through of family plans. Closing remarks should be similar in structure to the welcoming remarks (i.e., they should be brief, informal, and encourage audience participation). For example, following up on questions or issues raised in the welcoming remarks is recommended. Directing at least some questions to each of the "categories" of workshop participants (i.e., children, spouses, and veterans) helps to provide additional examples of the issues encountered in the workshop from different perspectives. The speaker should also emphasize that conflict is a normal part of most family interactions and can be a healthy way for families to grow and to understand each other better, especially if conflicts are solved in a manner that promotes better communication and understanding.

Post-Workshop

It is very important that staff allot some time immediately following the workshop for debriefing. During this time, issues discussed typically include staff perspectives and feelings about the various groups, including any countertransference issues that may have been evoked, and identification of any workshop participants who appear to be in need of additional intervention. It is critical that referral to community-based resources (e.g., referring a child for individual therapy in his or her home town) occur immediately following the workshop or shortly thereafter. It is also helpful to provide prospective clients with information on mental health services. Any aspects or activities of the workshop that could be improved on or modified, as well as aspects or activities of the workshop that seemed to be particularly helpful to participants, should be identified and discussed.

The final aspect of the workshop consists of two main follow-up activities. First, it is recommended that within a week of the workshop, an evaluation form be sent to all family members. Separate forms for adults and children should be used. If time permits, it is also helpful to contact families by phone and ask for general and specific feedback regarding their perception of the workshop. Second, it is desirable to conduct further follow-up (via mail or phone) at one-, two-, and three-month intervals. The focus of this contact should be on the family plans (e.g., Are family members following through on their responsibilities or goals? In general, is the family plan working? Is it time for new goals to be identified? etc.).

Conclusion

As clinicians become more aware of the risk factors involved in the psychosocial transmission of traumatic phenomenon, a wide range of interventions and services must be available to families. The Living Together/Learning Together PTSD Family Workshop represents a first step in acknowledging and attending to the interpersonal impact of PTSD. Insofar as this psychoeducational model is time limited, it is cost-effective, especially when compared with more long-term interventions. In addition, it can be effectively used as a screening aid for identifying families who need and want more intensive follow-up services. Most importantly, however, this psychoeducational workshop may help develop a sense of optimism that systemic changes within the family are possible—provided that each family member follows through with developing the behavioral tools they learned about in the workshop.

References

Emery, R. 1989. Family violence. *American Psychologist* 321-328.

Figley, C. 1987. Post-traumatic family therapy. In *Post-traumatic Therapy,* ed. F. Ochberg. New York: Brunner/Mazel.

Hardley, G., and B. Guerney. 1989. A psychoeducational approach. In *Treating Stress in Families,* ed. C. Figley, 158-181. New York: Brunner/Mazel.

Harkness, L. 1989. Children of war: A study of the offspring of Vietnam veterans with post-traumatic stress disorder. Unpublished doctoral dissertation, New York University.

Jordan, B., C. Marmar, J. Fairbank, W. Schlenger, R. Kulka, R. Hough, and D. Weiss. 1992. Problems in families of male Vietnam veterans with post-traumatic stress disorder. *Journal of Consulting and Clinical Psychology* 60(6):916-926.

Matsakis, A. 1988. *Vietnam Wives.* Kensington, MD: Woodbine House.

Rosenheck, R., and P. Nathan. 1985. Secondary traumatization in children of Vietnam veterans. *Hospital and Community Psychiatry* 36(5):538-539.

Solomon, Z. 1988. The effect of combat-related post-traumatic stress disorder on the family. *Psychiatry* 51:323-329.

van der Kolk, B.A. 1988. Trauma in men: Effects on family life. In *Abuse and Victimization: Across the Life Span*, ed. M. Straus, 170-186. Baltimore, MD: Johns Hopkins Press.

Williams, C., and T. Williams. 1987. Family therapy for Vietnam veterans. In *Post-traumatic Stress Disorders: A Handbook for Clinicians*, ed. T. Williams, 221-231. Cincinnati, OH: Disabled American Veterans.

Families of Vietnam Veterans with Post-Traumatic Stress Disorder: Child Social Competence and Behavior

Laurie Harkness, Ph.D.
Veterans Affairs Medical Center
West Haven, CT
Yale University School of Medicine, New Haven, CT

Earl L. Giller, M.D., Ph.D.
Pfizer Incorporated
Groton, CT

Abstract

Aspects of combat-related post-traumatic stress disorder (PTSD) in Vietnam veterans may affect their children's development. In this study, researchers assessed the influence of the severity of the father's PTSD symptomatology, level of family functioning, and the presence or absence of violent behavior in the veteran father on the child's social competence and behavior patterns. Forty families involving eighty-six children ages six to sixteen were recruited for the study. Fathers were assessed through various instruments to determine combat exposure and severity of PTSD symptoms. Both veteran fathers and their wives independently completed family function assessments and child behavior questionnaires. The children's teachers also completed child behavior questionnaires.

Results indicate that many children demonstrated problematic behavior and were at risk for developing more severe psychiatric disorders. A child whose father is violent is more likely to have additional behavior problems, poorer school performance, and lower social competence than a child whose father is not violent. Violence is most strongly related to lower socioeconomic status, larger family size, and unemployment or underemployment. Violent behavior in the father has a great impact on general family functioning, which has significant influence on the child's functioning. Clinicians should identify high-risk families and children and treat children by emphasizing their separateness from their father and that they are not responsible for their father's behavior or pain. Longitudinal follow-up studies should be conducted to assess the risks in various age groups and examine the family outcome following treatment.

***Laurie Harkness, Ph.D.,** is chief of the Psychiatric Rehabilitation Program at the West Haven VA Medical Center and assistant clinical professor of social work in psychiatry at the Yale School of Medicine. She has published numerous articles on PTSD and community-based treatment for the homeless and chronically mentally ill. **Earl L. Giller, M.D., Ph.D.,** is associate director for central nervous system research at Pfizer Incorporated.*

The relationship of a father's war experiences and subsequent post-traumatic stress disorder (PTSD) to family life has generated growing concern. Flashbacks, nightmares, and startle responses, along with irritability, violence, depression, and substance abuse are among the most common and most disturbing symptoms of combat-related PTSD. These all have an impact on interpersonal and family relationships. Many of these families appear to have suffered from the well-known profound and prolonged psychological effects that many veterans experience. However, relatively little has been done to investigate the characteristics and problems of the children in the families that Vietnam War veterans formed in the post-war period. This study examines aspects of PTSD in Vietnam veterans that may affect their children's development. Investigation of these children is essential in order to comprehend the long-term implications of the experiences of veterans with combat-related PTSD.

Studies of children of Holocaust survivors and children of psychiatrically disturbed parents have clearly suggested that the psychological reverberations of traumatic events may persist into the next generation. An individual's PTSD becomes part of the entire family system and can affect other family members. The effects of trauma on the second generation can occur in many ways, both subtle and overt. Children can experience the impact of their parent's traumatic symptoms of anxiety, depression, withdrawal, or anger (Beardslee et al., 1983; Weissman et al., 1984; Krystal, 1968), hear repeatedly about their father's war experiences (Robinson and Winnik, 1978), observe how other people treat their father, be overprotected (Sonnenberg, 1974), adopt their parent's reactive attitudes of bitterness or suspicion, or feel pressure to compensate for their parent's deprivation and suffering (Levine, 1982). Deficits in the children have been documented in many areas, including cognitive-intellectual functioning (Rolf, 1972; Erlenmeyer-Kimling et al., 1981), social-interpersonal functioning (Beisser, Glasser, and Grant, 1967; Erlenmeyer-Kimling, 1975), and affective functioning (Weissman et al., 1984; Beardslee et al., 1983). However, some research with trauma survivors has shown that the consequences are not necessarily pathologic (Krell, 1982). Some children can shelter themselves from the negative impact of the environmental and familial sequelae of traumatic experience. They have the capacity to elicit positive responses from parents, friends, and teachers. The risks associated with parental PTSD can also be buffered by constitutional characteristics of the child.

Recently, several authors have reported their clinical impressions on the impact of combat-related PTSD on the children of Vietnam War veterans. Haley (1983) observed that child-rearing seems to emphasize the veteran's working through the transition from the "reflex" of combat aggressiveness to adaptive, nondestructive aggression in their current lives. Her emphasis is more on how to help the veteran father deal with the young child than on actual child developmental issues. Rosenheck (1985a), after encountering several troubled and symptomatic children whose fathers were being treated for PTSD, described a process he called "secondary traumatization" to characterize the relationship between the father's combat experiences and subsequent stress disorder and children's problems.

In cases of secondary traumatization, the child, exposed to the father's symptoms of PTSD, especially the flashbacks, nightmares, and vivid memories that the veteran father continuously relives and often even reenacts, identifies with the parent and experiences in fantasy the same kinds of events his or her parent actually lived through. This study investigates these impressionistic findings through empirical research.

To date, the only published empirical study to investigate the impact of PTSD on children has been the National Vietnam Veterans Readjustment Study (NVVRS) (Kulka et al., 1990). The NVVRS found that children of Vietnam veterans with PTSD do tend to have more behavioral problems than do children of Vietnam veterans without PTSD and that they resembled a clinic-seeking sample of age mates rather than a normative sample. That study also found that these families reported more marital problems, more problems related to parenting, lower family adjustment, and more family violence than is found in families of those without PTSD. That study concluded that living with a veteran suffering with PTSD appears to have a significant negative impact on the psychological status and well-being of their spouses or coresident partners and their children (Kulka et al., 1990, p. 20). We examined which variables contributed to the variance in child behavior scores: the severity of specific PTSD symptoms or other associated problems. Results of this study are important in helping clinicians identify where to focus their clinical interventions: on PTSD, on the family, or on violence.

In an unpublished paper, Harkness and Giller (1992) reported the results of a study that examined spousal reports of their marital relationships in a group of forty Vietnam veterans with PTSD and their wives. Many of the couples reported problems in family functioning, including communication patterns, expressions of intimacy (cohesion), and problem-solving abilities (adaptability). A large number of couples described their family patterns of interaction as disengaged and rigid. Variables that most influence the level of family functioning were identified and discussed.

A major finding of the study was the powerful effect in the family of current violent behavior. Violent behavior was found to be even more influential than either the severity of a father's PTSD or the level of family functioning. The presence of violence not only makes the family system as a whole at risk for extreme dysfunction but the individual children in these families at risk for developing maladaptive behaviors and dysfunction (Harkness and Giller, 1992). This present study assessed the influence of the severity of the father's PTSD symptomatology, the level of family functioning, and the presence or absence of violent behavior in the veteran father on the child's social competence and behavior patterns. These independent variables (severity of PTSD, level of family functioning, and violence) have been proposed in the clinical literature to be important to a child's development.

Subjects and Procedure

After describing the study to the veteran father and obtaining his informed consent, he received the Structured Clinical Interview for DSM III-R (SCID) (for PTSD) (Spitzer and Williams, 1985) and Schedule for Affective Disorders and Schizophrenia (SADS) (Endicott and Spitzer, 1978) diagnostic interviews. If the veteran was diagnosed as having PTSD by DSM III-R criteria and did not meet research diagnostic criteria (Spitzer, Endicott, and Robbins, 1978) for schizophrenia or bipolar illness and gave written informed consent, he was further interviewed about his war experiences using the Jackson Interview (Keane et al., 1985), Figley's Structured Interview for PTSD (Figley, 1977), Horowitz, Wilner, and Alvarez's Impact of Events Scale (1979), and the VESI Stress Questionnaire (Wilson and Drauss, 1980). These instruments were used to assess combat exposure and severity of PTSD symptoms. He was also asked to complete a demographic questionnaire that included questions about psychosocial adjustment since the war.

A time was then scheduled to meet with the other members of his family, including all children above the age of six, pending the willingness of the wife and children to participate. These meetings occurred either at a local U.S. Department of Veterans Affairs Medical Center or at a Vietnam Veteran Outreach Center (Vet Center).

Of the forty-eight veterans recruited from Vietnam Veteran Outreach Centers, Vietnam Veterans of America chapters, and from the local VA Medical Center's Outpatient Mental Hygiene Clinic, forty-two met the inclusion criteria. Two wives refused to participate in the study. In the forty families who completed the study, all eighty-six children ages six to sixteen participated.

After explaining the purpose of the study to the family and obtaining informed consent, each member was asked to complete the Family Adaptability Cohesion (FACES II) (Olson et al., 1982) and the Parent-Child Communication Scale (Olson et al., 1982) as the measures of family function. To assess child functioning, two variations of the same form were used: the Achenbach Child Behavior Checklist (CBCL) (Achenbach and Endlbrook, 1983) and the teacher's form of the Child Behavior Checklist, the TBCL (Achenbach and Endlbrook, 1983). Both self-administered questionnaires measure the social competencies and behavioral problems of children ages four to sixteen, as reported by their parents or teacher. The nine behavior scales derived from the 118 behavioral problem items are schizoid or anxious, depressed, uncommunicative, obsessive-compulsive, somatic complaints, social withdrawal, hyperactive, aggressive, and delinquent. Derived from these are two more general factors called internalizing and externalizing behaviors.

With the parents' signed release of information, each child's teacher was asked to complete the TBCL. The TBCL behavior and competence scales that teachers score differ from those the parent scores. Behavior and competencies not evident to parents may be of great concern to teachers. Therefore, teachers are asked to provide competence information that focuses on the provision of special services, repetition of grades, ratings of academic performance, and on four general adaptive characteristics: how hard the child works, how appropriately the child behaves, how much the child is learning, and how happy the child is. Although the parents' and teachers' scores cannot be directly compared, together they give a better picture of child competence and behavior patterns. The higher the child's score for any scale, the more problematic the child's behavior.

Data are presented in two ways. Raw subscale scores are used to report on specific sex and age groups and to compare them with both a normative and clinic-seeking group of age mates. Second, to compare groups other than by age and sex, e.g., by severity of PTSD, T scores were used to allow comparison across age and sex groups.

Results

The children in this study resembled a clinic-seeking sample on many of the CBCL scales. For girls ages six to eleven, all but one behavior scale score was similar to those of a clinical sample. For girls ages twelve to sixteen, all the subscale mean scores were in the clinical range except the immature/hyperactive, schizoid, and delinquent scale scores, which were between the clinical and nonclinical values. For boys ages six to eleven, all the behavior scale scores were in the clinical range; and for boys ages twelve to sixteen, most of the behavior scale scores were in the clinical range. The only scales not in the clinical range in the male ages twelve to sixteen group were the immature behavior and obsessive/compulsive behavior subscales, which fell between the nonclinical and clinical scores. For all groups, internalizing and externalizing factor scores were in the clinical range (Table 1). On the total competence scale, this sample scored in the clinical range mainly due to their low activity subscale scores (Table 1). On both the social and school competence subscales, this sample scored between the clinical and nonclinical scores.

Effect of Severity of PTSD

To examine the effect of the severity of father's PTSD symptoms and level of family functioning on CBCL scores, several additional analyses were performed. Using T scores, a 2 x 3 ANOVA (severity x level of family functioning) showed a main effect of level of family functioning on both the Internalizing and Externalizing Behavior Scale scores (Table 2). Tukey post-hoc t-tests revealed that children from lower-functioning families (as measured by the FACES II), regardless of the severity of the father's PTSD symptoms, scored significantly

Table 1. Child Behavior Checklist Scale T Scores for This Study and Other Normative and Clinical Samples (Values Are Mean ± SD)

	Current Study	Clinical Sample	Nonclinical Sample* (n = 300)
Girls 6–11 (n=46)			
Internalizing	63.4 ± 9.7*	67.0 ± 9.1	51.3 ± 9.1
Externalizing	63.5 ± 11.1*	68.1 ± 9.5	51.0 ± 9.5
Social competence	40.3 ± 1.51*	36.7 ±10.0	51.1 ± 9.7
Girls 12–16 (n=34)			
Internalizing	60.0 ± 8.7*	64.3 ± 8.4	49.8 ± 8.0
Externalizing	57.4 ± 8.6*	64.0 ± 8.6	49.4 ± 7.5
Social competence	44.7 ± 16.9*	36.9 ± 9.8	50.9 ±10.0
Boys 6–11 (n=22)			
Internalizing	63.6 ± 9.7*	65.6 ± 8.9	51.2 ± 9.1
Externalizing	65.5 ± 9.9*	68.1 ± 8.7	51.0 ± 9.3
Social competence	39.8 ± 13.4*	37.0 ± 9.0	51.0 ±10.0
Boys 12–16 (n=22)			
Internalizing	62.0 ± 9.3 *	64.7 ± 8.2	51.3 ± 9.0
Externalizing	59.6 ± 10.1	66.2 ± 8.1	51.4 ± 8.9
Social competence	40.8 ± 11.0*	35.5 ± 9.2	50.9 ±10.1

* Ratings comparable to a clinical sample as reported by Achenbach and Endlbrook, 1983.

Table 2. CBCL Individual Children T Scores Compared by Severity of Father's PTSD Symptoms and Level of Family Functioning (Values Are Means ± SD)

	Low	Mild	High	F	P
Internalizing					
Mild PTSD	65.4 ± 10.2	59.2 ± 8.2	57.0 ± 7.8	7.26	.0001
Severe PTSD	66.7 ± 8.5	59.1 ± 7.1	58.3 ± 7.8		
Externalizing					
Mild PTSD	63.8 ± 12.2	60.3 ± 9.3	56.3 ± 8.8	4.22	.001
Severe PTSD	65.3 ± 9.0	60.1 ± 8.9	55.4 ± 8.0		
Social Competence					
Mild PTSD	39.4 ± 19.6	44.2 ± 14.8	42.9 ± 10.0	0.59	.711
Severe PTSD	39.6 ± 10.1	41.8 ± 12.8	41.9 ± 12.9		

higher (more problematic) than children from higher-functioning families on both the Internalizing and Externalizing Behavior Scales. No significant main effect of severity of PTSD or interaction between severity of PTSD and level of family functioning was found on any of the other scores. When family mean CBCL T scale scores, rather than individual child T scores, were used, a 2 x 3 ANOVA (severity of PTSD x level of family functioning) showed a main effect of level of family functioning only on the internalizing behavior factor (Table 3). Tukey post-hoc t-tests revealed that children from lower-functioning families, regardless of the severity of PTSD symptoms, scored significantly higher than children from higher-functioning families on the internalizing behavior scale. No significant main effect of severity of PTSD or interaction between severity of PTSD and level of functioning was found on this scale. No significant difference was found among groups on the externalizing behavior or social competency scale T scores.

Table 3. CBCL Family T Scores Compared by Severity of Father's PTSD Symptoms and Level of Family Functioning (Values Are Means ± SD)

	Low	Mild	High	F	P
Internalizing					
Mild PTSD	61.5 ± 10.2	58.6 ± 5.2	57.9 ± 5.0	3.35	.015
Severe PTSD	67.9 ± 7.0	59.0 ± 4.0	58.3 ± 6.7		
Externalizing					
Mild PTSD	59.1 ± 10.2	60.0 ± 7.3	58.4 ± 6.5	1.43	.240
Severe PTSD	66.3 ± 6.9	58.5 ± 9.7	55.4 ± 4.8		
Social Competence					
Mild PTSD	43.9 ± 13.6	41.6 ± 9.2	44.7 ± 8.3	0.39	.851
Severe PTSD	38.9 ± 5.4	43.9 ± 12.2	41.9 ± 14.0		

Violence

Because of the effect of paternal violent behavior on family functioning found in the previous study (Harkness and Giller, 1992), children were grouped by presence or absence of current violent behavior in the father. Significant differences were found on the Internalizing and Externalizing Behavior Scale T scores (Table 4), the school performance scale T score, and total competency scale T score. Children ages six to eleven from families with a violent father were more aggressive and delinquent; girls this age were more socially withdrawn. These problems seem to increase for the older children. Not only were both boys' and girls' behavior scale scores in the clinic-seeking sample range, but the scores of boys ages twelve to sixteen were *higher* than the clinic-seeking sample.

Table 4. CBCL Scale T Scores for Children from Families with Violent vs Nonviolent Fathers as Reported by Fathers and Mothers (Values Are Mean ± SD)

	Nonviolent (n=102)	Violent (n=70)	t	p
Behavior Scales				
Internalizing	59.2 ± 7.9	67.1 ± 9.5	5.73	.0001
Externalizing	58.7 ± 9.1	66.0 ± 10.5	4.76	.0001
Social Competence Scales				
Activity	41.5 ± 12.0	39.4 ± 10.2	1.28	.201
Social	44.6 ± 9.2	41.5 ± 14.0	1.59	.114
School	46.8 ± 12.7	42.2 ± 13.9	2.16	.032
Total competency	43.3 ± 14.5	37.9 ± 12.7	2.59	.011

School

Of the eighty-six children who participated in the study, 64 percent of their teachers completed and returned the teacher's TBCL. In terms of their overall social competence and behavior mean scale scores, these fifty-five children were similar to the full sample of the eighty-six.

When teachers' and parents' internalizing and externalizing scores were compared, it was found that the teachers saw these fifty-five children as significantly less internalizing and externalizing than did either of their parents (Table 5), i.e., less anxious, less socially withdrawn, less nervous, less inattentive, and less aggressive. When compared with scale norms, the teachers' scores saw this group of children as falling between the non-clinic-seeking and clinic-seeking sample. On the behavior subscale scores, when teacher's mean T scores for each behavior scale were compared first by severity of father's PTSD and then by level of family functioning, no significant differences were found between groups.

Table 5. Comparison among Mother's, Father's, and Teacher's Mean T Scores on CBCL Internalizing and Externalizing Behavior Scales (Mean ± SD (n=55))

	Mother	Father	Teacher	F	P
Internalizing	62.6 + 9.6	60.3 + 9.2	54.0 + 9.0	12.60	.0001
Externalizing	61.2 + 10.9	60.1 + 10.6	52.8 + 11.9	9.39	.0001

Comparison: Mother=Father>Teacher

When teacher's mean scale T scores for each behavior scale were compared by presence or absence of violent behavior in the father, however, significant differences were found in many behavior scale scores (Table 6). Children from families with violence were significantly more anxious, unpopular, inattentive, and aggressive. There was also a strong tendency for them to be more socially withdrawn, immature, and self-destructive. In the area of social competence, teachers reported a tendency for the children of fathers with severe PTSD to perform less well academically than children of fathers with mild PTSD (p=.065). Teachers also reported that these children do not learn as much (p=.087). No difference was found between groups on comparison of hard working, appropriateness of behavior, or happiness. Teachers reported no significant differences in social competency scores among children from low-, middle-, or high-functioning families. A tendency (p=.085), however, was found for children from low-functioning families to be less happy than children from higher-functioning families.

Table 6. Teacher's CBCL Behavior Scale T Scores for Children from Families with Nonviolent and Violent Fathers (Values Are Mean ± SD)

	Nonviolent (n=33)	Violent (n=22)	t	p
Anxious	56.9 ± 3.3	59.9 ± 5.5	2.31	.025
Social withdrawal	57.4 ± 4.2	60.9 ± 8.3	1.84	.072
Unpopular	57.4 ± 4.8	62.5 ± 8.9	2.47	.017
Obsessive/compulsive	59.0 ± 6.8	62.8 ± 9.0	1.15	.262
Inattentive	56.9 ± 3.7	60.8 ± 7.8	2.17	.035
Immature	56.6 ± 2.7	62.7 ± 7.6	1.90	.070
Self-destructive	59.3 ± 5.2	62.8 ± 7.1	1.97	.054
Aggressive	57.0 ± 4.4	62.5 ± 10.1	2.42	.019
Nervous	60.6 ± 10.2	61.6 ± 7.6	.31	.760

There were a number of significant differences between the violent and nonviolent groupings (Table 7). Children from families with violent fathers performed significantly more poorly academically, did not learn as much, and tended to be less happy. There was a tendency for them to behave less appropriately. Thus, as with the parents' reported scores, violence seems to be more of a discriminating variable in children's social competencies than severity of PTSD symptoms.

Table 7. Teacher's TBCL Social Competency Scale Scores for Children from Families with Nonviolent and Violent Fathers (Values Are Mean ± SD)

	Nonviolent (n=33)	Violent (n=22)	t	p
Academic performance	3.5 ± 0.8	2.7 ± 0.7	3.70	.0001
Externalizing	4.4 ± 1.7	3.7 ± 1.8	1.33	.190
Behaving appropriately	4.5 ± 1.6	3.6 ± 1.6	1.88	.066
Learn much	4.8 ± 1.4	3.8 ± 1.7	2.25	.029
Happy	4.6 ± 1.3	3.8 ± 1.6	1.98	.058

Discussion

This study of eighty-six children from forty families found that many children resemble a clinic-seeking sample of age mates on many problematic behavior scales, and are, therefore, identifiable as children "at risk" for developing more severe psychiatric disorders. In general, parents saw their children as depressed, anxious, somatizing, schizoid, uncommunicative, hyperactive, aggressive, and delinquent, with boys being perceived as having slightly more problems. Within this "high-risk" group, a lower level of family functioning and current violent behavior in the father were found to be significantly associated with the behavior problems of the children.

It is important to note that teachers saw a subgroup of fifty-five of these eighty-six children as significantly less behaviorally problematic than did the children's parents, rating them as more similar to the non-clinic-seeking normative sample. This may reflect parental concerns and preoccupations that heavily weigh on their observations. It may also be that when the child is in the family environment, he or she is triangulated into a dysfunctional family role, but outside the family, the same child, without role expectations, may behave differently.

Parental perceptions can influence children's behavior; if parents see their child as problematic, the likelihood of the child behaving that way is increased. In this study, very few differences were found between fathers' and mothers' perceptions of child behaviors and social competencies. This was surprising because in the survivor literature, particularly in researching the Holocaust, several writers (Rakoff, Sigal, and Epstein, 1965; Sigal, Silver, and Rakoff, 1973) hypothesized that the survivor parent(s) tended to be either overly harsh and judgmental, to hold high expectations for their children, or to be overly lenient in their perceptions of them.

A major finding of this study, supported by both the parent and teacher ratings, was that children from families with a violent father were significantly more likely than children from families where the father was not violent to have more behavior problems, poorer school performance, and lower social competence. Girls ages six to eleven years with violent fathers were more frequently perceived as socially withdrawn and delinquent. All mean scores for girls ages twelve to sixteen from families with a violent father were in the clinical range, with externalizing behavior aggressive scale score and *all* internalizing behavior scores (anxious/obsessive, schizoid, depressed/withdrawn, and immature/hyperactive) significantly higher than for girls with nonviolent fathers. For younger boys with a violent father, all externalizing behavior scores were significantly higher than for boys ages six to eleven with a nonviolent father; boys ages twelve to sixteen with a violent father showed all behavior scale scores higher than even the clinic-seeking mean.

Teachers' scores corroborated this perception. They reported these children as demonstrating poorer academic performance, not learning as much, not behaving appropriately, and less happy than their peers. They also reported them as more anxious, socially withdrawn, unpopular, inattentive, immature, self-destructive, and aggressive. Violent behavior has a powerfully destructive effect on children, and this effect in these families appears to be more influential than either the father's PTSD or the level of family functioning. In this study, violence was most strongly related to lower level of family functioning (families with lower cohesion and adaptability), lower socioeconomic status, larger family size, and unemployment or underemployment. In addition, a prominent symptom of PTSD, social isolation and alienation, is another social and family factor that often increases the likelihood of family violence (Steele, 1978). Violent behavior in the father was shown to have a great impact on general family functioning, which, in this study, has significant influence on the child's function. Research has shown that veterans with PTSD experience a high incidence of marital discord and domestic violence as well as higher unemployment, drug and alcohol abuse, and social isolation (Figley, 1977). The causal relationship among these variables is unclear. For example, does the unemployment lead to increased symptoms (substance abuse, violence, and social isolation) or does an increase in symptoms lead to unemployment and thus influence general family functioning and child behavior?

Clinical Implications

To date, the connections between violent behavior, PTSD, and child development have not been a focus of significant professional attention. This study represents the first work to examine the transgenerational effects of combat-related PTSD on the veteran's family system, especially on children's social competence and behavior patterns. The findings of this study raise questions about preventive programs not only for children of combat veterans with PTSD who are from lower-functioning families or whose fathers are violent, but also raise questions about children in general from families where there is violence. Effective intervention and treatment begins with identifying these families and, therefore, the children in these families as "high risk" and identifying, through an early comprehensive assessment, specific problem areas. This assessment needs to focus on individual and family dynamics, including violence, which always has a negative effect on family stability and emotional tone. Individual, couple, and family therapy may all be necessary, dependent upon the individual case and family circumstances. Clearly, treatment considerations will vary depending on who is the focus of treatment.

Many child behaviors reported by the parents resemble behaviors exhibited by the father, e.g., depression, anxiety, low frustration tolerance, and outbursts of anger. In working with these children, clinicians need to be sensitive to the presence of these behaviors in the father as they diagnose and treat the child. The strengthening of ego functions should be a major focus of treatment with these children with an emphasis on reality-testing, increasing frustration tolerance, and encouragement of verbalization as an alternative to reenactment. These children need to recognize their separateness from their fathers and be helped to discover that being different from their dad would be what would make him most proud. They need to become aware that they are not responsible for their parents' behavior and pain and do not need to feel guilty about it. They can thus gain needed distance from the intensity of family interactions and begin to address their own developmental concerns more appropriately.

The whole question of family and its role in the psychosocial generational transmission of trauma needs to be more clearly explored. During development, a child is subjected to an array of factors that affect him or her. These factors include the quality of the parents' interaction with each other and with the child, the mother's personality and her reactions to the father's PTSD, and the influence it has on the family life, the family dynamics, the child's constitution, and other life circumstances. These factors may aggravate or ameliorate particular potential problems.

From the studies of Holocaust survivors, children of psychiatrically disturbed parents, and this study, it is clearly important to continue to identify early those factors that make these children "high risk" and also continue to develop a knowledge base for the future that will guide clinicians toward more optimum interventions. Finally, longitudinal follow-up studies are needed that both assess further the risks in the different age groups and examine what happens to these families and children with treatment.

References

Achenbach, T., and C. Endlbrook. 1983. *Manual for the Child Behavior Checklist and Revised Child Behavior Profile*. Burlington, VT: Queen City Printers Inc.

American Psychiatric Association. 1980. *Diagnostic and Statistical Manual of Mental Disorders III.* Washington, DC: American Psychiatric Association.

Beardslee, W.R., J. Bemporad, M.J. Keller, and G.L Klerman. 1983. Children of parents with major affective disorder: A Review. *American Journal of Psychiatry* 140(7):825-832.

Beisser, A., M. Glasser, and M. Grant. 1967. Psychosocial adjustment in the children of schizophrenic mothers. *Journal of Nervous and Mental Disease* 145(2):429-440.

DeFazio, V., and M. Pascucci. 1984. Return to Ithaca: A perspective on marriage and love in post-traumatic stress disorder. *Journal of Contemporary Psychotherapy* 14:76-89.

Endicott, J., and R.L. Spitzer. 1978. A diagnostic interview: The schedule for affective disorders and schizophrenia. *Archives of General Psychiatry* 35:837-844.

Erlenmeyer-Kimling, L. 1975. A prospective study of children at risk for schizophrenia: Methodological considerations and some preliminary findings. In *Life History Research in Psychopathology* 4, ed. R. Wirt, G. Winokur, and M. Roff. Minneapolis: University of Minnesota Press.

Erlenmeyer-Kimling, L., Y. Marcuse, B. Cornblatt, D. Friedman, J. Rainer, and J. Rutschmann. 1981. The New York high risk project. In *Children at Risk for Schizophrenia: A Longitudinal Perspective*, ed. N.F. Watt, E.J. Anthony, L.C. Wynne, and J. Roff. New York: Cambridge University Press.

Figley, C.R. 1977. *The American Legion Study and Psychological Adjustment Among Vietnam Veterans*. Lafayette, IN: Purdue University.

Figley, C.R., ed. 1978. *Stress Disorders Among Vietnam Veterans: Theory, Research and Treatment*. New York: Brunner/Mazel.

Figley, C.R. 1980. Lecture delivered at the VA REMC, St. Louis, MO.

Figley, C.R., and S. Leventman. 1980. *Strangers at Home: Vietnam Veterans Since the War*. New York: Praeger.

Garmezy, N. 1974. Children at risk: The search for antecedents of schizophrenia. Part I. Conceptual models and research methods. *Schizophrenia Bulletin* 8:55-125.

Haley, S. 1983. The Vietnam veteran and his pre-school child: Child rearing as a delayed stress in combat veterans. *Journal of Contemporary Psychotherapy* 14(1):114-121.

Harkness, L.L., and E.G. Giller. 1992. Families of Vietnam veterans with post-traumatic stress disorder: Cohesion, adaptability and communication in the family. Unpublished manuscript.

Horowitz, M., N. Wilner, and W. Alvarez. 1979. Impact of event scale: A measure of subjective distress. *Psychosomatic Medicine* 41:209-218.

Keane, T.M., J.A. Fairbank, J.M. Caddell, R.T. Zimering, and M.E. Bender. 1985. A behavioral approach to assessing and treating PTSD in Vietnam veterans. In *Trauma and Its Wake*, ed. C.R. Figley. New York: Brunner/Mazel.

Kestenberg, J. 1980. Psychoanalyses of children of survivors from the Holocaust: Case presentations and assessment. *American Journal of the Psychoanalytic Association* 28:775-804.

Krell, R. 1982. Family therapy with children of concentration camp survivors. *American Journal of Orthopsychiatry* 36:513-522.

Krystal, H., ed. 1968. *Massive Psychic Trauma*. New York: International Universities Press.

Kulka, R.A., W.E. Schlenger, J.A. Fairbank, R.L. Hough, B.K. Jordon, C.R. Marmar, and D.S. Weiss. 1990. *Trauma and the Vietnam War Generation: Report of Findings from the National Vietnam Readjustment Study*. New York: Brunner/Mazel.

Levine, H. 1982. Toward a psychoanalytic understanding of children of survivors of the Holocaust. *Psychoanalytic Quarterly* LI:70-92.

Matsakis, A. 1988. Survey results: Effects of PTSD on family life. *Vet Center Voice* 9:10-12.

Niederland, W.G. 1981. The survivor syndrome: Some further observations and dimensions. *American Journal of the Psychoanalytic Association* 29:413-425.

Olson, D., D. Sprenkle, and C. Russell. 1979. Circumplex model of marital and family systems: Cohesion and adaptability dimensions, family types and clinical applications. *Family Process* 18:3-15.

Olson, D., D. Sprenkle, and C. Russell. 1983. Circumplex model of marital and family systems: VI. Theoretical update. *Family Process* 22:69-83.

Olson, D., H. McCubbin, H. Barnes, A. Larsen, M. Muxen, and M. Wilson. 1982. *Family Inventories*. Beverley Hills, CA: Sage Publishing.

Rakoff, V., J. Sigal, and N. Epstein. 1965. Children and families of concentration camp survivors. *Canada's Mental Health* XIV:24-26.

Robinson, S., and H. Winnick. 1978. Second generation of the Holocaust. *Israel Journal of Psychiatry* 18:99-107.

Rolf, J.E. 1972. The social and academic competence of children vulnerable to schizophrenia and other behavior pathologies. *Journal of Abnormal Psychology* 80:225-243.

Rosenheck, R. 1985a. Father-son relationships in malignant post Vietnam stress syndrome. *American Journal of Social Psychiatry* V(1) Winter: 19-23.

Rosenheck, R. 1985b. Malignant post Vietnam stress syndrome. *American Journal of Orthopsychiatry* 55(2):166-176.

Rosenheck, R. 1986. Impact of post-traumatic stress disorder of World War II on the next generation. *Journal of Nervous and Mental Disease* 174:319-327.

Rosenheck, R., and P. Nathan. 1984. Secondary traumatization in children of Vietnam veterans with post-traumatic stress disorder. *Hospital and Community Psychiatry* 36:538-540.

Sigal, J., D. Silver, and F. Rakoff. 1973. Some second generation effects of survival of the Nazi persecution. *American Journal of Orthopsychiatry* 43:320-327.

Sonnenberg, S. 1974. Children of survivors. *American Journal of the Psychoanalytic Association* 22(1).

Spitzer, R.L., and J.B. Williams. 1985. Instruction manual for the structured clinical interview for DSM-III (SCID). New York: Biometrics Research Department, New York State Psychiatric Institute.

Spitzer, R.L., J. Endicott, and E. Robbins. 1978. Research diagnostic criteria. *Archives of General Psychiatry* 35:773-782.

Steele, B. 1978. The child abuser. In *Violence: Perspectives on Murder and Aggression*, ed. I. Katash, S. Katash, and L. Schesinger. San Francisco: Jossey-Bass.

Strauss, M., R. Gelles, and S. Steinmetz. 1980. *Behind Closed Doors: Violence in the American Family*. New York: Doubleday/Anchor.

Weissman, M.M., J.K. Leckman, D.G. Gammon, and B. Prusoff. 1984. Depression and anxiety disorders in parents and children. *Archives of General Psychiatry* 41:845-852.

Wilson, J.P., and G.E. Drauss. 1980. *Vietnam Era Stress Inventory*. Unpublished inventory.

Art as a Therapeutic Technique: Addressing the Clinical Issues of Children of Vietnam Veterans

Holly Theodore Finan, M.A., and Michele McCutcheon, B.A.
Skagit Community Mental Health Center
Mount Vernon, WA

Abstract

This paper examines the use of art as a therapeutic technique for addressing the clinical issues of children of Vietnam veterans in a community mental health center program funded by the Agent Orange Class Assistance Program (AOCAP). Children of many veterans who have experienced post-traumatic stress disorder (PTSD) often encounter multiple stressors during extended periods in their lives. Within the therapeutic process these children may have difficulty expressing themselves verbally or may deny feelings because they do not want to betray the trust of their parents. Inclusion of artistic expression in the therapeutic design has been helpful in addressing the emotional content of the child's life.

Case studies of three children who have participated in this technique illustrate the five elements of the therapeutic process: family history, nonverbal behavior, form and style of artistic expression, child's description of the art, and the therapeutic intervention. The researchers conclude that art can be an effective bridge between a child's inner symbolic representations and the more direct experiential content in his or her everyday life.

Holly Theodore Finan, M.A., *received a master's degree in clinical psychology and child, family, and marriage counseling from Antioch University, Los Angeles, CA. She has worked extensively in the field of trauma for the past ten years, including work with veterans and disaster relief.* ***Michele McCutcheon, B.A.,*** *is currently completing a master's degree in cultural anthropology at Western Washington University with a curriculum emphasis on childhood and cultural diversity. She has worked with children in foster care services and with victims of domestic violence and sexual abuse.*

When children of Vietnam veterans experience emotional and psychological difficulties in their lives, they may currently apply for services through the Vietnam Veterans Family Service Program. By focusing exclusively on the needs of children and the family unit, this program fills a gap not previously addressed. The purpose of the Skagit Community Mental Health Center program is to provide short-term support services, including counseling, to children and family members of Vietnam veterans: to provide assessment, education, and case consultation through the use of a multidisciplinary team; to address the special mental health needs of children with disabilities, be they physical, developmental, or learning in nature; to act as advocates for children with special needs; and to provide referrals to other community resources.

As a result of an affiliation with the Mental Health Center, much of our client contact focuses on providing children of Vietnam veterans with individual and family counseling. We have seen that many of the clinical issues exhibited by these children, such as anxiety, depression, isolation, lack of trust, low self-esteem, and concern with personal safety, are indirectly related to the readjustment issues and post-traumatic stress disorder (PTSD) symptoms surrounding the parent's combat exposure in Vietnam.

Unlike many other kinds of trauma, such as the exposure to a single event, or the overt pain of more long-term kinds of abuse, traumas that children of Vietnam veterans experience are often not as obviously or as easily defined. The children we treat in our Agent Orange Class Assistance Program (AOCAP) have experienced multiple stressors and significant losses over a long period. They are forced to learn a multitude of coping skills in order to adapt to the constant change in their lives. These children often live with the results of prolonged exposure to, or perpetration of, traumatic incidents by their veteran parents. This can create special difficulties for the children of Vietnam veterans.

One of the greatest challenges for our program has been to encourage these children to examine the traumatic events and emotions they have experienced within their family system. For a variety of reasons, Vietnam veterans' children, especially those who are very young, often have difficulty addressing these issues in traditional therapeutic settings. We have found that these children may deny their feelings in the therapeutic session because they do not want to betray the trust of their parents. This is one reason why we have incorporated artistic expression into our therapeutic design. The free expression of the artwork allows the child to identify problem areas nonverbally for the therapist. Not only does the artwork become the medium through which the child can examine the emotional content of his or her life, it also allows for the separation of self from the trauma, making the therapeutic setting emotionally safe.

This paper examines three children from our program to illustrate the uses of art for addressing the clinical issues of children of Vietnam veterans. We have combined five elements of our therapeutic process into a single technique. These elements include a working knowledge of the family history, the child's nonverbal behavior, the form and style of artistic media, the child's description of the art, and the therapeutic intervention employed. This paper has not been written or intended to perpetuate the stereotype that all Vietnam veterans suffer from chronic PTSD symptoms or recurrent readjustment issues. Rather, it is intended to show through example how the use of this technique has had an impact on the quality of the therapeutic process within our program.

Combat Trauma and Its Impact on the Family

Although the Vietnam War has been over for almost two decades, combat traumas continue to affect Vietnam veterans in the form of readjustment issues and PTSD symptoms. Horowitz and Solomon (1978) were among the first to predict that stress response syndromes, such as PTSD, may periodically resurface throughout a trauma victim's life. PTSD, as outlined in the DSM III-R Statistical Manual (1987), is often the diagnosis associated with the particular stress response syndrome experienced by Vietnam veterans. Veterans diagnosed with PTSD may have some or all of the following symptoms: intrusions of trauma, emotional numbing, recurrent nightmares, isolating behaviors, anger, and hypervigilance. Recent studies indicate that stress responses can be reactivated many years after the initial trauma exposure (Solomon, Garb, Belich, and Grupper, 1987; Van der Kolk and Greenberg, 1987; and Scaturo and Hayman, 1992).

The reactivated traumas are not always triggered by specific events related to the initial combat exposure. Many mental health professionals believe that significant life changes, associated with stressful family readjustments, can reactivate the veteran's combat traumas (Stanton and Figley, 1978; Haley, 1984; and Scaturo and Hayman, 1992). Such a mechanism might contribute to the apparent delay in onset of symptomatic behavior. This is one explanation for the delayed response syndromes that many veterans experience.

Although family adjustments may reactivate the veteran's combat traumas, the veteran is not the only one affected. The family also reacts to the veteran's PTSD symptoms. The veteran's coping mechanisms often become enmeshed in the functioning of the family, and thereby perpetuate and institutionalize PTSD symptoms into the family system (Stanton and Figley, 1978). In extreme cases, the veteran's coping mechanisms are expressed in the form of physical, sexual, or emotional abuse.

It has only been in recent years that the impact of these combat traumas on the children and families of Vietnam veterans has been recognized in the literature (Rosenheck and Nathan, 1985). Parsons, Kehle, and Owen (1990) conducted a study of the children of PTSD-rated Vietnam veterans. Their results indicated a possible connection between the child's emotional and social functioning and the veteran's PTSD symptoms.

The problem with the priorities of many therapeutic approaches is that the focus of the treatment centers is on the individual veteran. By ignoring the family system, the therapeutic design allows for the perpetuation of the veteran's issues by the family members. To effectively treat PTSD, the entire family must be involved in the therapeutic process (Terr, 1989; and Figley, 1988). Not only is it important for the veteran to learn new skills for coping with family stress, but the individual family members must learn to recognize the patterns that perpetuate and enable the veteran's PTSD symptoms (Hendrix, 1989).

During the course of our work with children in the AOCAP program, we observed that many clients had difficulties expressing themselves verbally. In an attempt to identify and treat the psychological and emotional issues of clients who had problems talking in session, we began encouraging them to express themselves using various artistic media. We soon noted that art could be an especially effective means of establishing rapport with clients, ultimately allowing us to address deeper issues with them.

The Therapeutic Method: Five Elements

We have combined five elements into a therapeutic method that uses art for addressing the clinical issues of children of Vietnam veterans. These elements include: family history, nonverbal behavior, form and style of artistic media, description of the art, and the therapeutic intervention. The goal of our method is to provide a safe environment that engages children in examining and communicating the clinical issues and dysfunctional patterns within their family systems. We have designed these elements to incorporate the perspectives of the child, the family, and the therapist in order to provide holism to the therapeutic process.

The family history includes the initial assessment conducted with one or both of the parents. This element includes a general history of family functioning, the veteran's PTSD symptoms, and the issues surrounding the child's referral to our program. This information provides us with a working knowledge of the child's history and incorporates the family perspective into the therapeutic method.

The nonverbal behavior element consists of direct observation of the client's behavior during the actual drawing of the artpiece. We have found that this is an important component of the child's communication about his or her issues. Although the child may not be ready to verbalize feelings regarding specific traumas, he or she communicates through body posture the kinds of emotions experienced while drawing a picture of a traumatic event. This elicits important information that the therapist can use in determining the appropriate therapeutic interventions.

The form and style of artistic media is examined in relation to the child's control and commitment of the media used in the artpiece (Wadeson, 1987). We provide the child with a variety of materials and allow him to choose the types of media used in the artwork. The media available to the children include clay, watercolors, paint, finger paint, pens, crayons, pencils, sand, and various types of paper. The child's choice of media, as well as use of space, balance, organization, and color, tells us something about the child's mood and intent of the artwork.

One of the most important elements of our method is the child's description of the completed artwork. This element provides the therapist with the child's perspective regarding his or her clinical issues. On completion of the task, the therapist asks the child to describe the artpiece in detail. This element elicits more relevant information that may not be readily recognizable to the therapist. The information provided may range from the description of symbols that have personal meaning to the child to the portrayal of personal objects.

The therapeutic intervention, the final element of this method, combines the family, child, and therapist's perspective. The therapist examines all of the information collected and establishes the appropriate interventions that need to take place during the course of the child's therapy. These interventions can have myriad functions such as aiding in the initial intake of the child, the establishment of the therapeutic goals of the service plan, the identification of medically related issues, the termination of the therapeutic alliance, or the transfer of a case to another therapist. The following case studies illustrate the use of this method in the treatment of children of Vietnam veterans within our AOCAP program.

Case Study 1

Art was used in our first sessions as a therapeutic technique for assessing the client's current emotional state and in identifying core issues and therapeutic goals. Earlier family therapy had been unsuccessful. The client was instructed to draw something of his own choosing (Figure 1, Figure 2, Figure 3, and Figure 4).

Family History

The ten-year-old male client lives with his mother, stepfather, and two sisters. He is the middle child. His parents divorced when he was two years old and he has had minimal contact with his biological father since that time. Both his father and his stepfather are Vietnam veterans. His stepfather suffers from PTSD and has received both inpatient treatment and outpatient counseling. The stepfather was physically abusive to the client in the past and a restraining order was issued against him. After a time he returned to the home with no reported abuse since that time. His own unresolved issues involving the death of children in Vietnam are exacerbated by conflicts with his stepson.

Figure 1

Figure 2

Figure 3

Figure 4

The client has become the focus of family problems with energy spent trying to "fix" him. It is the expressed belief in the family system that "fixing" the child's behavior will improve the overall family dynamics. Concerns had been voiced regarding the client's propensity for getting hurt, as had fears that he might be suicidal.

Nonverbal Behavior

The client was visibly distressed at our first meeting. His body was tense and his eye movement hypervigilant as he scanned the room. Once instructed to draw, he became single-mindedly intent and worked with silent diligence for the majority of our session. He made no attempts at any kind of contact until he finished his drawing.

Form and Style of Artistic Media

The client drew from left to right (Figure 1) before adding the fourth figure at the bottom of the page. He drew with a pencil, highlighting certain areas with darker lines, perhaps to show with intensity parts of his body that have been hurt in the past: an eye, a leg, and an arm. By using different colored permanent markers, including red, blue, black, and green, he shows commitment to the words the characters are trying to communicate.

"GO! GO! Rob" appears sad, mixed with a slight snarl of anger, while "Mr. Bun" may say something about the client's own ability to perceive that something is wrong. "Boo!" has proportional advantage and, larger than life, he insists on being noticed. Note that everything leads to him while at the same time "Death" emerges from him, joined together by common lines in the drawing. Although everything leads to "Boo!," "Death" is given the pivotal place in the drawing.

Child's Description of the Art

On completion, the client handed over the picture and said, "'Go! Go! Rob!' is what I think about being born, 'Mr. Bun' tells about getting hurt, 'Boo!' about being scared, and 'Death' about when the Grim Reaper comes to take me away."

The client went on to say that he might get robbed and sometimes it hurts so much it feels like he doesn't have an arm or a leg and he wants to die.

Therapeutic Intervention

Figure 1 set up a therapeutic framework that served as a reference point for the client throughout the course of treatment. Subsequent sessions focused on helping the client to name his fears and to work with them one by one.

As therapy continued over the weeks the client drew many other pictures. It became clear that he learned and communicated most effectively by what he could visualize. This visual method of communicating became a vital strength of the therapy. For the next few weeks he drew cartoon characters or creatures from movies and stories that depicted a sense of power for him (Figure 2). These characters possessed special powers, special weaponry, advanced intelligence, and forcefulness that they were willing to share with the client while he was feeling particularly helpless and vulnerable. Unable to speak about his hurts directly, the client seemed to benefit by giving life to the characters he drew on paper. These creatures helped him to continually confront and redefine "Go! Go! Rob," "Mr. Bun," "Boo!," and "Death."

Approximately six weeks into the treatment, the client was instructed to draw a picture about how he was feeling. He hurriedly drew a smiling face (Figure 3), reporting that "I am fine." He was then instructed to draw what it looked like before he was fine. He turned the paper over and drew a person falling into a hole (Figure 4), which he labeled "200 Feet." Returning to Figure 3, he finished his "After" drawing. The hole had been covered over by dirt and by flowers, yet the hole was still there. A figure is jumping up in the air, saying, "Yah! Hoo!," while he is falling over backwards.

Using a multidisciplinary team, the client was subsequently diagnosed with Attention-Deficit Hyperactivity Disorder (ADHD). Art became an effective monitor in determining an appropriate dosage of Ritalin. Lines were drawn in random, hurried scribbles when he had forgotten to take his medication during the day. This contrasted sharply with more focused, detailed drawings when the medication was properly used. The client became impatient with his mother's repeated emphasis on the importance of taking his medication. He was more receptive to the benefits he could experience himself by observing the content of his art. The use of art continues to create the continuity by which meaningful communication can take place in the therapy sessions.

Case Study 2

At our second meeting, the client reported that "everything is just fine" and she didn't have anything else to talk about after the disclosures of our first session. The client was instructed to draw a picture of her own choosing. The use of art at this stage of the therapeutic relationship was intended as a method to engage the client in further relevant dialogue, thereby indirectly enhancing the process of information gathering and problem assessment, which was critical at this stage of therapy (Figure 5).

Family History

The eleven-year-old client's parents have been divorced for several years. Until the mother's recent remarriage, the family all lived relatively close to one another in their home town. On moving to a town several hundred miles away with her mother, stepfather, and younger brother, the client was separated from her older brother and father, resulting in less-frequent contact with them. The client had been struggling with recent adjustment difficulties after returning from a prolonged visit with her father over the summer.

The client's stepfather served in Vietnam and has difficulties with anxiety and depression, which have been reactivated since becoming a stepfather. He has no children of his own. The family has been experiencing readjustment issues revolving around the veteran's behavior, which alternates between anger and withdrawal. Communication style also has been an issue in the family dynamic, with his use of put-downs and in his dismissing or belittling the client's feelings and physical hurts with his own, "bigger" misfortunes.

Nonverbal Behavior

The client was immediately purposeful. She began to draw in the lower section of the paper after announcing the subject of her artwork. Concentrating intently in silence while drawing the head and the body of a horse (Figure 5), she worked with quick and steady strokes. She momentarily observed her work and commented on it with confidence. When she moved on to the horse's legs, she started and hesitated several times, erasing and drawing again, while beginning to talk apologetically. She spent a great deal of time drawing the barn and the fence, then hesitantly drew the mountains in the background, almost as an afterthought. She smiled on completion of her picture, made eye contact, and handed over the picture.

Form and Style of Artistic Media

Figure 5

The client chose pencil for her drawing, showing a lack of commitment to the subject matter. The thin lines outlining the horse were contrasted by the heavier markings of the mane and tail, adding intensity to the animal's overall effect. The dense hair might be perceived as a metaphor for the client's own need to "cover things up" that day. We observe that, proportionally, the legs are too thin to hold up a horse of the size in her drawing, perhaps emphasizing her own feelings that there was little beneath to support her in her own life. The fence boldly divides the picture, separating the horse and the barn from the mountains beyond.

Child's Description of the Art

When the client was asked to draw a picture, she said, "Yes, I will draw you a horse." While drawing the head and body, she stated that she was a good artist. She indicated that she had learned by watching her older brother, who is "very talented" artistically. She mentioned that watching her brother draw had been an important part of their relationship and that she misses him very much. She commented that she is not good at drawing legs and still has more to learn from her older brother.

She also said that the picture was not any particular place that she knows, but that it reminds her of home and her friends. She talked about her interest in horses and the beauty she sees in the animal.

Therapeutic Intervention

At our initial meeting, the client had been eager to disclose her current life situation. She was able to clearly articulate her dilemma, to cry, and to share her feelings. Her need to be with her father was quite problematic because her mother had made it clear to the client that it hurts the mother's feelings when the client talks about wanting to be with her father. In meeting with the mother separately, it became clear she had intense feelings and unresolved anger towards her ex-husband and little patience with her daughter's affection towards him. It appeared that the client experienced real emotional consequences when she expressed positive feelings about her father to her mother. This was a tremendous weight that the client carried: aching to be with her father while fearful of losing her mother's affection and approval because of those feelings. Ameliorating this dynamic was identified as one of our therapeutic goals.

In this case study, the process of drawing became a vehicle for obtaining valuable information about an important relationship with her older brother, reminding her of an alternative source of support. Shifting the focus of communication away from the client's father and onto her brother accomplished several significant things. First, the client was able to articulate her brother's importance in her life. She identified him as an ally in her difficult life circumstances. And she talked about him without risking negative emotional consequences and loss of relatedness with her mother. She was able to share these feelings of loss and affection with her mother while holding the family honor in place by not directly discussing family issues with someone outside the family.

This experience allowed for a method of continuing the therapy in a way that was supported by the mother and less threatening for the client. Because the mother valued the artistic abilities of her children, using our therapeutic time in this manner was acceptable to her. It provided an avenue for continuing the therapeutic tasks of enhancing communications within the current family system and validating the content of the client's emotional life in a way that felt safe for her.

Case Study 3

During the course of therapy, there are times when it is necessary for a case to transfer to a new therapist. This is usually a difficult process for the client as well as the therapists. Case transfers are often emotionally complicated for the client because they involve the termination of the relationship with the previous therapist and the development of a relationship with the new therapist. Part of this process involves a period of getting to know the client's background and relevant issues. This process, if successful, will ensure that the new therapist will continue to meet the current therapeutic goals. This was the purpose of the therapeutic intervention for Figure 6. The client was instructed to draw a picture to express his emotions and issues to the new therapist.

Family History

The client is a fifteen-year-old male child of an in-country Vietnam veteran. His veteran father, who has been absent from the home for most of this boy's life, continues to struggle with readjustment issues concerning isolation and employment. Although he continues to have occasional contact with his father, he reports feeling disconnected from him. The client currently lives with his mother and two siblings. The family background consists of continual moves, resulting in a lack of stability and structure throughout his childhood.

This client was referred to our program by a school counselor who was concerned with his preoccupation with death. The client readily admits that much of his artistic endeavors and activities revolve around this theme, and are often accompanied by thoughts of suicidal ideation.

Figure 6

Nonverbal Behavior

There was no hesitation on the part of the client concerning the subject matter of the artwork. As soon as he was given the instructions he readily began selecting the media for his picture and immediately began drawing the scene. It was evident that the subject matter he had chosen for the scene appeared to be one with which he was quite familiar. He was very quiet and thoughtful while drawing and did not attempt to interact verbally until the picture was completed.

Form and Style of Artistic Media

The client chose a dramatic combination of two media for the artwork. His use of black and white contrast adds to the intensity of the scene. The bold permanent marker, used on the window frame and bed, gives commitment to these items in the picture, while the use of pencil, which is lightly used for the walls and top of the bed, adds to the lack of commitment to the room's structural components, namely the walls. Note that the shading does not come to the edges of the paper, which elicits a lack of boundaries for the scene. Perhaps this lack of commitment to the structural components of the room could be attributed to his own issues of lack of structure in his home life, representing his absent father and continual relocations.

The scene itself is well balanced with the bed and window placement at adjacent areas of the paper. The bed provides the scene with a three-dimensional quality, giving the observer the feeling of looking into this room and perhaps into the way the client feels about the current state of his life.

Child's Description of the Art

On completion of the drawing, he appeared to be very satisfied with his picture and was eager to share it with the new therapist. The disposition of his speech was more relaxed and descriptive than prior to the assignment of the art project. Initially, the client began the session by briefly describing the events in his life. He did not describe any emotions connected with these events. However, in the discussion of his artwork, the client was more descriptive about his feelings. When asked about the personal meaning that the scene had for him the client said, "I've been there before," giving the impression that the place he had depicted was a recurrent theme in his life.

Therapeutic Intervention

This therapeutic intervention not only allowed the client to express his feelings about his current clinical issues, but also served as a way of physically looking at those feelings. This process provided him with a graphic way of expressing his feelings to the new therapist, which may not otherwise have been verbalized by the client during an ordinary talk-therapy session. By understanding the client's perspective and combining this with the information provided by his family, the therapist was able to integrate an appropriate therapeutic service plan that could focus on his issues of depression and isolation and improve skills in family communication and peer relationships.

Discussion

Children and stepchildren of Vietnam veterans may have a multitude of difficulties and challenges that they face each day that are too overwhelming, undifferentiated, or complex to effectively communicate to another person. Many have made multiple moves with their families, hindering their ability to form lasting friendships. Some have had to adapt to multiple stepparents, have experienced physical abuse (Matsakis, 1988), or have lived with an alcoholic (Kulka, Schlenger, Fairbank et al., 1990) or withdrawn parent (Williams and Williams, 1987; and Matsakis, 1988). These compounded pressures over a prolonged period can sometimes interrupt a child's ability to recover from any single traumatic event in his life. They also create special challenges for those in the helping professions. Establishing communication in a way that is meaningful to both the child and the therapist becomes very important.

Because art can facilitate communication at the conscious and unconscious levels simultaneously (Erickson and Rossi, 1980), it is possible for the therapist to stay apprised of both verbal content and the child's inner experience. These two levels do not always have a direct relationship to one another. When viewed together, they give a more accurate "read" on the issues for any particular child.

Many of the children we have seen in our program have very rich, active inner lives and are well served in communicating that inner life to the therapist through the use of art in our sessions. Art is able to give outward visual form to inner feelings and sensations (Mills and Crowley, 1986), breaking through the insular barrier surrounding the feelings a child may have carried silently for many years. This gives the therapist the opportunity to gather important information about what is going on for the child beyond what the child may be able to articulate verbally.

Some children appear to have become desensitized to verbal communication, perhaps learning at an early age to "tune out" too much stimuli. They may have learned this as a coping mechanism to deflect the veteran's own discontentment, which he may project onto the child. In these situations, nonverbal methods of expression can be important, both as an effective tool of communication and as a means of providing temporary relief from current stressors.

Artistic content lends itself to the expression of personal metaphors. These metaphors can help children visualize problems as well as solutions while providing assistance in activating inner strengths and fostering confidence in one's own abilities as was illustrated in Case Study 1. Artwork also allows a child to go somewhere else in his or her imagination, to somewhere more pleasant or peaceful as illustrated by Case Study 2 or to a place where the child does not want to be as was illustrated in Case Study 3. When there is a high level of confusion and turmoil within the structure of the family unit, finding a quiet place can be a challenge. By providing a quiet, neutral space, with uninterrupted time and materials for self-expression, children can often find their own solutions to difficult problems in their lives by reworking their problems through the artistic process.

Through the use of our five-element method, we have had positive results in working with children of Vietnam veterans, discovering that art can be an effective bridge between a child's inner symbolic representations and the more direct experiential content in the child's everyday life.

References

American Psychiatric Association. 1987. *Diagnostic and Statistical Manual of Mental Disorders,* 3d ed. Washington, DC: American Psychiatric Association.

Erickson, M., and E. Rossi. 1980. Two-Level Communication and the Microdynamics of Trance and Suggestion. In *The Collected Papers of Milton H. Erickson on Hypnosis*, Vol. I:430-451. New York: Irvington.

Figley, C. 1988. A Five-Phase Treatment of Post-Traumatic Stress Disorder in Families. *Journal of Traumatic Stress* 1:127-141.

Haley, S. 1984. The Vietnam Veteran and His Preschool Child: Child Rearing as a Delayed Stress in Combat Veterans. *Journal of Contemporary Psychotherapy* 14:114-121.

Hendrix, C. 1990. "The Effects of Post-Traumatic Stress Disorder on Marital Cohesion, Expressiveness and Conflict: A Study of Vietnam Veterans." Doctoral dissertation, Kansas State University, KS.

Horowitz, M., and G. Solomon. 1978. Delayed Stress Response Syndromes in Vietnam Veterans. In *Stress Disorders Among Vietnam Veterans: Theory, Research, and Treatment,* ed. C. Figley, 268-280. New York: Brunner and Mazel, Pub.

Kulka, R., W. Schlenger, J. Fairbank, R. Hough, B. Jordan, C. Marmar, and D. Weiss. 1990. *Trauma and the Vietnam War Generation*. New York: Brunner and Mazel, Pub.

Matsakis, A. 1988. *Vietnam Wives: Women and Children Surviving Life with Veterans Suffering Post-Traumatic Stress Disorder.* Washington, DC: Woodbine House.

Mills, J., and R. Crowley. 1986. *Therapeutic Metaphors for Children*. New York: Brunner and Mazel, Pub.

Parsons, J., T. Kehle, and S. Owen. 1990. Incidence of Behavior Problems Among Children of Vietnam War Veterans. *School Psychology International* 11:253-259.

Rosenheck, R., and P. Nathan. 1985. Secondary Traumatization in Children of Vietnam Veterans. *Hospital and Community Psychiatry* 36:273-288.

Rubin, J. 1984. *Child Art Therapy*. New York: Van Nostrand Reinholt, Inc.

Scaturo, D., and P. Hayman. 1992. The Impact of Combat Trauma Across the Family Life Cycle: Clinical Considerations. *Journal of Traumatic Stress* 5:273-288.

Solomon, Z., R. Garb, A. Belich, and D. Grupper. 1987. Reactivation of Combat-Related Posttraumatic Stress Disorder. *American Journal of Psychiatry* 144:51-55.

Stanton, M., and C. Figley. 1978. Treating the Vietnam Veteran within the Family System. In *Stress Disorders Among Vietnam Veterans: Theory, Research and Treatment*, ed. C. Figley, 281-290. New York: Brunner and Mazel, Pub.

Terr, L. 1989. Family Anxiety After Traumatic Events. *Journal of Clinical Psychiatry* 50:15-19.

Van der Kolk, B., and M. Greenberg. 1987. The Psychobiology of the Trauma Response: Hyperarousal, Constriction, and Addiction to Traumatic Reexposure. In *Psychological Trauma,* ed. B. Van der Kolk, 63-88. Washington, DC: American Psychiatric Press.

Wadeson, H. 1987. *The Dynamics of Art Psychotherapy*. New York: John Wiley and Sons.

Williams, C., and T. Williams. 1987. Family Therapy for Vietnam Veterans. In *Post-Traumatic Stress Disorders: A Handbook for Clinicians,* ed. T. Williams, 221-231. Cincinnati: Disabled American Veterans.

Acknowledgments

The authors gratefully acknowledge the following individuals for their editorial comments and support in the development of this paper: Terence Finan, Jim Shoop, Jeremy Wolf, and our AOCAP Advisory Board. We would also like to take this opportunity to thank the Skagit Community Mental Health Center for its support of Vietnam veterans and their families.

Storytelling: A Tool of Healing for Vietnam Veterans and Their Families

Tina Alston, Ph.D.
Base Camp, Inc.
Nashville, TN

Abstract

Storytelling has been used in many settings involving clients recovering from post-traumatic stress disorder (PTSD), addiction, child abuse, and other forms of trauma. This paper describes a new methodology for working with veterans and their families around the issues of alienation, anger, and loss using what may be the oldest form of therapy—storytelling. Using classic stories, the author describes simple techniques that can be adapted by the peer counselor, the "wounded healer" who has been through a similar journey of coming home from war.

Using the story of Odysseus to introduce the theme of return from alienation, this paper describes how storytelling can be an effective therapeutic option for helping families of Vietnam veterans. Theoretical considerations include: the basic structure of the folk tale, the function of story as a template for the symbols of unconscious life, and the necessity of learning to frame certain experiences as "play" or symbolic. A review of applied work on storytelling includes: therapeutic use of storytelling in clinical practice; the "mutual storytelling" technique; and the uses of personal narrative among self-help groups. Following these observations, four methods developed while working with persons recovering from war and other trauma are described: storytelling gatherings; a projective technique for exploring feelings (story-imaging); a technique for remembering stories of special people and their blessings; and improvised stories. Suggestions for further research and practice include the necessity of keeping methods simple and free of interpretation.

Tina Alston, Ph.D., *directs the Special Children's Program at Base Camp, Inc., an organization that serves Vietnam veterans and their families. She has more than twenty years' experience using storytelling as a tool for performing, teaching, counseling, and training in the corporate environment.*

Each fairy tale is a magic mirror which reflects some aspects of our inner world, and of the steps required by our evolution from immaturity to maturity. (Bettelheim, 1977)

The stories that our ancestors have given us were not just stories constructed to teach. They were not principally meant to socialize the listener. They did all of these things, but they also did much more. Stories of the past beyond written history represented the emergence of form out of the chaos of the inexplicable. They gave meaning to the tempest and storms of the universe surrounding humankind and provided intuitive understanding of the swirling within, the tempests of our feelings and emotions.

Homer's *Odyssey* is the story of a warrior who returned home after being gone for twenty years. The battle for Troy lasted ten years and his return home took ten years. His wife Penelope struggled to keep her suitors from taking over the bed and home of her husband Odysseus, the warrior. The journey home was perhaps more costly than the long battle. Odysseus faced the perils of sea monsters, the alluring invitations of the Sirens who offered him knowledge, and the temptations of the Lotus Eaters who offered him mind-erasing drugs. When he wandered into their home, at first, Penelope didn't recognize him. Here we find parallels to the story of the Vietnam veterans, some of whom are still on the way home after more than twenty years. Like Odysseus, they have been facing demons in the psyche that are as threatening and alluring as the fantastic creatures in the ancient Greek story.

When Odysseus finally returned, his wife Penelope thought he was yet another impostor trying to trick her. Finally she tested him by casually mentioning that she had moved their great bed. This would have been an impossible task because the bed that Odysseus had made for her was built around a great olive tree: it could not have been moved without destroying the tree. When she saw his outrage, she recognized him. She actually saw his great love for her in his anger at the apparent destruction of their beautiful marriage bed. Along with his father, son, and larger family, she bade him enter his own home and return to the life of the hearth and the community. Such a story of war, alienation, and return is timeless and finds echoes in the stories of Vietnam veterans and their families (Homer, Shaw translation, 1972).

Statement of Purpose

This paper describes a new methodology for working with veterans and their families around the issues of alienation, anger, and loss using what may be the oldest form of therapy—storytelling. The use of classic stories, this "first encyclopedia of knowledge" (Keen and Fox, 1974) offers simple techniques that can be adapted by the peer counselor, the "wounded healer" who has been through a similar journey of coming home from war. It has been used in many settings involving clients recovering from post-traumatic stress disorder (PTSD), addiction, child abuse, and other forms of trauma (Branyon-Ward and Ward, 1983). Storytelling also has become a vital means of reaching out to children of veterans and their teachers in school settings. "Mom, there was a lady telling stories today at school, and she gave me this special letter for families of Vietnam veterans."

The methods described in this paper have evolved from a study of this classic story and a review of the therapeutic uses of storytelling. Three main types of stories are the basis of this work: folk tales and myths, the personal story, and improvised stories mixing the language of folk or fairy tales with true-life themes and experiences. From a study of the basic structure of the folk tale, scholars point to the function of the story as a template for symbols of the unconscious life. Following these observations, it is easier to select methods that fit the needs of this population—those recovering from war and other trauma. Following a brief overview of therapeutic uses of storytelling by professionals and self-help groups, four methods that provide people with better access to their feelings and memories within a safe context are described.

Theoretical Perspectives

Stories and Dreams: From a Common Cauldron

If what the masters of dreams tell us is true—that stories come from a common font of dream and myth—the development of the species and that of the individual are interdependent (Munroe, 1955; Freud, 1965; Sanford, 1978; Johnson, 1986). Because dreams predate stories, the archetypal symbols of the species have arisen from the repetition of countless dreams of individuals. The rhythms of the cradle, of the warrior, the mate, and the family are repeated again and again. Traditional folk tales become the source of symbols with which we can all identify. A story may speak for us that which is unspeakable. As Jung said, "The forms which the (archetypal) experience takes in each individual may be infinite in all their variety, but like the alchemical symbols, they are all variants of certain types and they occur universally" (as quoted in Hall and Nordby, 1973).

Storymaking and Play

In addition to dreams and stories, other forms of art grow out of this cauldron of the unconscious storehouse. In the child, such art forms begin as play. For the adult they may find additional expression as "head play"—storymaking, poetry, and theater. In the study of play over the life cycle, it is easier to see some of the healing functions of storytelling and storymaking. Gregory Bateson (1972) describes the importance of play as a distinguishing characteristic of humans as a species, and further describes the healthy aspect of being able to set aside an event as pretend or not ordinary.

Framing an Experience

Bateson maintains that the more advanced the species, the more sophisticated their repertoire of play behaviors. For instance, monkeys engage in a type of mock combat in which they use and interpret a symbolic gesture that denotes "this is play," thereby avoiding intra-species destruction, which would threaten the entire group. This setting apart of experience through some sort of meta-communication is called a "frame." As children grow and develop this ability to stand above the immediacy of their experience, they begin to acknowledge that "this is play" or say, "we're only pretending." When they are unsure of the boundary between pretend and reality, they may ask, "Is this real or pretend?" Those who fail to develop this framing ability are haunted by the demons of the nursery into adulthood. A person may develop such dislocation of function and identify totally with the symbol or identify completely with the fantasy—as in the schizophrenic who fails to recognize the "metaphoric nature of his fantasies" (Bateson, 1972).

William Mahedy (1986), who served as a chaplain in Vietnam, contends that the normal ways of operating in war (another type or frame) were absent in Vietnam. Many others have also argued that there was no ritual of homecoming and decompression, which has long served to give a frame—an ending—to the horrors experienced in war. Instead of coming home as a group and being hailed as war heroes by family, friends, and "the tribe," veterans returned alone—often to ridicule. This lack of framing may also speak to the issues of PTSD, which affects families as well as veterans (Matsakis, 1988; Mason, 1990).

How does this ability to frame an experience as pretend relate to the value of stories and healing? Bruno Bettelheim (1977) follows the argument of Bateson and others in suggesting that in the fairy tale a child (and adults in therapeutic settings) can find a safe place to express feelings of outrage, pain, anger, etc. More recently, Joseph Campbell, in the television series based on his book *The Power of Myth* (1988), celebrates the wisdom in stories. Using this model, we will look more closely at the structure of stories and their function as a safe tool for healing (Branyon-Ward and Ward, 1983).

Structural Elements of the Hero Cycle

The Importance of a Protecting Power

Classic folk tales usually follow a pattern known as the hero cycle. The hero or heroine leaves home, encounters dangers, receives aid from one of another realm, faces more trials, and returns home. The following folk tale from Korea contains the essentials of the hero cycle described by Campbell (1975, 1988).

"The Tiger's Whisker" (synopsis): A young wife journeys up a mountain to visit a healer who lives as a hermit. She asks the healer for a potion to help her minister to her husband, who has returned from a great war. She complains that her husband hardly speaks, angrily tosses food aside when she tries to serve meals, and sits looking out at the sea. The hermit instructs her to pluck a whisker from the face of a tiger. Although dismayed at first, she finally comes up with a plan. She takes food to the cave of the tiger, remaining a safe distance when the tiger comes out to eat. For six months the woman takes food to the cave, each day coming closer to the tiger, until she is able to pat the tiger's head. On the next visit, while the tiger cuddles his head in her lap, the woman tenderly snips a whisker and returns triumphantly to the hermit with her prize. Instead of using the whisker to mix a magical cure, the hermit tosses it into the fire. The woman cries out in alarm, questioning what seems a cruel and absurd gesture. The hermit replies, "A woman who has tamed a tiger no longer has need of a potion."

After hearing this reply, the woman returns to her home, mulling over in her mind what she has learned (Courlander, 1959).

This tale needs no interpretation. The themes in this story are common to all families who have taken back into the hearth one who has faced hell on Earth. There are no magic cures for such soldiers and their families. Instead, each family member must journey up his or her own mountain and face his or her own tiger.

An important element in the story is the figure of the wise hermit, who listens to the wife's story and gives her the strength to do a great task. His wisdom was his "potion." Leaving the woman to ponder his words, he reflects the quiet knowledge of elders in traditional cultures such as the Cherokee, who tell stories with little or no interpretation (Awaikta, 1993). This wisdom has often been missing in our society, especially in families of Vietnam veterans who were and are often still isolated from sources of such wisdom.

Before the descent into the "dark belly of the whale" and the period of trials and initiation in a story, there comes the possibility of aid from another: a fairy godmother, or a wise mentor such as Obi Wan-Kenobi (*Star Wars*). This figure represents what Campbell (1988) called the "benign, protecting power of Destiny." How can counselors, volunteers, teachers, and others develop the role of the wise healer, especially in the context of storytelling?

Homecoming and the Importance of Positive Endings

Although most folk tales do not contain all the sub-elements of the Campbell model, all adhere to a basic structure—separation, initiation, and return. In the complete folk tale, there must be a thorough resolution of conflict: the enemy must be vanquished. Brian Sutton-Smith (1975, 1976), the developmental psychologist, made reference to anthropologists and others such as Levi-Strauss in describing the evolution of children's storymaking. It is not until the middle years of childhood (ages seven to twelve) that stories contain this completeness. The stories of younger children contain what Sutton-Smith calls "failed mediation" or "incomplete mediation." In the still-embryonic ego, the wild forces of impulse are too strong to be overcome—these impulses being the dragons from within, projected outward to become monsters. To a young child, it is important to know that the evil dragon in the story is really dead. If a story has an incomplete or unsatisfactory ending, a child may ask, "What happened to the troll?"

Similarly, the ending of the first episode of the *Star Wars* trilogy has an incomplete ending: the voice of Darth Vader promising to return. It is not until the third episode of the series that complete resolution of the ancient conflict occurs.

Clinical Applications

Projective Testing

Based on the theoretical construct—that a story contains expressions of the unconscious life—researchers have designed projective tests in which stories are used. The Thematic Apperception Test (TAT) gives the subject a set of photographs for which they make up a story—one for each picture. Advocates argue that looking at stories gives a more holistic, comprehensive measure of a person as well as providing a large amount of data to analyze the complexity of human behavior (Bronfennbrenner and Ricciuti, 1960).

Storytelling as Therapeutic Intervention

Since the time when Freud, Jung, and others saw the connection between stories, dreams, and the unconscious life, therapists have used stories and anecdotes (Stone, 1992). This paper discusses storytelling in the context of group settings and with peer counseling, limiting its view to those who have suggested less obtrusive ways of using stories. Richard Gardner (1971, 1975, 1993) has used stories in his work with children, coining the term "mutual storytelling technique."

Basically, mutual storytelling borrows the tools of acting—improvisation ensemble. One person begins a story and passes it along to one or more persons, all of whom add their parts. Gardner works with a child, starting a story and passing it back and forth. When the child falters or comes up with a weak ending, thus expressing a sense of helplessness, Gardner suggests a new, more powerful character to intervene or complete the story with a positive resolution to the plight of the hero or heroine. The need for positive intervention agents, such as the fairy godmother or wise mentor, recalls Sutton-Smith's work with the developmental progression of stories. According to Gardner, leaving a vulnerable child in a story with a bleak ending may reinforce this sense of helplessness.

Storytelling as a Format for Support Groups: Twelve-Step Groups and the Narrative Format

Ernest Kurtz (1979), an historian who has studied the evolution of Alcoholics Anonymous (AA), asserts that the paradigm of wounded healers telling their stories to each other is an important contribution of our society to the larger world community. When members reach out to one another, they simply tell stories of their "experience, strength, and hope." Such stories follow a three-step format modeled on the founder's story (Bill Wilson, or "Bill W."), who shared "what we used to be like, what happened, and what we are like now." The narrative format contains the basic elements of the classic hero story of transformation. "How it was" refers to the departure from natural goodness into addiction. "What happened" refers to that point of grace when someone reached out, from the fellowship or elsewhere, after the alcoholic had "hit bottom." In these stories, the supernatural agents are fellow sufferers—wounded healers who act as agents of the "higher power"—a generic term for the Deity.

Many other groups for persons recovering from trauma or other addictions have been formed—Al-Anon for the family members and Overeaters Anonymous, for instance. In *Recovering from the War*, Patience Mason (1990), the wife of a Vietnam veteran, describes her journey of healing. Like the woman in the story "The Tiger's Whisker," Mason sought help from others in the hope of finding a "potion." Instead she found the wisdom of the twelve-step groups she attended. She has adopted the opening and closing rituals of Alcoholics Anonymous as a suggested format for groups of family members of veterans.

Story as a Beacon of Change: Women's and Men's Stories

Recently, leaders of both men's and women's movements have used folk tales as beacons of change. Clarissa Pinkola Estes, a Jungian analyst and professor of women's studies, collected a rich series of stories in *Women Who Run With the Wolves* (1992). Likewise, the poet Robert Bly adapted the "Iron John" story and other fairy tales in lectures and workshops on men's changing roles. His book *Iron John* (1992) has, like Estes' book, become the most popular text of the men's movement.

Collections of such stories are important because they encourage adult readers to experience stories at ever-deeper levels of unconscious learning. These collections, however, can give the reader another set of authoritative meanings for stories (Hutton, 1993). How does this happen? When an authority (someone with a degree, a reputation as a renowned artist, etc.) interprets a story, it keeps one from experiencing it afresh, or from going within for one's own meanings. Stories act as dreams: just as universal symbols are a part of dream work, so too symbols are a part of stories. In dreams, however, not all meanings are universal. Some dream material may simply be left-over processing of the day's events, or material with only a personal meaning (Sanford, 1977; Johnson, 1986). With stories, as with dreams, it may be best to begin at the personal level as in the exercise called "story-imaging" described below.

Dangers of Interpreting Stories for Trauma Victims

When individuals have been subjected to stress and trauma over an extended period, their developmental fabric often becomes weak, and even tears. These adults often behave immaturely when making choices, either ignoring rules or following rules and authorities without question (Rutledge, 1990). In the case of spouses who have lived with addiction as well as the fallout from war, there is often a tendency toward self-doubt and denial of feelings. Spouses and children of such families often rely on authoritative answers—they expect the "magic potion" from without. They may be overly dependent on authority or may reject any outside authority (Matsakis, 1988; Mason, 1990).

Similarly, persons trained in warfare have learned to ignore their inner wisdom. A combat veteran who has been taught to move from threat to violence has been programmed to follow orders, and to ignore his own instincts. When faced with dilemmas, such persons react immediately with war-trained rather than problem-solving behavior. They have lost the ability to listen to the voice of intuition—a type of seeing, knowing, and understanding that is beyond military training (Goodwin, 1987; Mason, 1990; Washington, 1993).

Experts, therapists, and other professionals who deal with families of such veterans need to respect this wounding and nurture the inner wisdom of their clients. Instead of interpreting stories (as do Bly and Estes), they would do well to function like the wise hermit in the Korean story. They need to give clients the psychic armor to go off and face their own "tigers," to cheer them on, and to welcome them on their return.

People who have experienced trauma may have an even greater need for support in listening to their own voice. They need to hear stories with characters like the wise old hermit in the Korean story who taught the woman to discover her own resources. The next section suggests methods that storytellers and group leaders can use to nurture the inner wisdom of persons recovering from trauma.

Method

Storytelling Sessions

A pleasant introduction to storytelling is just an evening or hour of storytelling, preferably in the late afternoon. Irish poet Padraic Colum (1972) observed that storytelling in traditional societies occurred in the dim light around fires, after the work of the day had been completed. This nonwork setting acts as a "frame" to signify "this is storytelling," to borrow from Bateson regarding the "frame" of fantasy, which acts as a signal to the listener. The leader can be the sole teller, choosing stories that would reflect themes appropriate to the age group.

Another variation is a storytelling gathering where each participant is asked to arrive with an oral story as a ticket of admission. Numbers are distributed at the door, just as at a busy restaurant ("take a number"). After the meal is over (assuming a potluck meal accompanies the gathering) the leader assembles the group. He or she has a set of numbered cards and draws numbers at random. In this way, guests are not as tempted to mentally rehearse their story. Because no one knows who is next, it is easier to attend to the story at hand (Turner, 1989).

Other suggestions for storytelling gatherings come from Robert Akeret's *Family Tales, Family Wisdom* (1991). Akeret's method focuses on interviewing an elder (an older family member or colleague). Using memorabilia and photos, a facilitator works with the elder to recall significant events in his or her life.

Once, while jogging along a canal trail in England, this writer met a retired teacher painting scenes along the canal. During a brief conversation, the teacher mentioned that he liked storytelling as well, especially stories of the "Great War" (World War II). "I happen to have some pictures. Would you like to see them?" he said as he reached into a leather satchel for worn photos of D-Day and the Normandy invasion. In other wars, when heroes were welcomed home, this was a normal occurrence. Perhaps it is not too late to try some of Akeret's methods within a family or a veterans' center. A good beginning might be to start with stories of their community or families.

Storytelling gatherings create a sense of community. Because isolation is one of the most common elements in families of Vietnam veterans, a light-hearted activity of coming together to tell stories can be a good starting point.

Story-Imaging Groups

Story-imaging is a projective tool without norms, developed by the author for group work and counseling with individuals. Ultimately, it can become an aid to journaling as well as a self-help method. Story-imaging is a way of viewing a story as if it were a dream. Through story-imaging a person can learn a story by listening and can identify with all the aspects of the story instead of just the hero's or heroine's role. As a healing tool it raises awareness that there are many, often conflicting, parts of the self, just as there are different characters in a story. The recovering person learns that no one feeling is the whole person.

The story "The Tiger's Whisker" can be outlined with this technique. After the story is told or read aloud, the leader selects ten to fifteen important symbols from the story (usually characters, but key objects such as a cave or a whisker can be included). Using selected symbols from the story, the facilitator asks participants to complete the following phrase (to themselves or on paper): "I am the soldier's wife seeking help from the hermit, I feel ____________________" or "I am the soldier returning from war, I feel ______________" (see Figure 1 for a story-imaging worksheet). The facilitator makes it clear that there are no norms or correct answers. The exercise is meant to draw out feelings in a safe context, in the absence of judgment—even the benign judgment of norms. At the end of the exercise, a discussion can take place showing that a variety of feelings are possible for any situation—that there are no correct feelings. Those recovering from trauma often suffer a depletion of available feelings. At the beginning of recovery, a few feelings may be mentioned over and over, such as "depressed," "mad," "excited." With continuing personal work, however, those recovering from trauma develop a broader palette of feelings analogous to the infinite variety of colors in a rainbow.

Participants can put a star next to their most intense feelings, and others can call out their response for the same item. For instance, one person may have commented that the woman seeking help from the hermit felt "fear," while others might have named "embarrassed," "awed," or "depressed" as their feelings when identifying with the same person. At the conclusion, each participant is asked to repeat his or her own list of feeling words, using an introductory statement: "I am Jane, I feel 'happy,' 'alarmed,' 'worried,' 'peaceful,'" etc. "Recovery" literally means recovering the ability to feel and to act freely. This exercise may be seen as a practice session for identifying and specifying feelings.

Figure 1. Story-imaging Worksheet: "The Tiger's Whisker"

Directions: Leader calls out the incomplete sentence, and listener completes the sentence silently, then fills in chart: "I am the [symbol] in the story, and I feel [feeling]." Group leader will fill in names at the top of each column; individuals using this for a journal exercise may label columns with dates.

Symbol	Name or Date	Name or Date	Name or Date	Name or Date
Husband returning from war				
Woman going to hermit				
Hermit hearing the story				
Woman bringing food to tiger				
Tiger finding food				
Woman touching the tiger				
Tiger letting her pat him				
Whisker of the tiger				
Woman cutting off the whisker				
Woman returning to hermit				
Hermit throwing whisker into fire				
Woman crying at hermit				
Woman hearing his explanation				
Woman returning home				

True-Life Stories: Recalling "Angels"

The following technique has been adapted from a writing exercise designed to help a recovering person get in touch with inner wisdom (*The Twelve Steps: A Way Out*, 1987). To tap into that source of wisdom, participants are asked to recall people who have given them special blessings, such as "heroes you worshipped, wisdom figures you thought to be wise, or people you wanted to imitate." This writer has adopted the term "angels in disguise" to encompass all agents of change.

Before inviting people to tell stories of blessings and positive role models, the leader demonstrates by telling a personal story of someone who passed on special blessings, such as forgiveness and generosity. The participants then make a list of special people in their own lives, including extended family but avoiding nuclear-family members. The list can be expanded to include four-legged or feathered angels. (Pets are often a favorite topic, especially among those who have been abused or grew up with a distrust of adults.) Participants then list the blessings they received from such angels. Discussion of such angels can occur in a group setting or between a teller and listener (Alston, 1993).

An important feature of a group storytelling session involves the telling of a favorite angel story, first to a partner and then to the larger group. After hearing the partner's story, each listener retells that story to the larger group (not more than eight). The luxury of hearing one's story told by someone else makes it easier for more memories and feelings to emerge. At the conclusion of this activity, the leader asks, "How do we think that (name of the original teller) is passing on the blessing of his grandmother?" Each participant can provide feedback to the original teller as to how they see the blessings of the angel incorporated in his or her own life.

In contrast to many group methods for work on past trauma or abuse, the concept of recalling one's angels or mentors creates a self-nurturing, hopeful tone advocated by current writers in the field of recovery (Rutledge, 1990; Whitfield, 1990). There may be dangers of reinfecting wounds by retelling a painful story without a sense of transformation. When a person recalls a story of power and positive mediation, they can truly identify with the hero in the classic sense of the folk tale and the Campbell model.

Veterans and their families have used this technique to discover the blessings they have received throughout their lives, even during the "dark night of the soul." One veteran of the Korean War recalled "the image of my grandmother appearing to me, just before I ran ahead into what had been billed as a suicide mission. She must have saved me, because here I am." This process of recalling the light during a period of darkness can be coupled with other therapeutic techniques of going back to blocked memories.

After recalling her angel (a protective grandfather who didn't put up with the family's neuroses), one incest survivor was able to unlock additional memories that had blocked her recovery. Her therapist remarked that it would have taken many more months to work through her memory block, had she not first recalled this story of her grandfather.

Storytelling allows paradox. Remembering blessings can make way for painful memories to find resolution and healing. Laughter can often make it more comfortable to cry. A sense of safety can lead to new acts of courage.

Improvising Stories

A storytelling leader who is well versed in the language of folk tales can work with individuals or groups to create stories based on that individual's personal story. One way of creating a story ensemble is to use a piece of yarn about a yard long. The teller wraps the yarn around a finger while starting a story and continues to speak until there is no more yarn. When he or she runs out of yarn, and consequently runs out of words, it is the next person's turn. The second teller adds on to the story while winding the yarn around his or her finger. If there are only two tellers, the tale goes back and forth; if there is a group of tellers, the tale travels around the circle several times.

While visiting patients in Vanderbilt Children's Hospital, this writer met a young boy, about twelve years old, who appeared fairly healthy. Sam (a fictional name) was from a small town with a rich storytelling tradition, and was fluent and highly imaginative: he caught on to the storytelling technique immediately. The two of us wove a tale about a young man landing on a strange planet and visiting a cave full of perils. A mermaid in the underground waters came to his aid and helped him avoid danger. At the end of the improvised tale, Sam told the mermaid that he had another fear worse than the monsters in the cave—a fear of losing his friends because of their fear of AIDS. Sam told the mermaid he didn't have AIDS but was HIV positive as the result of blood transfusions. The mermaid responded that a friend of hers, a brave warrior named Prince Stefano, actually had that scary disease. He had told his close friends, and none of them ran away. They even took him on trips, did his laundry, and bought ice cream for him. The boy smiled.

Sam died of AIDS, as did the real-life counterpart, Prince Stefano. Although neither of them ever met the other, both of them were connected and got to hear about their fictitious counterparts. The boy was a child of a Vietnam combat veteran; the man was a combat veteran of Vietnam. Both died surrounded by friends (Alston, 1990).

Suggestions for Research and Practice

Storytelling therapy blends the world of folk art and healing. Keeping fresh this healthy mixture of sources requires a balance between methods that are free of formalized systems and methods that can be duplicated and observed by others. The following suggestions assume such a marriage between the arts and social science.

- **Use folk tales and real-life stories instead of therapeutic protocols.** Although the fields of social science have taught us much about storytelling, there is more to learn from the world of the folk arts and theater. Those who have only heard of therapeutic stories in the context of social sciences would do well to acquaint themselves with professional storytellers who are helping bring back the art of storytelling.

This revivalist movement had its origins in 1972, with the National Storytelling Association (NSA). At its annual storytelling festival in Jonesborough, Tennessee, NSA brings together storytellers from around the country and the world. The Association produces several important resources for the storytelling enthusiast: a journal—The Storytelling Magazine—several books on storytelling, collections of recorded stories, a directory of storytellers and events, and an extensive archive of taped performances (Smith, 1988; NSA, 1993).

At the 1993 festival, several tellers featured stories about Vietnam veterans, including the work of Elizabeth Ellis and Rod McQueary. Jon Spelman, who has been featured at previous festivals, has conducted a one-man show in Washington, D.C., featuring letters written by Vietnam veterans (NSA, 1993). The most important contribution of these professional tellers and national festivals may be the example they provide for smaller gatherings, such as local festivals or the storytelling parties discussed previously in this paper, for the real center of storytelling is still the heart, the family.

- **Develop data-collection methods that are simple and that can be recorded by the subjects themselves.** (See Figure 1 for a sample worksheet for the story-imaging exercise.)
- **Use gross measures for change instead of normative data.** For instance, record changes in the fluency of "feelings words" associated in the story-imaging exercise, or the numbers of new angels a participant lists within a storytelling session.
- **Use observational data recorded by others such as teachers or therapists and healers.** For example, after completing the exercise of recalling angels and blessings, some participants or their therapists may notice new breakthroughs.
- **Train paraprofessionals as storytelling leaders who have personally experienced their own healing from the war.** Equip such storytelling leaders with tools that discourage intrusive questions or discussions that encourage dwelling on the pain of the past. Develop a variety of referral sources of health care professionals for those who get in touch with powerful feelings.
- **Combine oral storytelling with journal writing and publishing.** Telling and hearing one's own stories brings up more feelings; writing often brings a greater degree of clarity and insight. Assembling collections of personal stories or traditional stories that echo themes of Vietnam can be a community-building activity for families. Teachers can implement such activities, incorporating concepts of both the social studies and language-arts curricula.
- **Combine stories of Vietnam with other personal stories.** Families that have experienced stress often become too preoccupied with each others' struggles. This is what family-systems experts call fusion (Bowen, 1971; Karpel, 1976). Spouses of Vietnam veterans often become so enmeshed in the struggle of their veterans that they neglect their own feelings and needs (Mason, 1990). Recovery from the war for many families may ultimately lead them to tell many other stories, instead of the story of one struggle.

  As spouses learn to separate their feelings and their story from those of their veterans, they become open to the process of goal-setting. Spouse-support groups have used workbooks that encourage writing about their own lives and their own goals for the future. It may take several months of such journal writing for a spouse to even conceive a personal rather than joint vision, such as "I see my husband get a job" or "I envision my child in remission from cancer." Developing personal affirmations and repeating them aloud with others in a patient process requires several months to come to fruition. Books that have been helpful for such spouse groups include Charles Whitfield's *A Gift to Myself* (1990), Thom Rutledge's *Simple Truth* (1990), and Louise Hay's *Love Yourself, Heal Your Life* (1990).

Summary

Storytelling as a Means of Coming Home

What is storytelling? It is practicing the art of using stories as a tool of wisdom and healing. It is telling stories and teaching others to discover and share their own memories. It is experiencing the fun of performance, entertainment, creativity, and imagination. It is rediscovering traditions, values, history, one's own power, and, finally, one's own story—the self. Storytelling is truly an ageless experience—as important for the adult as for the child.

How is storytelling particularly important for the families of Vietnam veterans? It is a way to pass on history and a way to process events that happen, with laughter or with tears. Old stories are told to heal wounds of the past and empower the present. New stories are full of possibilities to influence and energize the future. Soldiers recall their angels from the dark night of war and offer themselves anew for the grace or blessings from the future. Spouses find courage by facing their own "tigers" or fears with the support of others who have walked through such fears. Children hear stories of heroes and heroines, finding new faces in the eyes of their parents or others who provide them with mentoring and guidance.

Like the hero or heroine who returns transformed to the starting point of the journey, so do we return to that which is both primeval and present—the symbols of our dreams and our stories.

> We had the experience but missed the meaning
> And approach to the meaning restores the experience
> In a different form, beyond any meaning
> We can assign to happiness. I have said before
> That the past experience revived in the meaning
> Is not the experience of one life only
> But of many generations (Eliot, 1952, p. 133)

References

Akeret, R.W. 1991. *Family tales, family wisdom.* New York: Henry Holt & Company.

Alston, T. Fall 1990. Storytelling as therapy. *Vision: A Vanderbilt Nursing Quarterly.* Nashville, TN: Vanderbilt University.

Alston, T. 1993. Unexpected blessings in the stories of your angels. *Storytelling World* 2(2).

Awiakta, M. 1993. *Selu: Seeking the corn-mother's wisdom.* Golden, CO: Fulcrum Publishing.

Bateson, G. 1972. *Steps to an ecology of the mind.* New York: Ballantine Books.

Bettelheim, B. 1977. *The uses of enchantment: The meaning and importance of fairy tales.* New York: Vintage Books.

Bly, R. 1992. *Iron John: A book about men.* New York: Vintage Books.

Bowen, M. 1971. The use of family theory in clinical practice. In *Changing families: A family therapy reader,* ed. J. Haley. New York: Grune & Stratton.

Branyon-Ward, J., and J.R. Ward. 1983. Healing through stories. *Thanatos* 8(1): 8-9.

Bronfennbrenner, U., and H. Ricciuti. 1960. The appraisal of personality characteristics in children. In *Handbook of research methods in child development,* ed. Paul H. Mussen. New York: John Wiley & Sons.

Campbell, J. 1975. *The hero with a thousand faces,* 3d ed. New York: Meridian Books.

Campbell, J., with W. Moyers. 1988. *The power of myth,* ed. B.S. Flowers. New York: Doubleday.

Colum, P. 1972. Introduction. *The complete Grimm's fairy tales.* New York: Pantheon Books.

Courlander, H. 1959. *The tiger's whisker, and other tales and legends from Asia and the Pacific.* New York: Harcourt Brace.

Eliot, T.S. 1952. "Four Quartets: The Dry Salvages," in *The Complete Poems and Plays: 1909-1950*. New York: Harcourt Brace.

Estes, C.P. 1992. *Women who run with the wolves: Myths and stories of the wild woman archetype*. New York: Ballantine Books.

Freud, S. 1965. *The interpretation of dreams*. Translated by J. Strachey. New York: Basic Books.

Gardner, R.A. 1971. *Therapeutic Communication with Children: The Mutual Storytelling Technique*. New York: Science House Inc.

Gardner, R.A. 1975. *Psychotherapeutic approaches to the resistant child*. New York: Jason Aronson.

Gardner, R.A. 1993. *Storytelling in psychotherapy with children*. Northdale, NJ: Jason Aronson.

Goodwin, J. 1987. *Readjustment Problems Among Vietnam Veterans*. Cincinnati, OH: Disabled American Veterans.

Hall, C.S., and V.J. Nordby. 1973. *A primer of Jungian psychology* (rev. ed.). New York: New American Library.

Hay, L. 1990. *Love yourself, heal your life workbook*. Carson, CA: Hay House.

Homer. 1972. *The Odyssey*. Translated by T.E. Shaw. New York: Oxford University Press.

Hutton, R. 1993. *Warrior Nostalgia: The Flaw in the Men's Movement*. Unpublished paper.

Johnson, R. 1986. *Inner work*. San Francisco: Harper San Francisco.

Karpel, M. 1976. Individuation: From fusion to dialogue. *Family Process* 15(1):65-82.

Keen, S., and A.V. Fox. 1973. *Telling Your Story: A guide to who you are and who you can be*. Garden City, NY: Doubleday.

Kurtz, E. 1979. *Not-God: A history of Alcoholics Anonymous*. Center City, MN: Hazelden Educational Services.

Mahedy, W. 1986. *Out of the night: The spiritual journey of Vietnam vets*. New York: Ballantine Books.

Mason, P.H.C. 1990. *Recovering from the war*. New York: Penguin Books.

Matsakis, A. 1988. *Vietnam wives: Women and children surviving life with veterans suffering Post-Traumatic Stress Disorder*. Kensington, MD: Woodbine House.

Munroe, R.L. 1955. *Schools of psychoanalytic thought*. New York: Holt, Rinehart & Winston.

National Storytelling Association (NSA). 1993. *National Directory of Storytelling*. Jonesborough, TN: National Storytelling Association.

Rutledge, T. 1990. *Simple Truth*. Nashville, TN: Total Concepts.

Sanford, J. 1977. *Healing and wholeness*. New York: Paulist Press.

Smith, J.N. 1988. *Homespun*. New York: Crown Publishers.

Stone, R. 1992. *The family storytelling starter kit*. Winter Park, FL: Author.

Sutton-Smith, B. 1975. Play as novelty training. In *Once child indivisible,* ed. J.D. Andrews. Washington, DC: National Association for the Education of Young Children.

Sutton-Smith, B. (December 1976). The development of story making. Speech given at East Tennessee State University.

Turner, E. 1989. Homespun yarns. *Storytelling Magazine* Summer:4.

The Twelve Steps: A way out. 1987. San Diego, CA: Recovery Publications.

Washington, J. Feb. 1993. Creative uses of anger for PTSD veterans. Workshop presented at Base Camp, Inc., The Veterans Center.

Whitfield, C. 1990. *A gift to myself*. Deerfield Beach, FL: C. Whitfield.

In the Aftermath: Meeting the Special Needs of the Children of Vietnam Veterans

Margot B. Stein, Ph.D.; and Mary Ann Kimball, M.S.W.
The University of North Carolina at Chapel Hill

Michelle M. Macias, M.D.
Medical University of South Carolina

Abstract

This study examines biological dysfunction, including immunological dysfunction and genetic conditions, social-emotional problems, and levels of stress and dysfunction within families of Vietnam veterans, particularly as they relate to the children in these families. It presents a descriptive analysis of the major health, family, psychological, and learning issues of fifteen female and twenty-three male children of Vietnam veterans evaluated at a University Affiliated Child Development Center. Data are presented on medical problems, neurodevelopmental findings, emotional and behavioral problems, and family dysfunction.

Medical findings indicated higher percentages of diseases, including asthma, allergic rhinitis, recurrent rash, and attention deficit disorder than in the general population. However, the families sampled were self-referred because of developmental or school problems, and hence, the sample is highly biased. Higher levels of behavioral and social-emotional difficulties were noted, and appeared to be related principally to the father's occupational status. Learning disabilities contributed to the children's school and social problems. Although the parents described prolonged, intense stress, they did not perceive themselves as different from normal families when rated on standardized measures. These findings suggest the need for individualized, intense, long-term family services for some Vietnam veterans and their families.

Margot B. Stein, Ph.D., *is a clinical assistant professor in the Department of Psychiatry of the University of North Carolina School of Medicine, Chapel Hill, NC. She received her Ph.D. in school psychology from Duke University.* ***Mary Ann Kimball, M.S.W.,*** *is social work section head at the Center for Study of Development and Learning (CDL), Chapel Hill, NC. She holds a master's degree in social work from the University of North Carolina at Chapel Hill. Ms. Stein and Ms. Kimball also serve as co-principal investigators for the Agent Orange Projects at CDL.* ***Michelle M. Macias, M.D.,*** *is an assistant professor of pediatrics at The Medical University of South Carolina, where she is also developmental pediatrician and medical director of the Division of Genetics and Child Development.*

Evidence of the link between exposure to Agent Orange and disabilities in children of Vietnam veterans has not yet been scientifically determined to be significant, but research on the effects of exposure to Agent Orange continues. Nearly one-half million Vietnam veterans are adversely affected by war-related psychological stressors. A large percentage of this population can be considered to be of low socioeconomic status, with limited knowledge of or access to agencies that provide health care and other related services. Because of limited access to services many of these veterans are unable to receive treatment for psychological problems.

A variety of family stressors are inherent when a member of the family suffers from these psychological stressors. Vietnam veterans often demonstrate problematic relationships within the family unit, particularly when the veteran has post-traumatic stress disorder (PTSD). Jordan et al. (1992) described more problems with marital, parental, and family adjustment among veterans with PTSD than those among veterans without PTSD. It is widely accepted that environmental variables of the family unit affect the social and affective development of children (Thomas and Chess, 1977). If the final product of the developing child is the result of genetic endowment and environmental interaction, children of some Vietnam veterans are at risk for high- or low-severity developmental dysfunctions. A child is at risk for failure within the educational system when the family unit is functioning inadequately: that risk is compounded when less-than-normal biological attributes are added to an inadequately functioning family unit.

The Clinical Center for the Study of Development and Learning (CDL) developed an interdisciplinary family and child evaluation program and statewide network of services to provide resource management services to eligible Vietnam veterans and their families residing in North Carolina. The project had three main objectives: first, provide an interdisciplinary and comprehensive developmental evaluation for any child currently living in North Carolina whose parent served in Vietnam or the waters adjacent thereto between 1961 and 1972; second, establish an Agent Orange hotline designed to identify eligible clients and provide information services to veterans and their families; and third, conduct workshops—statewide—to increase the awareness of the problems and solutions available to Vietnam veterans and their families.

Although AOCAP provided the funding for direct services, research activities were undertaken using other university resources and contributions of many individuals' time and efforts.

The hypotheses prior to starting this Agent Orange Class Assistance Program (AOCAP) project were threefold. First, it was hypothesized that the population referred for evaluation would have evidence of significantly increased biological dysfunction, including immunological dysfunction and genetic conditions, when compared with the general population. Second, the referral population would have more social-emotional problems than a normative sample. Third, the families of Vietnam veterans would have significantly increased levels of stress and dysfunction within the family unit when compared with the general population.

Medical Findings

The combination of possible subtle biological anomalies created through transmission of dioxins to the fetal environment and environmental stressors created by a psychological disorder can be considered to adversely affect development and increase possibilities of low-severity developmental dysfunctions. Although teratogens are generally transmitted to the fetus maternally, evidence suggests that adverse effects of paternal exposure to teratogens may be transmitted to the fetal environment. It has been inferred that paternal teratogens may be transmitted to the fetal environment and may be a causative factor in severe or subtle damage to the developing fetus during critical developmental periods (Joffe, 1979).

Methods

Subjects

The Center for Development and Learning is a University Affiliated Program that provides interdisciplinary evaluations of children and adolescents with developmental and learning problems. This study sample included thirty-eight children of Vietnam veterans who reported that they might have been exposed to Agent Orange during the Vietnam conflict. The children were evaluated over a two-year period in the AOCAP project. The subjects consisted of a consecutive sample of children. Referrals were made by parents, and children were recruited through the Agent Orange hotline; there were no requirements other than that a parent had served in or near Vietnam between 1961 and 1972. The subjects included twenty-three males and fifteen females.

Procedures

Using the ANSER system (Levine, 1980) of parent, teacher, and child questionnaires, extensive information was obtained on each child, including past medical and behavioral history, demographics, developmental history, and academic performance ratings. Each patient underwent a complete medical history, physical and neurologic examination, and neurodevelopmental examination. A neurodevelopmental assessment instrument—the Pediatric Early Elementary Examination II (PEEX II) or Pediatric Examination of Educational Readiness at Middle Childhood (PEERAMID)—was administered to each child. These two instruments comprise a set of neurodevelopmental assessment procedures that survey eight broad areas: minor neurological indicators, fine motor function, language processing and production, gross motor function, temporal sequential organization, visual processing, memory, and selective attention. Both the ANSER system and PEEX II and PEERAMID are widely used by pediatricians and other health professionals: reliability and validity issues associated with these instruments have been addressed elsewhere.

Results

The medical problems of children in the study group were categorized into fourteen groups (see Table 1). A child with more than one diagnosed condition contributed one observation to each relevant group. The study group had higher percentages of diseases, including asthma (estimated at 8 percent of the general population), allergic rhinitis (estimated at 5 to 10 percent in the general population), and recurrent rashes—atopic dermatitis, eczema, urticaria, and psoriasis—(estimated at 7 percent in the general population). The other significant area of increased disease was attention deficit disorder, which occurs in approximately 5 to 10 percent of the general population but was found in 37.5 percent of the study population.

Neurodevelopmental testing was completed on thirty-eight children, and profiles were constructed in terms of neurodevelopmental strengths and weaknesses. An area was defined as being a weakness if the raw score fell below the normative range, and a strength if the raw score fell above the normative range (see Table 2). In summary, the data showed an increased incidence of memory problems, specifically in the various aspects of auditory memory (auditory active working memory, auditory sequential memory, and retrieval memory), and an increased incidence of language processing weaknesses (44.4 percent). The third major area of dysfunction was attention, with deficits occurring in 41.7 percent of children tested.

Discussion

It is commonly accepted that exposure of women to certain substances (teratogens) during pregnancy can result in altered embryogenesis and subsequent major or minor malformations, but the potential for paternal transmission of teratogens is not specifically known. In this study, several different medical conditions were found in higher percentages than in the general population. These conditions included various types of atopic disease, including asthma, allergic rhinitis, and recurrent rash. In addition, a significantly higher percentage of

Table 1. Medical Diagnoses of Children Referred to the AOCAP Project (n=38)

Diagnosis	Number of Cases	Percent
Maternal miscarriages	12	31.6
Asthma	9	23.7
Allergic rhinitis	14	36.8
Recurrent rash (atopic dermatitis, eczema, urticaria, psoriasis)	12	31.6
History of recurrent otitis media	13	34.2
Cardiac disease	0.3	7.9
Classic migraine headaches	2	5.3
Cerebral palsy (left hemiparesis, mild spastic diplegial)	2	5.3
Autosomal chromosomal defect	1	2.6
Syndactyly	1	2.6
Enuresis	5	13.2
Encopresis	2	5.3
Hearing impairment	2	5.3
Attention deficit disorder	15	39.5

Table 2. Neurodevelopmental Profile (n=36)

Neurodevelopmental Function	Strength Number	Strength Percent	Weakness Number	Weakness Percent
Memory				
Active working memory	0	0	21	58.3
Retrieval memory	1	2.7	12	33.3
Visual memory	4	11.1	5	13.9
Auditory sequential memory	2	5.5	15	41.7
Language processing/production	7	19.4	16	44.4
Fine motor function	20	55.5	5	13.9
Gross motor function	12	33.3	4	11.1
Visual processing	19	52.8	3	8.3
Temporal-sequential organization	2	5.5	8	22.2
Attention	2	5.5	15	41.7

children were diagnosed with attention deficit disorder. Five of the children in the study group had structural birth defects, including autosomal chromosomal abnormality, congenital heart disease, and syndactyly.

Attention deficit disorder was diagnosed in a significant percentage of the children studied. This disorder is generally believed to have a genetic component, but is usually considered multifactorial in origin.

Although high rates of attentional and other conditions were found in the study sample, the sample is self-referred because of developmental or school problems, and hence, highly biased. Thus, further evaluation of this at-risk population is essential: a carefully designed epidemiologic study could address the possibility of an association with these disorders.

Family Findings

Many families of Vietnam veterans have been characterized by their social isolation, marital instability, maladaptive coping such as violence and substance abuse, and lowered self-esteem of family members (Maloney, 1988). When a father suffers with PTSD, the level and intensity of stress within the family often increases (Figley, 1978).

The families represented in this group were also coping with the stress often associated with having a child with a learning or developmental disorder. According to Wikler (1981), families with children that are mentally retarded or have another type of developmental disability are more likely to experience stress than families with normal children. Dane (1990) also has described chronic stress in families with children who have learning and attention disorders—milder forms of developmental disability. Because learning difficulties are usually less obvious to persons outside the family, families whose children have learning difficulties often receive less understanding and support than families with children who have obvious disabilities. In addition, parents may be blamed for a problem with learning that may be confused with poor motivation or poor parenting. The families in this sample of Vietnam veterans could be experiencing both the stress of the child's problem as well as the stress of the Vietnam experience.

A parent interview was conducted by the social worker on the evaluation team to assess the critical issues affecting these families. The interview focused on: parents' current concerns about the child being evaluated; past and current family functioning; the history of how the fathers have coped with the Vietnam experience; and the history of the parents' own problems with school and emotional difficulties. In addition to the interview, data were gathered from a parent questionnaire and from the Family Environment Scale (Moos, 1981).

Thirty-five families were represented in this sample because three sets of siblings comprise the thirty-eight subjects. Ten interviews were conducted with mothers only: the remainder included both parents. Two fathers were in prison, one was deceased, and the whereabouts of two others were unknown. Most families were from rural areas of North Carolina. Many were still living in areas where they grew up. Many of the referrals were made because fathers, who were seeking treatment to cope with the Vietnam experience, had heard about the project from professionals. Most parents were very open in discussing their concerns and family problems. Fathers were asked about their Vietnam experience but were not asked probing questions if they indicated a reluctance to discuss it.

Families in the sample presented with a number of strengths that have lent stability. Approximately one-third had been married more than fifteen years, although another one-fourth were currently divorced. Both parents were relatively well educated; more than 80 percent had at least a high school education and more than 50 percent had completed some college courses. In addition, the families were sufficiently organized to complete the referral process, fill out the questionnaires, and get transportation to a large medical center for the required evaluation.

Despite their educational attainments, a large number of the fathers (35.5 percent) were unemployed, 36.8 percent had a history of PTSD, and approximately 40 percent had substance abuse problems. The prevalence of substance abuse is likely an underestimate, because fathers for whom little information was available were described as having a variety of psychiatric disorders. Forty-six percent of the fathers reported learning or attention problems in school, and at least 30 percent had repeated a grade. Those who had repeated a grade were likely to have later adjustment problems: 55 percent were now receiving treatment for PTSD.

A large majority of the mothers in this group were employed (almost 80 percent), and had fewer mental health problems than their husbands. Twenty percent suffered depression, but only one case of substance abuse was reported. Approximately one-third of the mothers, however, had learning difficulties in school, although only 14 percent had repeated a grade.

Based on these data and the clinical interview, several themes are apparent in these families:

- Prolonged and chronic stress was described throughout most of the years since Vietnam, although a few families believed that the war had not been a significant factor in their lives. Although a large number of the marriages were long term, several of the couples had separated and reunited a number of times. The husband's mental health and unemployment seemed to be a greater cause for stress in the family than the child's problems. Whereas many parents of a disabled child have tended to express primary concern about the impact of the child's problem on the family, the reverse was true for these veteran parents who worried and felt guilty about the impact of the family problems on their child.

- Mothers appeared to have assumed a great deal of the responsibility for the family, and often were trying to compensate for their husbands' difficulties. In many cases, the wives were working outside the home and making the primary parenting decisions while their unemployed husbands had few family responsibilities. This was not viewed as highly unusual by the wives who completed the Family Environment Scale (Moos, 1981). They described their families as being similar to other families in all measures, including cohesion, independence, conflict, and organization.
- The reported problems of fathers in this sample were consistent with the findings of other studies of veterans suffering with PTSD (Card, 1987). Alcoholism, mental health problems, and unemployment were highly represented in this group in which many of the men had heard about the program because they were seeking treatment related to their Vietnam experience. PTSD symptoms have been associated with combat experience. Level of combat has been related to other factors such as family socioeconomic status and school experiences (Cordray, Polk, and Britton, 1992). In this sample, the impact of combat experience was difficult to assess because many fathers were reluctant to talk about their combat experiences in a one-hour interview. Many expressed a preference for speaking only with other veterans about their war experience. Many of these fathers, however, reported school difficulties and grade retentions prior to military service in Vietnam, which raises questions about their vulnerability and resiliency in coping with the trauma of Vietnam. The issue of exposure to Agent Orange was discussed, but most veterans were uncertain about their exposure to the defoliant. Only one veteran was receiving disability payments for Agent Orange exposure.
- Although these families did not see themselves as socially isolated, many lacked the resources needed to cope with the ongoing stresses in their lives. A number of families relied on religious affiliations for support; others described a lack of social density where there were few support systems surrounding the family (Bronfenbrenner, 1979). When asked about supportive persons in their lives, several fathers could identify no one with whom they could talk about their problems. The ongoing stress related to the father's problems, and to a lesser degree, the child's problems, seems to have usurped much of the family energy for seeking resources outside the family. This was demonstrated by four families who elected to teach their children at home, rather than advocate through the school system for appropriate services.
- Despite the family problems reported and concern expressed about the impact of these problems on their children, mothers who completed the Family Environment Scale see their families as within the mainstream of how families function. This may be partially explained by the high number of rural families who may tend to see conflict and struggles as a normal part of life. Indeed, one family in which both parents had college degrees but suffered chronic mental illness had been homeless intermittently throughout their twenty-year marriage. Both were eloquent, but resigned, as they described their problems. Family distress was described by many of the parents, but there seemed to be little expectation that the current level of functioning, or the family unit itself, would change much in the future. Many of the families seemed to believe that they would continue to rely on one another in time of need.

How much of the distress in these families may be related to the problems of their children, the Vietnam experience itself, their socioeconomic status, or indirectly related to prior school difficulties is still unclear (Cordray et al., 1992). Forty percent of the fathers had at some point sought treatment related to their service in Vietnam, and a large number were unemployed. Many mothers were providing financial and emotional support for the family. Some families were under great stress and dysfunctional, while others were doing well and did not believe that the Vietnam experience was a major factor in their lives. For the families in this sample, the children's problems dictated different family interventions. The needs of the families were highly varied, and adequate services to address those needs have not yet been developed. As the children in these families grow up and their needs change, a comprehensive network of family members will be needed to assess and provide appropriate and ongoing services both for the children and other family members.

Psychological Findings

Extensive literature concerning the impact of the Vietnam war on veterans and their families exists. Yet, despite growing evidence that parental exposure to intense stress, aggression, fear, and anxiety may place their children at increased risk for social and emotional problems (Silverman et al., 1988), few studies of the social-emotional functioning of children of Vietnam veterans have been conducted. As Parsons et al. (1990) pointed out, in many countries parents are struggling to cope with the severe stress of constant and pervasive violence. By examining the social-emotional functioning of children of Vietnam veterans, we may be able to better address not only the needs of these children and their families, but those of a broader population as well.

This study was conducted to answer three questions:

1. Is the social-emotional functioning of the children of Vietnam veterans significantly different from that of other children?
2. Does the presence of psychiatric disturbance in the father place his children at greater risk for social-emotional difficulties?
3. Is a veteran's child with a learning disability at greater risk for emotional behavioral problems?

Methods

Subjects

The sample consisted of thirty-eight children referred by the child's father or mother for evaluation at a University Affiliated Child Development Center in North Carolina. These children were referred because of concerns related to academic, emotional, and medical problems, often in combination. They ranged in age from six to eighteen, with a mean age of eleven years, eight months, and included fifteen girls and twenty-three boys. Five children were African American, one was biracial, and thirty-two were Caucasian. The socioeconomic status of the families was highly varied, with about two-thirds of the fathers either semiskilled, unskilled, or unemployed, and about one-fourth working in a medium business, minor professional, craftsman, clerical, or sales position.

Procedure

Information regarding social-emotional functioning was obtained using a test battery developed to assess children with learning and psychosocial problems. This battery consisted of the Achenbach Child Behavior Checklist or CBCL (Achenbach, 1986), the Revised Children's Manifest Anxiety Scale or RCMAS (Reynolds and Richmond, 1990), and the Children's Depression Inventory or CDI (Kovacs, 1985). The CBCL is a well-standardized instrument that contains a list of behavioral problems and competencies that are rated by parents or parent surrogates. The instrument includes nine separate clinical scales for the six-to-sixteen age group that are grouped into two factors: internalizing and externalizing. The RCMAS is a thirty-seven-item self-report instrument designed to assess the level and nature of anxiety in children and adolescents from six to nineteen years old. It yields a Total Anxiety score as well as four subscale scores. Finally, the CDI is a twenty-seven-item self-rating instrument aimed at measuring depression in children and adolescents between the ages of eight and seventeen. It yields a total score for depression. The CBCL was filled out by the mother in twenty-seven cases, by the father in six cases, and by both parents in six cases. The RCMAS was completed for twenty-six of the children, and the CDI for only fifteen children.

Frequency-level data was initially collected for all thirty-eight children on a total of thirty-six variables. These consisted of the child's age in months, race, gender, father's level of education, mother's level of education, father's occupation, mother's occupation, home status (with whom the child was living), marital status of the parent with whom child resided, father's psychiatric status, child's current grade placement, special education status (children who were already certified as learning disabled (LD) in their school system, or children who met the criteria for LD (versus non-LD) status after their evaluation at the Center, and those who had dropped out of school), and actual or estimated Intelligence Quotient (IQ). Frequencies were calculated on key variables, including parental level of education, father's occupation, child's home status, child's special education status, and anxiety as presented by child's self-report.

Means and standard deviations were then obtained on each of the thirty-five variables. Tests to determine whether the means obtained on each of the subscales for the CBCL were statistically significant were calculated.

In addition, group comparisons were made to determine the difference between CBCL means for: (1) younger children (i.e., under the age of twelve) versus older children (i.e., twelve and over); (2) fathers with and without a psychiatric diagnosis; and (3) children with and without a learning disability. In each comparison, selected demographic variables were examined between groups to determine the need to control for the influence of those variables.

Results

Demographics

As mentioned above, 35.5 percent of the fathers were unemployed, and an additional 25 percent were employed in unskilled or semiskilled occupations. These figures testify to the financial stress experienced by a significant number of the families seen and are all the more striking when one considers that 42.9 percent of the fathers had attended college, although few (3.6 percent) were college graduates. In contrast, twenty-five of the mothers had completed college.

The father's psychiatric status is also noteworthy—57.9 percent of the veterans had a psychiatric diagnosis. Of these, 36.8 percent were diagnosed with PTSD and 21.1 percent had another diagnosis, frequently substance abuse, depression, or anxiety. Of the fathers with PTSD, 35.7 percent were currently unemployed, and 28.6 percent were employed in unskilled occupations.

Referral concerns involving children's learning problems were generally corroborated by evaluation findings, although not all the children qualified for LD services according to the criteria established for local public school systems. Of the children referred, 39.5 percent met all the criteria for an LD diagnosis. In addition, several of the children with learning problems who did not meet eligibility criteria but were diagnosed with attention deficit disorder or another medical disability were recommended for placement as "Other Health Impaired."

Question 1: Is the social-emotional functioning of the children of Vietnam veterans significantly different from that of other children?

These children of Vietnam veterans, self-referred for developmental and school problems, differed from normal expectancies in terms of their higher scores on the CBCL, (Figure 1 and Table 3), but not on the RCMAS or CDI. Although none of the mean values obtained achieved clinical levels, they all approached clinical levels on the CBCL. Of the thirteen youngsters who completed the CDI, only two reported clinical levels of depression, and the mean score was 99.53, falling solidly in the average range. On the self-report ratings, however, an individual

Figure 1. Mean Scores on Parent-Completed Child Behavior Checklist

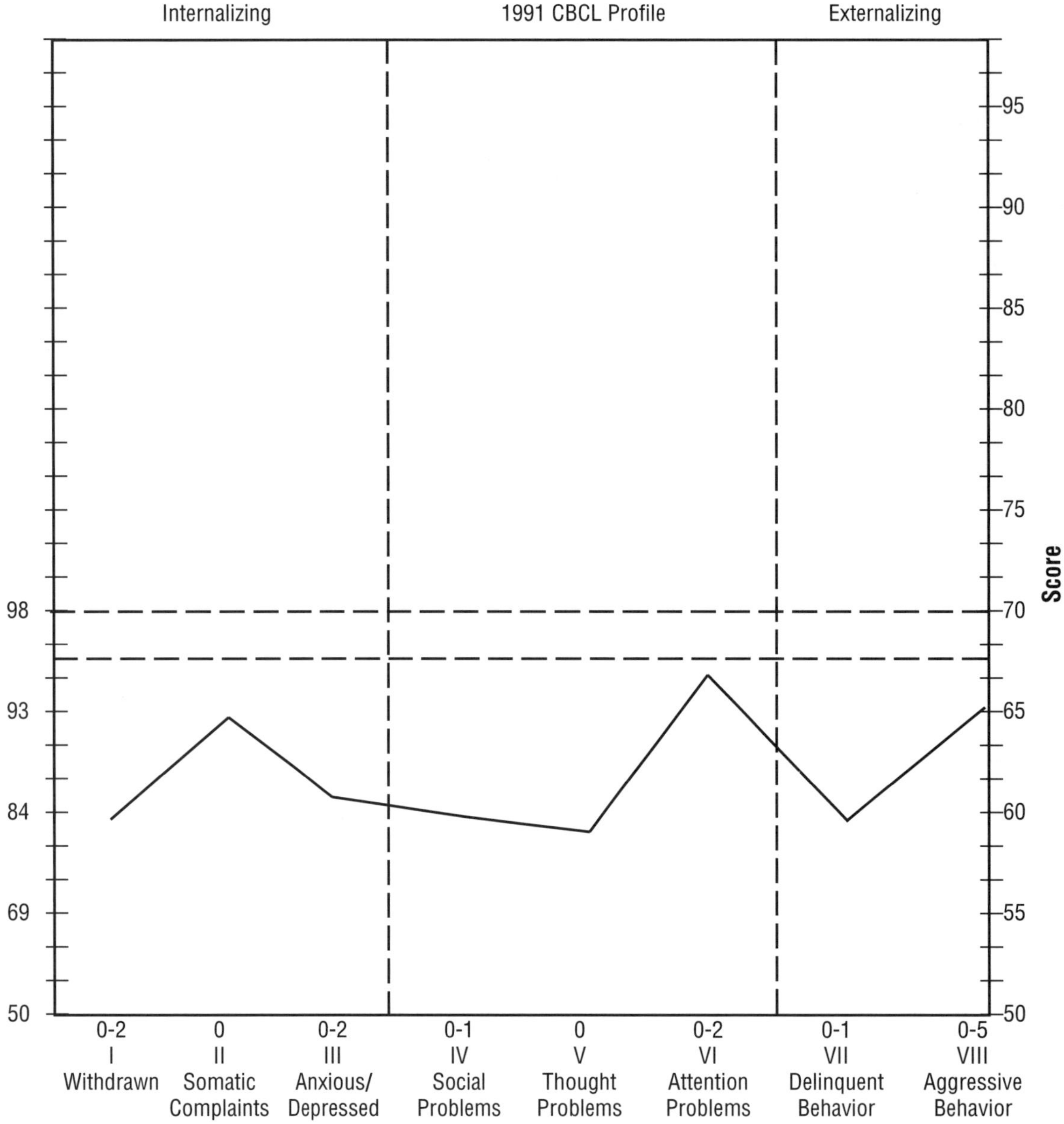

case analysis showed that 26.9 percent of the youngsters had elevated physiological anxiety, and 23.1 percent had elevated worry/oversensitivity (Table 4).

Question 2: Does the presence of psychiatric disturbance in the father place his children at greater risk for social-emotional difficulties?

Initial group comparisons of social-emotional status for children with fathers with and without psychiatric disorder revealed a significant difference between groups on the variables of father's occupation, (t(1) = -6.01, p>.0001), and this variable was covaried on subsequent analyses on ANCOVA. As can be seen in Table 5 (see page 424), the only scale that approached significance was the CBCL school performance, and was in the expected direction. Thus the

Table 3. Obtained Social-Emotional Ratings on Children of Vietnam Veterans

CBCL Scale	Mean	SD	t-value
Withdrawn	62.7105	0.42241	.4226*
Somatic	65.7105	9.97341	9.5819*
Anxious/depressed	63.5000	10.25914	8.0047*
Social problems	63.5789	10.81089	7.6406*
Thought problems	61.5000	0.61962	6.5872*
Attention problems	67.7895	0.31901	10.4866*
Delinquency	60.4474	9.68639	6.5607*
Aggression	64.7632	12.06438	7.4437*
Internal	65.2105	0.44070	9.1838*
External	61.8684	12.76956	5.6535*
Total	65.9474	1.13777	8.7096*
Activities	45.2778	1.5058	-3.1360
Social	37.8571	1.8526	-6.5545
School	34.0870	1.7147	-9.2803
Total	**39.4783**	**2.0428**	**-5.1506**
RCMAS1	10.2692	3.7371	
RCMAS2	9.8462	2.8284	all these are
RCMAS3	9.4615	2.2228	insignificant
RCMAS4	9.5769	2.7759	
RCMASTOT	51.1538	9.9409	
CDITOT	99.5333	10.6261	

*Significant t-values at the .001 level.

Table 4. Anxiety as Presented by Child Self-Report (n=25)*

RCMAS Anxiety Scales	Percent
Physiological anxiety	26.9
Worry/oversensitivity	23.1
Social concerns/concentration	7.7
Social desirability	19.2
Total anxiety	11.5

*Children obtaining scaled scores of 13 or higher on the Revised Children's Manifest Anxiety Scale

father's occupational status, rather than his psychiatric status, appeared to have a significant impact on the child's social-emotional functioning.

Question 3: Is a veteran's child with a learning disability at greater risk for emotional behavioral problems?

Initial group analyses between children with and without LD revealed no group differences on key sociodemographic variables. Consequently, a test was used that indicated no significant differences between groups. Children with a learning disability, however, did appear to be at increased risk for school and social problems (Table 6, page 425). Similar trends were evident with respect to lowered social competence, increased delinquent behavior, and an increased tendency to respond in a socially undesirable manner.

Table 5: Obtained Social-Emotional Ratings on Children of Fathers with and without Psychiatric Disorders

	Nonpsychiatric		Psychiatric		
CBCL Scales	**Mean**	**SD**	**Mean**	**S**	**F**
Activities	46.50	8.54	44.66	9.02	0.18
Social	40.54	11.27	36.62	10.34	0.08
School	30.44	5.35	36.42	8.59	3.55+
Total competence	41.88	10.58	37.92	8.52	0.13
Withdrawn	61.00	10.31	63.5	10.37	0.79
Somatic	63.6	7.79	66.65	10.70	0.04
Anxious/depressed	58.91	7.34	65.61	10.71	0.99
Social problems	65.66	10.59	62.61	10.77	0.60
Thought problems	57.91	8.46	63.15	11.09	0.52
Attention problems	66.83	8.91	68.23	10.87	1.10
Delinquency	59.00	9.21	61.11	9.82	0.60
Aggression	58.25	8.56	67.76	12.25	0.55
Internal	61.66	10.13	66.84	10.17	0.26
External	56.00	12.68	64.57	11.86	0.18
Total	**62.33**	**10.44**	**67.61**	**11.05**	**0.25**
RCMAS1	8.55	2.94	11.17	3.79	0.56
RCMAS2	9.22	2.61	10.17	2.87	0.04
RCMAS3	8.77	1.93	9.82	2.28	0.33
RCMAS4	9.44	2.45	9.64	2.92	0.13
RCMASTOT	47.44	8.82	53.11	9.93	0.43
CDITOT	94.00	7.01	102.3	11.36	0.07

+ $p<.08$

Discussion

The picture that emerges from these data is of a group of children who are subject to multiple, severe stresses. Many of these youngsters must grow up struggling to cope with significant financial and social-emotional difficulties that affect the entire family unit, and that are beyond their control. In particular, the father's occupation, specifically his unemployment and under-employment, appears to have a major impact on the child's social-emotional functioning. Indeed these data suggest that even the father's psychiatric problems (i.e., depression, PTSD, anxiety, and substance abuse), so emphasized in the literature on families of Vietnam veterans, may be eclipsed by the nature of the father's employment. In this regard, the discordance between the father's education and his subsequent employment may greatly contribute to family stress.

The sharp contrast between parents' perceptions of their children as significantly anxious and the children's denial of significant anxious symptomatology as a group also is noteworthy, and merits further exploration. It is also true, however, that slightly more than one-fourth of these children reported elevated anxiety on the RCMAS. These perceptions would be consistent with instances of intergenerational transmission of problems reported by Rutter (1966), Weismann et al. (1984), Danieli (1985), Signal et al. (1988), and Silverman (1988).

A case study will serve to conclude this paper. By fleshing out the statistical skeleton presented above, it may convey a more complete image of some of the children seen by the AOCAP project at the CDL.

P. was a pleasant, attractive, socially poised and cooperative fifteen-year-old girl whose parents' own academic problems had led to their retention in high school. Referral concerns

Table 6. Obtained Social-Emotional Ratings on Children with and without Learning Disabilities

	With LD		Without LD		
CBCL Scales	**Mean**	**SD**	**Mean**	**SD**	**P**
Activities	44.20	7.48	45.60	7.75	.656
Social	34.00	11.23	39.70	9.34	.128
School	29.12	6.84	37.21	7.37	.025*
Total competence	34.37	9.13	41.42	8.44	.097
Withdrawn	63.33	11.23	62.18	10.03	.753
Somatic	64.53	10.21	66.63	9.92	.547
Anxious/depressed	62.86	10.76	64.00	10.10	.753
Social problems	69.73	11.26	59.59	8.52	.005*
Thought problems	62.53	11.78	60.68	9.91	.619
Attention problems	70.46	10.65	66.00	9.92	.213
Delinquency	63.60	9.86	58.40	9.19	.120
Aggression	67.60	14.16	62.81	10.26	.255
Internal	64.53	11.43	65.68	9.93	.754
External	64.13	12.68	60.27	12.16	.387
Total	**67.53**	**11.30**	**64.81**	**11.13**	**.486**
RCMAS1	9.50	3.50	10.60	3.87	.495
RCMAS2	8.90	2.77	10.26	2.69	.251
RCMAS3	8.80	1.77	9.86	2.44	.267
RCMAS4	8.40	2.72	10.20	2.58	.123
RCMASTOT	48.10	7.70	52.60	10.85	.288
CDITOT	98.50	12.28	100.87	9.66	.714

* Note: CBCL = Child Behavior Checklist, with a mean of 50 and a standard deviation of 10; With LD = with a learning disability; Without LD = without a learning disability; RCMAS = Revised Children's Manifest Anxiety Scale, with a mean of 10 and a standard deviation of 3 for subscales; RCMAS1 = physiological anxiety subscale; RCMAS2 = worry/oversensitivity subscale; RCMAS3 = social concerns/concentration subscale; RCMAS4 = lie subscale; RCMASTOT = total score; CDITOT = Children's Depression Inventory total score.

included recurrence of the skin disorder urticaria, learning and behavioral issues. P.'s father had been exposed to the defoliant Agent Orange in Vietnam, and had a history of PTSD and substance abuse, but had been sober for the past nine years. Her mother had a history of depression. In school, P. was somewhat distracted and disorganized, and often seemed restless. The school observed that sometimes she did not study or complete her homework, but she was described by her parents and teachers as a sociable, well-liked adolescent who enjoyed a leadership role and was engaged in numerous extracurricular activities. Both she and her mother described their relationship as close.

During the evaluation, P. seemed tense, spoke rapidly, cracked her knuckles, and popped her chewing gum. Glancing out the clinic window at the rain, she quietly commented that rainy weather often reminded her father of Vietnam. She also observed that her dad had a really bad temper and always had his gun with him. P. added that until recently, she feared that he would wake up in the middle of the night and, thinking he was still in Vietnam, would "go off." She described close, emotionally warm relationships with both of her parents, and seemed highly attuned to their emotional states and individual needs. On the CBCL, P. obtained elevations well into the clinical range on all except one (social problems) of the eight scales, as well as significant elevations on the physiological anxiety and worry/oversensitivity scales of the RCMAS. Although her total score on the CDI was within the normal range, P. reported vegetative symptoms of depression and past suicidal ideation. Her comments indicated poor self-esteem. In spite of her ongoing concern for her father, in particular, and her tendency to worry about many aspects of her life, her academic difficulties, and her bouts of sadness and discouragement, P. displayed excellent motivation to do well in school and excellent interpersonal skills.

P. represents a combination of the vulnerability and resilience found among many children of Vietnam veterans. As she moves through adolescence towards adulthood she, like a significant number of other children of Vietnam veterans, will continue to require close monitoring and social supports in order to realize her promise.

References

Achenbach, T.M. 1986. *Child Behavior Checklist and Youth Self-Report.* Burlington, VT: University of Vermont.

Bronfenbrenner, U. 1979. *The Ecology of Human Development.* Cambridge, MA: Harvard University Press.

Card, J.J. 1987. Epidemiology of PTSD in a National Cohort of Vietnam Veterans. *Journal of Clinical Psychology* 43:6-17.

Cordray, S.M., K.R. Polk, and B.M. Britton. 1992. Premilitary antecedents of post-traumatic stress disorder in an Oregon cohort. *Journal of Clinical Psychology* 48:271-280.

Dane, E. 1990. *Painful Passages: Working with Children with Learning Disabilities.* Silver Spring, MD: NASW Press.

Erickson, J.D., J. Mulinaire, P.W. McClain, T.J. Fitch, L.M. James, A.B. McClearn, and M.J. Adams. 1984. *Vietnam Veterans' Risk for Fathering Babies with Birth Defects.* Atlanta, GA: U.S. Department of Health and Human Services.

Figley, C.R. 1978. *Stress Disorders Among Vietnam Veterans: Theory, Research, and Treatment.* New York: Brunner/Mazel.

Goodwin, J. 1990. *Readjustment Problems among Vietnam Veterans.* Cincinnati, OH: Disabled American Veterans.

Joffe, J.M. 1979. Influence of Drug Exposure of the Father on Perinatal Outcome. *Clinics in Perinatology* 6(1): 21-36.

Jordan, B.K., C.R. Marmar, J.A. Fairbanks, W.E. Schlenger, R.A. Kulka, R.L. Hough, D.S. Meiss. 1992. Problems in families of male Vietnam veterans with post-traumatic stress disorder. *Journal of Consulting and Clinical Psychiatry* 60(6):916-926.

Kelly, D.P., M.S. Levine, and M.R. Burchinal. 1988. Identifying attention deficits which impair cognition and spare activity (abstract). *Journal of Developmental and Behavioral Pediatrics* 9:103.

Kovacs, M. 1985. The Children's Depression Inventory (CDI). *Psychopharmacology Bulletin* 21: 995-998.

Levine, M.D. 1980. *The ANSER System.* Cambridge, MA: Educators Publishing Service.

Levine, M.D. 1985. *Pediatric Examination of Educational Readiness at Middle Childhood: Examiner's Manual.* Toronto: Educators Publishing Service.

Levine, M.D. 1990. *Pediatric Early Elementary Examination-II: Examiner's Manual.* Chapel Hill, NC: Clinical Center for the Study of Development and Learning.

Levine, M.D., L. Rappaport, T. Fenton, et al. 1988. Neurodevelopmental readiness for adolescence: Studies of an assessment instrument for 9-14-year-old children. *Journal of Developmental and Behavioral Pediatrics* 9:181-188.

Maloney, L.J. 1988. Post-traumatic stresses on women partners of Vietnam veterans. *Smith College Studies in Social Work* 58:122-143.

Moos, R.H., and B.S. Moos. 1981. *Family Environment Scale Manual.* Palo Alto, CA: Consulting Psychologists Press

Parsons, J., T.J. Kehle, and S.V. Owen. 1990. Incidence behavior problems among children of Vietnam war veterans. *School Psychology International* 11:253-259.

Piaget, J. 1970. Piaget's theory. In *Carmichael's Manual of Psychology,* ed. P.H. Mussen. New York: Wiley.

Reynolds, C.R., and B.O. Richmond. 1990. *The Revised Children's Manifest Anxiety Scale.* Los Angeles, CA: Western Psychological Services.

Rutter, M. 1966. *Children of Sick Parents.* London: Oxford University Press.

Signal, J.S., V.F. DiNicola, and M. Buonvino. 1988. Grandchildren of survivors: Can negative effects of prolonged exposure to excessive stress be observed two generations later? *Canadian Journal of Psychiatry* 27:779-784.

Silverman, W. K., J.A. Cerny, and A.E. Burke. 1988. Behavior problems in children of parents with anxiety disorders. *Journal of the American Academy of Child and Adolescent Psychiatry* 27:779-784.

Thomas, A., and S. Chess. 1977. *Temperament and Development.* New York: Brunner/Mazel.

Upton, A.C., and B.D. Goldstein. 1984. Human health and environment: Some research needs. *Report of the Third Task Force for Research Planning in Environmental Health Sciences.* NIH Publication No. 86-1277.

Weissman, M.M., J.F. Leckman, K.R. Merikanges, G.D. Gammon, and B.A. Prusoff. 1984. Depression and anxiety disorders in parents and children. *Archives of General Psychiatry* 41:845-852.

Wikler, L. 1981. Chronic stresses of families of mentally retarded children. National Council on Family Relations. Reprinted with permission, from *Family Relations* 30(2):281-288.

Acknowledgments

This research was an outgrowth of clinical services funded by grants awarded to the Clinical Center for the Study of Development and Learning by AOCAP, the Maternal and Child Health Bureau, and the Administration on Developmental Disabilities.

In addition, the authors wish to thank Benedicia Harris, Stephen R. Hooper, Zelma Myers, Ed Taylor, and Thomas J. Wasileski for their assistance in the preparation of this project.

Vietnam Veterans and Family Decision Making

Annette Richards, B.S., with Kristina Handy, M.A.
The Cottage Program International
Salt Lake City, UT

Abstract

This study attempts to determine why Vietnam veteran families have difficulty with decision making, how this affects their family functioning, and how decision-making problems can be resolved. The paper compares decision making among fifteen Vietnam veteran families, fifteen high-risk families, and a sample of fifteen families from the general population. Studies show that the psychological effects of combat trauma place veteran families at risk for unhealthy decision-making and problem-solving processes.

We postulate that both Vietnam veterans and high-risk families will score the lowest overall in decision making. The scores are taken from the Family Profile that assesses family functioning on seven different levels (decision making being only one of the levels). This paper studies differences among the three populations in overall decision-making scores as well as relative scores among the seven different levels for each population.

Annette Richards, B.S., *is a prevention specialist/counselor at The Cottage Program International and a coordinator of the FIF Utah State Family Prison Parenting Program. She holds a B.S. in psychology from the University of Utah. Most recently,* ***Kristina Handy, M.A.****, was associate editor for the International Studies Association in Provo, UT. She earned her M.A. in international and area studies and B.A. in international relations and Spanish at Brigham Young University.*

The Cottage Program International's (CPI) Vietnam Veteran Family Services Program (VVFSP) addresses the needs of veterans and their family members. One of our assessment tools, the Family Profile (FACES III), aids each family in determining its level of balance and healthy family functioning. Initially, when the VVFSP administered the Family Profile we discovered a trend: each Vietnam veteran family scored lowest, out of seven categories, in decision making. Questioning these results, we began a study using a group of Vietnam veteran families, high-risk families, and a sample of families from the general population to determine why Vietnam veteran families have difficulties with decision making, how this affects their family functioning, and how the problem can be resolved.

Studies have shown how the psychological effects of combat trauma may affect the veteran and place his or her family at risk for unhealthy problem solving and decision making. On this premise, we hypothesize that both Vietnam veterans and high-risk families will score the lowest overall in decision making when compared with the general population.

Background of Instruments

The Cottage Program International began in 1972 as an alcohol and drug abuse prevention service. Since its inception, the program has been replicated, and its approach adopted, by organizations throughout the United States. In 1987 The Cottage Program International developed the Families in Focus Program (Boswell, 1992). Families in Focus was the culmination of seventeen years of applied research and professional experience with high-risk individuals and families. The insights, principles, and programs for positive change included in this work were derived from the experiences of thousands of families we have worked with over the years.

The Families in Focus project came about as a result of a desire to help families learn the skills necessary to have a healthy and positive family life in today's environment. It is also a result of the recognition that the environment today's children and youth are exposed to is an increasingly dangerous one. Rates of substance abuse, teenage pregnancy, runaways, suicide, and gang violence are all alarming indicators of the problems that threaten young people. Families in Focus is based on the following principles:

- The family needs to be the focus of our efforts to prevent these problems;
- Families need to focus their energies on a healthy family life if they are going to have one; and
- Families who are in focus will be a positive influence in our community and society.

Developed along with Families in Focus is a family assessment tool called the Family Profile. This tool originated from the Circumplex Model of Marital and Family Systems (FACES II) (Olson and Wilson, 1985). Three central dimensions of family behavior are integrated in the Circumplex Model: cohesion, adaptability, and communication (Figure 1).

Family cohesion refers to the level of emotional bonding that family members have toward one another (Olson, Russell, and Sprenkle, 1983, p. 70). There are four levels of family cohesion ranging from extreme-low cohesion to extreme-high cohesion. These are disengaged, separated, connected, and enmeshed. The disengaged and enmeshed levels are considered extreme. The separated and connected levels represent a more balanced family.

Family adaptability is defined as the "ability of a marital or family system to change its power structure, role relationships and relationship rules in response to situational and

Figure 1. Circumplex Model of Marital and Family Systems

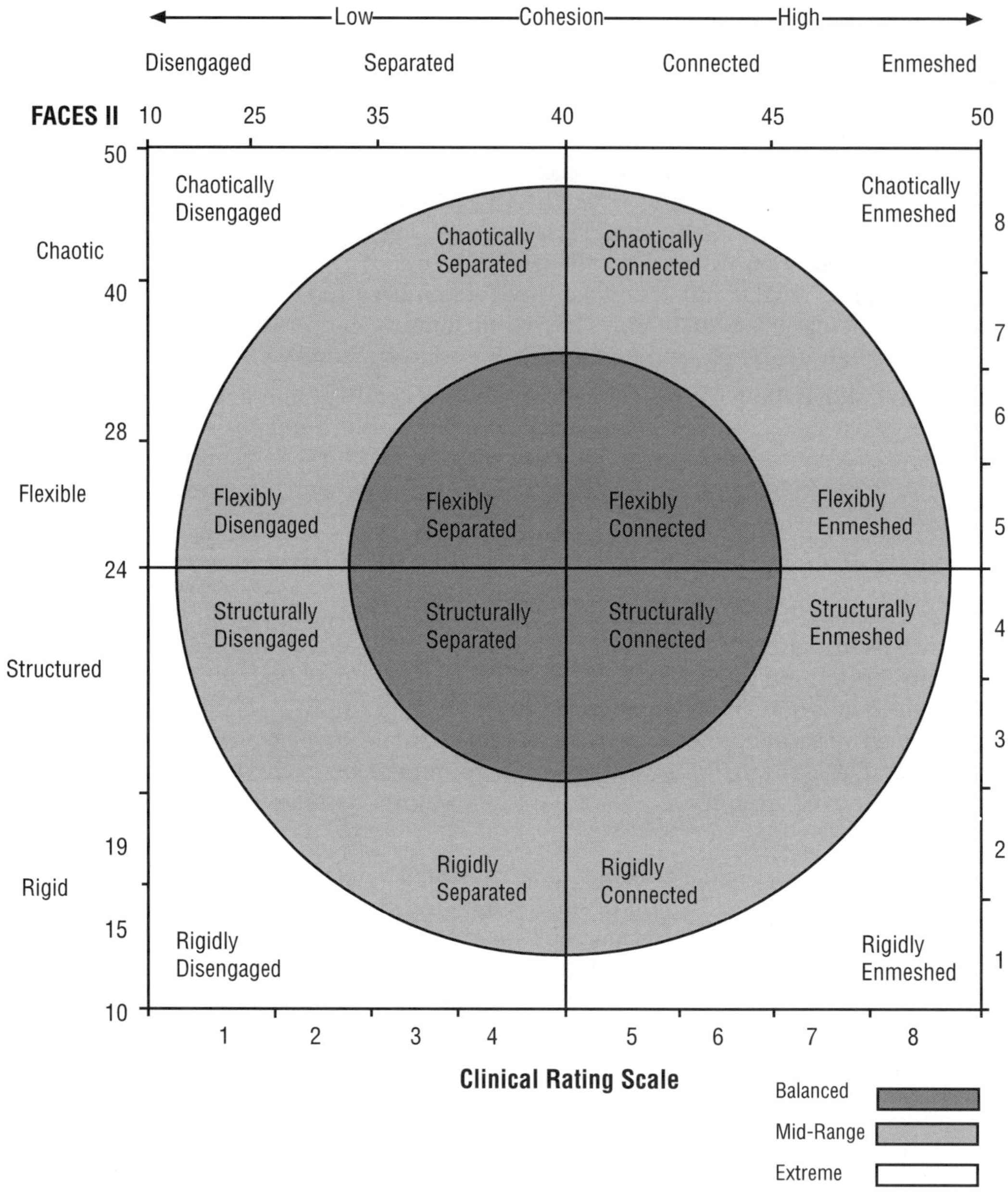

In plotting the couple or family into the Circumplex Model, mark the specific location that most accurately reflects the actual scores.

developmental stress" (Olson, Russell, and Sprenkle, 1983, p. 70). There are also four levels of family adaptability. These levels range from extreme-low adaptability to extreme-high adaptability. The four levels are identified as rigid, structured, flexible, and chaotic. The two moderate or balanced levels are structured and flexible. For each dimension, the balanced levels (low-moderate levels) have been demonstrated to be most viable for healthy family functioning (Olson et al., 1985).

Family communication, the third dimension, assumes that families who are balanced have better communication skills than families who are not balanced (Olsen et al., 1985).

The Families in Focus assessment tool, the Family Profile (FACES III,) addresses seven areas of family functioning: family fun, family decisions, family pride, family values, family feelings, family communication, and family confidence. Much like its predecessor, the Circumplex Model, the Family Profile also assesses homeostasis (balance) within the family. However, more areas of family functioning are assessed with the Family Profile.

The Family Profile assesses four areas of functioning. Each area of functioning is based again upon the seven keys to a healthy family. The Profile assesses balance within the marital relationship, sibling balance, family balance, and self-awareness as to individual balance. Family members assess themselves as to balance within their own family. If balance is extreme, the family then begins to assess what their problem is according to how they scored on the Family Profile.

In the study "Problems in Families of Male Vietnam Veterans With Post-traumatic Stress Disorder" (Jordan et al., 1992), the Circumplex Model of Marital and Family Systems (FACES II) was used to assess both adaptability and cohesion and the degree of balance in both areas. The findings showed that "men with PTSD were 2.5 times more likely to fall into the highest category (extreme) for family adjustment (all couples). Among theater veterans with children, over half of those with PTSD described their families as poorest in functioning on both adaptability and cohesion (couples with children)" (Jordan et al., 1992).

This study also notes that "[a] variety of problems that can negatively affect the family have been found to be associated with combat-related PTSD: difficulties with family cohesion and expressiveness (Solomon, Mikulincer, Fried, and Wosner, 1987); the veterans' problems with intimacy and sociability (Roberts et al., 1982); the veterans' problems with self-disclosure, expressiveness, physical aggression and relationship adjustment (Carroll et al., 1985); and the veterans' deficiencies in interpersonal problem-solving skills (Nezu and Carnevale, 1987)."

Along with deficiencies in problem-solving skills, it appears that Vietnam veteran families struggle with decision making. According to Dr. T.I. Rubin (1985), there are two types of decisions: abdication and real decisions. He states, "in abdication, people either resign completely from the decision-making process or so pervert the process as to almost negate it." He explains further that in making real decisions the individual self is involved completely, "nothing is held back." Abdication is the result of decision blockers or "decision killers." Three of these blockers are described below.

Decision Blocker 1: Losing Touch with Feelings

"In psychoanalysis, losing touch with feelings is known as alienation. It serves as a major defense against anxiety, and is pervasive and devastating to the decision process." (Rubin, 1985, pp. 28-29)

There has been a great deal of research on how stress affects the coping mechanisms of Vietnam veterans. "Vigilant individuals tend to be hyper-alert to threats in their environment, whereas avoidant individuals are likely to deny such threats" (Breznitz, 1983). Working from Wilson's "disruptive" framework, vigilance or avoidance often become a function of dynamic interactions with the environment. Where vigilance or avoidance may serve as a survival mechanism during massive trauma, that same vigilance during the post-traumatic event may no longer serve a useful function (Wilson, in press). Vigilance or avoidance from past trauma results in detachment from the environment. Such avoidance from a previous life-threatening experience (combat) activates the animal flight or fight instinct. Many veterans fall into the flight category where they tend to shut down emotionally or "numb" themselves to their surroundings.

Veterans' inability to assess the present-day environment enhances their vigilance or avoidance. By avoiding their surroundings, veterans create a false sense of emotional safety. Security for veterans is reinforced each time they lose touch with their feelings.

As the veteran becomes emotionally detached, the spouse interprets the behavior as rejection. Avoidance in the marital relationship along with the veteran's decreased sexual activity is interpreted as rejection by the spouse (Haley, 1978; Williams, 1980). To escape the painful issues of rejection, the spouse in turn loses touch with her or his feelings.

Furthermore, avoidance of the veteran's surroundings creates additional responsibility for the spouse. According to Solomon's study, the veteran's spouse often takes on the child care and the financial and psychological well-being of the family (Solomon, 1988). Overwhelmed by responsibility, the spouse gravitates toward emotionally numbing herself or himself.

With both parents becoming detached from their feelings, the children's emotional growth becomes stunted. The veteran's behavior (aggressiveness or retreating emotionally) becomes detrimental to the emotional well-being of the child. According to Haley (1978) "vet aggression is manifested in the parent/child relationship." Combat memories intensify the aggression and the veteran either acts out or avoids the child so as not to hurt her or him. Displayed feelings of aggression or avoidance confuse the child. Healthy parent-child relations become stifled and psychological growth is hindered. The child suffers. Acceptable behavior for the child is physical acting out or emotional numbing. The child becomes immobilized psychologically and growth for the child is grounded by indecisiveness.

Decision Blocker 2: Hopelessness, Depression, and Severe Anxiety

Combat veterans commonly suffer from depression and anxiety. "PTSD patients often experience sadness, anger, guilt, and anxiety" (Pitman et al., 1991). Though depression and anxiety are not represented in the diagnosis of PTSD (DSM III-revised), the veteran's life is nevertheless complicated by these disorders. Generally the veteran is faced with maintaining control when experiencing a severe panic attack. The need to either fight or flee emerges. Again the veteran becomes immobilized by past trauma and the ability to make realistic assessments of his or her environment is diminished. Depression for the veteran decreases his or her everyday ability to function. Problems of severe anxiety and depression have a negative result upon the spouse and children.

The spouse begins to exhibit the same affective disorders as her husband. "Clinical reports have described the wife of the PTSD veteran as chronically distressed, overwhelmed, helpless, hopeless, depressed, anxious, guilty, feeling worthless, hurt, rejected, or angry" (Herndon and Law, 1986). Overwhelmed and fatigued by such emotion, the spouse begins avoiding painful feelings. Every day becomes a struggle for spouses as they try to hold the family together. Additional responsibility creates greater hardship for the spouse and escape for her or him is found in indecisiveness.

Anxiety and depression also become evident in the children. One case study involved a male child who exhibited symptoms similar to those "reported in children of Holocaust survivors, [including]: deficient development of his ego boundaries; high levels of guilt, anxiety and aggressiveness" (Rosenheck and Nathan, 1985). Again the children suffer from a lack of parental stability. Children respond by mimicking their parent until affective disorders begin to emerge in their own lives. Continued anxiety or depression creates additional problems with indecisiveness. This is represented in the final decision blocker.

Decision Blocker 3: Lack of Confidence or Poor Self-Esteem

Continuous depression or anxiety destroys self-esteem particularly when lacking the necessary skills to deal with such affective disorders. According to Solomon et al. (1992), in "From front line to home front," veterans with PTSD have problems trusting others because of this lack of self-esteem. As Solomon notes, "if the veteran avoids his surroundings he escapes hypervigilance. This enables him to always be in control. However, he silently fears his ability to control his surroundings, resulting in a lack of confidence. Distrust and lack of confidence hinders the family from moving forward."

Distrusting the spouse slowly chisels away at the marital relationship. Once again the spouse is overwhelmed by the veteran's lack of intimacy and trust. The spouse's self-esteem is destroyed as she or he interprets the veteran's behavior as rejection. Soon the spouse retreats into herself or himself by cutting off additional relationships. The spouse often "alienates herself from extended family, friends, and helping institutions. Soon the family becomes a tightly closed off, somewhat fortified unit" (Solomon, 1988). Stagnation emerges as the spouse closes herself or himself off to the world. The veteran's preoccupation with the environment, along with the spouse's poor self-esteem, hinders emotional growth for the children.

A survey was conducted by a Vet Center counselor involving children of veterans. "The most commonly reported problems for children of Vietnam veterans were loss of self-esteem; aggressiveness; developmental difficulties; impaired social relationships; and symptoms mirroring those of the veteran" (Jordan et al., 1992). Another study supports this: "Children experience considerable distress, depression and self doubts" (Solomon, 1988). If children perceive their father's or mother's behavior as rejection, they will very likely grow up with poor self-esteem. Anything that represents failure (reinforcing low self-esteem) threatens the child until she or he becomes indecisive.

San Marcos, Texas, Study of High-Risk Groups

FACES III was used previously to assess a high-risk population in San Marcos, Texas. This study showed that the high-risk population assessed scored the lowest in decision making. This may be so for several reasons. High-risk individuals or families are usually categorized as not being resilient in unsafe or dangerous situations such as those involving alcoholism, drug abuse, gang involvement, etc. Human service providers and professionals tend to initially view high-risk individuals as powerless and void of coping and decision-making skills.

The only study involving FACES III (Family Profile) involved twenty-one High-Risk Families. Low-income (high-risk) Hispanics participated in a San Marcos, Texas, Housing Authority study. The Family Profile scores showed the following results for the twenty-one families who completed the Family Profile. Family Decisions (with a mean of 16.3), followed by Family Communication (with a mean of 17.2), Family Fun (with a mean of 17.7), Family Feelings (with a mean of 18.6), Family Confidence (with a mean of 18.9), Family Values (with a mean of 19.0), and Family Pride (with a mean of 20.0). According to this study, high-risk families scored lower in Family Decisions than in the other six keys of family functioning.

Results of the Vietnam Veteran Family Study and Prescriptive Analysis

Table 1 below shows the scores in each category of family functioning for the three populations. As the numbers of participants for each population vary, the absolute numbers listed

Table 1. Family Functioning for Three Populations

Family Profile's Seven Keys	Vietnam Veteran Families	High-Risk Families	Sample of General Population
Family fun	1,067	643	1,058
Family decisions	899	578	876
Family pride	1,229	745	1,162
Family values	1,133	684	1,067
Family feelings	1,138	699	1,078
Family communication	1,051	680	1,041
Family confidence	1,158	755	1,139
	n=58	*n=42*	*n=53*

here do not represent average scores. An analysis was performed to determine statistical significance of the differences shown here. Results are given below.

Vietnam Veteran Group Results

The veteran families scored lower in decision making on average than the general population surveyed, but higher than the high-risk group. Their scores respectively were 15.5, 16.53, and 13.76. These results imply, first of all, that the field of decision making in the Vietnam veteran family is open to additional research. Decision making plays such an integral part in daily living that "empowerment" becomes limited as the decision-making process slows. Second of all, by understanding the veteran family and decision making, efforts can be made to develop successful treatment techniques.

Our veteran families displayed certain types of behaviors that interfere with decision making. Control for the veteran is necessary to life. He or she is subject to the fight or flight instinct at any time. By making decisions outside of their safety zone (limited solely to aggression or avoidance), veterans are jeopardizing their own survival. To allow their spouses' power in the decision process, veterans use control in hopes of preventing the spouses from leaving the relationship. The child in our estimation suffers the most. He or she is prohibited from making decisions with the family (refer to Family Profile decision-making questions). The children's psychological growth becomes retarded because their parents don't involve them in family matters. The child strays from making decisions and finds it difficult to even attempt making appropriate decisions.

The veteran's lack of self-esteem filters through the entire family. The spouse interprets the veteran's actions of avoidance as rejection. She or he soon begins to lose touch with feelings to cover painful issues of rejection. The spouse becomes uncomfortable in making decisions because it may result in greater failure.

In the psychoeducational group we provided for spouses of veterans with PTSD, we found that an underlying theme in their discussion was either avoidance or aggression within the marital relationship. Each wife had put her needs last in the family. With time the wife's self-esteem began to whittle away. The wife's social life was nonexistent unless she worked, and typically she associated almost exclusively with her immediate family. The women's group gave us a greater understanding of what actually occurs in the veteran family.

With both parents exhibiting low self-esteem, the child grows up lacking the confidence to make decisions. The child's behavior often becomes representative of the father (veteran). The child becomes locked into a cycle of either aggression or avoidance. Any behavior deviation results in turmoil for the child. The child fears stepping out and making decisions because any failure means rejection from the father.

Statistics

An analysis of variance was performed on the Family Profile test scores of the three participating populations. Decision-making scores among the three groups showed no significant difference, F=.053. However, in each of the other six categories, there was a significant difference found among the three groups' test scores.

We attribute these results to the questions pertaining to decision making in the Family Profile. The questions asked may represent a more difficult ideal to obtain than the questions in the other six categories. Further research will help us ascertain the appropriate evaluative abilities of these questions.

Problems and Biases with Research and Methodology

This study was the first to use FACES III to assess Vietnam veterans and their families. The validity of the results remain questionable for the following reasons. Olson's Circumplex Model studying balance within the family does not specifically address veteran populations.

The Circumplex Model shows the balance among veterans and their family members was extreme, and that among PTSD Vietnam veterans' families, adaptability and cohesion are poor. Although Faces III addresses balance, decision making among Vietnam veteran families has never been assessed with the Family Profile.

Several biases were present with this FACES III study. None of the families was randomly selected. The dropout rate in the Family Profile was difficult to determine because several of the children weren't present at the time the Profile was administered. Also many of the children were under eight years old and did not participate. Another noticeable problem involving FACES III was that initially it was difficult to get the family to fill out the Family Profile. One reason for this was that family members weren't always present when completing the Profile. It is not until the Family Profile is completed that an understanding of balance within the seven keys is generally understood.

The fact that this was not a numerical match study pertaining to age and number of children creates yet another bias. Also, additional information was gathered from the veterans, creating greater rapport with them and their families than with the high-risk and general population families. One bit of knowledge that was obtained concerning the veterans was whether they had been exposed to additional trauma in their life besides Vietnam. Another bias was that only one (FACES III) instrument was used to assess the three groups. Additional assessment tools would have ruled out some of the biases.

Subjects

Vietnam Veterans: Fifteen Vietnam veteran families participated in this study. Each veteran served in Vietnam for at least one tour during 1961–1972 and all were combat veterans. The veterans were all male. They had all been exposed to combat while in Vietnam. Of the fifteen, eleven had been diagnosed by either the VA Hospital or by a private psychiatrist as having symptoms of PTSD. Their average age is 44.4 years old, all were married (two were separated), and they had an average of 2.6 children.

High Risk: Participants representing our high-risk population were taken from the Salt Lake County Housing Authority. Low income, limited education, and substance abuse qualify as high-risk factors. As indicated by the study, several of the high-risk families had fewer children participate in the questionnaire, and there was less parental participation because of the higher incidence of single-parent families. This particular population scored the lowest in decision making because high-risk individuals often lack the necessary skills to make appropriate decisions.

General Population: Participants representing the general population had a relatively higher income and more education. All participants were part of two-parent families.

Conclusion

Of all the participating groups, the general population showed the most surprising results. We postulated that veterans and the high-risk population would score lowest in decision making while the general population would not score lowest in any particular area. However, this population also scored lowest in decision making compared with the other six categories. Many factors can explain this. First, this population may represent many risk factors that were not taken into account, placing them in a higher-risk category. And second, as stated above, the Family Profile instrument may not accurately assess healthy decision making. This study using the general population is the first of its kind. Additional research or revamping the decision-making questions found in the Family Profile may shed further light on decision making in the general population.

Veteran families scored lower than the general population in decision making but not as low as the high-risk population. We focused on three reasons why veterans struggle with making decisions: losing touch with feelings, depression or severe anxiety, and poor self-esteem.

When treating the Vietnam veteran who suffers from secondary symptoms of PTSD (depression or severe anxiety), medication can play a role in controlling both depression and anxiety. According to Turchan et al., tricyclic antidepressants and benzodiazepines (anti-anxiety) have been shown to be helpful in treating PTSD (Turchan, Holmes, and Wasserman, 1992, p. 400).

Due to severe depression and anxiety, the therapeutic process is stifled. Depression for the veteran can range from mild to severe and chronic. As depression and anxiety intensify, the veteran soon becomes dysfunctional. With the veteran's depression out of control, it is difficult if not impossible to address his PTSD. But through the use of drug therapy, the veteran's depression and anxiety can decrease, making the veteran more capable of working on his PTSD. Tricyclic antidepressants also help when a person is losing touch with feelings. According to Susan L. Mejo (1990), "tricyclic antidepressants are often considered a firstline medication for symptoms involving re-experiencing, numbing, hyperalertness, sleep disturbances and memory difficulties."

Once drug therapy takes effect, making the veteran more functional, the veteran and therapist can then focus on coping skills, empowerment, and understanding trauma. Also, Families in Focus home visits or seminars can be introduced to the veteran's family. This program will strengthen the veteran family by teaching them how to achieve balance within the family. It will also serve as a tool to fall back on when the family is struggling or in crisis.

The question still remains, once the veteran's PTSD is under control, will decision making in the family increase? Once a family is alerted to its decision-making problems, the Families in Focus program can then be utilized to strengthen healthy decision-making processes. However, additional research into Vietnam veteran families or the Family Profile in decision making would lend greater understanding into an area that has been studied very little.

References

American Psychiatric Association. 1987. *Diagnostic and Statistical Manual of Mental Disorders,* 3d ed. (revised), Washington, DC.

Boswell, B.N. 1992. *Families in Focus,* 3d ed. Salt Lake City, UT: Cottage Program International.

Breznitz, S., ed. 1983. *The denial of stress.* New York: International Universities Press, Inc.

Carroll, E.M., D.B. Rueger, D.W. Foy, and C.P. Donahoe, Jr. 1985. Vietnam combat veterans with post-traumatic stress disorder: Analysis of marital and cohabiting adjustment. *Journal of Abnormal Psychology* 94:239-337.

Haley, S.A. 1978. Treatment implications of post-combat stress response syndromes for mental health professionals. In *Stress disorders among Vietnam veterans,* ed. C.R. Figley, 281-295. New York: Brunner/Mazel.

Herndon, A.G., and J.G. Law. 1986. Post-traumatic stress and the family: A multimethod approach to counseling. In *Trauma and its wake, Volume II: Traumatic stress, theory, research and intervention,* ed. C.R. Figley, 264-279. New York: Brunner/Mazel.

Jordan, K.B., C.R. Marmar, R.A. Kulka, R.L. Hough, D.S. Weiss, J. A. Fairbank, and W.E. Schlenger. 1992. Problems in families of male Vietnam veterans with post-traumatic stress disorder. *Journal of Consulting and Clinical Psychology* 60(6):916-926.

Mejo, S.L. 1990. Post-traumatic stress disorder: An overview of three etiological variables and psychopharmacological treatment. *Nurse Practitioner* 15(8):41-44.

Nezu, A.M., and G.J. Carnevale. 1987. Interpersonal problem solving and coping reactions of Vietnam veterans with post-traumatic stress disorder. *Journal of Abnormal Psychology* 96:155-157.

Olson, D.H., C. Russell, and D. Sprenkle, eds. 1983. *Circumplex Model: Systemic Assessment and Treatment of Families.* New York: Haworth Press.

Olson, D.H., and M. Wilson. 1985. *Family Inventories.* St. Paul, MN: Family Social Science, University of Minnesota.

Pitman, R.K., B. Altman, E. Greenwald, R.E. Longpre, M.L Macklin, R.E. Poiré, and G.S. Steketee. 1991. Psychiatric complications during flooding therapy for post-traumatic stress disorder. *Journal of Clinical Psychiatry* 52(1):17-20.

Roberts, W.R., W.E. Penk, M.L Gearing, R. Robinowitz, M.P. Dolan, and E.T. Patterson. 1982. Interpersonal problems of Vietnam combat veterans with symptoms of post-traumatic stress disorder. *Journal of Abnormal Psychology* 9:440-450.

Rosenheck, R., and P. Nathan. 1985. Secondary Traumatization in Children of Vietnam Veterans. *Hospital and Community Psychiatry* 36(5):538-539.

Rubin, T.I. 1985. *Overcoming indecisiveness: The eight stages of effective decision making.* New York: Harper and Row.

Solomon, Z. 1988. The effect of combat-related post-traumatic stress disorder on the family. *Psychiatry* 51:323-329.

Solomon, Z., M. Mikulincer, B. Fried, and Y. Wosner. 1987. Family characteristics and post-traumatic stress disorder: A follow-up of Israeli combat stress reaction casualties. *Family Process* 26:383-394.

Solomon, Z., M. Waysman, G. Levy, B. Fried, M. Mikulincer, R. Benbenishty, V. Florian, and A. Bleich. 1992. From front line to home front: A study of secondary traumatization. *Family Process* 31:289-302.

Turchan, S.J., V.F. Holmes, and C.S. Wasserman. 1992. Do tricyclic antidepressants have a protective effect in post-traumatic stress disorder? *New York State Journal of Medicine* 92(9):400-402.

Williams, C.M. 1980. The veteran system—with focus on woman partners: Theoretical considerations, problems, and treatment strategies. In *Post-traumatic stress disorders of Vietnam veterans,* ed. T. Williams, 73-124. Cincinnati, OH: Disabled American Veterans.

Wilson, J.P. (in press). *Understanding and treating the Vietnam veteran.* In *Post-traumatic therapy,* ed. F. Ochberg. New York: Brunner/Mazel.

Zeitlin, S.B., R.D. Lane, D.S. O'Leary, and M. J. Schrift. 1989. Interhemispheric transfer deficit and alexithymia. *American Journal of Psychiatry* 146: 1434-1439.

Object Relations Family Therapy and PTSD: Family Therapy with Four Generations of a Vietnam Veteran's Family

Nancy E. Errebo, Psy.D.
Vet Center, Missoula, MT

Abstract

Four generations of a Vietnam veteran's family were seen for family therapy by the Post-traumatic Stress Disorder Clinical Team (PCT) at a large urban U.S. Department of Veteran Affairs (VA) Medical Center (VAMC). Therapy focused on family dynamics, individual issues of family members, the impact of the war on the veteran, and the impact of the veteran's PTSD on family members. Object relations family therapy (ORFT) is discussed as a transition between psychoanalytic psychotherapy and systemic family therapy.

This case had several positive outcomes, although the veteran continued to experience serious problems. Family members achieved greater understanding of the veteran, who was the identified patient, and each improved individual functioning as a result of examining family dynamics. The veteran, who initially was unable to discuss his war experiences, was able to tolerate the intensity of the inpatient treatment program. He discontinued using narcotics for pain management and formed good relationships with other Vietnam veterans.

In the case presentation, family dynamics, individual issues, and therapeutic interventions are described at length.

***Nancy Errebo, Psy.D.**, was staff psychologist for the Post-traumatic Stress Disorder Clinical Team (PCT) at the Phoenix VAMC, where she served as training coordinator for the Psychology Service. She is currently on the staff of the Vet Center in Missoula, MT.*

A growing body of literature indicates that psychological trauma has intergenerational consequences. Boszormenyi-Nagy (1985) points out that therapists have an ethical responsibility to make an effort to protect future generations from the effects of their patients' trauma.

Cross-generational effects of trauma have been shown in studies of the children of parents incarcerated in internment camps during World War II. Authors who conducted in-depth interviews with forty children of Holocaust survivors found the imprint of trauma on the deepest levels of the children's character structure (Szilagyi, Cserne, Peto, and Szoke, 1992). Last (1988-89), in reviewing the literature on psychopathological symptoms in children of Holocaust survivors, found that the severity of parental trauma was associated with low assertiveness, low active coping modes, high levels of preoccupation with nurturance, and avoidance of inferiority in the children of survivors. Nagata (1990) compared children of Japanese Americans interned during World War II with children of Japanese Americans who were not interned. Subjects whose parents were interned were found to be less secure about their rights in the United States. Psychiatric problems of children whose parents were interned in Japanese civil internment camps in the Dutch East Indies appeared to be related to their parents' feelings about the past (Doreleijers and Donovan, 1990).

Although the cross-generational effects of combat-related trauma have not been studied as extensively as the traumas discussed above, many authors have noted that families are affected by the post-traumatic stress disorder (PTSD) of veterans (Figley, 1988; Williams, 1987). Several studies have examined the effect of veterans' PTSD on women partners (Maloney, 1988; Verbosky and Ryan, 1988; Coughlan and Parkin, 1987). Effects of veterans' PTSD on their children have not been as systematically studied or described.

Models of Family Therapy with Veterans' Families

Most of the literature on the etiology, conceptualization, diagnosis, and treatment of combat-related PTSD centers on the individual, but family therapy is often recommended. Several therapeutic models have been proposed, most of which center on couples therapy. Most models are structured and time limited.

Throughout this paper, I will refer to the Vietnam veteran as he. The reader should be aware, however, that women did serve in combat zones of most wars and do suffer from combat-related PTSD.

Candis Williams (1987) authored a thorough and useful systemic conceptualization of Vietnam veterans' marriages from the point of view of women partners. Many of her ideas apply to the treatment of other family members. She advocates therapy with the veteran's family of origin when possible.

The women Williams treated found it difficult to cope with their male partners' episodes of rage, substance abuse, emotional isolation, emotional demands, suicide threats, and constant crises. The women had assumed responsibility for all areas of family life and were physically and emotionally exhausted. Their self-esteem was as low as the men's. Williams tried, via women's support groups, to help them focus on taking care of themselves. The women found education about PTSD very helpful and drew great support from problem solving with other women. They found it more difficult to move to the next stage of therapy and accept that their own behavior may have contributed to the problem. Williams and Williams (1987) identified the following tasks in family therapy: remove the veteran from the identified patient role; address the family's methods of handling anger; find a way to deal with war experiences; educate the family about PTSD; develop skills of communication and supportiveness; and explore a shift in roles and values.

Craine, Michael, Hanks, and Stevens' (1992) family adaptation theory model (FATD) stresses the role of interpersonal factors in the maintenance of PTSD. Scaturo and Hayman (1992) observed that the consequences of combat trauma have different impacts at different stages of family life. Brooks (1991) noted shortcomings in the literature of systemic perspectives as applied to families of Vietnam veterans. He discussed the impact of the U.S. Department of Veteran Affairs (VA) system on the veteran's actual family. Figley (1988) proposed a five-step model for family therapy.

Obstacles to Effective Family Therapy

As a VA psychologist, I have encountered problems in working with Vietnam veterans' families that I have not been able to overcome through the use of these models. First, families may be invested in viewing the entire problem as the fault of the war. Part of the combat veteran's task is to integrate wartime experiences with the rest of his life. It is a complex, time-consuming process that requires looking at the family in which he grew up. Veterans and their families often reject interpretations based on childhood experiences because of normal resistance. It is important to remember, however, that they observed profound personality changes in the veteran after the war; any problems he had before Vietnam may seem pale in comparison.

Another problem is the different styles of individual insight-oriented therapy and family therapy. It is sometimes confusing for the veteran with whom I have been working individually to adjust to the more directive style I assume in family sessions.

Most important, these models do not challenge the family to work at the same deep introspective level at which the veteran is working. These models do not reach the deep levels of character structure that Szilagyi (1992) and her partners believe were affected in children of Holocaust survivors. Although it is unrealistic to expect the VA to provide as much therapy for veterans' children as they provide for veterans themselves, I do think that it can help families work at a deeper level without overloading their resources.

Object Relations Family Therapy (ORFT)

Sussal (1992) found the same sorts of problems as I did in making transitions from individual to family therapy. She suggests that therapists can easily apply knowledge of individual psychoanalytically oriented psychotherapy to families using object relations family therapy (ORFT), a flexible approach that incorporates work with the entire family, couples, and individuals. She found that ORFT eliminates "switching from hat to hat" (p. 315) when working with individuals and families.

Based on the ideas of British object-relations theorists, ORFT has the potential to help families work at the kind of depth I advocate. The creators of ORFT, Scharff and Scharff (1987) and Slipp (1988), use object relations concepts of projective identification, repressed ego systems, mother-infant relationships, and group theory. Their techniques include dynamic listening and interpretation of transference, countertransference, resistance, and unconscious collusive forces. Complete definitions and discussion of all of these concepts are beyond the scope of this paper, but projective identification is described below as a major family dynamic.

I use projective identification as Siegel (1991) defines it in her discussion of ORFT. Unconscious conflicts originating in earlier internalizations are often reenacted in intimate relationships through the process of projective identification. Parts of the personality that were formed by internalization of abusive or neglectful objects are projected onto a partner who actually takes on feelings and behaviors that permit the self to reexperience a traumatic relationship. The partners in the relationship seem to unconsciously choose each other for this reenactment.

Object Relations Family Therapy and PTSD

The ideas of Scharff and Scharff and Slipp complement current psychoanalytic thinking about PTSD (Ulman and Brothers, 1988; Haley, 1974; Horowitz, 1986; Krystal, 1978 and 1984; Rose, 1991). Rose's (1991) model for psychodynamic psychotherapy with rape victims is particularly compatible with ORFT and is adaptable to the conceptualization of combat-related trauma.

Rose postulates that the experience of rape, which, like combat, is a stressor outside the expectable range of human experience, overwhelms adaptive techniques for coping with stress. Because these techniques were developed and internalized from the early supportive environment, the traumatic experience shatters internalized object relations. The maternal introject is perceived as failing, abandoning, and betraying. Victims then feel contempt and rage towards maternal figures and their own adaptive techniques. When these feelings are projected, relationships can be distorted, damaged, or destroyed.

ORFT provides a framework within which the traumatized individual and the family can examine how the veteran's perceptions of the traumatic event were shaped by early object relations. Thus, the model helps overcome resistance to interpretations that emptiness and alienation may have predated Vietnam.

ORFT even aids the exploration of the veteran's relationship to the VA, a most complex system. Feelings of rage, inadequacy, and contempt are often projected onto the VA system and constitute a powerful resistance in therapy.

Object relations therapy has helped me write about the family described below—although I had not heard of ORFT at the time I treated them. At that time, I was searching for a way to combine psychoanalytic and systemic thinking. I noticed that projective identification seemed to be a strong family dynamic. That observation helped guide my conceptualization. In describing this case, I will present systemic considerations and discuss projective identification as a major interpersonal dynamic. Names and identifying information have been disguised.

The Thomas Family

Michael, a forty-two-year-old, white, divorced, male Vietnam veteran, was referred to the Post-traumatic Stress Disorder Clinical Team (PCT) of a large urban VA Medical Center (VAMC). Though softspoken and polite, Michael was guarded. Tattooed arms folded over his chest, he regarded the therapist through narrowed eyes. His tense face bore many scars. His ear looked as if it had been stitched on after being cut or bitten off in a fight. He complained of nightmares, sleepwalking, intrusive thoughts of Vietnam, flashbacks, rage, exaggerated startle response, suicidal ideation, and a sense of a foreshortened future. He was reluctant to speak of his two tours in Vietnam as a Marine from 1967 to 1969, but he did tell me that many of his friends had died and that he had "accidentally killed a couple of kids" while attacking a village. Clearly, a diagnosis of PTSD was indicated. Complicating the clinical picture was Michael's addiction to the narcotics prescribed for chronic pain that resulted from a self-inflicted gunshot wound to the stomach six months after his return from Vietnam.

Michael led a hard life before and after the military. The oldest of his alcoholic mother's six children, he was physically abused by several of her eight husbands. His mother often left him with his grandmother for long periods.

His alcoholism and his wife's infidelity ruined his marriage. After his wife left him he "assaulted three guys" and served three years in prison. While he was in prison, his grandmother rescued his three children from their alcoholic, promiscuous mother. He gave his grandmother power of attorney, and the children have lived with her ever since. Michael lived with his children and grandmother, although from time to time he would move out in a rage, often taking one of the children with him. Together, he and his grandmother operated a small horse ranch for a living.

Michael attended two group therapy sessions and then canceled, stating that he was depressed and suicidal. I encouraged him to come in and talk with me, but he declined.

That afternoon, his mother appeared at the clinic and asked me to call her son. She was convinced he would take his own life unless he was hospitalized. She looked distraught and physically ill but was determined to persuade me. She told me what a sweet, helpful little boy he had been, how intelligent and funny he was. She begged me not to tell her son she had contacted me. I stated my reluctance to keep secrets, but she insisted that her "stubborn" son would never enter the hospital if he knew she had initiated it. She left as suddenly as she came. I never saw her again, for she soon died of cirrhosis of the liver.

I did call Michael, who arrived at the PCT in one hour's time accompanied by his eighty-year-old grandmother, a sturdy, bright-eyed woman I will call Rachel. Michael was admitted to the psychiatric unit. We also scheduled a family session for the following week.

The family session was attended by Michael's grandmother, brother, and three children. The family apologized for Michael's absence. He had obtained a pass to leave the psychiatric unit to care for his mother. Forty-year-old Robert, dressed in western clothing and boots, said he had "sensed something was wrong" and had driven from Texas to be with the family. Young Michael, seventeen, was tall and erect with a shy, serious demeanor. He looked much as I imagined his father had looked when he was an idealistic young Marine. Jessica, fourteen, was a pretty, stylish brunette with a sweet smile. Brian, twelve, had a stooped posture and walked with a limp. His slow, painstaking speech made me think he might have a developmental disability. Rachel told me, though, that he had some neurological problems and tended to be "lazy," but that he, like the rest of the family, was highly intelligent.

Indeed, all family members did seem to be uncommonly intelligent. They were attractive, engaging, articulate, eccentric, and humorous as well. They told the family history with relish, especially Rachel's rescue of Michael and Robert from their alcoholic mother and, in the next generation, Rachel's rescue of young Michael, Jessica, and Brian from their mother, "the alcoholic slut." Everyone agreed that, "We owe everything to Grandma."

The children described the fear, anger, and helplessness they felt when their father tore up the house and berated them. He often threatened to kill himself because "no one loves me." The children were exhausted by their efforts to prove their love for him. Despite his behavior the family expressed devotion for Michael. Robert said he had always idolized his older brother and envied Michael's special relationship with their grandmother, Rachel.

The family pronounced the session a success. They proposed one individual session for each of them and then weekly family sessions to be attended by the entire family or groups of twos or threes. They wanted Michael to have group and individual sessions as well. Their plan sounded as good as any I might devise, so I agreed. I got to know them well during the next year.

Systemic Considerations

From a systemic point of view, the most striking feature of the family was its hierarchy. Michael had never left his family of origin. He had brought his children into it and was now, in effect, married to his grandmother. Rachel had been the parental figure for three generations, but it was clear that she probably would not be available to the children as long as they needed her. Michael had too many problems to take care of them. The children, in fact, took care of him. This crisis brought them to therapy.

The hierarchy needed rearranging and boundaries needed defining. This was accomplished by the treatment team assuming the role of authority and caretaking which had been performed by his grandmother and children. I didn't see much hope of Michael being able to take care of his children. I did hope that his children might be helped to stop taking care of *him* so that they could better take care of themselves.

To that end I urged them to set limits with their father and to let him pay the natural consequences of his behavior. I encouraged them to call the police if he frightened them. Jessica did call the police one night and her father was taken to jail.

Soon thereafter, he appeared in my office angry at her and at me. I confronted him about his children's fear of him. He retorted angrily that they had no reason to be afraid of him because he had never hit them as he had been hit. I expressed sorrow that he had been hit and said that I admired his ability to break that pattern. Nonetheless, I stated firmly, his rages, name calling, substance abuse, suicide threats, and prison sentences had indeed made the children afraid. I urged him to commit to solving his problems in therapy and to allow the treatment team to help him. He quietly acknowledged that I was right. The next week he attended the family session for the first time.

After that meeting I saw more of Michael and less of his family. He attended group and individual therapy at the PCT and prepared himself for the intensity of the inpatient PTSD program.

Projective Identification as a Family Dynamic

I arrived for Michael's first family session to find the PCT in an uproar. Michael had called his daughter a "slut" and she had returned his insult. Our secretary and a psychology intern had sequestered Jessica in the secretary's office and were considering calling security when I arrived.

I ushered the family into the conference room, thanked them for demonstrating to me how things really are with them, and invited them to continue being themselves. Michael and his grandmother engaged in a ferocious exchange about Michael's competence as a father. The children intermittently interjected their thoughts in a spirited fashion. I thought I noticed veiled amusement on the part of the grandmother, which indicated to me that some sort of central dynamic was operating. So I intervened for the first time.

I said it saddened me to hear Michael's verbal abuse of his children, but observed that they appeared to be able to talk back and stick up for themselves. Therefore, I concluded, they must not be totally intimidated, and thus he must have done something right as a father. Everyone agreed.

I noted further that I saw no evidence that Jessica was a "slut," and I asked Michael if he really wanted her to play that role. Without waiting for an answer, I wondered if any other important person in his life fit the description of "slut." The answer was obvious to the whole family. I didn't have to explain projective identification to them. The family quickly understood that the process had long been a dynamic in their system. They responded well to insight-oriented interpretation. After all, one of their pastimes was analyzing their interactions.

As a result of neglect, abandonment, and abuse, Michael had felt worthless, helpless, inadequate, and empty since he was a small child. He was able to find some comfort and security in his relationship with his grandmother, to whom he was "special."

Michael found mastery, competence, and a strong father figure in the Marine Corps, which, he stated, "was the only family I'd ever known." He excelled in his first tour in Vietnam. On returning to the States, he felt betrayed when he learned that the Marines had lowered their entrance standards and reduced the length of training. He knew these "brothers" didn't stand a chance in Vietnam. To "save" them, he volunteered for a second tour.

His second tour was a nightmare. On the worst day of his life, he found his two best friends mutilated and castrated. He was pinned down while trying to get their bodies to safety, and his unit was forced to abandon him. It was a miracle he wasn't killed himself. During this dreadful episode he experienced a sense of profound fragmentation and dissociation.

In bits and pieces and parts, he projected all of the distressing, confusing mixture that was his inner experience onto his family, especially his children. His alliances shifted constantly. One of them would assume the role of the special, favored child. Another would play the inadequate, helpless part of Michael. Still another would act as the persecutor. Readers will probably be able identify other projections.

Projective identification seemed to have been a longstanding dynamic. A poignant moment in therapy was Rachel remembering harsh treatment at the hands of her adored father. She claimed not to have been hurt, but we all wondered together why she had always surrounded herself with so many hurting people.

In fact, the first instance of projective identification in this case was Michael's mother inducing me to play the part of her that was a loving, powerful mother to Michael. His ambivalent feelings towards her were played out in the transference.

Treatment Outcome

After a year, Michael was admitted to the inpatient PTSD program. He courageously endured chronic pain without narcotics while completing the three-month program. I accepted a job in Montana, and he and I said good-bye just before he was discharged. He attended the Aftercare Group at the PCT for four months with good maintenance of his therapeutic gains. He terminated group when he moved to another state.

I wish I could say that the story ended on that positive note, but a year later he was referred to the PCT from the intensive care unit. He did not keep his appointment. I do not know where he is now, how he is, or even if he is alive.

References

Boszormenyi-Nagy, I. 1985. Commentary: Transgenerational solidarity—therapy's mandate and ethics. *Family Process* 24(4):454-456.

Brooks, G.R. 1991. Therapy pitfalls with Vietnam veteran families: Linearity, contextual naiveté, and gender role blindness. *Journal of Family Psychology* 4(4):446-461.

Coughlan, K., and C. Parkin. 1987. Women partners of Vietnam vets. *Journal of Psychosocial Nursing and Mental Health Services* 25(10):25-27.

Craine, M.H., R. Hanks, and H. Stevens. 1992. Mapping family stress: The application of family adaptation theory to post-traumatic stress disorder. *American Journal of Family Therapy* 20(3):195-203.

Doreleijers, T.A., and D.M. Donovan. 1990. Transgenerational traumatization in children of parents interned in Japanese civil internment camps in the Dutch East Indies during World War II. *Journal of Psychohistory* 17(4):435-447.

Figley, C.R. 1988. Post-traumatic family therapy. In *Post-traumatic Therapy and Victims of Violence,* ed. F. M. Ochberg, 278-294. New York: Brunner/Mazel.

Haley, S.A. 1974. When the patient reports atrocities. *Archives of General Psychiatry* 30:191-196.

Horowitz, M.J. 1986. *Stress Response Syndromes*, 2d ed. Northvale, NJ: Jason Aronson.

Krystal, H. 1978. Trauma and affects. *Psychoanalytic Study of the Child* 33:81-116.

Krystal, H. 1984. Psychoanalytical views on human emotional damages. In *Post-traumatic Stress Disorder: Psychological and Biological Sequelae,* ed. B. Van der Kolk, 1-28. Washington, DC: American Psychiatric Press.

Last, U. 1988-89. The transgenerational impact of Holocaust trauma: Current state of the evidence. *International Journal of Mental Health* 17(4): 72-89.

Maloney, L.J. 1988. Post-traumatic stresses on women partners of Vietnam veterans. *Smith College Studies in Social Work* 58(2):122-143.

Nagata, D.K. 1990. The Japanese American internment: Exploring the transgenerational consequences of traumatic stress. *Journal of Traumatic Stress* 3(1):47-69.

Rose, D.S. 1991. A model for psychodynamic psychotherapy with the rape victim. *Psychotherapy* 28:85-95.

Scaturo, D.J., and P.M. Hayman. 1992. The impact of combat trauma across the family life cycle: Clinical considerations. *Journal of Traumatic Stress* 5(2):273-288.

Scharff, D.E., and J.S. Scharff. 1987. *Object Relations Family Therapy*. Northvale, NJ: Jason Aronson.

Siegel, J. 1991. Analysis of projective identification: An object-relations approach to marital treatment. *Clinical Social Work Journal* 19(1):71-81.

Slipp, S. 1988. *The Technique and Practice of Object Relations Family Therapy.* Northvale, NJ: Jason Aronson.

Sussal, C.M. 1992. Object relations family therapy as a model for practice. *Clinical Social Work Journal* 20(3):313-321.

Szilagyi, J., I. Cserne, K. Peto, and G. Szoke. 1992. A masodik es a harmadik generacio: Holocaust tulelok es gyermekeik/ Survivors of the Holocaust: The second and third generation in Hungary. *Psychiatria-Hungarica* 7(2):17-129.

Ulman, R.B., and D. Brothers. 1988. *The Shattered Self: A Psychoanalytic Study of Trauma.* Hillsdale, NJ: The Analytic Press.

Verbosky, S.J., and D.A. Ryan. 1988. Female partners of Vietnam veterans: Stress by proximity. *Issues in Mental Health Nursing* 9(1):95-104.

Williams, C.M. 1987. The veteran system with a focus on women partners. In *Post-traumatic stress disorders: A handbook for clinicians*, ed. T. Williams, 169-192. Cincinnati, OH: Disabled American Veterans.

Williams, C.M., and T. Williams. 1987. Family therapy for Vietnam veterans. In *Post-traumatic stress disorders: A handbook for clinicians,* ed. T. Williams, 221-231. Cincinnati, OH: Disabled American Veterans.

The Children of Vietnam Veterans: Complex Concerns and Innovative Solutions

Phillip R. Kraft
Family Health Counselor
Vietnam Veterans Agent Orange Victims, Inc.

Abstract

An organization was created in 1978 by Paul Reutershan, who filed suit against the chemical companies that manufactured Agent Orange, to provide direct case management and support services for the thousands of Vietnam veterans and their families who came to him for help. Since that time, the organization has focused most of its attention on providing those services for the veterans' children and families as well as the veteran. The nonprofit Vietnam Veterans Agent Orange Victims, Inc. (VVAOVI) presents some models of how outreach services can assist individual families in learning new empowerment skills and strategies to obtain what they need. The organization has helped thousands of families in thirty-eight states. The following principles guided VVAOVI's projects: (1) accepting the veteran's negative feelings about Agent Orange exposure develops a sense of caring and trust in the relationship between the individual and the organization from which he or she is seeking help; (2) an array of medical and social challenges may confront children with disabilities and chronic health conditions, and these challenges must be addressed for the long term; (3) an ambivalent attitude on the part of veterans in their dealings with various health care and social systems requires outreach and support to the family in navigating these systems; and (4) service needs must be tailored to the individual situation and to the resources of the family's community.

Case studies representing five families are used to illustrate the principles of the VVAOVI projects. Results of the projects include the following lessons: (1) the presenting crisis that motivates a family to seek services usually represents only a portion of more complex problems the family is facing; (2) income eligibility requirements of health insurance companies often limit access to services the family needs; (3) social service organizations are not always aware that the U.S. Department of Veterans Affairs (VA) does not care for the families of veterans and as a result those agencies need to develop more outreach strategies for this population; and (4) assisting veterans to negotiate directly with health care providers and others concerning the expense of services often results in less economic impact on the family. The project advocates continued proactive interventions on the part of veterans and those supporting them in order to integrate the families successfully into their communities.

Phillip R. Kraft *is a family health counselor at Vietnam Veterans Agent Orange Victims, Inc., where he provides ongoing family services for Vietnam veterans and their families. He served in Vietnam in 1970 with the U.S. Army.*

Each person's journey is singular. No two journeys are identical. For Vietnam veterans who were exposed to Agent Orange the journey they have made with their families forms a mosaic of adversity and challenges as well as strengths and successes. For the past sixteen years, Vietnam Veterans Agent Orange Victims, Inc. (VVAOVI) has journeyed with many veterans and their families in seeking the supports and services as well as the healing they need. There are no simple solutions or instant cures. But along this journey there is sorrow and joy, frustration and success, and the beginning of a broader vision for ourselves and the families: a vision based on pride, dignity, and self-respect.

How We Began

In 1978, Paul Reutershan founded VVAOVI, a nonprofit organization, to spearhead the cause of the Vietnam veteran exposed to Agent Orange. In its early days, VVAOVI was responsible for getting the names and addresses of thousands of Vietnam veterans into the agency's files. This information was used to support the suit that Reutershan filed in 1978 against the chemical companies that manufactured Agent Orange. This suit became the foundation of the larger class action suit that resulted in the Agent Orange Class Assistance Program (AOCAP). Reutershan died that year, but his legacy is this organization.

The mission of VVAOVI is to create a holistic perspective of both the veteran and the family member. This approach is supported by the fact that the problems encountered by veterans and their families are rarely simple and easily resolved. Rather, many of the medical, health, and social challenges seem to be intertwined with the veteran's service in Vietnam and concomitant exposure to Agent Orange.

With this orientation, VVAOVI assisted veterans' claims with the Veterans Administration (now the U. S. Department of Veterans Affairs (VA)), provided counseling to veterans with post-traumatic stress disorder (PTSD), assisted veterans in acquiring services for additional problems, and collected and distributed data pertaining to the medical conditions and disabilities that impacted the veterans.

From the program's inception, it was evident that veterans were concerned not only with their health problems but were beginning to question whether Agent Orange could have contributed to congenital conditions or chronic health problems in their children. With increasing efforts across the United States focused on establishing the impact of exposure to Agent Orange on the veterans, programs were now challenged to move into a previously unexplored arena—the needs of children. By the time Hank Schieb approached VVAOVI in 1985, it was apparent that although conclusive answers to the effect of Agent Orange exposure might never be forthcoming, the children could not wait for medical or other therapeutic services. VVAOVI could not provide definitive answers, but in collaboration with families, we joined them on their journey.

Here, in Hank Schieb's own words, is his story and that of his daughter, Brandie.

> Hi,
>
> Here is a short history lesson I hope you will read. My name is Hank Schieb, and I have a young daughter named Brandie. I may be just a little bit prejudiced, but I feel she is the greatest girl there is. She has not only grown to become a lovely young lady, but through her I have come out of the cave I've been living in since I came home from Vietnam, back in 1971. You see, she was born with some serious birth defects that I've been shown came from my exposure to Agent Orange. At that time, I was a mechanic for a construction company, and although my wife and I were crushed by the problems

of dealing with the defects, at least I had medical coverage through the union. Five years later, my lifelong dream of opening my own repair garage presented itself. I took the chance and opened my garage in my hometown of Winsted, CT. Soon after opening, I found that there was no insurance company anywhere that would take Brandie in any type of policy for health insurance. Soon I had three mortgages and several huge personal loans to cover her medical bills. I was about to lose my home, business, and everything I have worked for. All seemed lost until three other 'Nam vets heard of my problem. Frank McCarthy and Jim Sparrow of VVAOVI, and Tom Condon, a columnist for the *Hartford Courant*, without my knowledge started the "Brandie Schieb Fund" within the veteran community. I soon found out that I was not the only vet in trouble. There were thousands and thousands of vets in the same boat as I was.

The result was that enough money was raised so that Brandie got the medical attention she so badly needed. In fact, there was a small amount left. Then I was asked if we could possibly help another vet with what we had. Of course we said yes. Well, then another and another and so on. We discussed this all with Brandie, and her response was to change the name of the fund to "The Brandie Schieb Children's Fund" and try to raise money on a larger scale. Well, it worked. To date, the fund has given financial help to hundreds of vets' kids all around the country. VVAOVI asked for nothing from me but to feel proud of myself for having served. The issue of Agent Orange and children has dimmed in the eyes of the American people in the past few years. These kids are still people and need your help. Most are now teenagers and are forming the impressions now that will last a lifetime. I want them to have the impression that America cares about them and is willing to help. I also want them to grow up knowing we do not turn our backs on our veterans.

VVAOVI has developed an array of strategies to help families obtain the services they need for their children. To date, empowerment and assistance have been provided to thousands of children's families; actual funds have been expended to assist more than 270 children from thirty-eight states. These children may have medical, learning, and behavioral problems ranging from congenital conditions that are readily identified and corrected (e.g., cleft palate, hypospadia (a misplaced opening of the urethra), and strabismus) to conditions that will require multiple operations, procedures, and intervention over a period of years (e.g., spina bifida, Treacher-Collins,* and club foot). Some of the children have had medical conditions that resulted in death. Other children have less evident problems such as learning disabilities and attention deficit hyperactivity disorder. VVAOVI provides services to all of the children, regardless of the presence or extent of a disability or health condition because all children's needs deserve recognition and response.

Principles of a Responsive Agency

Journeys have no meaning if learning does not occur. The odyssey of VVAOVI with Vietnam veterans and their families has yielded some important principles in providing effective supports and services. Four principles set the framework for our interaction with these families:

- First, effective communication and the development of trust with Vietnam veterans is facilitated by accepting the veterans' feelings about Agent Orange exposure. The scientific community may be hesitant to assign definitive causal attributes to dioxin exposure, but the veterans' feelings must be accepted and respected. Whether an irrefutable link is ever made, veterans' children have problems and their needs are real. To debate the scientific data with veterans is counterproductive. Acceptance of feelings

---

*Cranio-facial condition often requiring constructive surgery to provide external ear structure, eyelids, and jawbones. This is what Brandie Schieb has.

of guilt, anger, frustration, and anxiety communicates the message, "We hear you and we care." The journey can be made easier by having someone who cares with you.

- Second, children with disabilities and chronic health conditions do not exist in a vacuum. They may live in families challenged by lack of consistent, affordable, available health care, economic disadvantage, or educational and attitudinal barriers within their communities. Marital conflict, abuse of alcohol and other drugs, or the effects of PTSD may also be present. Within this complex mixture, it must be understood that supports and services are often needed over an extended period of time and that short-term solutions must be accompanied by strategies to increase the confidence and skills of the family in their interactions with providers and agencies.

  Families often seek services when they are confronted with a crisis and all of their other resources are exhausted. VVAOVI acknowledges their concerns and works collaboratively with them to find workable short- and long-term solutions. The crisis that moved the family to seek assistance may not be the most complex one, and VVAOVI has seen the value of both patience and tenacity. Complex health, financial, educational, and emotional problems require careful coordination and active involvement of the family members.

- Third, ambiguity and ambivalence will be companions on the journey. Vietnam veterans may request assistance for themselves and their families, but they resent what they perceive as charity. To obtain what they feel they are entitled to because of their service to their country is acceptable. Often, however, the solutions presented to veterans may make them feel like they are asking for charity. For instance, veterans may find it demeaning to ask a hospital to forgive a portion of their bills or to complete exhaustive applications that are intrusive and often result in services that are difficult to access.

  Veterans want definite answers about their own health and their children's health. But there may never be clear answers, and recognizing this may only serve to increase negative feelings about themselves and the future. In acquiring services, the veteran must interact with multiple state and local agencies and service providers. The veterans may be distrustful of any system and yet acknowledge that the services they need for their families are available in these same systems. To both acknowledge the ambivalence and simultaneously support the family in learning the skills and gaining the confidence needed to navigate bureaucratic mazes is a requirement of a proactive agency.

- Fourth, VVAOVI worked with families to find solutions for some of the challenges they face in ensuring that their children have all of the medical, educational, and technological services they need for full community participation for the past sixteen years. These solutions include linking families with a variety of programs and resources; creating coordinated service arrays and seeking innovative ways to find funding sources. There is no pattern of service needs; so, services are sought and tailored on an individual basis. Families bring varying economic resources, skills in negotiating for services, and levels of energy to the process. VVAOVI has the responsibility of offering support at the level of intensity needed as well as suggesting possible solutions that respect the diversity of each family.

Profiles of Families

The application of the principles of a responsive agency is best illustrated by sharing portions of the journey that VVAOVI has taken with families and their children. The families that are profiled are not weak, helpless, or incompetent. On the contrary, they have been faced with major challenges in their lives and responded with ingenuity and perseverance. When traditional methods had been exhausted, these families sought help from VVAOVI. These profiles represent the multidimensional needs faced by the family as a whole as well as individual family members and the complexity of resources required. (To protect privacy, personally identifiable information about these families has been edited.)

Andy

Since birth, Andy has experienced a variety of health and developmental problems, including feeding difficulties and delays in language and social development. Although his parents had obtained numerous diagnostic evaluations, specialists had been unable to provide a label for his condition. Autism had been suggested, and Andy was receiving special education services. Children with autism often have difficulty in expressing themselves verbally and in relating to other people. The family had health insurance, although with the mother in school and the father able to obtain only part-time work, they had to pay the full cost of the premiums.

Through the years, the parents had used various strategies to help Andy learn and were determined to seek additional ways to assist him in connecting positively with the world around him. When the family contacted VVAOVI, they were trying to locate three nontraditional services that had been useful for children with autism: swimming therapy, hippotherapy,* and audio enhancement training (AET). These services were not covered by insurance because AET is considered experimental. We linked the family with a swim therapist and helped them negotiate for lessons. A local equestrian program provided its services free. VVAOVI assisted the parents in their search for a qualified AET provider. AET is a program originally developed in Europe that retrains the brain to accept as painless those sounds ordinarily perceived by persons with autism as painful. Andy (after AET) now enjoys the town's church bells, which had previously terrified him.

Hospital bills for Andy often exceeded the insurance benefits and were of significant concern to the family. The family was encouraged to negotiate with the hospital administration to accept insurance payments as sufficient. With support, the parents not only accomplished this but learned to analyze their hospital bills carefully and refuse to pay for procedures that did not actually occur. The family learned skills to address more assertively areas of concern and were delighted with Andy's increased ability to interact with others and enjoy more of his environment.

Suzy and Frank

VVAOVI was contacted by a Vietnam veteran who was in prison and worried about his wife and children. The family was located and their health needs were identified. Suzy, who is seventeen, had a severe to profound bilateral sensori-neural hearing loss. Her hearing aid needed repairs, but because her mother was employed, the family did not qualify for public assistance programs. Civic organizations that often aid in obtaining assistance devices chose not to help the family of a convict. In addition, Frank, a younger brother, had no vision in his right eye and needed a current opthalmological examination and a prescription for corrective lenses.

By linking the family to traditional providers, hearing aids and an opthalmological examination could be obtained, but time was a serious issue. Suzy had spent the previous year without an aid, and her schoolwork had been affected. VVAOVI assisted both Suzy and her mother in understanding how to use the system. Relying on the system, however, would mean a delay of at least six to nine months while income determinations and eligibility re-

---

*Hippotherapy is horseback riding for children with developmental challenges. It instills a sense of balance and self-confidence by providing children with a freedom of movement that they have difficulty accomplishing independently.

quirements were conducted, and it was imperative for Suzy's schooling to get the hearing aids as soon as possible. In collaboration with the mother and Suzy, VVAOVI negotiated with an audiologist and a hearing aid dealer for both an examination and immediate delivery for the hearing aid at a reduced cost.

Based on these efforts, Suzy was able to complete high school successfully and enroll at a university. Through these activities, VVAOVI reaffirmed its commitment to reach out to families and to assist them in finding the resources they need.

Milly

Milly's journey was particularly challenging. Raised in the Ozarks, she has limited vision and requires glasses with special corrections. Her greatest challenge, however, is a condition known as alopecia totalia, which is the absence of any hair. VVAOVI was contacted by Milly's mother in 1991. Milly was confronting several problems that are painful for adolescents. She needed to connect with others who had the same condition, and, more immediately, she needed a wig that appeared more natural and could not be pulled off easily. Milly was linked to the National Alopecia Areata Foundation. Through this resource, she learned about support groups across the United States and receives current information about this condition as well as strategies for coping emotionally with it.

The strategies for coping were especially helpful because Milly had been traumatized by the verbal and physical assaults of her peers. She decided to quit school while she waited for the specially designed wig, which required several months to complete.

Her mother was worried about the impact that missing school would have on Milly's grades. With encouragement, Milly's mother visited the school principal to fully explain the situation. Because he now understood the situation more clearly, the principal arranged for counseling for Milly to prepare her for school reentry and also allowed Milly to move ahead with her class even though she had not been able to complete her finals. The next school year, Milly, with her new wig and increased self-confidence and coping skills, became a member of the National Honor Society.

Robin, Christopher, and Nancy

Sam had three children, all with significant cranio-facial problems. Robin (age fifteen) and Christopher (age eleven) had already had corrective procedures on their lower jaws. As an infant and toddler, Chris had to wear a cranial helmet. Nancy (age nine) had the same jaw malformation as her siblings. All three required ongoing treatment. Sam had a high-intensity career in investment banking, and he had never received assistance for his PTSD. Given the multiplicity of challenges he faced, he often felt overwhelmed. Confronted with increasing pressures, he became despondent and was unable to continue with his job. Sam telephoned VVAOVI for assistance. After two weeks of long telephone conversations with Sam, he recognized that he needed to seek treatment for PTSD. Sam was linked to a team leader at a local Vet Center where he began group therapy sessions. The Vet Center team leader and VVAOVI supported Sam in his decision to receive additional individual therapy at the VA Medical Center.

Robin was receiving extensive orthodontia treatment, and Sam could not discuss the steadily mounting bills with the orthodontist without having severe anxiety. With assistance from VVAOVI, the orthodontist was contacted and provided with additional background information. The orthodontist agreed to accept half of the balance and write off the rest as a charitable donation to VVAOVI. Because he now understood more about the extensive medical needs of this family, the orthodontist agreed to absorb additional costs incurred for ongoing treatment. Resolving this issue was critical to Sam. It allowed him to have some peace of mind and to focus on strengthening his own life.

Randy

Many of the families who contact VVAOVI do not qualify for government assistance based on income. Often, they consider themselves to be middle-class families for whom the added medical- and health-related expenses have become insupportable. The Judsons are an example of a family caught in this dilemma. The father had been an officer in the military and had a reasonably good job. The mother worked until she had an accident. Randy has immune system problems including an Epstein-Barr-type condition and is allergic to almost all man-made chemicals used in the manufacture of medications. This presents a significant problem for an adolescent who is highly susceptible to infections.

As a result of these problems, Randy missed school frequently. Because Randy's absences did not usually extend for ten days and he did not have a disability that the school system recognized, he had not been eligible for in-home tutoring. Randy's parents had spent extensive time and energy in convincing the school system that this was unfair. After lengthy negotiations, the school system agreed to provide Randy with in-home tutoring immediately when his missed a single day of school because he had developed another infection.

By the time this was resolved, Randy had already missed too many days of school and was directed to complete a three-week science course in summer school in order to successfully complete his junior year. One major barrier remained: the summer school had a policy that one day's absence meant failure of the entire course. The family was told that another option would be to enroll Randy in the summer session of a nearby private school at their own expense.

The additional expense of the private school was more than the family's already strained budget could handle. The mother contacted VVAOVI for information and some proactive problem solving. We assisted her in talking to the principal at the private school to ensure that they understood the implications of Randy's condition in reference to attendance. The private school was willing to work with the family and Randy and also discounted half of the tuition fee as a charitable contribution to the organization.

With the support and understanding provided, Randy's mother returned to her quest to ensure appropriate educational opportunities for her son. Randy is currently attending an out-of-state university. He has good financial support, and the university recognizes his needs for specific accommodations and adaptations.

His mother has since volunteered her services to work with other families facing similar challenges. She has reached out to others with her wisdom, strategies, and insights into how systems can be encouraged to be more responsive.

Lessons for Systems

The years of experience at VVAOVI in collaboration with Vietnam veterans and their families provide valuable lessons that could benefit systems. First, a crisis may motivate the family to seek help, but the immediate crisis is usually only part of more complex issues that require multiple solutions over a period of time. Too often, families have been provided a single response to a crisis, but those in the health care system did not take the time to develop trust with the family and to understand more holistically what the pervasive issues were and how the family might want them addressed. Helping a veteran receive assistance for PTSD is important, but this alone does not resolve the medical and financial concerns facing the family.

Second, because many veterans and their families are employed and have some insurance, they often face a series of barriers to acquiring services. Income eligibility frequently restricts access. Medical and educational systems must identify ways to provide needed services, not limit them. Families with one or both parents employed and who are covered by some health insurance are at the greatest risk for denial or limitation of medical and health benefits. Insurance companies should assist those families by modifying existing rules or establishing more flexible funding systems.

Third, there is an ongoing need for the multiple health and social service systems to recognize that the VA does not provide comprehensive services to veterans and certainly not to their families. Consequently, professionals in these systems must learn about the issues surrounding Vietnam veterans and their families and develop strategies that respond to those needs. This has policy implications for the various systems because they need to develop more outreach strategies for veterans and their families as well as provide the services and supports that are required to address the families' concerns.

Fourth, resources can be leveraged. The use of proactive strategies to help families talk directly to private health care providers has identified a number of options: reduced payments, encouraging medical providers to write off medical bills as charitable deductions, developing extended payment schedules, and obtaining *pro bono* services.

Health and social service systems can become more responsive. With continued proactive interaction with veterans and their families, advocacy through AOCAP grantees, and examination and incorporation of the models used by programs that have successfully supported veterans and their families, the children of Vietnam veterans can become full participants in their communities.

Acknowledgments

I would like to acknowledge the support of Frank McCarthy, Patricia Carstens, Jimmy Sparrow, and Judith Holt.

Transition to Independent Living: Challenges Facing Vietnam Veterans' Families Having a Child with a Developmental Disability

Susan R. Leibold, M.S., R.N.
Spina Bifida Association of America
Tucson, AZ

Abstract

The experiences of the Spina Bifida Association of America's Project Independence have been to empower Vietnam veterans' family systems to support the individual with spina bifida to move towards independence. The purpose of this program has been to help the child or young adult develop techniques to learn that "I can do it myself" and to support the veterans' families in letting go of their developmentally disabled child.

The intervention strategies discussed in this paper are based on the needs of the family, the age and abilities of the child, and the complexities of their learning disabilities. The strategies include bowel continence training, camp for school-age and early adolescent young people, a young adult program on independence, and a home accessibility program.

Results of the program can be generalized to families with other types of developmental disabilities. The implications for policy makers and public agencies are great as our society is faced with the largest number of young adults with a developmental disability and few affordable resources for assisting them into a productive and independent life.

Susan R. Leibold, M.S., R.N., *is project director of the Spina Bifida Associations of America's Project Independence. She received an M.S. in nursing from the Medical College of Virginia at Virginia Commonwealth University.*

Preparation for independence, a goal for all people with disabilities, begins at birth. In striving for this goal, numerous barriers are encountered, including ones created by the parents of the person with disabilities. Additional barriers face a child born with disabilities into a family with a parent who is a Vietnam veteran. Products from the war include family isolation, domestic violence, and post-traumatic stress disorder (PTSD) with its symptoms of depression, difficulty concentrating, isolation, irritability and rage, avoidance of feelings or alienation, survival guilt, anxiety reaction, sleep disturbances or nightmares, and intrusive thoughts (Figley, 1989). Many families experience these symptoms and seek treatment. Others, unaware of the symptoms of PTSD, seek no treatment. Some families experienced the birth of their child with spina bifida as a traumatic life event; subsequently, symptoms of PTSD develop in one or both of the parents. A still smaller number of families experience symptoms that originate from the war and are reactivated by the birth of their child. This complicates the process of helping children with spina bifida to become independent. Unfortunately, no published research could be found that explores the relationship among PTSD, the Vietnam War, and the birth of a child with a physical disability.

Description of Families

Currently, 403 families throughout the United States have a child with spina bifida and a parent who served in Vietnam and are enrolled in the program. Three of those families have lost their child since the program began. Both parents were living in the home in 67 percent of the families; parents were separated or divorced in 15 percent of the families; and in 2 percent of the families, the father had died. The status of the remaining 16 percent of fathers was unknown (they may not have been married, etc.). Of the families in the program:

- 62 percent of the fathers and 84 percent of the mothers were employed at least part time.
- 9 percent of the families had no health care coverage.
- 29 percent had Supplemental Security Income (SSI) and 27 percent received handicapped children's services (the old crippled children's programs).

The remaining families had some type of health care coverage, but it may not have included durable medical equipment. The health of family members other than the child with spina bifida was remarkably good:

- 6 percent of the mothers had health concerns, including miscarriages, diabetes, deafness, arthritis, and heart problems.
- 8 percent of the male siblings had health concerns ranging from hyperactivity, dyslexia, seizures, asthma, speech problems, scoliosis, and club feet.
- 6 percent of the female siblings had health problems, including hydrocephalus, learning disabilities, allergies, asthma, depression, and other developmental disabilities.
- 16 percent of the fathers had health care concerns related to PTSD, skin rash or sores, allergies, ulcers, heart problems, and high blood pressure.

Seventy-five percent of the families reported that there has been no one to help them since the birth of their child with spina bifida. Several mothers responded that they felt this was their burden to bear and didn't feel it was appropriate to ask for help. Family members may have been of some support, but many of the parents felt that they couldn't leave their child with spina bifida with a family member. This sense of social isolation permeated through the majority of families around the country. This social isolation may be partly attributed to the aftereffects of the Vietnam War. Yet only a small percentage of the fathers reported symptoms of PTSD. Guilt and shame may be additional explanations that made it difficult to relate to society with their child (Loebig, 1990; McCubbin, 1988; Samuelson, Foltz, and Foxall, 1992). Of the families who said they were receiving help, the most frequently mentioned source was the local chapter of the Spina Bifida Association.

The Spina Bifida Association of America had the opportunity to identify family needs in coping with a child with spina bifida and develop a program on independence to meet those unique needs. The programs included a camp focusing on aspects of independence for children of school age and in their early teens; a weekend workshop for young adults age seventeen and older and their parents; bowel continence training; and a home accessibility program.

Independence Programs

The programs were developed based on the needs identified when completing the initial assessment of the family and on the learning disabilities. Independence issues were the primary concern identified within the family and were not being addressed within the developmental disability community. Independence is the acquisition of knowledge that is gained from life experiences and the achievement of the interrelationships of dependence-independence-interdependence. Dependency occurs in varying degrees throughout life. Interdependence and independence emerge as a person is able to separate emotionally from the parent, make decisions based on his or her own values, learn to live on his or her own, and provide or know how to obtain assistance with self-care, health care, transportation, vocation, peers, and recreational activities (Monson, 1992; Wright, 1982).

Spina bifida is a birth defect that occurs in the first month of fetal development when the spinal cord is forming. An interruption in the formation of the spinal cord causes an infant to be born with an open cyst on the back, which contains spinal fluid and remnants of the spinal cord. The resulting paralysis affects the ability to ambulate and to control the bowel and bladder. Problems with skin breakdown also occur because of the lack of sensation in the paralyzed areas. Hydrocephalus and associated learning disabilities occur in 80 percent to 90 percent of all people afflicted with spina bifida. These learning disabilities include perceptual motor skills—which are needed to drive a car—and comprehension, attention, hyperactivity or impulsivity, memory, organization, sequencing, and decision making or problem solving—all of which are needed for employment, relationships, and living way from home (Lollar, 1993).

Families raising a child with spina bifida find that achieving independence is particularly difficult because of the numerous self-care skills that must be learned and the comprehensive medical needs that must be managed (on top of the complex learning disabilities that impact achievement of these skills). A lack of vision or dreams as to what a child with spina bifida can accomplish in later life is common on the part of parents: this is a very different view from what they have for their other children (Ward, 1991). Families couldn't identify anyone willing to address these needs in a holistic fashion.

The first two programs developed were the bowel continence program and the camp program. As these issues of the young person and family were addressed, others arose, and the young adult program and the home accessibility program were developed.

Bowel Continence

The bowel continence program is a focus for intervention because bowel incontinence is a significant problem in steps towards independence. Most children are bowel continent by the age of three. A recent study found that one-third of the adolescents were dependent on their parents' involvement in their bowel program (Blum, Resnick, Nelson, and St Germaine, 1991). To have an adolescent still requiring his or her parent to assist him or her in completing a bowel program or to do it for him or her prevents true independence. Bowel continence also remains an ongoing problem because it is not addressed in an organized and consistent approach at the multidisciplinary spina bifida clinics; therefore, parents are not receiving the education or support to begin this process. The program focus in this area was to train each clinic nurse coordinator in continence protocols that were developed based on age-related successful continence strategies. Two hundred staff of the 202 clinics have been trained;

unfortunately, if a clinic nurse was responsible for other clinics or the medical director or clinic administration was not interested in helping families achieve continence, the family did not receive assistance through the clinic. These families had to rely on the Agent Orange Class Assistance Program (AOCAP) nurse consultant for continence training. This situation may have delayed the family receiving continence training initially, but if a family was motivated, they were able to receive assistance over the phone by the AOCAP nurse consultant. Follow-up of a family's progress is ongoing.

Camps for Independence Skills

Many children with spina bifida do not associate with any peers outside of school due to therapy, environmental barriers, parental attitudes, and exclusion by neighborhood children. Their learning disabilities can make it difficult to remember rules to games and even appropriate social communication. Camps for special-needs children offer the opportunity to get away from parents, spend time with peers dealing with the same issues, experience new levels of independence, and have fun. This camp program is designed to expose children to age-appropriate independence skills as well as normal social experiences. Camps were provided an orientation program that focused on the social skill development and learning issues confronting people with spina bifida. The camps were also given an overview summary of the camper's current level of independence as well as goals the parents or child would like to accomplish. At the end of camp, the counselors completed an independence evaluation, which allowed for pre- and post-camp comparisons.

Young Adults' Issues in Independence Program

Young adults completing high school or out of school have a particularly difficult time with independence because they have lived dependently for such a long time. There has not been the encouragement or the expectations by the parents to learn independence skills. Many young adults still are not bowel continent, have never paid for a meal in a restaurant, do not know how to order refills on medication, do not know how to use public transportation, or do not know how to seek appropriate help when a problem arises.

The Issues in Independence program was developed to help these young adults, with the support of their parents, identify their current levels of independence and determine what existing strategies would best help them reach their individual highest potential. The program includes lessons on what constitutes independence and the impact of learning issues, vocational skill development, social skill development, and sexuality on independence. It provides experiences of planning social outings in coed company that the young adult has not been able to do within his or her own communities. The parents have a separate meeting to discuss these topics and how to help their young adult children achieve independence. These discussions have been very beneficial for the parents as they have remained very isolated from other parents (especially the fathers) and their experiences.

Home Accessibility Program

Environmental barriers provide difficulty in achieving independence. Many parents live in older homes that have steps to get into the house and very small bathroom doors that will not accommodate a wheelchair. As a result, the young adult cannot use the bathroom without the assistance of an adult to carry him or her into it. It is difficult to achieve independence if one's home is not designed to support the effort. A program to help families make their homes more accessible was developed and is based on identifying community assistance for materials and labor to modify a home's entryway or bathroom. It involves local fundraising, setting up a trust fund or escrow account for the child, and distributing the funds to contractors once construction is completed. Because of the recession, it has been difficult to mobilize resources quickly. It has been helpful to network with ACCESS, Christmas in April, and Habitat for Humanity. We have also been identified by Vietnam Veterans of America as a group that they would recommend to their local chapters for local fundraising.

Results of These Programs on the Veteran and Family

Working with families on the bowel continence training program was the first glimmer into a family's concept about independence. Many parents were reluctant to begin a bowel program because they "had tried them all before and nothing had worked." Others did not believe they needed to change what they were currently doing, even if the young persons were not doing their bowel program by themselves. Several mothers would not relinquish the responsibility for doing the bowel program to their young person because they "knew he just wouldn't be able to do a good enough job." A lot of work was needed by some of the families to meet some of their more pressing needs (veterans issues, other health care issues, and obtaining durable medical equipment, for instance) before a discussion about bowel continence could take place. One of the other problems identified by the families was that many of the teenagers could not get into the bathroom unless their fathers carried them in, which raised issues of developing sexuality, boundaries, privacy, and independence. The home accessibility program was designed to address the issue of access. It became clear that many of the families experienced similar problems; it had not occurred to them that a school-age child in a small wheelchair that fit through the bathroom door could not fit through the door when he or she began using a larger wheelchair. Even more surprising to program staff was the small number of children who were able to get in and out of their houses by themselves. Most families had not even considered inquiring about having a ramp built for their main entryway.

In working with these families, it became clear that they had no idea how to contact contractors, get estimates, or even identify what they needed. The majority of these families had little expertise in connecting with community resources and needed step-by-step instructions on how to get the information needed to begin a local fundraising effort.

The camping program was a very positive experience. Parents responded most favorably to the respite from their child with spina bifida, noting that they could do "normal activities with their other children," or that "it was just a relief to get a break from all the caretaking responsibilities." Several families refused to let their child go to camp because of separation anxiety on their part. Strong overprotection on the part of the parents was very difficult to break through and possibly stemmed from their social isolation. Over the course of the program, a few parents did relent in the past year and allowed their child to attend camp: both parent and child were pleased with the experience. Skills taught at the camp included bedmaking, social skills, learning to work on a project independently without having someone nearby, and dressing. A few became independent in their bowel and bladder programs while at camp.

The young adult program identified the greatest number of needs because independence was expected from the young adult. Parents were becoming exhausted by the continuous caretaking aspects, and the young adult was very lonely and wanted to be doing something of worth. The issues that the parents raised were:

1. Frustration that the young adult was not performing his or her own health care behaviors;
2. Fear of injury if left alone;
3. Lack of a dream or vision for the future for the young adult; and
4. Inability to see the young adult as a sexual being.

The issues that surfaced for the young adult included:

1. No opportunity for peer interaction;
2. No opportunity to participate in a team effort; and
3. The degree that the learning disabilities hampered attempts at independence.

Conclusions

These programs needed to be developed because of the unmet needs facing these families. Neither the developmental disability community nor the veteran community have addressed the habilitative or independence issues children with developmental disabilities face. The trauma the veteran and the family face following the birth of a child with a developmental disability needs to be assessed and addressed as part of the ongoing care the family receives. This proactive approach may prevent many of the problems parents face in helping their child become independent.

The Spina Bifida Association of America adapted a brochure describing the effects of the Vietnam War and of having a child with a developmental disability on families. It lists several recommendations that the developmental disability and veteran community can use to begin to address this problem. The brochure has been sent to social workers within these institutions.

Recommendations

It is evident that the stress experienced by the Vietnam veteran cannot be isolated from the status of the child or family. It is imperative that the U.S. Department of Veterans Affairs:

- Study the effects of the Vietnam War and the effects of the birth of a child with a developmental disability on the family;
- Identify the stressors that the Vietnam War and the disability bring to the family and what community resources are available to assist the family;
- Establish the practice for the local offices to inquire on intake whether any of their children have a developmental disability or chronic illness;
- Ascertain whether the child is receiving medical services and if the child has funding for medical services; and
- Have local offices build relationships with program facilities that offer pediatric services for referral purposes.

The developmental disability community needs to:

- Study the effects of having a child with a developmental disability and any service connection with Vietnam within the family;
- Ascertain on intake if either parent served in Vietnam and how they are coping; and
- Develop relationships with Vet Centers, workers in PTSD clinics at local VA hospitals, local veterans' groups, and the state office for the Division of Veterans Affairs for information regarding benefits, counseling, and advocacy.

References

Blum, R.W., M.D. Resnick, R. Nelson, and A. St Germaine. 1991. Family and peer issues among adolescents with spina bifida and cerebral palsy. *Pediatrics* 2:280-285.

Figley, C.R. 1989. *Helping Traumatized Families*, 1-10. San Francisco: Josey-Bass Publishers.

Loebig, M. 1990. Mothers' assessments of the impact of children with spina bifida on the family. *Maternal-Child Nursing Journal* 3:251-264.

Lollar, D.J. 1993. Learning among children with spina bifida. *Spina Bifida Spotlight*, 1-6.

McCubbin, M.A. 1988. Family stress, resources, and family types: Chronic Illness in Children. *Family Relations* 37:203-210.

Monson, R.B. 1992. Autonomy, coping, and self-care agency in healthy adolescents and in adolescents with spina bifida. *Journal of Pediatric Nursing* 7(1):9-13.

Samuelson, J.J., J. Foltz, and M.J. Foxall. 1992. Stress and coping in families of children with myelomeningocele. *Archives of Psychiatric Nursing* 5:287-295.

Ward, M.J. 1991. Self-determination revisited: Going beyond expectations. *Transition Summary* 7:2-4, 12.

Wright, B.A. 1982. What is wrong with the concept of independence/What will make it right? *Pediatric Social Work* 4:99-103.

Advocacy and Resource Leveraging to Effect Change for the Children of Vietnam Veterans

**Bonnie W. Webb, Sharon Meek, Rita Larrabee,
Carla Putnam, and Roger Jones**

**The Access Group
United Cerebral Palsy Associations, Inc.
Atlanta, GA**

Abstract

The Access Group is a national program that addresses the assistive technology needs of the families of Vietnam veterans who have children with disabilities. This family-directed program, based on leveraging and collaboration, is targeted to outcomes for the child and family and toward change at the individual and systems levels. Within the first two years, the Access Group handled 3,122 inquiries at the information and referral level. This paper reports on a subset of 454 families nationwide, with children ranging in age from birth to thirty-eight who were served at an intensive family support level. The importance of the project's basic philosophy and outreach strategies is addressed, while its success in collaboration and leveraging of resources is reported in terms of financial impact, personal impact, and systems change.

The paper covers implications for future service coordination and policy development, including needs for individual and family training options, protection and advocacy support needs, resource allocation, legislation, regulation change, collaboration, professional training, and family empowerment. Unmet and ongoing family needs for assistive technology supports include computer technology, technology-related advocacy, home modifications and environmental adaptations, adapted recreation and leisure, communication devices, and transportation and mobility. The paper concludes with ten family-defined issues related to assistive technology service delivery with recommendations for policy change and implementation.

***Bonnie W. Webb** is a speech/language pathologist who maintains a private practice and also works in home health care, hospital, nursing home, school, and community settings. She worked with United Cerebral Palsy Associations, Inc. (UCPA) to establish the Access Group. **Sharon Meek** is director, and **Rita Larrabee** is project manager of the Technology, Learning and Collaboration (III) Project of UCPA. **Carla Putnam** is information coordinator for UCPA's Technology Related Technical Assistance Project. **Roger Jones** is technology distribution coordinator for the Access Group. Previously he was co-founder and president of the adult section of the Georgia Association for Children and Adults with Learning Disabilities.*

Vietnam was a strange experience for the United States. A war that was called a conflict. An effort without commitment. A war affecting civilians and soldiers. New and advanced technology against primitive but effective tactics. Soldiers who were courageous and loyal, but who were never welcomed home.

With each war, technology plays a more important role. Experts have argued that "because the technological resources existed, it was virtually impossible not to use them" and have called the Vietnam War "a great technological proving ground." In its usual contradictory way, Vietnam served to prove both the "grave limitations in the ability of technology to affect the political overtones of a war," while ensuring that the impact of such technology "would be felt for many years to come." (Bonds, 1988, p. 17)

In this light, it becomes even more interesting that technology and war are still playing a role in the lives of the soldiers who fought more than twenty years ago. Young soldiers came home and tried to go on with their lives. They had families. Many of those soldiers had children with disabilities. Now, instead of needing to know how to transport personnel, how to use surveillance devices, or how to detect communications—they needed to know how to transport a child in a heavy wheelchair, how to help a child communicate, or how to use a computer with their child. They had learned well in Vietnam and knew how to fight a war without front lines. They brought these lessons home to the new front lines that their children and families would encounter daily. It would take a "hearts and minds" campaign to meet the assistive technology needs of their children.

Through Agent Orange Class Assistance Program (AOCAP) funding, technology has become a tangible symbol of commitment to Vietnam veterans and their families; a tool through which the community can become involved in disability and veterans' issues; and a visible response to the needs of Vietnam veterans' families who have children with disabilities.

Three wives of Vietnam veterans created this project: two are parents of children with disabilities. Long before the workscope for this project was written, they proposed such a program. They outlined plans that would document needs for technology, identify barriers, map out strategies and action plans, increase access to technology, and then determine whether this made any difference in the lives of children and adults with disabilities. As the Access Group began to work together, the project began to unfold and surpassed even the team's expectations.

The Philosophy

> *Philosophy and identity are inexorably tied together for any company. What you do defines who you are, and what you believe in should be a basis for how you act.* (Ehrenfeld, 1993, p. 59)

A critical first step in the establishment and implementation of this family-directed program was clarification of basic beliefs that would govern all future goals and activities. The following core tenets were adopted and reaffirmed throughout the life of the project:

- We as individuals, parents, persons with disabilities, and professionals can make a difference for individual children.
- We believe that an individual with a disability should be respected as a human being and encouraged to shape his or her own life.
- Project hallmarks are innovation, creativity, and enthusiasm.

- We value impact and outcome and believe in minimizing resources devoted to planning, while maximizing resources devoted to implementation.
- We believe that change is most effective when individual needs and system barriers are addressed at the same time.
- Everyone who is eligible for the project's services should get them.
- Through the quality and impact of our activities, service to a few will have implications for many.
- We will help families find solutions to their assistive technology needs and will not accept less than complete success in our efforts.
- We will choose the problems and barriers the project confronts, rather than letting fear or tradition direct activities.
- Actions are only limited by vision.

Project Profile

The Access Group, a joint national project of United Cerebral Palsy Associations, Inc., and the Agent Orange Class Assistance Program, was established in October 1991 to meet the assistive technology needs of families of Vietnam veterans who have children with disabilities. By increasing family access to devices such as adapted toys, computers, powered mobility, communication devices, home adaptations, vehicle lifts, and educational software, the project was expected to impact an individual's ability to learn, compete, work, and interact with family and friends. The achievement of such impact was designed around three platforms as a response to requests for assistance:

- Establishing an assistive technology peer support information and resource center to provide basic information and referral;
- Developing a technology-related family support system for technical assistance and individual problem solving; and
- Conducting technology-related advocacy, systems change, and networking activities.

Requests for Assistance

Within the first two years, the Access Group responded to 3,122 inquiries at the information and referral level. A total of 2,000 families and AOCAP professionals were served through the distribution of the project newsletter, *Under Lock and Key*, and the *Keynotes*, individual fact sheets on assistive technology topics. As families identified unmet assistive technology needs, they entered a case management level of service. They received intensive technical assistance and individual problem solving, including access to advocacy support, resource mobilization, and support in information utilization. At the end of the first two years, 454 families entered this level of assistance. This level of service is ongoing as the Access Group believes, and families have confirmed, that obtaining information, services, and resources is a life-long activity. As individuals within the family become more knowledgeable and sophisticated, their needs and involvement levels change. Experienced families serve as mentors and peer supports to others, while children grow up to learn strategies and become self-advocates and advocates within the community.

Families from forty-seven states and the District of Columbia were served during the first two years (Chart 1). The largest number of families were served in four regions: the Southeast, Southwest, Mid-Atlantic, and Northwest. These numbers reflect the location of the project, general population trends, and areas of most active referral from other AOCAP projects.

Chart 1. Family Support, by Region

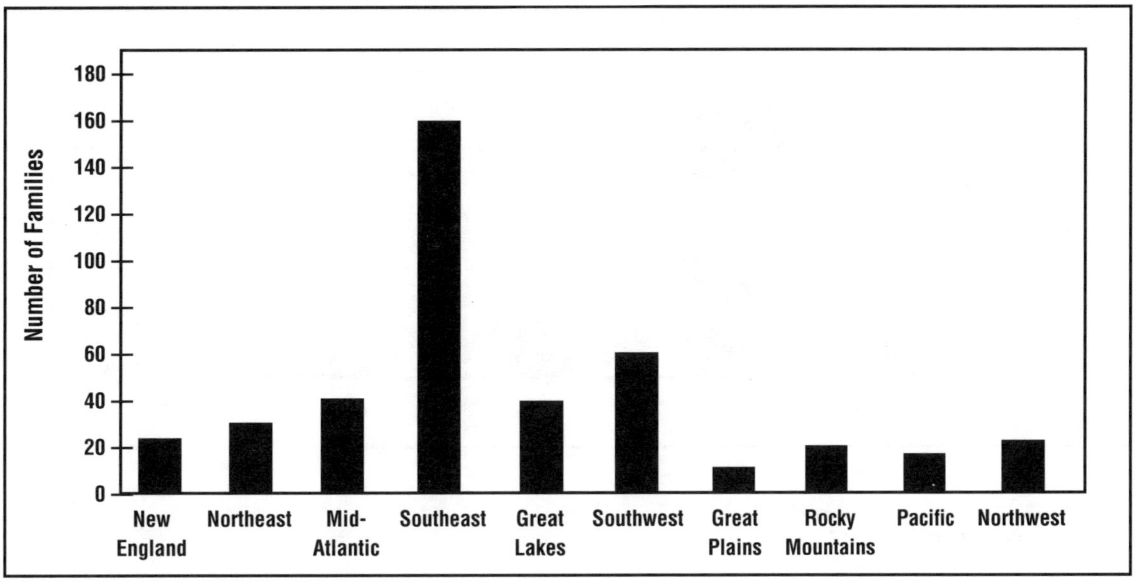

Individuals served ranged in age from one to thirty-eight. The majority were age six to sixteen (Chart 2).

The majority of families served had children with movement-related disabilities, including cerebral palsy, spina bifida, quadriplegia and paraplegia, and degenerative muscular conditions. The category of communication disorders included only those individuals who listed this as their primary disability. Many children included in other categories had accompanying communication disorders but were not included in this category for the sake of clarity (Chart 3).

Technology-Related Case Management System

As families entered the level of individual technical assistance and problem solving, a four-stage process was implemented:

Phase 1: Documentation of needs and setting of priorities. Families prioritized their needs including communication, mobility, environmental design, etc. Needs were identified in the thirty-nine areas reflected in Table 1. Many families identified more than one area of need. The most frequently listed were computers, computer accessories, software, and computer training. A related area included requests for augmentative or alternative communication devices or device training.

More than 50 percent of the families requested technology-related advocacy assistance, either in the areas of education, rehabilitation services, medical, insurance, Supplemental Security Income (SSI), or legal services. Families were unfamiliar with their rights or the strategies needed to access entitlements to goods and services within education and rehabilitation settings. In this context, families requested assistance in getting devices or services written into their individualized plans; they wanted to know how to access appropriate assistive technology evaluations; and they asked for support in encouraging schools and agencies to conduct professional training activities.

Other major areas of need included bath and home modification, vans, lifts, ramps, recreational devices and adapted toys, wheelchairs and positioning equipment, and equipment related to vision and hearing. Less requested, but of critical need, were diapers and formula. These needs, though insignificant in number, had reached almost crisis proportions.

Chart 2. Individuals Served, by Age

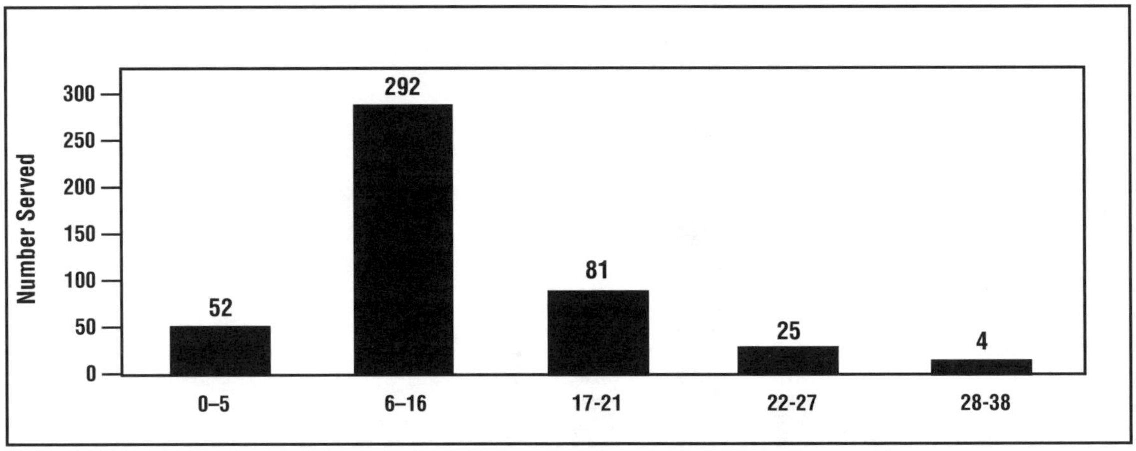

Chart 3. Disability Type

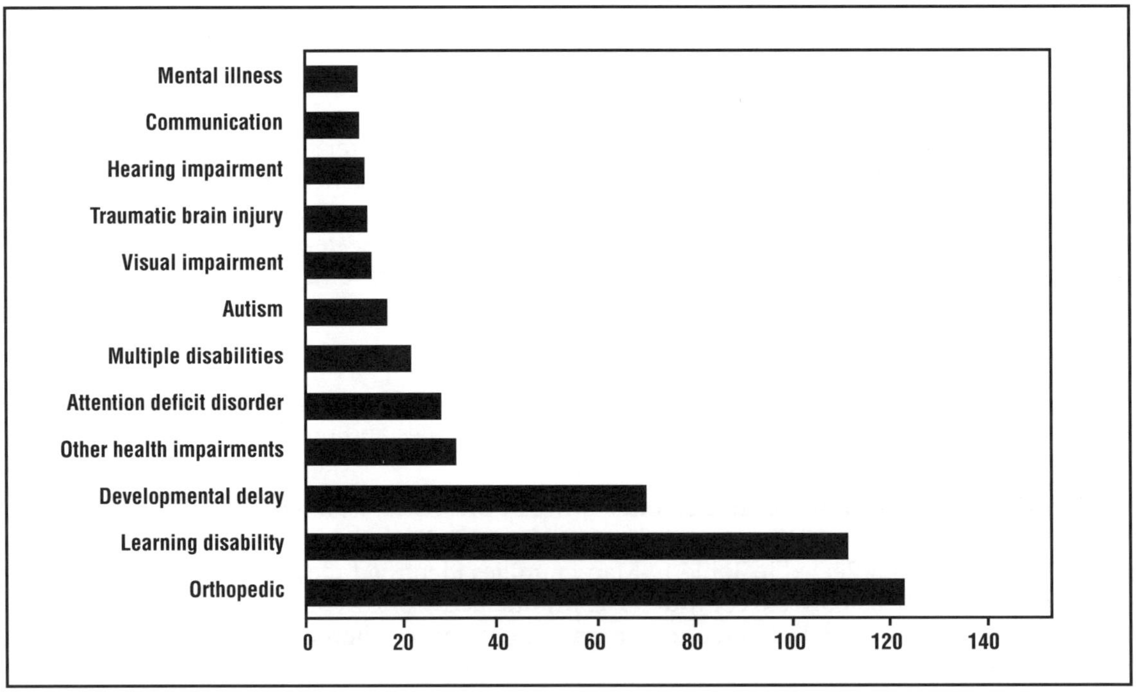

Phase 2: Identification of barriers to assistive technology. Staff members were assigned to work with individual families. It should be noted that Access staff, like many families, are not fond of the term *case management*. Staff consider themselves as supporting the families' efforts to gather information, manage, and coordinate their own services. Given these concerns, staff will be referred to as support specialists in the remainder of this paper. Each support specialist reviewed the priority form with the family, documented all barriers that families were experiencing, and assisted them in choosing strategies to meet their technology needs.

Families reported that, by far, their two greatest barriers to obtaining assistive technology were lack of personal financial resources and lack of information on devices and services

Table 1. Needs Identified by Families

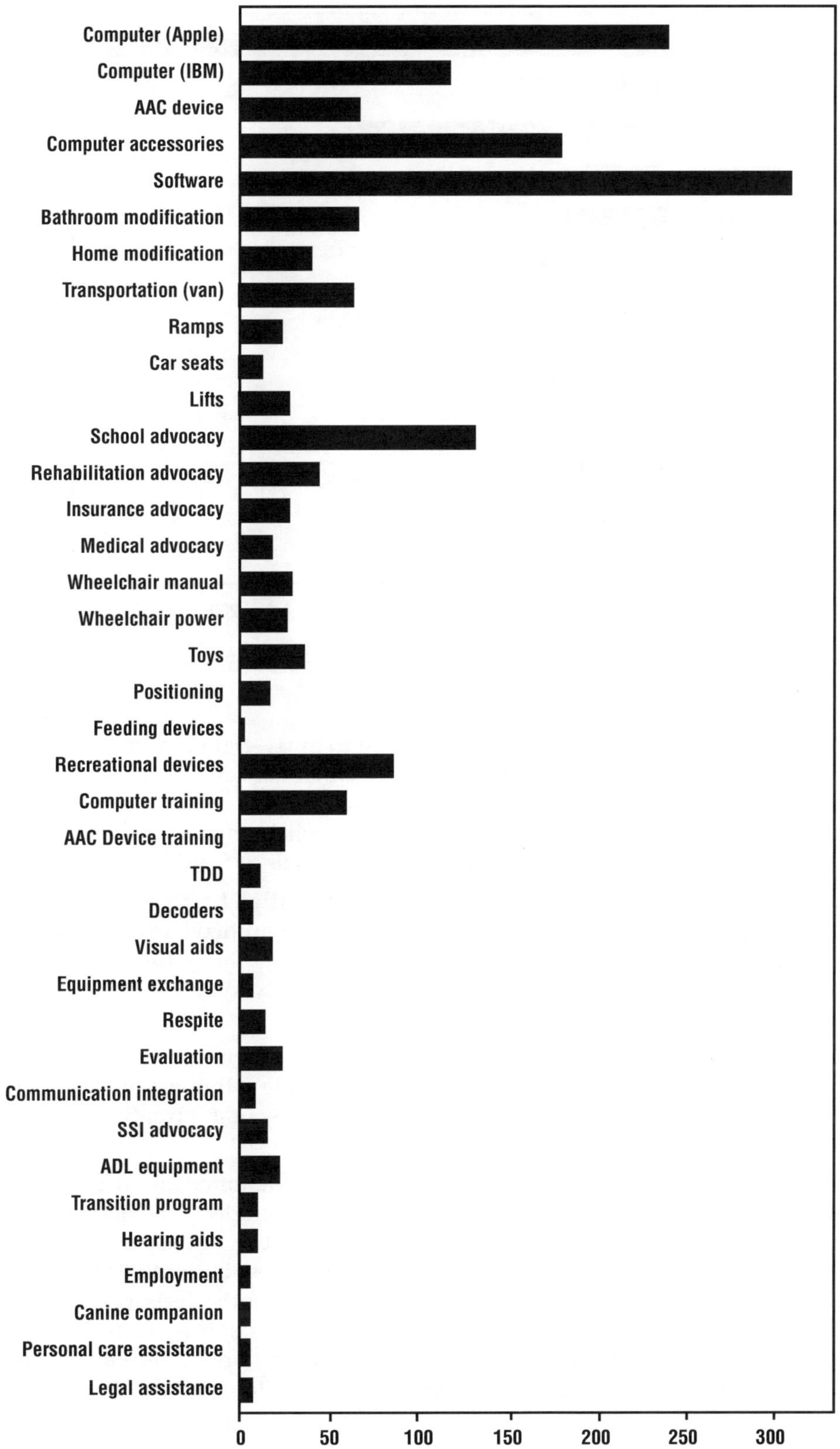

Chart 4. Barriers to Technology

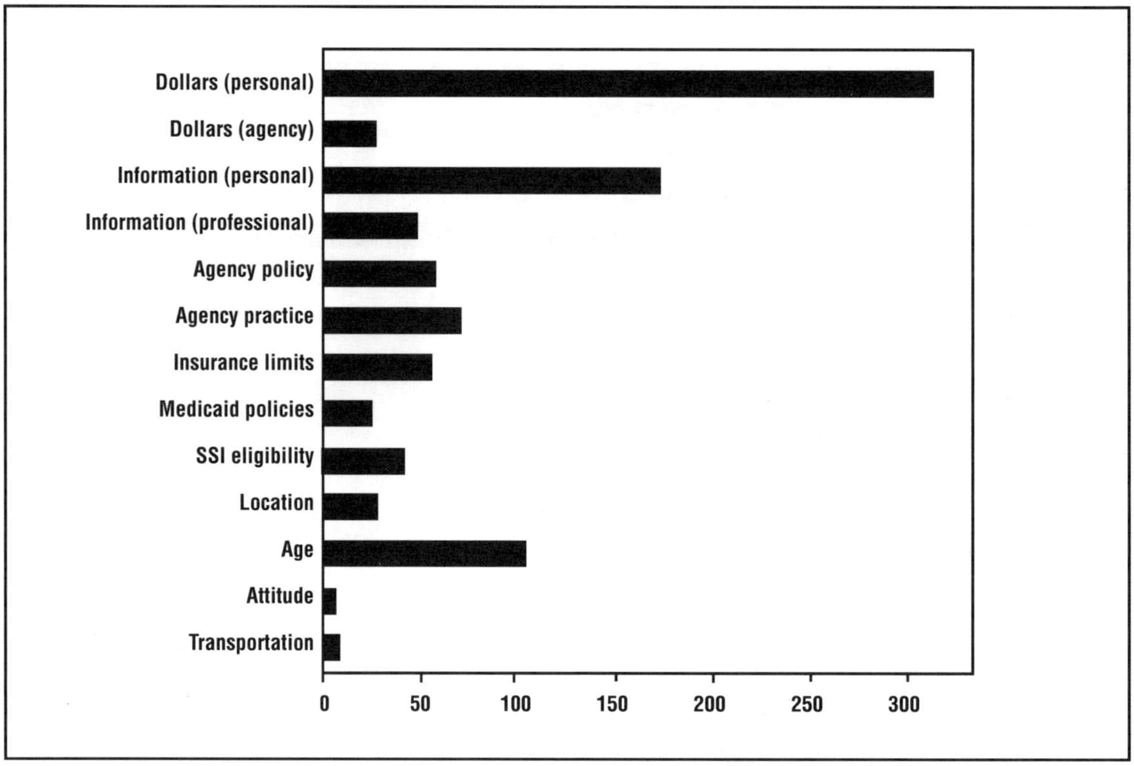

(Chart 4). Almost all of those individuals age seventeen to thirty-eight reported that their age was a barrier to obtaining access to services or devices. Other barriers encountered, in order of frequency, included agency practices, insurance limits, agency policies, lack of information or knowledge of professionals, SSI eligibility criteria, Medicaid policies, agency funding resources, geographic location, transportation, and attitudes (of professionals or family members).

Phase 3: Development of strategies for overcoming identified barriers. Families and staff worked together to plan effective ways to overcome the identified barriers. This process involved helping families recognize all of the options available, gather information and resources, expand documentation, and feel supported sufficiently to initiate or reinitiate their attempts to meet their needs.

Strategies that had not been successful for one family worked well for others, and many families vigorously pursued strategies while suggesting possible solutions for others. This phase was regarded by both families and staff as a two-way flow of information. When the process worked well, everyone was able to learn and benefit.

Thirteen referral points and eighteen other strategies were identified and used with families during the first two years (Chart 5). These referral points included consultants; the National Information System; local AOCAP projects; Brandie Schieb Foundation; service agencies such as rehabilitation services and local departments of education; individuals who were recognized as experts in a particular area; programs funded under the Technology-Related Assistance for Individuals with Disabilities Act of 1988, or Tech Act;* the United Cerebral Palsy Association's network of local affiliates; Protection and Advocacy programs; Parent Training and Information programs; Lekotek and Compuplay programs (toy lending library programs);

* Pub. L. 100-407, 102 Stat. 1044 (1988). The Tech Act was amended in March 1994 (Pub. L. 103-218).

Chart 5. Strategies Used by Families to Obtain Technology Devices or Services

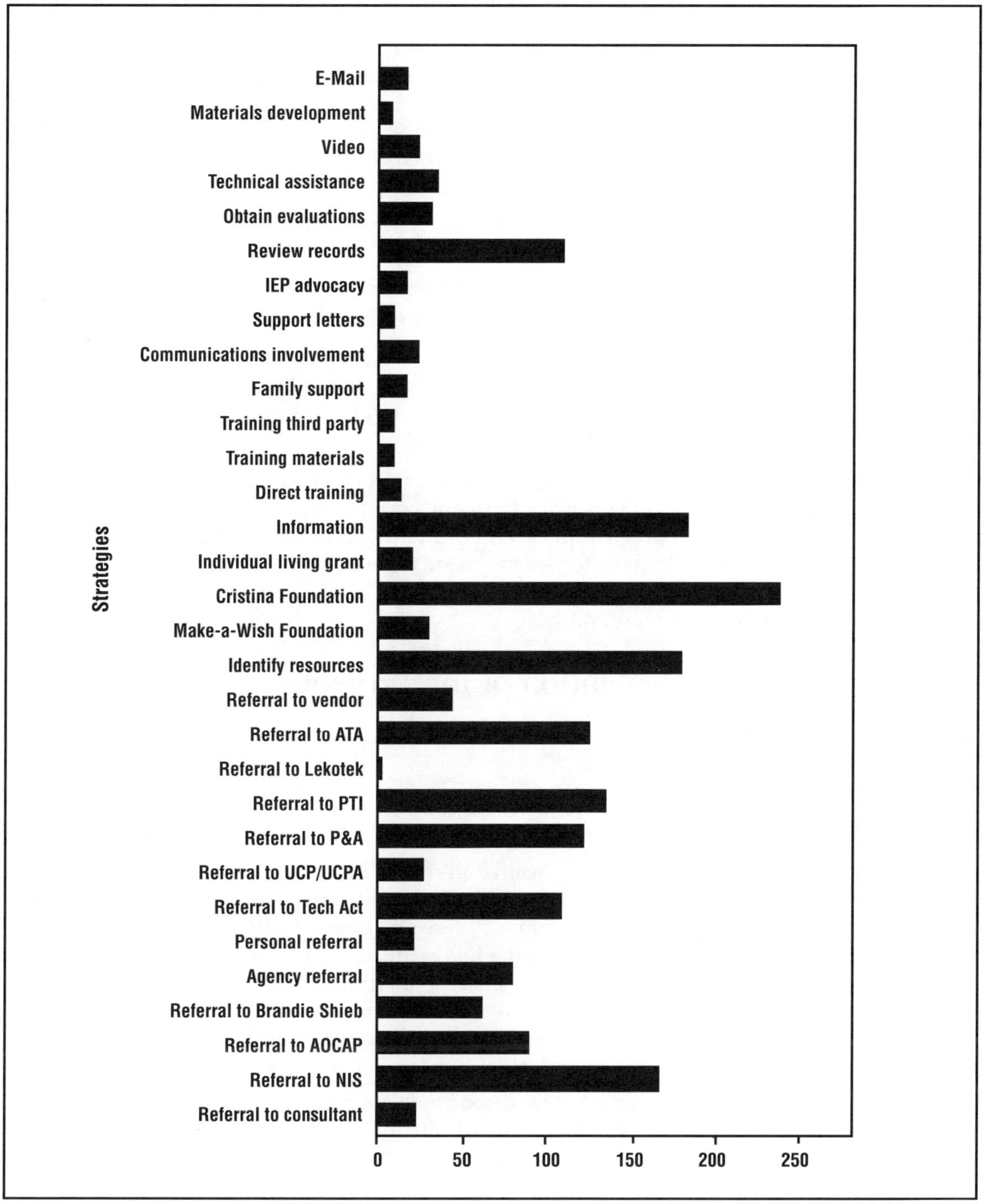

Alliance for Technology Access projects (technology resource and demonstration centers); and individual vendors or distributors of devices or products. Families were also assisted in identification of disability- or age-specific resources in their local area. Families were connected with wish foundations such as Make-a-Wish, Dream Factory, Sunshine, and Starlight when appropriate.

Training needs were met by direct training in the Access Group offices, by development of training and independent learning materials, and by identification of third-party training resources. Family support options and community involvement were also used effectively for some families, while others benefited from advocacy at individual education program meetings, review of records, technical assistance, and purchase of evaluation services. Some families successfully used support letters from the Access Group outlining their needs, rights, and resources. Other families videotaped their child in different settings, had the tape and records reviewed by "technology experts," and used the resulting recommendations from them to leverage resources from their system. Still others were able to use e-mail systems, such as KitNet, an AOCAP-funded program that enabled children to keep in touch by electronic mail, to network and find information and peer support.

Phase 4: Documentation of impact and outcome. The entire process would have been considered incomplete without evaluation of outcome. This was attempted at three levels:

- **Customer Satisfaction**. Were family expectations being met? Were families pleased with the service? Could changes be made to improve services?
- **Financial Impact.** The financial value of goods and services obtained by families as the result of implemented strategies was compiled on an annual basis. In addition, financial value of goods and services leveraged to support the project and utilized to expand and maximize project activities was documented.
- **Personal or Functional Impact.** A dollar value cannot be assigned to outcomes such as increased independence, enhanced self-esteem, social integration, educational access, or expanded employment opportunities, and evaluating the extent of project impact in such areas takes time. Initial efforts were made to evaluate the impact that the acquisition of a device had on families. Surveys completed on this topic were most useful after a family had a device for six months.

Evaluation of the Project

As the project gathered information in the process outlined above, several questions were addressed.

Were the Families Satisfied?

A random survey of customer satisfaction was conducted during the first quarter of the second year. At that time 160 families were receiving individualized service support. Seventy-one families responded to the survey, although many were still on the waiting list for equipment at the time of the survey. Survey results reflect the following answers from families: 39 percent of the families reported that the Access Group made a difference in their ability to obtain equipment, while 46 percent reported that there was a difference in the amount of technology-related services they received. An additional 77 percent declared that the Access Group increased their knowledge and understanding of assistive technology.

When asked if they had received a timely response to their inquiries or requests, 68 percent reported a response within two days; 21 percent within one month; 1 percent over a month; and 4 percent reported that the response took too long.

When asked whether the technology information supplied by the Access Group was understandable and useful, 68 percent of the respondents said that the information they received was Very good; 15 percent Okay; 6 percent Could be better; 1 percent Terrible; while 10 percent reported that this question was not applicable to their inquiry. Eighty-two percent of the families reported that they would recommend the project to another family.

Results

Generally, families were satisfied with the Access Group services. However, the survey pointed out four areas for change:

1. Staffing patterns were changed and additional staff and volunteers improved response and delivery time;
2. The equipment exchange and computer recycling programs were fully implemented and refined;
3. Efforts were made to identify increased opportunities for peer support and family networking;
4. New families entering the individual support level were given more specifics about the computer recycling process, the expected wait for equipment, ways in which they could contribute or participate, and a status report on vans, lifts, and home modification strategies.

Customer satisfaction surveys have both benefits and drawbacks. Even though a survey reflects positive responses, individuals who have not received any assistance related to assistive technology may have low expectations of what a project should or could provide. As a result, they may rate any response favorably if they have nothing else with which to compare it. Therefore, the Access Group asked: Have you been able to get technology-related assistance from other groups? If so, what groups? Forty-six percent of the families responding reported that they had not accessed other technology-related supports, while six families did not answer this question or replied that it was not applicable (Chart 6). Those who did report receiving assistance from other groups often accessed multiple sources (Chart 7).

Chart 6. Families Who Had or Had Not Accessed Technology Support from Other Sources

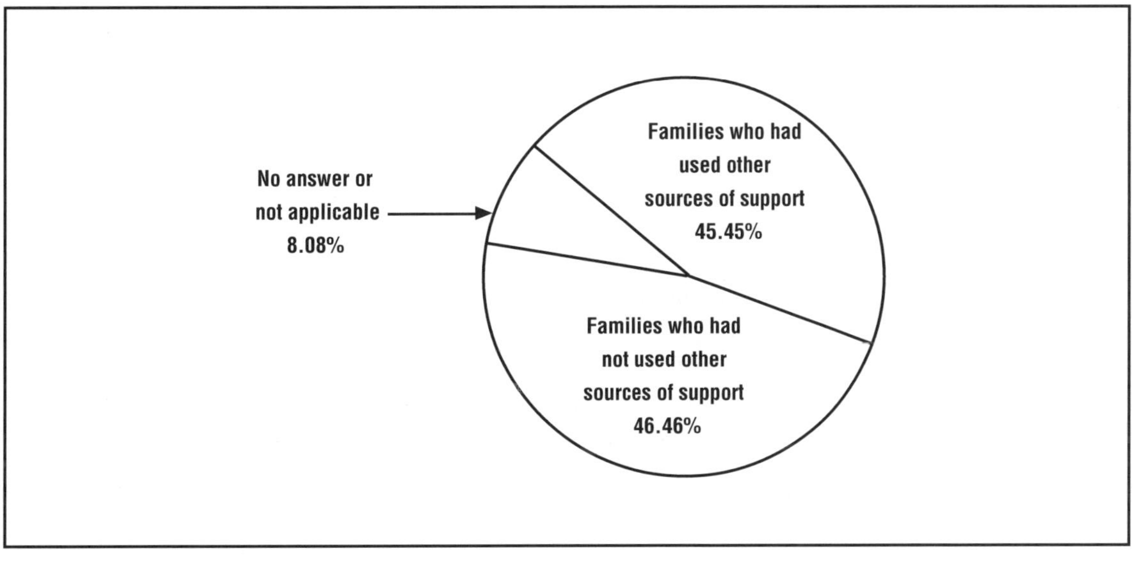

Did It Make a Difference?

Although AOCAP funding was the catalyst for implementation of the project, it was clear from the beginning that leveraging resources would be the springboard for the Access Group to accomplish its goals.

This project was supposed to serve families throughout the United States in an efficient and effective manner with AOCAP funding equivalent to about one-half of the amount of federal funds available to serve individual states operating under the Tech Act. During the first year, $15,119 worth of goods and services were donated to the project to supplement administrative and operating costs: furniture, software, equipment for office use, office supplies, open house

Chart 7. Other Sources of Technology Information and Support Used by Families

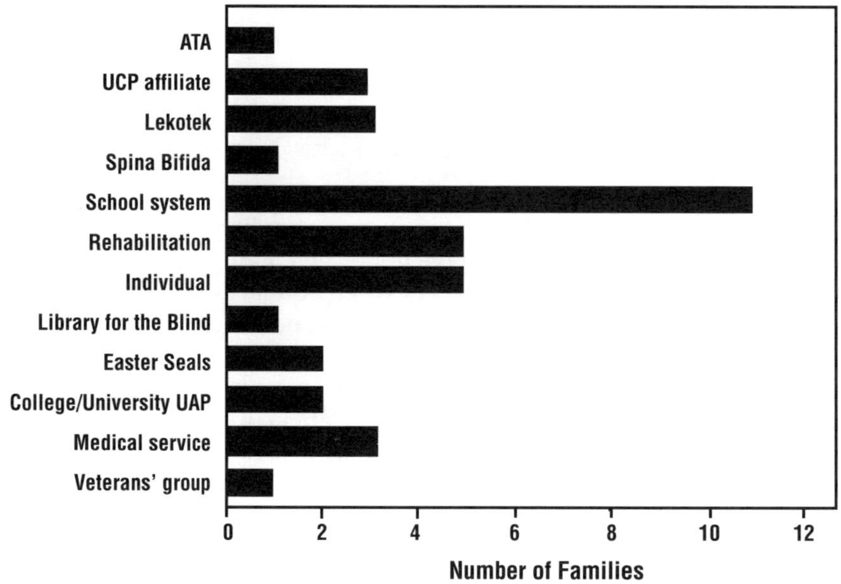

donations; volunteer time for one staff position helped get the project started effectively. During the second year $6,860 in goods and services were donated, and an additional $3,177 was raised through an "Accessible Alternatives" Concert. Funds from this concert were used to repair donated equipment and to purchase supplemental equipment for families.

The project had no funds to purchase equipment outright, but about 80 percent of the families had identified needs for computers. As a result, the computer recycling program was established during the third quarter of the first year. Through this program, use of consultants, referral to other agencies or organizations, and community donations, families received $34,545 worth of technology-related goods and services during Year 1, and $87,165 during Year 2. (These estimates are very conservative.)

During a two-year period, the AOCAP grant totaled $582,516. During this period Access leveraged additional direct goods and services for families, valued at $121,710. These resources supplemented the basic project services for a return rate of 20.9 percent. If administrative re- sources, concert profits, and donations are included, the return rate rises to 25 percent (Chart 8).

Even more important than the financial impact however, and more basic to the existence and philosophy of the project, is the answer to this question: Did it make any difference to the family? Approximately 157 families received devices or technology-related services at this level during the first two years (Chart 9).

The Access Group asked those families who had received a computer whether it had made any difference in their lives. Of the eighty families who had their equipment for four to six months, twenty-one responded to a phone survey. These families had received Apple, Macintosh, and IBM-compatible computers. They were using them for school work, homework, games, stimulation, and self-therapy. Fifty-seven percent of the families reported that their child was able to work more independently as a result of obtaining the computer. Sixty-two percent reported that their child's basic skills level had increased as a result. Parents said,

Chart 8. Value of Resources Leveraged During the First Two Years of the Project

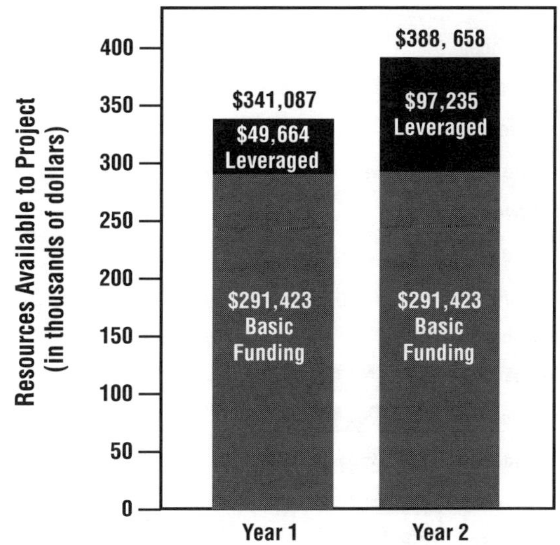

"He is doing great in spelling, his reading skills have gone up." "He has passed the basic skills test for graduation and I believe the computer is partially responsible. His teacher sees improvement."

Forty-eight percent reported that their child played more independently with the computer, while 38 percent reported that the parents had more free time as a result of their child having the computer. Families said, "We have a lot more free time. She is able to work by herself." "I hope this will enable him to do work without me having to write for him."

Sixty-two percent believed that their child's self-concept had improved as a result of increased independence with the computer. "It has helped him deal with his feelings and keep his feelings under control." "She doesn't have to depend on someone else to take her to school to use their computer."

When asked what the most important change for the child had been as a result of having the computer, parents cited "speech improved"; "improvement in school work"; "he pays attention"; "the computer is a friend for him since his disability keeps him from being able to play outside with other children"; "math skills are greatly improved"; "he is much more independent"; "he is beginning to understand cause and effect"; "he is more aware of his abilities"; "other methods of teaching have not worked, the computer has."

Twenty-nine percent of the families surveyed reported that their child's teacher viewed the child differently since he or she began using the computer, while 33 percent reported that the child's siblings and peers reacted more favorably to the child because he or she had a computer. "He controls the computer, they have to ask him if they can use it, and this gives him a feeling of importance." "She is deaf and the kids in the neighborhood can now play games with her." "He is teaching his younger brother how to use it. Dad sometimes brings one home from work and they can compete."

Eighty-one percent of the families reported that they did not believe they could have acquired this equipment if they had not contacted the Access Group. While some families said that they had always realized the importance of a computer for their child, 62 percent of the families stated that their attitude regarding the importance of the computer had changed since their child received it.

Chart 9. Impact and Outcomes for Families During the First Two Years

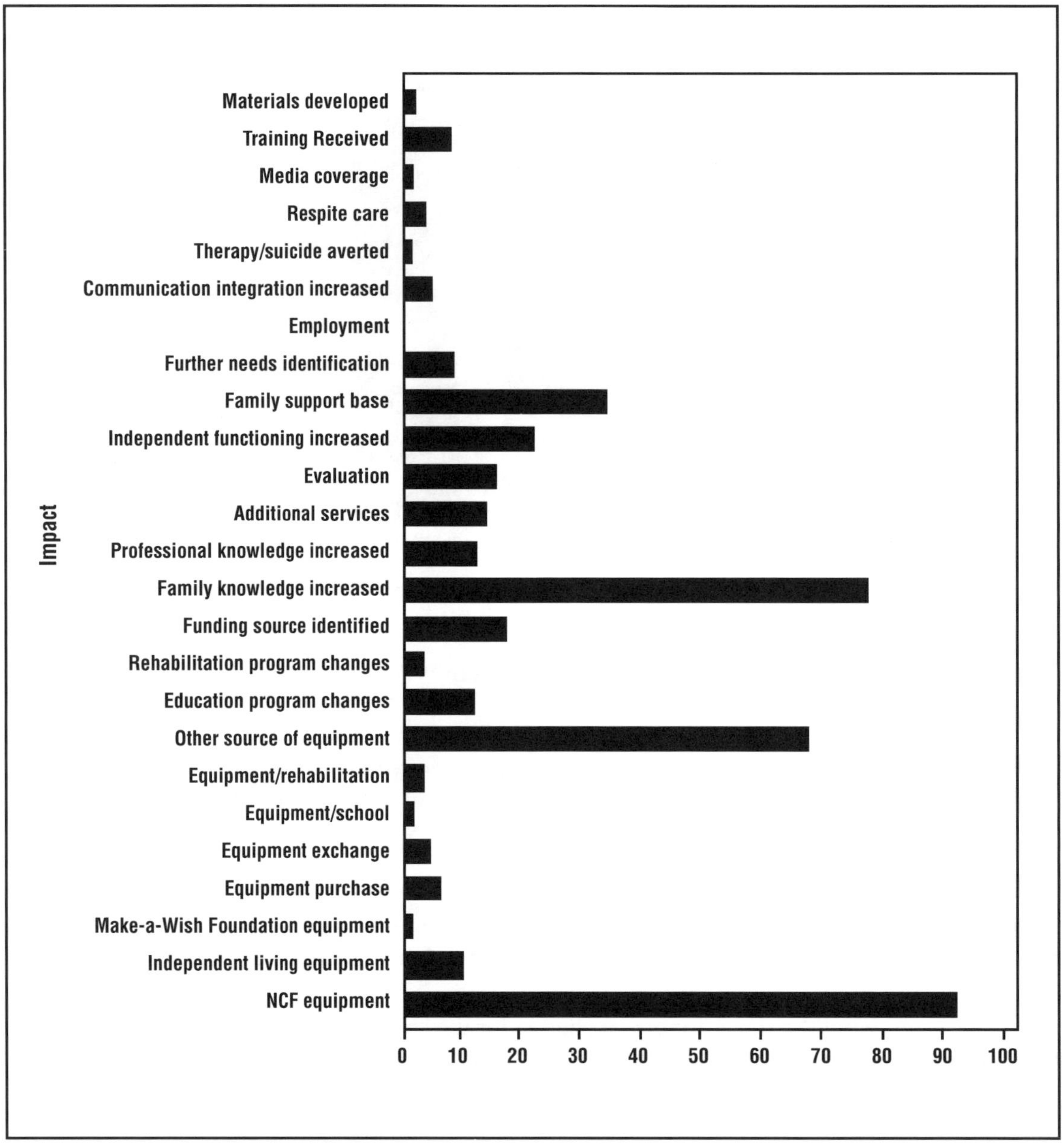

Many families reported that the presence of the computer had changed their interactions with their child. It changed things, "especially for Dad, we can use it with them." "We spend more time with our kids with very positive results." "We feel more confident in his ability to learn because the computer has shown he can count. We did not know this before receiving the computer."

Fifty percent of the families volunteered that they had never received any services from any other Agent Orange programs or veterans' programs. Many also reported secondary disabilities that they felt were a direct result of their child's disability. "I (Mom) am having back and arm pain due to lifting the wheelchair and helping E." "Our backs are very bad because of lifting." Overall, families were enthusiastic about the use of technology and the impact it had had on their family. Many families were excited about the prospect of other technology supports, "if a computer can make this much difference."

Implications

So what does it all mean? If we ask, families will tell us what they need and the barriers they are experiencing. If we listen, families will tell us what they see as the solutions to problems with the system. The Access Group has tried to ask and to listen. Families have told us:

Issue 1. Both families and professionals are asking for information and training. Training is provided for individuals with disabilities and their families or for professionals. In some instances, the professionals are taught first, in the belief that they will then train the families with whom they work.

Recommendations:

- All training events should include individuals with disabilities and family members. Training should be planned with the belief that individuals are equal participants on an Individual Education Plan (IEP) or Individual Written Rehabilitation Plan (IWRP), or similar team, and need equal access to information and training.

Issue 2. Families do not have sufficient access to informed advocates in the area of assistive technology.

Recommendations:

- Protection and Advocacy programs, University Affiliated Programs (interdisciplinary programs of training, research, and service), and Developmental Disabilities Planning Councils should present at all training events sponsored by Tech Act programs and explain how they can assist individuals and families in accessing technology-related advocacy and training programs.
- Protection and Advocacy programs should actively become involved in training on strategies for accessing assistive technology, both for advocates and self-advocates.
- All individual program plans should incorporate a written notice to participants concerning their rights to assistive technology services and devices.

Issue 3. Families do not know how to access vendors and manufacturers directly. Most assistive technology information is filtered through the professional.

Recommendations:

- Vendors and manufacturers should be educated to the buying power of the individual and family. Training, demonstrations, displays, articles, and direct marketing to disability- and family-oriented groups and conferences should be expanded. Potential customer groups such as independent living programs, self-advocacy and parent groups, and peer support groups should initiate ongoing dialogues related to existing and developing products.

Issue 4. Families have lifelong information needs. Knowing how to use information is as important as knowing where to find it. Many families may not be ready to pursue a particular issue or service at the same time their case manager is ready. They can still benefit from support and validation that they are right in setting their own agenda and that support will still be available to them at some future date if it is needed.

Recommendations:

- Formalized peer networking is an invaluable resource to families. Families have repeatedly asked for a vehicle by which they could talk directly to each other. They regard newsletter and magazine pen pal systems as limited; few have access to modems or can pay for on-line time; and most specifically want to "talk" to another parent about their concerns. There is a great need for a formal nationwide information exchange that is supported by toll-free phone access.

Issue 5. Twenty-one percent of the families responded that vans, lifts, and ramps are a critical issue as a child grows older and becomes too heavy to lift. Often the shift from using a manual wheelchair to a heavy electric wheelchair precipitates a crisis. Because of travel to keep medical and other appointments, mileage on a van or other vehicle accumulates rapidly. Reliable transportation is a vital link to acquiring medical care. Lifting and transporting a child with a disability has resulted in family members acquiring secondary disabilities such as knee or back injuries.

Families often have one parent stay home to care for the child with a disability, therefore limiting the income available for items such as vans and lifts. In addition, many families report extremely high medical bills that affect their ability to finance expensive items. Families may not be able to afford an initial down payment or they express fear of committing to payments for a van and lift because of other medical expenses.

Lack of appropriate transportation results in social isolation and impacts recreational options available to a family; it adds stress and affects the self-esteem of the family, and can be a barrier to employment and independent living options.

A new 1994 Dodge Grand Caravan converted, with climate controls, runs about $35,400.

Recommendations:

- Seek support of auto manufacturers and encourage avenues for families to provide input to designers and engineers. Create a forum for discussion of these needs at the national level or between consumer groups and auto manufacturers.
- Expand existing rebate programs to include funds for lifts or modifications; establish incentive programs to encourage the donation of equipment; set up matching funds; and encourage vehicle financing programs to establish low-interest, no interest, no down payment, or low-payment options for families.
- Investigate fleet buying programs to offer reduced-cost vehicles to families who have members with disabilities. Identify equipment recycling options through car rental programs or through hotels or other groups that purchase great quantities of vehicles. For example, would Avis or Hertz donate used vans? Would Radisson or Marriott donate one van for every 100 they purchase?
- Expand efforts to create a national clearinghouse for used vans, lifts, and other vehicle modifications.
- Recognize corporate giving programs linked to auto manufacturers that might set up a fund to help families with vehicle purchase and modifications.

Issue 6. Computer recycling offers a viable method for families to acquire entry-level or supplemental devices. Few opportunities exist for families to receive training on computer use with their child. Families face a choice of getting the equipment and then finding the training, or getting the training and then finding the equipment.

Recommendations:

- Legislation and regulations for disposal of government surplus equipment should offer priority to programs that are recycling equipment to individuals with disabilities. Computers, vans, and lifts are sitting idle or being purchased by re-sellers at auction, when they could make significant impact on the technology needs of individuals with disabilities.
- Incorporate both "how to get it" and "how to use it" information as basic components of any technology-related core curriculum.
- Conduct an awareness campaign targeted to businesses and individuals, focusing on the equipment recycling process, its benefits, and recipient agencies such as the National Cristina Foundation. Offer a toll-free number for donations.

Issue 7. There is a need for a nationwide equipment exchange database for individuals or agencies wishing to sell, buy, rent, or borrow used equipment. Individual organizations, Tech Act programs, and others have attempted to conduct such programs but have encountered the following barriers:

a. With donations given to a central location, there are immediate considerations of warehouse space, insurance, inventory, showcasing, and repair.

b. Groups who have attempted to exchange equipment have either had to limit the territory covered to state and local, or to limit the types of equipment (for example, wheelchairs or vision products). This limitation has resulted in situations in which a product may be available in Virginia, but the person who needs it is in Florida and never knows about it.

c. Attempts to directly match equipment owners and potential users have often run into problems even when a successful match is made because neither can afford to pay the cost of shipping nor for minor repairs that might be needed.

d. There is no central national forum through which equipment owners and potential users can share information, and there is no centralized system through which Tech Act projects, Alliance for Technology Access sites, user groups, Parent Training and Information projects, and others can acquire and disseminate information beyond agency or geographic barriers.

A successful nationwide equipment exchange program would have the following characteristics:

a. Outreach to and identification of potential donors;

b. Identification of members of a dissemination network (individuals, groups, agencies) that could use the system on both an input and output basis, and that could, in turn, further market and disseminate the database subject and content in a multitude of formats;

c. Extensive range and scope of equipment to be included;

d. Technical assistance to users in listing and searching equipment information and access in all formats; and

e. Resources to fund shipping, refurbishment, and repair.

Recommendations:

- A national equipment exchange network should be established and should include all potential participants, building upon but reaching beyond the already implemented efforts of individual Tech Act states.
- Equipment recycling involving Medicaid equipment is vital, but mandating such equipment recycling and having it governed or operated through Medicaid itself should be approached cautiously. Many states are now looking at having Medicaid pay vendors to refurbish such equipment, thereby adding considerable cost to the operation. In addition, clear guidelines need to be established as to when such recycled or refurbished equipment will come into play as Medicaid attempts to meet technology needs. Will families be required to accept used rather than new equipment? Will equipment availability become a determining factor, or will Medicaid use this as another strategy to avoid meeting the individualized needs of families? Similar questions arise related to the need for recycling equipment issued by the U.S. Department of Veterans Affairs.

Issue 8. Families recognize that home modifications are time- and labor-intensive. There is generally a discrepancy between the initial recognition of the need for home modifications and the length of time it takes to resolve the problem. The family makes do by lifting, pushing, pulling, and hauling. As secondary disabilities appear, the situation becomes a crisis.

Recommendations:

- Home modifications and environmental control issues cannot be addressed completely without the collaborative assistance and involvement of financial institutions, contractors, and building materials suppliers and manufacturers. There is no national forum at present in the disability community for discussing individual housing issues (i.e., in the manner in which the Tech Act addressed technology issues). Dialogue is limited largely to architects or Americans with Disabilities Act (ADA) compliance specialists and seldom involves all the potential players. A national conference with participation of families and individuals with disabilities and other players to document needs and outline strategies would be a good starting place.
- Specific modifications to the Community Reinvestment Act (CRA) to include individuals with disabilities and their families among defined minority groups who are eligible for CRA consideration would be beneficial.
- Education of financial professionals about disability-related issues and education for customers on strategies to access financing for home modifications would be a good place to start.
- Families should be encouraged to apply for Medicaid to support device acquisition, home modifications, or specialized transportation needs. Many families are not aware of their rights in this area and have not even attempted to utilize the supports of Medicaid or family support funds.

Issue 9. National sports and recreation organizations often have narrow eligibility for participation, so that many children and adults are still excluded from services. When providing access for individuals with disabilities, sports and recreation programs have followed the old education model by providing segregated programs, rather than inclusive activities. Many families have little knowledge of how they can participate in their local sports and recreation programs. Even those who do know how to become involved in programs have low expectations of what they will do for their families. Adapted toys and recreation devices are seldom covered by insurance or Medicaid.

Recommendations:

- Parents and individuals should be encouraged to access vendors and manufacturers directly, and vendors should be encouraged to expand their loan and preview policies for adapted toys and recreation equipment.
- Local sports and recreation organizations should audit their own programs for both physical and programmatic accessibility.

Issue 10. Families are still experiencing difficulty in getting communication devices written into individual plans (Individual Education Plans, Individualized Family Service Plans, or Individualized Written Rehabilitation Plans). Loan or demonstration programs are just now being established in many locations and are nonexistent in others, so families and professionals seldom have an opportunity to try or become familiar with a variety of devices. As a general rule, the system still "owns your child's voice" if they pay for the device, and many children are not allowed to use a device outside the school setting, in the evenings at home, or over the summer months. Few families have requested communication devices through Medicaid, and it is rare that families or professionals regard this as a viable strategy for obtaining a device.

Recommendations:

- Training events related to augmentative or alternative communication and other sensory aids including telecommunication devices for the deaf (TDDs), hearing aids, and learning tools should include training for individuals, parents, and professionals at the same time and on an equal basis.

- Protection and Advocacy programs should conduct specific outreach programs to identify individuals who are nonverbal and do not have communication devices.
- Families and individuals should be made aware that Medicaid is an option for funding communication devices.

Conclusion

The blending of veterans' issues and the issues of children with disabilities can only benefit both groups. All individuals who experience disability have encountered barriers to service delivery and have sought and learned strategies to overcome such barriers. Combining and expanding circles of influence can only serve to extend the impact and outcomes achieved by both groups.

The terms *market-driven* and *consumer-controlled* have been gaining prominence in disability networks and business settings. Veterans' groups have always been clear about who was in control and what was to their best interest. They made decisions for themselves. The network set up for information dissemination and service delivery for this project could benefit veterans with assistive technology needs, just as it has benefited their children.

Veterans' groups and disability groups are two of the most powerful special interest groups in the United States. If these groups were able to identify common needs and issues, and were willing to work together to resolve them, the potential for change would be unmatched. If nothing else, AOCAP projects have proven that both veterans and children should be served as part of a family and as part of a community. Never again should their needs be evaluated or their services be delivered in an isolated manner.

It is clear from the experience of the Access Group that many families with children with assistive technology needs received services and support for the very first time because information was specifically given to them in the context of veteran support. It is also clear that some Vietnam veterans, who would never seek support or services for themselves, gladly accepted the resources and support of the Access Group on behalf of their children. Some fathers who had not had any contact with their children for years initiated the process to obtain goods and services for their children, without intruding on their lives. Others expressed the hope that the technology could represent more: the healing of old scars and the beginning of new relationships.

Traditionally the mother is the service manager when a family has a child with a disability. The Access Group has found that the link to the veteran has resulted in the father becoming more involved and serving as the primary contact in the service management process. Once the veteran has initiated the contact and developed a relationship with the project, the contact is maintained with the father. Many fathers had never before been the one to represent the family in talking about their child. As a general rule, fathers are considered by most training and information programs as an underserved and underrepresented group. This could not be said about the participants of most AOCAP projects.

Many Vietnam veterans express the feeling that they supported their country but that their country let them down. This project and others like it will not change that, but for the first time veterans can feel that their contribution is being recognized. The Access Group always tells veterans, "We will tell your child, and we want you to know, that this device or service is a direct result of your service in Vietnam. Welcome home."

References

Bonds, R., ed. 1988. *The Vietnam War: The illustrated history of the conflict in Southeast Asia.* New York: Military Press.

Ehrenfeld, T. 1993. The (Handbook) Handbook. *Inc.* 15(11):57-64.

Afterword

The accomplishments of the Agent Orange Class Assistance Program (AOCAP) network of community-based, family-focused service providers are well documented in the preceding pages. More than 200,000 Vietnam veterans and their family members have received services since the program began in 1989.

Perhaps a more important measure of the network's success, however, is the qualitative change that has occurred in the lives of individuals and families served by the network.

Working in partnership with Vietnam veterans and their families, the network has enabled children with severe disabilities who were once excluded from regular classrooms to learn side by side with their nondisabled peers. Children's surgical and other critical health care needs have been met. Families with staggering medical bills have received cash assistance or aid in negotiating reductions in balances and more realistic payment plans. Youngsters and their parents have been provided with computers and modems and linked to friends across the country. Homes, wheelchair ramps, and adapted bathrooms have been acquired. Therapeutic counseling has been provided to veterans, their spouses and children. Jobs, Supplemental Security Income, veterans' benefits, and independent living skills training and a vast array of other human services have been accessed.

The dedication of the AOCAP programs' staff has been remarkable. Hundreds of human services professionals have striven to provide highly individualized, comprehensive services to class members. They have worked hard continually to hone their service coordination skills and increase their knowledge of the complex veterans' and public disabilities services systems.

Staff have peered into the Internet to seek the latest medical information for class members with rare and often deadly diseases. They have devoted countless evenings and weekends to meeting with community groups to find solutions for those they serve. They have braved Alaska's bush in single-engine aircraft to share information on the symptoms of post-traumatic stress disorder with families and health aides in remote villages. And they have immersed themselves in others' cultures, eating sea worms and joining in native healing ceremonies to learn, to understand, and better to serve.

The AOCAP network is committed to the continuation of the efforts begun by AOCAP funding. The symposium was a powerful precipitant and served to galvanize the resolve to continue the unique, cost-effective, and efficacious work begun under AOCAP. This commitment led to action in September 1994 with the establishment of the National Alliance of Veteran Family Service Organizations (NAVFSO). The Alliance is an interactive network of family-focused, community-based programs for veterans and their families with special needs.

The Alliance provides important services and benefits to member organizations: advocacy to develop funding resources to continue and expand support for community-based, family-focused veterans' service programs; technical assistance to develop program resources at the state and local level; and networking among member organizations' staffs to facilitate the ongoing exchange of information and expertise. The Alliance also offers training and education to member organizations' staffs to enhance best practices in working with veterans and their families; and information dissemination and public education on the needs and issues of veterans and their families.

The establishment of the Alliance stands as evidence of that characteristic that has been key to the success of the AOCAP network—perseverance. Staff simply will not let the important and innovative initiatives begun under AOCAP die. Although few resources for ongoing funding are immediately available, the NAVFSO leadership is committed to a comprehensive search for all possible funding sources.

The strength of the Alliance is in its members. This strength will be tested in light of recent political changes. The Alliance looks forward to addressing the challenges posed by decreasing fiscal resources in the face of ongoing or increasing human need. We have demonstrated the efficacy of what we do. We provide unique services to populations who, in part because of a distrust of government and other human services providers that stems from their wartime and other experiences, would otherwise not have received needed services.

The overall fiscal impact has been the leveraging of substantial additional resources that have reduced ongoing dependence upon Alliance resources. The impact in human terms has been the attainment of more autonomous functioning for tens of thousands of individuals.

Gary E. May
President
National Alliance of Veteran Family Service Organizations

Appendices

Appendix A

National Symposium Agenda

Monday May 16:	**National Symposium Welcome and Opening Session**
Plenary Session 2:00—2:45 PM	**Administrative announcements and other business for AOCAP project personnel:** Dennis K. Rhoades, Executive Director, Agent Orange Class Assistance Program
Plenary Session 3:00—5:00 PM	**Formal Opening Session Introductory Remarks:** Dennis K. Rhoades, Executive Director, Agent Orange Class Assistance Program **Address:** Honorable Hershel W. Gober, Deputy Secretary, U.S. Department of Veterans Affairs **Welcome:** Dennis K. Rhoades, Executive Director, Agent Orange Class Assistance Program; and William E. Jones, Ph.D., Executive Director, American Association of University Affiliated Programs for Persons with Developmental Disabilities **Remarks:** Congressman Lane Evans (D-Ill.), Co-chair, Vietnam Era Veterans in Congress; Honorable Jack B. Weinstein, Senior Judge, U.S. District Court, Eastern District of New York; and Frank McCarthy, Member, Board of Advisors, Agent Orange Class Assistance Program **Overview of the AOCAP Network of Services in Film:** *The Legacy of Vietnam Veterans and Their Families*
Poster Session and Reception 6:00—8:00 PM	**Displays by projects in the AOCAP Network**
Tuesday May 17th:	**Veterans Affairs and the Broader World of Human Services**
Plenary Session 10:00—10:40 AM	**Keynote Presentation:** "The Evolution of Veterans Benefits and Services: The Contribution of AOCAP in Historical Perspective"—*Wilbur J. Scott, Ph.D., Professor of Sociology, University of Oklahoma*
Discussion Panel 10:45—11:45 AM	**Moderator:** David F. Addlestone, Esq., Co-Director, National Veterans Legal Services Project **Panelists:** Honorable Mary Lou Keener, General Counsel, U.S. Department of Veterans Affairs; Jeff Lande, Legislative Assistant, Office of Congressman Lane Evans; and John F. Sommer, Executive Director, Washington Office, The American Legion

Plenary Session
1:30—3:15 PM

AOCAP in a Systemic Context
Moderator: Honorable Matt M. Railey, Chief Judge, 4th Judicial District, State of Colorado; and Member, Board of Advisors, AOCAP

Presentations:

"Impact Analysis of the AOCAP Network of Services"—*Bryan Smith, Ed.D., Project Director, National Information System for Vietnam Veterans and Their Families (NIS), University of South Carolina*

"New Lamps for Old: The Potential for Systemic Change in the Delivery of Services to Vietnam Veteran Families"—*Gary May, A.C.S.W., Assistant Professor of Social Work, University of Southern Indiana; and Member, Board of Advisors, AOCAP*

"Between the Courts and Congress: Leveraging VA Benefits for the Agent Orange Plaintiff Class"—*Barton Stichman, Esq., Co-Director, National Veterans Legal Services Project*

Discussion Panel:
Honorable Edward P. Scott, Assistant Secretary for Congressional Affairs, U.S. Department of Veterans Affairs; Richard E. O'Dell, Co-Author, *Veterans Benefits: The Complete Guide*; and Wayne Smith, Development Director, Vietnam Veterans Memorial Fund

Concurrent Sessions
3:30—5:00 PM

Community Service Provider Perspectives
Moderator: Bryan Smith, Ed.D., Project Director, NIS

Presentations:

"Rural Veterans: Traumas and Transitions"—*Wayne Price, L.C.S.W., Team Leader, Veterans Readjustment Counseling Center*

"Sea Worms, Northern Lights, and Vietnam: The Other Forgotten Warrior Project in Alaska"—*Tima Priess, M.A., Project Director, The Other Forgotten Warrior Project, University of Alaska, Fairbanks*

"A Report from the Front: The Collected Perspectives of AOCAP Project Field Staff"—*Dawn Sudduth, M.Ed., Assistant Project Director, National Information System for Vietnam Veterans and Their Families, University of South Carolina*

Veterans' Services in a Broader Context
Moderator: Gary May, A.C.S.W., Assistant Professor of Social Work, University of Southern Indiana; and Member, Board of Advisors, AOCAP

Presentations:

"A Shock to the System: Training Advocates under the Veterans' Judicial Review Act"—*Ronald B. Abrams, Esq., Director of Training, National Veterans Legal Services Project*

"Ameliorating the Adverse Consequences of VA Benefits Law for Survivors of Vietnam Veterans"—*Michael Wildhaber, Esq., Staff Attorney, National Veterans Legal Services Project*

Evening Session
6:00—7:30 PM

Community Veterans' Services: From The American Legion to the Grassroots

Moderator: Michael Blecker, Executive Director, Swords to Plowshares

Panelists: W. Charles Clay, Ph.D. Candidate, University of Oklahoma; Peter Cameron, Executive Director, Vietnam Veterans of California; Thomas M. James, Esq., Managing Director, Community Outreach to Vietnam Era Returnees (COVER); Ralph Cooper, Executive Director, Veterans Benefits Clearinghouse; and Stephen Pederson, Program Coordinator, Vietnam Veterans Family Assistance Program/ The American Legion, South Dakota

Wednesday May 18th: Families of Veterans: A Resource for Healing

Plenary Session
10:00—11:00 AM

Keynote Presentation:
"For Those Who Bore the Battle: Family-Centered Veterans' Services"—Charles R. Figley, Ph.D., Professor of Social Work, Florida State University

Discussion Panel
11:00—11:45 AM

Moderator: Karen Gould, Ph.D., Assistant Director, E.K. Shriver Center, University Affiliated Program

Panelists: Mary James, M.Ed., L.P.C., Executive Director, Community Outreach to Vietnam Era Returnees (COVER); Martha Zeigler, Executive Director, Federation for Children with Special Needs; and Charles T. Hagel, President, McCarthy & Co.; and Member, Board of Advisors, AOCAP

Plenary Session
1:30—3:15 PM

Family-Centered Policy, Planning, and Systems Change

Moderator: Ron Gardner, Assistant Vice Chancellor, Louisiana State University Medical Center; and Member, Board of Advisors, AOCAP

Presentations:

"Designing Veteran Family Assistance Services to Meet the Needs and Preferences of Vietnam Veterans Who Have Children with Special Needs"—*Jean Ann Summers, Ph.D., Associate Director, Institute for Human Development, University Affiliated Program, University of Missouri, Kansas City*

"A Consortium for Services to Vietnam Veterans and Their Families: An Innovative Model for Serving the Veteran Community"—*Frank Scott, Ph.D., Vietnam Veterans Family Services Project, E.K. Shriver Center University Affiliated Program*

"AOCAP Service Coordination: Conceptual Framework, Outcomes, and Policy Implications"—*Judith Holt, Ph.D., Interdisciplinary Training Director, University of Arkansas University Affiliated Program*

Concurrent Presentation Sessions 3:30—5:00 PM

Program Evaluation
Moderator: Frank McCarthy, President, Vietnam Veterans Agent Orange Victims; and Member, Board of Advisors, AOCAP

Presentations:

"Service Evaluation Outcomes for Families of Vietnam Veterans with Children with Disabilities in the Baltimore Metropolitan Area"—*Peter LaCount, M.Ed., Project Coordinator, Vietnam Veterans Family Support Project, Kennedy Krieger Institute*

"Geographic and Demographic Influences on Three University-Based AOCAP Projects in the Gulf South Region"—*Susan Turner, M.S.W., Project Coordinator, Mississippi Vietnam Veterans' Family Support Network, University of Southern Mississippi*

Service Models

Moderator: Honorable Matt M. Railey, Chief Judge, 4th Judicial District, State of Colorado; and Member, Board of Advisors, AOCAP

Presentations:

"Helping Families Understand Post-Traumatic Stress Disorder: A Psychoeducational Workshop Model"—*Lisa Cosgrove, Ph.D., Vietnam Veterans Family Services Project, E.K. Shriver Center University Affiliated Program*

"PTSD and Family Decision Making"—*Annette Richards, Caseworker, VetLink, The Cottage Program*

"A Family Focused Resource Coordination Model for the U.S. Department of Veterans Affairs"—*Gordon Hollingshead, M.P.A., Project Director, Vietnam Veterans' Children's Assistance Program, University of Montana*

Service Delivery

Moderator: Gary May, A.C.S.W., Assistant Professor of Social Work, University of Southern Indiana; and Member, Board of Advisors, AOCAP

Presentations:

"Vietnam Veteran Family Assistance Program: A Collaborative Private Agency and Public University Student Intern–Assisted Service and Education Delivery"—*Larry Braden, M.S.W., Executive Director, Community and Family Services*

"An Effective Multimodal Priority Model for Counseling Hispanic Vietnam Veteran Families Adversely Impacted by Agent Orange"—*Patricia A. Fox-Whipple, M.A., Project Director, American GI Forum*

"Specific Cultural and/or Ethnic Sensitivity Issues That Service Providers Must Address When Serving Navajo Vietnam Veterans"—*Helen Mitchell, Ph.D., Agent Orange Family Assistance Program, Utah State University*

Concurrent Presentations and Activity Sessions
6:30—8:00 PM

Service Programs

Moderator: Diane Carlson Evans, R.N., Chair and Founder, Viet nam Women's Memorial Project; and Member, Board of Advisors, AOCAP

Presentations:

"Transition to Independent Living: Challenges Facing the Vietnam Veteran Family with a Child with Developmental Disabilities"—*Sue Leibold, R.N., M.S., Project Director, Spina Bifida Association of America*

"Triple-Stress Jeopardy of Agent Orange Class Members and a Collaborative, Multidimensional Service Model"—*Duane Schielke, Associate Director, United Cerebral Palsy Association, New York State*

Case Studies

Moderator: Lisa Cosgrove, Ph.D., Vietnam Veterans Family Services Project, E.K. Shriver Center University Affiliated Program

Presentations:

"Object Relations Family Therapy and PTSD: Family Therapy with Four Generations of a Vietnam Veteran's Family"—*Nancy Errebo, Ph.D., U.S. Department of Veterans Affairs Readjustment Counseling Center*

"'Hidden Clients' of Domestic Violence"—*Eileen Pencer, M.Ed., C.S.W., Vice President, Chief Program Officer, Lower Eastside Service Center*

Workshop

"Storytelling: A Tool of Healing for Vietnam Veterans and Their Families"—*Tina Alston, Ph.D., Project Director, Base Camp*

Roundtable Discussions

"Issues, Problems, and Solutions for Vietnam Veterans and Their Families Living in Rural Areas"

Chair: Leslie Ann Snow-Pond, Service Coordinator, Agent Orange Family Assistance Program, Utah State University

"Vietnam Veteran Wife Burnout: Spouse/Partner Relationships"

Chair: Marijane Goonan, T.R.T., Assistant Department Director, Sunshine Terrace Foundation

Thursday May 19th:

Children of Vietnam Veterans and the Legacy of the War

Special Plenary Session
9:00—10:15 AM

"Health Care Reform: Its Potential Impact on Our Children"—*Allan I. Bergman, Deputy Director, Community Services Division, and Director, State-Federal Relations, United Cerebral Palsy Associations—Guest Speaker*

Keynote Presentation
10:25—10:55 AM

"Turning Today's Lesson Into Tomorrow's Hope for the Future: How Can We Best Help Our Children"—*Honorable Bob Williams, Commissioner, Administration on Developmental Disabilities, U.S. Department of Health and Human Services*

Discussion Panel
10:55—11:45 AM

Moderator: Carl F. Calkins, Ph.D., Director, University Affiliated Program for Persons with Developmental Disabilities, Institute for Human Development, University of Missouri at Kansas City

Panelists: Brandie Schieb, Student; Marijane Goonan, T.R.T., Assistant Department Director, Sunshine Terrace Foundation; and Curtis Kelly, Student

Concurrent Sessions
1:30—3:00 PM

Post-Traumatic Stress Disorder: Its Impact on Children
Moderator: David Lloyd, Esq., Director, National Center on Child Abuse and Neglect

Presentations:

"Families of Vietnam Veterans with Post-Traumatic Stress Disorder: Child Social Competence and Behavior"—*Laurie Harkness, Ph.D., Chief, Psychiatric Rehabilitation Program, U.S. Department of Veterans Affairs Medical Center*

"A Clinical View of Children of Veterans and Post-Traumatic Stress Disorder"—*Mary James, M.Ed., L.P.C., Executive Director, Community Outreach to Vietnam Era Returnees (COVER)*

Physical Conditions and Mental Health Issues Affecting Children of Vietnam Veterans

Moderator: Mark E. Swanson, M.D., Director, University of Arkansas University Affiliated Program

Presentations:

"Some Lingering Consequences of the Vietnam War on Veterans and Their Families"—*Bryan Smith, Ed.D., Director, National Information System, University of South Carolina*

"In the Aftermath: Meeting the Special Needs of the Children of Vietnam Veterans"—*Margot Stein, Ph.D., Psychologist, The Clinical Center for the Study of Development of Learning, Biological Sciences Research Center, University of North Carolina at Chapel Hill*

Systems Development on Behalf of Children with Special Needs: Collaborative Policy and Planning Implications

Moderator: Ray Sanchez, M.S.W., Program Manager, Administration on Developmental Disabilities, Administration for Children and Families, U.S. Department of Health and Human Services

Panelists: Marvin Fifield, Ph.D., Director, Center for Persons with Disabilities, Utah State University; John G. Reiss, Ph.D., Director, National Center for Policy Coordination at the Institute for Child Health Policy, University of Florida College of Medicine; and Barbara Spoor, M.P.A., AOCAP Project Coordinator, American Association for University Affiliated Programs for Persons with Developmental Disabilities

Concurrent Sessions
3:15—4:45 PM

Post-Traumatic Stress Disorder: Treatment and Other Service Issues

Moderator: Diane Carlson Evans, R.N., Chair and Founder, Vietnam Women's Memorial Project; and Member, Board of Advisors, AOCAP

Presentations:

"Art as a Therapeutic Technique: Addressing the Clinical Issues of Children of Vietnam Veterans"—*Michele McCutcheon, Case Manager, Skagit Community Mental Health Center*

"Children of Vietnam: A Third Generation"—*Mary Moyer, M.S., Executive Director, The Next Step*

"PTSD and the Family: Secondary Traumatization"—*Lisa Cosgrove, Ph.D., Clinical Psychologist, E.K. Shriver Center University Affiliated Program*

Programs That Work

Moderator: Judith Holt, Ph.D., Interdisciplinary Training Director, University of Arkansas University Affiliated Program

Presentations:

"Advocacy and Resource Leveraging to Effect Change for the Children of Vietnam Veterans"—*Bonnie W. Webb, Director, The Access Group, United Cerebral Palsy Associations*

"The Children of Vietnam Veterans: Complex Concerns and Innovative Solutions"—*Phil Kraft, Family Health Counselor, Vietnam Veterans Agent Orange Victims*

"Serving the Children of Vietnam Veterans"—*Susan Pincus, M.D., Co-Director, Agent Orange Program, Department of Pediatrics, Albert Einstein College of Medicine*

"Project Independence: Homes That Work for Vietnam Veterans' Children with Disabilities"—*Kenneth S. Holmes, Housing Accessibility Coordinator, Project Independence, Spina Bifida Association of America*

Children's Domain Policy Recommendations Working Group

Co-Facilitators: William E. Jones, Ph.D., Executive Director, American Association of University Affiliated Programs for Persons with Developmental Disabilities (AAUAP); and Carl Calkins, Ph.D., Director, University Affiliated Program for Persons with Developmental Disabilities, Institute for Human Development, University of Missouri at Kansas City

Friday May 20th:	**The Legacy of the AOCAP Network**
Plenary Session 9:00—10:30 AM	**Building on the Experiences of the Agent Orange Class Assistance Program as a Catalyst for Systems Change** William E. Jones, Ph.D., Executive Director, American Association of University Affiliated Programs for Persons with Developmental Disabilities (AAUAP); and Barbara Spoor, M.P.A., Project Coordinator, AOCAP Training and Technical Assistance Project, AAUAP
Plenary Session 10:45 AM—12:00 Noon	**Report on the Symposium:** Dennis K. Rhoades, Executive Director, and Members of the Board of Advisors, Agent Orange Class Assistance Program **National Symposium Closing Remarks**: Dennis K. Rhoades, Executive Director, and Members of the Board of Advisors, Agent Orange Class Assistance Program

Appendix B

National Symposium Planning Committee

Dennis K. Rhoades, Chair
Agent Orange Class Assistance Program (AOCAP)

David F. Addlestone
National Veterans Legal Services Project (NVLSP)

Carl F. Calkins
University of Missouri at Kansas City

Marvin Fifield
Utah State University

Karen Gould
E.K. Shriver Center

William Jones
American Association of University Affiliated Programs (AAUAP)

Michael Nicastro
AOCAP

The Honorable Matt M. Railey
4th Judicial District Court
State of Colorado

Florentino Zamora
AAUAP

Veterans Affairs

David F. Addlestone, Chair
NVLSP

Thomas Goonan
Utah State University

John Hanson
The American Legion

Thomas James
Community Outreach for Vietnam Era Returnees (COVER)

Michael Leaveck
AOCAP

Gary E. May
AOCAP Advisory Board

Wayne Smith
Vietnam Veterans Memorial Fund

Families

Karen Gould, Chair
E.K. Shriver Center

David Ewing
Swords to Plowshares

Ronald Gardner
Louisiana State University

Mary James
COVER

Cynthia Kaufman
Kennedy Krieger Institute

Susan Leibold
Spina Bifida Association of America

James Stuart
AOCAP

Developmental Disabilities

William T. Jones, Co-Chair
AAUAP

Carl Calkins, Co-Chair
Missouri Vietnam Veterans Education and Resource Center

Peter T. Cameron
Vietnam Veterans of California

Deborah Crane
Federation for Children with Special Needs

Frank McCarthy
AOCAP Advisory Board

Babette Polzer
AOCAP

Bryan C. Smith
University of South Carolina

Barbara J. Spoor
New York Office for Mental Retardation and Developmental Disabilities

Logistics

Florentino Zamora, Chair
AAUAP

Sally Allman
AOCAP

Kenneth Boggs
Action to Rehabilitate Community Housing (ARCH)

Marlene K. Fridley
NVLSP

Judith Holt
University of Arkansas

Mary Lou Keener
AOCAP Advisory Board

Robert Van Keuren
Vietnam Veterans of San Diego

Publications

Marvin Fifield, Chair
Utah State University

Mary E. Cadette
NVLSP

Julie Clark
Bazelon Center for Mental Health Law

James C. Hudson
AOCAP

Diane Smoyer
AAUAP

Solomon Watson
The New York Times

Appendix C

Agent Orange Class Assistance Program
Board of Advisors

Steve Champlin
Washington, DC

Diane Carlson Evans
Northfield, MN

Ronald Gardner
New Orleans, LA

Charles T. Hagel
Omaha, NE

Gary E. May
Indianapolis, IN

Frank McCarthy
Orlando, FL

The Honorable Matt M. Railey
Colorado Springs, CO

Helen Phillips
Poland, OH

Dr. Oscar Salvatierra
San Francisco, CA

Solomon B. Watson
New York, NY

Appendix D

Agent Orange Class Assistance Program Staff

Dennis K. Rhoades
Executive Director

Michael R. Leaveck
Deputy Director

Evelyn J. Anderson
Director of Finance

Lisa Buono
Systems Manager

Sally Allman
Grant Representative

James C. Hudson
Grant Representative

Michael Nicastro
Grant Representative

Babette Polzer
Grant Representative

James L. Stuart
Grant Representative

Appendix E

Agent Orange Veteran Payment Program Advisory Board

Charles T. Hagel
Omaha, NE

Donna-Marie Boulay, Esq.
Minneapolis, MN

Albert S. Dandridge, III, Esq.
Philadelphia, PA

John L. McElrath
Fairfax, VA

Vincent J. Martin, Jr.
Summit, NJ

Appendix F
National Symposium Participants

Ronald Abrams
National Veterans Legal Services Project
Washington, DC

Rena Acha
Lower Eastside Service Center
New York, NY

David Addlestone
National Veterans Legal Services Project
Washington, DC

Martin Aelmore
The American Legion
Vietnam Veterans Family
Assistance Program
Wichita, KS

Joyce Aide
Association of Birth Defect Children
Orlando, FL

Teddy Aires
Clean & Sober Streets
Washington, DC

Barbara Aliza
Association of Maternal & Child Health
Programs
Washington, DC

Sally Allman
Agent Orange Class Assistance Program
Washington, DC

Tina Alston
Base Camp Inc.
Nashville, TN

Edna Amuimuia
Learning Disabilities Association of Hawaii
Honolulu, HI

Evelyn Anderson
Agent Orange Class Assistance Program
Washington, DC

James Archie, Jr.
ARCH Training Center Inc.
Washington, DC

Jim Bailey
Logan County Vietnam Veterans Inc.
Mt. Gay, WV

Cosme Barcelo
American GI Forum, NVOP
San Antonio, TX

Patricia Barger
Kennedy Krieger Institute
Baltimore, MD

Kirk Bauer
National Handicapped Sports
Rockville, MD

Paul Beals
University of Alaska Fairbanks
College of Liberal Arts
Fairbanks, AK

El Belish
Life Quest (RENEW)
Sheridan, WY

Gerald Bender
Minnesota Department of Veteran Affairs
St. Paul, MN

William Bennett
National Vietnam Veterans Coalition
Washington, DC

Ken Berez
Vietnam Veterans of America Foundation
Washington, DC

Gary Berg
The American Legion
Vietnam Veterans Family Assistance Program
Portland, OR

Allan Bergman
United Cerebral Palsy Associations
Washington, DC

Robert Biehl
University of Illinois
Division of Special Care for Children
Springfield, IL

Lee Bitsui
Navajo Agent Orange Family
Assistance Program
Fort Defiance, AZ

Donald Bjornstad
Association for Retarded Citizens/GA
East Point, GA

Thomas Blake
New York State Department of Health
Albany, NY

George Blatchley
United Cerebal Palsy Association
Canton, NY

Michael Blecker
Swords to Plowshares
San Francisco, CA

Ken Boggs
ARCH Training Center, Inc.
Washington, DC

Thomas Boland
The American Legion
Vietnam Veterans Family Assistance Program
St. Paul, MN

Edward Borg
Vietnam Veterans of California, Inc.
Santa Rosa, CA

Thomas Bourne
Vietnam Veterans of California, Inc.
Sacramento, CA

Larry Braden
Vietnam Veterans Family Assistance Program
Community & Family Services, Inc.
Portland, IN

James Bradshaw
The American Legion
Vietnam Veterans Family Assistance Program
New York, NY

Mary Brady
Vietnam Veterans Family Services Project
E.K. Shriver Center
Waltham, MA

Pearl Brandes
Lower Eastside Service Center
New York, NY

Patricia Braun
Spina Bifida Association of America
Melrose Park, IL

Michael Brauner
Second Start Inc.
San Jose, CA

Bill Brew
U.S. Senate Committee on Veterans Affairs
Washington, DC

Lisa Buono
Agent Orange Class Assistance Program
Washington, DC

Larry Butcher
VETS Inc.
Fraserse City, MI

Mary Cadette
National Veterans Legal Services Project
Washington, DC

Carl Calkins
Missouri Vietnam Veterans Education and Resource System
Kansas City, MO

Randi Cameon
Institute for Child Health Policy
University of Florida at Gainsville
Gainsville, FL

Peter Cameron
Vietnam Veterans of California, Inc.
Santa Rosa, CA

Diane Carlson Evans
Agent Orange Class Assistance Program
Washington, DC

Patricia Carstens
Vietnam Veterans Agent Orange Victims
Darien, CT

Glendon Casto
Center for Persons with Disabilities
Utah State University
Logan, UT

Andrea Censky
Paralyzed Veterans of America
Washington, DC

Richard Christian
The American Legion
Washington, DC

William Christoffersen
National Executive Committee
American Legion UT
Salt Lake City, UT

Joseph Clark
Vietnam Veterans of Brevard, Inc.
Veterans Family & Children Assistance
Melbourne, FL

Julie Clark
Bazelon Center for Mental Health Law
Washington, DC

W. Charles Clay
University of Oklahoma
Norman, OK

Jeane Cole
Spina Bifida Association of America
Orlando, FL

Corky Condon
Sons & Daughters In Touch
Arlington, VA

Ralph Cooper
Veterans Benefits Clearinghouse Inc.
Roxbury, MA

Patrick Cork
Family Service Association of Brown Co.
Green Bay, WI

Lisa Cosgrove
Vietnam Veterans Family Services Project
E.K. Shriver Center
Waltham, MA

Thomas Courtney
The American Legion
Vietnam Veterans Family
Assistance Program
Indianapolis, IN

Melvin Cozzens
ATC Program Development
Front Range Community College
Westminister, CO

Deborah Crane
Federation for Children with Special Needs
Westfield, MA

Dulcie Dana
National Handicapped Sports
Rockville, MD

James Daniels
Vietnam Veterans of California, Inc.
Santa Rosa, CA

Gail Davies
Florida State University
Vietnam Veterans Family Program
Tallahassee, FL

Jacqueline DeCarlo
Lower Eastside Service Center
New York, NY

Joseph DeResta
Vietnam Era Veterans Association of
Rhode Island
Providence, RI

Mary DeVivo
Albert Einstein
College of Medicine
Bronx, NY

Jeanette DeVolt
American GI Forum, NVOP
San Antonio, TX

Melanie Deffendall
Louisiana State University
Medical Center/VVFSP
New Orleans, LA

Daniel Denault
Veterans Outreach Center Inc.
Pittsfield, MA

Dianna Denboba
Maternal & Child Health Bureau
Rockville, MD

Patty Dimond
National Veterans Foundation
Los Angeles, CA

Thelma Ductor
AOCAP, Family Member
Nokesville, VA

Michael Dunn
Veterans Benefits Clearinghouse Inc.
Roxbury, MA

Dwight Edwards
VVHIC
Pennsylvania Department of Health
Harrisburg, PA

Hayley Edwards
American Association of University
Affiliated Programs for Persons with
Developmental Disabilities
Silver Spring, MD

John Eeckhoudt
Vietnam Veterans Leadership Program
Project Access
Pine Bluff, AR

Ruth Eisenberg
National Veterans Legal Services Project
Washington, DC

Elaine Eklund
American Association of University Affiliated Programs for Persons with Developmental Disabilities
Silver Spring, MD

Bill Elmore
Missouri Veterans Leadership Program
St. Louis, MO

Judy Elton
Vietnam Veterans Family Assistance Program
Muncie, IN

Dorothy England
Community Service Programs of West Alabama Inc.
Tuscaloosa, AL

Nancy Errebo
Vet Center
Missoula, MT

Daniel Evangelista
Vietnam Era Veterans Association of Rhode Island
Providence, RI

The Honorable Lane Evans
U.S. House of Representatives
Washington, DC

David Ewing
Swords to Plowshares
San Francisco, CA

Gwen Ewing
Bazelon Center for Mental Health Law
Washington, DC

Laura Facciponti
The First Occupational Center
Vietnam Veterans Children's Services
Orange, NJ

Luis Falcon
Puerto Rico Vietnam Veterans Assistance Program
San Juan, PR

Leslie Felton
Vietnam Veterans Family Support Project
Kennedy Krieger Institute
Baltimore, MD

Marvin Fifield
Utah State University
Logan, UT

Charles Figley
Florida State University
Tallahassee, FL

Holly Theodore Finan
Skagit Mental Health Center
Mount Vernon, WA

Charles Fontaine
North Dakota Vietnam Veterans Children's Assistance Program
Minot, ND

Elizabeth Forsythe
National Veterans Legal Services Program
St. Louis, MO

Ethel Foulks
National Information System
Center for Developmental Disabilities
Columbia, SC

Patricia Fox-Whipple
American GI Forum NVOP/LA
El Monte, CA

Enrique Franco
Aliviane, Inc.
El Paso, TX

Ronald Gardner
Louisana State University Medical Center
Clinical Affairs
New Orleans, LA

Jacqueline Garrick
U.S. Army
Silver Spring, MD

James Gavin
Family Service Association of Central Connecticut
Meriden, CT

The Honorable Hershel W. Gober
U.S. Department of Veterans Affairs
Washington, DC

Michael Goldsmith
NE Vietnam Veteran Outreach and Family Support Program
Omaha, NE

Tony Gonzalez
Rock Island County Council on Addictions
Rock Island, IL

Marijane Goonan
Agent Orange Family Assistance Program
Logan, UT

Thomas Goonan
Agent Orange Family Assistance Program
Logan, UT

Pattie Gorham
Nebraska Vietnam Veteran Outreach and Family Support Program
Omaha, NE

Karen Gould
E.K. Shriver Center
Waltham, MA

Kathleen Gould
Learning Disabilities Association of Hawaii
Honolulu, HI

William Greaver
Universal Family Connection, Inc.
Chicago, IL

Catherine Greene-Stansell
Vietnam Veterans of America, Inc.
Ohio State Council
Columbus, OH

Charles T. Hagel
McCarthy & Company
Omaha, NE

Michael Hahn
Florida Department of Veterans Affairs
Tallahassee, FL

Kristina Handy
Cottage Program International, Inc.
Salt Lake City, UT

Laurie Harkness
Psychiatric Rehabilitation Program
West Haven VA Medical Center
West Haven, CT

Margaret Harlow
Vietnam Veteran's Children's Assistance Program
Missoula, MT

Colleen Harrigan
Louisiana State University Medical Center/VVFSP
New Orleans, LA

Lawrence Helm
St. Louis Vietnam Veterans Leadership Program
St. Louis, MO

Susan Hirshfield
Penngrove, CA

Elizabeth Hodges
Veterans' Support Service, Inc.
Portland, ME

Bruce Hoem
Institute for Disability Studies
University of Southern Mississippi
Hattiesburg, MS

William Holcomb
Vietnam Veterans Family Services Project
E.K. Shriver Center
Waltham, MA

Gordon Hollingshead
Montana Vietnam Veterans Children's Assistance Program
Missoula, MT

Kenneth Holmes
Spina Bifida Association of America
Home Accessibility Program
Walnut Creek, CA

Judith Holt
University of Arkansas-UAP
Little Rock, AR

John Honeywell
Community Outreach to Vietnam Era Returnees
Charlottesville, VA

Karen Horn
Missouri Vietnam Veterans Education and Resource System
Kansas City, MO

James Hudson
Agent Orange Class Assistance Program
Littleton, CO

Art Hughes
Artist
Penngrove, CA

Millie Hughes
Logan County Vietnam Veterans Inc.
Mt. Gay, WV

William Isetts
Vets Inc.
Traverse City, MI

Mary James
COVER
Charlottesville, VA

Thomas James
COVER
Charlottesville, VA

Charles Jensen
Vietnam Veterans of California, Inc.
Santa Rosa, CA

Susan Johnson
National Information Systems for Vietnam Veterans and Their Families
Columbia, SC

William Jones
American Association of University Affiliated Programs for Persons with Developmental Disabilities
Silver Spring, MD

John Kahler
National Veterans Legal Services Project
Washington, DC

The Honorable Mary Lou Keener
U.S. Department of Veterans Affairs
Washington, DC

Curtis Kelley
AOCAP, Family Member
Nokesville, VA

Bonnie Kelly
Louisana State University
Medical Center/VVFSP
New Orleans, LA

Leslie Snow Kemblowski
Utah State University
Center for Persons with Disabilities
Logan, UT

Mary Ann Kimble
Clinical Center for the Study of Development and Learning
Chapel Hill, NC

Phillip Kraft
Vietnam Veterans Agent Orange Victims Inc.
Darien, CT

Peter La Count
Kennedy Krieger Institute
Baltimore, MD

Greg Lais
Wilderness Inquiry Inc.
Minneapolis, MN

Jeff Lande
Office of U.S. Congressman Lane Evans
Washington, DC

Vonda Lauritzen
Agent Orange Family Assistance Program
Logan, UT

Douglas Lay
Vietnam Veterans of America, Inc.
Ohio State Council
Columbus, OH

Amy Lazar
Missouri Vietnam Veterans Education and Resource System
Kansas City, MO

Leon LeBorgne
Paralyzed Veterans of America
Washington, DC

Lisa LeGrave
Family Service Association of Brown County
Green Bay, WI

Michael Leaveck
Agent Orange Class Assistance Program
Washington, DC

Ignacio Leija
American GI Forum, NVOP
San Antonio, TX

Carol Lett
COPIN Foundation
Niagara Falls, NY

Susan Liebold
Spina Bifida Association of America
Tucson, AZ

Cathy Liles
University of Arkansas-UAP
Little Rock, AR

Patrick Lindsay
North Dakota Vietnam Veterans Children's Assistance Program
Minot, ND

David Lloyd
National Center on Child Abuse and Neglect
Washington, DC

Roger Lloyd
Vietnam Veterans Family
Assistance Program
Muncie, IN

Walter Long
Veteran Benefits Clearinghouse Inc.
Roxbury, MA

Roland Loudenburg
American Association of University
Affiliated Programs
Silver Spring, MD

Edward Lowry
Philadelphia Veterans Multi-Service Center
Philadelphia, PA

Melissa Lyon
Vietnam Veterans of San Diego Family
Assistance Program
San Diego, CA

Michelle Macias
Dev. Pediatrics, Vince Mosely Center
Medical University of South Carolina
Charleston, SC

Jack Maloney
Suffolk County Youth Bureau
Children of Vietnam Veterans
Hauppauge, NY

Maria Martinez
Agent Orange Veteran Payment Program
Hartford, CT

Denise Matthews
Institute for Child Health Policy
University of Florida at Gainesville
Gainesville, FL

Gary May
University of Southern Indiana
Evansville, IN

Edward McCann
Family Services of Tidewater Inc.
Norfolk, VA

Frank McCarthy
Agent Orange Class Assistance Program
Orlando, FL

Vernon McCarty
Life Quest (RENEW)
Sheridan, WY

Michele McCutcheon
Skagit Mental Health
Psychiatric and Behavioral Health Services
Mount Vernon, WA

Sharon McGrath
COPIN Foundation
Niagara Falls, NY

Anita McKelroy
Team of Advocates for Special Kids
Anaheim, CA

Mike McKelroy
Team of Advocates for Special Kids
Anaheim, CA

Betty Mekdeci
Association of Birth Defect Children
Orlando, FL

Shad Meshad
National Veterans Foundation
Los Angeles, CA

Kenneth Miller
The American Legion
Vietnam Veterans Family
Assistance Program
Louisville, KY

Beverly Mitchell
Vietnam Veterans of Brevard, Inc.
Vietnam Veterans Child & Family Program
Melbourne, FL

Helen Mitchell
Utah State University
Agent Orange Family Assistance Program
Logan, UT

Maureen Moran
Veterans' Support Services, Inc.
Portland, ME

Margaret Morrow
Senate Committee on Veterans Affairs
United States Senate
Washington, DC

Connie Morse
Seattle Veterans Action Center
Seattle, WA

Donald Moses
U.S. Department of Veterans Affairs
Washington, DC

Mary Moyer
The Next Step, Inc.
Albany, NY

Robert Muller
Vietnam Veterans of America Foundation
Washington, DC

Debbie Murtagh
Vietnam Veterans Children's
Assistance Program
Missoula, MT

Zelma Myers
The University of North Carolina–
Chapel Hill
Chapel Hill, NC

Denise Neal
Association for Retarded Citizens/GA
East Point, GA

Deborah Neas
Family Services of Milwaukee
Milwaukee, WI

Michael Nicastro
Agent Orange Class Assistance Program
Washington, DC

Kathy Norris
University of Arkansas
Little Rock, AR

Valerie Nowak
Vietnam Veterans Family
Counseling Program
Dallas, TX

Richard O'Dell
Roanoke, VA

Dottie O'Donnell
Saratoga County Rural Preservation Co.
Ballston Spa, NY

Clay O'Neil
Aliviane, Inc.
El Paso, TX

Patrick O'Toole
Port Jefferson, NY

Mimi Okino
Lower Eastside Service Center
New York, NY

Robert Ortiz
Swords to Plowshares
San Francisco, CA

George Otto
U.S. Department of Veterans Affairs
Washington, DC

John Page
The American Legion
Vietnam Veterans Family
Assistance Program
Winston-Salem, NC

Patricia Peck
Vietnam Veterans Family Services Project
E.K. Shriver Center
Waltham, MA

Stephen Pederson
The American Legion
Vietnam Veterans Family
Assistance Program
Sioux Falls, SD

Eileen Pencer
Lower Eastside Service Center, Inc.
Vietnam Veterans Family Service Center
New York, NY

Twyla Perry
Vietnam Veterans of San Diego
Family Assistance Program
San Diego, CA

Paula Peterson
Spina Bifida Association of America
Salt Lake City, UT

Teena Petro
Vietnam Veterans Family
Assistance Program
Muncie, IN

Helen Phillips
Agent Orange Class Assistance Program
Poland, OH

Susan Pincus
Albert Einstein College of Medicine
University Affiliated Program
Bronx, NY

Nick Pointon
The American Legion
Vietnam Veterans Family
Assistance Program
Belleville, IL

Babette Polzer
Agent Orange Class Assistance Program
Washington, DC

Wayne Price
Grants Pass Vet Center
Grants Pass, OR

Tima Priess
University of Alaska Fairbanks
College of Liberal Arts
Fairbanks, AK

Carla Putnam
The Access Group/UCPA
Atlanta, GA

Janis Quackenbush
COVER
Louisa, VA

The Honorable Matt Railey
Agent Orange Class Assistance Program
Colorado Springs, CO

Gershon Ratner
National Veterans Legal Services Project
Washington, DC

Milton Reaves
COVER
Charlottesville, VA

Frank Reiger
Children of Vietnam Veterans
Assistance Program
Inglewood, CA

John Reiss
National Center for Policy Coordination
Gainesville, FL

Kris Retlin
The First Occupational Center of NJ
Orange, NJ

Dennis Rhoades
Agent Orange Class Assistance Program
Washington, DC

Annette Richards
Cottage Program International, Inc.
Salt Lake City, UT

Charles Ritter
Missouri Vietnam Veterans Education
and Resource System
Edgar Springs, MO

Elinor Roberts
Swords to Plowshares
San Francisco, CA

Virginia Rogers
Farragut North Productions
Washington, DC

Leonard Rubenstein
Bazelon Center for Mental Health Law
Washington, DC

Walter Russell
United Cerebal Palsy Association
Canton, NY

Lee Saffold
Community and Family Services of
West Alabama
Tuscaloosa, AL

Joe Salas
American Red Cross
Mid-Rio Grande Chapter
Albuquerque, NM

Jesse Sanchez
The American Legion
Vietnam Veterans Family
Assistance Program
Albuquerque, NM

Ray Sanchez
ACF/ADD
Washington, DC

Billy Sandlin
CHS Phase 2
Laytonville, MD

Daniel Sandstrom
Wilderness Inquiry Inc.
Minneapolis, MN

Francisco Santiago
Puerto Rico Veterans Assistance Program
Office of the State Advocate for VA
Han Rey, PR

Jennifer Saylor
COVER
Charlottesville, VA

Linda Schaffner
Base Camp Inc.
Nashville, TN

Brandie Schieb
AOCAP, Family Member
Winsted, CT

Michele Schieb
AOCAP, Family Member
Winsted, CT

Duane Schielke
United Cerebral Palsy Assoc. of NY
New York, NY

Richard Schneider
Non Commissioned Officers Association
Alexandria, VA

Thomas Schroeder
Rock Island County Council on Addictions
Rock Island, IL

Linda Schwartz
Vietnam Veterans of America, Inc.
Washington, DC

Richard Schwartz
The American Legion
Vietnam Veterans Family Assistance Program
Orlando, FL

The Honorable Edward P. Scott
U.S. Department of Veterans Affairs
Washington, DC

Frank Scott
Vietnam Veterans Family Services Project
E.K. Shriver Center
Waltham, MA

Wilbur Scott
Department of Sociology
University of Oklahoma
Norman, OK

Jan Scruggs
Vietnam Veterans Memorial Fund
Washington, DC

Betty Searles
VA Medical Center
Compensation & Pension
Seattle, WA

Ginny Shelton
Office of U.S. Congressman Lane Evans
Moline, IL

James Shoop
Skagit Mental Health
Psychiatric and Behavioral Health Svc.
Mount Vernon, WA

John Schwab
Maternal & Child Health Bureau
U.S. Public Health Service
Rockville, MD

Betty Siemer
Second Start Inc.
San Jose, CA

Ynes Simon-Alvarez
Veterans Benefits Clearinghouse Inc.
Roxbury, MA

Bryan Smith
National Information System
Center for Developmental Disabilities
Columbia, SC

David Smith
Vietnam Veterans Children's Assistance Program
Missoula, MT

Frederick Smith
The American Legion
Vietnam Veterans Family Assistance Program
Wilkes-Barre, PA

James Smith
The American Legion
Vietnam Veterans Family Assistance Program
Muskogee, OK

Michael Smith
Philadelphia Veterans Multi-Service Center
Philadelphia, PA

Wayne Smith
Vietnam Veterans Memorial Fund
Washington, DC

Phyllis Sneirson
Federation for Children with Special Needs
Boston, MA

Efrain Soto Cruet
Puerto Rico Vietnam Veterans Assistance Program
San Juan, PR

Barbara Spoor
American Association of University Affiliated Programs
Silver Spring, MD

Peggy St. Clair
UAP/Project Access
Mnt Home, AR

Catherine Stansell
Vietnam Veterans of America, Inc.
Ohio State Council
Columbus, OH

Margot Stein
University of North Carolina–Chapel Hill
Chapel Hill, NC

Charles Stewart, Sr.
The American Legion
Vietnam Veterans Family
Assistance Program
St. Louis, MO

Adrian Stilson
COVER
Charlottesville, VA

Barton Stichman
National Veterans Legal Services Project
Washington, DC

James Stuart
Agent Orange Class Assistance Program
Washington, DC

Yolanda Suarez
American GI Forum, NVOP
San Antonio, TX

Dawn Sudduth
National Information System
Center for Developmental Disabilities
Columbia, SC

Jean Summers
Missouri Vietnam Veterans Education
and Resource System
Kansas City, MO

Mark Swanson
University of Arkansas-UAP
VVLP-ARK
Little Rock, AR

Richard Szymanski
Suffolk County Youth Bureau
Children of Vietnam Veterans
Hauppauge, NY

Joseph Taggart
Philadelphia Veterans Multi-Service Center
Philadelphia, PA

Sherry Tatro
Vietnam Veterans Mobile Family Service
Project/Veterans Outreach Center Inc.
Pittsfield, MA

Max Tenberg
The American Legion
Vietnam Veterans Family
Assistance Program
Washington, DC

John Terzano
Vietnam Veterans of America Foundation
Washington, DC

Teresa Thompson
Navajo Agent Orange Family
Assistance Program
Fort Defiance, AZ

Wayne Thompson
Community Health Center, Inc.
Oklahoma City, OK

Susan Turner
Institute for Disability Studies
University of Southern Mississippi
Hattiesburg, MS

Mary Wallace
Bayaud Industries, Inc.
Denver, CO

Marsh Ward
Clean and Sober Streets
Washington, DC

Katy Warner
Seattle Veteran Action Center
Seattle, WA

Jerry Washington
Base Camp Inc.
Nashville, TN

Bonnie Webb
The Access Group/UCPA
Atlanta, GA

The Honorable Jack B. Weinstein
U.S. District Court
Eastern District of New York
Brooklyn, NY

Muria Whitaker
UAP/Project Access
Springdale, AR

Michael Wildhaber
Law Office of Wildhaber & Associates
Washington, DC

Kelli Willard
Vietnam Veterans of America, Inc.
Washington, DC

Arlene Williams
Southern California Veterans Services Council
Inglewood, CA

The Honorable Robert Williams
Administration on Developmental Disabilities
Washington, DC

Mindy Winningham
Vietnam Veterans Family Assistance Program
Muncie, IN

Donald Wirth
Saratoga County Rural Preservation Co.
Ballston Spa, NY

Leroy Woods
Community Health Center, Inc.
Oklahoma City, OK

Francine Zambrana
Team of Advocates for Special Kids
Orange, CA

Florentino Zamora
American Association of University Affiliated Programs for Persons with Developmental Disabilities
Silver Spring, MD

Martha Zeigler
Federation for Children with Special Needs
Boston, MA

Edward Zipeto
ARCH Family Services
Washington, DC

Appendix G

Legal History of Agent Orange Litigation

Listed chronologically:

In re "Agent Orange" Prod. Liab. Litig., 475 F. Supp. 928 (E.D.N.Y. 1979) (dismissing federal constitutional and statutory claims, reserving possible federal common law claims, denying motion to limit communications to third parties).

In re "Agent Orange" Prod. Liab. Litig., 506 F. Supp. 737 (E.D.N.Y. 1979) (finding subject matter jurisdiction on basis of federal common law issues), *rev'd*, 635 F.2d 981 (2d Cir. 1980), *cert. denied*, 454 U.S. 1128 (1981).

In re "Agent Orange" Prod. Liab. Litig., 28 Fed. R. Serv. 2d (Callaghan) 993 (E.D.N.Y. 1980) (granting motion of terminally ill plaintiff to videotape his own deposition).

In re "Agent Orange" Prod. Liab. Litig., 506 F. Supp. 750 (E.D.N.Y. 1980) (ordering government to refrain from destruction of documents pursuant to internal procedure).

In re "Agent Orange" Prod. Liab. Litig., 506 F. Supp. 753 (E.D.N.Y. 1980) (resolving issues relating to modification of complaint and answers).

In re "Agent Orange" Prod. Liab. Litig., 506 F. Supp. 754 (E.D.N.Y. 1980) (ordering videotaped deposition).

In re "Agent Orange" Prod. Liab. Litig., 506 F. Supp. 756 (E.D.N.Y. 1980) (establishing agenda for status conference).

In re "Agent Orange" Prod. Liab. Litig., 506 F. Supp. 757 (E.D.N.Y. 1980) (requiring plaintiffs to file individual notices to retain right to bring actions against federal government).

In re "Agent Orange" Prod. Liab. Litig., 506 F. Supp. 762 (E.D.N.Y. 1980) (dismissing claims against government as third-party defendant, establishing case management plan, conditionally certifying Rule 23(b)(3) class, and denying defendants' motion for summary judgment).

In re "Agent Orange" Prod. Liab. Litig., 91 F.R.D. 616 (E.D.N.Y. 1981) (establishing committee to review procedures for videotaped depositions).

In re "Agent Orange" Prod. Liab. Litig., 91 F.R.D. 618 (E.D.N.Y. 1981) (allowing motion to amend caption, denying motion to amend complaint, denying defendants' motion for summary judgment on "government contractor" defense).

In re "Agent Orange" Prod. Liab. Litig., 93 F.R.D. 514 (E.D.N.Y. 1982) (allowing defendant to proceed with scheduled destruction of documents).

In re "Agent Orange" Prod. Liab. Litig., 534 F. Supp. 1046 (E.D.N.Y. 1982) (denying reargument on dismissal of government as third-party defendant, denying interlocutory appeal, provisionally dismissing claims against non-manufacturer defendants, denying motion to form steering committee for plaintiffs' counsel, denying motion for decertification of class, deferring decision on statute of limitations issues, and establishing elements of government contractor defense).

In re "Agent Orange" Prod. Liab. Litig., 537 F. Supp. 977 (E.D.N.Y. 1982) (provisionally dismissing claims against non-manufacturer defendant).

In re "Agent Orange" Prod. Liab. Litig., 94 F.R.D. 173 (E.D.N.Y. 1982) (appointing special master to supervise discovery).

In re "Agent Orange" Prod. Liab. Litig., 544 F. Supp. 808 (E.D.N.Y. 1982) (denying motion to disqualify defense attorneys, provisionally dismissing claims against certain non-manufacturer defendants, and denying motion to implead suppliers).

In re "Agent Orange" Prod. Liab. Litig., 95 F.R.D. 191 (E.D.N.Y. 1982) (clarifying that denial of motion to implead suppliers was without prejudice).

In re "Agent Orange" Prod. Liab. Litig., 95 F.R.D. 192 (E.D.N.Y. 1982) (affirming special master's ruling as to location of depositions).

In re "Agent Orange" Prod. Liab. Litig., 96 F.R.D. 578 (E.D.N.Y. 1983) (adopting special master's protective order for discovery of government documents).

In re "Agent Orange" Prod. Liab. Litig., 96 F.R.D. 582 (E.D.N.Y. 1983) (rejecting first amendment challenge to protective order).

In re "Agent Orange" Prod. Liab. Litig., 96 F.R.D. 587 (E.D.N.Y. 1983) (adopting with modifications special master's order regarding videotaped depositions).

In re "Agent Orange" Prod. Liab. Litig., 97 F.R.D. 424 (E.D.N.Y. 1983) (adopting protective order).

In re "Agent Orange" Prod. Liab. Litig., 97 F.R.D. 424 (E.D.N.Y. 1983) (adopting special master's protective order for Department of Agriculture documents).

In re "Agent Orange" Prod. Liab. Litig., 97 F.R.D. 427 (E.D.N.Y. 1983) (adopting special master's procedures for discovery of documents possibly subject to executive privilege).

In re "Agent Orange" Prod. Liab. Litig., 97 F.R.D. 541 (E.D.N.Y. 1983) (denying interlocutory appeal of decision deferring certification of class and determination of appropriate notice).

In re "Agent Orange" Prod. Liab. Litig., 97 F.R.D. 542 (E.D.N.Y. 1983) (affirming special master's denial of discovery request).

In re "Agent Orange" Prod. Liab. Litig., 565 F. Supp. 1263 (E.D.N.Y. 1983) (granting summary judgment for four defendants on government contractor defense; denying summary judgment for other defendants).

In re "Agent Orange" Prod. Liab. Litig., 98 F.R.D. 522 (E.D.N.Y. 1983) (adopting order of special master concerning discovery of government documents).

In re "Agent Orange" Prod. Liab. Litig., 98 F.R.D. 539 (E.D.N.Y. 1983) (adopting special master's order to unseal documents in connection with summary judgment motions).

In re "Agent Orange" Prod. Liab. Litig., 98 F.R.D. 554 (E.D.N.Y. 1983) (denying request for reconsideration of order to unseal documents).

In re "Agent Orange" Prod. Liab. Litig., 98 F.R.D. 557 (E.D.N.Y. 1983) (ordering special master to review discovery decisions in light of court's decision to try causality and liability issues).

In re "Agent Orange" Prod. Liab. Litig., 98 F.R.D. 558 (E.D.N.Y. 1983) (approving special master's order of additional discovery to clarify circumstances surrounding document destruction).

In re "Agent Orange" Prod. Liab. Litig., 570 F. Supp. 693 (E.D.N.Y. 1983) (clarifying program for discovery).

In re "Agent Orange" Prod. Liab. Litig., 571 F. Supp. 481 (E.D.N.Y. 1983) (granting motion of law firm to be relieved as lead counsel for plaintiffs and appointing new plaintiffs' management committee).

In re "Agent Orange" Prod. Liab. Litig., 99 F.R.D. 338 (E.D.N.Y. 1983) (approving discovery recommendations of special master).

In re "Agent Orange" Prod. Liab. Litig., 99 F.R.D. 645 (E.D.N.Y. 1983) (lifting prior protective order applying to government documents obtained during discovery).

In re "Agent Orange" Prod. Liab. Litig., 100 F.R.D. 718 (E.D.N.Y.) (certifying Rule 23(b)(3) and Rule 23(b)(1)(B) classes), *appeal denied,* 100 F.R.D. 735 (E.D.N.Y. 1983), *mandamus denied,* 725 F.2d 858 (2d Cir. 1984), *aff'd,* 818 F.2d 145 (2d Cir. 1987), *cert. denied,* 484 U.S. 1004 (1988).

In re "Agent Orange" Prod. Liab. Litig., 100 F.R.D. 778 (E.D.N.Y. 1984) (denying motion to implead suppliers of chemical components).

In re "Agent Orange" Prod. Liab. Litig., 580 F. Supp. 690 (E.D.N.Y. 1984) (finding national consensus law on issues of liability, government contractor defense and punitive damages).

In re "Agent Orange" Prod. Liab. Litig., 580 F. Supp. 1242 (E.D.N.Y.) (reinstating third-party plaintiffs' claim for indemnity against government with respect to claims of veterans' wives and children), *mandamus denied,* 733 F.2d 10 (2d Cir.), *appeal denied,* 745 F.2d 161 (2d Cir.), *cert. denied,* 465 U.S. 1067 (1984).

In re "Agent Orange" Prod. Liab. Litig., 101 F.R.D. 97 (E.D.N.Y. 1984) (ordering *in camera* disclosure of names of scientists deleted from government report).

In re "Agent Orange" Prod. Liab. Litig., 597 F. Supp. 740 (E.D.N.Y. 1984) (approving settlement of class action subject to fairness hearings).

In re "Agent Orange" Prod. Liab. Litig., 603 F. Supp. 239 (E.D.N.Y. 1985) (dismissing claims of veterans' wives and children against government), *aff'd in part, vacated in part,* 818 F.2d 201 (2d Cir. 1987), *cert. denied,* 484 U.S. 1004 (1988).

In re "Agent Orange" Prod. Liab. Litig., 104 F.R.D. 559 (E.D.N.Y. 1985) (modifying protective orders).

In re "Agent Orange" Prod. Liab. Litig., 105 F.R.D. 577 (E.D.N.Y. 1985) (affirming with modification magistrate's order that defendants in two non-settled cases produce deponents).

In re "Agent Orange" Prod. Liab. Litig., 611 F. Supp. 1221 (E.D.N.Y. 1985) (dismissing defendants' claim for indemnity from government for settlement payments to veterans' families), *aff'd,* 818 F.2d 204 (2d Cir. 1987).

In re "Agent Orange" Prod. Liab. Litig., 611 F. Supp. 1223 (E.D.N.Y. 1985) (ruling as to admissibility of opt-out plaintiffs' scientific evidence and expert testimony and granting summary judgment in favor of defendants for plaintiffs' failure to establish causation), *aff'd,* 818 F.2d 187 (2d Cir. 1987), *cert. denied,* 487 U.S. 1234 (1988).

In re "Agent Orange" Prod. Liab. Litig., 611 F. Supp. 1267 (E.D.N.Y. 1985) (same), *aff'd,* 818 F.2d 187 (2d Cir. 1987), *cert. denied,* 487 U.S. 1234 (1988).

In re "Agent Orange" Prod. Liab. Litig., 611 F. Supp. 1285 (E.D.N.Y. 1985) (dismissing action brought by Hawaiian civilians), *aff'd in part, vacated in part,* 818 F.2d 210 (2d Cir. 1987), *cert. denied,* 484 U.S. 1004 (1988).

In re "Agent Orange" Prod. Liab. Litig., 611 F. Supp. 1290 (E.D.N.Y. 1985) (dismissing claim of civilian physician for failure to demonstrate exposure to herbicides), *aff'd in part, vacated in part,* 818 F.2d 210 (2d Cir. 1987), *cert. denied,* 484 U.S. 1004 (1988).

In re "Agent Orange" Prod. Liab. Litig., 611 F. Supp. 1296 (E.D.N.Y. 1985) (determining class action plaintiffs' attorney fees and reaffirming settlement), *aff'd in part, rev'd in part,* 818 F.2d 226 (2d Cir. 1987).

In re "Agent Orange" Prod. Liab. Litig., 611 F. Supp. 1396 (E.D.N.Y. 1985) (establishing plan for disbursement of settlement fund pending appeals), *aff'd in part, rev'd in part,* 818 F.2d 179 (2d Cir. 1987).

In re "Agent Orange" Prod. Liab. Litig., 611 F. Supp. 1452 (E.D.N.Y. 1985) (denying motion to set aside attorney fee-sharing arrangement), *rev'd in part*, 818 F.2d 216 (2d Cir.), *cert. denied*, 484 U.S. 926 (1987).

In re "Agent Orange" Prod. Liab. Litig., 618 F. Supp. 623 (E.D.N.Y. 1985) (approving settlement of class action and dismissing with prejudice claims of class members).

In re "Agent Orange" Prod. Liab. Litig., 618 F. Supp. 625 (E.D.N.Y 1985) (approving plan for Australia and New Zealand).

In re "Agent Orange" Prod. Liab. Litig., 787 F.2d 822 (2d Cir. 1986) (dismissing claims of non-class plaintiffs against defendant not named in complaints).

In re "Agent Orange" Prod. Liab. Litig., 800 F.2d 14 (2d Cir. 1986) (denying motion to disqualify plaintiffs' attorneys from appealing settlement).

In re "Agent Orange" Prod. Liab. Litig., 804 F.2d 19 (2d Cir. 1986) (denying repeal of stay on settlement funds pending appeal).

In re "Agent Orange" Prod. Liab. Litig., 689 F. Supp. 1250 (E.D.N.Y. 1988) (modifying class assistance program as required by 818 F.2d 179 and granting opt-out plaintiffs opportunity to opt into class for purposes of benefiting from settlement fund).

Uniroyal, Inc. v. Home Ins. Co., 707 F. Supp. 1368 (E.D.N.Y. 1988) (holding insurer must indemnify Agent Orange defendant).

In re Ivy, 901 F.2d 7 (2d Cir. 1990) (declining to vacate order transferring case from Eastern District of Texas to Eastern District of New York).

In re Agent Orange Fee Application of Yannacone, 139 F.R.D. 581 (E.D.N.Y. 1991) (upholding magistrate's decision in attorney's fee dispute).

In re "Agent Orange" Prod. Liab. Litig., 781 F. Supp. 902 (E.D.N.Y. 1991) (holding that settlement bars class members from litigating Agent Orange claims in state court, and that plaintiffs who did not know definitively whether they were included in class as of the first opt-out deadline are bound by settlement), *affirmed*, 996 F.2d 1425 (2d Cir. 1993), *cert. denied*, 114 S. Ct. 1125 (1994).

In re "Agent Orange" Prod. Liab. Litig., 781 F. Supp. 934 (E.D.N.Y. 1992) (remanding civilian plaintiffs' claims to Texas courts).

In re "Agent Orange" Prod. Liab. Litig., 996 F.2d 1425 (1993) (affirming 781 F. Supp. 902), *cert. denied*, 114 S. Ct. 1125 (1994).

Appendix H

AOCAP Grantees by State

National Support Projects

American Association of University Affiliated Programs for Persons with Developmental Disabilities
Bazelon Center for Mental Health Law
National Veterans Legal Services Program
National Information System, University of South Carolina UAP
United Cerebral Palsy Associations, Inc.

National Service Projects

National Handicapped Sports
Spina Bifida Association of America
Vietnam Veterans Agent Orange Victims, Inc.
Wilderness Inquiry, Inc.

State	City	Program
Alabama	Tuscaloosa	Community Services Program of Western Alabama
Alaska	Fairbanks	University of Alaska
Arizona	Ft. Defiance	Utah State University, Navajo Agent Orange Family Assistance Program
Arkansas	Little Rock	University of Arkansas UAP, Vietnam Veterans Leadership Program
California	Anaheim	Team of Advocates for Special Kids (TASK)
	Berkeley	Veterans Assistance Center
	Los Angeles	Southern California Veterans Services Council
		American GI Forum
	San Diego	Vietnam Veterans of San Diego
	San Francisco	Swords to Plowshares
	San Jose	Second Start, Inc.
	Santa Rosa, Sacramento	Vietnam Veterans of California
Colorado	Denver	Bayaud Industries
Connecticut	Meriden	Family Services Center
Delaware		*Veterans Multi-Service Center (Philadelphia, PA)*
District of Columbia		ARCH Training Center, Inc.
		New Way, Inc.

Italics indicate that a grantee located in another state also operates in this state.

State	City	Program
Florida	Melbourne	Vietnam Veterans of Brevard
	Orlando	Legion Vietnam Veterans Family Assistance Program
	Tallahassee	Florida State University
Georgia	Atlanta	Association for Retarded Citizens
Hawaii	Honolulu	Learning Disabilities Association
Idaho		*Utah State University (Logan, UT)*
Illinois	Chicago	Universal Family Connection
		Woodlawn East Community and Neighbors
	Rock Island	Rock Island County Council on Addictions
	Springfield	Legion Vietnam Veterans Family Assistance Program
Indiana	Indianapolis	Legion Vietnam Veterans Family Assistance Program
	Portland	Community Family Services, Inc.
Iowa	Des Moines	Easter Seal Society
Kansas	Wichita	University of Kansas
Kentucky	Louisville	Legion Vietnam Veterans Family Assistance Program
	Paintsville	Mountain Comprehensive Care Center
Louisiana	New Orleans	Louisiana State University UAP
Maine	Portland	Veterans Support Services, Inc.
		E.K. Shriver Center (Waltham, MA)
Maryland	Baltimore	Kennedy Krieger Institute
Massachusetts	Belmont	McLean Hospital
	Boston	Federation for Children with Special Needs
	Pittsfield	Veterans Outreach Center
	Roxbury	Veterans Benefits Clearinghouse
	Waltham	E.K. Shriver Center UAP
Michigan	Detroit	Legion Vietnam Veterans Family Assistance Program
	Muskegon	VETS, Inc.
Minnesota	Minneapolis	Wilderness Inquiry, Inc.
		Legion Vietnam Veterans Family Assistance Program

State	City	Program
Mississippi	Biloxi, Hattiesburg, Jackson	University of Southern Mississippi UAP
Missouri	Jefferson City Kansas City St. Louis	Legion Vietnam Veterans Family Assistance Program University of Missouri at Kansas City UAP Vietnam Veterans Leadership Program
Montana	Missoula	University of Montana UAP
Nebraska	Omaha	Great Plains Paralyzed Veterans of America Charitable Foundation
Nevada		*Utah State University (Logan, UT)*
New Hampshire		*E.K. Shriver Center (Waltham, MA)*
New Jersey	Orange	Occupational Center *Veterans Multi-Service Center (Philadelphia, PA)*
New Mexico	Albuquerque	American Red Cross Legion Vietnam Veterans Family Assistance Program *Utah State University (Logan, UT)*
New York	Bronx Canton Hauppauge New York City Saratoga Springs Niagara Falls	Albert Einstein College of Medicine United Cerebral Palsy Association Suffolk County Youth Bureau Lower Eastside Service Center Legion Vietnam Veterans Family Assistance Program Saratoga County Rural Preservation Copin Foundation
North Carolina	Chapel Hill Winston-Salem	University of North Carolina UAP Legion Vietnam Veterans Family Assistance Program
North Dakota	Minot	Minot State University UAP
Ohio	Columbus	Vietnam Veterans of America Ohio State Council
Oklahoma	Oklahoma City	Community Health Centers, Inc. Legion Vietnam Veterans Family Assistance Program
Oregon	Salem Chiloquin	Legion Vietnam Veterans Family Assistance Program Southeast Oregon Rural Health Network

State	City	Program
Pennsylvania	Philadelphia Harrisburg	Veterans Multi-Service Center Legion Vietnam Veterans Family Assistance Program
Puerto Rico	San Juan	Puerto Rico Vietnam Veterans Assistance Program
Rhode Island	Providence	Vietnam Era Veterans Association
South Carolina	Columbia	National Information System
South Dakota	Sioux Falls	Legion Vietnam Veterans Family Assistance Program
Tennessee	Nashville	Base Camp, Inc.
Texas	Dallas El Paso San Antonio	American GI Forum Aliviane, Inc. American GI Forum
Utah	Logan Salt Lake City	Utah State University UAP The Cottage Program International, Inc.
Vermont		*E.K. Shriver Center (Waltham, MA)*
Virginia	Charlottesville, Front Royal, Staunton Norfolk	 COVER Tidewater Family Services
Washington	Mt. Vernon Seattle	Skagit Community Mental Health Center SEAVAC
West Virginia	Mt. Gay	Logan County Vietnam Veterans *COVER*
Wisconsin	Green Bay Madison	Family Services of Brown County Vets House, Inc.
Wyoming	Sheridan	RENEW

United States Government INFORMATION

Charge your order. It's easy! MasterCard VISA

Order Processing Code:
* 7762

Fax your orders (202) 512–2250
Phone your orders (202) 512–1800

❑ **YES,** send me _____ copies of **The Legacy of Vietnam Veterans and Their Families — Survivors of War: Catalysts for Change**, SN 028–004–00090–7 for $34 each ($42.50 foreign).

The total cost of my order is $ __________. Price includes regular shipping and handling and is subject to change.

Company or personal name (Please type or print)

Additional address/attention line

Street address

City, State, Zip code

Daytime phone including area code

Purchase order number (optional)

Check method of payment:

❑ Check payable to Superintendent of Documents

❑ GPO Deposit Account ☐☐☐☐☐☐☐ – ☐

❑ VISA ❑ MasterCard

(expiration date) ***Thank you for your order!***

Authorizing signature 8/95

Mail To: Superintendent of Documents
P.O. Box 371954, Pittsburgh, PA 15250–7954

Important: Please include this completed order form with your remittance.

United States Government INFORMATION

Charge your order. It's easy! MasterCard VISA

Order Processing Code:
* 7762

Fax your orders (202) 512–2250
Phone your orders (202) 512–1800

❑ **YES,** send me _____ copies of **The Legacy of Vietnam Veterans and Their Families — Survivors of War: Catalysts for Change**, SN 028–004–00090–7 for $34 each ($42.50 foreign).

The total cost of my order is $ __________. Price includes regular shipping and handling and is subject to change.

Company or personal name (Please type or print)

Additional address/attention line

Street address

City, State, Zip code

Daytime phone including area code

Purchase order number (optional)

Check method of payment:

❑ Check payable to Superintendent of Documents

❑ GPO Deposit Account ☐☐☐☐☐☐☐ – ☐

❑ VISA ❑ MasterCard

(expiration date) ***Thank you for your order!***

Authorizing signature 8/95

Mail To: Superintendent of Documents
P.O. Box 371954, Pittsburgh, PA 15250–7954

Important: Please include this completed order form with your remittance.

For sale by the U.S. Government Printing Office
Superintendent of Documents, Mail Stop: SSOP, Washington, DC 20402-9328
ISBN 0-16-048205-4

ISBN 0-16-048205-4